CREATIVE
WAYS
TO
TEACH
ENGLISH

Grades 7 to 12

CREATIVE
WAYS
TO
TEACH
ENGLISH

Grades 7 to 12

SECOND EDITION

DON M. WOLFE
Brooklyn College

THE ODYSSEY PRESS INC. NEW YORK

Acknowledgments

The author wishes to express his gratitude for the following permissions to reprint the various selections which appear in the text: to Simon D. Campbell, for lines from "The Old Woman," by Joseph Campbell; to Melville Cane, for his poem, "Snow Toward Evening"; to Nathalia Crane, for lines from "The Flathouse Roof," originally published by Thomas Seltzer & Company in *The Janitor's Boy and Other Poems;* to J. M. Dent & Sons, Ltd., for the passage from *Youth,* by Joseph Conrad; to Harcourt, Brace & World, Inc., for "Primer Lesson," by Carl Sandburg, from *Slabs of the Sunburnt West,* copyright, 1922, by Harcourt, Brace & World, Inc., renewed, 1950, by Carl Sandburg; to Holt, Rinehart and Winston, Inc., for sixteen lines from "The Sleeper," by Walter de la Mare, from *Collected Poems, 1901–1918,* copyright, 1920, by Holt, Rinehart and Winston, Inc., copyright, 1948, by Walter de la Mare, reprinted by permission of the publisher; to Houghton Mifflin Company, for twelve lines from "Songs for My Mother," from *The Shoes That Danced,* by Anna Hempstead Branch; to Alfred A. Knopf, Inc., for "Mother to Son," from *The Dream Keeper and Other Poems,* by Langston Hughes, copyright, 1932, by Alfred A. Knopf, Inc.; to the National Council of Teachers of English, for "The Most Common Grammatical Errors," from *The English Journal,* Vol. 19 (1930), pp. 440–45; to Dr. L. J. O'Rourke, for two pages from *Rebuilding the English-Usage Curriculum;* to Dr. Robert C. Pooley and Appleton-Century-Crofts, Inc., for pp. 194–98 and 218–23 from *Teaching English Usage,* by Robert C. Pooley, copyright, 1946, by the National Council of Teachers of English, reprinted by permission of the author and publishers; to Scholastic Magazines, for materials reprinted from *Best High School Writing,* copyright, 1941, by Scholastic Magazines, Inc.; to the L. W. Singer Company, Inc., for materials reprinted from the *Enjoying English* series, by Don M. Wolfe and Ellen M. Geyer; to The Stackpole Company, for material from "Elements of a Reading Program," also six experience themes, from *The Freshman and His World,* by Wolfe, Donahue, and Firor, copyright, 1955, by The Stackpole Company; to Dr. M. J. Stormzand for material from *How Much English Grammar?* by Stormzand and O'Shea, copyright, 1922, by Warwick & York.

to Mary Stormont Wolfe

PREFACE

Even from our own experiences as students, each one of us shapes several definitions of the term "good English teacher." At one time a good English teacher is one who sets minds on fire with the desire to read, not only the good books, but the great books and poems of the world. The great books and poems trace the images of greatness by which a youth may decide a destiny pregnant with meaning for generations to follow. A good English teacher is a miner: a miner of the gold of greatness in himself and in his students. If one has known the bracing clash of free minds, he may define a good English teacher as one who leads a discussion of those realities that agitate the minds of his class, a discussion so exciting that even the most timid member of the class suddenly speaks with a fearless eloquence.

Each one of us places his definitions of a good English teacher in a hierarchy of values from great to small. Where, for example, should we place this definition? "A good English teacher is one who in one year teaches the grammar of the simple sentence so imaginatively, so thoroughly, that even the weakest student does not need to learn grammar again." Those teachers who reject this definition may nevertheless find value in this one: "A good English teacher is one who patiently collects the peculiar combination of errors in the themes of each member of his class, helping each one to recognize and banish his deficiencies, all without a knowledge of grammar." One can imagine a class of ninth-graders invincibly hostile to grammar values, but willing to accept the English teacher who gives individual attention to each student's collection of errors in usage. How vital is this definition as compared with still another? "A good English teacher is one who makes his students aware of the healing or destructive nature of the word or epithet carelessly uttered; of the irrationalities blazing up behind the facade of language; of the responsibility one has to use his language for the furtherance of social enlightenment and the discharge of one's duties in the home, the school, the community." To encompass the variegated demands of English teaching, each of us needs many skills and disciplines; perhaps in a single memorable hour we may exemplify half a dozen definitions that gave us that rare inner glow of triumphant unity with our class.

In this book, as in my own experience, one definition of the good English teacher seems to me paramount in validity: "The good English teacher is one who, week by week, draws from his students stories or themes that reveal to each the unique coloring of his personality and the unique dignity of his experiences." All correctness, grammatical abstractions, semantic search, invaluable as they often appear, are to my mind subordinate to this function. Such a definition is first in the order of time and first in the order of validity. It engages the whole personality of the student, not one small intellectual part of him. This English teacher draws from the weakest student experiences as intense and shaking and memorable to the class as those of the most brilliant boys and girls. Only by this function can each student become a teacher of everyone in the class, achieve that community of closeness and growth with others inseparable from the beauty of honest self-inspection. Self-expression means also the sharing of fun, frolic, delight; it means the training of the emotions as well as the training of the mind; and each poignant sally of self-expression has not only its unique illumination of the individual but also a parallel significance in social illumination and semantic search. "What is a daughter?" "What is a son?" One can define such words only in terms of his own experience; but the class' synthesis of the good son, the good daughter, for a strong family and a strong society, may bear a rich fruit of social meaning as well.

The ways to teach English embodied in this volume owe their origins to many teachers, first to my teachers years ago at the University of Pittsburgh: Florence M. Teagarden, whose warm humanity and priceless insight into the art of friendly questioning worked a unique magic in my outlook as teacher and person; Percival Hunt, who gathered round him memorable colleagues, teachers whose voices and ideas still haunt the mind and linger in the ear—

Roger Sergel, George Carver, H. W. Schoenberger, Frederick Mayer; Mrs. Lela Hamilton, the most resourceful and imaginative classroom teacher I have had the good fortune to observe; Ellen Geyer, my teacher and collaborator on *Enjoying English*, a tower of dignity and enlightenment to a whole generation of English teachers; J. Ernest Wright, master composition teacher among all his fellows, a man who brought to each class a wealth of riches in ideas on the art of writing, a new vision of the growth possible in tracing the patterns of the masters in themes from our own experience. In more recent years, I am indebted to my colleagues on *Enjoying English*, Gertrude Unser, Harold von Arx, Don Mahan, Hannah Bechtel, and most of all to Dr. Charles Glicksberg, my friend and colleague at Brooklyn College, author of *Writing the Short Story* and many other vital books, whose friendship from year to year has been an increasing reward and delight.

D.M.W.

Preface to the Second Edition

In the years that have passed since the publication of *Creative Ways*, its principles have found enhanced acceptance by teachers of Grades 7–12 across the country. The additional chapters and appendices of the present edition extend these principles in fresh applications, such as Appendix 18, "A Realistic Writing Program for Culturally Diverse Youth," pages 514–522. Increasingly the most vital and rewarding task of the English teacher is to prove to each student, however handicapped or brilliant, that his deepest experiences have a unique dignity and vividness that he can portray in burning images of sensory diction. The most deprived student has this language at his tongue's end; also he has feelings as deep as the most talented boy, that great well of energy from which to draw many hours of eager labor. Moreover, he has in his mind records traced by his eyes, his ears, his finger tips, his tongue, his nose, as selective and differentiated as the sense impressions of the most sophisticated and intellectual boy. We must help him to realize the value of these memories in building memorable paragraphs no one else could write. This appeal to the senses and memory of sense impressions were the basis of the famous English A course at Harvard (alas, now no more!), which required from the student a short daily theme a day, to be deposited, as Walter Prichard Eaton writes, in the teacher's mail box by ten o'clock each morning. With sensory language the gifted student can soar to heights he has not dreamed of; this diction is the most explosive resource of the deprived student as well. To tap the vast energy of the student, whether deprived or gifted, the teacher needs to read model themes to her classes from her former students or other teachers' students. The best model themes are *expository paragraphs* developed by images of color, sound, and touch.

Over the country, since the advent of *Creative Ways*, the use of model themes in sensory diction has been greatly intensified, not only in high school classrooms but also in college classes in the teaching of English. The best way to learn to teach writing is to write oneself about the indelible impressions of recent days and crucial moments deep in one's youth. Hence the new chapter in this text, "Classical Principles in Action: The Teacher as Writer and Critic," below, pages 397–422. The teacher-to-be must prove to herself that she can write. The best assignments on the high school level are almost always the most explosive assignments on the college level and more often than not on the graduate and elementary levels as well. But no assignment can be fully persuasive without the reading and discussion of student themes (or suitable professional models), representing experiences familiar to the class and gradually reaching deeper, week by week, into the life of the student teacher.

Though the ways and means to the improvement in high school writing is the main emphasis of *Creative Ways*, many new resources have been included in various fields, together with annotated bibliographies which include many of the latest books and articles on the subject at hand. An analysis of structural linguistics (pages 345–360); a chapter on the sentence-building game and its relation to transformational grammar (pages 214–228); a new chapter on transformational grammar by Dr. Gladys Haase, of Brooklyn College (pages 361–370); a revised chapter on student problems (pages 36–49), written in the main by Mr. Eugene Doherty, of the Princeton Township Public Schools; special appendices on the dramatization of statistics (pages 505–506), analysis of aspirations (pages 510–513), literary sentences for grammatical analysis (pages 507–509).

In sending forth this second edition, I am indebted not only to my old teachers and colleagues, as named in the preface of 1958; I am especially grateful to Mr. Eugene Doherty, Miss Ruth Popofsky, and Miss Josie Lewis, my colleagues on *Enjoying English;* to the many teachers who collaborated in the anonymous identification of student problems (see pages 37–38). Finally, I am especially indebted to Sister Mary Paul Catherine, formerly of Marian College, Morogoro,

Tanganyika, whose students wrote of incandescent moments in African villages of their childhoods, moments which revealed the fundamental identity of their problems with those of young people in other lands, other countries, across the globe.

D.M.W.

Princeton
May 30, 1966

CONTENTS

PART II USAGE AND GRAMMAR

PART III THE TEACHING OF LITERATURE AND SEMANTICS

PART IV   RESOURCES IN BOOKS AND IDEAS

APPENDICES

Part I

EXPERIENCE RESOURCES IN SPEAKING AND WRITING

1 How to Begin:
The First Writing Assignment

IN MEETING a high school writing class for the first time—let us say, a ninth-grade class—how can we best show that we understand some of their deeper feelings and reflections? The student needs to write from his own definition of the word *experience*, not from ours. Only thus can he gain that confidence from which will flow his unique sentence rhythms. The question is, then, what writing assignment can you and I make that will show we understand the need every boy and girl has for self-expression on a meaningful level? The average boy or girl often expects life and school to be dissonant and separate entities, with life the reality and school the make-believe. Some students and many teachers are uncomfortable when the deeper life of the student enters the classroom. One main aim in the first writing assignment, then, or in the first two or three assignments, is to achieve in the student's mind a burning coalescence of life and the English classroom.

In order to make a fruitful writing assignment, we must begin with the student's experience, choosing a branch of his life that we know has deep emotional roots. In emotional rootage and potential, the poor student of limited intelligence is equal to the brightest. We must tap these deep springs with their streams of feelings, bitter, sweet, humorous, whimsical. If we begin with family life, for example, we know we tap some of the source feelings of his personality. In taking family life as the first topic, we take the chance that some students are locked and barred emotionally, and will neither write

3

nor speak. But when we are in doubt, it is better to risk this failure with a few students than to take a chance on a topic less certain to inspire strong response. Here, then, are some possible theme ideas:

My Dad Is a Funny Guy	My Mother Is Patient
They Brought Me Up Wrong	They Don't Understand Me
Dad Brought Me Up by Hand	They Treat Me as a Kid
A Family Problem	We Have Hilarious Times
A Fight with My Brother	I Look Out for My Sister

Of course we do not begin by writing these topics on the board. We have them written down ready to suggest when the time comes, when the class is emotionally ready.

One excellent way to begin a discussion of family life is with the problem of discipline. "How were you brought up?" we ask. "Did your dad or mother ever whip you? Were you brought up, as Dickens says, by hand? How should boys and girls be punished, if at all?" Such questions usually start a discussion with many humorous overtones. If the discussion lags, you and I must tell how we were brought up. What punishment really worked? What punishment did not work? Little stories of scoldings and punishments make an excellent beginning. When we see a student has a story, we should bring him up front to tell it in detail. We ask him to tell when and where the incident took place. In what town was he living? How old was he? What school was he attending? As he tells the story, we interrupt to draw him out more completely. This is all preparation, a series of hints and reminders, for the theme he may wish to write on family life.

Crucial Motivation: Student Models

In such a discussion you and I show the class that we want to begin with their lives and problems, rather than with topics interesting only to us. The next step, which we may decide to take on a second day, is much more vital. That is the reading of student models of the seriousness and variety that we wish the class to achieve. These student models should be ones that we have carefully saved from the year before. If we have not saved them, then we must rely upon other teachers' student models. Here are two of the kind we mean:

MY BIGGEST FEAR

Since my father's death when I was six years old, my biggest problem has always been, "What will happen if my mother dies?" It is a terrible thought, but it comes to my mind once in a while, especially while I am lying in bed with a fever. When I have a high fever, it seems as if I am lying in a gigantic room. I feel as if needles are pricking me. Things are coming at me, as if in a dream. Finally I come to my senses with a start. I say to myself, "What would happen if Mother died? Where would I go? What would I do?" I am dependent on my mother because she is both father and mother to me. She is always willing to hear my problems and help me in any way she can. I dread to think of her not being with me. I hope it won't happen.

Mary Jane Kielty

FAMILY PUZZLE

Growing up with my family has two sides to it, like a penny you sometimes flip. If I choose heads, heads don't always come up. I like to reach for the flour can from the shelf for Mother or run to the store for anise seed when she makes cookies. But I don't like to set the table for a chicken dinner on Sundays, or drain the washtubs in the cellar on washdays when I get home from school. Blackening Dad's shoes so he can wear them to church on Sunday morning hasn't been fun like helping him wash the car or nailing boards around the kitchen sink. Even that isn't always fun. Sometimes I can take my kid brother Immie up on the roof and set traps for pigeons, but sometimes Dad slaps my ears for that. He doesn't always give me a dollar for a Saturday movie, and sometimes Mother insists on buying me tennis shoes instead of loafers. I've had a few whippings, and I've been sent to bed early, but growing up at home hasn't been all pain or all pleasure. As I said, it's like flipping a coin.

Terry Quinn

After reading such a student model as one of these, we ask the class, "What is good about this story?" Mary Jane had this deep fear about her mother. Do all boys and girls have fears about their parents? We may say to the class, "If you have a fear about your father or mother, that might be a good theme topic." The more class talk about each pupil model, the more emotional as well as intellectual motivation for the assignment. It would not be disproportionate, in the first assignment, to take a whole hour for the reading and discussion of three student models. In such an hour of conversation, we may ask the students to suggest topics that these models remind them of. Theme topics that spring spontaneously from such discussions make the richest kind of student writing. After exchange of impressions about student models, we read to the class or write on the board topics we have saved, like the ones listed on page 4, also topics suggested by the class. Only this kind of emotional preparation for the first assignment can show boys and girls that in the very first theme we want a burning record of the life they think has the deepest meaning. Again we must remember that in this appeal to the emotions no two students will respond with exactly the same experiences. We appeal to the uniqueness of each student. We remember, too, that the poor student, however different his experiences, has the same intensity of feeling as the brightest. Unless we can switch into action this emotional electricity, the writing program cannot be a fulfillment either for us or for the student.

For the Weaker Student: One Hour in Focus

A few students in the class may find themselves emotionally blocked against the family assignment. Here, then, is another way to begin, related to the family theme but easier to crystallize for the weak student. Call the title of such a theme, "My First Hour This Morning." Even by the poorest student such a topic is easily focused and crystallized because he can rely completely on the chronology of events too recent to be forgotten. Normally speaking, this topic brings a sharp, clear writing response. In such a theme we may ask for sounds, colors, sensations of touch, smell, and taste. The reason for this is that usually in the first hour a person will rise and put on clothes of a specific color, go down to breakfast, taste orange juice, milk, bacon, or toast, and hear sounds of the kitchen around him before he grabs his hat and leaves the house. To show our students the possibilities of such a theme as this, we may wish to read a student model like the following:

A LONELY HOUR

My first hour this morning was lonely. Just now my father is away on a business trip and my mother is sick with influenza. At seven-thirty the alarm clock tingled in my ear. I shut it off quickly, so my mother wouldn't hear it. In the September wind outside my window the brown leaves were floating down from our big oak tree. I could hear the leaves swish as the branches swayed. Closing my window, and washing quickly, I slipped on my nylon stockings, red shoes, and gray corduroy suit. Then I tiptoed down the stairs and out into the kitchen. There I boiled two eggs, toasted two slices of bread, and squeezed some orange juice for myself. While the eggs boiled, I ran outside for the morning paper, propped it up before me as I ate, and flipped on some music. I wasn't so lonely then, except when I heard my mother coughing. Usually she gets my breakfast and drinks a cup of coffee with me. I hope my mother gets well soon and we can have breakfast together again.

Zelda Mastin

How Can the Student Capture His Audience?

In the reading and discussion of student models we have taken, then, the first crucial step: tracing the roots of familiar experience in such a realistic way that each boy and girl in the room has emotional readiness to write.

For our next step, the question is this: What kind of language can the student use to capture his readers? We must emphasize that each student is writing with his own class in mind. They are his readers, his audience, the best judges of his writing. What language will capture them, make them relive his own experience? The answer to this is easy: "Appeal to your reader's eye, ear, finger tips. Use sights, sounds, colors. As a picture is worth a thousand words, so a word picture such as 'sizzling hamburger' or 'flaming red leaf' is worth a thousand words such as *food* and *autumn*."

Making a Moment Real

To teach the use of sensory language, the visualization of one moment is an indispensable device. When is a moment dramatic and real? How does one moment of life come alive in words? This is the problem. We may ask our students to write a few sentences about a moment of the present class hour. We may say, "Now we shall take about five minutes to write about the things you see, hear, and touch at or around your desk. Use two words such as 'September afternoon' to give the setting in time, the season of the year, and the time of day. Then tell what you see, what you hear, what you touch." Here is a short student model to illustrate:

ENGLISH-CLASS MOMENT [1]

It is a warm September afternoon at South Side High School, Rockville Centre, Long Island. As I sit at my desk in Mr. Barber's room, I see a tall, black-haired young man sitting in the desk in front of me. He has blue eyes, black hair, and very long arms. I hear his fingers tapping on a blue book he is holding in his hand. As I move, I hear my old desk squeak. I hear my pen scratching on the paper. I feel its smooth roundness, a little sweaty now from my nervous fingers. Now and then I hear the clock tick on the yellow wall to my right. As I look around, I see a lovely black velvet ribbon on Sonia's yellow hair. As I move my paper, my left hand slides over two little ridges in my smooth brown desk.

Harry Reid

Anticipating the Crucial Errors

As the class writes its rough draft in pencil, we may be able to pass through the room and see a number of the most common errors. The misspelled words we may write in our class record book and dictate them in a little spelling lesson before the final draft. If we see in the rough draft certain key sentence errors, we may put these on the board before the final draft is made. In the ninth grade about one-third of all errors are sentence errors. By the senior year this proportion has dropped to perhaps ten per cent. By the second year of college perhaps only one student in thirty makes the sentence error. As we examine the run-on errors, we see that they are concentrated in the use of the adverbs *then, there, however, therefore, finally,* and in the use of pronouns between complete thoughts, *he, they, it, she, we, I.* In the ninth grade it is usually advisable to drill on these sentence errors involving adverbs and pronouns. If we can have a mimeographed sheet ready to show these common errors, we can make the student conscious of the need of reading each of his sentences aloud in order to hear each period fall into place. When a student has very persistent sentence-sense troubles, we may urge him to read aloud the last sentence of his theme first (and so on backward) in order to separate each thought with complete auditory as well as semantic distinctness.

[1] For other themes about classroom moments, see below, pp. 66, 72.

Dramatizing Manuscript Clarity

Only when the student is emotionally prepared to write do we turn to the problem of manuscript requirements and the avoidance of common errors. We know that once a student feels the flow of his personality into language, correctness will have a new meaning. The more vital the experience he is recording, the more urgent it is to him to write neatly, in whole sentences, and to spell correctly. To make our point about manuscript neatness, we hand out theme paper and dictate a few sentences to be written in ink as the beginning of a paragraph. Before we dictate the sentences, however, this picture (or a similar one) goes on the board.

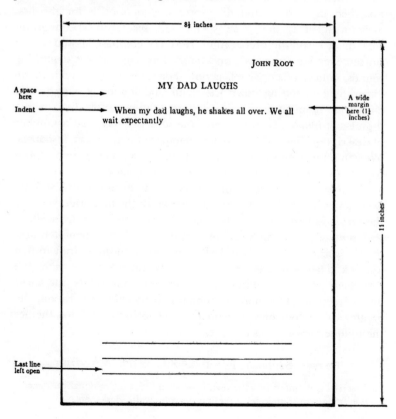

As we dictate the sentences, we go from seat to seat and point out penmanship errors. Here is a boy with no space after periods. Here is another who makes capital letters look like small letters. We say, "Leave a space about as wide as your little finger after each period." "Make a capital T like this, just two lines, no curlicues." "Poor handwriting can look neat if you leave white spaces between the words and especially between sentences."

*   *   *

The emotional preparation of the class is easily the most vital ingredient of the first writing assignment. By reading and discussing student models, we can show the class that we understand the deeper levels of their thoughts. Even if two classroom hours are absorbed in reading and discussing student models for the first assignment, it is time well spent. The second most important ingredient is stylistic preparation. Here the emphasis should be not on sentence structure, but on sensory language: words describing sounds, colors, touch, smell, action. For such sensory vividness an experiment in setting down the sights and sounds of a particular classroom moment is invaluable preparation. After five or ten minutes of making such a record, the students may read a number of descriptions in a brief time and compare their sensory responses. We can show even the weak students that of all sensory impressions sounds are the most easily crystallized in language.

In avoidance of common errors, as in avoidance of stylistic weaknesses, prevision is the key to success. In the first draft, we note the errors as best we can. The two skills we stress most are spelling and sentence recognition. Then we turn to manuscript requirements, insisting upon a first draft in pencil and a final draft in pen and ink. The more preparation in manuscript requirements for the first theme, the more emphasis on a few common errors, the fewer our corrections. The more emotional and stylistic preparation, the greater will be our own enjoyment in exploring in the first themes the unique personalities of the class.

To the Student Teacher: Suggested Activities

1. Describe a moment in your own classroom like that assigned on page 8. Use images of sound, color, action, people, walls, desks, etc.

2. Make a list of ten or twelve suggested theme topics about family life like those on page 4. Gauge your topics to one grade level, and name this level. Under each topic write a few sentences to show why students of the age level you select would be interested in the topic. Give your topics variety of mood and liveliness of phrase.
3. Write a paragraph of your own (200–300 words) about a moment in your own family. Use images of several senses as in the themes on pages 5, 6, and 7. Use images of both place and person. Follow the manuscript requirements outlined on p. 9.
4. Write a paragraph about a moment in a class with the teacher who best understood you. Show in this sketch what she did or said that appealed to you. Make clear the season of the year, the time of day, and the name of the town. Use images to describe your teacher and suggest with images the classroom itself. Experiment with sounds. Remember that sounds are easier to make real than images of color, touch, or smell.
5. Visit a teacher recommended by your professor. Visit one of her classes. Ask her for hints about the first writing assignment. Then write a brief report about her advice, using several sentences of her exact words.

Suggested Readings

APPLEGATE, MAUREE: *Freeing Children to Write*, Harper & Row, Publishers, 1963

Rich and fruitful suggestions set down in inimitable style by a highly gifted teacher.

BENNETT, ROBERT A.: "Unit Ideas for the New School Year," *English Journal*, Vol. 49 (September, 1960), pp. 400–08

Full of specific suggestions for units in literature, such as (Grade 8) "The Many Faces of Courage," "Pioneers! O Pioneers!," "The Family Team," (Grade 9) "In a Mirror," (Grade 11) "The Pursuit of Happiness," (Grade 12) "What Men Live By."

BRUNER, JEROME S.: *On Knowing. Essays for the Left Hand*, Harvard University, 1963

A series of exciting essays beginning with the "Conditions of Creativity." Another interesting chapter: "The Act of Discovery."

"But What Are We Articulating With?" *English Journal*, Vol. 51 (March, 1962), pp. 167–79

The NCTE committee reports on the freshman English offerings in ninety-five colleges and universities. A valuable, realistic article.

CARRIAR, SHIRLEY M.: "One Use of Theme Files in Junior High School English," *English Journal*, Vol. 51 (March, 1961), pp. 195–97

Valuable suggestions for the many uses of a theme folder for each student.

DAKIN, DOROTHY: *How to Teach High School English*, Heath, 1950
This book contains many useful suggestions about ways to begin. See especially pp. 28–59.

DEBOER, JOHN J., KAULFERS, WALTER V., and RAND, HELEN: *Teaching Secondary English*, McGraw-Hill, 1951
A very thoughtful book, containing many suggestive ideas in all branches of the teaching of English. See pp. 19–47.

GROSE, LOIS M.: "Teaching Writing in the Junior High School," *English Journal*, Vol. 49 (February, 1960), pp. 89–94
Realistic emphasis on the single full paragraph, identification of writing errors, use of the theme folder for each pupil, variety of rich assignments.

HOOK, J. N.: *The Teaching of High School English*, Ronald Press, 1950
The first three chapters of this book contain many suggestions on student-teacher relations that both the beginning and the experienced teacher will find useful.

JOHNSON, ERIC W.: "Avoiding Martyrdom in Teaching Writing: Some Short Cuts," *English Journal*, Vol. 51 (September, 1962), pp. 399–402
Realistic suggestions for improvement of themes before the teacher begins to mark them.

LOGAN, EDGAR: "Physical Words," *English Journal*, Vol. 43 (April, 1954), p. 196
A writing assignment which prompted this teacher's discovery that "*physical words* carry an impact that sometimes releases real creative teen-age skill."

MCGUIRE, EDNA: "College Freshmen on Writing in High School," *English Journal*, Vol. 51 (April, 1962), pp. 256–58
A valuable sampling of opinion in response to specific questions, such as, "How often should high school students write? How should the teacher mark the themes?"

MINTON, ARTHUR: "Design for Composition," *English Journal*, Vol. 30 (February, 1941), pp. 136–146
This article outlines in detail four steps to be used as guides for students in the writing of compositions, and further explains how these steps can be used by the students to evaluate their work.

MIRRIELEES, LUCIA B.: *Teaching Composition and Literature in Junior and Senior High School*, Harcourt, Brace, 1952
This important book should be read by every high school teacher of English. See particularly Chapter 19, "Motivating Composition in Relation to Pupils' Experience," pp. 269–299.

REDFORD, GRANT H.: "Of Teachers, Students, and 'Creative Writing,'" *English Journal*, Vol. 42 (December, 1953), pp. 490–496
Both teachers and students must value a "desire to share one's experiences with others, and by means of this intimate communication to

transcend the isolation of self," before students can make meaningful writing contributions.

RINKER, FLOYD: "Priorities in the English Curriculum," *English Journal*, Vol. 51 (May, 1962), pp. 309–12

This article names the development of the teacher as the first priority: ability to write is a fundamental element in teacher preparation. Writing by the students should take one-third of the school week. Grammar is not high in the list of priorities, but: "The Commission recommends that grammar be retained as an essential part of the English curriculum."

SMITH, DORA V.: "A Curriculum in the Language Arts for Life Today," *English Journal*, Vol. 40 (February, 1951), pp. 79–85

The use of real problems in the classroom to meet the needs of today's students. A useful list of books for student reading is appended.

SONKE, DOROTHY: "Growth Experiences in Theme Writing," *English Journal*, Vol. 42 (May, 1953), pp. 246–50

An article rich in specific helps to the teaching of vital self-expression.

SQUIRE, JAMES R. and others: *The National Interest and the Teaching of English*, NCTE, 1961

An indispensable analysis of English teaching in America; deficiencies, achievements, perspectives based on answers to questions by teachers in every state. Selected conclusions: (1) Teachers are not receiving quality training in English proper (2) Sixty percent of high school courses in English are now taught by teachers who lack even the minimum requirements of a major in English (3) Only forty-one percent of the colleges require prospective teachers to take an advanced course in composition. See also *The National Interest and the Continuing Education of Teachers of English*, by James R. Squire and others, NCTE, 1964.

"The First Assignment, A Symposium," *English Journal*, Vol. 43 (September, 1954), pp. 287–296

Seven experienced high school teachers suggest practical first assignments, each designed to be challenging for the student and to give the teacher information about the hidden talents and interests of individual students.

WHITE, ELIZABETH S.: "Tips for the Beginning English Teacher," *English Journal*, Vol. 47 (September, 1958), pp. 349–53

A useful checklist of workable principles and assignments for the first weeks of school.

2 Marking and Returning the First Set of Themes

OFTEN WE TEACHERS view with dread the prospect of marking thirty or sixty or ninety compositions. If we use the resources of emotional preparation and anticipation of common errors, however, we may gradually make the marking of themes a rich experience in exploration of unique student personalities. When our time is taken primarily with correction of errors, we have two strikes against us: 1. In marking errors, we lose time in which we could make constructive stylistic comments. 2. It is a dreadful drudgery to read papers mainly for errors, knowing that these same errors will appear again and again, however assiduous our toil. In general, then, pleasurable theme reading requires the following:

(1) a strong emotional preparation of the class,
(2) the writing of a first draft in class,
(3) drill in class on two or three common errors,
(4) rewriting in pen and ink.

When we meet these conditions, we can often look forward to the reading of even sixty papers in perhaps two hours or less.

Marking and Criticizing the First Themes

In marking any student's theme, the first questions we must bear in mind are these: What kind of comment will encourage the student to give more time to and do better work on his second theme? What kind of comment will help him to build upon whatever stylistic excellence he possesses? Important as correctness is, we may be certain that the student is not going to be primarily interested in the correction of mistakes, even when a mistake brings the penalty of a lower grade on this theme or the next. We may also be certain that such words as "trite," "poor," "dull," "weak," or "absurd" are going to make him lose rather than gain confidence in himself, especially if no *particular words* are pointed out as trite and no specific phrase is marked as dull or weak.

Our main asset in helping the student give more time to his next theme is to comment favorably on something in the theme, even if it is only a single active verb such as *wobbled* or *sparkled*, or a comparison, such as "like the bark of the oak tree in our back yard." If the student has dug down to a rich vein of experience, beginning his theme, say, with the sentence, "A quarrel with my mother yesterday made me very unhappy," this is a wonderful chance to comment sympathetically and tactfully in words perhaps like these: "You have chosen to write on a vital, moving topic. Even though your theme lacks images, your language has a rhythm and dignity comparable to the depth of this experience." Such comments, when we write them clearly in red ink, are so cherished by a sensitive youth that he eagerly turns to another vital subject which he feels will meet with similar commendation. The important thing about such appreciation is that it is individual attention to a unique personality. No other student has given us freely of himself on this topic. If there is one thing above others we as teachers can do to provide for individual differences, it is to make unique comments of praise on our students' papers. Often, of course, it is not the comment at the end of the paper that is the most important. When we star a word or a phrase and write above it "a sparkling word" or "This gives it punch," we encourage the student to use vivid phrasing again and again. Bit by bit he sees in his own language the foundation stones on which to build a style. In the first papers our best procedure is to minimize all destructive comments in favor of commendation of some kind, even on such superficial things as margins, handwriting, or spacing.

Another creative approach to theme criticism is to tell the student what improvement to aim at in his next theme. Many students, for example, will write a whole series of themes without sounds such as "a bell tinkled" or "a truck rumbled and clattered down the alley." Of all sense impressions, sounds are easiest to describe. On a theme containing no sound images we may write: "In your next theme try for at least four sounds, such as 'I heard a typewriter click-clacking in the principal's office.' " When a student is deficient in color images, we may say, "Use three or four color words in your next theme." The same principle of anticipating the next paper may be followed for all theme problems. For example, we may write, "In your next theme stick closely to the point of your topic sentence." Many students have a habit of writing six or seven sentences instead of fifteen or twenty. To them we may say: "In your next theme use at least fifteen sentences." Such an approach to theme criticism often helps the student to surpass himself; it gives him a sense of growth that is infinitely more constructive than the satisfaction of excelling his fellow-students.

When the student knows that on each paper carefully written he will find words of praise, our practice of deducting for specific errors will not upset him. If we have explained that the sentence error is the most crucial kind of mistake, if we have illustrated it on the board, if we have had a mimeographed drill on the most prevalent kinds of sentence errors, normally the student will not object if we deduct ten per cent on the first theme for this error, fifteen per cent after the first month, and twenty per cent after the second month. If we have drilled on forty or fifty demons, such as *receive*, *separate*, etc., the average student will not object to our deducting five per cent on the first paper, eight per cent on the second paper, etc., for errors in spelling. It is a wise plan for us to explain each error carefully before we show a numerical deduction for it on the paper. Some teachers start with low deductions for errors and increase them several times a semester, as shown below.

	September Per Cent	November Per Cent	January Per Cent
Sentence errors	10	15	20
Misspelled words	5	8	10
Poor margins	5	8	10
Capitalization errors	5	8	10
No italics for names of books	5	8	10
No space under title	5	8	10
Last line of theme page not left open	5	8	10
Faulty penmanship	5	8	10
Insufficient space after periods	5	8	10
Its and *it's*, *there* and *their*	5	8	10

Such a plan is most effective, of course, when the class can discuss and agree upon the reasons for different penalties.

Returning the First Papers

Except for the days spent in emotional preparation for the first theme, no composition time is more crucial than the day we return the first batch of themes. On that day we establish the first principles of class criticism. We show by our approach to each theme whether the criticism will aim merely at finding fault, or at discovering in each paper an idea, a sentence, a phrase, a word that communicates a vivid sense impression or an emotional reality to weak students as well as strong ones. In general, from the seventh through the twelfth grade, we know that it is disastrous to hold up a paper to ridicule or irony. The only possibility of fostering growth, either by the class or by the individual whose theme is criticized, is to show what merit and what elements of writing skill a student has achieved.

At the beginning of the period, however, before reading papers to the class or asking the students to read them, it is sound practice to dictate in rapid succession words and phrases wrongly written in their themes. This is a group problem, not a personal one. Here is a sample of such a rapid dictation drill:

1. Spell *disappoint*.
2. saw its color. Spell *its*.
3. Write this title: My Job after School.
4. Write this construction: I saw a bird just then. It had white wings and a white tail.
5. I like tennis. Spell *tennis*.
6. I like autumn. Spell *autumn*.
7. going to high school. Spell *high school*.
8. going to Smith High School. Spell *High School*.
9. Write a capital T on your paper.
10. Write and punctuate the following: We looked around. There stood Jim.
11. their house. Spell *their*.
12. this summer. Spell *summer*.
13. I said, "It's too late." Write the whole sentence.
14. Spell *across*.

As illustrated above, the most diverse errors can be dramatized in this kind of practice. Capital letters, sentence errors, spelling problems, penmanship, punctuation, possessives, all these may be drilled on and drawn together in one drill from one batch of themes. We may even say, "Use a specific term for the general term *fruit*. Avoid the general when you can use a specific term." As we dictate, we may pause to make explanations or answer questions. When we have finished dictating, each student keeps his own paper until we have made corrections. We may ask those students who have misspelled words to spell them correctly aloud. We may ask a student to write phrases or words on the board. Such a dictation period requires the close attention of everyone in the class. It may be long or short, depending upon the time available or the number of errors. It allows for flexibility of plan. The students are not distracted by having their own themes before them as they write. In some cases we may mimeograph sentences from student themes containing errors for correction by the class. This method, however, is probably not so effective as dictation, though it has the advantage of allowing us to quote longer passages than we can dictate in class. A correction period normally should not require more than twenty minutes after we have handed back the first few sets of themes. Even with the first batch of themes, we can afford to neglect some errors for the stimulation of reading themes aloud.

Nothing is more delightful to a class than to hear the various students read papers aloud. We have selected, let us say, six or seven papers that we wish to be read by the students themselves. After each paper is read, we ask in effect, "What phrase is best in the story? What idea is fresh and original to you? At what point does the writer describe life as you know it to be? At what point was the writer looking at the object as he described it?" When the first question is, "What is commendable about the paper?" no student writer objects to having faults pointed out. Commendation in class discussion should invariably precede negative comments. In handling the first set of themes, we may even omit negative criticism altogether in favor of building up an atmosphere of commendation. As each student reads his paper, we should encourage the class to take notes on specific words. A general comment, such as "The paper is lively," or "The theme is like a moving picture," is lifeless and uninstructive compared to specific comments, such as, "I liked his comparison when he said, 'My bunk was as hard as a table top,'" or, "I thought his most vivid sentence was the one containing the words, 'The bacon was sizzling and the coffee perking.' " As one theme after another is read, we may ask, "What quality does this theme have that the others lack? Does this theme have more sounds than the ones read before? Does this theme have a more exact topic sentence? Which of the themes read has the most lively colors? Does this theme have more action words than the others? Which of the themes read was written with the deepest feeling?"

When should we return and discuss the first class themes? For the sake of motivation of a new set of lively papers as well as for improvement in accuracy, no timing problem is more important than this one. We should give back the papers and read some aloud in class *just before the next theme is due.* This has several constructive effects: 1. It stimulates the students who have done well to write even better themes. 2. The reading in class gives hope to other students that this time their themes will be selected and discussed. 3. The class discussion points out lively words and phrases that may help other students to surpass themselves stylistically. 4. The errors discussed will help the weak students to avoid particular pitfalls in spelling, punctuation, spacing, and sentence errors. In the weeks to come, we should return themes regularly and promptly, not allowing ourselves to assign more papers than we can mark and criticize. A *regular day*, whether once a week or once every two weeks, when students can count on theme return, is a substantial psychological incentive to richer and regularly written compositions.

*   *   *

The marking and returning of the first class themes, like all succeeding sets of papers, should be carefully timed to assure greatest interest and motivation. The ideal time is just the day or two before the next theme is due. In the marking of themes, we need to show the student what quality his language has on which he can build. Can he strike off original comparisons? Does he strike deep into the reality of his problems of home, school, or friendship? Does he use verbs that leap out at us from the page? Does he open sentences with past participles or a pair of adjectives or an absolute construction? For easy reading of his handwriting, does he place his words far enough apart? Does he have even one striking sound, color, or touch impression? We commend something in his paper, if only one word. We avoid hackneyed general impressions such as "trite," "confused," "generalized" in favor of such specific comments as, "Use *hobbled* instead of *walked*," "Hooray! A fresh, original comparison!" "Add sounds here to make it real, such as, 'Her heels clicked on the tile floor,' " "What color? Red, green?"

In handing back themes, we shall put emphasis on the achievements, not on the deficiencies, on the subject matter, not on correctness. We shall gather the errors together at the beginning of the period. We shall save the reading of themes for the last part of the period. In the discussion, especially of the first few batches of themes, we shall put the emphasis on language achievement, however unimportant, to show what the student can build on in future themes. His only competitor worth considering is himself, and each week, with diligent effort and the motivation the class provides, he has a good chance to surpass his own best work.

To the Student Teacher: Suggested Activities

1. Exchange themes with a fellow student. Read his or her theme and correct and comment on it as you would a student paper, keeping in mind the principles set forth in this chapter. Use red ink only.
2. Read your classmate's theme to your class (only, however, with his or her permission) and comment on it as you have in your red-ink markings. Ask for comments from the class. Have you evaluated it fairly and constructively?
3. If your professor prefers, he may mimeograph one or more themes on good paper and distribute them to the class for marking and evaluation. This is one good way to compare standards of judgment. Use only red ink in writing your comments.
4. Ask a local high school teacher to let you read and evaluate a set of her themes. To save time, you may need to make your comments very brief. Write grades in pencil so the teacher can change them if she wishes. Ask her to go over the papers with you and make suggestions about your criticisms.
5. Make a list of the errors in context from a set of thirty high school themes. Which errors are most numerous? What is the percentage of sentence errors? Have the errors mimeographed if possible and distributed to the class.

SUGGESTED READINGS

A Scale for Evaluation of High School Student Essays, published by the NCTE (1960), 508 South Sixth Street, Champaign, Illinois

BISHOP, ERNEST G.: "To Improve the Student's Technique in Theme Correction," *English Journal*, Vol. 24 (December, 1935), pp. 835–36
How students can be helped to make careful theme corrections.

BURKE, VIRGINIA M.: "A Candid Opinion on Lay Readers," *English Journal*, Vol. 50 (April, 1961), pp. 258–64
While recognizing the value of lay readers, the author warns against a cold analysis by a reader who does not know the corrector, nor the corrector him. The lay correction plan has many advantages, but must be used with caution.

CARRIAR, SHIRLEY M.: "One Use of Theme Files in Junior High School English," *English Journal*, Vol. 51 (March, 1961), pp. 195–97
Valuable suggestions for the many uses of a theme folder for each student.

CARROLL, JANE Z.: "A Plan for Meeting Individual Differences in Composition and Reading," *English Journal*, Vol. 48 (November, 1959), pp. 466–72, 479
"Another drawer of my filing cabinet holds a manila folder for each pupil. These folders are the pupils' English notebooks. I used to find that pupils often lost papers or forgot to bring them to class. I myself forgot to check notebooks, and found their varying sizes and vast bulk a problem when I collected them for close examination. Now we keep the folders, each class separate in alphabetical order, in the classroom at all times. They are instantly available to me for checking, or for exhibiting a pupil's work to a parent."

CRAWFORD, S. C. and PHELAN, MARIE C.: "A Summary of Methods in Composition Work," *English Journal*, Vol. 19 (October, 1930), pp. 616–20
Interesting material on pupil self-correction and criticism.

DAKIN, DOROTHY: *How to Teach High School English*, Heath, 1947
See Chapter 10 for some instructive advice on theme writing and theme criticism.

DUSEL, WILLIAM J.: "Some Semantic Implications of Theme Correction," *English Journal*, Vol. 44 (October, 1955), pp. 390–97
An arresting appraisal of the unpredictable power of many traditional grading symbols to mislead or upset the young person, with suggestions for constructive marking procedures.

GROSE, LOIS: "Essential Conditions for Teaching Written Composition," *English Journal*, Vol. 50 (April, 1961), pp. 247–251
Concrete suggestions, with emphasis on the suggested teaching load of one hundred pupils, the creative evaluation of pupil themes, classroom arrangement and equipment.

GROSE, LOIS M., MILLER, DOROTHY, STEINBERG, ERWIN R.: "Suggestions for Evaluating Junior High School Writing," NCTE, 704 South Sixth Street, Champaign, Illinois, 1959

Evaluating Ninth-Grade Themes: Illinois English Bulletin, March, 1933
> Twenty pupil themes with practical, realistic suggestions for evaluating student writing. Order from NCTE.

HOOK, J. N.: *The Teaching of High School English*, Ronald Press, 1950
> See Chapter 9 for some stimulating remarks on the selective correction of students' papers.

"Improve Your Writing," Department of the Army pamphlet, January, 1959
> Write to Headquarters, Department of the Army, Washington 25, D.C.

JOHNSON, ERIC W.: "Avoiding Martyrdom in Teaching Writing: Some Short Cuts," *English Journal*, Vol. 51 (September, 1962), pp. 399–402
> Realistic suggestions for improvement of themes before the teacher begins to mark them.

JUDINE, SISTER M., IHM, ed.: *A Guide for Evaluating Student Composition*, NCTE, 1965
> A rich and valuable group of essays on evaluation of themes, by gifted teachers and supervisors.

KEENE, KATHARINE, "Students Like Corrections," *English Journal*, Vol. 45 (April, 1956), pp. 212–15
> A helpful explanation of why students want and need defined methods of theme correction.

KOCLANES, T. A., "Can We Evaluate Compositions?" *English Journal*, Vol. 50 (April, 1961), pp. 252–57
> A perceptive article, with cogent reasons why lay readers may hinder, not help, the teacher in "the most important and demanding single task the teacher is called upon to perform."

MCCAFFERTY, JOHN: "Beginning Composition in the Senior High School," *English Journal*, Vol. 49 (December, 1960), pp. 636–38
> An ingenious plan for the gradual elimination of errors in tenth-grade themes. Lists of priorities in correctness given to the class and attacked cumulatively one by one.

MCCLURE, E. ISABELLA: "English in the Experience Curriculum," *English Journal*, Vol. 36 (January, 1947), pp. 7–11
> This article has an excellent "Code Sheet for Technical English" to be given to each student to use in checking the mistakes in his composition.

MIRRIELEES, LUCIA B.: *Teaching Composition and Literature in Junior and Senior High School*, Harcourt, Brace, 1952
> The teacher will find Miss Mirrielees' first chapter on the problem of the correct attitude toward student composition, correction, and evaluation very informative.

OGGEL, ELIZABETH: *Thoughts into Themes*, Holt, Rinehart and Winston, 1963
Excellent analysis and rating of student themes, with helpful suggestions for teacher commentary.

PALMER, ORVILLE: "Sense or Nonsense? The Objective Testing of English Composition," *English Journal*, Vol. 50 (May, 1961), pp. 314–20
An analysis of testing procedures by a specialist in the field. Mr. Palmer staunchly defends the objective test.

PALMER, ORVILLE: "Seven Classic Ways of Grading Dishonestly," *English Journal*, Vol. 51 (October 1962), pp. 464–67
Realistic and imaginative analysis of grading procedures.

ROBINSON, MARY: "Using the Opaque Projector in Teaching Composition," *English Journal*, Vol. 35 (October, 1946), pp. 442–45
Projecting student themes on a screen as a useful way to show structural faults, misspellings, etc. A valuable article.

ROODY, SARAH I. and LYMEN, BESS: "Managing Student Writing," *English Journal*, Vol. 44 (February, 1955), pp. 75–79
Two teachers present their time-saving methods of planning assignments and grading papers.

SAUER, EDWIN H.: *The Use of Lay Readers in the High School Composition Program*, Harvard University Press, 1962
Authoritative and impartial statement about the use of the lay reader program in Concord and Newton High Schools, Massachusetts.

3 Sequence of Theme Topics: How Shall I Decide?

WE HAVE NOW RETURNED the first set of themes on family life. To the student, whether in the seventh grade or the twelfth, no department of experience is so earthy and crucial as this. Perhaps after a month or two we shall return to a family topic. When our students write autobiographies near the end of the semester, many of them will want to deal with a critical family problem, tracing it from early years to the present time. However, thinking of the semester ahead, we ask ourselves, "How shall I decide upon a sequence of topics? What shall I plan to assign this week, next week, or a month from now?"

Can I Bring to Class Provocative Student Models?

The choice of the second and third theme topics to be assigned depends in good part upon student models. In response to what assignment in the past have we received the most sparkling themes? Unless we have two or three student models that will provide the rich emotional preparation that we have achieved with the family unit, we cannot expect a warm response from the class. The second assignment is crucial because we are still gaining the confidence of the class, confidence based upon our understanding of what problems mean most to them. If we have student models on one of the following topics, we are sure to keep close to the feelings of the class.

1. *A Day in My Diary.* This topic provides an opportunity to concentrate on the crucial moments of experience. What was a growing-up moment of a day I remember? What was my first comprehension of death? What was the crucial moment of a day of discovery? What was a moment of love and understanding? What was a day of disappointment? What was a moment of frustration? What was a day of catastrophe?

2. *School Memories, School Problems.* An assignment on school experience is usually very fruitful, especially if we can encourage the student to speak freely about a moment of frustration, embarrassment, happiness, or hatred. If this assignment is used, we can make it one of reminiscence of earlier school years or one of recent school problems, depending upon the student models we have at hand.

3. *Friendship Tried, Friendship True.* The topic of a moment of friendship is meaningful on all levels. If we have student models about a broken friendship, first romance, a friend lost, a friend gained, a moment of companionship, a happy moment with a friend, a sad moment with a friend, a definition of a friend, then we are sure of an electric fusing of classroom expression and student experience.

Visualization of a Moment

As in the first assignment, so in the second and third we need to emphasize the concept of a moment. To make any theme of personal experience very real, the student must pin down his feeling to one time. The question is, then, "How can I visualize one moment?" The necessary elements of full visualization are as follows:

1. What were the time of day and the season of the year? Tell the reader in two words, such as "August morning," "June evening."
2. What was the name of the place? Tell this in such words as "near the playground on York Avenue," or "in Miss Flynn's alegbra class," or "at our cabin on Long Lake."
3. What sounds did you hear at that moment? Was the clock ticking, a pan clattering, a student coughing?
4. What colors did you see around you?
5. What did someone say at that moment? What did you say at that moment? What were your thoughts?

The following student model shows the full expansion of a moment, visualized mainly in sensory language.

A SECRET MISSION

Miss Brill was gone. Now was my chance! I tiptoed into my kindergarten room, closed the door quickly behind me, and stood listening for a second to be sure that there was no one in the room or in the hall outside who would come in. After scampering across the front of the room past Miss Brill's formidable desk to my aisle, I stopped suddenly. One of the word-charts hanging on the wall had given a disgruntled flop against the blackboard. It seemed to be showing its dissatisfaction with my actions and looked down from the wall as sternly as the two tables of stone glared at the Israelites of old. After assuring myself that it was not really Miss Brill's black eyes that stared at me, but only the large black letters and curious markings of the word-chart, I hurried up the aisle. I passed the sand-table where a prosperous Eskimo village was modeled. The cotton snow and the paper houses were reassuring, and the company of the little paper Eskimos gave me courage. But as I looked down into the frozen sea, a pane of glass, I nearly cried out with fright as the eyes of a terrified little boy stared up at me from the bottom. I hurried on past the little circular table where I had so often cut out my green paper dolls and molded my clay men. I started, suddenly, at a faint tap on a near-by window. The tapping noise, I discovered to my great relief, was only the window shade slapping the window lightly in intermittent raps. Lest my "jittery" nerves should get the better of me, I hurried on to my battered brown desk in the farthest corner of the room. Inside, in the corner where I had kept it for nearly a week, was the precious treasure. Snatching it out and carefully concealing it in my hand, I tiptoed to another little desk, brighter and glossier than mine. This was the desk I worshiped as an altar. And here I came with my treasure, a pair of brightly polished scissors with shiny red handles that would cost ten cents at any of Woolworth's famous stores, to offer it as my first sacrifice to the little goddess I so adored. The ritual over, my journey to Mecca completed, I crept stealthily from the room. I had given my first present to my childhood sweetheart.

Duane Mitchell

When a moment is fully rounded, as in "A Secret Mission," the student's paper will contain a high proportion of concrete words. Stylistically speaking, the aim of the student should be to intensify his language from week to week. The more often he concentrates on a single moment and the more fully he develops this moment in the ways shown above, the more concrete his language will become.

What Are the Student's Problems?

One way to help choose a semester sequence of topics is to find out through anonymous statements what the students believe to be their most pressing worries and problems. For the students of our class to be completely frank in stating their problems, we must ask that their statements be anonymous. We may say to them, "In this class I should like what you write about to be as close to your daily thoughts and feelings as possible. I know that the more deeply you feel, the more eloquently and skillfully you will write. I know that the more pressing your problem, the more interest you will have in writing about it and the more interested anyone will be in reading about it. Would you be willing to state what your chief problems are without giving your name? All I am interested in is to know what the deepest worries and most persistent problems of this class are. Would you be willing to write down in class ten or twelve sentences that tell what your chief problems are? Print your sentences so that your handwriting will not be recognized. Do not sign your name. Put the word *boy* or *girl* at the top of your paper."

Some students will prefer to give more time than we can allow for this work in class. They will prefer to type their comments at home, perhaps to expand several of their statements to show some details of their problems. In experiments conducted in New York City schools, under the direction of Gertrude Unser and Harold von Arx, this approach to problems has proved fruitful and productive beyond all expectations. The results of this experiment are set forth at length in Chapter 4, pp. 36–49.

What Topic Is Searching and Timely?

One secret of any sequence of topics is knowledge of the students and the daily shifts and changes in the flow of their emotional energy. We all know the necessity of disregarding a perfectly logical progression in a course in order to capture in talks or papers the passing mood of joy, despair, or enthusiasm.

From day to day, moods of high school boys and girls fluctuate violently and unpredictably. Attitudes toward teachers and parents veer from love to hate, contempt to hero-worship, in a few short hours. What was a momentous worry upon awakening this morning vanishes with the warm look of a friend or a kind teacher's hand upon one's arm.

When, in a single class hour, we are able to channel into a theme the energy of any transient intense mood, writing miraculously improves. In inviting such expression, we may say, "What are you worried about today? What happened that made you angry, sad, joyful, hateful? What happened that made you laugh? What would you change in your life just now? What person would you like to love and respect you? What happened today that you wish you could erase from memory? What moment of today would you like to live over again?"

We may invite one or two students to speak on today's worry, today's joyful moment, today's surprise. In making such an assignment, we may read one or two student models, and suggest a number of topics such as the following:

1. A Black Look from My Father
2. Everything Went Wrong This Morning
3. I Should Have Stayed Home Today
4. I Didn't Have My Assignment
5. Why Didn't They Stop to Pick Me Up?
6. This Is My Lucky Day
7. A Teacher's Unkind Words
8. That Class Was So Boring
9. What That Teacher Said Made Me Happy
10. My Brother Made Me Cry
11. I Came off without Breakfast
12. I Am Living in the Clouds Today
13. A Moment with My Boy Friend
14. My Girl Friend Laughed

How Can I Give a Sequence of Topics Variety?

However serious may be our purpose in inviting a flow of personality from the deep springs of experience, it is wise to provide periodically a complete change of mood in writing and speaking assignments. From time to time we shift to topics releasing fancy and frolic, topics of escape from serious realities; we encourage the easy flow of wit, humor, and exaggeration that are the essence of adolescent ebullience.

One way to achieve this end is to suggest a theme on person-ification. We may say, "Describe one hour in the life of a clock on your classroom wall, a penny, a flashlight, a mirror, a refrigerator door at home, a door knob on your classroom, a shoe on your little sister's foot, your teacher's desk. If one of these could live and breathe and tell his story, what would he say about one hour of life? What people would he see? What feeling would he have?"

In assigning a theme on personification, we suggest first a number of topics like the ones above, then read and discuss in class a student model such as the following:

A BLINKER

The life of a blinker on such a cold December day as this is more in-teresting than my observers imagine. My job is to warn the motorists of the dangerous intersection and sharp curve at Fifth Avenue and South Negley, Pittsburgh. All I do day in and day out is to blink, blink, blink. But my life is not without variety, for I see many strangely different people watch for my warning blinks. Here comes a truck with a colored man driving; I suppose he is an ashman, because with every jar of the truck I see bits of blue dust and ashes fly out behind. Just behind the truck is a big Lincoln sedan carrying men in shiny black suits and women in green, yellow, and blue dresses. Here come some college boys in a car without a top; it is all pasted with yellow "Wreck Tech" stickers and daubed with red paint. As they pass me, one of them, a little redheaded chap, playfully doffs his cap to me, and says, "Good evening, sir." I guess he noticed me because I just received my new overcoat today; I feel so much warmer now, quite prepared for the winter. I do not like winter, however, because I see so many accidents. Machines try to take this corner too fast, and sometimes one skids and turns over. Often I myself suffer from the scraping of a fender, but I have not yet been sent to the hospital, as was one of my brothers who is now blinking again at Wightman and Forbes. But one can never tell what the winter will bring forth, especially with the schoolboys throwing snowballs at me. Here they come now, tossing a football around to each other. I must warn them about this big Hermes ice-cream truck coming up Fifth Avenue. Yes, life for a blinker is not without its thrills and responsi-bilities. Blink! Blink!

Curtis Garner

In analyzing this theme, we ask, "Why does Curtis locate the blinker at a particular corner and give the names of the streets?

How does he tell the season of the year? To boys and girls living in Pittsburgh, what college or university would the words 'Wreck Tech' suggest? What images do you like best? What sentence makes the blinker seem most alive?'' These questions point out the qualities of Curtis' theme that we wish for many papers. The more time spent in such discussion, such *prevision*, the less thought we need to give to *revision*. Boys and girls do delightful things with this assignment particularly if we provide a plentiful supply of lively topics like the following:

The Moon Looks Down	A Wastebasket Reminisces
The Chimney on Our School	My Old Tennis Shoes
The Leather Button on Miss Marks's Dress	A Football's Exciting Life
	The Mirror on My Dresser
A Windshield Wiper Speaks	My Father's Old Hat
A Red Leaf Takes a Tumble	A River Leads a Sad Life
Our Mail Box Tells His Story	A Highway Billboard
My Dog Looks at Life	

What Topics Have Social Meaning?

A theme based on actual sensory experience is easier to write and almost always more intense in interest to the class than a theme of social meaning, such as, "What Do I Mean by *The American Way of Life?*" Yet to become more mature intellectually, the student must advance sooner or later to a social topic and be prepared to dramatize his conclusions from the vicarious experience he finds in books as well as from vivid moments of his own life. Some topics, such as "What Is Happiness to Me?" lend themselves easily first to a personal experience of a happy moment, and then to the consideration of such social topics as "Poverty as a Cause of Unhappiness," or "Disease and Ill Health as Main Factors in Unhappiness."

In the upper years of high school, and often in the ninth and tenth grades, students have jobs after school and in the summer months. These jobs are very personal experiences. From this starting point the class may decide to make reports from actual observation on other jobs in the community, each student choosing one of the occupations he thinks he might like to pursue. Such a theme sets the student's imagination to work about the future and his eventual choice of a life work. Such a theme topic projects the student's thinking also into the field of employer-worker relations, hazards of particular occupations, civic responsibility for occupational dangers.

One way to initiate the discussion of jobs is to ask each student to tell about a job he has held, as in the following talk.

MY JOB IN THE FLOORING FACTORY

Last summer I had a job I didn't like. For the first time I worked eight hours a day along with men older than I. The day seemed long and tedious. Promptly at eight o'clock a mournful whistle blew, and I was at my bench. Above me was a high rack with hundreds of thin pieces of wood two inches wide and about a foot long. These pieces of wood I took down, forty or fifty at a time, and fitted into a wooden rack on my bench. Then I tightened a wooden screw that pressed the blocks together. After this I glued a piece of heavy paper to the wood. When the glue was dry, I cut the paper at one-foot spaces. Each square contained six pieces of wood, which was then sawed square and used for parquet flooring. The same thing over again a thousand times a day: That was what I didn't like. I kept looking at the clock and thinking, "I'm going back to school. I'm going back to school. It won't last forever" I couldn't see how the older men had stood it all those years.

Ken Fitzgerald

After several such talks we may have a panel discussion in which one or more of the following topics might be used.

What makes people dread to go to work?
What is meant by a creative job?
How can people express themselves creatively with an assembly line job?
Should a bricklayer attend college?
Should a waitress attend college?

On the topic of happiness, the student may first describe a happy moment of his own, then engage in a discussion of such a topic as "What Is One Thing that Makes Adults Happy?" Such topics as the following may open the discussion:

1. Getting Engaged
2. Getting Married
3. Having Children
4. Going to College
5. Having a Creative Job
6. **Having Job Security**
7. Having Good Friends
8. Owning Your Own House
9. Having Strong Faith
10. Working in the Earth
11. Being Out-of-Doors
12. **Traveling in a Car**

This topic may then be followed by "What Makes People Unhappy?" These topics may help to pin down discussion:

1. Not Enough Money	7. Disease and Disability
2. Not Enough Food	8. Quarrels in the Family
3. Out of a Job	9. Job of Drudgery
4. Marriage Unhappy	10. Loss of Religious Faith
5. Fear of Unemployment	11. Not Enough Education
6. Death in the Family	12. Working Too Long and Hard

Choosing a Sequence of Topics

In choosing a sequence of topics for oral and written composition, our main concern should be the experiences and moods of the students, not the imposition of our own ideal hierarchy of topics. We should try first to choose the topics that the student can take hold of with electric intensity: family, school life, friendships, frustrations, handicaps, moments of ecstasy and moments of victory and defeat. To give our weekly themes variety and delight, we should veer away from the serious now and then for a sally into the whimsical, the humorous, the imaginative. Finally, we should gradually choose topics with a social and intellectual implication so that our students can put their own personal experiences in perspective and attain greater maturity in social outlook.

On the basis of these principles, here is a suggested outline of topics for the tenth- or eleventh-year level:

1. Streets and Neighbors
   Social concomitant: What Is a Good Neighbor?
2. Growing Up in Our Family
   Extension in social criticism: What Makes a Happy Family?
3. School Moments, School Memories
   Social concomitant: What Makes a Good School?
4. Holidays and Dinner Bells
   Social concomitant: Holiday Customs in Other Lands
5. When Stop Lights Tell Their Tales: Personification
6. Do Animals Act Like People?
7. Friendship's Steel
   Social topic: What Is a True Friend?
8. A Happy Moment in My Life
   Social concomitant: What Makes a Happy Man? What Things Make People Unhappy?

9. The Automobile in Your Life and Mine
   Social correlation: How Can Driving Be Made More Safe?
10. This I Believe
    Extension in ideas: What Is a Patriot? What Is an American?
11. Hopes, Heroes, and Horizons
    Extension in ideas: How Does a Great Man Get Started?
12. The Next Step in Your Future
13. Links in My Life's Chain: Autobiography
14. Jobs for Today, Jobs for Tomorrow
    Social concomitant: When Is a Job Creative? How Can Leisure Be Creative?

To the Student Teacher: Suggested Activities

1. Make a list of fifteen topics most vital to you at this moment, arranged in order of decreasing interest. Ask yourself, "If I were teaching this class of student teachers to write about themselves, what topics would I choose?" Make any notes necessary in order to explain your choices.
2. Make a list of twenty specific theme topics that you think would be well liked at a particular grade level, say eighth year or eleventh. Then interview a student, or several students if possible at that level, and ask them if these topics would be interesting. Summarize your findings in a brief annotation under each topic.
3. Examine four different textbooks such as *Enjoying English, English in Action, Building Better English*, for a particular school year. Make a list of fifteen or twenty specific theme topics suggested, showing what textbooks suggest the ideas. Arrange the theme topics in the order of their interest for the student, as you picture his response.
4. Make a list of theme topics for every two weeks of the school year of a particular grade level, following the idea presented on pp. 32–33. Under each theme topic show why in your opinion the students would respond constructively to the subject you suggest.
5. Read three or four articles in the *English Journal*, among those listed on pp. 33–35 or others of your own choice. Quote a passage from each article and show what constructive idea you derived from it.
6. Ask in your library for the exciting book, *Reading Ladders for Human Relations*, 1963 (American Council on Education, 1785 Massachusetts Ave. N.W., Washington 36, D.C.), by Muriel Crosby and others. How does this book reveal the topics of intense vitality we should be suggesting for high school themes?

Suggested Readings

ANDERSON, LORENA A.: "Ways and Means of Teaching Writing," *English Journal*, Vol. 51 (December, 1962), pp. 621–24

An informative summary of teaching resources used in the junior and senior high schools of Charleston, West Virginia.

BLAISDELL, THOMAS C.: *Ways to Teach English*, Doubleday, 1930.
Suggestive and imaginative experience theme topics, pp. 521–28.

BROWN, FRANCES: "Students Consider Their Futures," *English Journal*, Vol. 39 (November, 1950), pp. 515–17
The use of the student's concern for his future career or vocation to initiate a related series of compositions.

CLARK, HELEN MACDONALD: "Suggestions for Themes," *English Journal*, Vol. 40 (June, 1951), pp. 332–36
A series of related subjects that have been found to be stimulating to the imagination of students.

DOMINCOVICH, H. A.: "Composition in the Short Short," *English Journal* Vol. 30 (April, 1941), pp. 294–98
Description of a carefully worked out plan for developing interest and skill in writing short stories.

FOX, MARJORIE E.: "A Thousand Topics for Composition," *Illinois English Bulletin*, Vol. 39 (December, 1951). Copies from the IATE Treasurer, 109 English Building, Urbana, Illinois.

GROVER, LOUISE ROWLETT: "The Interview Helps the Student," *English Journal*, Vol. 37 (February, 1948), pp. 85–88
How an interview with a person of prominence or interest in the community provides a basis for a series of assignments.

HOARD, JEAN: "An English Workshop in a Wisconsin High School," *English Journal*, Vol. 30 (February, 1941), pp. 154–56
Working with a small class of "B" or "A" students in an intensive writing project, this teacher achieves some rewarding results.

HUSSEY, EDITH L.: "We Plan Together," *English Journal*, Vol. 40 (January, 1951), pp. 16–22
This article contains a detailed description of a growing sequence of topics based upon the actual needs of the students gathered from classroom discussion.

JENKINS, KENNETH D.: "Towards a New Awareness of Creative Writing," *English Journal*, Vol. 54 (January, 1965), pp. 21–22
Fresh and vigorous statement of five fundamental principles.

JOSEPHS, LOIS: "A Disciplined Approach to Creative Writing," *English Journal*, Vol. 51 (October, 1962), pp. 468–73
A suggested progression in terms of proved disciplines, beginning with description of the concrete object and one-paragraph character sketches and going on to forms of exposition.

LOWE, LEE FRANK: "Writers on Learning to Write," *English Journal*, Vol. 53 (October, 1964), pp. 488–95
Questions put to writers with brief but fascinating replies to each query.

Illuminating and unexpected sidelights on the growth of talent in school experience.

MARTIN, HAROLD C., and others: *Freedom and Discipline in English*, Report of the Commission on English, College Entrance Examination Board, 1965 (Princeton, N. J.)

Comments on the teaching of composition based upon countrywide *End-of-Year Examinations for College Bound Students*, Grades 9–12.

POLEY, IRVING C.: "A Spiral Approach to Composition," *English Journal* Vol. 33 (December, 1944), pp. 532–38

A detailed account of a week's preparation for writing a composition. This article should be read carefully by the teacher of composition on any level.

SISTER MARY THEODORA, CSA: "The Daily Writing Assignment," *English Journal*, Vol. 40 (April, 1951), pp. 226–27

The use of the daily "stint" in writing; interesting one-word titles are listed that may prove suggestive.

SMITH, LUJEAN C.: "A Ninth Grade Writing Program," *English Journal*, Vol. 50 (May, 1961), pp. 348, 354

A program woven around the topics, "My Identity," "My Impressions," "My Experiences," "My Achievements," "My Hopes."

Studies in the Teaching of English, *Illinois English Bulletin*, Illinois Association of Teachers of English, May, 1961

Useful and illuminating articles by Chicago teachers in service. In describing an anthology of creative writing gathered from the Chicago public schools, Rita Ellen Hansen writes (p. 35) that the student work reflected the general theme, "A Student Experiences Life," with the following subdivisions:

He grows up.	He appreciates beauty.
He examines the world around him.	He examines the arts.
	He wonders.
He meets many kinds of people.	He loves his country.
He laughs.	He awaits the future.

THOMAS, CHARLES S.: *The Teaching of English*, Houghton Mifflin, 1927

List of over a thousand theme topics, pp. 525–53, divided into suggestive experience categories, including lines of poetry as theme ideas such as "O world, thy slippery turns!"

WOLFE, DON M.: "A Realistic Writing Program for Culturally Diverse Youth," *Improving English Skills of Culturally Different Youth*, U.S. Office of Education, Washington, 1964

WOLFE, DON M., with JOSIE LEWIS and LELA T. HAMILTON: "Making It Come Alive: How to Personify," *Enjoying English 9*, Singer, 1966, pp. 344–50

4 The English Teacher and Student Problems[1]

By Eugene N. Doherty and Don M. Wolfe

EACH OF US is aware of the gap between the literature or grammar we teach and the burning thoughts of the students who face us daily. Each one lives with his own images of *life, love, delight, despair;* lives also with definitions of *happiness* and *ambition.* The lanky boy with legs sprawled in the aisle, gazing intently out the window: perhaps a moving line from *The Red Pony* has turned a key in the lock of his memory, and his anguished mind relives a quarrel with his father or sharp blows with his brother. We may say to ourselves: "What problems are they wrestling with? Are Joe's parents about to separate? Is someone's family hungry? Which student is desperately in love? What student hates school? Does he hate my class, too?" When the teacher in some way can get answers to these questions, he will be better able to bridge the gap between life's stark realities and the often artificial life of the classroom. Of all the keys to eloquent and spontaneous expression, none gives surer release than the conviction that the topic the student is writing about is a burning reality. Moreover, more than any other instructor, the English teacher realizes that the first step to the solution of any problem is tracing its boundaries and meaning for another human being. This chapter is an attempt to show how one resource was used in some ninety classrooms to identify the patterns of deepest feeling most persistent in adolescent life.

[1] My gifted and generous colleague, Mr. Eugene Doherty of the Valley Road School, Princeton, New Jersey, has rewritten this chapter to incorporate and analyze the findings of the 1964 experiment.

Over a decade ago two of my gifted colleagues, Miss Gertrude Unser and Mr. Harold von Arx of Flushing and Bay Ridge High Schools, New York City, asked several of their teachers to cooperate in securing anonymous answers to the problems harassing the students in their classes. The students were asked merely to print or type in sentence form their ten most pressing problems, or, if they preferred, to describe one or more problems in some detail. The teacher asked each student to identify himself merely by sex and age: "Boy, 15" or "Girl, 16." The responses to this request were more frank and explicit than anyone expected. When assured of anonymity the students apparently felt free to unburden their feelings even in an impromptu manner. In the spring and autumn of 1952 the experiment was repeated in thirty classrooms in New York City, Ohio, and Pennsylvania. Some 1,244 students, ranging from fourteen to eighteen years of age, gave responses. The ten most crucial categories thus identified were identified as shown in the chart on page 38.

In 1964 the same experiment was extended to some 1,804 students in sixty-two classrooms of Ohio, Florida, Georgia, Texas, New Jersey, Kentucky, Pennsylvania, Michigan, New Mexico, Arizona, and New York.[2] The 1964 experiment confirmed the

[2] Teachers who have collaborated in the 1964 experiment are: Dr. Andrew J. Beeler, Director, Division of Curriculum, Louisville, Kentucky; Mrs. Mary Anne Reiss, Ahrens Trade High School, Louisville; Miss Betty Miles, Atherton High School, Louisville; Mrs. Alice Baird, Barret Junior High School, Louisville; Mrs. Marie Miller, Eastern Junior High School, Louisville; Mrs. Anne Habich and Mr. Louis J. Torstrick, Manly Junior High School, Louisville; Mr. Frank Ross, Supervisor, Secondary English, Detroit Public Schools, Detroit, Michigan; Mr. Charles Hohner, Chairman, Department of English, Cooley High School, and Miss Wilma Chapin, Cooley High School; Mr. Peter J. McLaughlin, Coffey Junior High School, Detroit; Mr. John White, Grant Junior High School, Detroit; Mr. B. Earl Sloan, Taft Junior High School, Detroit; Mr. Frank A. Doggett, Principal, Duncan U. Fletcher Junior-Senior High School, Jacksonville Beach, Florida, and members of his staff: Mr. Daniel Richardson, Chairman, English Department, Miss Barbara Davies, Mrs. Margery Fouraker, and Mrs. Ann Herlong; Miss Louise Kershner, Glen Rock High School, Glen Rock, New Jersey; Mrs. Jeanette H. Ryan, Chairman, Department of English, New Providence, New Jersey; Mr. Allen R. Kirschner, Chairman, Department of English, Princeton High School, Princeton, New Jersey; Miss Josie Lewis, Bainbridge High School, Bainbridge, Georgia; Sister Mary Austin, Saint Saviour High School, Brooklyn, New York; Mrs. Elaine Berger, Flushing High School, Flushing, New York; Mrs. Ruth Nelson Quinche, Hewlett High School, Hewlett, New York; Mr. John Sanford Joy, Mamaroneck

selection of the ten main categories of student problems identified in the 1952 findings. A comparison of the two experiments, which we feel now should be much more widely extended, appears from the following table:

Ten Categories of Student Problems

1. *School problems:* grades, homework, tests, study habits, impersonal teachers. 1952: 416 students, 33%; 1964: 945 students, 52%.
2. *Family problems:* conflicts with parents, arguments with siblings. 1952: 289 students, 24%; 1964: 929 students, 51%.
3. *Personal problems:* shyness, nervousness, etc. 1952: 295 students, 24%; 1964: 805 students, 45%.
4. *Concern about the future:* college, career, success. 1952: 103 students, 13%; 1964: 451 students, 25%.
5. *Boy-girl relations:* dates, going steady, popularity. 1952: 219 students, 16%; 1964: 401 students, 24%.
6. *Recreation:* leisure time, need for car, sports, etc. 1952: 81 students, 6%; 1964: 318 students, 18%.
7. *Moral issues:* smoking, immorality, purposefulness. 1952: 64 students, 5%; 1964: 236 students, 13%.

High School, Mamaroneck, New York; Miss Francine Fettman, Mount Vernon High School, Mount Vernon, New York; Miss Sara Sherman, Chairman, Department of English, and Mr. Walter Mendoza, Southside High School, Rockville Centre, New York; Mr. Albert Craz, Tarrytown High School, Tarrytown, New York; Mr. Jack Fields, Great Neck High School, Great Neck, New York; Miss Alice Buskirk, Chairman, Department of English, Albuquerque High School, Albuquerque, New Mexico; Mrs. Roberta Redding, Miss Carla Sperling, Highland High School, Albuquerque; Mrs. Elaine Greenspan, Manzano High School, Albuquerque; Mr. Tillman L. Hale, Mrs. Jean Wylder, Sandia High School, Albuquerque; Mrs. Kathryn Hearn and Miss Marion Geesman, Hayes High School, Delaware, Ohio; Mrs. Elba Kerrick, High School Supervisor, Language Arts, El Paso, Texas; Mrs. J. H. Abbey, El Paso High School; Mrs. Jacqueline Brown, Burges High School, El Paso; Miss Lois Grose, Supervisor of Language Arts, Pittsburgh, Pennsylvania; Mrs. Ethel L. Hubbard, Carrick High School, Pittsburgh; Miss Ellen W. Booth, Chairman, Department of English, Miss Dorothy Hill, Mrs. Elaine Cohen, Mr. Carmen Accetta, Mrs. Gladyce Petersen, Mrs. Marva Harris, and Miss Corinne Yoder, Langley High School, Pittsburgh; Mr. Wayne H. Mong, Principal, Peabody High School, Pittsburgh; Mrs. Elizabeth H. Trumbull, Schenley High School, Pittsburgh; Sister Mary Paul Catherine, Rosary College, Mwanza, Tanganyika, Africa; Mr. Edward F. Meany, Sleepy Hollow High School, North Tarrytown, New York.

8. *Money:* financial problems, part-time jobs, etc. 1952: 144 students, 12%; 1964: 264 students, 12%.
9. *Problems of appearance:* complexion, clothes, weight. 1952: 66 students, 5%; 1964: 216 students, 12%.
10. *Fears and restlessness:* death, religion, war, etc. 1952: (as "world tensions"): 66 students, 5%; 1964: 220 students, 13%.

The responses in both surveys were astonishingly frank. Many students remarked, "Writing about my problems and seeing them on paper make them seem less formidable and overwhelming." One eleventh-grade boy, confining himself to one main problem, wrote, "The problem that confronts me daily is getting along with my family and friends. I am the only boy in a family of six. I feel compelled to pretend stoicism and refrain from revealing my true emotions for fear my sisters will notice that I'm no superman, that I'm afraid and weak. I'm in the added dilemma of being a student leader. When conflicts arise between groups, I am fearful of jeopardizing my position or my friendships. I'm never willing to reveal my true self because I feel people would be shocked and disappointed with me. I'm constantly afraid of what others think of me." This statement shows the frankness that generally prevailed in the answers.[3]

One student in two listed a school problem among his most pressing. Of the 858 students commenting about school problems, 199 listed grades as crucial. Time after time the students respond, "Will my grades improve?" Several students noted that parents, teachers, and colleges put so much significance on grades that pressure mounts. One Princeton junior wrote, "I try not to work only for grades, but I've been brainwashed the other way." Other com-

[3] A startling confirmation of the main categories of student problems comes from African girls attending Rosary College, a secondary school in Mwanza, Tanganyika. The teacher is Sister Mary Paul Catherine. "I cannot study hard without despairing," wrote one girl (eighteen). "When I ask pocket money from my father," wrote another, "he never gives it to me. He tells me I am wasting his money. Many times he has told my mother that educating girls is no profit. Therefore I had better stop school and marry." An eighteen-year-old girl wrote: "My parents don't want me to marry somebody outside my tribe." Another: "I have trouble in my heart because my parents do not want me to follow modern civilization." A nineteen-year-old: "I don't know how to choose a future **partner.**"

ments include: "I can't stand the pressure of competition for grades." "Grades are too important. Not enough attention is given to developing the individual." "If I'm to get into college, I have to keep up my grades." "My parents pressure me so much to get high grades I feel I must cheat on tests." Only one student suggested any unfairness in the general grading practices: "An 85% in one room would be 15% lower from my teacher." Homework problems plagues 197 students. Their protests centered around trivial assignments for which the student could comprehend no useful purpose. Several students remarked, "Homework instructions are not exact. The assignment is made as we pass out the door." "Each teacher thinks his subject is the only one and piles on the homework." "Some evenings I have no homework, and others I have so much I cannot finish." "Too many long-range assignments are made at the same time." In 141 responses the students spoke of study-pattern problems. One ninth-grade girl said, "I have poor study habits. I never know what point to emphasize when I study for a test. I get so discouraged when I study hard and then fail because I studied the wrong material." Other school problems dealt with inability to concentrate on subjects, inadequate reference facilities, lack of proper study space at home, and the nuisance of constant interruptions and distractions.

One in two, or 813 students, listed a distressing family problem. Of the 1800 papers, about 561 included inability to communicate with parents. Startling statements like "I hate my father," or "I dislike my mother intensely," occur over and over again. Many students wrote, "My outstanding problem is in the home — maintaining a loving relationship with my mother. My family has no togetherness." Other students commented: "I resent my father's constant constructive criticisms." "My parents are loathe to realize that I've grown up, that I have ideas of my own." "For years I have not been able to bring my problems to my parents." "My father looks at me as though he's ashamed of me, as though I'm stupid." A Pittsburgh sophomore girl wrote, "My parents ask me leading questions when I come home from a date. They don't believe I'm trustworthy." Girls complained of parental interference or strife twice as frequently as boys. In two hundred responses the students spoke of serious domestic problems. "I worry about my father. I don't know how he can stand living with my mother. She treats him like dirt all the time." "My biggest problem is worrying about my father. He has heart trouble and diabetes." A New York girl told of a fear about her mother: "My mother isn't an alcoholic, but two or three times a year she drinks and leaves the house for a month at a time. We don't know where she is or anything about her." Remarks about divorce and separation occur very frequently. "My parents argue constantly and are on the verge of a divorce." "My parents are separated, and carrying on individual relations with each of them is a problem." One senior girl wrote, "My stepfather comes home late at night and quite drunk." A Detroit freshman boy told of severe quarrels between his grandparents: "Grandpa drinks, and Grandma is going to see her lawyer. I feel guilty because my living with them has started the quarreling." Other comments include: "My mother has recently divorced her fourth husband. I love my mother, and I love my father, too. Their problems bother me. I'm forbidden to see my real father." Constant bickering between brothers and sisters was listed as a major problem by many students. Household chores, such as babysitting, housework, and putting younger children to bed were common complaints by girls. One senior wrote, "I'm the oldest of three children. My parents have been divorced since I was six. I have the responsibility of running the household." A sophomore boy said, "I'm continually compared to my nearly perfect brother. When my parents tire of that, they compare me to my friends." A twelfth-grade girl confessed, "My father has a nervous problem, and people laugh at him. I'm terribly embarrassed, and I laugh, too. This makes me feel guilty and disloyal."

Of the 742 students who included personal problems on their lists, 321 set down shyness, lack of confidence, or nervousness as serious problems. Frequently recurring themes are: "I have no confidence in myself." "I'm so shy in the presence of adults I stutter." "How can I be less sensitive to criticism?" "I'm very nervous when I speak before the class." These feelings of personal inadequacy have neither a socioeconomic nor a geographic identity. Students from wealthy urban areas noted concern as frequently as students from rural or economically depressed areas. On seventy-three papers appeared the statement, "I worry about what others think of me." A Princeton junior said, "I play different roles around the school. I wear one face for my teacher, one for my friends, and still another for my parents. None of these is the real me." An Albuquerque senior wrote, "I maintain different images of myself. I never reveal my true self. I'm afraid of what people will think of me." This attempt to swallow oneself in the shadow of conformity has its off-setting faction. In sixty-nine responses students complained of surrendering their individualism. One Long Island senior wrote, "I cannot be myself. My family tries to strangle my independence by telling me what to do, when to do it, and how. People pry into everything that I do. They want to know everything that happens to me." Another wrote, "I am prevented from being myself. I must pretend I am what I am not, and pretend I am not what I really am." The problems of relationships with fellow students was a frequent theme. The problem of getting along with friends was noted by 139 students. "I make cruel remarks and then regret them." "My temper flares up, and I say things I don't mean." "Little things upset me." Concern about having at least one true friend appeared sixty-two times. "I have many acquaintances but no true friend." An Albuquerque student wrote, "Sometimes I think I'll go crazy if I don't talk to someone about my problems." Other personal problems which the students felt were pressing include selfishness, jealousy of classmates with more fashionable clothes or with friendlier personalities, moods of depression, and inarticulateness in mixed groups.

Approximately one student in four expressed a serious concern for the future. In 389 responses, 207 students, primarily boys, expressed worries about college acceptance and successful performance in college after acceptance. Many students had grave doubts that family resources would be adequate to cope with college costs. "Shall I get a scholarship to help finance college?" "Will the college of my choice accept me?" "I've been accepted to Smith, but I worry about the high academic standards." Seniors are deeply concerned about careers after graduation. "Am I too young to decide on a career?" "What jobs are there for teenagers in a small town?" "I've never been good at anything. I've developed no skills in school. What job am I prepared for?" "I've taken only college courses, but I'm not going to college. What kind of job shall I have?

Shall I be able to support a family?" It is remarkable that each student, consciously or not, accepted the blame for poor preparation or poor guidance. Not one paper accused the school, the guidance department, or the parents for the student's dilemma. Several students commented on the irony of being forced to make lifelong decisions at a time in life when the student is least able to decide. One senior put it, "My values and standards are still changing. I don't know what I want in life, what I want to do; but I must make decisions now, and live with them."

Boy-girl friendships were listed by 334 students, or one in five, as depressing problems. In the ninth grade almost all the dating problems were listed by girls. In the upper grades the dominance of girls continued, but not in the same degree. Among the problems listed by boys were the following: "Who should speak first?" "I'm too shy in mixed company. I can never think of anything to say." "I can't tell if it's love or infatuation." "There isn't any place boys and girls can go except to the movies." "I never have enough money for dating." "I don't know how to meet girls. I get tongue-tied in their presence." Girls' responses were far more numerous and surprisingly candid. "I'm worried about moral questions. Is it wrong to French kiss? Should I let a boy kiss me on the first date?" "Finding a boy who respects a girl is quite a problem these days." A sophomore girl said, "I've been going with a boy for three months. Now a girl is interfering. She isn't attractive, but she has a car and takes him where he wants to go." A senior wrote, "I'm looking for a Prince Charming. I'm not in love and I wish I were." Another girl remarked, "I want to truly love someone other than members of my family." Several girls spoke obliquely of sexual dilemmas: "I like a boy very much, but the only girls he likes are those who go all the way. I know I should leave him alone, but I love him too much. What can I do?" Another wrote, "How far should I let my boy friend go? We seem to be quarreling all the time." "What's the difference between a good girl and a bad girl? When does a good girl become a bad girl?" Many girls complained of the difficulty of meeting boys or nervousness in their company. "Whenever I dance with a boy, my hand gets soaking wet." "I lack experience with boys and feel ill at ease with girls who date a lot." "I tend to be always playing a part, an imagined role; and I find it especially difficult to

talk seriously with boys." Several students identified parental interference in boy-girl friendships as disturbing problems. "My parents
object to my dating outside my religion." "Grandma is prejudiced
against my boy friend's nationality and forbids me to see him."
"My parents ask me questions after every date. I'm sure they don't
trust me." "My boy friend's parents have forbidden him to see me
anymore because of my mother's drinking."

Only 257 students, one in six, felt recreation time a serious
problem. Of this number 226 students, predominantly boys, were
disturbed by the lack of time to do anything but school work. One
junior said, "I feel frustrated by the lack of free time. Homework
takes up my week nights, and weekends seem too short to accomplish anything. I love music, but I can't spare the time to practice.
I would like to write stories or see plays, but I simply cannot afford
the time." Another student complained, "Trivial assignments take
up all my time. I can never read the books that I want to read."
Other comments include: "School is not the only laboratory for
learning." "My most serious problem is finding more hours in the
day without endangering my health." "I have no time for visiting
museums, walking in the woods, reading for pleasure, or working
on my hobby." A Detroit boy wrote, "The best media for learning
is living, but the mountains of homework prevent me from engaging
in any activity other than school work." A number of boys complained of car problems. "I'm old enough to get my license, but
I'm not allowed to drive." "I wish I had a car of my own." Less than
ten students listed after-school sports as a problem, though one
junior wrote, "Playing football drains my energy. When I get home
I'm very tired, but I must begin my homework." Another boy confessed, "I had to prove to myself I wasn't chicken; so I went out for
football. I made the team, but I didn't play often."

A surprising number of students, 228, or one in eight, commented on moral issues. The problem of smoking ranked approximately equal to concern about world politics. Several students
wrote, "I know I shouldn't smoke, but I can't break the habit."
A Louisville girl said, "My mother feels my friends are wild because
they smoke." Many students remarked that they felt out of place
in a group because they did not smoke. A tenth-grade boy, reflecting
recent health campaigns, said, "I like to smoke, but now I'm worried

about lung cancer. I don't smoke to act big; just to calm my nerves when my family drives me crazy." Both boys and girls indicated concern about world politics. "The image of America throughout the world worries me." "I am disturbed by the attitude of other nations toward our nation." In twenty-eight responses students mentioned worries about racial discrimination. Not one student in the eight states polled advocated continuance of segregation. A Pittsburgh girl wrote, "I am confused about racial discrimination. We all live by the same basic code. Why should color make a difference?" Several students, but only girls, noted a growing evidence of moral decay in school and society. "The *Adults Only* signs never keep kids away from sex pictures." "Everyone is obsessed by sex." Cheating, stealing, lying, gambling, or deceiving one's parents were not listed as problems by boys or girls. Many students regarded acquiring a more mature philosophy of life, a genuine purposefulness, as their most crucial problem.

Money problems were listed by 216 students, or one in eight, as pressing dilemmas. Wealthy urban areas as well as rural and economically depressed areas felt the press of finances. Girls were essentially concerned with family finances, not personal. "My father works two jobs, but we still have to struggle to make ends meet." "I know that my parents cannot afford to send me to college." "My father has not worked in nineteen months. No money is coming in except when my mother sells a painting." "My parents are both ill, and Dad's business is in bankruptcy." Boys were primarily concerned with their own personal financial dilemmas. "I don't know how I will get money to repair the car." "I never have enough money for dates." "I find living in a wealthy community is very difficult when my father's income barely permits us to exist." "Where can I find a summer job?" "I must work after school to bring money home." A senior boy wrote, "My family's financial situation makes me feel guilty to spend money except for absolute necessities." A number of students, both boys and girls, complained of the scarcity of jobs, whether after school or during the summer.

Appearance, though a problem to only one in eight, was regarded as critical by the 211 students who listed it, especially girls. In seventy-five responses the students were worried about being overweight; only twelve students thought they were too thin. "I cannot seem to lose weight." "Those extra ten pounds worry me." Boys as well as girls listed complexion problems in twenty-eight responses. One eleventh-grade girl wrote, "When I have an important date, my skin is certain to break out."

An unusual number of students were beset by disturbing fears, doubts, and anxieties. They felt a confusion and restlessness and a seeming inability to cope with their fears. One senior girl wrote, "On cold dark nights I look at the stars and wonder if we are the only humans in the universe. I'm afraid." In 167 responses, or one in twelve, the students had serious questions about God, religion, or a life after death. A New York boy wrote, "My mother grew seriously ill and I found myself questioning God's existence and the usefulness of prayer. I'm afraid that I'm losing my faith." Another student said, "My mother and father are not religious, but I want to join a church. I'm afraid to speak to them about it." "Is there a God? A life after death?" Many students included anxieties about identifying themselves with some purposefulness or utility in life. One senior boy stated, "I'm worried because the little fruits of this wretched life disgust me." Other students included: "Depression creeps into my life whenever the going gets tough." "I'm terribly inconsistent. I hold a position of leadership; yet I'm disorganized and fearful of making errors. I must learn to analyze more deeply."

How Can the English Teacher Help?

In coping with the manifold problems described on the preceding pages, the high school student needs first of all the opportunity for writing and speaking. Only by describing his problem and citing dramatic moments in which it harassed him most intensely, can a boy or girl be expected to objectify his experience. Among all his instructors, only the English teacher has the opportunity and the equipment to elicit this first step toward a mature self-analysis.

In initiating such a search for problem realities, the teacher may well ask the class for anonymous typed or printed statements such as those which formed the basis for the present investigation. Problems thus identified may then be presented anonymously for discussion by the class or by panels of five or six students each. The ideal problem for such a discussion is one besetting many members of the class — not one or two only — such as, "After graduation, should I get a job or try to go to college?" Or: "When you like a girl or boy who doesn't like you, what is a mature way to cope with the problem?" Discussions of such questions will almost invariably help the individuals in the class to grapple more constructively with their own particular problems. Furthermore, such class discussions lead to many fruitful conversations among friends outside of class.

After identification of several main problems in generalized form the teacher may then call for personalized descriptions of problem moments written in vivid concrete language. In this assignment no embarrassment need arise for this reason: Each student is permitted to select his own problem which may be humorous, superficial, or profound. If any student wishes to avoid a boy-girl problem, a family problem, a deep-seated fear or anxiety, he is free to do so and concentrate on less dangerous ground.

It may well be asked, "As fascinating as these problems are in themselves, why should the English teacher deal with them at all? Are they not the problem of the counselor or the school psychologist?" To this I would reply that as English teachers we have not fully realized either our usefulness to our students or our own feeling of creative labor until we have invited from each student an expression of his feelings on topics that call upon him to trace the roots of his personality, his obstacles, his conflicts, his values. Not until we as English teachers fulfill this aim will our students enrich their themes with the whole range of personality in the same way that each great author of English or American literature has unfolded to his readers some of his most crucial conflicts and ideas.

The mere self-listing of student problems shows the tremendous gap that exists between the invitations to write and speak in the English class and the problem realities of each individual student. Each student has a right to expect that he can write or speak about some uprooting realities of his life for this reason: Until he traces the conflicts that torture his mind and drain his emotional energy, he has not realized the writing power and talent of which he is capable. When Emerson said, "Every man is eloquent once in his life," he was too restrictive of man's creative energies. Were he alive today, he might well change his dictum to read: "Every man is eloquent each time he speaks from a deep cavern of himself as if to his only trusted friend." Until American English teachers assume, then, a responsibility for finding out the deep-running problems, fears, and obstacles of each student and encourage him to express his feelings as freely as he can about each one, the student cannot find the natural level of his writing power nor make the first crucial step toward the mature answers to the questions that rack his brain and plague his sleepless hours.

To the Student Teacher: Suggested Activities

1. From the chapter you have just read copy ten or twelve statements by high school students that you feel represent their most pressing problems. Show these statements to a high school friend and ask him to comment on each problem. Which ones are most crucial for him? Which are only incidental?
2. Ask a teacher in your community to perform the experiment described on p. 46 and give you permission to examine the anonymous answers. The class should be one you have reason to know is responsive and sympathetic to the teacher. Observe the class as the teacher performs the experiment. If the teacher is willing you may wish to present the suggestions to the class yourself, but normally a class will be more responsive to a teacher they know well. Write a report in which you show what the particular problems are in this classroom and grade level. Other members of your class may suggest the same experiment to teachers of other grade levels.
3. Write a theme describing a persistent problem you grappled with in high school. Describe one moment in which the problem was most painful or baffling. Round out the moment with many images.

Suggested Readings

ARBUCKLE, DOUGALD S.: "Can English Teachers Be Counselors?" *English Journal,* Vol. 42 (December, 1953), pp. 490–96
> Because he knows his students, the English teacher can be a uniquely useful counselor.

BURTON, DWIGHT L.: "Books to Meet Students' Personal Needs," *English Journal,* Vol. 36 (November, 1947), pp. 469–73
> The relation of the home problems of the students to their school work. Contains a useful list of student home problems as well as a list of novels centered about these problems.

ELKINS, DEBORAH: "Students Face Their Problems," *English Journal* Vol. 38 (November, 1949), pp. 498–503
> Description of an experiment in the use of literature to help students

come to terms with their own problems. Useful list of helpful books appended.

FINDER, MORRIS: "Teaching English to Slum-dwelling Pupils," *English Journal*, Vol. 44 (April, 1955), pp. 199–204

A program of stimulating learning experiences in literature, language study, speaking and writing particularly appealing and meaningful to slum-dwelling students.

GESELL, ARNOLD, ILG, FRANCES L., and AMES, LOUISE BATES: *Youth. The Years from Ten to Sixteen*, Harper and Brothers, 1956

See "Wishes and Inclinations," ages 14–16, pp. 374–75; "Self-Evaluation," ages 14–16, pp. 370–71; "Father-Child," ages 14–16, pp. 398–400.

GILLESPIE, CLARE M. and ZLOTNIK, HAROLD: "What Makes Me Tick? A Unit in Attitudes," *English Journal*, Vol. 40 (September, 1951), pp. 374–78

How, by working with the guidance department of a large high school, theme writing was used effectively to clarify student problems.

Intergroup Relations in Teaching Materials, American Council on Education, 1948

Analysis of problems related to various ethnic, racial, and religious groups in American society today. Excellent list of teaching materials in history, geography, citizenship, literature, and reading.

LABRANT, LOU: *We Teach English*, Harcourt, Brace, 1951

Chapter II, pp. 171–89. Here the problem of teacher-student relations is analyzed with much insight.

MARSH, PHILIP M.: "Simplifying and Humanizing English Composition," *English Journal*, Vol. 29 (December, 1940), pp. 819–25

Excellent practical suggestions about making friends with students by means of composition assignments.

MINTON, ARTHUR C.: "Thinking-Composition," *English Journal*, Vol. 40 (January, 1951), pp. 7–11

The use of themes about problems bearing on personal ethics and responsibility.

PEEL, LEE S.: "The Teen-Ager Looks at Himself," *English Journal*, Vol. 42 (November, 1953), pp. 459–60

A striking unit: a class divided itself into committees to poll student opinion on teen-age problems and then write lucid reports of its findings.

SHELLHAMMER, LOIS B.: "Solving Personal Problems Through Sociodrama," *English Journal*, Vol. 38 (November, 1949), pp. 503–05

How to act out situations or problems in the classroom to clarify the conflicts involved.

WHITFIELD, RUTH M.: "The Therapeutic Value of Letter-Writing," *English Journal*, Vol. 33 (November, 1944), pp. 489–91

The author tells of a letter-writing experiment in which the student presents his problems to the class.

5 For Better Themes: Student Models Point the Way

WHETHER WE ENJOY the hours we spend each week on student themes depends entirely upon the depth of experience and the intensity of language the students use in their papers. For the teacher who says, "I dread to mark themes; they are so dull," there is only one answer: a collection of dull themes is almost never the fault of the students. An alert, sympathetic teacher can insure himself against this kind of boredom and drudgery. The more time we give to the writing assignment proper, preparing the student emotionally for his task, showing in detail the ways and means of handling his topic, etc., the more likely we are to enjoy the hours spent with class themes. The questions arise, then, "How can I inspire my students to write themes that I will read eagerly? How can I bring themes to my desk each week that will make me feel closer to my students, help me to understand them, achieve a rapport with each boy or girl?" The one certain way to accomplish this is to motivate the writing of student papers by the reading and discussion of student themes. When you and I read a student theme to the class, we must ask them to discuss its most arresting sentences; we must ask them, "What kind of boy or girl wrote this theme?" We arouse interest with the mere knowledge that this is a student theme, not a literary model impossible of imitation.

Theme on Personality

To be specific and practical, let us examine a student paper and show how it would be presented to a class of juniors or seniors. The topic assigned for discussion and writing is "My Disposition." As we open up this subject to the class, we may ask, "What trait of yours do you feel makes you a little different from all other boys and girls of your type?" We may show the kinds of topic sentences other boys and girls in years past have used to open their themes. These sentences in themselves show the rich variety of topics and how these topics may be narrowed. At the same time, reading these topic sentences to the class will call to mind almost at once sentences that the students may use about themselves. In the topic sentences below the italicized words are those that express the key impression of one element of personality:

I take myself *too seriously*.
I am *orderly* to the point of exasperation.
I am a *happy-go-lucky* fellow.
I *lose* my *temper* quickly.
Little things *discourage* me.
I wish I were a less *reticent* person.
The things I like best are the *sparkling* things.
I am too *frank*.
Everyone, they say, has an *inferiority complex*, but mine takes peculiar forms.
A dog's antics always *delight* me.
I am *superstitious*.
I have a lot of *determination*.
I am happiest when I can make people *laugh*.
When I am overwrought, music is a wonderful *medicine* for me.
I am a *loyal* friend.

Class Criticism of a Student Model

After reading these topic sentences to the class, we may say, "Now I wish to read a theme to illustrate this assignment. Years ago there was a girl in my class named Sophia Polovina. She was a talented and charming girl. After you have heard this paper, I would like you to give me your impressions of Sophia. Is she really as lacking in sensitivity as she says?" Then we may read Sophia's paper as follows:

SENSITIVITY

Sensitivity, my childhood companion that sulked when teased, wept bitterly when insulted or belittled, grew angry at trivial injuries and grieved at others' misfortunes, is dead. I remember a time when I stormed and fussed over a ten-cent purple comb that Nicky used for the knotted shag of White-Paw, his six-months-old puppy; but two months ago, looking upon a memento of a classmate who died of meningitis, a never-used white linen handkerchief now black-blotched with iodine, I was calm. There was a time when I would have stamped with rage, fumed, and missed several meals at such a sight, but I did not even inquire who the vandal had been. I recall vividly my thirteenth birthday when in self-pity I locked my bedroom door and, holding my breath valiantly, longed for death because Papa had not brought the fiery red satin gown that he had faithfully promised me three weeks before. But how lightly I bear the expected broken promises of today! I remember how my nose pinched, my lower lip quivered, the tears burned my eyes the day my civics teacher gave me an "E" for misbehavior. Today I am so unaffected when an instructor criticizes my work as "flamboyant and insincere," that I can even muster a lukewarm smile. Last week I chanced upon a seventh-grade schoolmate who disclosed to me the brutishness of her husband. How hard and unsympathetic she must have thought I was in my response! But her troubles stirred no emotion within me; I knew that many a man cruelly beats his wife. And I remember many times shuddering at poverty as it clung to a lean hungry man who stared with listless but longing eyes at store windows. I remember hurriedly covering my eyes and accusing God at the sight of a legless man wheeling his way through a crowd of his indifferent, hustling fellow-men. Now, accustomed to pitiful misfortunes, I accept them as common patterns woven into life. Not even the sight, last week, of a dead, black-striped kitten, its sunken belly bathed in blood turned black in the snow, moved me to quick pity. Having lost my sensitivity through surfeit, I am like a clam which when irritated strikes not, but recoils within its protective crust.

Sophia Polovina

After reading this paper to the class and repeating our question, "Has Sophia lost her sensitivity?" we have various answers. Some believe she was only fooling herself, that in reality she has not lost her sensitivity. Others may point to the image of the dead kitten to show that she is still extremely sensitive. Still other students may say that she is only protecting herself against being hurt. Then we may ask the class if it is necessary as each person grows older that he make himself to some extent immune to the suffering that he sees around him. A drunken man lies on the subway steps. In New York most people pass by him with no more than a glance. A man has a heart attack, lies on the sidewalk at two in the morning. In any big city many people pass him by. As we grow older, we see much suffering that we cannot relieve. What would happen if we tried to help everyone who needs help or everyone who is sick or has had an accident? Why do we not stop for people whose cars have broken down? Sophia's problem is not a unique one. It is only that she has expressed her problem in a unique way with images that no one else would use.

Variety in Mood and Appeal

Perhaps only a few people in the class, however, will want to write a theme as serious and searching as that of Sophia. When we read student models to the class, we need to present a variety of both technique and mood. If we read a whimsical, humorous theme on disposition, we shall encourage the students who are gifted with a whimsical or humorous vein to express themselves. For our own well-being, we teachers need the tonic of humor as we read our papers each week. The class needs to hear them, too, when we hand back their papers. A humorous model, then, helps to give variety to the response of the class. It provides a cushion, a relief against too serious a class mood. The following theme on disposition is whimsical and humorous. That it was written by a boy is an advantage to class morale. Each time we shall we wise to read models appealing to both boys and girls.

JUST OLD TENNIS SHOES

I shall always remember what chums my old tennis shoes were to me. The minute we were released from school, I would rush home to put on my old clothes and sneakers. Putting on these old gym shoes boosted my spirits and self-confidence sky-high, made me sure-footed, sure of myself, even cocky. Let me explain. It is a great feeling to run at a mile-a-minute clip, then with a shriek of tortured rubber, to stop triumphantly on a dime. Say, no right-minded boy would think of robbing old Mr. Gerlensmicher's grape arbor wearing stiff, unyielding leather shoes. No, Sirree! If you dared to walk under the window where Mr. Gerlensmicher sat with a shotgun full of rock salt, would you do it in leather shoes? Well, not any of the boys I know would; but if you had tennis shoes on, then you could take that dare. That's why buying a pair of tennis shoes would always bring a catch to my throat. After all, the old pair had been on so many glorious escapades with me that the idea of replacing them with a new uninitiated pair saddened me. Nevertheless, I would look forward to the purchase of a new pair of tennis shoes far more than I would to the purchase of a new suit. Anybody can have a new suit, but to have a pair of shoes that understand your every move — well, that is something. Like every real boy, I had an admiration for athletic prowess. The association between sports and tennis shoes is very close; this is another reason for believing that the wearing of tennis shoes is symbolic of red-blooded youth. I still retain my love for my old sneakers; I think that love will be part of the bubbling joys of my boyhood memories. If ever you want to put me into a mellow mood, just bring out a pair of my old tennis shoes. Dirty, odorous, and filled with holes, they could tell many a story. But like true pals, they don't.

Ben Hild

The selection below is well liked for its series of humorous images:

THINGS I DISLIKE

Things displeasing to me are: the sun shining in my eyes when I awaken; three or four stations at once on a radio; the change in a person's voice when he uses a telephone; fried halibut; the harsh hungry cheeping of birds on a cold winter day; the number three; the manner in which men chew gum and look self-conscious at parties and dances; a person who shakes my hand, says "Hello," and then can't remember my name; walking downhill; the sound of steel guitars; detective stories; the hypocritical welcome in church of a person who does not speak to me six days of the week; children reciting or performing; any speaker who talks more than thirty minutes; large, thick-lipped mouths; the use of bright finger-nail dyes by women; and, finally, the way trousers stick to a seat in a warm theater.

Thomas Mitchell

Another fruitful model for the theme on disposition is one presenting a series of sights and sounds suggestive of one mood, as illustrated in these topic sentences, in each of which the italicized word shows the key impression to be supported in the paragraph:

Some sounds *grate* on my nerves.
The sounds I *like* are the tinkling sounds.
My *favorite* color is yellow.
I *like* loose-fitting clothes.

The things I *like* best are the quiet things.
I *like* maple wood.

Below is a model to illustrate images of sight and sound. Though written by a college student, it has marked literary value. A theme of literary power is expected now and then in the upper high-school years, and especially from a class of gifted students. Nevertheless, this theme is well liked and appreciated by all levels of students. The use of sights and sounds in a series, all blending into one mood, forms a fruitful class experiment.

QUIET THINGS

The things I like best are quiet things. First there is the quietness of the sky at night over Duna, purple in the winter and apple green in the summer; twilight with its haze of gray and stars that push through the dark with steady yellow light; the quiet of two cypresses opposite my window; willows dripping after a rainstorm; smoke from chimney tops, and blue wood smoke of campfires in the fall; our old hall clock that is wound too tightly to run; fog over the city; pools of water where pebbles and white sand show through a span of reflected sky; leaves flitting down from maples when there is not any wind; sheep that browse on a distant hillside; two kittens asleep in a basket of hay; the sound of somebody's breathing at night; an old man in a doorway, sifting sunlight through his knotted fingers; afternoons in August when piles of feathery clouds trail shadows over the hills; the quiet of my grandmother's hands; Badger, our St. Bernard, stretched full-length on the sunny lawn; a house where someone has died; moonlight shadows on my bedroom floor; trampled grass; the broken stems of tall white daisies; day dreams, wistful and impossible; the lights in one of Whistler's Nocturnes; locusts buzzing in the alley behind our house; a ridge of straight dark pines against the sky; my nephew asleep among his toys on the floor; some violets; dust motes floating in a bar of sunlight; myths of Arcadia, and Pan piping strange music by a riverside; a cherry tree snowy white in Uncle Jim's orchard; the faded photographs in our family Bible; the *Faerie Queene*, full of slow rhythm and rich imaginings; a set of dust-covered harness on the granary door. These are only some of the quiet things I like.

University of Pittsburgh, *Student Themes*

In reading this paper to the class, we may say, "What kind of person is the writer? How do these images suggest his personality? Which image to your mind is most revealing of one aspect of his disposition?" We may suggest to the class that no two people beginning with this same topic sentence would select the same images to dramatize their conception of "Quiet Things." Similarly, no two people who like yellow things, brown things, sparkling things, or golden things would select from the life around them the same images to support their impressions of themselves. This is why a series of images reflects uniqueness of personality. On the technical side we may point out in "Quiet Things" that many of the images contain rather exact place words which help us to visualize the object. For example, it is not only the sky at night but it is "the sky at night over Duna;" it is not only the two cypresses but it is "the two cypresses opposite my window;" it is not only a clock but it is "our old hall clock." Any word which makes an image more exact or complete makes it more appealing to the reader and reflects more fully the individuality of the writer. For example, the writer does not write merely "leaves flitting down" but "leaves flitting down from maples when there is not any wind."

To ask each member of the class to write even a very short theme using only images of sight, sound, or color as a prelude to the longer theme on disposition is very helpful as an extension of our training in sensory language and, incidentally, of the class' appreciation of the technical aspects of literary style. The best path to appreciation of literature is not the study of literature *per se:* it is the experience of communicating one's expressions of life with the *same means* the author uses, i.e., with one's own unique images, that makes the machinery of literary power and insight come alive.

The Play of Imagination: Personification

The younger the student, the more delight he takes in personification, wherein lies the continuing charm of all animal cartoons of the *Alice in Wonderland* and Walt Disney tradition. Most adults, indeed, have a childlike side which makes a theme on personification appealing to them as well. To assign a ninth-grade class a theme on personification, we may first read and discuss such a model as "A Blinker," on page 29.

In discussing this theme, we may say, "How does the author weave in motion, time, and place? Do time and place help to make this story real? What is the effect of using such proper names as

Fifth Avenue, Hermes, Lincoln?" We may point out Curtis' images of person, images of action, the effective bit of dialogue. As we discuss the theme, we may list on the board the virtues we seek in the class' papers, such as:

1. Specific mention of time and place.
2. A bit of monologue: inanimate object speaking.
3. Images of action: "ashes fly out behind."
4. Images of person: "red headed chap."
5. Humorous touches: "one of my brothers . . . now blinking again."
6. Lively ending: "Blink! Blink!"

Introducing a Mood Sketch

In introducing a mood sketch, we may read a theme like the following, which traces the thoughts and feelings of the writer over a period of several minutes. In "Six O'clock" William Leigh communicates his feelings mainly by suggestion through the use of images. In the mood sketch we have two worlds, the internal world of the writer and the external world in which the thoughts took place. William Leigh makes the external world so real with sights and sounds that it easy for the reader to imagine his feelings. It is impossible to suggest the technique of writing a mood sketch except by use of a pupil model that the students feel is not too far removed from their own potential achievement.

SIX O'CLOCK

It is six o'clock in the morning. Another night of work is over. How strange the silence is to my ears, after listening to the roar of machines and the crash of steel for eight hours. The *snap, bang, bang* of the shears still resound dully within my aching head. Slowly we stumble out through the steel shop into the welding room. Our footsteps echo hollowly amid the now quiet machines. Those electric welders, whose iron tongues were spitting out flaming sparks a short ten minutes ago, are now cold and silent. Overhead the pale dawn shines dimly through the grimy skylights. My feet feel like leaden weights, my eyes burn, my head bobs wearily up and down, my shoulders ache. Slowly we trudge down the long sloping hall by the office. Those posters on the wall. How gaudy, how futile they look now! They read, "Taxes on your bread," "Safety-First Week." Who the hell cares about taxes and safety at six in the morning? The door swings open on creaking hinges. A breath of cool sweet air brushes against my hot cheek. It feels like the refreshing touch of spring water upon a dusty throat. I'm tired, so tired. Bed will feel like heaven today. The door bangs shut after me, bringing a feeling of quiet relief. We hasten across the drive, our feet making crunching sounds amid the black ashes. Into the office we pour. Where's my card? Four fifty-nine, four five nine. Ah, there it is. Bong, bong, bong. There goes the hurried ring of the time clock. It swallows our cards, punches them, and vomits them out in a split second. It's my turn now: *bong.* One minute after six. I shove it quickly into the box on the night shift board. I say, "Mornin', Dutch," to the watchman, and hustle out the gate. Free at last! It feels good, climbing the long ash hill toward home and rest. Five minutes after six, and the sun shoving his flaming head over the foggy hills. Another weary night is over.

William Leigh, Jr.

A Theme about Family

To invite worthwhile themes about family life, we need to pierce very deep into the consciousness of the class. In order to show what haunting reality is possible in a theme like this, our main resource is a pupil theme. Here are two pupil models, one serious and one whimsical.

DESERT OF SILENCE

I do not know my family. Day after day, year after year we live under the same roof; but beyond the barest fundamentals of companionship, my family and I are total strangers. They do not think as I, nor do they know what I think. And neither they nor I seem to care. We plan and live without each other, our paths coinciding only by chance. In times of stress alone do we join, and then briefly; our mutual interests soon vanish, and unity recedes into the shadows. . . . This state of affairs has not mushroomed out overnight; rather, it has grown like the giant black oak, slowly but inexorably. As I write this, I find myself wondering what caused this schism in a bond that should be so utterly firm and complete. There can be only one reason: Silence. Forbidding and bleak it rose between us, built layer on layer of suppressed emotions and welded with unspoken thoughts. Perhaps the family too wonders what has happened; but I do not know, for they never tell. If we had shared our hopes, dreams, and ambitions long ago, we might not be stranded in this emotional desert. But then I was too shy to make advances; now I am too proud. In our family, however, pride has been less terrible than indifference. Long ago one kind word or act might have spanned the gulf, but because no attempt was ever made we drifted apart like similar poles repelling each other, dimly realizing what was happening, at first not daring to act, and finally not caring. . . . Our destinies, like parallel lines, run side by side, never meeting. As far as the eye can see, they do not join; but the eye cannot see into infinity. . . .

John Harbison

MY FATHER'S PIPE

My father's pipe is an unerring barometer of his moods. Smudged with brown stains and gnarled by his constant chewing, it is not attractive except in Dad's mouth, where it assumes wonderfully varied positions. When he is happy, it bobs up and down like a buoy at sea, short, decisive puffs of smoke shooting from the bowl. Without looking, I know that my father's face is relaxed in a broad grin. After a good meal of his favorite dish, baked macaroni, his pipe assumes a new angle, sagging droopingly from the corner, sending toward the ceiling long slow streams of smoke. Occasionally when in this mood my father removes his pipe and scans it in a quizzical, loving manner. When my father is angry, however, his pipe juts out taut and firm between his teeth; now and then it jerks up and down, spilling ashes over the wide expanse of his vest. Short nervous puffs rise from the bowl; large swirls of smoke stream from his mouth, reminding me of the legendary fire-spouting dragons of fairy-tale lore. After a tiresome day at the office my father's pipe suggests a weary spirit and exhausted body. Then it remains stationary in his mouth, puffs of smoke streaming out at long intervals. Very often the pipe goes out, and my father reaches wearily into his wrinkled pants pocket for a match. Yes, whatever his mood, there is no surer indicator than that battered old briar from which he derives daily pleasure.

John Rutledge

*   *   *

The student theme is a priceless resource in the teaching of writing. For motivation that brings to our desk themes brimming over with life's intensity, humor, and pathos, it is indeed the only indispensable resource. By means of the student theme we pierce deep into the lives of the class before us. We show by reading a student theme not only that we understand their problems and feelings. We also show that other students like themselves have been willing to set down in vivid form not the flimsy and superficial experiences usually reserved for school compositions but rather those indelible experiences reserved for one's close friends. The use of such pupil themes very often shapes a class into a community of mind and spirit, a class in which friends become accustomed to speaking freely and easily to each other. When students see that other boys and girls before them have opened deep recesses within themselves, they find it easy to break the habit of schoolroom reticence. Furthermore, even the reading of a pupil model inspires discussion which in itself must evoke expressions of profound meaning for the class. The more discussion of student models flowing from such comments and questions, the richer and more profound will be the themes of the class.

Gradually, then, each teacher of English must build for herself a reserve of student models cherished year after year, models which she knows will bring yet more splendid papers to her desk. Gradually each teacher forms a habit of speaking a little about the student who wrote this theme maybe last year, two years ago, or five years in the past. These student themes are the most treasured resource of the English teacher who looks forward each week to reading her papers, knowing that each will be a further revelation of a unique boy or girl.

To the Student Teacher: Suggested Activities

1. Read several student themes in a high school literary magazine or in books such as *University of Pittsburgh: Student Themes; Give Me a Pen; Pupils Are People; Young Voices; They All Want to Write;* or *The Freshman and His World*, by Don M. Wolfe, Ruth Firor, and Thomas Donahue (Stackpole, 1954). Copy one of these student themes on your paper. Then show in a critique of this theme why in your opinion it would bring a response from the class level of your choice. What quality does it have that would make it more appealing than professional writing?

2. Read a portion of a book of autobiographical writing, such as *The First Years*, edited by Theodore Baird, or one of the following:

   Experiment in Autobiography, by H. G. Wells
   Autobiographies, by William Butler Yeats
   The Harbor, by Ernest Poole
   Pioneer's Progress, by Alvin Johnson
   Look Homeward, Angel, by Thomas Wolfe
   Autobiography of Lincoln Steffens
   My Experiments with Truth, by Mahatma Gandhi

   What story or passage in your book appealed to you especially as being the closest in style to student writing? Copy a passage of two or three hundred words and read it to your teaching-of-English class. Show why in your opinion this short selection would be appealing to high school students. See then if your judgment is verified by class discussion of the selection you have read.

Suggested Readings

A Student Experiences Life, published by Chicago Public Schools (1961). Copies available from Taft High School, 5605 N. Natoma, Chicago 31, Illinois.

Vital student expression some of which shows explosive development of writing power.

BARNES, RUTH M.: "An Approach to Composition in the High School," *English Journal*, Vol. 35 (November, 1946), pp. 483–86

This article contains some arresting, lively examples of student autobiographical writings.

Best High School Writing, Scholastic Corporation, Dayton, Ohio, 1941

Invaluable collection of prize stories, poems, essays, autobiographical sketches, humor, by the winners of *Scholastic* awards.

BURROWS, ALVINA T., et al., *They All Want to Write: Written English in the Elementary School*, rev. ed., Prentice-Hall, 1952

Full of timely suggestions for the teaching of writing on every level.

CROSS, E. A. and CARNEY, ELIZABETH, *Teaching English in High Schools*, Macmillan, 1950.

See pp. 515–30 for useful pupil poems and themes.

Evaluating Twelfth-Grade Themes, Illinois English Bulletin, April, 1953

Twenty senior themes analyzed and evaluated. Invaluable suggestions. Order from NCTE.

From Chicago: A Student Experiences Life, Chicago Board of Education, 1961

An unusually rich anthology of student writing from Chicago high schools. The book is divided into such sections as "He Grows Up," "He Examines the World Around Him," "He Meets Many Kinds of People," "He Laughs," "He Appreciates Beauty," etc. Write to Miss Rita Hansen, Taft High School, 5605 N. Natoma, Chicago 31, Illinois.

Give Me a Pen, Publication 608, Los Angeles Public Schools, 1956

Lively pupil writings, mainly poems, from the second grade to the twelfth.

KLEIN, ANNA LOU: "Expository Writing for Amateurs," *English Journal*, Vol. 53 (January, 1964), pp. 16–22

Note the use of concrete illustrations and concrete details for developing exposition. Some critics have the false impression that images are not used to develop exposition.

MIRRIELEES, LUCIA B.: *Teaching Composition and Literature in Junior and Senior High School*, Harcourt, Brace, 1952, pp. 623–48

Excellent appendix of pupil themes and poems.

Rhyme and Reason, Poetry Written by Boys and Girls in the Elementary Grades, Louisville, 1953–54

A delightful and suggestive compilation. For a copy of this booklet, address Miss Bonnie C. Howard or Miss Mary Browning, Louisville Public Schools, Louisville, Kentucky.

ROUNDS, ROBERT W.: "Creative Writing and Living Language," *English Journal*, Vol. 31 (June, 1942), pp. 454–62
How to develop a feeling for words through creative compositions. Interesting examples of students' work.

"Some of the Best Illinois High School Prose of 1960," *Illinois English Bulletin* (April, 1961), 109 English Building, Urbana, Illinois.

"Some of the Best Illinois High School Prose of 1962," *Illinois English Bulletin* (April, 1963). Copies from the IATE Treasurer, 109 English Building, Urbana, Illinois.

STAPP, HELEN I., and others: *Teaching Aids in the English Language Arts, Illinois English Bulletin*, Vol. 50 (February, 1963)
Descriptions of several hundred useful resources for the English teacher. This book is a service of distinction to the profession. Address: IATE Treasurer, 109 English Building, Urbana, Illinois.

Student Themes, edited by Percival Hunt, University of Pittsburgh, 1942
One of a series of collections formerly used by all freshman classes at the University of Pittsburgh. Distinguished student writing in expository and creative form, many of them showing genuine literary power.

Student Writer, monthly publication devoted expressly to student writing. Each issue contains student stories, poems, and articles, as well as essays on the teaching of writing by experienced teachers. Address: 2651 N. Federal Highway, Fort Lauderdale, Florida

WEBSTER, EDWARD HARLAN and SMITH, DORA V.: *Teaching English in the Junior High School*, World Book, 1927
Strikingly good examples of models from professional writers, with analysis of qualities appealing to boys and girls, pp. 128–44. Pupil models, pp. 348–63.

WOLFE, DON M., with LELA HAMILTON, DON F. MAHAN, EUGENE DOHERTY, BETTY MILES, JOSIE LEWIS, and RUTH NELSON, *Enjoying English, 7–12*, 1966

Young Voices, A Quarter Century of High School Writing Selected from the *Scholastic* Awards, ed. Kenneth M. Gould and Joan Coyne, Harper, 1945
An invaluable collection of student writing selected from *Saplings*, an annual volume containing the *Scholastic* Awards (1926 to 1941), and *Best High School Writing* (1941).

6 The Art of Seeing:
Training the Five Senses

TEACHING A STUDENT how to use sensory language is to some of us the most economical and rewarding of all activities in the teaching of English. What magic color and sound and image perform for the moving picture, sensory words accomplish for language. As Conrad wrote, "My task which I am trying to achieve is, by the power of the written word to make you hear, to make you feel — it is, before all, to make you see." A single page of Conrad will show how consistently he maintains a higher proportion of sensory language than any novelist since Dickens. Sensory language is preferred in literature and life because it communicates with picture words which instantly form images, thus conserving the energy of the reader. The principles of sensory language are rewarding because they are easy to communicate to the class. The poor student can understand the meaning of "A picture is worth a thousand words." Similarly in the use of language a picture word, such as "red raspberries," may be worth a hundred abstractions, sucy as "fruit" or "food." Though it is a principle easy to comprehend, the use of sensory language has numerous repercussions in the art of reading and the comprehension of literary merit. Only by the use of sensory language as a norm of reference can the teacher of literature pin down for his class the essence of literary language. At no other point do the teaching of writing and the teaching of literature coalesce so effectively as in teaching the student how to use sensory language.

What Is Electrical Language?

I have said that sensory language is easy and fascinating to teach to weak students as well as to strong. We may begin with a phrase that everybody understands, such as "sizzling hamburger." We ask the class, "Each of us has five senses. Which of the five senses does this phrase appeal to? Let us say *sizzling* appeals to the ear. What other senses does the word *hamburger* appeal to?" In examining the phrase, we find that the word *sizzling* strikes the ear and brain with electric speed. The word *hamburger* appeals simultaneously to the tongue, the nose, and the eye. We may ask each member of the class first to write a phrase like "sizzling hamburger," one word of which appeals to the ear, the other word to the tongue, the eye, or the nose, such as "crackling popcorn," "pattering rain," "rustling corn," "rumbling fire engine." To make sure a phrase is still more intense in its sensory appeal, we may add a color, such as "rumbling red truck," "rustling green corn." As we call on members of the class to read their phrases, we may write them on the board and decide which of the phrases is most original or exact in its sensory impact.

Still another opening to the problem of sensory language is to show why the senses respond to certain words and not to others. For instance, in speaking of a person with an unpleasant expression, we may use the term, *sour face*. A more emphatic expression than *sour face* is *sour puss*. A still more emphatic expression is *pickle puss*. The ancestor of *pickle puss* in Shakespeare's language is "vinegar aspect." Why, we may ask, is the word *pickle* or the word *vinegar* more emphatic than the word *sour?* The reason is that as soon as the word *pickle* is mentioned, we see the green color and taste the pickle, and perhaps smell it, whereas when we use the word *sour*, each person has to call up his own simile to make the abstraction more real. The word *sour* does not appeal to the senses, at least not instantaneously. The words *pickle, vinegar, sauerkraut,* on the other hand, communicate instantaneously an exact sense of sourness as well as an image of the object in the mind of the reader.

To show the class further how language may communicate instantaneously to the senses, we may ask each one in the class to write a sentence describing something in the very room where we are sitting. The sentence may begin, "I see," "I feel," "I hear," "I am touching." After the sentences are written, we may ask the students to read them to the class. To make each sentence more real, we may ask each student to try to use (1) a color, (2) a sound, or (3) a name of a boy or girl in the room. Here are sentences typical of what may be expected, let us say, at a tenth-grade level:

> I see the sun shining on the red curls of Barbara's hair.
> I hear the squeaking of Joe's desk behind me.
> I hear the click-click of Miss Bryant's heels on the wooden floor.
> I feel the sweaty barrel of my fountain pen between my fingers.
> I see a long crack in the green plaster above Longfellow's picture on the wall.
> I hear the crumple of paper as Eleanor squashes it into a ball and lays it on her desk.
> I smell the odor of baked beans as it drifts up from the cafeteria below our room.
> I hear Ruth whisper behind me, "Lend me your eraser."
> I see a broad blue wall.
> I see boys and girls writing.

Of the sentences above, the last one presents a picture too broad and general for anyone to see it clearly. When a sentence such as this is read aloud, we need to ask the class, "What does Harold need to add in order to make his picture clear? Could he take one girl and visualize some particular thing about her, such as a green ribbon or a gold ring?" Further, as other boys and girls read their sentences aloud, we may ask, "What sentence makes us taste most easily? What sentence makes us hear something very exactly?" In each sentence read aloud we may pick out at least one word that is more intense than any other. We may ask, "What are the most intense words in Harold's sentence?" "What are the weak words in his sentence?" "What words do not appeal instantaneously to the senses?" In an experiment of this kind it is often possible for ten or fifteen students to write their sentences on the board so that they may be analyzed more quickly. The value of this approach to sensory language lies mainly in the specific criticism of individual words and phrases that a number of students in the class have written. Thus we may give some individual instruction to as many as fifteen students in a single class period, meanwhile clarifying the meaning of such words as *intensity* and *instantaneous* in the use of sensory language. A further benefit is that in such a procedure the students are likely to name a number of their fellow-students, thus enhancing the personal and concrete appeal of the sentences written by the class.

Sights and Sounds in the Classroom

After this experiment in single-sentence imagery of the class-room, we may carry the process a step further by asking each member of the class to write a theme describing the sights and sounds of the classroom. In order to pin down specific achievements we wish the students to accomplish, we may write on the board certain requirements for this theme, such as the following:

1. Three sounds you hear
2. Three colors you see
3. Two things you touch
4. The names of two fellow-students
5. Three movements or actions observed in the class
6. Time of day and season
7. An image of some part of a person's face or clothing

In order to clarify this assignment, we may read a student model such as the following:

BARBARA TO MY LEFT

As I glance around, I see the October sunlight glistening in Barbara's yellow hair to my left. This morning she is wearing a salmon-colored sweater with a white scarf. Now and then I can see the flash of her serious blue eyes as she reaches across to borrow my eraser. "May I?" she asks, with just a hint of flirtation in her voice. In front of me my friend Mack, his pencil clamped in a huge fist, struggles with his theme word by word. I hear him shuffling his feet and tapping the pencil on his desk. From behind me I hear a sudden sneeze, a whisper, a crackle of paper as some one wads it in his hand and makes a new start. I feel my hands begin to sweat as Miss Parish looks over my shoulder, saying, "Why, Fred, this is your best theme yet!" Then Barbara goes by to sharpen her pencil, her high heels clicking on the floor. I catch a whiff of her apple blossom perfume. At last the bell rings, and people around me begin to shuffle toward the door.

Fred Bowers

Meanwhile we may ask the class to form groups of three or four students each for the purpose of visiting a place in the community and recording multiple sense impressions. By multiple sense impressions we mean to make a record in phrases of the actual things seen, tasted, heard, smelled, and touched in the place. Excellent places to make a record of sense impressions are the five-and-ten-cent store, the school cafeteria, the local drug store or luncheonette, the railway or bus station, any corner of a busy street, the kitchen at breakfast time, the dining room at meal time. We may ask each group, or each individual, if we prefer, to make a record while actually looking at the place. The student will write phrases to show what he is tasting, seeing, smelling, or touching. When he goes home, he will revise the language to make it sharper and clearer in its sensory appeal. In order to make this assignment vivid, we may write on the board the kind of sense chart we prefer, showing examples of sensory phrases. Here is a sense chart for a ninth-year class:

Place: Five-and-Ten-Cent Store   *Time:* Wednesday Afternoon.

Things I Saw	Sounds I Heard	Things I Smelled	Things I Touched
(1) banks of chocolate kisses snugly wrapped in shining tin foil with a few of their white paper streamers sticking out (2) trays of white buttons fastened on cards (3) the gleam of glass counters	(1) the zing of the cash register (2) the crackling of wrapping paper (3) the clinking of ice in glasses at the soda fountain (4) the drone and buzz of voices (5) the rattle of a toy machine gun	(1) the warm roasted peanuts (2) cheap perfume (3) moth balls (4) cheap soap (5) hot coffee (6) roasted frankfurters	(1) cold padlocks at the hardware counter (2) hot porcelain as I drank some coffee (3) crisp, smooth Christmas cards (4) smooth, soft wax candles

For Each of the Senses: A Brief Record

Still another fruitful assignment is to ask each member of the class to write one or two sentences of description for each of the five senses, these short descriptions to be based upon actual observation, the student taking notes with his eye on the object. The usual temptation here is for the student to attempt a description from memory rather than from close, repeated observation. Actually, though the student has seen a geranium in a pot on the window sill, he has never observed it for the purpose of creating exact pictures of its appearance. The most difficult task in the teaching of sensory language is to convince the student that repeated and renewed observation for the purpose of writing brings dividends of freshness and originality that can be acquired in no other way. It is easy for the experienced teacher to spot instantly the description written from observation and the description written from hazy memory. In order to show the students in dramatic form what we mean by this assignment, we may read and discuss student descriptions like the following:

A. Sight

Three tumbling, rolling kittens were chasing a tiny green maple leaf over the back yard as the leaf turned over and over, fluttering in the wind.

Dorothy Hawthorne

I take infinite delight in watching bacon fry. From an uncolorful lifeless appearance, it takes on an appetizing, crispy, brown look. Its distinct straight pieces change into many shapes. Its sides curl up just like the broad grin on a clown's face.

Charlotte Weinberger

B. Touch

As I sat miserably in a barber's chair, some short pieces of hair slid down my back. They tickled, itched, scratched, and burned; as though filled with life, they wriggled, squirmed, stung, and bit furiously at my skin.

Charles Turek

C. Sound

The attention of the crowd centered on the man as he skillfully counted out the new money, which crackled, rustled, crackled again.

Robert Morrow

The rather flat monotones of the everyday dishes are followed by the fierce, crashing notes of the pots and pans, and the final crescendo of the frying pan as it *bongs* upon the hook from which it is to hang.

Virginia C. Barber

D. Taste

I love the taste of fried chicken, with the crisp, crunchy skin and the tender meat bursting with juice. When my mother rubs a little garlic into the chicken, I can taste its delicate, spicy flavor for hours afterward.

Helen Mason

E. SMELL

It seeps insidiously under doors, upstairs, and under my pillow: a rusty odor like that of scorched soles on hot registers. Someone has burnt the beans.

Jeanne Reilley

When the papers in response to this assignment are handed in next day, we may ask each student to read aloud one of his descriptions. The class may again select the most vivid and original images. Who has used a striking simile? Who has used both color and sound in one sentence? Who has described something that no one else thought of describing? One of the problems we always encounter in this assignment is the tendency of a student to select a large object instead of a small object. We need to say, "You cannot describe a house in one sentence. You can only describe a fingernail of your own hand or an eraser on your pencil or a bottle of ink on your desk."

A Model before the Class: A One-Sentence Impression

Another experiment in sensory language that brings quick results is to ask one of the students in the room to rise and act as a model. Each student may first write one sentence of description about the model. We may say: "In your sentence use an image of your friend's hair, eyes, clothes, or movement. Try for one significant image." Discussion of these one-sentence impressions is very useful in preparing the class for longer descriptions. We may ask, "What words in Tom's sentence are the most exact?" "What phrase in Mary's sentence appeals instantly to the senses?" "What has Joan noticed about our model that no one else noticed?" A person is difficult to describe, but in a single sentence one can communicate a particular image of significance to the observer, such as an image of a bracelet, an earring, a shoelace, a curl of hair, a watch, an eyebrow, a scarf.

A Model before the Class: Describing a Person

After this practice in using images of person, we may ask another student to act as a model for a short theme of description. Students are almost invariably fascinated by observing and describing one of their friends. As Joe stands before the class, we may ask such questions as the following:

1. What is one word that interprets Joe's personality to you? Is he *graceful, neat, nervous, friendly, poised, eager?* In the first sentence of your description use one word that suggests his personality. Underline this word.
2. In your second or third sentence you need to suggest Joe's general appearance, his approximate age, height, and coloring. You may say, for example, "Joe is a tall, brown-faced boy of seventeen."
3. What colors bear out your impression of Joe's personality? Be sure to name colors and kinds of clothes. Remember shoes and socks as well as his shirt, his tie, his belt, his trousers.
4. What movement bears out your impression of Joe? What about his posture, his hands, the tilt of his head?
5. Now come to the face, the hair, the eyes. Name colors. Show how these things reveal Joe's personality.
6. What one thing (movements, hands, shoes, sweater, ring) is most significant in revealing Joe's personality? Put this description last.

After discussing the order of images and perhaps writing them on the board, we may wish to read and ask the class to analyze a student model before they write descriptions of the boy or girl standing before the class. Here is such a model:

A LOOSE GREEN SWEATER

Joe is an easygoing boy of eighteen, short and plump, wearing a loose green sweater as he stands before us, his blue eyes blinking with good humor, his red hair sticking up in patches, his grin widening under his freckled nose. The sunlight plays lazily over his brown corduroys, a gray shirt with a gay green tie, and a pair of loose brown loafers. Joe's knuckly hands swing easily as he pulls himself up and sits down slowly, his lips curving in a wide lazy smile over his sparkling white teeth.

Marjorie Watkins

Degrees of Concreteness

Often in teaching sensory language we must make several approaches to the central concept before we achieve full and explicit explanation. To show the difference in exactness and fullness among images, we may put on the board a single word such as *paper*, and ask "What does this word make you *see?*" If each member writes his answer to this question, the answers will vary widely: each boy or girl must complete a picture connected with the word *paper*. The concept most frequently associated with paper is *whiteness*. To be very exact, we need to particularize paper by saying *white linen paper* or *scented pink paper*. But even this image is not so appealing or exact as "white linen paper with blue edges and the gold initials L G in one corner." The more complete the image, the more exact its communication.

We distinguish among images, then, by referring to them as *low, middle,* and *high* concrete details. *Paper* is a low concrete detail. *White linen paper* is a middle concrete detail. An image expanded to achieve greatest fullness and exactness, therefore most originality and differentiation, we call a *high concrete detail*. To *white linen* paper we may add *blue edges and gold initials,* thus making the paper different from all others of its kind.

In general, the more fully a student can expand an image, the more original and creative he becomes in the art of writing. We may ask the class to experiment with a number of words to illustrate this principle. We may say, for example, "For tomorrow write images of middle and high concreteness for four of the following words, representing four different senses":

light	apple	candle	water
pipe	pencil	moan	ice
candy	sand	laugh	meat

Sensory Language in Similes and Metaphors

One of the special resources of sensory writing is the use of simile and metaphor. Here the first aim is to encourage the student to use a comparison based on observation rather than upon the figurative language he hears and reads. For example, the student often takes over into his themes such trite figures as "hungry as a bear" and "quick as lightning" from daily speech and reading. To make a beginning in class, we may ask each student to use a simile based on something that he actually sees in the classroom. For example, Howard may write, "Joe's crew cut just in front of me sticks up like the bristles of a brush." Another student may write, "Helen's eyes are milky blue." When these sentences are written, we may ask a number of students either to read their comparisons aloud or to write them on the board for discussion. We may ask, "Who has the fresh, the original simile, one that you have not heard in conversation or read in a book?" Contrary to popular thought, it is not difficult to make similes and metaphors. Our job is to convince each student that he can conceive similes and metaphors from observation. Each student is capable of creating not only sentences but also from time to time a theme of literary value.

To help the student expand his use of simile and metaphor, we may read some good models for discussion as the basis of tomorrow's assignment. Brief descriptions like the ones following provide effective motivation:

FADING INTO A HUM

There I reclined, with the sibilant hiss of the leaky radiator lulling me to sleep, the low rise and fall of Professor Brown's lecture fading into a muffled hum. Through the dimness of my half-closed eyes I could see his hand, like a piston rod, stroking his jaw. In the kaleidoscope of my clouded brain the red, blue, and yellow of the dresses blurred with the dark grays and browns of the suits, and the sharp glint of varnished wood wove itself through the images like a red thread through a manila rope.

John Hough

A CLOUD OF STEAM

As the thick wooly blanket winds through, the mangle hums softly, releasing a cloud of steam which greasily grasps my hand and suddenly leaves it cold and clammy, much as would the grip of a too-casual friend.

Jeanne Reilley

IN THE LIBRARY

A boy sat in the library reading his book. His eyes traveled back and forth across the printed page like the carriage on a typewriter.

Virginia Barber

In discussing these models, we may point out that the reason a simile or metaphor appeals to the readers is that almost invariably it presents an intense image. The sharper and clearer the image in a simile, the more suggestive it becomes as in the very ending of John's description, "like a red thread through a manila rope." Students find it easy to pick out the most intense and colorful language in any piece of writing. We need to convince them also that they are good literary critics even though they have not had the formal preparation. In no department of the teaching of writing is this approach more fruitful than in class criticism of sensory language.

As a final step in the use of simile and metaphor, we may ask a class of juniors or seniors to write an imaginative theme based upon an extended comparison. For example, in what way is life like a river, a candle, a hotel? In what way is a human being like a tree, like a book, like music? To show the charm and variety of sensory language in a theme of analogy, we may read to the class one or two themes like the following:

RAIN AND PEOPLE

To me there are as many different kinds of rain as there are people. You may never have thought of it, or you may not agree, but I always feel a personality in the rain. There is the miserable drizzle that comes sometimes with fog and seems to spread its depressing influence as freely as its dampness seeps through a watertight raincoat. This kind of rain reminds me of a poor itinerant beggar who brings chill reality to the animated happy beings around him. Then, unexpectedly interrupting the calm, pleasant weather at the point when we are preparing for some picnic or summer expedition, comes that blustery, noisy rain with roaring thunder and flashing lightning. Haven't you seen people like that, noisy boastful people who come breaking in on your dearly loved solitude without warning and sometimes frighten you with their noise and wildness? But often the rain is quiet and gentle as it falls on the roof in a hushed patter. At such a time it is like a mother, soothing, hushing, comforting. Do you know anyone brisk, businesslike, and always right? I do. There is a kind of rain to match just such people; that steady downpour which is so useful to growing things and which rather coldly and heartlessly pelts down on the tender, growing, green things on the earth. Finally there are those gay, sparkling drops that dance fitfully before the breeze and can never be depended on for any real use because they usually end in a lovely rainbow. These are like lively, gay people who are not practical or useful, but who are often the most dearly loved. Perhaps you see now that rain is like people: changeable, chatty, quiet, merry, or sad.

Kathryn Reynolds

To initiate ideas for the analogy theme, we may put on the board suggested topics like the following:

Life and a Rose	Education and a Book
Life and a Candle	Going to School and
A Tree and a Man	Building a House
Football and Life	Life and a River
Wages and Grades	Money and Knowledge
A Baby and a Flower	A Child and a Piece of Clay
Rain and People	A Sunset and Life

*   *   *

No other resource in English, then, is more adaptable to various age and intelligence levels than the teaching of sensory language. Whether in the fourth grade, the eighth, or the twelfth, we can teach a student to intensify his language with simple sounds, colors, and smells. We can teach him to look at objects or people in the classroom and describe them. To make a language record *as we look or hear* is the key to the training of the senses as well as to the intensity and freshness of phrase. In such a process no two boys or girls in the room will describe a person, a rose, a desk in just the same way. Gradually a new world opens to the students, a world they have looked at a thousand times, but never visualized for the purpose of telling another person: the drops of water on the petals of a rose, a large brown freckle under Joan's right eye, the knuckled forefinger of Dad's right hand that he can't quite straighten out. The more skilled our students become in sensory writing, the more riches they find, not only in self-expression, but also in literature. When our students examine literature after training in sensory writing, they see the life of a book afresh and anew: the first images of Magwitch in *Great Expectations*, the description of Black Dog in *Treasure Island*, the many shades of brown Wolfe saw in the Hudson River, the first lines of "The Great Lover." For the first time they see that the images of the writer are the essence of his art. More valuable still, the students see that by this same reliance on fresh images they also may create American literature, if only a phrase, a sentence, a page, a sketch, that only one person could write from his unique outlook on the world.

When Sherwood Anderson wrote, "No man can quite make himself a camera," he showed why any person writing with his eye on the object must communicate some deep part of himself in the choice or order of images, in the use of simile or metaphor, in the suggestion of his emotional response. In this process lie the root and flowering of creativeness in the use of language.

The best way to become skillful teachers of writing is to train ourselves to engage in the same techniques and processes of observation and writing that we ask of our students. The suggestions below are all in keeping with this principle of correlation.

1. Sit down at a table in the library or cafeteria and write a description of the sights and sounds of that place as Fred did in his description of Barbara in the classroom on page 66. Try to fulfill all the requirements of this assignment. The only difference between your achievement and that of a high school student is that your own writing is more mature, your sentences a little longer, and your exactness of observation more fully developed.

2. Go to a place such as the five-and-ten, a cafeteria, or the kitchen of your home and make a chart of sense impressions like those listed on page 67. Remember that though you have seen a place a hundred times, you probably have never looked at it for this particular purpose of making a record. The whole art of training the senses is seeing things and hearing things as if you had never experienced them before and for the purpose of making a record. See *Enjoying English 12* (1955), Unit 1, "Sharpening the Senses: The Art of Being Alive."

3. Write five short descriptions like those on pp. 68–69, one for each of the five senses. If you do not believe in training your five senses, you can make up these descriptions from your imagination. An experienced teacher, however, can spot a faked observation as far as he can see it. The thing to do is to write at least the notes for these sentences with your eye actually on the object, as Wordsworth wrote many of his poems.

4. Appoint a model to stand before your class. Then describe him as directed in this chapter, pp. 69–70. As your model stands before you, you may ask him questions. This often requires him to make movements and certainly to let you hear his voice and see his face in movement. If your class is a friendly one, you may ask him some very searching questions about his personality. See *Enjoying English 12* (1955), Unit 13, "A Key to His Character."

5. Choose five of the words on p. 71 and write phrases of high concreteness for each word.

6. Write two descriptions of students in your class like those on p. 70. In each of your descriptions use both a simile and a metaphor. Use several figures of speech if possible.

7. Write a theme based on an analogy or comparison like "Rain and

People," by Kathryn Reynolds, on p. 73. Note the suggested topics for this kind of theme on p. 74.

SUGGESTED READINGS

"Autumn Is Back Again," by boys and girls of the sixth grade, Bloom School, Louisville Public Schools, Louisville, Kentucky, 1954

Sparkling result of cooperative observation of sights and sounds. Copies may be secured from Miss Dorothy Dreisbach, Louisville Public Schools.

EICHENBERG, MARY ANN: "Bringing a Class to Its Senses," *English Journal*, Vol. 54 (September, 1965), pp. 515–18

Another realistic experiment that proves every child can use the language of the senses, that is, the language of the poet and the novelist, though with lesser skill.

GALLANT, JOSEPH: "A Program for English Study," *English Journal*, Vol. 30 (May, 1941), pp. 396–401

Sets forth the idea that writing exercises should require precision in observation, concreteness in detail. Contains a long list of readings which will help the student become more conscious of his environment.

LITTWIN, MAXWELL F.: "Three Methods of Developing Imagination in Pupils' Writing," *English Journal*, Vol. 24 (October, 1935), pp. 654–61

Excellent suggestions on how to stimulate the imaginations of the class.

LOGAN, EDGAR: "Physical Words," *English Journal*, Vol. 43 (April, 1954), p. 196

A writing assignment prompted this teacher's discovery "that *physical words* carry an impact that sometimes releases real creative teen-age skill."

MIRRIELEES, LUCIA B.: *Teaching Composition and Literature in Junior and Senior High School*, Harcourt, Brace, 1952

See pp. 273–78 for a detailed plan to motivate work in sense impressions in the freshman year.

STUART, MRS. MILO H.: "Teaching Young Writers to Be Seers," *English Journal*, Vol. 32 (May, 1943), pp. 253–56

How to teach students to master the art of exact observation.

TREANOR, JOHN H.: *Treanor's English Series*, Pamphlet Number Three, "Ideas for Composition," Boston, 1954

Invaluable concrete suggestions for training the five senses and increasing the proportion of sensory diction in pupil themes.

WOLFE, DON M., HAMILTON, LELA, and DOHERTY, EUGENE: "Your World Here and Now: Writing Sense Impressions," *Enjoying English 7*, 1965, pp. 249–54

WOLFE, DON M., with JOSIE LEWIS and LELA T. HAMILTON, *Enjoying English 10*, Singer, 1966, "Vivid Moments, Vivid Words," pp. 37–44

WONNBERGER, CARL G.: "Writing — A Way of Life," *English Journal*, Vol. 48 (February, 1959), pp. 66–73

"Another way to improve the powers of observation is to practice frequent and detailed recall of what one says, does, experiences, and thinks. Our grandfathers kept journals and diaries for this purpose."

7 Fruitful Long Paper:
The Autobiography

THROUGHOUT THE high school years no long project in writing (from 1200 to 2500 words) is so persistently fruitful as the autobiography. The idea of such a project has a connotation of superior dignity and worth in the mind of the student beyond that of any other assignment. But the word *autobiography* has so many meanings that for each level on which it is assigned it must be defined anew. To many students on the ninth-grade level an autobiography means a book tracing one's life from the day he was born. To other students the word *autobiography* may mean a book tracing only a section of one's life, such as Carl Sandburg's *Always the Young Strangers*. At age fourteen a student cannot consider writing an autobiography in this sense. He can only write an autobiographical sketch or theme which the teacher illustrates or defines, a sketch describing only a few vivid moments or experiences having one central meaning.

Even a section of one's life, unless it is reduced to a day, a week, or a summer, perhaps a year, is too broad a compass for the high school autobiography. The first problem, then, is one of selection. We need first to help the student narrow the time span, second to help him narrow the topic itself to that point in which a few vivid moments or experiences will dramatize the central meaning. For example, "Friends Who Have Influenced Me" may be reduced to "A Friend Who Influenced Me." Even then we may say to the student, "Influenced you in what way?" He may reply, "To leave the gang I was running around with. It all happened in one summer." The word *summer* suggests the suitable time span; the word *influenced* is reduced to "influenced me to leave the gang." Thus we have a narrowing that enhances the dramatic quality and helps the student to avoid the pale, weak language of generalized narration.

To show ninth graders how to limit autobiographical topics, we may discuss in class some of the ways of making a selection described below. We may read aloud these possible subjects, then in a round-the-class discussion ask various members of the class to name topics suggested by the discussion. These autobiographical topics suggested in class talks would not, of course, be final choices. The class is merely exploring the possibilities in terms of each student's resources. The autobiographical resource that the student first suggests may not be his final one, but it will help to suggest other resources to fellow-students. We may say, "Why would you like to read Abe's paper on this topic? What moments would you put in? How could Tom make his topic more appealing? Would you advise Laura to change her topic? Is it too broad to be visualized in four or five moments? "In this way we open the discussion of the autobiography by getting immediately into the potential topics. Moreover, as each topic is suggested, the class has an opportunity to evaluate it in terms of its originality and depth of meaning for the writer.

Autobiographical Approaches: Narrowing the Topic

One person: What person has had a great influence on the student's life — father, mother, brother, sister, boy friend, girl friend? What moments dramatize this influence?

One sport: What moments of experience with basketball or football or other sport have made a deep impression on the student? How did they influence his life?

One summer: How did it change the student? What moments were most important?

One year: What happened to make the student grow up in one year? What four or five moments gave him greater insight and maturity than he had hitherto possessed?

One day: What day was most important in the student's life? What day was full of fun, emergencies, sadness? The student may describe five moments of one day and why they were important to him.

One fear: Each of us has had a fear as a child. At what moments was this fear most intense? In what way has this fear changed or disappeared?

One death: Almost everyone at age fourteen has had an experience with death, perhaps the death of a pet or friend, or even the death of a stranger. What moments connected with this death are most vivid to the student? What main meaning did he derive from the experience?

One pet: How did the student get the pet? What was the first moment of acquaintanceship? What did the pet look like? What moments with it were most delightful?

One hope or dream: What dream or hope for the future does the ninth-year student have? Would he like to have a certain job? What has been his acquaintanceship with the job as he observed other persons working at it? What moments of observation can he use?

One automobile: What was the first moment of seeing the automobile? What moments of good times has the student had in it? Has the automobile suffered any collisions? What were the narrow escapes in this car? Does the car have a name, a personality?

One place: Every student has spent many happy times in one place, such as a farm, a cabin, a porch, a kitchen, a living room, a school room. What moments in this place does he remember joyously?

Student Models Indispensable

Meanwhile, to show what other boys and girls have accomplished in the autobiography, we may read one or two selections each day from our treasure chest of student themes. Our own student themes are the most valuable motivation we can use for the autobiography. A student autobiography shows not only how other boys and girls have handled opening paragraphs; it shows the depth of meaning that some students have been willing to put into their long papers. High school students naturally assume that school is an artificial existence, sometimes a utopia, sometimes a purgatory. The essence of life, sad or bright, is for them outside the classroom, not in it.

Their most baffling problems, their most poignant fears and hopes, they cannot put normally into their English themes. But the auto- biography gives us and the student a chance to make English and life a coalescent unity. He sees that another student has not only had a deep fear, a family problem, an intense love like his own, but also that another boy or girl like himself has been willing to write about it freely. We cannot tell a student, "Write about what's troubling you most," and expect him to respond. But invariably if we read an autobiography about a student's most harassing dilemma, other students will respond by first thinking deeply about their own prob- lems and many also by writing about them. For these reasons, no motivation can possibly be so strong as that of student themes. Even half a dozen such themes read in part or in whole are the most valuable resource we can have in assigning the autobiography.

Framework of Organization

The next step in assigning the autobiography is to show the student a useful framework of organization for him to follow. One such useful frame is as follows. In an opening paragraph of three or four sentences the student sets forth the key idea, the kernel or heart of his long paper. This short topic paragraph the student then fol- lows with a series of five long paragraphs, each of them describing a single vivid moment. Finally at the end of the paper, the student writes a short concluding paragraph, drawing together the main ideas of his autobiography into a summarizing statement. This makes a total of seven paragraphs, five of them describing the moments, ranging in length from 150 to 200 words. A useful diagram to show this framework of organization is as follows:

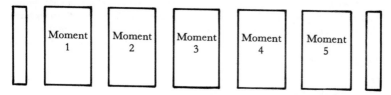

With this topic and frame of organization in mind, the student can now proceed to writing in a few sentences an introductory paragraph to his own autobiography for a discussion with the class. Here are several illustrations of opening paragraphs:

A TEACHER WHO CHANGED MY LIFE

Miss Oliver was the most inspiring teacher I had. In my year with her, the sixth grade, she changed my outlook in many ways. In this theme I expect to show how her gentleness and patience and understanding of me helped me to become more grown up.

MY CHILDHOOD DAYS ON THE FARM

Of my childhood days I liked best those spent on the farm, from the time I was five until I was eight. My memories of these early years, memories of home folks, school, tramps in the woods, and of Bird, my dog, are as clear as my memories of yesterday.

GOOD TIMES IN OUR JALOPY

Our family has had some wonderful good times in our old jalopy which Dad brought for $50 five years ago. It is a 1941 Mercury. Dad and I worked on it together. He taught me how to take a motor apart. We painted it a fiery red. Then it was ready for family trips and good times which I shall never forget.

MY SISTER SUE

My sister Sue is now four years old. From the time she was born I have helped take care of her. My experiences in taking care of Sue have been very delightful. In this paper I shall show what taking care of Sue has meant to me.

MY HOBBY: ELECTRIC TRAINS

When I was eight years old, my father bought me a small electric train for Christmas. Since then my family has given me five other trains. From this hobby I have learned many things about railroads, electric motors, and railroading signals. In this theme I shall describe five moments when this hobby gave the greatest pleasure.

A TRIP TO THE GRAND CANYON

Last summer our family took a trip to the Grand Canyon. My father had seen the Canyon when he was a boy and wanted his children to have the same experience. We left Pittsburgh August 1 and returned August 20. In those three weeks I had some exciting and wonderful moments I shall never forget.

Writing the First Paragraph

The next step in the autobiography project is to ask the student to hand in his first long paragraph containing a description of one moment. When I use the word *moment*, I do not mean necessarily one moment of time, but simply the dramatic focus of an experience, lasting perhaps one moment, several minutes, or even a half hour. The student can make the dramatic point of any experience vivid in a number of different ways. He can make the setting real by the use of time and place references such as "one July afternoon at Jones Beach." or "at the rim of the Grand Canyon during an August sunset." Still another way to visualize the dramatic moment is to use colors such as "streaks of red in a bright blue sky," or an image combining color and taste, such as "brown buttered toast and blueberries and cream." Often a single image of touch will help the reader to share the writer's experience unforgettably, as when Conrad writes in *Youth*, "I have the feel of the oar in my hand." We may also ask the student to use several sounds in each moment, such as "I could hear the jingling of his keys and the swishing of his corduroy trousers," and such single phrases as "*pattering* footsteps," "*clicking* heels," "*sputtering* and *hissing* of the fire." The weakest ninth-grade boy or girl can make a scene more real with such use of sounds and colors. Still another intensifying element is the use of a bit of dialogue: "Jim, you scurry for some fire wood. Susie, put some bacon in the skillet." To illustrate these ways of making a moment vivid, we may read to the class two opening paragraphs from an autobiography:

MY CHILDHOOD DAYS ON THE FARM

Of my childhood days I liked best those spent on the farm, from the time I was five until I was eight. My memories of these early years, memories of home folks, school, tramps in the woods, and of Bird, my dog, are as clear as my memories of yesterday.

Having come into the world on Friday, April 13, I was oppressed as a boy by the dangers that are thought to accompany that unlucky day. Near the time of my sixth birthday, while I was attending a country school near Pittsburgh, the boys told me that because I had been born on Friday, the thirteenth, I was related to the "Old Witch." Unless I did something to break her power over me, I was doomed. Though I did not believe them at first, they persuaded me, after much recess discussion, to carry a black cat with me all day, even to school. Carrying this black cat would break the spell of the "Old Witch." On that memorable morning, clad, I remember in new red suspenders, corduroy trousers, and new copper-toed shoes, I shuffled hesitatingly along the cool road, gripping my lunch pail in one hand and a kitten black as coal in the other. Tucking the kitten into my shirt as I approached the door, I peeped in. Mr. Brandt had his back turned, placing some books in a case near his desk. Slipping in quietly, I pushed Blackie into my desk and tried to look cool. During writing class, which was just before lunch hour, Blackie began to mew. When Mr. Brandt took one look and started toward me, his black eyes sparkling with anger, all my old fears about the "Old Witch" rushed upon me. He was going to take my cat and allow the spell to continue. Pulling Blackie out, I dashed from the school and, with tears streaming down my cheeks, ran all the way home. There Mother calmed me and told me that it was all a joke, and that Friday, April 13, was just the same as any other day. But I shall never forget my fear of the "Old Witch."

Junior and Senior Autobiographies

In the junior and senior years of high school, the autobiography takes on a realistic usefulness unattainable or perhaps undesirable in the ninth year. In the class of a sympathetic teacher the boy or girl at seventeen can use the autobiography to grapple with one of his main problems. Perhaps a siege of sickness or hospitalization following an automobile accident has forced upon him a maturity of thought hitherto unrealized. Perhaps he has fallen in love with a girl he sees every day; he is amazed at the beautiful new coloring his life now holds. In all departments of life he has more knowledge of himself than ever before. Often, by seventeen, a boy in his reflective moments can put his finger unerringly on the central weakness of his disposition and write about it with utter frankness, tracing its growth over a period of years. In the junior and senior years many boys and girls have held jobs that brought them face to face with harsh realities of the working world. For the first time, perhaps, they know the mood of drudgery and the attrition of spirit imposed by useless or boring labor. An autobiography about a particular job, a trait of disposition, a fascination for music, a friendship, a sweetheart, a teacher, a father, a single game that taught an athlete a lesson, an accident, a sickness — all these topics have the inherent value of requiring a realistic appraisal of one of life's central patterns.

Perhaps the deepest value of the autobiography on the junior or senior level is the opportunity it offers for searching self-appraisal. The older the high school student, the less he can afford the luxury and delight of writing for escape. The problems that beset him are too many and too baffling for him to postpone his grappling with them. Indeed, the teacher who probes one by one the key problems of her class and in one way or another gets the class to write about them is doing her students an inestimable service. Of all themes about problems, the autobiography is the most searching. As many students say, "This theme was painful to write, but I felt a great sense of relief when I finally got it down on paper."

Suggestive Topics for Class Discussion

The following topics may suggest the scope and depth of upper-year autobiographies:

1. Anger Was My Waterloo
2. A Friend Who Helped Me Grow Up
3. A Book That Helped Me Grow
4. I See My Dad in a New Light
5. My Definition of Love
6. An Automobile Accident: What It Taught Me
7. A Game That Taught Me a Lesson
8. A Job That Taught Me the Meaning of Drudgery
9. What This Year Has Taught Me
10. Music Is My Delight
11. Five Moments of a Happy Summer
12. This I Believe: Five Moments of Illumination

Conference a Vital Need

On the junior and senior levels we can perform a service sometimes of lifelong value by sitting down with each student for even five or ten minutes before he chooses the topic of his autobiography. If he wishes to write an autobiography of escape, we may direct him to a more rewarding subject, though still not painful. If he prefers a superficial topic to one of depth, we have a chance to help him face and describe a dilemma of deep meaning. Moreover, a student often wishes to choose an autobiographical topic of crucial private meaning but is perhaps afraid that the teacher will be shocked by his revelations. In a conference we can often assure the student indirectly that a searching honesty, wherever it leads, is our goal, not a moral judgment of his behavior. If we wish to be good teachers of composition, we must keep ourselves shockproof to each student's revelations, helping him to feel free to write the truth, however painful. If he describes one of his own problems fully and intensely, he will probably see for himself the necessary solution. If, as often happens, a student possesses a magical strain of humor and is plagued by no baffling dilemma, we may encourage him in conference to let his humor flow with new zest and whimsy over a school problem that nags or worries the whole class. On the technical side, a few words in conference may help the student to reduce his topic to one day instead of one summer, to one friend instead of several, to full visualization of one failure or success rather than a generalized picture of several crises. Usually a series of such conferences about the autobiography means long hours before or after school. If one is willing to pay this price, he may discover a priceless reward in fascinating long papers and the esteem and affection of his classes.

Reading Literary Autobiographies

A substantial parallel benefit in work on the autobiography may be the reading of an autobiography or an autobiographical novel. To interest the class in these books, to show also how other writers have dealt with problems and moments similar to our own, we may read such passages as Francie's Saturday trip to the junkman in *A Tree Grows in Brooklyn;* the incident in Sherwood Anderson's *Tar* when Tar discovers a man weeping at his wife's grave, the same man who day after day cheated him of pennies when he bought a paper; Anderson's remarkable sketch called "Discovery of a Father," about his endlessly garrulous father who came home silent one rainy night and took his son swimming in the nearby pond, all the while saying not a word; the delightful chapter in *Life with Father* titled "Father Sews on a Button"; the story of the pony Lincoln Steffens asked for at Christmas, in his *Autobiography;* the Christmas morning in *Of Human Bondage* when Philip Carey, after long prayer, waits for God to make his club foot whole; part of the story of Eugene's wonderful high school teacher in *Look Homeward, Angel;* a passage from Dreiser's *Dawn* describing the dire poverty, the quest for coal, the fried potatoes, of the Sullivan winters in his early years; a passage from

Twain's *Autobiography* describing the sights and sounds of the farm: the lilacs, the sumacs "luminous with crimson fires," the rustle of fallen leaves, the wild grapes, the carving knife splitting the watermelon, the frozen apples in winter. Each teacher has his own treasure of such books and passages; the very wealth of autobiography testifies to the persistent rewards of this assignment.

Day-by-Day Plan

In assigning the autobiography in the junior or senior year, we may use a plan somewhat like the following:

First Day. Discuss the definition of *autobiography* we shall use in the course, using a diagram (see page 81) to show frame of organization. We read several opening paragraphs to show the range and significance of topics.

Second Day. We read aloud one complete autobiography on a serious problem applicable to many students, then ask for class discussion of the problem as well as the autobiography. If time permits, we read further from our collection of student autobiographies.

Third Day. We call for brief talks about tentative topics by a few members of the class. Then we may ask the students to write in class opening paragraphs on tentatively chosen topics. We may say, "Write on your paper, 'Please do not read,' if you would rather not have your opening read aloud." Some students may be willing to have their openings read anonymously. We collect these, but read only those we have permission to read.

NOTE: During the first three or four days we endeavor to assign as many conferences as possible to discuss final choice of topics. One simple way to assign conferences is to draw up a schedule of the hours we are willing to give, divided into ten-minute periods. The students then write their names in the spaces representing the times they prefer.

Fourth Day. We read aloud a paragraph or two to illustrate the meaning of *moment* and the ways and means of making a moment vivid. If time permits, we read several introductory paragraphs already handed in, and discuss them with the class.

RETREAT FROM PEOPLE

From earliest youth I have had a deep conviction that I am not like other people, that I am inferior, marked for defeat. Although to some extent, as the years pass, I am overcoming this feeling, it often, even now; governs my personality completely.

Following an accident on the public playground near my home I felt for the first time the scorn of my friends and family. As a child of five I lived in Brackenridge, Pennsylvania, a town which owed its existence to the presence of the Allegheny Steel Company. One of my chief delights in life at this time was to "pump up" on the swings in the playground to see if I could "go over." ("Going over" consisted of swinging higher than the steel bar to which the swing was attached.) On one June afternoon, while I was swinging away at a high rate of speed and singing so loudly that my voice drowned out all other sounds, little Johnny Valesek ran out in front of my swing. I saw him coming and screamed, but I could not stop in time. The heavy wooden seat of the swing hit his head with a terrific impact that knocked him over and pitched me out head first into the cinders underneath. After I had revived somewhat, I staggered dizzily to my feet, only to see the senseless body of the little boy several feet away with no color whatsoever in his face and a huge, ugly gash on the side of his head; from this gash a spurt of blood issued, trickled down his neck, and formed a dull splotch of color on the ground. Soon the frantic yells of the bystanders brought a crowd. The boy's mother, crazed by the sight of her son, called me a murderess, threatened to call a policeman, and made a dash at me as though to beat me. I was thoroughly terrified. With the women wagging their heads and shaking their fingers at me, and with the accusing eyes of my playmates upon me, I left the scene. Fearing that I would be taken to jail, or that I would have to kneel with bared knees upon chicken feed (my father's favorite mode of punishment), I crept down into the cellar and hid behind a washtub. Here I picked the cinders out of my knees and leaned my throbbing head against the cool, damp cellar wall. It was a long time before my father discovered me. At the supper table I ate under the hostile gaze of my family; then with a promise of "You're gonna get it; just you wait," ringing in my ears, I was marched off to bed. It was several days before I ventured any farther than the back porch. From a distance I watched all the other boys and girls solicitously catering to Johnny, who was encased in bandages like a mummy. I got the reputation of being a mean, nasty, vicious little girl. Mothers called their children indoors when I passed; stones met me at every corner. I got into the habit of making mud cakes alone and of playing house in the shed. It gave me a mournful satisfaction to sit in the sunlit doorway of the shed with my rag doll and chant over and over again, "Nobody likes me. Why don't I die?" I even made up a little tune to go with it. Once my older brother happened to overhear me. From then on, every time I cried or even looked as though I wanted to cry, he'd mimic me to perfection,

"Nobody likes me. Why don't I die?" This taunt did not cure me. Filled with deep sorrow for myself, I went about more melancholy than before, avoiding everyone. This incident was the beginning of my difficulty in associating with and in being accepted by other people.

Helen Vronsky

Fifth Day. We assign for tomorrow the rewritten introductory paragraph and the first main paragraph, reading one or two more models. We emphasize again the ways of using sight, sound, touch, and dialogue to make a moment come alive. Good autobiographical moments may be read from Ernest Poole, *The Harbor*, or Mark Twain, *Autobiography*, or from such remarkable adolescent writing as *Diary of a Young Girl*.

Seventh Day. We return first paragraphs, reading several aloud when permission is given. Then we assign the long paper for the following Monday.

Eleventh or Twelfth Day. Long papers due. We collect them and ask if some are willing to read selected moments, one paragraph each. Later, in the days that follow, we hand back the autobiographies, reading (with permission) some intense passages to show the achievement of the class.

*   *   *

Of the factors that make for the success of the autobiography assignment, the most life-giving is the emotional preparation achieved by the student by meditation upon intense moments of experience with a single central meaning. For this emotional preparation the reading and discussion of student papers is signally fruitful; only by such a process can the student begin to search through the patterns of his past and select the one that arouses his deepest feelings. If he is inhibited from using this topic, he knows which topics are alternatives. If he feels free to speak to his teacher in private, we can perhaps help him make a wise choice. In the achievement of writing correctness and writing vividness, the most productive process is prevision: a part of the long paper handed in, some such papers discussed in class, the probable errors anticipated, the enlargement of sensory language to make a moment real, the consistent use of time and place references. In tracing the use of sensory language, as he reads an autobiography or autobiographical novel, the student may take on a new dimension of critical insight, finding that he himself is now attempting the same means toward stylistic intensity as that used by the author. For a climax of solid achievement the junior or senior student needs to allow himself eight to fifteen hours of solitary thinking and writing. Afterward, when those who are willing read their best paragraphs in class, rich rewards will begin to appear; the students view each other with new interest, sympathy, and insight. Moreover, in our solitary hours of reading, we may finish one autobiography after another with a new conviction that the teaching of writing in high school can be more exciting and rewarding than the teaching of literature.

To the Student Teacher: Suggested Activities

1. Read the first several chapters of *Always the Young Strangers*, by Carl Sandburg, or *Pioneer's Progress*, by Alvin Johnson. Then select a passage in which the author makes his early life extremely real. Read your selection to the class and explain why you like it.
2. Read a portion of Theodore Dreiser's *Dawn*, the autobiography of his early years. Copy a passage of 200–300 words that you think is especially revealing. Read your passage and explain why you selected it.
3. Make an outline of your own autobiography, limiting the topic as shown on pp. 79–80, using a single sentence for each paragraph. Then write the introductory paragraph, showing your main idea and how you intend to develop it. Does the theme represent a really fundamental part of yourself? Before you write, read Helen Vronsky's autobiography, "Retreat from People," in *Enjoying English 11* (1955), pp. 104–12, or the opening chapter of Ernest Poole's wonderful book, *The Harbor*.

   Ideally speaking, you should complete the writing of this paragraph and outline in order to be better prepared to make this assignment in a high school class. Perhaps your teacher will permit you to complete your autobiography to be handed in as your term paper.
4. For grades 7–10, an ideal choice for student reading is Anne Frank, *Diary of a Young Girl*, one of the most remarkable records written by an adolescent girl in the past several decades. Anne was a Dutch girl of Jewish background who, with her family, hid in an Amsterdam warehouse for several years during World War II to escape persecution and annihilation by the Nazis. Anne wrote her diary in the midst of danger and despair. Finally the family was discovered and sent to a concentration camp, where Anne died. Anne's father, who survived until the Americans reached the concentration camp, afterwards found Anne's

diary and permitted it to be published. Read a portion of this diary and make a report of ten minutes to the class, showing what passages you think high-school students would find compellingly real.

5. Would pupils of the seventh grade like *Diary of a Young Girl?* See if you can get acquainted with a seventh-grade pupil, and ask him to read a portion of the book. Then tell the class of the seventh-grader's response to this autobiography. Or, better still, bring the seventh-grader to your teaching-of-English class and ask him to make the report himself.

6. Bring to class a chapter from Clarence Day's *Life with Father* and read several paragraphs to show how you would communicate the hilarity of this book to a high school class.

7. Read a portion of Mark Twain's *Autobiography.* Copy five passages of extreme sensory intensity and write a brief annotation under each passage showing why you selected it.

Suggested Readings

BARNES, RUTH M.: "An Approach to Composition in the High School," *English Journal*, Vol. 35 (November, 1946), pp. 483–86
  This article contains some exciting and searching examples of student autobiographical writing.

BUCKINGHAM, LEROY H.: "Creative Writing Based upon Experience: Some Psychological Values," *English Journal*, Vol. 30 (September, 1941), pp. 553–57
  The use of the autobiographical composition to help the student come to a clearer view of himself and his world.

COOK, LUELLA B.: "Writing as Self-Revelation," *English Journal*, Vol. 48 (May, 1959), pp. 247–53
  "To help pupils become aware of this deeper self and then to explore this inner part of their being is one of the special privileges of the teacher of English."

DAKIN, DOROTHY: *How to Teach High School English*, Heath, 1947
  See Appendices, pp. 491–92, for an autobiographical unit used at Pullman, Washington, High School.

DOMINCOVICH, H. A.: "Composition in the Short Short," *English Journal*, Vol. 30 (April, 1941), pp. 294–97
  How a study of the short story can lead to the student's writing of autobiography.

EBERHART, WILFRED: "Humanizing the Evaluating of Written Composition," *English Journal*, Vol. 29 (May, 1940), pp. 386–93
  The student's composition as a reflection of his own world.

Essays on the Teaching of English, ed. Edward J. Gordon and Edward S. Noyes (Appleton-Century-Crofts, 1960), pp. 79–136, "Creative Writing"

"Creative writing forces a student to isolate and examine his own experiences, as against analyzing the experiences in a book or newspaper."

HENRY, GEORGE: "How to Get Interesting Themes," *English Journal*, Vol. 33 (September, 1944), pp. 348–55

Interesting examples, with useful suggestions, of autobiographical material written by students.

KAPLAN, MILTON A.: "Look into Thy Heart and Write," *English Journal*, Vol. 43 (January, 1954), pp. 13–18

Arresting and practical motivation for writing autobiographies, with excellent selections from student writing.

LAZARUS, ARNOLD L.: "English XL," *English Journal*, Vol. 43 (February, 1954), pp. 71–74

Suggests an interesting approach to autobiographical writing: a daily journal for recording experiences and reactions. See especially 'The Journals' on p. 72.

MILLER, WARD S.: "We Write Our Life Stories," *English Journal*, Vol. 29 (June, 1940), pp. 490–93

A step-by-step account of a classroom experience in the writing of autobiographies.

REEVES, RUTH E.: "The W in RWS," *English Journal*, Vol. 49 (April, 1960), pp. 256–59

Exciting ideas for keeping a journal, the students writing only in class (ten or fifteen minutes, three times weekly). Questions: "What interesting thing did I see yesterday? What interesting thing did I hear today or yesterday? What did I think about? What trouble did I have?"

ROSS, FRANK E.: "For the Disadvantaged Student—A Program that Swings," *English Journal*, Vol. 54 (April, 1965), pp. 280–83

A program for writing and speaking that brings the realities of the disadvantaged youth and the classroom together.

The English Language Arts in the Secondary School (New York: Appleton-Century-Crofts, 1956), Chapter 2, "The Adolescent the Teacher Faces."

A too brief but realistic profile of adolescent traits.

TRAINOR, FRANCIS X. and MCLAUGHLIN, BRIAN K.: "An Inductive Method of Teaching Composition," *English Journal*, Vol. 52 (September, 1963), pp. 420–25

Excellent analysis of common personal experiences as a strong point of expository writing.

WOLFE, DON M.: "A Realistic Writing Program for Culturally Diverse Youth," *Improving English Skills of Culturally Different Youth*, U.S. Office of Education, Washington, 1964

WOLFE, DON M. (with RUTH NELSON and LAURADA OSBORN), "Links in My Life's Chain: My Autobiography," *Enjoying English 11*(Singer, 1966), pp. 329–42

WOLFE, DON M., ed. *The Purple Testament,* preface by John Dos Passos (New York: Doubleday & Company, 1949)

Life stories of disabled veterans of World War II, beginning with sketches of home towns and home places, and ending with moments of combat and hospitalization.

8 Speech Resources in the Democratic Classroom

ONE OF THE MOST difficult tasks of the English teacher is to create in her classroom the kind of atmosphere in which boys and girls feel free to speak their spontaneous impressions of life, books, and ideas. Each pupil comes to our classroom inhibited in speech by his family, his friends, or his former teachers. Already he may have learned to say to his father what his father wants to hear rather than what the son feels in the depths of his personality. Already he may have learned to voice an idea or an impression of a book that he knows his teacher wants to hear. Less acutely, perhaps, is he inhibited by his friends in the class. They understand the necessity for his speaking at times not from his most vital thoughts but from the exigencies of classroom diplomacy. To build up among our students a pervasive conviction that we really want free and truthful expression of opinion in our class is the first prerequisite to the growth of the unique student in his speech activities. Our willingness to attain this prerequisite we may gauge by the following question: On the very issues on which our own ideas are most decisive and dogmatic, do we encourage our students most imaginatively to speak opinions to the contrary?

One way to create a democratic atmosphere for the growth of speech skills is to have several discussions early in the year in which we welcome differences of opinion among all members of the class. On the junior high school level we might present a question such as "How late should boys and girls of our age be permitted to stay out?" or "Why do students cheat?" or "How would you improve our school?" The first of these questions requires for profitable discussion an exciting diversity of opinion and our willingness to hear criticism of parental discipline. The second question, on cheating, requires us to listen to explanations if not justifications of cheating on the part of our students, referring, of course, not to our own classroom but to experiences of preceding years. The third question requires us to listen respectfully to criticism of the methods and practices prevailing in our school.

The essential ingredient of our earliest discussions is our own apparent impartiality toward ideas, an impartiality that prevents any of our students from knowing exactly what we think about these crucial issues. Our task here is to be a skillful chairman, not a judge. The moment we suggest a commitment to one idea or the other, we set up a new inhibition upon the speech of our class, an inhibition that may have consequences lasting over months or even a whole year of academic work. It is easy for us to assume the role of the wise admonisher, settling questions by the authority of age and experience, and this approach to training children has many advantages if we expect silence and acceptance. But if we expect a free flow of truthful speech in our class, we must convince our students that we are open to the evaluation of all ideas impartially, drawing out each opinion as fully as we can without stating our own. The older our students, the more ingrained their inhibitions on classroom speech. In the upper years of high school it is more difficult to convince our students of our open-mindedness than in the seventh or eighth grade. By this time they are more cautious, less trusting, one may say more realistic in their evaluation of motives. Nevertheless, in the high school years we must attempt to show in such a discussion as described above that we welcome the most diverse judgments and opinions. "The opinion of good men," wrote Milton, "is but knowledge in the making." Controversial questions like the following may draw from our class dozens of answers and qualifications to which we are equally impartial: "Should juniors or seniors work after school?" "Should a boy or girl go steady against parental wishes?" "What is a mature definition of *citizen, student, teacher, happiness?*" Our persistent aim is to show that we welcome in our class the most diverse and contradictory judgments.

In evoking discussion, we aim also to encourage originality and the growth of independent thinking on the part of each one of our students. If we are teaching Thoreau, "On Civil Disobedience," we may ask, "Who is a nonconformist? In what way are you a nonconformist?" For the encouragement of individual thought and speech, Emerson's essays are invaluable, particularly "Self-Reliance." "A man should learn to detect and watch," wrote Emerson, "that gleam of light that flashes across his mind from within more than the lustre of the firmament of bards and sages." One great advantage of free speech in a democratic classroom is that in speaking his opinions without inhibition the student's mind becomes electric with other thoughts, some of which may be highly creative. An atmosphere of discussion in which many differences of judgment and opinion clash with each other is of inestimable efficacy in the most profound educational sense.

TECHNIQUES OF SELF-EXPRESSION

What Is the Ideal Discussion?

The ideal discussion is one to which every pupil of the class has contributed not from imitation but from conviction. In the ideal discussion the teacher as chairman seeks to draw out the timid boys and girls. If five or six vocal students attempt to monopolize a discussion, the teacher calls upon the timid members to speak, appealing to the sportsmanship of the talkative members. We ask, "What are the qualities of a democratic discussion?" partly to show the vocal students how they sometimes prevent less confident students from bringing something of value into the class conversation. At the end of an ideal discussion every pupil will have spoken. Our own opinion we still hold in reserve. We may point out several questions which have not yet been answered or problems that the discussion has not dealt with. Each teacher, I grant, is inevitably a propagandist for his values, and perhaps there is no way for a teacher to prevent his class from knowing some of his private opinions by the end of the school year. Meanwhile, however, by refraining from dogmatism, we shall have gained the confidence of the class in our determination to welcome diverse and contradictory opinions.

The One-Minute Talk

The one-minute talk is especially useful in drawing the timid student into a speech situation. When we have one-minute talks, we may ask each student to come to the front of the class and speak in a formal way. It is important that he come up promptly, stand on both feet with his heels together (contrary to public speaking technique, but the surest way to achieve reasonably good posture), and lock his hands behind his back if he does not know what to do with them. We avoid talks five minutes long or even three minutes long. It is infinitely preferable to have five one-minute talks from each student than to have one student give a five-minute talk. In five one-minute talks he has five opportunities to come to the front of the room promptly, face the class, and speak loudly enough for the pupils in the back row to hear. Meanwhile he becomes accustomed to looking into the faces of his fellow-students, speaking on his feet, achieving an erect and natural posture.

It is easy to make opportunities in the early weeks of the year for one-minute talks. For instance, in the eighth grade we may say to the class, "For tomorrow I would like each pupil to speak for one minute about a recent moment when he had fun." Or we may say, if the class by this time is friendly and we have discussed some problems, "For tomorrow I would like each pupil to make a one-minute talk beginning this way: 'One of my problems is . . .' " In choosing a moment when he had fun, the average eighth-grade pupil will not have difficulty. For him to speak on one of his problems, however, requires a climate of free speech and friendliness which our class may not yet have acquired. Still another question we may present to an eighth-grade class is this: "What is a growing-up pain? What do you mean by *growing up?*" Each pupil, then, would be free to speak on the important or the unimportant growing-up pains. We do not, of course, in such a required talk, wish our students to be embarrassed. We want them to have a choice of topics so that each may speak from a deep level or a light level of his experience.

The Panel Discussion

When one-minute talks involve serious problems, it might be well for us to suggest a panel discussion to precede the talks. Panel discussions are becoming increasingly popular as a means of opening to the class diverse and contradictory opinions about fundamental experience. For example, we might have in an eighth-grade class a panel entitled "My Biggest Growing-Up Problem." The discussion may open in a form somewhat as follows:

MODERATOR: Today we shall have a panel discussion on the topic, "My Biggest Growing-Up Problem." The first speaker will be John Wilson. John's subject is "Staying Out at Night."

JOHN: My biggest problem is staying out after ten o'clock. If I come in from a movie at ten-fifteen instead of ten o'clock, my dad raises a rumpus. Dad comes from the old country, and he is very strict. He doesn't realize that American boys and girls have more freedom to come and go than he did when he was a boy.

MODERATOR: Ann Scott will talk about "Going Out with the Family."

ANN: Nearly every Sunday my family goes to visit relatives. I like to stay home and have girls in to chat and listen to records. Mother insists that I go with her and Daddy. She can't understand how boring those visits are to me.

(Later, after other panel members have spoken)

PUPIL: John, how do you handle the problem of getting in late, knowing your dad is going to be angry?

JOHN: Well, usually I listen to my mother and come home before ten, even though I miss part of the movie. Every now and then, though, the movie is so exciting, I just can't get up and leave it. But I'd do almost anything to keep Dad from raising a rumpus.

After six or seven members of the class have spoken in a panel discussion, it is much easier for us to assign one-minute talks for the whole class. Gradually, as the class becomes better acquainted, we may assign more and more crucial topics for both one-minute talks and panel discussions.

As our students advance from one high school level to another, the panel discussion becomes more and more vital as a speech activity in which diverse and contradictory opinions are encouraged.

On the sophomore or junior level, for example, we might open a discussion of family problems with single sentences spoken by various members of the class. We may even suggest openings to single sentences, like the following:

1. The main problem in my family is . . ..
2. My dad is jolly when . . ..
3. When my dad is upset . . ..
4. Every Sunday afternoon . . ..
5. A special time in our family is . . ..
6. At the dinner table . . ..
7. In my family we always have fun when . . ..
8. My mother does not understand that . . ..

Following this speaking of sentences, we may ask our students to comment on one of the problems suggested by this list on the board:

Wearing my clothes	Too much noise
Nagging me about things	No privacy at home
Not enough clothes	Too much make-up
Wrong kind of clothes	Manners not good
No place to study	Grades too low
Coming in late	Not allowed to drive
Too young for dates	Not enough money
Wrong kind of dates	Friends unwelcome
Too many dates	Friends not "right"
Careless around the house	Quitting school

Following the discussion of home problems in which we encourage the class to identify some of their particular worries, we assign one-minute talks for the next day in which each student tells a story about a problem. Here is a story about a home problem written by a tenth-year student:

SMOKING IS NOT FOR ME

My mother has a strong prejudice against smoking. She doesn't even like my dad to smoke, but not for the usual reasons. My mother hates a mess. Especially does she hate stale cigarette butts in the living room after company leaves. Last Sunday as my dad was reading the paper, he said, "Molly, do the girls in your class smoke? Are you going to smoke yourself?" I knew my dad was just curious. He expects me to smoke sooner or later. My mother, who was sitting by the fire, sewing on buttons, was immediately on edge. "Molly," she said, "I hope you never touch a cigarette. Don't you see how much worry and work and mess such a filthy habit causes? Besides, have you considered how much it harms your health?" Mother's face was flushed and angry; her brown eyes were full of worry and trouble. Dad takes such things more lightly because he is a smoker himself. "No, Mom," I said, "I am not going to smoke for a while yet. Maybe not at all, though I do like the smell of Dad's cigarettes." My mother's face smoothed out. She looked relieved as she picked up her needle and thread again. Dad just winked at me and turned to the sports page again.

Molly Barrow

The speech resources thus far discussed, the discussion, the panel discussion, the one-minute talk, may be used as ends in themselves, in which no written work follows. The excitement generated in a discussion, however, may be channeled very creatively into a theme (or several themes) containing the considered reflections of each student on the problem at hand. When we have selected a topic of central significance, and when each one in the class has contributed to the discussion, we have an ideal climate of motivation in which the best thoughts may be crystallized in written form. In fact, it may be said that almost invariably the quality of student themes will be enhanced in proportion to the time and energy devoted to class discussion of the topic.

Oral Definitions of Controversial Words

In speech activities as in writing we look first to the sensory life of the student for experience topics and afterwards progress to intellectual experiences and social ideas. This progression we may follow on every level from the seventh grade through the twelfth, first asking the students to record their own experiences, whether in family, school, or community, and then leading each discussion toward an intellectual and social evaluation. After a discussion of family life, for example, we may ask, "What can the citizen do to make family life happier? Does a better job with a higher salary give a father a better chance to make his family happy? Does a better chance for an education mean that when boys and girls grow up they can become wiser parents?" Discussion of the social concomitants of personal experience always embodies a fascinating transition from the concrete to the abstract, from incidents to principles.

In this situation we can help our students crystallize a number of judgments by asking them to define such words as the following: *adolescent, adult, son, daughter, education, kindness, fairness, honesty, citizen, cheating, friend, peace, family.* In asking for oral definitions of such words as those above, we shall hear strikingly different impressions of the same word, as in the following three definitions of the word *education:*

JOE: Education to me means going to school to learn to make a living.

HELEN: To me education is a special chance to see if I can develop my talent in music.

MAX: Education to me means getting well acquainted with some wonderful fellows. I think you learn more from people than you do from books.

The Interview: Practical and Realistic

A practical, realistic speech activity is the interview. Nowhere is the art of conversation dramatized more effectively than in the questions used in an interview. The interviewer must repress his own desire to converse, must efface, in fact, his own personality, in order to invite the fullest expression of personality from his partner. Realistic interviews may be acted out before the class, interviews in which one student asks questions which reveal to the class the most interesting facts about and opinions of the student interviewed. This is appealing to the class because the subject at hand is the personality of the student, in which everyone is interested. After each member of the class has acted out an interview with a partner, we are ready for interviews with men and women of the town. The following list of townspeople who might be interested in interviews is only suggestive (a few unusual occupations should be explored):

the major	a garage mechanic
a lawyer	a second-hand car dealer
a physician	a hospital superintendent
a postman	a garbage collector
a nurse	a music teacher
a secretary	a television repair man
a clergyman	a housewife with children in school
the postmaster	a policeman

We may ask teams of two pupils each to call citizens of our community by telephone and make appointments with them. We ask each team to visit the citizen at his office or place of business; he should be a stranger to each of the interviewers, but engaged in an occupation in which the interviewers are interested. In a few instances the interviewers may ask the person whom they meet to come to class and respond to more questions, so that the whole class can hear the interview. The success of an interview depends upon the imagination of the interviewer, especially in knowing what questions to ask in order to evoke responses of self-revelation.

Spontaneous Dialogue

Another speech resource is acting out rehearsed or unrehearsed conversation before the class. Below are brief descriptions of a number of emergencies. We may ask the students of our class to divide into couples or teams and choose one of these problems to act out before the class. A committee may be appointed to criticize the conversations, analyzing the constructive qualities of what they consider to be the two or three best ones.

MEETING EMERGENCIES

1. Believing that they have received unfairly low grades, two sophomore students see the history teacher after school and politely but firmly state their case.
2. Two boys who are close friends want to ask the same girl to a dance. They talk it over.
3. Two girls who are close friends want to invite the same boy to an "All Men Broke" or "Sadie Hawkins" party. How do they solve the problem?
4. As you are leaving a train, you see an elderly lady carrying a large suitcase. Show how you would greet her, carry on a short conversation, and take leave of her after reaching the waiting room.
5. On a train or bus you suddenly discover you do not have either ticket or money. You and the bus driver talk it over.
6. Two sophomore boys make plans to earn enough money to go to camp together.
7. A very shy freshman boy asks you a question on the first day of school. Show how you would make him feel at ease. Draw him out with questions about himself.

8. A student who has been caught cheating on an exam talks the matter over with his teacher after school. The boy explains why he cheated.
9. While your father is away, a friend of his comes to the house. You have never met him before. Show how you would welcome him and draw him out to make him feel at home.
10. A father and mother are worried about their son's low grades at school and about his sullen disposition at home. They talk the matter over with him. How does the son show he really appreciates his parents' concern for him?

SPEECH ACTIVITIES IN THE STUDY OF LITERATURE

In the study of literature the speech resources described above are effective means of clarifying both the reading itself and the student's impression of the masterpiece. In addition to this correlation, however, there are other speech activities especially suited to the study of literature:

1. Memorized readings of single lines or sentences
2. Memorized readings of stanzas or passages
3. Memorized readings of longer poems
4. Choral speaking of poems
5. Statement of the author's purpose in one sentence
6. Acting out scenes from a play
7. Television or radio broadcasts
8. Reports on lives of authors or analysis of play
9. Panel discussion of poem, play, short story, or novel
10. Imaginary conversations or interviews with characters from literature

A number of the activities named above will be discussed in Chapters 17, 18, 19, 20, and 22, below. In this chapter we can consider only a few of the speech resources that the teacher correlates with the study of literature.

Memory Quotation

One of these resources is the memory quotation of a single line of poetry in answer to the roll call. It is amazing how expressive a single line of poetry can be when recited in this way. When we are studying a novel, a short story, or an essay, we may likewise ask each student to quote in answer to the roll call a single sentence or part of a sentence that he feels is exceptionally beautiful or provocative. Often at the beginning of the period we may have a lively discussion of several of the quotations recited to the class.

A similar correlation is, of course, the recitation of memory passages which are discussed at length in the chapter on the teaching of poetry (below, pp. 258–59). When we ask a student why he has selected certain lines from among the poems we have studied, we have a clue to his unique response to a poem. In such a poem as the following, for example, when we ask, "What to you is the most electric line in this poem?" we may have several different responses.

SONNET XXXIII

The world is too much with us; late and soon,
Getting and spending, we lay waste our powers:
Little we see in Nature that is ours;
We have given our hearts away, a sordid boon!
This Sea that bares her bosom to the moon;
The winds that will be howling at all hours,
And are up-gathered now like sleeping flowers;
For this, for everything, we are out of tune;
It moves us not. — Great God! I'd rather be
A Pagan suckled in a creed outworn;
So might I, standing on this pleasant lea,
Have glimpses that would make me less forlorn;
Have sight of Proteus rising from the sea;
Or hear old Triton blow his wreathed horn.
                                        William Wordsworth

In a class that I observed one boy chose "sight of Proteus rising from the sea" because he loved mythology. Another student chose "Little we see in Nature that is ours" because he had always lived in the city and felt that he was cheated of nature's gifts. Still another boy chose "The winds that will be howling at all hours" for its description of sound. Then the teacher chose her line, which was "And are up-gathered now like sleeping flowers." This she preferred, she said, because of the beautiful comparison and the word *up-gathered*. Each person, then, might choose a different line in each poem as the most appealing. It might be intense in idea, in image, or in bringing to memory a particular moment. Such responses make very fruitful discussion because every criticism forces each student to re-examine his own preference. Though all preferences are welcome, we cannot engage in such a discussion without coming to a deeper appreciation of the poet's purpose.

Stating the Main Point

When we are studying an essay or a short story, one excellent device is to ask each student to speak in one sentence the point of the story or the essay. It is amazing how many opinions exist in a single class about the main point of even the simplest essay. To clarify the main point, we then write on the board a number of answers and consider them one by one. Which are subordinate points of the essay? Which is the main point? Gradually we eliminate the subordinate points and come to an agreement on the principal idea the author had in mind. This discussion of the main point of an essay or a short story does a great deal to clarify reading analysis.

Acting a Scene from a Play

In teaching a play, no exercise is more expressive or illuminating than to ask several boys and girls to stand at the front of the room and read the lines of the various characters in an important scene. This kind of reading, however deficient in individual expression, does a great deal to make the scene come alive in the minds of the class. After all, a drama is meant to be acted, not to be read. This is one reason why plays are so much more difficult to read than novels or short stories.

* * *

Ideally speaking, in a year's time we should invite the student to speak first about himself, his thoughts and feelings, his intense moments of experience, his ideas, beliefs, superstitions; then, later, his impressions of books and social ideas, each of which has a relevance in his daily life and memories. Our aim is to make him so relaxed and spontaneous that the unique part of himself will appear not only to himself and us, but also to his fellow-students, whose words and actions are to him, in turn, an intense education.

In these invitations to speak we must be careful to repress our own self-expression in favor of the expression of the unique boy or girl unfolding before us. "Respect the child," wrote Emerson. "Wait and see the new product of Nature. Nature loves analogies but not repetitions. Respect the child. Be not too much his parent." Emerson also wrote, it is true, "Trespass not on his solitude." To carry out our purpose, we must trespass on his solitude, or at least we must make him feel that he no longer wishes to keep his ideas to himself. We must make him feel that the classroom is a happy place that welcomes all shades of experience and differences of opinion as the essence of growth and challenge. We do not wish to reproduce in a child another person like ourselves. We wish him to be a rich, unique individual in his own right. The heart of a democratic classroom is the conviction on the part of the class that the teacher is eager to hear opinions hostile to his own or those of the class. Of the many speech activities conducive to emotional and intellectual growth, the discussion is the most fruitful, especially when it can draw out the timid as well as the expressive members of the class. To encourage the backward boys and girls, we ask them questions or ask them to come to the front of the room and speak. The one-minute talk is an ideal assignment for this purpose. By a wise use of panel discussions we can also encompass some of the backward students of the class and enable them to develop leadership as a group speaking in cooperation with each other and evoking questions and comments from the class. In the use of the interview we have the essence of the richest kind of conversation, which is repeated and persistent invitations to the other person to express himself. The essence of conversation is imaginative listening and questioning. No one can participate in a successful interview without learning something of this art.

Among speech activities in the study of literature the discussion is again our most fruitful resource. Though we are superior in learning to the student, we must encourage him to express his ideas and opinions of literature in much the same manner that we encourage him to express his idea of sensory life around him. In the study of literature the most important thing is the link between the child and the life described in the masterpiece. When we enable a student to recognize this link in the writing before him, we have helped him to take a big step in the appreciation of literature. Literature has meaning for the average student only so far as it is related to a moment, a conviction, an image, in his own life. For advanced critics of literature this is not intellectual enough. Nevertheless, in a democratic classroom we do not expect to make of our students critics of literature in a professional sense. To us the attainment of enjoyment is more precious than the attainment of critical insight on the high level of Aristotle's *Poetics* or Horace's *Ars Poetica*. Without pain or anguish the child can speak lines of poetry from memory, sentences or passages of beautiful prose, which leave an indelible impression on his memory because, selected by himself, they represent in his mind a link to intimate experience. The acting of a scene from a play and imaginary interviews with characters from novels are also fruitful and provocative resources in the study of literature. Moreover, whenever a writing project is the main assignment, whether based upon experience or the reading of literature, speech activities provide greater energy of motivation than any other resource.

To the Student Teacher: Suggested Activities

1. Let us imagine you are teaching a ninth-grade class. What several topics might you choose from for a sure-fire discussion about the second week of class? Choose a topic of varied significance, one which is certain to invite difference of opinion. In a paragraph of about 150 words show how you would present this topic to the class and encourage a lively discussion.
2. Interview one of your fellow-students before the class. Show by your questions what qualities of interviewing you would emphasize in your classroom.
3. Lead your teaching-of-English class in this discussion: How were you brought up? Were you brought up by hand, by admonition, by stern looks, or by a combination of these three? Draw out each person in the class to answer these same questions, so that at the end of the hour each of your fellow-students will have made a contribution to the discussion.
4. Appoint a panel of five to discuss a poem such as Robinson's "Ben Jonson Meets a Man from Stratford." The panel members may meet several times if necessary to prepare their discussion, decide upon their topics. The leader of the panel will then introduce each speaker and lead the discussion that follows the panel talks. A stern timekeeper should be appointed to limit each of the panel speakers to five minutes of his main speech.

5. Speak from memory lines from a poem which has a deep meaning for you. Then describe a moment in your life which pinpoints the meaning of the lines for you.

6. Speak a sentence or a passage to the class from a great prose work such as Milton's *Areopagitica* or Joseph Conrad's *Youth*, such as the passage beginning, "And this is how I see the East," or a favorite sentence from Melville's *Moby Dick* or Hardy's *The Mayor of Casterbridge*, such as, "And in autumn airy spheres of thistledown floated into the same street, lodged upon the shop fronts, blew into drains; and innumerable tawny and yellow leaves skimmed along the pavement, and stole through people's doorways into their passages with a hesitating scratch on the floor, like the skirts of timid visitors." Explain why the passage is explosive or appealing to you.

Suggested Readings

APPY, NELLIE: *Pupils Are People*, Appleton-Century-Crofts, 1941
This book consists of a series of essays dealing with the uniqueness of each student. Important.

Artistry in English, a series of studies in brief pamphlets to assist in an appreciation of literature as transmitted by the spoken word on records. Record study guides thus far issued include biographical data, suggestions for further reading, a summary of the recording, and suggestions for use. The pamphlets are issued by the Educational Record Club, 355 Lexington Avenue, New York, under the general editorship of Dr. Joseph Mersand, Chairman of the English Department of Jamaica High School, New York. The pamphlets thus far issued include "Sonnets From the Portuguese," "Great Scenes From *Macbeth*," "Palgrave's Golden Treasury."

BENNETT, ROBERT A., ed.: *Speech in the English Classroom*. NCTE
Ten leaflets of rich suggestiveness and concrete classroom applications.

BURROWS, ALVINA, FEREBEE, JUNE, and others: *They All Want to Write*, Bobbs-Merrill, 1939
While this book deals only with children from the first to fourth grades, it has many ideas of general interest on the subject of student individuality.

Discussion Guide for Teachers of English, National Council of Teachers of English, 1952
An analysis of effective discussion, followed by a presentation of the aspects of English teaching to which it may be fruitfully applied.

ELLIF, GERTRUDE: "A Direct Approach to the Study of Listening," *English Journal*, Vol. 46 (January, 1957), pp. 20–27
An exciting classroom experiment based in part upon the "Brown-Carlsen Listening Comprehension Test." Students themselves participated in the development of listening materials.

FRAZIER, ALEXANDER: "Making the Most of Speaking-and-Listening Experiences," *English Journal*, Vol. 46 (September, 1957), pp. 330–38
    Concrete suggestions for speaking projects accompanied by listening assignments.

HAUGH, OSCAR M.: "The English Teacher as Teacher of Speech," *English Journal*, Vol. 44 (April, 1955), pp. 205–10

HOLBROOK, DAVID: *English For Maturity*, Cambridge University Press, 1961
    An invaluable summary of the most fruitful methods and values in the teaching of English in England's secondary schools. The author emphasizes "the very culture of the feelings." A book highly praised in England.

HOOK, J. N.: "Each Is an Island: Individual Differences in the English Classes of Littleville," *English Journal*, Vol. 37 (January, 1948), pp. 8–14

Instruction in English and Speech, Board of Education, New York City, 1952, pp. 89–138
    Unusually rich and suggestive descriptions of specific procedures and activities.

KEYES, GEORGE E.: "Creative Dramatics and the Slow Learner," *English Journal*, Vol. 54 (February, 1965), pp. 81–84
    A compelling report on a venture in creative dramatics and the highly promising results.

MIRRIELEES, LUCIA B.: *Teaching Composition and Literature in Junior and Senior High School*, Harcourt, Brace, 1952, pp. 239–69
    A lively, comprehensive survey of speech activities with a wealth of sources and specific helps.

POLEY, IRVIN C.: "Drama in the Classroom," *English Journal*, Vol. 44 (March, 1955), pp. 148–51

SHANE, HAROLD G.: *Research Helps in Teaching the Language Arts*, Association for Supervision and Curriculum Development, 1201 Sixteenth Street, N.W., Washington 6, D.C., 1955
    Chapters on spelling and creative writing of special interest to seventh- and eighth-grade teachers.

SONKE, DOROTHY E.: "English Workshop," *English Journal*, Vol. 43 (October, 1954), pp. 363–66
    Devised to help teachers meet the individual needs of slower students, this workshop utilized the insight and talents of superior students, giving them valuable leadership-training opportunities as student-teachers.

Speech in the English Classroom. NCTE Portfolio, 1961, 508 S. Sixth Street, Champaign, Ill.; edited by Robert A. Bennett, Richard Corbin, Wilmer A. Lamar, Mary Marjerrison, Ruth Reeves, and Lorietta Scheerer.
    Twelve exciting essays by master teachers, among them Helen F. Olson, Margaret Painter, Alexander Frazier, Wilmer A. Lamar, P. Merville Larson, and others. Rich in ideas and values.

The English Language Arts in the Secondary School (New York: Appleton-Century-Crofts, 1956), Chapter 7, "Developing Competence in Speaking."
    See especially suggested unit, "Living with Others," used at Erasmus Hall High School, Brooklyn, by a tenth-grade group taught by Evelyn M. Hill. Excellent teacher contributions on teaching of literature, pp. 221–36.

TREANOR, JOHN H.: *Treanor's English Series*, Pamphlet Number One, "Oral Drill," Boston, 1953
    Useful concrete suggestions for classroom activities in pronunciation and correct usage.

WHITTAKER, CHARLOTTE C.: "Television and a Senior Literature Program," *English Journal*, Vol. 43 (April, 1954), pp. 183–86
    Television programs provided a background of common experience for discussing great themes and ideas in the theatre, the structure of plays, and dramatic production.

9 Philosophy of Life: This I Believe

HIGH SCHOOL YEARS are an ideal time for the tentative crystallization of beliefs and credos. "The study of faiths and utopias," wrote William James, "is the noblest exercise of the human reason." Though James was thinking of great books already written, we as teachers can also serve "human reason" by helping each student to write his own statement of even one belief or ideal. What do I believe about loyalty to my country? What do I believe about family life? What do I believe about religion? What do I believe about friendship? What do I believe about war, democracy, human nature, happiness, love? To formulate a credo on any of these topics is a life-long task. Nevertheless, the earlier we help a student to grapple with even tentative statements of belief, the better his chance for earlier maturity as a citizen, friend, husband, son, or brother. As our discussions advance, we emphasize again and again the need for tentative and cautious judgment, for leaving the mind open to new light that may change a credo. But to state and dramatize and discuss tentative beliefs have a fascination for the high school boy or girl that he may never feel again. Many students will never afterward seek the essence of truth in so many different departments of life as in these formative years. Their beliefs are intensely real and often unqualified. One of the benefits of stating a credo is to pin down its meaning and qualify its application.

Sentences to Live By

In the ninth or tenth grade the simplest kind of credo is a series of sentences, most of them beginning with "I believe," encompassing varied facets of experience. Any boy or girl can write such a series of statements with a great deal of profit to himself and to the class. The value of such a project is the fresh, individual quality of each statement, which has a dignity of self-expression that few students can resist. Here we are seeking from the student the blunt truth, not consistency of outlook.

WHAT I BELIEVE

1. I believe in going to church, but I don't go very often.
2. I believe in helping take care of my crippled brother. In the summer I make some money to help pay his doctor bills.
3. I believe in being careful about what I say. I can't always say what I think in school.
4. I believe a healthy man should fight for his country. My dad fought in World War II.
5. I have only one friend. I believe in being loyal to him and fighting for him when the chips are down.
6. I believe in taking my own part in an argument and using my fists when necessary.

Jerry McTavish

One beneficial extension of this assignment is to ask two or three friends to join together in writing a group credo. Though a group credo cannot be freshly individual, it has the merit of encouraging three or four friends, perhaps of different religious faiths, to state the beliefs they possess in common. Below is an example of such a creed:

A CREED

1. I believe in respect for, but not worship of, my ancestors because I need to help make a better world than they knew.
2. I believe my duty to my family is to be honest, so that I will never bring shame to them.
3. I believe I need religion because I do not know everything there is to be known, and only religion can answer some of my questions.
4. I believe the world needs religion to find peace.

5. I believe faith is believing what we know to be right, even though we cannot prove it; just as we cannot see the wind, but we know it is there.
6. I believe every man is my brother. I should put no stumbling blocks in his path, and I should help him on his way.
7. I believe my country has given me the opportunity for my life, and if it asks me, my life is what I owe it.
8. I believe most great deeds have been performed by one man with an idea, who, because he truly believed in himself, could make others believe in him, too.

Tony Grieco, Tom Washington, Ruth Johnson, and *Rachel Cohen*

As the high school student idealizes his teacher or his pastor, so he sometimes idealizes his credo, often to unworkable extremes. When the idol falls, from the cracking clay in its feet, that ideal teacher or pastor or friend suffers a final and ignominious eclipse. There is no halfway ledge for the idol to cling to; there is no shading in the adolescent's judgment. Similarly, when an adolescent sees reasons to doubt a belief he has firmly held in years past, he may pass quickly to total rejection. One of the fruitful effects, then, of stating a credo in the high school years, is to see that our allegiance to a belief, like our allegiance to a person, may change in color and application and intensity with the passing years.

Prelude to Writing a Credo: A Story for Class Discussion

In the upper years one of the best ways to dramatize the shaping of a credo is to read to the class a story that lends itself to varying interpretations. For instance, in the story below, Art says, "Doesn't everybody get away with something?" This is his excuse for not giving Doc the change for the five dollars. We know from Art's statements that his father's words have taught him to shave the corners of honesty on the theory that everybody else does it, too. Joe does not deny, for example, that he has cribbed in Miss Olson's class. This situation then raises the question not only of whether or not one is suspicious or trusting of human nature; it also requires a student to examine the applications of his own credo. "Change for Five Dollars" is a story, then, we may read to the class with the assurance that it will inspire no easy answers or one-sided conclusions. As teachers we want no easy, premature solutions; we know from experience that black-and-white judgments do not usually satisfy the mature mind.

CHANGE FOR FIVE DOLLARS

One December afternoon in Massillon, Ohio, Art Mason, Virginia Purillo, and Joe Pulaski were having chocolate floats together at the Corner Drug Store. Art was a chunky boy with a square chin and black eyes; Joe was a quiet lanky boy, with blue eyes and yellow hair; Virginia was everybody's friend: a slim, straight girl with long black hair and large brown eyes.

Art left his friends to buy some razor blades for his dad. Old Doc Williams came puffing out from the prescription laboratory, his hazy blue eyes peering at Art through thick-lensed glasses. Art handed him a dollar bill.

"A box of blades. O.K. Say, there's the phone." Doc hurried back to his prescription desk. When he returned, he absentmindedly gave Art change for a five-dollar bill. Art sauntered back to Joe and Virginia, his nimble feet dancing. "Look! I'm in luck. The old miser gave me change for a five."

"But you're just kidding, aren't you, Art?" asked Virginia, her brown eyes soft and calm.

"Certainly not," replied Art. "You don't know Doc the way I do. I worked for him last summer at fifty cents an hour and no pay for overtime. He's an old skinflint. This is just back pay."

"Get wise to yourself," disagreed Joe. "You can't get away with that." Through the prescription window he glanced at Old Doc's gray head.

"You'll see," said Art. "You get away with cribbing in Miss Olson's class, don't you? Doesn't everybody get away with something? In this world you are in a game every day to beat the game, get away with something. My dad says you gotta take in this world, and give as little as you can."

"Is that all you believe, Art?" asked Virginia.

"Do you believe that everybody has a heart of gold?" Art answered. "In this world you have to be tough. Old Doc was tough with me. Now I'm going to be tough with him."

For a while Art sat in moody silence. Then suddenly he jumped up and gave back the change to Old Doc. Swaggering back to the table, he told his friends, "Just to please you two. Besides, I thought you might tell on me," he added with a wry grin. "See you later." He dashed away, his square shoulders bobbing up and down.

"Do you know what makes him that way?" wondered Virginia.

"Yes, partly," Joe answered. "I lived next door to him when we were little. His dad was always tough with him, cuffing him around. When Art was fifteen, he started to cuff back. Now the only one he's really nice to is his mother. He would do anything for her, but his dad made him believe you have to be tough."

"Gosh," said Virginia, "my parents have given me so much love all my life. They just never let me down."

"Well," Joe commented, "I take human nature as it comes. I guess I'm ready for the worst, but I'm always hoping for the best. Let's ask Art to ask Margie to the dance, and we'll all go together. What do you say?"

"Sure," said Virginia enthusiastically. "Maybe he will believe in us yet."

Philip Karant

After reading this story to the class, we may ask questions like the following:

Do you believe that Art is right in saying, "Doesn't everybody get away with something?"

Does Art have a just comeback in his accusation that Joe has been guilty of cribbing?

Do you believe it would have been right for Virginia and Joe to tell on Art if he had not returned the money?

Do you believe that Joe and Virginia are doing the right thing at the end of the story?

What do you think would help Art?

Class Assignment: Answer One Question

Our next task is to assign a one-paragraph theme on the story, in which we ask the student to answer one question such as the following:

What is going to happen to Art?

What is your opinion of Joe?

Is it a reasonable approach to human nature to ask, as Virginia does, "Do you know what makes him that way"?

To illustrate how other students have answered questions about this story, we may read the following student themes to the class:

ART IS TOUGH

I believe Art is going to keep on being tough and suspicious as he is now. He was really afraid that Virginia and Joe would tell on him. No matter what a friend has done that is wrong, I don't believe in being an informer. But Art knew that they would consider it honorable to tell on him. If they take him to the dance, that won't change Art. No matter how much they try to befriend him, he is going to stay tough. If his dad is tough with him, how can he expect other people to befriend him? I believe that human nature tends toward suspicion. I find it in almost everyone I know.

Roy Pitkin

THE HOME SHAPES HUMAN NATURE

I believe human nature is as good as the home you come from. Take Virginia, for instance. She says her family has always given her love. She can count on her mother to tell her the truth, wipe her tears away, and get her a warm dinner on a rainy night. For this reason it is easy and natural for Virginia to love. If Art had his father's love, he would be just as kind as Virginia and Joe are. I guess for Art love from just his mother and not his father is not enough. Therefore I believe human nature is just what the family makes it. Even if Virginia has some hard knocks later, her first impulse will be love and trust of other people.

Georgia McCabe

We may now read to the class a few short themes about the story, "Change for Five Dollars." In the discussion of the themes many people are sure to volunteer many differing opinions about Art and Joe and their contradictory opinions of human nature. In such a conversation the differentiated personality of each student comes into focus on one idea. What causes each one to have a slightly different definition of the term, "human nature"?

If time permits, we may now continue the discussion on the philosophical level, citing, as we proceed, statements by great thinkers about the term, "human nature." One of the most fruitful ideas comes from Thomas Gray's "Elegy Written in a Country Churchyard." When the poet asks, in effect, "Why is it that this village has produced no Milton, Cromwell, or Hampden?" he gives an answer that many people have since laughed at as romantic nonsense, an answer, however, that is finding more and more acceptance among students of human nature in the twentieth century. In brief, Gray says, "This tiny village did have potential great men, but two conditions prevented their flowering. These two conditions were ignorance and poverty":

> Knowledge to their eyes her ample page
> Rich with the spoils of time did ne'er unroll
> Chill Penury repressed their noble rage,
> And froze the genial current of the soul.

Almost every writer has left an implied or explicit impression of the nature of man. For example, Robert Owen said, "The character of man is made for him, not by him." Emerson was almost always optimistic: "Man is a fagot of thunderbolts." "Man is a dwarf of himself." "Man is a stream whose source is hidden." Machiavelli wrote, "All men are bad and ever ready to display their vicious nature." Plutarch wrote, "The soul has a principle of kindness in itself." Father Flanagan said, "There is no such thing as a bad boy." We may say to the class, "Do you believe that human nature is merely the result of early childhood environment, or do you think that evil is fixed in human nature?" The discussion then may lead back to the story itself or to the individual comments of the class; and finally again to the philosophical definition we know will be important to them in future years.

What Do You Believe about Happiness?

Perhaps the most important concept for each of us to define is *happiness*. To begin a discussion of happiness, we may ask the class to describe in a theme of a few sentences a single moment of happiness like the following:

CHRISTMAS MORNING

When I was seven years old, the thing I wanted most was a brown cocker puppy just like the one my friend Tony across the street had. On Christmas morning I woke up at six o'clock and slipped down the stairs without a sound. Under the tree was a wooden box with a red ribbon around it. Inside, on one of my old sweaters, lay a cocker puppy. He looked up at me, stood up unsteadily, and wagged his tail sleepily. Quickly I took him in my arms and stroked his pretty brown fur. He had a big white spot on one ear. Then we romped together all through the house, and I fed him some warm milk. That was one of my happiest moments.

Fritz Waller

Happy moments of the past lead naturally to the discussion of happy experiences in the adult world. As our students look forward to adult life, what are the elements they believe now will bring them happiness? Here are some possibilities to discuss now with the class:

Owning a farm	Having good friends
Getting rich	Working in a garden
Getting engaged	Being a creative worker
Getting married	Owning your own house
Rearing a family	Having religious faith
Going to college	Traveling where you wish
Having a secure job	Becoming a civic leader

One effective approach to the topic of happiness is to ask the class to discuss the chief causes of unhappiness in the adult world. Which of these causes of unhappiness is most crucial? Which of these causes are preventable? Which of these causes are preventable by individual action? Which are preventable only by social action?

Not enough money	Wrong kind of job
Not enough food	Disease and disability
Family broken by war	Death in the family
Unemployment	Quarrels in the family
Unhappy marriage	Loss of faith in one's self
No encouragement at home	Loss of faith in religion
Fear of losing a job	Lack of educational opportunity

Finally in our discussion of happiness we may strike a more intellectual level by presenting to the class definitions and opinions conceived by thinkers of former centuries. Here are a few:

1. Aristotle, *Nicomachean Ethics*. Happiness is a life of contemplation, a life in which one is not compelled to earn a living but can devote his whole time to intellectual pursuits. "We conclude that happiness is coextensive with speculation, and that the greater a person's power of speculation the greater will be his happiness."
2. Emerson: "Happiness is a perfume you cannot pour on others without getting a few drops on yourself."
3. Happiness is the companionship of two people in love.
4. Happiness is the feeling of being a useful, efficient worker, whether or not the work is enjoyable.
5. Happiness is popularity with one's friends.
6. Happiness is the pleasure of being physically alive, sound in body, responsive to the pleasures of eating, dancing, enjoyment of nature.
7. Happiness is appreciation of beauty, whether in books, personality, architecture, painting, or nature.
8. Old Chinese proverb: "If you would be happy for an hour, get drunk. If you would be happy for a year, get married. If you would be happy always, cultivate a garden."

9. "Happiness is the faculty for being surprised."
10. Hardy, *The Mayor of Casterbridge*. Happiness is "but the occasional episode in a general drama of pain."

Writing a Long Theme: My Philosophy of Life

The general topic, "My Philosophy of Life," is much too broad to allow the student to describe particular moments in a long paper. When the time comes for this assignment, our first problem, as in other long papers, is to help the student narrow his topic. For instance, he may select for the central element of his philosophy of life his idea of friendship, his idea of marriage or courtship, his idea of happiness, his conception of democracy in human relations. The following suggest further possibilities:

My Definition of Love	I Am Afraid to Trust People
My Definition of Cheating	I Believe in Going Steady
I Am Always Hopeful	I Don't Believe in Going Steady
I Believe in Facing Facts	I Believe in Being Different
My Definition of Success	I Respect My Parents' Wishes
You Can't Buy Happiness	I Learn from My Mistakes
Lying Is Sometimes Justified	Getting Along with My Parents
Human Nature Can Be Changed	I Believe in Trusting My Friends
You Can't Change Human Nature	I Believe in Telling the Truth
Money Is the Root of All Evil	I Believe in Love at First Sight

Whatever the topic chosen, the student should endeavor to suggest the main idea of his theme in a series of vivid moments. For instance, in the theme below, "Facing Facts about Myself," George Graham limits his philosophy of life to a single facet, facing facts about himself. Then he describes several moments of self-revelation and understanding in which he came to see both mature and immature qualities in his personality.

FACING FACTS ABOUT MYSELF

I believe in facing facts about myself, both pleasant and unpleasant. Sometimes I am pleasantly surprised. At other times I am disappointed in myself. Here are a few critical moments in my life when I looked at myself in the mirror as honestly as I knew how.

At fourteen I realized that I was ashamed of my mother. One Sunday evening in November my mother asked me to go to church with her. Through my mind flashed a picture of my mother, gray-haired and wrinkled, in her dark old-fashioned clothes, walking down the long aisle of the church before the services began, while the organist played soft, solemn music. I saw all my friends looking at me, particularly Arlene Wilder, whose mother was always dressed in the most stylish fashion. Somehow her dresses were always bright, silky, youthful, filled with sunlight. As these thoughts flashed through my mind, I said, at last, "Well, Mom, I guess I'd better study my algebra for the Monday morning test." She didn't say anything; she just looked at me with her sad, aged, workworn face. After a while she brought me some orange juice at my desk. I remembered how she always insisted on my having two new suits every fall, and yet I was ashamed of her. Now, three years later, I am glad to say I always go to church with my mother.

The next winter, when I was fifteen, I learned a very pleasant fact about myself. I learned that I had steady nerves when the going was tough in a basketball game. We were playing Woodrow Wilson High School on their new, shiny, neon-lighted gymnasium floor. Up to that time I had been just a substitute, getting in a few games for a few minutes at the end. But in this game the coach suddenly called to me at the beginning of the last quarter, "Go in for Backer. Tell the team I said to feed you the ball for three shots in succession under the basket." Well, the team worked the ball down to me. I pivoted, feinted with my left, and scored two out of three baskets with my swift hook shot. The boys were counting on me to make a third basket to tie the score. The rooters in the stands were yelling, whistling, stamping their feet, cheering hoarsely, urgently. Well, I made that last shot without getting panicky. It skittered around the rim, bounced up, teetered precariously for a split second, and then whooshed through the net. I knew it would go in. That moment gave me a feeling of confidence in myself that was really a tonic. Now, whenever the going gets tough, the boys give me the ball.

Naturally I have some unpleasant facts to face. One is that up to now I haven't liked to work after school in order to have spending money. One evening last week Dad said, "Say, can't you get a job after school to earn yourself some spending money?" I had to admit to myself that I didn't want a job. I was willing to get the money from Dad for my one date a week with Alice. Dad just grinned. He understands me too well. Only yesterday I went to look for a job carrying groceries after school, sort of hoping I would not get it. I find that I don't like to keep asking Dad for a dollar here and a dollar there. I have learned that facing the truth about myself is the first step in overcoming my faults.

George Graham

Credo by Implication: A Religious Moment

One of the most rewarding assignments in high school teaching is to ask the class to describe a moment of religious experience.

A moment of religious feeling, unlike the intellectual statement of a credo, is not subject to challenge or discussion. The credo underlying the moment of religious mood can only be suggested. The problem is really to make it vivid, not to make it rational or consistent. If our classroom contains members of our three common faiths, the best approach to this topic is simply to read descriptions of three religious moments exemplifying vividness of image and completeness of feeling. The following themes will illustrate the kind of student models most useful in making this assignment.

MY CONFIRMATION

On Sunday evening, June 5, my confirmation became one of the most beautiful and significant events of my life. At the Beaver Falls High School auditorium I acknowledged my faith in Judaism and my willingness to abide by its principles. I was confirmed with eleven other boys and girls; they were my childhood friends. The scene itself was a lovely, inspiring one. The stage was decorated entirely in white with green flowers and shrubs. A bower for flowers on the platform was covered with fine white cloth, a silver star of David gleaming majestically from the top. As we slowly started to march from the rear of the darkened auditorium, a violin throbbed out the strains of that solemn, grand masterpiece, Mendelssohn's "March of the Priests." After we were seated, the rabbi, Benedict Glazer of the Rodef Shalom Temple in Pittsburgh, delivered a most inspiring talk on the way to keep our lives beautiful. As I sat there, my thoughts dwelled on my relationship with God. I wondered if He were watching over us tonight, if He were taking us, even as we gave ourselves. I thought of my companionship with those boys and girls, how I had gone to school with that girl, why I admired that boy. Oh, how proud I was to belong to the Hebrew religion! Then to soft music, four persons slowly marched to the rabbi, and he blessed us. That benediction I shall never forget; it was the crowning happiness of my confirmation. In my heart I resolved to be a true Jewess, that I might be worthy of my great ancient race. Such was my confirmation; I shall remember and cherish it always.

Miriam Saul

MORNING WATCH

Summer before last, at the Young People's Christian Conference at Kiski, I had my first true glimpse of the wonder and majesty of the Creator's handiwork. At first we thought holding morning watch, as our counselors called it, was a little silly and sissified, but we soon came to love those few minutes before breakfast as the richest of the day. Immediately after rising, with a little pamphlet of a few Bible verses, a prayer, and perhaps a poem or a beautiful thought, every boy and girl wandered off across the fields, sometimes in groups, oftener alone. One morning I wandered away to a grassy plot on a high bluff, a spot that became to me the loveliest of the countryside. Below me lay the town of Saltsburg in the midst of a wide green valley. Around me grew mock orange bushes and stunted pines, wet now with dew in the bright morning sunshine. The glistening dew outlined delicate webs on the stunted pines and waving uncut grass. As it fell from the leaves of the tall poplar trees behind me, the constant *drip, drip* was as soothing as a stroking hand. Through the breaks in the drifting mist I could see the silent streets and houses of Saltsburg in the valley below; far beyond the rising sun outlined in vivid orange, red, and purple the shadowy hills. Looking up, I could catch glimpses through the trees of the cloudless blue sky. In this beautiful spot I felt a rush of gratitude. My heart quieted. A new serenity swept over me, and I felt closer to the Creator than ever before. In my memories the image of that moment still clings like a benediction.

Maxine Rhodes

THE ROSARY

One of the most comforting forms of prayer advocated by the Catholic Church is, to me, the Holy Rosary. The Rosary is a simple method of prayer originally used by faithful Catholics who were unable to read Psalms. The Rosary consists of a repetition of Our Father and ten Hail Mary's, five or fifteen times. When my mind is sorely troubled by earthly matters, I instinctively reach for my Rosary. I begin with the Apostle's Creed. Slowly my fingers slip across the gleaming beads. Softly I repeat Our Father, then three Hail Mary's. Lovingly I repeat these beautiful prayers to myself; not mechanically, but with reverence; not with empty soul, but with a soul filled with love and understanding. So complete is my concentration that it shuts out my immediate surroundings. As the fifteen mysteries pass majestically through my mind, I seem to be a part of them. The Annunciation brings joy to me, a joy that makes me weep at the Nativity. Faintly I feel Christ's intense agony on the Cross; I accompany the Virgin as she sorrowfully beholds him. Joyfully I witness the Descent of the Holy Ghost and the Assumption. I, too, join in the beautiful Coronation of the Blessed Virgin. Thus in a little blessed string of beads one can see and feel the beautiful story of the Gospels. As I lift the Cross to my humble lips in finality, my thoughts slowly return to earthly cares. But a new glow has entered my being — a feeling of content and safety that gives me courage to carry on in the troubled sea of life. Above all, the Rosary soothes me and strengthens my faith. Almost unconsciously I end with, "Oh God, make me a better Catholic!"

Blanche Orpelli

Useful and Suggestive Topics

Very often merely the reading of a series of topics will help the student to select a moment of his own pregnant with meaning.

*   *   *

Throughout the high school years, a student's statement of one or more of his beliefs gives him an opportunity to express something of the essence of his personality. Beginning with single sentences, some of them perhaps inconsistent in thought and mood, the student advances to an analysis of a story involving fundamental differences of opinion about a realistic dilemma of two or three boys or girls his own age. Our next step is to invite definitions of key words such as *happiness, love, human nature, democracy, maturity.* As in all writing, it is wise for us to encourage definitions of private importance before we proceed to definitions of social and intellectual significance. In high school years the creed a boy lives by is often bound up with attachment to particular people, sometimes members of his family, a girl he is in love with, or a teacher he admires. Nevertheless each of these attachments in itself has a social concomitant that sooner or later we must ask the student to crystallize for the sake of his maturation as a citizen. The word *success* may have a purely private meaning for a boy or girl but a social meaning for his or her classmates. For example, if a boy says in class, "My idea of success is to be the wealthiest man in this town," the social meaning of this ambition may be destructive. The class can help such a student to see the social consequences of his private belief. Similarly if a boy says, "You can't change human nature," it is the duty of the classroom to help him see that what he means is, "You can't change the depravity of human nature." When such a statement of a credo appears, the class must be prepared to analyze it sympathetically and realistically for the benefit not only of the writer, but also for the benefit of the class. In no other department of composition are the values of citizenship more fundamentally examined than in the formulation of a credo. As the culmination of his analysis, a student may select among his values one that he considers most crucial and extend it for the reader by describing a number of dramatic moments in which his belief was violated or sustained.

A theme of religious experience, though the most suggestive and enlightening of credos, is not subject to class analysis and appraisal by the criteria of intellectual consistency. Such a theme should be merely descriptive, its riches lying for the class in the exchange of memorable moments rather than in the testing of ideas. Yet in this exchange of memorable moments we often find the essence of private communication becoming in fact a citizen's opportunity to enter imaginatively into the life of neighbors with backgrounds different from his own. Certainly to comprehend the value and meaning of our three common faiths is an end we are all seeking without desiring to subject each other to rational tests in the field of faith. Some time in the high school years we wish to give an opportunity to each student to describe a moment in which his religious faith was most intense. In this moment we may find the core of his faith; but around this core of faith are many secular beliefs which in free discussion may lead our students to more mature and enlightened concepts of a democratic way of life.

To the Student Teacher: Suggested Activities

1. Teachers of English are notoriously weak in anthropology. Literature is the study of man, yet most English teachers do not have a scientific point of view about human nature. Read a portion of Alfred Kroeber's *Anthropology;* Ruth Benedict's *Patterns of Culture;* Henry George's *Progress and Poverty*, on heredity and environment, Book IX, Chapter IV; or Otto Klineberg's *The Negro and Selective Migration*. Quote a passage from one of these books that in your opinion gives a scientific view of human nature.
2. Write your own definition of *happiness* by describing a moment when you were completely happy. Follow the suggestions given on pp. 117–18.
3. Choose one of the statements about happiness on pp. 118–19. In a paragraph of about 200–300 words show why you think this is false or true.
4. Write a theme about a religious moment in your life, defining the word *religion* in your own way. Build up your moment with images of color, sight, sound, and touch. All of us have been influenced by religious customs or ideas. Your theme may represent a hostile point of view toward religion, a friendly point of view, or even an indifferent point of view.

But your moment should be so vivid that your attitude toward religion at that moment can be clearly visualized by the reader.

5. Write your own definitions in single sentences of the following words: *success, maturity, creativity, student, college.*

SUGGESTED READINGS

BERTRAM, JEAN DESALES, "Books to Promote Insights into Family-Life Problems," *English Journal*, Vol. 45 (November, 1956), pp. 477–82
Describes fruitful results with particular novels and student response to particular passages.

BRUNER, JEROME S.: *The Process of Education*, Harvard University Press, 1963
Searching and exciting examination of fundamental theories. Chapters on "Readiness for Learning," "Intuitive and Analytic Thinking," "Motives for Learning," and "Aids to Teaching." On memory Professor Bruner writes, "Unless detail is placed into a structured pattern, it is rapidly forgotten. Detailed material is conserved in memory by the use of simplified ways of representing it."

BURTON, DWIGHT L.: "Books to Meet Students' Personal Needs," *English Journal*, Vol. 36 (November, 1947), pp. 469–73
Contains a useful list of student problems as well as a list of novels centered around these problems. An illuminating study.

ELKINS, DEBORAH: "Students Face Their Problems," *English Journal*, Vol. 38 (November, 1949), pp. 498–503
Description of an experiment in the use of literature to help students come to terms with their own problems. Useful list of helpful books appended.

FIDONE, WILLIAM G.: "The Theme's the Thing," *English Journal*, Vol. 48 (December, 1959), pp. 518–23
Grouping great books by themes, such as "Man and Nature," "The Utopian Dream," "The Jazz Age," "Religion and the Search for Certainty in a World of Doubt." Exciting and fruitful article.

FRANK, ROBERT: "An Experiment in Senior English," *English Journal*, Vol. 38 (January, 1949), pp. 10–12
Description of an actual classroom experience in which "cynical," bored students were aroused to active participation by presenting them with problems and projects that were closely related to their lives.

GILLESPIE, CLARE M. and ZLOTNIK, HAROLD: "What Makes Me Tick? A Unit in Attitudes," *English Journal*, Vol. 40 (September, 1951), pp. 374–78
Working with the guidance department of a large high school, these teachers use theme writing effectively to help students clarify their problems.

HORST, J. M.: "English in Human Relationships," *English Journal*, Vol. 37 (December, 1948), pp. 524–29

How a "sense of human relationships" was introduced into a program for students of the eleventh year.

MACKINTOSH, HELEN K.: "The World of the English Teacher," *English Journal*, Vol. 47 (March, 1958), pp. 111–17

The central necessity of English teaching is awareness of the personal problems of the students. Miss Mackintosh believes that such questions as, "Three times happy," "Three times afraid," "Three times angry," and "Three times ashamed," make writing a deeper and richer experience than is possible with more conventional topics. One student said to a teacher, "Why don't you sound our depths?"

MINTON, ARTHUR C.: "Thinking-Composition," *English Journal*, Vol. 40 (January, 1951), pp. 7–11

The use of themes with problems bearing on personal ethics and responsibility.

RUSSELL, EDNA F.: "What Should I Do?" *English Journal*, Vol. 32 (September, 1943), pp. 382–86

Account of an interesting classroom experience in motivating students towards statements of their philosophy of life.

SHELLHAMMER, LOIS B.: "Solving Personal Problems through Socio-drama," *English Journal*, Vol. 38 (November, 1949), pp. 503–05

How students acted out situations or problems in the classroom to clarify the conflicts involved.

WERF, LESTER V.: "Textures in the Teaching of English," *English Journal*, Vol. 40 (December, 1951), pp. 559–61

Interesting discussion of social purpose of learning and group work; "digging into life-values."

WHITFIELD, RUTH M.: "The Therapeutic Value of Letter-Writing," *English Journal*, Vol. 33 (November, 1944), pp. 489–91

The use of letter writing as a more direct means to achieve honesty and sincerity in themes, as well as an outlet for students' emotional and moral problems.

WOLFE, DON M. and GEYER, ELLEN M.: *Enjoying English 10*, Singer, 1954, Experience Unit 9, "Yet All Experience Is an Arch"

Suggested theme assignment on religious experience.

WOLFE, DON M. and GEYER, ELLEN M.: *Enjoying English 11*, Singer, 1955, Experience Unit 4: "This I Believe"

Writing a long paper on one pattern of one's philosophy of life. Introductions to specific problems: What do I believe about human nature? What do I believe about happiness?

10   Can Creative Writing
Be a Democratic Art?

ABOUT TEN YEARS AGO, at Brooklyn Polytechnic Institute, a short, stubby boy with yellow hair and a bumptious grin appeared in a freshman English class. His name was Karl Schultz. The stress in the class was on grammar and sentence structure, at which the teacher pounded away daily with little effect on the mind of Karl Schultz. Though always in a gay humor, his grin unfailing, Karl failed his usage tests regularly.

Meanwhile the teacher, in desperation, suggested a theme on family: father, mother, brothers, and sisters. From old files he read to his class a few of his best themes. The following week, when the thirty boys brought their papers to class, the teacher knew some of the patterns: the whimsical, mellow dad; the jolly moments; the mother waiting, late at night; the restraints, the bitter silences. Only a few students could fail; one of them would be Karl. But when the teacher came to Karl's theme about his father, it brought him up with a shock. As a little boy, wrote Karl, he found he could not brag about his father, a man who seemed just to mope around the house all day and never do anything. Talking with the gang at the corner, he longed to say that his father was a truck-driver, an engineer on a train, a policeman, a tavern-keeper. One day, unusually distraught, he ran into the house and burst out to his mother, "Why ain't my dad like other dads? Why couldn't he have been an aviator, anyway?"

"Well, son," replied his mother, "your father was an aviator, a pilot in the 187th Imperial German Squadron of World War I. But he was shot down over France, and he has never been the same man since."

From this time forth, wrote Karl, he was proud of his dad. He could brag, but now he didn't want to. When he came running in from school, he ran to his dad and talked eagerly, a throb of pride and wonder in his throat.

In One's Own Life: The Unique Vein

Though Karl's theme was full of errors, the teacher marked it a "B" and read it to the class anonymously as the best theme of the week. At the end of the semester, however, he was forced to fail Karl, who in four long months could not learn to distinguish an adverb from an adverbial clause or to put a period between two sentences, especially when the second sentence opened with *However*. For that teacher Karl's success in creative writing and his concurrent failure in grammatical terminology marked a milestone in his professional growth. Here was a boy who in one leap could bring to life a deep unique vein in his life; yet his mind was as impenetrable to the abstractions of language as the teacher's own mind to the abstractions of calculus or physics. From that time forth the instructor was convinced more than ever that the psychological unburdening of creative expression and especially the art of image-making are more easily attainable by the average student than the mastery of correctness and infinitely more valuable to him. Each year hundreds of teachers in America, like the Polytechnic instructor, are becoming more aware that the creative process, which can be learned more easily than grammar and punctuation, is of such dynamic impress on the student's mind that it will remain with him the rest of his life.

"Every man," said Emerson, "is eloquent once in his life." But this is to minimize man's powers. When a boy or girl feels deeply, eloquence appears as if by magic, if only a phrase, a metaphor, a sentence. Eloquence is the sure concomitant of the pouring-forth of the immense well of feeling. As Karl wrote about his father, his language suddenly acquired, the teacher found, a new individuality, a flow of vivid phrase and rounded sentence, stinging with an intensity remote from his past themes of perfunctory topics.

Again and again the theme of family life, when presented by a sympathetic teacher, calls forth papers remarkable as emotional therapy, as well as for stylistic intensity. From my friends, as well as from my own classes, I have culled a number of stories that suddenly tie in one great knot teacher and student, school and life.

"Until recently," wrote Mary Holt, "I thought my mother hated me. From early childhood I sensed her hostility." Mary was the daughter of Russian immigrants in a western Pennsylvania steel town. She was an ugly child, brown and skinny. When she was six, her mother had sent her to school in Russian clothes. Not until near the end of high school did Mary's mother notice that Mary drew away when she came near. The harassed mother had had no time for Mary, who did not understand her mother's preference for her little brother.

In the prosperous district of Brooklyn, Henry Gilbert hated his father from the age of six, when as a punishment he was placed in the hallway of his apartment building wearing nothing but pajamas. A neighbor woman passed through the hall, saw him, and laughed. In Henry's mind the laugh was unforgettable and his father unforgivable. An obedient boy, he went his way, never crossed his father's will. Until his freshman year at college, when he wrote about this experience, Henry still hated his father. His hatred of his father was a deep cavern in his life, now lighted for the first time by a more rational searching and a more mature evaluation than he would have thought possible.

It is easy enough to say that in high school and college one should stimulate school themes on happy moments and pleasant memories. To pass by the deep conflicts of the student's life, however, instead of leading him to face and examine them, is to do the student a grave injustice, divorcing his deepest life from an outlet only the sympathetic teacher can provide. Every day the skillful school counselor listens eagerly and helpfully to students from homes broken by poverty, neglect, and despair. In such daily emergencies is the English teacher to be wanting, when he may invite to his desk papers that will haunt his dreams and summon a new patience, a new energy, to the task of meaningful composition?

The aims of correctness, however necessary, fall into appropriate focus when a pupil lays bare a deep-running stream of his daily life. To a pupil writing such a theme, however, correctness suddenly looms very important. When a sentence describes sorrow or heartbreak, a moment of ecstasy or despair, it suddenly becomes meaningful, as Ellen Geyer has said, to give it the dignity of correctness.

What is often forgotten is that each individual's life possesses a uniqueness communicable in the end by him alone. "The life of every individual," wrote Novalis, "should be a bible to us all." The problem, then, is to lead the pupil to explore one by one the patterns of his own unique life: his childhood fears and ecstasies, the places he knows well, friendships made and friendships broken, the events of death and birth in his family, first sweethearts, intense moods, peaks of feeling; the origin and growth of his prejudices, the changes in his religious outlook; the impact of his street, his gang, his school, his teachers upon his life; his moments of exhilaration, joy, despair; his dreams, his early mornings and his midnight hours. In the past most teachers and curriculum planners have not felt free to incorporate the most vital experiences of all in the so-called "experience curriculums." In the future, it is hoped that, as teachers and planners, we may grapple with these most fundamental experiences, relegating the more superficial experience patterns to their rightful subordinate roles in classroom time and attention.

Image-Making: The Indispensable Tool

To express his uniqueness, every boy or girl needs, it is true, at least one indispensable tool of the craft, skill in image-making. By image-making I mean the reproduction of sounds, colors, sensations of touch, taste, and smell. At any one moment each of us is alive to the world about him through the five senses. Any normal boy or girl can be taught to use color words, sound words, taste words, smell words, in describing a moment of his experience. A good preparation for this is to ask the pupil to write five brief descriptions, one emphasizing sound, another color, another taste, with as much mingling of the senses as possible:

Sight: LITTLE FROZEN FACES

Look closely at the ice cubes in a refrigerator tray. They are like so many little frozen faces in metal picture frames.

Sound: DISH-PAN HANDS

Not from the radio, but from the dish-pan rises the after-dinner music. The selection begins in light, airy moods and ends with sorrowful, deep bass notes. First, there is the *tinkle, clink, clink, tinkle* of the crystal glasses, which grows into a stronger, resounding tone — *kling, ping, kling, ping* — as the silverware flies from pan to drainboard. For variation the milk bottle adds its *glug, glug, glick* as it drowns in the foamy water and sinks to the bottom of the sudsy depths. The rather flat monotones of the everyday dishes are followed by the fierce, crashing notes of the pots and pans, and the final crescendo of the frying pan as it *bongs* upon the hook from which it is to hang. But wait, with the last piece completed and the water sliding from the tilted pan, one last spoon adds a tinkling note of hope as it slops into the sink. New hope — for what? It is a hope that someone other than I will enjoy the pleasure of the dishpan music tomorrow evening.

Virginia C. Barber

Smell: OF COOKIES AND GRANDMOTHERS

Perhaps your grandmother had an old rose-leaf jar, just as mine did. Then you, too, sniffed the odors of cookies and candies, and grandmothers, and flowers, and spices, all from one little pot.

Taste: STUFFED WITH RED PEPPER

Once I ate a stink bug. He was hidden in a luscious red raspberry, one of a handful which I should have put into the basket I was supposed to be filling. Instead, I popped the handful into my mouth and bit right into the middle of him. If he wasn't stuffed with red pepper, he certainly tasted like it. For hours afterwards the lining of my mouth was drawn and wrinkled and my tongue burned uncomfortably.

Touch: LIKE LOOSE WET PAPER

On a hot sultry morning I feel most uncomfortable. The collar of my shirt softens and clings to my skin like the loose wet paper on a billboard.

This process of sensory reporting of experience the average boy or girl grasps not only readily but eagerly. The colors and sounds of the moving picture, radio, television, reinforce the teacher's instruction at every step. The class may go hunting for sounds in the halls of any school, scattering to many places, returning in ten minutes with a rich record of varied sounds. The class may describe one of its own members as he stands in front of the room. Who can resist a puppy on a teacher's desk, held by his proud master as the class catches the puppy's antics in varied word portraits? The class may describe the sounds and colors of early morning, of a favorite meal, the smell of bacon and eggs, the reds and yellows and oranges of falling leaves in October.

Creativity within Reach

The person is rare who even without training never creates a phrase or a sentence of literary intensity. As Mrs. Poyser in *Adam Bede* struck off memorable similes in her daily conversation (". . . if you're to be corked up for ever, and only dribble your mind out by the sly, like a leaky barrel"), millions of humble people speak so creatively that the world would be richer for a record of their language creations. "To evoke in oneself," wrote Tolstoy in *What Is Art?* "a feeling one has once experienced and having evoked it in oneself then by means of movements, lines, colors, sounds, or forms expressed in words, so to transmit that feeling that others experience the same feeling — this is the activity of art." Few students are so limited as not to be able to use color words, sound words, touch words, in their own language. One sentence of real literature in a pupil's theme, moreover, is worth in appreciation the discussion of many pages of literature. In creating a single intense, original image, a student not only learns appreciation of literature with a clarity and insight not to be gained in appreciation classes but also gains a sense of unique achievement in the use of our common language: No other boy or girl could write those words, because no other boy or girl has felt exactly the same shading of experience or observed in the same light or with the same eyes a single house, a moon, a yard, a face.

A few years ago an instructor at American University, Washington, D.C., was called upon to teach English to fifty-three disabled veterans, eleven of them amputees. Though the teacher had been asked to teach letter-writing and grammar, he soon discarded this procedure in favor of the visualization of personal experience, beginning with simple descriptions of trees or fields or places the fifty-three veterans had known in their youth. From thirty states they had gathered, nervous and tense, full of hope for the future and eagerness to become counselors to disabled veterans like themselves. From home life to rookie days, to first combat, to the fateful moment of searing shell or blasting bomb, to hospitalization, to the return home and the struggle to find useful work again: these were the themes of their writing in a six months' course.

Week by week they wrote, dipping deep into bitter memories, calling up moments of eager laughter and hilarious horseplay. From this experience of writing week by week about things that desperately mattered came a book, *The Purple Testament*, for which each wrote at least one story. Of the fifty-three men and women in the class, no more than one or two failed to visualize sound by sound, color by color, and touch by touch at least one joyous or bitter moment.

Of the fifty-three men and women, only three were college graduates. Many had not yet graduated from high school. For this group of adults, creating images was a process easily learned and readily applied to the necessities of communication. Such image-making, the core of creative expression, is an art that any man or woman, any boy or girl, of normal intelligence can readily acquire.

Among his many tasks, the English teacher is forced day by day to make choices fateful for his students. Many teachers prefer an hour on a great poem to an hour on pupil themes. However vital to the student, the themes to such a teacher seem trivial and unimportant compared to "The Vision of Sir Launfal" or a soliloquy of Lady Macbeth. For the illumination of such great passages the English teacher has had special training. Actually, however, for perceiving each other's needs and troubles, an hour (in which the most vital themes must often be read anonymously) spent on first love, first hate, first disappointment, first disillusionment in a teacher or a friend, an hour on such topics, whatever the lack of literary accomplishment, is an experience to the class that may bestow crucial benefits for decades to come.

Appreciation of Literature: Creative Writing Points the Way

The most fundamental way, moreover, to the appreciation of literature is the attempt of the pupil to reproduce in his own way, however faint and faltering, the effects of the creative process by which the masters transmuted their own experiences into "something so written to aftertimes as they should not willingly let it die." The potentialities of creative writing as a democratic art, exemplified in such books as *The Purple Testament* and *They All Want to Write*, present an endless vista, largely as yet unrealized, of the professional growth and influence of the English teacher, whether he labors on the elementary, the high school, or the college level.

Like a good physician or the trained counselor, the English teacher dares not pass moral judgment on the stream of life that daily or weekly flows across his desk. In *Look Homeward, Angel*, Thomas Wolfe wrote of a high school teacher who understood that "every boy is to himself a monster." Should the stabs of guilt that daily press into his chest find a record in his class papers? Should the love life of the high school boy or girl, more intense and furious than any other he will ever know, find no voice in papers, but rather only on street corners or in locker rooms or the darkness of parked cars?

There are, of course, limits to frankness, even with the most sympathetic and tactful teacher. But it is no credit to our profession that our students must find ears other than our own for their terrifying secrets, secrets that somehow lose their power to poison and betray us when they find the clean record of pen and ink, even if only one confessor can read and understand.

If the teacher expects that memorable intensity that comes only from the deepest ecstasies and torments, he must be shockproof, a listener with impartial ears and open mind, eager to understand, reluctant to condemn. Once a pupil realizes that any facet of his own life brings a shock to the eye or a sudden pallor to the cheek of his teacher, he will never again return to that moment pregnant with insight into himself and illumination for the teacher.

Whether the pupil's age is eight years, twelve, fifteen, twenty, or fifty years, creative writing as a democratic art can be taught. Each person, however humble or limited, can learn gradually the dignity of his own experience, seeing in his life the unique materials of potential literature. This is the first step, a step that students of all ages can accomplish with ease under a sympathetic teacher and in a friendly group of fellow-students.

If this view is sound, English teachers in the United States, dealing each year more realistically with the meaning of experience materials, have a remarkable opportunity not only to participate in a movement that will bring intrinsic satisfaction over a lifetime to the pupils themselves but also to fertilize the growth of a new and more representative generation of young writers on the American scene than has hitherto appeared.

To the Student Teacher: Suggested Activities

1. Get a copy of Tolstoy's *What Is Art?* from the library. Look for sentences which illuminate Tolstoy's definition of art. Copy on your paper five or six such passages. Under each passage write a brief notation of your impression of Tolstoy's statement.
2. Borrow from the library George Eliot's *Adam Bede*. Read passages describing Mrs. Poyser. Bring to class a number of original bits of dialogue in which images and metaphors brighten her daily conversation.
3. Read a portion of one of the following books: *Creative Youth*, by Hughes Mearns; *They All Want to Write*, by Alvina T. Burrows, *et al.* Does Mr. Mearns believe that creative writing can be a democratic art? In a brief paragraph show the implications of the philosophy stated in one of these books.
4. What passage in the chapter you have just read do you feel will be most helpful to you as a teacher? Quote the passage and explain why you have selected it.
5. Read a portion of *Look Homeward, Angel* or *You Can't Go Home Again*, by Thomas Wolfe. How does Thomas Wolfe use images of sensory intensity? Quote a passage in which he appeals to several of the five senses. Then write a brief paragraph about this passage showing what means he has used to make his style electric. What metaphors or similes does this passage contain?

Suggested Readings

"Academy Awards in Writing for Students," *The Student Writer*, Vol. 2 (May, 1963), pp. 8–32

An exciting issue of a new magazine devoted entirely to creative writing by high school students. Address: 2651 North Federal Highway, Fort Lauderdale, Florida.

Appy, Nellie: *Pupils Are People*, Appleton-Century-Crofts, 1941

A series of essays on individual differences in children prepared by the Committee on Individual Differences of the National Council of Teachers of English. See particularly the essay by Paul Witty, pp. 37–58.

BROWN, ELEANOR F.: "Creative Expression via Student Journals," *English Journal*, Vol. 29 (September, 1940), pp. 582–85
> How the keeping of daily journals by the student may be used as a basis for interesting writing.

BRUNER, JEROME S.: *On Knowing, Essays for the Left Hand*, Harvard University Press, 1962
> Exciting chapters on the conditions of creativity, identity in the modern novel, art as a mode of knowing, and the act of discovery.

CHAPIN, G. ESTHER: "Help Them Create," *English Journal*, Vol. 38 (December, 1949), pp. 577–79
> This article has a number of good suggestions for the teacher who is interested in stimulating really creative writing by students.

Children Learn to Write, ed. Fannie J. Ragland, National Council of Teachers of English, 1944
> Various ways of encouraging children to write effectively, with many illustrations of pupil response.

English for the Academically Talented Student, ed. Arno Jewett, NCTE
> A useful survey of ways and means to expand the achievements of the gifted student on the high school level.

Four Quarters (ed. Brother Edward Patrick, La Salle College, Philadelphia 41), Vol. 10 (November, 1960)
> Contains valuable symposium on the question "Can creative writing be taught?" with responses by John F. Kennedy, Don Wolfe, Theodore Morrison, Malcolm Cowley, and others.

Four Quarters (ed. Brother Edward Patrick, La Salle College, Philadelphia 41), Vol. 10 (January, 1961)
> Valuable symposium on the teaching of creative writing by Anthony West, Ray Bradbury, John Knowles, John O'Hara, Katherine Anne Porter, Paul Bowles, and others.

GUILD, FLORENCE: "Maintaining a Creative Atmosphere," *English Journal*, Vol. 39 (March, 1950), pp. 154–58
> How to encourage the self-respect of the student and help him to realize the worth of his personality and experiences.

LABRANT, LOU: "Teaching High School Students to Write," *English Journal*, Vol. 35 (March, 1946), pp. 125–28
> The case for creative writing from personal experience is stated here with exceptional clarity and force.

MCKENZIE, BELLE: "The Demands of Creative Writing," *English Journal*, Vol. 29 (June, 1940), pp. 445–49
> Addressed to beginning teachers, this essay demonstrates that creative writing is the student's honest use of his own experience.

MERRIAN, H. G.: "Who Can Teach Creative Writing?" *English Journal,* Vol. 36 (November, 1947), pp. 464–69

> For the teacher who is doubtful of his ability to teach creative writing.

REDFORD, GRANT H.: "Of Teachers, Students, and 'Creative Writing,'" *English Journal,* Vol. 42 (December, 1953), pp. 490–96

> Both teachers and students must value the "desire to share one's experiences with others, and by means of this intimate communication to transcend the isolation of self," before students can make meaningful writing contributions.

ROODY, SARAH I. and LYMEN, BESS: "Managing Student Writing," *English Journal,* Vol. 44 (February, 1955), pp. 75–79

> Two teachers present their time-saving methods of planning and grading writing assignments.

THORNLEY, WILSON R.: "The Case for Creative Writing," *English Journal.* Vol. 44 (December, 1955), pp. 528–31

> A forceful evaluation of the need to include in school curricula the study of "creative communication in the language we live by."

WARREN, JAMES E., JR.: "The 'Brown Book': An Outlet for *Real* Writing," *English Journal,* Vol. 42 (January, 1953), pp. 11–15

> This resourceful teacher organized a publication for student creative writing, with issues devoted to "Science-Fiction and Fantasy," "Travel," "Arts," and "Interesting People."

———— "The Topic Sentence in Creative Writing," *English Journal,* Vol. 36 (December, 1947), pp. 530–32

> Instead of giving a subject for a composition, the author suggests giving a topic sentence which will stimulate the imaginations of the students. Interesting examples are given.

WESTON, JOHN: "A Case for Creativity," *English Journal,* Vol. 50 (May, 1961), pp. 346–48

> "All art appeals primarily to the senses, the five standard ones and the sixth one of the soul."

When Children Write, Association for Childhood Education International, 1955

> The situations in which children write willingly, and how to get them started.

WOLFE, DON M.: "Can Creative Writing Be a Democratic Art?" *English Journal,* Vol. 40 (October, 1951), pp. 428–32

> The value of the psychological unburdening of creative expression and the importance of the stimulation of image-making for students.

Part II

USAGE AND GRAMMAR

11 What Are Minimum Essentials?

To NO TWO TEACHERS does the term *minimum essentials* carry quite the same meaning. To one teacher the supreme essential might be to unlock the psyche of a boy who has never known what it means to speak or write freely about himself. To such a teacher in such a situation the boy's poor spelling may fade into insignificance. To another teacher *minimum essentials* may mean those elements of speech correctness which enable a boy to speak before the class without falling into the common habitual errors. To still another teacher *minimum essentials* are the elements of written correctness without which a student cannot represent himself in respectable English. Finally, whether one believes the search for minimum essentials should apply to written or to spoken English, there is some disagreement on the particular essentials that should receive priority in classroom time and attention.

Those teachers who claim that we should strive first for minimum essentials of correctness in speech will find an admirable analysis in *Teaching English Usage*, by Robert Pooley, who has tabulated lists of errors which should and should not be attacked on junior and senior high school levels (see below, pp. 471–77). Very few of the errors in Mr. Pooley's list are troublesome in written English, though they abound in speech. Should the teacher concentrate then on these speech errors and make them her first line of attack? Those who answer affirmatively point to the fact that students now speak a thousand times more often than they write, and will follow a similar pattern in adult life. By the same token, however, if a student speaks a thousand words for every one word or ten words he writes, his errors in speech will be proportionately more difficult to eliminate. This is a fact generally disregarded by those who believe that minimum essentials in speech should receive priority of classroom attention. The boy who says, "I did it" correctly in a classroom situation may say, "I done it" a dozen times on playground, bus, and telephone before the day is over. Indeed, as experienced teachers know, this is the normal pattern of things. Most students do not dare to speak correctly when their parents and friends speak incorrectly. The weight and drag of custom are a thousand times stronger than the correct speech pattern learned in the classroom. The child will not speak correctly until *he wishes to emulate the correct speech habits of the people around him.* But even if our students wish to speak correctly against the customs of their peers, their errors in speech are a thousand times more frequent than their errors in writing. To deal effectively, then, with minimum errors in speech on any level from the seventh grade through the twelfth would require a prohibitive allotment of classroom time.

It is a mistake to assume that drill on common speech errors will have a drastic effect on correctness in written English. A glance at Mr. Pooley's list for either junior or senior high school (below, pp. 471–77) shows that few of these errors occur in student themes. In almost every spoken sentence a student has a chance to make an error in pronoun usage; not so in written English. Though every written sentence contains a verb, the problem verbs do not appear nearly so frequently in writing; even when they do, the student often writes them correctly, contrary to his speech custom at home or among his friends.

I do not say that we should not attack the common errors in speech even when we feel we cannot crack the barriers of custom. This approach to speech correctness, however, can be most profiitably carried on in the elementary classroom from the third through the sixth grade, when pupils often take delight in language games. In junior and senior high school we can call attention to speech errors, but we cannot hope to eliminate them. A highly illuminating study of the *order* in which minimum essentials in both speech and writing should be dealt with in the elementary grades may be found in Mr. L. J. O'Rourke's *Rebuilding the English Curriculum.* Mr. O'Rourke identified fifty-one important elements of oral usage and twenty-seven problems of written usage (see below, pp. 479–81). Mr. O'Rourke's table of essentials, together with Mr. Pooley's selection of particular errors makes a highly useful checklist of speech problems from which the high school teacher may select the speech errors he wishes to attack in his particular classroom.

I would define *minimum essentials,* then, as the main elements of correctness in written usage. I do not deny that a boy's speech in later life is infinitely more important than writing skill. But mastery of errors in speech can come only when he *wants* to speak correctly, a condition that applies with less force to his errors in writing. Even when a boy is ashamed to speak correctly, he often wants very much to write correctly: he speaks for the esteem of his peers but writes for the esteem of his teacher. Mastery of minimum essentials in writing is a practical, attainable goal; mastery of minimum essentials in speech is as unattainable as Paul Bunyan's stride. Whatever our efforts, it is very difficult for us to make a record of class errors in speech. To make a record of class errors in writing, however, is a relatively easy task, simply by tabulating the mistakes in several sets of student themes. The written errors of our own classroom we may check with those tabulated in special investigations, of which two of the most useful are Stormzand and O'Shea, *How Much English Grammar* (below, pp. 482–83), and Harap, "The Most Common Grammatical Errors" (below, pp. 484–90).

When we read a set of thirty themes with appalling errors in spelling, sentence sense, and capitalization, not to mention manuscript and penmanship untidiness, how do we begin to pin down essentials? One way, as suggested above, is to make a list of all the errors in the first several collections of themes. For the time being, we exclude such things as dangling participles, which require some knowledge of grammar to cope with, also all comma errors. Knowing where to put a period is now and later a hundred times more important than knowing where to put a comma. When we begin to classify our errors, if the class is ninth grade, we may discover something like this:

1. Everyone has penmanship and manuscript faults.
2. Every student has some spelling difficulties, perhaps one-fourth or one-fifth of the total.

3. About one-fifth of the errors are derived from confusion about meaning, such as *it's-its*, *who's-whose*, etc.
4. Often one-third of the errors are sentence-sense errors.
5. About one-sixth may be capitalization errors, such as *Oak trees*, *Football*, etc.

By thus counting and classifying the errors in the first few sets of themes, we may define the term *minimum essentials* for our own students and give drill on those principles they now need in order to eliminate the greatest number of errors in the shortest time. Let us consider these classes of minimum essentials one by one.

Manuscript and Penmanship Essentials

A forceful way to dramatize minimum essentials in manuscript form is to hold up each paper in the first set and show in what way it has not met our requirements of the first assignments. This criticism we carry through in a firm, kindly way. "This paper lacks a margin on the right," we may say. "What is wrong with this paper?" Perhaps the writer himself answers: "I forgot to leave a space under the title," or "I forgot to leave the last line of the page open," or "I forgot to write on only one side of the paper." In the first papers and in many later ones these are common weaknesses. For the next assignment we may insist on a line in pencil for the right margin or a couple of X's in pencil on the last line to remind the writer himself to leave it open. When the first manuscripts come in, and we have held up each one for class criticism, it is often advisable to have them rewritten for the next day, even before we read them for other errors than manuscript ones. In showing some papers, we may say, "Make each capital letter a half inch high. Leave a half inch after each period. These two principles alone will make your penmanship readable." Of course, calling attention to manuscript requirements is not sufficient unless we follow through with specific penalties for specific violations. A reduction of five per cent or eight per cent for a poor margin, for too small a capital letter, or for failure to leave a space after a period, is the kind of reminder many students must have before they use the care necessary to overcome careless habits of manuscript preparation.

Spelling the Problem Words

When time permits concentrated drill, we turn first to spelling errors as the easiest to identify and correct in the shortest time. The many books and pamphlets written about spelling are relatively valueless unless they help to identify the words misspelled most frequently. Throughout the high school years and even in the first year of college, sixty of the most commonly misspelled words are these:

all right	disappear	its	quit	there
among	disappoint	later	receive	they're
athletics	doesn't	lose	relieve	together
beginning	embarrass	loose	sandwich	too
believe	experience	necessary	sentence	to
benefit	finally	occasion	separate	tries
clothes	forty	occurrence	shining	until
coming	friend	pleasant	similar	who's
deceive	grammar	principal	stopped	whose
definite	hoping	principle	studying	women
describe	hurriedly	quiet	surprise	writing
dining room	it's	quite	their	you're

Each problem word has a trouble spot. In the word *sentence*, for example, the trouble spot is invariably the second *e;* in the word *separate* the trouble spot is the *a* of the second syllable. The best way to drill on the demons, then, is to provide a mimeographed list of the trouble words with the trouble spots left blank, like this:

1. am g the trees	4. good in ath etics	7. com ng too
2. al ight with me	5. a ben fit to us	8. dec ve me
3. begin g now	6. beautiful new cloth s	9. def te time

When the method above is adopted, however, we need to see that there is plenty of space for the students to write the letters. Some teachers may prefer to give the student hints as to the number of letters, like this:

am − − g the trees   al − − ight with me   begi − − − ng now

If we feel that writing the full word is important, we may ask the class to write the whole words on a separate sheet of paper or on full spaces provided under each word on the mimeographed sheet.

To master the list of sixty demons by this method requires a repetition of the same drill (preferably in slightly different form) five or six times. After each drill the class may wish to make a list on the board of all the words missed. Gradually the list will diminish. The class' special list of demons still unmastered may be mimeographed and given separately. In the class list we may decide to include words being misspelled in the themes. We may also include other demons not included in the sixty above, such as *acquaint, optimistic, business, decision, government, immediately, interest, realize, recommend.*

Meanwhile, for variation we may wish to dictate sentences containing demons like the following:

1. *Among their* most *pleasant experiences* are those spent in *athletics.*
2. My *friend described* the *principal dining* hall in camp.
3. *Hoping* to sell the *woman's shining* new *clothes,* the *villain* was *disappointed.*
4. *You're quite* certain the *beginning* of the *sentence* is *all right?*
5. The wheel came *loose* and *later* was *separated* from *its* axle.
6. *They're studying* the *necessary principles* of *grammar too hurriedly.*
7. *It's too* late *to* know *whose sandwiches* have been *received.* We must not *lose* our list.
8. He *doesn't* want to *embarrass* or *surprise* us with a *definite* offer.
9. When the shouting *definitely stopped,* I yelled, "*Who's there?*"
10. *Until* this *occasion* it had not *occurred* to us to *deceive* him by *coming* home *together.*

Confusion of Meaning: The Key Problem Words

Other words difficult to spell and use correctly are those in which the meaning is confused, often because the two or three words are pronounced in the same or nearly the same way. Some of these difficult words are repeated in the spelling demons above. A confusion of *it's* and *its* is much harder to cope with than a misspelling of *occasion* or *believe.* Yet the use of *its* is also a spelling problem. Here are the main trouble words in this category:

1. there, their, they're
2. too, to, two
3. you're, your
4. it's, its
5. whose, who's
6. know, no, now
7. new, knew
8. quit, quite, quite
9. where, were
10. clothes, cloths
11. principle, principal
12. should of *for* should have
13. lose, loose
14. may, can
15. learn, teach
16. leave, let

Of these groups Numbers 1 to 5 and 11 are the most difficult essentials to master. Words 1 to 5 are of most frequent occurrence in student themes on all levels, hence the most urgent in our scale of priority. The confusion of *principal* and *principle* requires much more practice than most teachers can afford, especially in view of a chance of attainable mastery in the first five groups and all the others. We have no trouble in eliminating the confusion of *quit*, *quiet*, and *quite*, or of *clothes* and *cloths*, in which the ear easily differentiates one sound and one meaning from another. *Where* and *were* are also differentiated by ear, but with more difficulty.

Possessives as Problem Words

Possessives may also be considered a spelling problem. The simplest rule for forming the possessive is to add *'s* to any word not ending in *s: John's* tie, *men's* suits, *women's* hats. For words ending in *s*, add only the apostrophe: *Gladys'* coat, *Mr. Thomas'* house. This is the rule accepted by the United States Government *Style Manual*. If you think that the problem should be complicated by using an additional *s* as in *Jones's* house, many authorities will agree with you. Here is another instance of divided usage that all of us should prefer to be uniform. But few people that I know challenge the *Style Manual* preference as incorrect. We have enough complications without delving into all the exceptions noted on possessives by Webster's unabridged dictionary alone. Here are some representative problem possessives:

1. George's book	6. Burns' poems
2. one class' book	7. Dickens' novels
3. two classes' books	8. one sailor's shoes
4. one man's hat	9. two sailors' shoes
5. two men's hats	10. Mr. Thomas' lawn

The formation of the possessives above is comparatively simple for the high school student as compared with the formation of the possessive *its*. He has a hard time seeing why one should use an apostrophe with *John's dog*, but not with *its tail*. Yet I have never had a student use an apostrophe with the possessive *his*. Indeed one way to cope with the *its* problem is to say, "Is the word you want a possessive like *his*? When you say, 'its porch,' it is like saying, 'his porch.' Since you do not use an apostrophe with *his*, you do not use it with *its*. They are both possessive pronouns. It is only with nouns that we use the apostrophe to show possession."

Capital Letter Essentials

Why do many capitalization rules tend to confuse the student rather than aid him? The reason for this is plain: we fail to tell him what *not* to capitalize. Whether our experience is wide or narrow, the story is the same: students tend to use too many capitals rather than too few. We may always say about the capital letter, as Mark Twain did about the adjective. "When in doubt, leave it out." It is true that students fail generally (without rigorous drill) to capitalize the important words of a title or the first word of a quoted passage. But even these lapses are far less common than the exasperating *Sincerely Yours*, or such incorrect usages as *High School*, *Algebra*, and *Summer*.

To show the student most economically what and what not to capitalize, we can provide him with a Mastery Style Chart like the one opposite for the ninth grade. In this chart, as in all capitalization drills, we include the capital letter to open a sentence, keeping our inner eye on the most important minimum essential of all: sentence recognition.

How to Drill for Mastery of Essentials

In the preceding sections we have analyzed the meaning of *minimum essentials* as applied to the frequency and priority of written errors in spelling, capitalization, problem words similar in sound, and possessives. By a mastery of these essentials, the student can eliminate from fifty to seventy-five per cent of his theme errors thus far without any knowledge of grammar.

Before we go on to the most crucial minimum essential, sentence sense, it is fair to ask, "But how do you help the student achieve the mastery you aim at?" In answering this question, we can only add to the reservoir of suggested methods by which one teacher learns from others. The most effective method I have found for repeated

Mastery Style Chart: Capital Letters

I	II
algebra Spanish modern history American literature manual training	sophomore in high school junior class freshman King High School Freshman Class

III	IV
high school Mayfield High School senior in college Cleveland College	February Tuesday winter summer

V	VI
the Bible Greek gods and goddesses in His name the Almighty Father	My dear Sir: Dear Susan, Yours very sincerely, Very truly yours,

VII	VIII
We saw Dad a moment ago. *Or:* We saw dad a moment ago. He said, "We just saw my dad." I waited. We know Mother left. I know my mother is here. my aunt	the Far East the Middle West Go directly north. I traveled ten miles east.

IX	X
First Baptist Church Ohio River Eighteenth Street the Rocky Mountains	President Jones Mr. Jones, president of the college Coach Terry Mr. Terry, football coach

XI	XII
Pride and Prejudice Why I Like to Fish *The House of Seven Gables* My First Airplane Ride	tulips, roses, daisies oak trees, walnut trees tennis, basketball football, track

drill on various essentials is a dictated test lasting from five minutes to thirty minutes, with questions running through the scale of essentials, like this:

1. Spell *similar*.
2. Spell *its* as in the phrase "its color."
3. Spell *it's* as in the sentence, "It's my fault."
4. "It's their house." Spell *their*.
5. Spell *knew*. "I knew his name."
6. "Now is the time." Spell *now*.
7. Spell *all right*. Think of *all wrong*.
8. Spell *loose*, as in the phrase, "a loose wire."
9. "A quiet day." Spell *quiet*.
10. "He quit his job." Spell *quit*.
11. "He left *quite* early." Spell *quite*.
12. "I like Gladys' dress." Spell *Gladys'*.
13. "Who's the chairman?" Spell *who's*.
14. "Whose pen is this?" Spell *whose*.
15. "Too early." Spell *too*.
16. "I'm too tired now." Spell *too*.
17. "I know the principal parks in this city." Spell *principal*.
18. "We are learning the principles of grammar." Spell *grammar* and *principles*.
19. "Sincerely yours." Spell *yours*.
20. "We have many oak trees." Spell *oak*.

The first great advantage of this kind of drill is its flexibility: it permits a flexible time span, flexible choice of materials, flexible choice of emphasis. If ten minutes of a period are available after reading some themes in class, we may gather the errors together in this drill technique. If our class is weak in *too* and *their*, we may dictate as many as a hundred choices in fifteen minutes. We can give fifty questions to *principle* and *principal* or only five or six, as the occasion requires. Meanwhile we may turn to a particular student and say, "Jim, how did you answer Number 26?" We know from his papers that Jim hasn't straightened out *its* and *it's*. We know that a few others are weak, too. So we stop a few minutes for another explanation, asking for answers from other weak students. Thus this exercise makes possible effective adaptation to individual needs. Because our drill may run as high as a hundred questions, we are not concerned that we give the answers to several of them as we make explanations. Still another advantage, though an incidental one, is that this technique is a chatter-stopper and a concentration-starter. It enforces instant attention from everyone. When we wish the drill to be a formal test, we can ask that all answers be written with pen and ink. We may say, "Do not cross out your answer. One idea of this test is instantaneous correctness." Depending on the group, we may ask the students to exchange papers even though this may involve some hiking of grades. Soon we come to know the cheaters and how to deal with them individually. On this kind of test it is more difficult to cheat than on any other. The very speed of our dictation, when necessary, can prevent many glances at other papers.

Sentence Sense as a Primary Goal

Since various investigations and common experience show that failure of sentence sense in the ninth year accounts for about one-third of all errors, no other goal is so difficult or so highly prized as the attainment of unerring sentence recognition. Though it is first in importance, we place it last here in the sequence of minimum essentials only because many other errors are more easily erased in the early weeks of school. The sentence error is the most baffling of all errors, partly because it requires ultimately a fundamental comprehension of grammar, and partly because it has a mysterious and thus far unknown relation to maturing processes of thought that come automatically with the years. In high school years the proportion of sentence errors gradually declines, partly perhaps through a generally increasing awareness of the sentence as a unit of thought rather than through our own efforts in the classroom.

Nevertheless we can in a number of ways intensify and accelerate sentence awareness without as yet depending on grammatical resources. One of the most effective devices is to mimeograph eight or ten sentence errors from the first set of themes for discussion in class. If this is impracticable, we may ask eight or ten students to write on the board the fragments or run-on sentences that we have starred on their papers. In the ninth year and long after we must rely upon the student's ear to tell him where the old sentence ends and a new one begins. We must rely upon his ear to tell him the difference between a fragment and a whole thought. When the sentences from the class' own papers appear on the board, we may ask not the writer alone, but several other students also, to read the run-on or the fragment and tell the class how to correct it. One advantage is that these theme errors are personal; they involve language written about vital experience, not the language of text-book drills. Hence a discussion on the class' sentence errors makes an ideal beginning for the year-long struggle for sentence recognition.

The next step is to pin down the classes of sentence errors (with a few mimeographed drills if possible) by attacking first the most common run-on problems. Since they are the easiest to eliminate, we begin with the run-ons involving the pronouns *it, we, he, she,* and *they.* Of these the *it* run-on error is the most prevalent and the most difficult to banish:

> We soon spotted the house, it was the last one in the block.
> Please bring my sweater, it is on the bench.
> It was Jack, he was panting and sweating.
> Then we had a glimpse of Jane, she was sitting on the top row.
> Joan and I met at the corner, we went in together.
> Barbara had a cold, she couldn't come with us.
> Joe and Harold ran toward us, they were shouting and laughing.

Another kind of run-on error has its focus in an opening adverb of the second thought, usually *then, now, there, suddenly,* or *soon:*

> We opened the window and leaned out, then we heard a great shout.
> Suddenly there was a knock at the door, then we heard Jim's voice.
> We had only two minutes to play, now was the time.
> The sun was setting, soon it would be dark.
> Joe waited, suddenly he heard a loud crash.
> I turned around, there stood Dad.

Finally, of course, we have the run-on sentence that has no identifiable focus in either the adverb or the pronoun:

> We looked up at the sky, a cloud was sailing across the moon.
> We wrote far into the night, by that time we were all very tired.
> Where could Jack be, no one seemed to know.

We can deal with each of these classes of run-on errors in separate mimeographed drills. As they appear anew in themes, the students may write them on the board and read them aloud again. If the pronoun focus is the continuing trouble spot, we can give it additional time with a new drill. We may ask the students with the least sentence sense to make up drills for the class. We may read drills from textbooks and ask the class to write only the beginning words of the second sentence of each run-on. Still another approach to the run-on problem is to ask each student to do the following:

1. Write two complete thoughts, the second of which begins with the word *he*.
2. Write two complete thoughts, the second of which begins with the word *it*.

If time permits and the work seems fruitful, we may extend this kind of practice to all the pronouns and adverbs that appear in run-on constructions.

The fragment in either phrase or clause is much more difficult to deal with than the run-on habit. When a student writes, "Coming down the street and tipping his hat to Sadie," the thought appears fairly complete to him. Though we may struggle with him by asking, of course, "Who was coming?" the difference between his version and ours is often too subtle for him to grasp, particularly if he has named the hero for the third time in the sentence preceding. For those who comprehend, we can say that the fragment has neither subject nor verb, but this will not usually help the writer. Moreover such a clause fragment as the persistent "because he had always been my friend" has a subject and a verb. An effective drill, however, is to mimeograph a series of fragments with a sprinkling of whole sentences, and discuss them with the class. Though a student may often pay no attention to his teacher he will usually permit one of his fellow-students to give him insight. We may say to the class, "Here are ten word groups. Three of them are sentences. Seven of them are only pieces of sentences. First, then, which are whole sentences?" As the class identifies each fragment, we may call on the weak student to add words to it to make it a complete thought. Other students may complete the thought in different ways, thus reinforcing the concept more effectively than our own analysis can do.

Thus far in this program of minimum essentials, I have written nothing about grammar, or punctuation other than end signals. As long as a student cannot spot the end of a sentence, or tell a fragment from a whole, I cannot call comma pointing or a knowledge of transitive verbs a minimum essential. When I use the term *minimum essentials*, you may well ask, "For whom?" My concept of minimum essentials is the mastery of those principles which will allow the average student (who does not go to college) to write legibly and correctly in whole sentences, avoiding the most pervasive errors in spelling, capitalization, and problem words in possessives and contractions. I do not see how anyone can punctuate correctly or use pronouns correctly in speech without a pretty thorough grounding in grammar. But the teaching of grammar above and beyond the minimum essentials I have outlined is an impossible and unrealistic goal with the present pupil load carried by English teachers in America. If they each had fifteen pupils in a class instead of thirty to fifty, my program of minimum essentials would be more ambitious. As limitations now stand, however, I should be happy if every high school graduate could attain the goals of writing correctness outlined in this program of minimum essentials.

To the Student Teacher: Suggested Activities

1. Read Pooley's *Teaching English Usage* on minimum essentials, particularly pp. 191–240. Then make a chart of twenty-five errors (in the grade level of your choice) that you would concentrate on if you were dealing only with correct speech.

   What elements of usage does Mr. Pooley believe so disputable that they should not be taught? Make a list of twenty such usages that should be omitted from classroom teaching on the grade level of your choice.
3. Study carefully the selection from Stormzand and O'Shea, *How Much English Grammar?* (Appendix 11, p. 482). This chart shows, for example, that out of a thousand chances, the pupil fails to set off an introductory dependent clause with a comma 650 times. This is the most frequent error in student writing. Do you believe, therefore, that it should receive the greatest amount of drill as a minimum essential?
4. Name five errors in the list in Appendix 11, p. 408, that in your opinion should be given the greatest attention on the grade level of your choice. Give a reason under each selection for your judgment.
5. Ask a friend to give you the spelling test of words listed on pp. 417–18. Then list the words you missed, and for each word, name the grade level in which you remember first using this word.

6. Ask a teacher at the local high school or junior high school to permit you to mark a set of student themes. Be sure to get specific directions from her as to what errors you are to mark. Then, as you mark the papers, list the errors that you find and classify them as "spelling," "comma after adverbial clause," "sentence-sense error," etc. How many errors did you find in all? How many errors in each of the categories represented in the papers?

   From this analysis, what errors would you concentrate on in the grade level you have chosen?

7. Study the punctuation exercises in two or three ninth-grade books, such as *English in Action, Enjoying English, Building Better English*. Which exercise did you find that you think would be most useful in teaching seven or eight main comma rules? Then make a similar test of your own that you feel would be effective in teaching these rules.

Suggested Readings

BERRY, THOMAS ELLIOTT: *The Most Common Mistakes In English Usage*, Chilton Company Publishers, 1961

   A valuable book that pins down common errors in a realistic fashion, beginning with commonly confused words and including such chapters as "Errors in Using Prepositions," "Errors in Case," "Errors in Making Comparisons," "Redundancies," etc.

CROSS, E. A. and CARNEY, ELIZABETH: *Teaching English in High Schools*, Macmillan, 1950

   Chapter X, on spelling demons, capitalization, and vocabulary, is rich in specific helps.

End-of-Year Examinations in English for College-Bound Students, Grades 9–12. 1963. College Entrance Examination Board, Princeton, N. J.

   This valuable booklet contains sample questions in literature and composition, sample responses by students, and evaluations of the responses. Question 3, Grade 10, is alone worth a teacher's investment in this book.

FINCH, HARDY R.: "Some Spelling Problems and Procedures," *English Journal*, Vol. 42 (April, 1953), No. 4, pp. 190–92

   A useful review of resources and techniques.

FINCH, HARDY R., BELL, HARRISON B., and BROCHICK, ANNA: *Spelling for You*, Prentice-Hall, 1959

   Excellent progression of spelling lessons and cumulative reviews. Emphasis on trouble spots in difficult words. Appealing and effective drawings. Excellent sections also on handwriting and dictionary study.

HARAP, HENRY: "The Most Common Grammatical Errors," *English Journal*, Vol. 19 (June, 1930), pp. 440–46

   One of the three or four most useful summaries of common errors. See this list below, pp. 410–14.

HILDRETH, GERTRUDE: *Teaching Spelling*, Holt, 1955
See "Some Techniques of Word Study," pp. 256–66, and "Improvement of Spelling in High School and Beyond," pp. 267–85.

Improve Your Writing, U. S. Government Printing Office, Washington, D.C., 1959
A useful summary of minimum essentials (28 pp.).

MCGUIRE, EDNA: "College Freshmen on Writing in High School," *English Journal*, Vol. 51 (April, 1962), pp. 256–58
A valuable sampling of opinion in response to specific questions, such as, "How often should high school students write? How should the teacher mark the themes?"

MARCKWARDT, ALBERT H., and WALCOTT, FRED: *Facts about Current English Usage*, National Council of Teachers of English, 1938
An important list of established, disputable, and illiterate usages.

OGDEN, HERBERT V.: "Spelling Makes Friends," *English Journal*, Vol. 41 (October, 1952), pp. 468–73
Appealing new ideas for making spelling realistic by associating it with other skills.

O'ROURKE, L. J.: *Rebuilding the English-Usage Curriculum to Insure Greater Mastery of Essentials*, Washington, D.C., 1934
Invaluable study of minimum essentials for various grade levels. See special list of written and oral essentials, Appendix A, pp. 97–98.

POLLOCK, THOMAS CLARK: "Spelling Report," *College English*, November, 1954, pp. 102–09
This article shows clearly what words we should concentrate on from grade school to college. See spelling drill on problem words, below, pp. 417–18.

POOLEY, ROBERT C.: *Teaching English Usage*, Appleton-Century-Crofts, 1946
Lists particular errors in usage (mainly oral) to be attacked in junior high school, pp. 194–95; errors to be attacked in senior high school, pp. 218–20. See these lists in Appendix 9, below, pp. 397–404.

Reading Ladders for Human Relations, American Council on Education, Washington, D.C., 1964
Invaluable manual for reading guidance with seven reading ladders from easy books to the more difficult. Grouped around central problems such as "Patterns of Family Life," "Community Contrasts," "Differences between Generations." Valuable on every level of reading guidance.

ROSENSON, JULIUS S.: "The Oral Approach to Sentence Sense," *English Journal*, Vol. 47 (October, 1958), pp. 425–30
A delightful, practical, and down-to-earth analysis of ways to teach sentence sense.

ST. PETER, MARY: "A Sentence Strikes Out," *English Journal*, Vol. 50 (April, 1961), pp. 271–72

Delightful personification of Mr. Sentence by a graduate student. The mechanical teacher, says Sentence, "wants me paralleled, puncuated and varied!"

Selected Bibliography of the Teaching of Spelling, Hutchinson Council of Teachers of English, Hutchinson, Kansas, 1952

Informative annotated list of articles and books: a valuable cross-section of views. Address Miss Inez Frost, Junior College, Hutchinson, Kansas.

SHEFTER, HARRY: *Six Minutes a Day to Perfect Spelling*, Pocket Books, New York, 1954

A book filled with arresting ideas for the English teacher in the junior and senior high school. Mr. Shefter teaches spelling to adults in New York University's Division of General Education.

STAGEBERG, NORMAN C.: "Some Structural Ambiguities," *English Journal*, Vol. 47 (November, 1958), pp. 479–86

A valuable article with analysis of twenty ambiguities in phraseology and how to cope with them in the classroom.

"Standards for Written English in Grade 12," *Indiana English Leaflet* (October, 1960), 314 South Water Street, Crawfordsville, Indiana

STORMZAND, MARTIN J. and O'SHEA, M. V.: *How Much English Grammar?* Warwick and York, Baltimore, 1924

Authoritative listing of minimum essentials in writing. Substantiates findings of previous investigators. See especially Chapter 10, "The Relation between Use and Error," showing a number of errors on particular problems per thousand classes. See below, p. 408.

Teaching Aids in the English Language Arts, *Illinois English Bulletin* (February, 1963)

Comprehensive lists of standardized tests for sale, with publishers and prices named. Also: lists of films and filmscripts, recordings, and magazines.

WARD, CHARLES H.: *What Is English?* Scott, Foresman, 1925

Do not miss Mr. Ward's analysis of spelling problems, particularly his emphasis on demons and hard spots, pp. 45–59, 103–12.

WOLFE, DON M., with JOSIE LEWIS and LELA T. HAMILTON, *Enjoying English 9*, Singer, 1964, "One Hundred Errors in Usage," pp. 400–401

12 What Is Creativeness
in Usage Drills?

The Secret of Meaningful Practice

MOST OF US are looking for ways by which our students may master as painlessly as possible the minimum essentials they should have learned several years before they came to us. How is it possible to make usage drills a more indelible experience? The more realistically usage drills are linked with self-expression, the more intense, rapid, and meaningful becomes the learning process. By creativeness in usage drills I mean, then, that expression of personality or experience that one pupil, and one pupil alone, can bring to the classroom. But how is this possible?

On the most elementary level each student brings to the classroom unique information that may be the subject matter of his usage practices. If, for example, we ask a student to write an answer to such a question as "Where were you born?" or "When were you born?" we require him to show his knowledge of two capitalization rules and two comma rules. On a slightly more advanced level, if we ask him to write the name of a book he has seen most recently, or the name of the magazine he likes best, we require him to capitalize the proper words and underline for italics the title of a book. To the average student some one else's choice of a book, some one else's birthplace or birthday, is as bloodless as the moon. When this information is asked about his own life, his own preferences, his own origins, usage assumes a meaning the class has never known it could possess. To show more explicitly how drill in usage may be linked with unique experiences, here is a series of questions the answers to which embody a progression of usage principles from the elementary to the complex:

Answer only in Complete Sentences

1. What is your favorite day of the week?
2. In what town or city and state were you born?
3. What is your street address?
4. What is your favorite vegetable?
5. What is one of your favorite movies?
6. What did you bring to school today?
7. What is one of your favorite poems?
8. What is the color of sand? Use the possessive of *it*.
9. Quote something of interest you said today. Begin with the conversational tag, *I said*.
10. Write two complete thoughts about getting ready for school this morning. Begin the second thought with *then*.
11. Write a sentence beginning, "When I was ten years old." Use a comma after *old*. Tell something of genuine interest about yourself at age ten.
12. Did you walk, run, or ride to school this morning? Write a sentence opening with a participle, such as "Walking down Clifton Street, I . . ." Put a comma after the opening phrase. Tell something you actually did on the way to school.

For best results from such a drill the teacher himself should go over each of the papers. I can imagine that many teachers would want to read the answers of their students to these questions. The matter of usage then assumes a new importance for the teacher as well as for his class. Yet if we ask the students to exchange papers, we have the benefit of the students being interested in each other's answers and simultaneously asking questions about mechanics they had never been curious about before. It is true that in some instances a junior or senior student might feel that some questions, especially in the context of a usage drill, might be an invasion of certain areas of private experience. The creative approach to mechanics embodied in this procedure is limited by the very nature of the knowledge sought to areas of factual rather than emotional experience. Yet the factual materials themselves are personal in the sense that no other student could use precisely the same ones.

Applying the Creative Principle to Usage Practices

To see how this approach to usage works out in classroom application, let us break down the problems into departments and show examples of what questions we should ask. Ask for answers in words only, or complete sentences, as you choose.

Capital Letters

1. What is the name of your school?
2. What is the name of a store you know in this town?
3. What is the name of a bank you know in this town?
4. What is your favorite flower?
5. What is your favorite game?
6. On what railroad or airline have you traveled?
7. What is one river flowing through your state?
8. What is the name of one of your best friends in school?
9. What is the full name of your uncle or grandfather?
10. What is the title of your favorite novel?
11. In what school subject do you do your best work?
12. What three fruits do you like best?

Possessives and Contractions

In possessives and contractions the usage drill cannot be so closely related to experience as in capital letters. Nevertheless even if the student writes sentences of unimportant meaning to himself, the problem is much more dramatic than in some one else's sentences.

1. What is the color of your house? Use the possessive of *it*.
2. What is the population of your town? Use the possessive of *it*.
3. Use the possessive of *it* and the contraction of *it is* in one sentence.
4. Use the contraction of *you are* in a sentence.
5. What did you say today to a friend in school? Use the word *your* and the contraction of *you are*.
6. Use the possessive of the word *Dickens*.
7. Use the possessive of the word *Gladys*.
8. Use the possessive of the word *sailors*.
9. Use the possessive of *they* and the contraction of *they are* in the same sentence.
10. What is the color of your shirt or dress? Use the possessive of *it*.

Sentence Sense Improvement

One of the problems in usage drills is to get away from the purely mechanical analysis that most students fall prey to in examining drills written by other people. When a student writes his own sentences to dramatize the run-on problem, he must be imaginative. Here are assignments that require an imaginative approach to the run-on trouble spots:

1. Write two complete thoughts about a boy in this room, the second of which opens with the pronoun *he. Example:* "Joe sits behind me. He always shows me his theme before class."
2. Write two complete thoughts about a girl in this room, the second of which opens with the pronoun *she. Example:* "Ellen is one of my favorite people. She is the most cheerful person I know."
3. Write two complete thoughts about an object in this room. Open the second thought with the pronoun *it. Example:* "Near the end of the hour I always watch the clock. It gives a little click just before the bell rings."
4. Write two complete thoughts about two girls or two boys in this room. Open the second thought with the pronoun *they.*
5. Write two complete thoughts about you and a friend in this room. Open the second thought with the pronoun *we.*

Each of the sentences above deals with a pronoun trouble spot in the run-on. When we ask the student to write such sentences, we direct him to fresh, vivid subject matter of intense interest: the boys and girls of his own class. To clinch the interest as well as the principle, we may ask ten or twelve students to write their sentences on the board. If some students have used semicolons instead of periods, we have a chance to say, "This semicolon is correctly used. A semicolon is like a period; it is simply not quite so vigorous a separation. But you can get along very well without any semicolons at all. The semicolon is a vanishing mark of punctuation for most ordinary mortals. Even the New York *Times* uses the semicolon only rarely."

To relate the run-on problem even more realistically to immediate experience, we may ask the class to write a paragraph of six or seven sentences on topics of family or school life. Three of the sentences should open with different pronouns, such as *he, she, we, it,* or *they.* Here are a model theme and some suggested topics:

OUR NEW MASTER

We have a new master in our family. It is Prince, our blue-eyed, black-masked Siamese cat. He has made slaves of Mother, Father, and especially of me. It is impossible to ignore him. When he wants to eat, he walks right over to me, hits me with his front paw, whips his black-tipped tail about, and whines impatiently. If I don't rush to the refrigerator immediately, he digs his claws into my leg. It is his way of telling me that he is not playing. Cats are that way.

Frances Williams

Suggested Topics:

A Moment with a Family Pet	A Street Scene
A Traffic Jam	A Crowded Bus
Profile of a Television Program	A Shopping Trip

Another type of run-on we may trace to such adverbs as *then, however, finally, now, there, suddenly:*[1] "We had a pick-up game after supper, then we went to the movies." In dealing with these trouble spots, we may link experience to usage in the following way:

1. Write two complete thoughts about what happened before school this morning. Open the second thought with *then. Example:* "I looked at the clock by my bed. Then I gave a big leap toward the bathroom."
2. Write two complete thoughts about a disappointment of the past day or two. Open your second thought with *however. Example:* "I expected Jim to meet me after basketball practice. However, he did not come."
3. Write two complete thoughts about a change of mind or a change of feeling. Begin the second thought with *now* or *finally. Example:* "A year or two ago I felt very calm during an examination. Now I get very nervous."
4. Write two complete thoughts about a recent surprise. Begin the second thought with *suddenly* or *there. Example:* "We were just eating supper. Suddenly there was a knock at the door."

To make the problem of run-ons with adverbs more realistic, we may ask the class to write a story of four or five sentences involving a clear time sequence (and therefore adverbs of time) as in a scene from a motion picture. Most students will have a recent motion picture fresh in mind. We may say, "Write a sketch of five

---

[1] Some specialists would also include *so* and *yet*. Other specialists regard the comma as acceptable before *so* and *yet* in such a sentence as, "He saw me coming, yet he did not stop."

or six sentences about a scene from a movie. Open at least three sentences with one of the adverbs we have discussed." Then we may read an example like the following:

A PRINCE OR A SLAVE

The movie, *The Ten Commandments*, has many sad and thrilling incidents. For example, just as Moses is about to be made Prince of Egypt, he discovers he is a Hebrew by birth. Suddenly his whole life is complicated. If he tells the truth, he must become a slave. His sweetheart begs him to keep the secret and become a prince. Then his adopted mother tries to make him believe the story is not true anyway. However, Moses stubbornly goes to look for his true parents. When he finds them, he recognizes his mother, Jehoshabel, as the old woman who was almost crushed to death one day through the overseers' neglect. "You are the woman I saved!" he cries. Then he makes his decision. He will go back to his own people, even though they are only slaves.

Elsie Barnes

Punctuation Usage

Of all departments of usage, punctuation can be least linked to experience. Nevertheless even in punctuation drills the student learns more quickly from examples of his own invention than from exercises in the drill book, however skillfully devised. We may use other people's drills to establish a basis of minimum problems and minimum comprehension. Then we may go on to assignments like the following:

1. Write a sentence opening with an adverbial clause about something that happened to you yesterday. Open the sentence with *when, until, unless, because,* or *if.* Place a comma after the clause. *Example:* "Because I felt ill yesterday afternoon, I left school early."
2. Write a compound sentence with the conjunction *but* about a moment of yesterday. Be sure each clause is a complete thought. Place a comma before *but. Example:* "I was very hungry at noon, but I did not want to miss the test."
3. Write a sentence containing a series of nouns. Tell about three recent purchases. Place a comma after the first and second nouns. *Example:* "Last Saturday my mother and I bought apples, pears, and peaches at the market."
4. Write a sentence about coming to school this morning. Open it with a present participle. Place a comma after the phrase. Be sure your participle

does not dangle. *Example:* "Running along the rough sidewalk on Argyle Place, I tripped and fell."

5. Write a sentence using a comma with direct discourse. Use words you actually spoke. *Example:* I said to Miss Sherman, "May I borrow this book?"

Writing Conversation

Writing dialogue is a difficult problem from the third grade through the thirteenth and even beyond. We need first some ways of dramatizing the trouble spots, such as these:

DIRECT QUOTATION TROUBLE SPOTS

Use a comma after the tag.   Use quotes.   Use a capital letter.

> Tom said, "Wait for me at the corner."
> Tom said, "Will you lend me your gym shoes?"

Use a comma before the tag.   Use a small letter.

> "Wait for me at the corner," said Tom.
> "Will you lend me your gym shoes?" said Tom.

Do not use *both* a question mark and a comma.

To try to connect one's own experience with drill in this problem may seem somewhat artificial. Nevertheless we can require the student to use his own language even when the experience he speaks of is not vital in itself. Here are some possibilities:

1. What question did a friend or relative ask you today? Begin your answer with the name of the person, like this: My friend Joe said to me, "Will you wait for me after gym class?"
2. Now put the tag at the end of your sentence. Put the question first. Do not use both a comma and a question mark after the question.
3. What did your mother, sister, or brother say to you today? Open your sentence with the tag.
4. Now write the same sentence with the tag at the end.
5. What question about school work are you asking yourself now?
6. Write the same question with the tag after it.

From a quoted single sentence, we proceed to a single sentence interrupted by a tag, like this:

AN INTERRUPTED SPOKEN SENTENCE

"All truth asks," said Thomas Paine, "is the liberty of appearing."

Note the comma.   Note the small letter.

Here we may ask the student to blot out the tag with his fingers to see for himself how the interrupted sentence should be punctuated. The trouble spot is the first word after the tag interrupter.

The next step is to come to two complete sentences interrupted by a tag. Here also the key to comprehension is the blotting out of the tag momentarily to see how the two sentences would be punctuated. The problem spot is the first word of the second sentence:

> *"We need a new furnace,"*
> *said the principal. "Our old*
> *one is worn out."*

Notice how the   Begin the second sentence
tag is set off.   with a capital.

To give practice on these two problems, we may ask the students to do the following:

1. Write the following sentence from dictation: "If you will wait a minute," said Slats, "we'll go with you."
2. Now write a sentence you heard spoken in the hall today. Interrupt the spoken sentence with a tag such as *John said*.
3. Write the following from dictation: "Wait a minute," said Slats. "We'll go, too."
4. Now write two spoken sentences with an interrupter tag at the end of the first sentence.

Using Indirect Discourse

Changing indirect into direct discourse gives some help in mastering the technique of punctuating spoken sentences. In each sentence the student is required to add a few new words of his own choosing.

1. Max said that he knew the answer to this problem.
2. Marian asked Miss Harper if she could go to the library.
3. Fred said he had known Miss Perkins a long time.
4. Marlene shouted that Miss Hope was there today.
5. We asked him which door leads to the laboratory.
6. Dad asked me if I were going to the second show.
7. Mother told me that she would like me to come home early.

A Dialogue for Two

To emphasize the principles of usage in conversation, we may ask each student to write a short dialogue about a personal problem or a school problem. This kind of approach requires correct usage in entirely creative language. We may read an example or two like the following:

HAS HE ASKED YOU YET?

Tillie met me in the hall after chemistry class. "Has Nick asked you yet?" she said.

"No, he hasn't," I replied. "But he called me up last night. We must have talked a half hour, but not a word about the dance. The coach won't give him a break."

"He's mean," said Tillie. "He's just keeping you dangling. I hope some one else asks you first."

"Not a chance of that," said I. "Everybody thinks we're still going steady. Nick hasn't said anything. Neither have I."

"Oh, he's mean," said Tillie again, "and the good looking fellows always want to play the field."

"I still like him," said I. "Maybe he'll ask me yet."

Mabel Merriman

MORE SLEEP FOR JAKE

As the whistle blew toward the end of the practice scrimmage, the coach motioned to Jake, his senior forward. Jake plopped down on the bench and threw a sweat shirt around his shoulders.

"What's the matter with your wind?" asked the coach.

"Nothing. I'm all right," said Jake.

"You're not getting the rebounds," said the coach. "You're even dropping passes. I never saw you do that before. How much did you sleep last night?"

Jake didn't answer. He was a truthful guy with the coach. They had worked well together for three years.

"Well, try to do better tonight," said the coach, patting his shoulder. "Get your shower now. We've never needed you more than we do right now. Don't let us down."

Jake looked at the coach. "I'll get more sleep tonight," he said. "You can count on it." He ran slowly toward the shower."

Richard Hanson

*   *   *

Creativeness in usage drills means the use of the student's own unique materials and choice of language as the foundation of the learning process. In using such materials, we find that in some instances the linking of practice to experience is easy and natural, as in the direction, "Write the name of your physician," or

"Write a sentence telling when and where you were born." In other instances, such as, "Write a sentence opening with *when*. Tell something that you did before school this morning," the linking of experience to practice may seem artificial. Even more difficult, if not indeed inadvisable, is the linking of experience to usage drill in the spelling "demons" or possessives. Nevertheless, despite the unevenness of application, dramatizing principles of usage in one's own language and from one's own experience has the virtue of intensifying interest and accelerating the mastery of minimum essentials that no other approach can muster. A mistake in the language of a teacher's drill means little to the student. A mistake in a sentence of his own construction, however pale the experience represented, has the inestimable advantage of making the problem more immediate and dramatic. When, finally, a student makes an error in a theme of profound emotional portent, the problem of usage behind the error has an immeasurably heightened meaning.

To the experienced teacher the disadvantage of such creativeness in usage drills will be clear enough. We have a class, let us say, of thirty ninth-grade boys and girls. At other hours of the day, we may have three or four other classes in ninth-grade English. We need a practice drill that will serve for all these classes, a drill in capitalization or punctuation or sentence errors. It is the kind of drill we can mimeograph easily and talk about in class, each with his sheet before him. When necessary, we can ask the students to exchange papers, correct errors, and even to grade the papers. This traditional approach to usage has the added urgency that it saves time for teachers carrying twice or three times the load we should ask them to carry. Moreover, it has its uses in getting before our students certain fundamentals in the simplest form possible.

The creative approach to usage should follow and not displace the approach we have described above. Even so, it has the disadvantage of requiring thirty different answers for every problem posed. I do not minimize this disadvantage. Time does not permit us to correct creative usage drills in any great number. The advantage must be sought in the acceleration of interest and hence a quicker road to mastery. Moreover, such usage drills require each student not only to do his own work but also to write statements and short papers about himself that may heighten his respect for both the ideal of correctness and the resources of his daily experience.

To the Student Teacher: Suggested Activities

1. Give yourself the test on minimum essentials (below, pp. 467–69). Write one sentence for each construction called for, using punctuation marks correctly. Do this test in pen and ink. Before you hand it to your professor, ask questions in class about those constructions you do not understand. Would you consider this test creative in the sense described in this chapter?

2. Turn to the test on pp. 467–69, sentences 27–54. Which of these sections did you find most helpful or challenging? Write a 25-sentence test of your own, following the best ideas of sentences 27–54 or sentences of other sections of the Minimum Essentials Test.

3. Write a short paragraph fulfilling the assignment on pp. 161–62. Open three or four of your sentences with pronouns, as is done in the theme called "Our New Master."

4. Write a story about a moment in eight or ten sentences, in which several of the sentences open with such adverbs as *then, however, finally, suddenly, now,* and *there.* You will find a model for this kind of experimental theme on pp. 162–63.

5. Turn to "A Student's Grammar Profile" (below, p. 459). Under Test II, follow the directions for the first five problems. Then write a paragraph giving your impression of this kind of drill on punctuation usage. Is it effective learning to use your own participles and your own absolute constructions? Does this kind of drill on grammatical elements and punctuation usage have any creative function? Why is it more or less fruitful than correcting sentences printed in a workbook?

6. Choose a pair of difficult words, such as *principal* and *principle, to* and *too, whose* and *who's, their* and *there, its* and *it's.* Show your class how you would present one of these pairs of words to a class in grades 7–12. How would you dramatize your explanation?

Suggested Reading

STAPP, HELEN I., and others: *Teaching Aids in the English Language Arts, Illinois English Bulletin,* Vol. 50 (February, 1963)

Descriptions of several hundred useful resources for the English teacher. This book is a service of distinction to the profession. Address: IATE Treasurer, 109 English Building, Urbana, Illinois.

13 Teaching Grammar:
Formal and Creative
Use of Diagraming

THE TEACHING of grammar, even with the skill of the gifted teacher and the response of a receptive class, is possibly the most baffling problem of the English curriculum. It is baffling partly because in the time spent on grammar the student could learn, for example, a great deal about usage or much more profitable things in writing about himself. It is possible that grammar brings less real learning per hour spent than does any other phase of English. Then, too, it is difficult for us to do a thorough job with the principles of grammar and at the same time to relate these principles to actual errors in speech and writing. Finally, the problem is baffling because the principles of grammar require an intellectual quality on the part of the student which is not present in the lower third of many classes. Unless a weak student has one remarkably gifted teacher in one of his classes from the sixth grade through the tenth, he is likely not to learn grammar at all despite parts of five school years he will have spent on it before graduation from high school.

Nor do we yet know where grammar belongs in the curriculum. When can boys and girls learn about nouns with the least expenditure of mental power? This is still a mystery. When can they learn verbs with the least energy and the most permanent results? It is quite possible that at some time in the future a child will have no training in transitive and intransitive verbs (the most baffling element of grammar to learn and teach) until the tenth or eleventh grade. I can imagine a time when even the parts of speech would be postponed until the ninth or tenth grade and no complex sentences or verbals attempted until the eleventh or twelfth grade. Teaching children grammar before they are prepared by mental growth to absorb its difficult abstractions causes more waste than perhaps any other ill-timing in American education.

Nevertheless, facing these problems realistically, we know that most teachers will continue to teach grammar if only because most curricula still require it. It is familiar and respectable ground to more teachers than any other aspect of English. As long as the demand for grammar is a continuing tradition, we believe it can be taught with increasing skill decade by decade with fewer and fewer Latinized terms. Further, by the pooling of resources grammar can be taught more creatively and more thoroughly to more students than in preceding decades. Not only can grammar point more realistically toward speech and writing errors; it can give more and more emphasis to sentence synthesis, to the student's building his own sentences with his own parts of speech.

One thing more is certain: When we as teachers are required to teach grammar, it is worse than useless to tell us to teach it half-heartedly or superficially. When taught at all, grammar must be approached as a separate subject. It is agonizing to any conscientious teacher to see ten or twelve pupils out of a class of thirty floundering in a morass of grammatical terminology imposed for a period or two, a week or two, with a few bright pupils hurrying ahead, perhaps having mastered the principles some years back.

TEACHING THE PARTS OF SPEECH

Begin with Nouns

On the seventh and eighth grade level, we may wish to give separate attention to each part of speech. We cannot assume in the seventh or even in the ninth grade that our pupils will be able to identify the function of a noun, pronoun, or adjective.

The problem is to make the definition of a noun dramatic enough for the weak pupils to take new heart, convinced that they can learn now what they have failed to learn in the preceding grades. To begin well, we must make grammar personal. We may say to the class in order to dramatize the definition of a noun, "This row of boys and girls will please write on the board. The rest of you write the words I ask for at your seats."

1. Write the name of a person you know well.
2. Write the name of a town or city you like.
3. Now touch the sleeve of your shirt or dress. Write a noun that names a part of the clothes you are wearing today.
4. Write the noun *home*. Now write three nouns that name things you saw at home this morning.
5. Touch something on or near your desk. Write the name of something you have touched.
6. Write the name of something you cannot see or touch such as *courage* or *hunger*."

Such an approach requires each student to use his own noun resources. The names he writes are related realistically to his town, his friends, his home, his clothes, his school. No two students in the room will use exactly the same nouns.

This use of personalized nouns makes it easy to distinguish between common and proper nouns. This distinction, however, is not relatively an important one. In teaching grammar, we must keep wherever possible only to those principles that function for greater accuracy in either speech or writing. The distinction between common and proper noun does not function toward this end.

Teaching Verb Identification

The best way to teach the meaning of the word *verb* is to ask the students to supply several missing verbs for sentences like the ones below.

Jack _____ the garage door.
The farmer _____ us some corn and tomatoes.
The flag _____ in the wind.
Joe _____ a little black dog.
Where _____ the erasers?

We may point out that there are two main types of verbs, action and being; those that tell what somebody or something does, did, or will do; and those that tell what something or somebody is, was, or will be:

Some verbs tell what something or someone *does*, *did*, or *will do*:

The robin *hopped* across the grass. (*Hopped* is a verb telling what the robin *did*.)

Charles *sits* in the first row. (*Sits* is a verb telling what Charles *does*.)

Some verbs tell what something or someone *is*, *was*, or *will be:*

John *is* at home.
He *was* at school.
He *will be* at the movies tonight.

To pick out a verb in a sentence is very difficult for a weak student. We must constantly keep in mind that the teaching of grammar must be geared to the intelligence and imagination of the lower third of our class. Here is one sure-fire method of testing whether or not a word can be a verb:

A VERB FINDER

When you want to find out whether a word can be a verb, try this finder. Use *I, you, he* or *it* before the word you are checking. If the combination makes a sensible sentence, the word can be a verb. Notice the following:

| I window | he windows | you window | it windows |
| I apple | he apples | you apple | it apples |

At once we see that *window* and *apple* cannot be verbs. When used with *I, you, he* or *it*, they do not make sense.

In making the explanation above, we must keep before the class as much as possible the principle that a part of speech is *merely a job within the sentence*. When a word has the job of a noun, it is a noun as in the sentence, "The *work* was tiresome." When it does the work of a verb, it is a verb. "In this class we *work* enthusiastically."

The next step in identifying a verb is to put a number of words on the board and ask the class to use the verb finder on each one. Here is a list that will help the student see the difference between words that can be verbs and words that cannot have this function:

easily	red	here	bread
from	ask	hear	taste
go	write	high	peanut
candy	grass	hot	along

After we have used the verb finder with a number of words, the next step in teaching verbs is to ask the students to find the verb in each of a number of sentences like the following:

WHAT IS SPRING?

1. The creek flows along joyously.
2. Daisies blossom along the banks.
3. Sudden winds rage furiously.
4. Sharp lightning flashes across the sky.
5. The earth is soft and muddy.
6. Big black clouds cover the sky.
7. Strong gusts of wind wrap our coats around us.
8. Pussy willows show their soft fuzzy buds.
9. Tulips peep out of the grass.
10. Grass and trees turn green overnight.

In teaching the verb as a part of speech, we shall be wise to stay as long as possible with the one-word verb. The lower the grade level or the weaker the class, the more necessary it is to use one-word verbs.

A vital step for the student in learning each part of speech is to shift from mere identification to the use of his own words as parts of speech. For example, an exercise requiring the student to use three different verbs in each sentence is an excellent device; we may say, "Write three verbs on your paper for each of the subjects below. Make each verb as lively as possible. Do not use the same verb twice."

Example: A horse gallops, neighs, grazes.

A teacher _____	A car _____
My friend _____	A dog _____
My father _____	A tree _____
The coach _____	My brother _____
A boy _____	A baby _____
The policeman _____	A train _____

Teaching Adjectives

The first step in teaching adjectives is to break down the meaning of the definition: *An adjective is a word that describes or points out a noun or pronoun.* When we break down this definition, we find that adjectives answer these questions: *What kind? What color? What size? Which one? Whose? How many?*

The best way to show the various functions of an adjective is to put on the board boxes like the following, one group showing how adjectives describe, the other showing how adjectives point out. After we have drawn the boxes on the board and started a list for each box, the students themselves may fill in with other suggested phrases.

ADJECTIVES THAT DESCRIBE

What color?	*What color?*	*What size?*
brown hair *red* rose *black* dress *blue* skies	*green* leaves *purple* dusk *silver* moon *orange* light	*large* purse *tiny* beads *tall* tree *huge* castle

What kind?	*What kind?*	*What kind?*
suede shoes *tennis* courts *jolly* fisherman *readable* book	*Christmas* joy *American* food *Chinese* people *French* customs	*roaring* lion *swirling* snow *sputtering* motor *growing* grass

ADJECTIVES THAT POINT OUT

Which one?	*Which one?*	*Whose*
a coat *the* umbrella *an* apple *third* row	*this* dress *that* jacket *last* chance *those* books	*my* handkerchief *your* boots *his* skis *their* garage

How many?	*How many?*	*How many?*
three pennies *two* baskets *five* pennies *nine* rockets	*no* bananas *many* planes *few* mountains *several* men	*six* times *fifth* house *third* day *fourth* trial

The next step is to write on the board sentences like the following and ask the class to use different adjectives in each blank.

1. Today Mary is wearing a _____ _____ dress.
                           (What color?) *(What kind?)*

2. We ate _____ _____ sandwiches.
           (How many?) *(What kind?)*

3. Did you bring _____ _____ pencil?
               (Whose?) *(What kind?)*

4. _____ dog carried off my _____ shoes?
     (Which one?)   *(What kind?)*

5. We had a _____ time at _____ party?
         (What kind?)   *(Whose?)*

Teaching Adverbs

As in teaching adjectives, the first step in teaching adverbs is to break down the definition into understandable components: *An adverb is a word that modifies (changes the meaning of) a verb, an adjective, or another adverb.* Adverbs answer these questions: *How? When? Where? How much?*

To show immediately what words fulfill these functions, we put on the board five columns of adverbs, asking the pupils to suggest additional adverbs:

How Words	*When Words*	*Where Words*	*How Much Words*
noisily	often	there	*too* often
softly	once	away	*not* enough
easily	yesterday	forward	*never* ends
quietly	then	back	*quite* happy
gaily	today	outside	*very* easy

The next step is to use several different adverbs in the same sentence to show how each adverb modifies (changes) the meaning of the verb, adjective, or adverb.

How Lively Adverbs Help the Sentence

Think of several adverbs to fill each blank below. Speak your sentences to the class.

We all chattered _____. (Use *how* words.)
The boy ran _____. (Use *where* words.)
He was _____ anxious to go. (Use words telling *how much.*)

How Adverbs Modify Three Kinds of Words

To show how the adverb modifies three different parts of speech, we may write on the board a series of verbs, adjectives, and adverbs, with modifying opportunities like this:

Verbs	*Adjectives*	*Adverbs*
came _____	_____ bright	_____ early
saw _____	_____ tall	_____ skillfully
said _____	_____ angry	_____ softly
sang _____	_____ pretty	_____ politely
found _____	_____ attentive	_____ far

We may follow this kind of drill with the conventional identification drill like the following:

Can You Find Them?

There are adverbs in each of the sentences below. The number to be found is shown in parentheses. Find each adverb and tell what question it answers.

1. She walks most gracefully. (2)
2. Finally they walked very slowly into the house. (3)
3. He is quite ill now. (2)
4. The train came too soon. (2)
5. Instantly the driver slowed down. (2)
6. Softly and sweetly they sang. (2)
7. An extremely tall man received them quite graciously. (3)
8. Quickly and efficiently Mother packed the lunches. (2)
9. His mother was too old and feeble then. (2)
10. It was too bad he could not speak more confidently. (4)

As sentence openers, adverbs are rich in emphasis and variety. To illustrate this resource, we may ask the pupil to rewrite sentences in two different ways, each time placing the adverb in a different position. One of these positions should be at the opening of the sentence.

Example: The cat crept cautiously across the porch.
Revisions: Cautiously the cat crept across the porch.
            The cat crept across the porch cautiously.

To enable the student to use a variety of adverbs, we may ask him to write sentences using such adverbs as the following, especially as sentence openers:

too	once	upward	snugly	gracefully
often	soon	smoothly	largely	hopefully
very	less	swiftly	slowly	tomorrow
again	more	politely	seldom	anxiously
quite	late	smilingly	forever	courteously
never	most	nervously	angrily	instantly

Keep to a Few Pronouns Only

In introducing pronouns, we keep to the ones that cause errors and omit the ones that never cause confusion. We omit the possessives, also *you* and *it*. The only pronouns that cause errors in case are the following:

SUBJECT PRONOUNS

> I
> we
> she
> he
> they
> who

OBJECT PRONOUNS

> me
> us
> her
> him
> them
> whom

We now initiate class practice with the noun-and-pronoun subject, used in sentences about things that actually happened:

Yesterday *Joe and I* found a four-leaf clover.
Last evening *Helen and I* made some brownies.

To clarify the use of object pronouns, it is wise to introduce a few prepositions, even though we have not yet come to the preposition as a part of speech. It is easier to teach objective case through prepositions than through the very difficult concept of transitive verb. We may put these prepositions on the board and ask the class to put after each one a noun and pronoun object:

for John and me	under _____	to _____
with Harry and him	beside _____	with _____
against Joe and her	for _____	toward _____

The next step is to use these phrases in sentences. Always use double objects, a noun and a pronoun, in teaching objective case after prepositions. This kind of practice may be indefinitely extended in a more formal treatment of prepositions.

Teaching Prepositions

The best way to teach prepositions on the junior high school level is to ask the students to act out several prepositions as in the following sentences:

1. Joe walked into the room.
2. Joe walked across the room.
3. Joe walked around the teacher's desk.
4. Joe walked toward his own desk.

Here are other sentences easily acted out by each member of the class to show how a preposition changes the relationship between one word and another in the sentence.

1. Ralph held his book (under, beside, over, inside) his desk.
2. Helen stood (at, behind, outside, before) the door.
3. Jim held his paper (toward the light, before his friend, in his coat pocket).

The next step is to write a list of common prepositions on the board:

above	at	by	into	toward
across	before	down	like	under
after	behind	during	of	until
against	below	except	on	up
along	beneath	for	over	upon
among	beside	from	through	with
around	between	in	to	without

We now show how various prepositions used in the same spot within a sentence will change the meaning. We may work out with our students the following exercise, asking them to use several prepositions in each blank:

1. The farmer searched for the calf _____ his barn.
2. We walked barefoot _____ the creek.
3. The bell rang _____ noon.

4. Jerry waited _____ his bicycle.
5. A snake crawled _____ the porch.
6. Maud looked _____ the box of clothes.
7. Glen ran _____ us.

Our next step is to help the student establish his concept of a prepositional phrase. The easiest way to fix this concept in mind is to show a preposition and its object in diagrams:

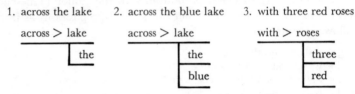

With the pattern above before them, the pupils may diagram perhaps twenty prepositional phrases that we write on the board. Here are a few samples:

into the water	between two trees	up a tall hill
except us	to my father	until noon
beneath the glass	without him	behind a red barn
beside an oak tree	over the prairie	against our team

We need to dramatize the principle that a preposition is not a preposition unless it takes an object, which object is usually a noun or pronoun. The use of the arrow in diagraming these prepositional phrases will emphasize and clarify the concept of the object. Diagraming the prepositional phrase will also help the student to see that in many prepositional phrases an adjective describes or points out the object.

Using Object Pronouns after Prepositions

Now is the time to stress the use of object pronouns after prepositions. This can be done on the seventh-grade level as the first step toward the concept of objective case. We may place the object pronouns on the board again.

OBJECT PRONOUNS

| me | us | her | him | them | whom |

1. Now the pupils may speak and write a number of prepositional phrases, always with a double object:

with Joe and me	beside Nellie and her	for you and him
for Sally and her	over Helen and us	between you and me
before Tim and him	against Joe and him	to Tom and us

2. Again the diagraming of phrases on the board will help clarify the concept of object:

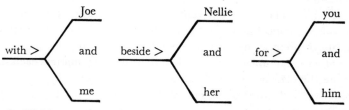

3. Writing and speaking sentences about the boys and girls in the class always helps to dramatize the concept. Telling about things that actually happened:

> Yesterday Frances went to the movies with Mary and me.
> Last night my little sister sat between my mother and me.

Unless the case of pronouns carries over to speech, it does not really function. Very few errors in pronouns are made in written work.

WHY IS DIAGRAMING USEFUL?

Teachers of the past two decades have turned again to diagraming as a means of visualizing the parts of speech and the structure of the sentence. As teachers we do not care particularly about the method of diagraming. We do care about having a picture, a cartoon, a dramatization, anything that can reduce the abstract to the concrete, especially for the weak students of the class. What a map is to geography and history, the chart to civics, the triangle to geometry, the graph to physics, the diagram is to grammar. The more abstract any principle, the more necessray some means of visualization. Yet many specialists in education are strong for visual aids in every field except in the teaching of grammar.

Like most methods, diagraming may be used creatively or mechanically. With it one may attempt to explain rare subtleties of language use (is any of us without his favorite ones?) or with it drive home the barest essentials of grammar in undress, keeping the sentences five or six years younger than the pupils (a necessity in all teaching of grammar until first principles are established), avoiding for the time being all confusing exceptions. Diagraming, like any other schematic device, may be either the beginning of sentence building by the pupil, or an end in itself, pursued by hunch or imitation.

In ideal classroom diagraming, the pupil will experience the pleasure of logical analysis; for diagraming, like geometry, requires clarity of premise, mastery of axioms, and logic of conclusion. On the other hand, unless care be taken that the pupil masters each step before the class advances ahead of him, the weaker pupils will lose initiative, and, worst of all, confidence in their ability to master the problems involved.

The use of diagraming has these specific values:

1. The weaker the pupil, the greater the need for a visual aid. Diagraming offers at least some kind of a picture, a map, or a chart of difficult language abstractions.

2. In a diagram the pupil thinks of each word in relation to the sentence. When the pupil diagrams "I fell down" and "The dog ran down the street," he has a chance to see how a word becomes a different part of speech each time it changes its essential function.

3. The placing of each word in a diagram represents ideally a decision in terms of grammatical principle. Pupils should be encouraged to omit words rather than to guess.

4. Boys and girls like this exactness of thought and the visual picture of each decision in relation to the sentence. Each decision is represented by a physical movement which is conducive to association.

5. Learning is cumulative. Each set of sentences to be diagramed may contain all the principles thus far studied.

6. For each sentence diagramed a pupil may be asked to write and diagram another sentence similar in structure and equally intense in diction.

USE OF DIAGRAMING:
SEVENTH- AND EIGHTH-GRADE LEVEL

Step-by-Step Approach [1]

VERB TESTER

I orange	I eat	I quietly
you orange	you eat	you quietly
he orange	he eats	he quietly

One easy way to approach diagraming on the seventh- or eighth-grade level is to begin with a three-word sentence such as "The horse galloped." After we write this sentence on the board, we may say, "The first step in diagraming any sentence is to find the verb." Then we may put this easy verb tester (shown above) on the board in a box.

Unless we show some clear-cut way like this for the weaker student to identify a verb, he will not be able to take the first and most important steps in diagraming a sentence.

1. Then we place the verb in the diagram, like this:

$$\underline{\qquad\qquad\qquad} \mid \text{galloped}$$

2. The second step is to find the subject. To find the subject we ask, "*Who* or *what* galloped?" This identifies the subject as the word *horse*.

$$\underline{\quad\text{horse}\quad} \mid \underline{\quad\text{galloped}\quad}$$

3. The third step is to find the adjective or adverb that modifies the subject. However, this raises a complication of defining the word *adjective*. We remind the class about the definition (see pg. 174). Several pupils may write it on the board. In the sentence we have

---

[1] See *Enjoying English 7* (1966), pp. 132–86, especially pp. 165–71.

cited, the word *the* is an adjective because it points out. It answers the question, *which one*. Now we place the adjective in the diagram:

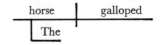

4. Then we add a second adjective.

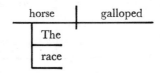

5. The next step is to diagram several sentences similar to the above sentence. Add a different adjective to each one. For example, we may write on the board from the students' suggestions, the following sentences:

> The black horse galloped.
> The frisky horse galloped.
> The old horse galloped.
> The tired horse galloped.

Here the students themselves may suggest many adjectives. We may help to establish the definition of the word modified by showing that modifies means *to change the meaning of*. In the sentence we are working with, an adjective such as *black* changes the meaning of the word *horse*.

6. The next step is to add an adverb to the diagram. We must remind the pupil about the definition of the adverb by writing a sentence on the board:

> The black horse galloped _____.

The students themselves may now suggest adverbs answering the questions *how*, *when*, *where*. Their sentences may come out like this:

> The black horse galloped *away*.   (*Where?*)
> The black horse galloped *far*.   (*Where?*)
> The black horse galloped *fast*.   (*How?*)
> The black horse galloped *slowly*.   (*How?*)
> The black horse galloped *again*.   (*When?*)

Then we may diagram these sentences as shown in the two samples below, writing after each adjective and adverb the question it answers.

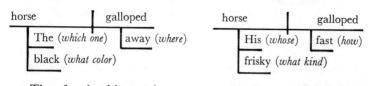

Thus far, in this step-by-step approach for seventh and eighth grades, some teachers may object that the sentences are too easy. It is a basic principle in all formal grammar instruction, however, that most sentences must be some years less mature than those the pupils speak or write. The language used by the seventh-grade pupil in speech or in writing is too complicated for him or for even much older people to analyze. Moreover, for the sake of the lower third of the class, we must not go too fast in the teaching of diagraming. It is much better to give the advanced students special tasks than to carry the lower third of the group forward when they are still uncertain about definitions or functions of these four parts of speech: *noun, verb, adjective, adverb.*

First Diagrams in Class[2]

With explanatory models on the board, we are now ready to proceed with the diagraming of perhaps twenty short sentences. For best results this work should be done in class where we can watch the approach of the weak students and be of help to them. It is wise to insist that each pupil use a ruler in making his diagram frames. It is also wise to say, "Work slowly. Make sure you understand each word's job. If you don't know where a word belongs in the diagram, leave it out. A word left out will not count the sentence wrong, but one word wrongly placed will count the whole sentence wrong." This kind of instruction encourages the student to work slowly and imaginatively. If pen and ink are available, it is wise to insist on their use in diagraming. Of course, only the pencil is used for the lines of the diagram.

Here are samples of the kinds of sentences to begin with:

[2] See *Enjoying English 7* (1966), pp. 165–71.

1. Alice giggled.
2. The candles flickered.
3. The wrens chirped sweetly.
4. We giggled too often.
5. She always dresses neatly.
6. Jack was here yesterday.
7. The white clouds moved slowly.
8. Connie laughed mysteriously.
9. The bell rang very loudly.
10. That small mirror fell down.
11. Three geese cackled busily.
12. A gray horse galloped away.

Before advancing further, we must be certain that everyone in the class can diagram easy sentences such as these. We assign many more easy sentences if necessary. A good student likes this work because he can do it easily and quickly. If we feel that we are wasting the time of the better students in waiting until the poorer ones catch up in diagraming skill, we can direct the better students to reading in the classroom library or to making up and writing on the board sentences for the weak students (and themselves) to diagram. The more time spent on the four parts of speech, the more certain our progress will be toward mastery of more difficult constructions.

If we wish to turn immediately to a creative aspect of grammar, we may ask each student to write five sentences of his own, each of them containing two adjectives, an adverb, a noun, and a verb. He could then diagram his own sentences.

Diagraming Prepositional Phrases

The next step in diagraming is to include prepositional phrases in the diagram. This is fairly easy if we can get the students to see that each prepositional phrase performs the function of either an adverb or an adjective; as in the sentence, "The light of the moon shone through the window."

We now begin to use pronoun objects of prepositions in diagraming prepositional phrases:

1. We worked with Bob and him.   2. I sat between Dad and her.

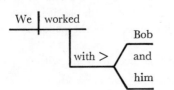

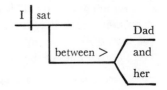

Intransitive Linking Verbs

Thus far we have been working only with intransitive non-linking verbs. Now we must turn to intransitive linking verbs and help the students to visualize predicate nouns, pronouns, and adjectives. These are typical sentences for predicate adjectives:

Orange juice is refreshing.   The shoes are very dirty.
These raw carrots are crisp.   The gentleman seemed nervous.
This magazine is interesting.   Blanche is lively.

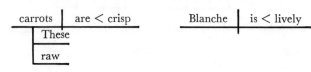

In teaching the diagraming of predicate pronouns, we try to make our sentences as natural as possible, linking them usually with predicate nouns:

Examples: The two boys were Joe and he.
The captains were Nelly and she.

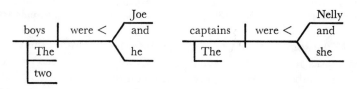

Teaching the Concept of Transitive Verb [3]

Thus far we have dealt only with intransitive verbs. We can best begin explanations of the transitive verb by asking the pupils to act out several transitive verbs. We may say, for example, "Will each person take a sheet of paper in his hand? Ready? Tear the paper in two. Now say with me, 'I tore the paper in two.'" To dramatize the word *transitive* further, we may say, "Touch your desk or touch your ear." Then ask the student to write on his paper, "I touched my ear." Very often an absurd or laughable sentence or

[3] See *Enjoying English* 7 (1966), pp. 205–11.

action will help to dramatize a grammatical principle more effectively than a sensible one.

We now advance to the most crucial problem in all grammar: showing the difference between transitive and intransitive uses. The best way to dramatize this difference is to ask the student to use a verb first transitively as in the sentence, *I wore this coat today* and then intransitively as in the sentence, *The coat wore out:*

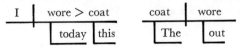

Here are some verbs that may be used for such an exercise:

stuck	turned	flew	studied
broke	played	swam	painted
wrote	tasted	felt	slammed
drank	opened	rang	ate

When the student has spoken and written sentences dramatizing the difference between transitive and intransitive uses, he is ready to complete and analyze such sentences as the following:

He cut	He howled	He hit	He laughed
He crawled	He slept	He sang	He painted

As the student completes each sentence, he underlines the verb and marks it *transitive* or *intransitive*. It is an excellent practice to have a number of such sentences written on the board.

The student is now ready for a further dramatization of transitive verbs by the use of diagraming. We ask him to diagram sentences like the following, in which the same verb is used transitively in one sentence, intransitively in another:

1. The wind blew the fog away.
2. The wind blew wildly.

3. May bought a new hat.
4. May bought wisely.

5. Jack opened the door.
6. The door opened quietly.

7. I washed my face.
8. The leaves washed away.

9. Dad stopped the car.
10. The car stopped at the curb.

11. Fred sang a new song.
12. Fred sang to the class.

13. Joe stopped the farmer.
14. Joe stopped at our house.

15. Jack painted the fence.
16. Martha painted for an hour.

Once the concept of transitive verb is established, we may reinforce the concept by asking the pupils to diagram pronoun objects, as in the sentence, *Dad found Mary and me.* In such sentences we also ask the student to make a choice of the correct pronouns. From now on, in all our diagraming we use both transitive and intransitive verbs. This is the most difficult distinction the student is required to make; hence we must give it more time and imagination than any other concept. Nothing clarifies objective and nominative case as effectively and permanently as persistent practice with pronouns after the verb *to be* and pronouns after transitive verbs.

So far, in dramatizing grammatical principles, we have dealt only with simple sentences. The time one has for grammar, in the seventh and eighth grades particularly, might well be spent on the simple sentence alone. One of the most persistent wastes in the teaching of grammar is the expenditure of teaching energy on a number of complicated principles when we should concentrate on a very few.

One way of concentrating teaching energy is by sticking to the simple sentence until the weakest student in the class stands on firm ground, feeling the security that comes from a sense of mastery and a sense of oneness, however short-lived, with his peers. When we have two months or three months in the seventh or eighth grade to spend on grammar, it is wise to spend the whole time on the simple sentence and its parts. Even then, we should not attempt participles and infinitives, but confine ourselves to parts of speech and the case of pronouns. If we can help our students master the case of pronouns, with the correlative knowledge of transitive verbs that it involves, our students will be forever grateful that by our instruction they have done a few things well.

USE OF DIAGRAMING: NINTH-GRADE LEVEL

By the time he enters the ninth grade, the student has had several bouts with grammar, often unsuccessful ones, as far back as the fifth year. When we say, then, that we are going to spend six or seven weeks on grammar, the student may groan, "Oh, not *again*." The inertia imposed by defeat and frustration in the study of grammar prevents most pupils who have failed before from making a fresh start now. Our problem is to overcome this inertia by convincing even the poorest student of the class that it is possible for him to learn grammar if he approaches it slowly and imaginatively and does not attempt too many things. If he does attempt too many things, we, as teachers, are at fault. It is much better to spend six weeks on five parts of speech in the ninth grade (nouns, verbs, prepositions, adverbs, and adjectives) than to spend this time on eight parts of speech or, worst of all, to attempt complex sentences as well as simple and compound ones. There are, of course, many ninth-grade classes in which it is possible in two months to teach the parts of speech and case, keeping the weak students with the class, giving them the satisfaction of learning principles they thought they could never master.

The Six Helpers[4]

Though some teachers do not approve of this formal procedure, many have found that the use of the Six Helpers given below can prove very compelling to the ninth-grade class. These Six Helpers are a synthesis of the most important principles of grammar. A full week spent in memorizing and explaining them will provide a common background the class needs for its weeks on diagraming. The longer we spend on these essentials, the surer we can be that the whole class will make progress, not the bright ones only.

The Six Helpers

HELPER NO. 1: MODEL DIAGRAM

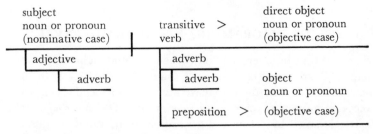

[4] See *Enjoying English 9* (1966), pp. 427–29.

Example: The very tall player threw the ball to him too quickly.

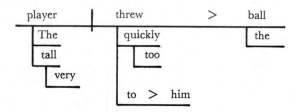

HELPER NO. 2: MODEL DIAGRAM

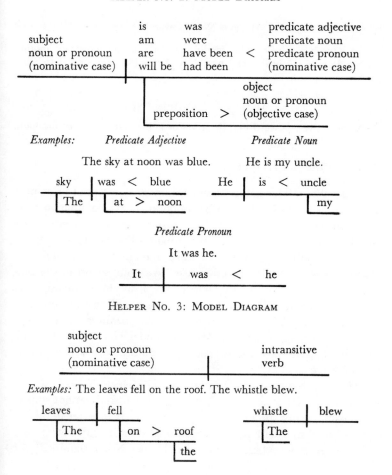

HELPER NO. 3: MODEL DIAGRAM

Examples: The leaves fell on the roof. The whistle blew.

HELPER No. 4: SIX PRONOUNS

Nominative Case	*Objective Case*
I	me
we	us
he	him
she	her
they	them
who	whom

HELPER No. 5: ADVERB

An adverb is a word that modifies a verb, an adjective, or another adverb. It tells (1) how, (2) when, (3) where, (4) why, or (5) in what degree.

HELPER No. 6: ADJECTIVE

An adjective is a word that describes or points out a noun or pronoun.

Teaching the Six Helpers

Helper No. 1. This helper shows a number of essential principles. The subject is always a noun or pronoun in the nominative case. But what is nominative case? We can answer this question effectively only by showing the uses of the six pronouns listed in Helper No. 4. After a transitive verb we must have a noun or pronoun in the objective case. What is objective case? We point again to the pronouns in Helper No. 4. In Helper No. 1 we have an adjective modifying a noun and an adverb modifying an adjective, a verb, and another adverb. We keep returning to the meaning of the word *modify*, and use the illustrative sentence under Helper No. 1 to this end. Finally, we have the prepositional phrase with a pronoun in the objective case.

This is a big dose of grammar in one Helper. Now, however, we are trying for a new approach to grammar and cannot stop to teach each part of speech. We must compress. It is better to memorize Helper No. 1 without understanding all of it than not to have some image of foundation principles. Helper No. 1 requires more work than any other. If the weak pupils write it from memory twenty times, it will not be too much when accompanied by more explanations to fortify the memory work.

Helper No. 2. Here we have the linking verb and the nominative case after it. We keep the prepositional phrase here because some pupils get the idea that the prepositional phrase with a linking verb takes the nominative case also, as does the linking verb!

Helper No. 3. This shows the intransitive non-linking verb. It helps to show that some verbs are complete in themselves.

Helper No. 4. We need constant reference to these pronouns in explaining the case used in other Helpers.

Helpers No. 5 and No. 6. On the ninth-grade level students easily forget definitions and must come back to them again and again.

Mastering the Six Helpers

To ask the students to write these Helpers from memory time after time may seem a waste of energy. However, many experienced teachers who have used them have not found it so. Each time the student writes a Helper again, he learns a little something, particularly if he hears explanations and makes some sentence diagrams between the writings. The Six Helpers go together and should be written together after they have been written separately. The students may begin with Helper No. 1 and write it until everyone in the class can write it perfectly before going on to Helper No. 2. Then we include Helper No. 1 as we write Helper No. 2, Helpers No. 1 and No. 2 as we write Helper No. 3, and so on. In this way the most important Helper has the most practice.

As the students memorize the Helpers, they may be diagraming sentences and referring to the Helpers as they diagram. This procedure will help in achievement of mastery.

After mastering the Six Helpers, the student is ready for the simplest exercise in diagraming: short sentences containing only noun, verb, adjective, and adverb. Typical sentences are: *The lanky boy swam easily. Then the back door closed softly. Joe always whistled merrily.* The longer the time spent on the simplest constructions, the easier the next steps in diagraming. From these sentences we go on to two-word verbs and questions such as *Did you listen carefully?* and *The brick wall has fallen.*

Thus far in this ninth-grade approach, we have used only those intransitive verbs that are complete in themselves. Now we advance to the intransitive linking verb, sticking closely to the forms of *to be* as shown in Helper Number 2. Here we combine in one exercise predicate adjectives, predicate nouns, and predicate pronouns with emphasis on the nominative case after the verb *to be* as in the sentence *It was Joe and she.*

One very effective way to clarify predicate nouns, pronouns, and adjectives is to present a series of incomplete sentences such as the following:

It was _____.	The sky is _____.
My dad is _____.	He is _____.
It is Joe and _____.	The team was Mary and _____.
The sun was _____.	The couple was Joe and _____.

The Diagraming Method: Order of Grammatical Problems [5]

In the first exercise, as explained on p. 193, the students on the ninth-grade level diagram only sentences with four parts of speech: noun, verb, adjective, and adverb. We may repeat this assignment several times if we feel that our weak students are still wobbly in comprehension. Fortunately the diagraming approach is cumulative: in dealing with a new problem the students never lose their grip on old ones. The following is a tested order of new problems to follow the easiest sentences in a scale of increasing difficulty:

1. Intransitive linking verbs, predicate nouns, pronouns, and adjectives. *Examples:* It was John and I. We were chilly.
2. Transitive verbs with noun and pronoun objects. *Example:* Dad took Mary and me.
3. Adjective and adverb prepositional phrases. *Example:* The roof of the house shone in the sun.
4. Pronoun objects after prepositions. *Example:* We ran toward Dad and him.

[5] See *Enjoying English 9* (1966), pp. 134, 183–87, 192, 173–82, 136–44, 147–50, 154–64, 194–205.

5. Verbs of two or more words, and questions. *Examples:* We shall see the circus. Have you seen Joe?
6. Agreement of subject and verb. Use of expletive *there*. *Examples:* There (are, is) many windows in our room. A basket of apples (is, are) on the porch. Neither of these trees (grow, grows) in California.
7. The present participle. *Example:* Jumping into the truck, he drove away.

To drill thoroughly on each of the problems named above takes more time in the ninth grade than most teachers can afford. In the tenth, eleventh, and twelfth grades, assuming a sound foundation in the ninth (which is rather optimistic), we may add the following:

8. The past participle
9. The infinitive
10. The gerund
11. The compound sentence

12. The complex sentence
13. The adverb clause
14. The adjective clause
15. The noun clause

In each of the topics outlined above, the student visualizes in diagrams sentences suggested by the teacher or his textbook. These sentences must be those that a child much, much younger might write or speak. The principles of grammar must be presented in terms of the easiest problems possible. Even then we must watch each sentence to be sure it does not contain an idiomatic expression irrelevant to our problems or too difficult to be coped with. The student advances with pleasure and confidence only when he grasps each step, each grammatical principle, as he grasps arithmetic. Few people, young or old, find pleasure in grappling with problems they can never quite solve for want of a solid foundation. When we English teachers hear many people of professional distinction use such phrases as "you and I" after prepositions, we have an inkling of what difficulties we face in teaching "you and me" to boys and girls of fourteen to eighteen. This is why, whatever the age level of our students, it is usually wiser, when in doubt, to deal with the fundamental principles of the simple sentence rather than the complicated business of gerunds, noun clauses, and other perfectly valid problems. When our class, grammatically speaking, is still in the seventh grade, we have little choice but to begin at that level of knowledge and advance with as many short, sure steps as possible. When, however, the curriculum leaves us no alternative but to teach more complicated constructions, my own judgment is that the diagrammatic approach should not be attempted. The teaching of grammar by diagraming requires six to eight weeks of daily work to become cumulatively effective.

Functional and Creative Applications

Thus far we have dealt with the formal teaching of grammar: a procedure required in many schools even when the teacher is not sympathetic with its purpose. In such an approach to grammar it is impossible for the student to see all the useful applications of his grammatical knowledge. It is true that he sees the relation of objective case and nominative case to errors in speech. It is also true that we can teach him incidentally the usefulness of opening a sentence with an adverb, a prepositional phrase, or a past participle. It is certain, too, that we can teach him incidentally the building of sentences made up of his own choice of words, but our choice of grammatical elements. For instance, we may say after dealing with participles in diagrams, "Write a sentence opening with a present participle." The student is required to use his own participle; at the same time he learns the use of another grammatical element as a sentence opener. When a student diagrams a well-constructed sentence, we may ask him to write a sentence of similar grammatical construction with his own words. These are all ways and means of making grammar function in speech and writing. One difficulty, however, in making these applications, is that most of us who are required to teach grammar do not have the time to teach both the fundamental principles of our subject and their manifold applications to style. It is logical to teach the punctuation of the adverbial clause when we teach the recognition of the adverbial clause. However, the time element often prohibits us from mingling as we should like the stylistic and individual applications of grammar with the mastery of primary principles.

Can Diagraming Be Creative?

I would agree with those who say that analysis of grammatical relationships is not creative thinking, though certainly it is training in logical thinking comparable to that required in arithmetic or geometry. But diagraming becomes creative the moment the student *diagrams his own sentence.* This kind of creative approach is possible from the very first day of our work on diagraming. We may ask each student to make up his own sentence of four parts of speech and diagram it on the board. We may ask him to write five sentences with only four parts of speech and add them to his diagrams of textbook sentences. Furthermore, we may ask the brilliant students to make up lively sentences about each member of the class, sentences that can be diagramed easily by weaker ones of the group. Perhaps these superior students can improve upon the sentences in the book. We may suggest to them that they use livelier verbs, more exact nouns, more words describing color, sound, and taste. Such a sentence as "A brown hamburger sizzled in the skillet" can show the class that a sentence to be diagramed may have a punch of its own; it doesn't have to be as dead as a fish on the butcher's slab. Moreover, we may send our students scurrying to the poets and prose masters, to Shakespeare, Longfellow, Millay, Lincoln, Sandburg, Stevenson, and a host of others for sentences which the class may diagram with much profit. I do not agree with those who believe that this analysis of great words, phrases, and patterns is destructive to the love of literature. Having once found a few such sentences to diagram, the student can make a further creative sally by creating sentences of similar intensity of diction and phrase. In these and many other ways, diagraming can become a creative action. When a class combines distinguished sentences and its own attempts at similar distinction with diagraming analysis, it cannot fail to approach language with more pleasure and comprehension than ever before.[1]

To the Student Teacher: Suggested Activities

1. On the teaching of transitive verbs, examine three textbooks on the ninth-grade level, such as Tressler, *English in Action,* Wolfe, Hamilton, and Lewis, *Enjoying English 9,* Blumenthal, Roberts, *English Syntax.* Then present a twenty-minute lesson to your teaching-of-English class.

[1] See Appendix 16, below, pp. 507–509, "Golden Sentences for Grammatical Analysis," for practical applications of ideas expressed here.

In this class combine the best methods you have found for teaching transitive and intransitive verbs.

2. Examine suggestions in three or four textbooks about the teaching of present participles in the tenth grade. Then write a short lesson showing how you would introduce present participles to a tenth-grade class. In your lesson be sure to have the students use their own present participles in sentences.

3. Examine *How Much English Grammar?* (Baltimore, 1924), by Stormzand and O'Shea. Cite five or six conclusions presented in this book which are still timely and useful.

4. Read *The English Language Arts* (Appleton-Century-Crofts, 1952), pp. 286–301, on the teaching of grammar. Quote five statements from this treatment that you feel are important for the teacher.

5. An important book now out of print is *English Evidence*, edited by C. H. Ward, consisting of selections from 180 essays by teachers on various aspects of the teaching of English. Read the section on grammar, pp. 211–22. Make a list of eight or ten constructive ideas you find in this selection.

6. A controversial book still suggestive and valuable is C. H. Ward's *What Is English?* (Scott, Foresman, 1925). Read a portion of Chapter 26, "Grammar for Composition," or Chapter 7, "The Teaching of Grammar." Ward's writings are always readable and provocative. Make a list of six or eight statements or examples that you feel would be of help in the teaching of English.

7. Make a list of ten grammatical principles that you feel are necessary for correct speech. Illustrate each principle with one or two sentences containing the possible error resulting from a lack of grammatical knowledge.

8. Write a brief essay showing why grammar is more important or less important in speaking correctly than in writing correctly.

9. Using the model diagrams on pp. 190–92, make up fifteen sentences and diagram them. Use all the grammatical principles illustrated in the Helpers 1, 2, and 3.

10. Compare these two books on grammar for college students, each of which uses diagraming as a tool of explanation: Dorothy Dakin, *The Mastery of the Sentence* (Harper, 1932) and House and Harman, *Descriptive English Grammar* (Prentice-Hall, 1931). Write a paragraph about each book and a third paragraph showing which you would prefer as a reference book.

11. Complete the assignments in "A Student's Grammar Profile" (below, p. 459). Do this work slowly and conscientiously. What value does this approach to grammar have that is not present in the analysis of textbook sentences?

Suggested Readings

BERTLING, LOIS B.: "English Grammar and the Thinking Process," *English Journal*, Vol. 35 (December, 1946), pp. 544–50
A reconsideration of the presentation of the elements of formal grammar.

BLAISDELL, THOMAS C.: *Ways to Teach English*, Doubleday, 1930
Helpful suggestions for teaching the transitive verb to upper grades, pp. 212–14. Excellent specific helps throughout this book.

BORGH, ENOLA M.: "The Case for Syntax," *Elementary English*, Vol. 42 (January, 1965), pp. 28–34
Some realistic applications of transformational grammar. The English teacher needs many more articles of such splendid calibre as this one.

BRYANT, MARGARET M.: *A Functional English Grammar*, Heath, 1945
Authoritative and enlightening view of grammar by a distinguished scholar.

————: "The Psychology of English," *English Journal*, Vol. 36 (October, 1947), pp. 407–12
A basic consideration of grammar as function.

COOK, LUELLA B.: "An Inductive Approach to Language," *English Journal*, Vol. 37 (January, 1948), pp. 15–21

COWSAR, MARGARET I. and TEER, MARGARET: "How Does Grammar Mean?" *English Journal*, Vol. 50 (December, 1961), pp. 596–600
"Teaching the time concept of our verbal system — pointing out clearly where time *is* involved with tense and teaching *how* time tends to become involved with tense even when it is *not* the same — may be a step forward toward clear thinking."

DAKIN, DOROTHY: *Mastery of the Sentence*, Harper, 1932
The most useful, succinct, yet comprehensive, treatment of grammar for the teacher. All constructions explained by both exposition and diagrams. About 110 pages in length.

DEBOER, JOHN J., and others: *Teaching Secondary English*, McGraw-Hill, 1951
Chapter 6 of this book has a thorough consideration of the present situation of conflicting ideas about the teaching of grammar.

Essays on the Teaching of English, ed. Edward J. Gordon and Edward S. Noyes (Appleton-Century-Crofts, 1960)
The chapter on grammar, pp. 34–56, written by a committee of five, four of them from private academies, opens thus: "Let us begin by stating unequivocally that this Committee believes grammar should be taught in the secondary schools."

FARNSWORTH, BURTON K.: "The Reading Approach to English," *English Journal*, Vol. 32 (October, 1943), pp. 435–37
Developing interest in correct grammar through projects conducted by students on subjects they find absorbing.

HARAP, HENRY: "The Most Common Grammatical Errors," *English Journal*, Vol. 19 (June, 1930), pp. 440–46
One of the best summaries of links between grammar and correctness.

HATFIELD, W. WILBUR: "Using Grammar for Correctness and Style," *English Journal*, Vol. 31 (February, 1942), pp. 137–42
Showing the student that there is a grammar problem in correct expression, and helping him to solve the problem.

HERMANS, MABEL C.: *Studies in Grammar*, Holt, 1924. Revised, 1946
For a thorough study of grammar as a separate subject, this textbook is singularly useful. Each grammatical principle keyed to a problem in correct speech or writing.

LEONARD, J. PAUL: "Functional Grammar: What and Where?" *English Journal*, Vol. 22 (November, 1933), pp. 729–35
A practical outline for a four-year high school course based on ability to use grammar rather than on the mere acquisition of grammatical names.

MAKEY, HERMAN O.: "A Means or an End?" *English Journal*, Vol. 42 (March, 1953), pp. 159–60
A brilliant and perceptive article showing the constructive uses of diagraming.

NEUMAYER, ENGLEBERT and RUTAN, EDWARD: "A Grammar of Meaning," *English Journal*, Vol. 30 (October, 1941), pp. 628–33
Very useful examples of teaching grammar along with meaning. These examples should be very useful to the teacher.

NEWSOME, VERNA L.: "Expansions and Transformations to Improve Sentences," *English Journal*, Vol. 53 (May, 1964), pp. 327–35.
The main benefit of this article is its application of theory to particular problems of style. The expansion principle is especially well handled. The author realizes that application of principles is a hundred times more needed than new grammatical theory or terminology. She returns often and effectively to the nomenclature of traditional grammar.

POOLEY, ROBERT C.: *Teaching English Usage*, Appleton-Century-Crofts, 1946
See pp. 43–77 for illuminating discussion on certain basic problems in English grammar.

POOLEY, ROBERT C.: "What Grammar Shall I Teach?" *English Journal*, Vol. 47 (September, 1958), 327–33
A constructive article illuminated by specific examples of effective teaching of grammatical principles.

SALISBURY, RACHAEL: "Grammar and the Laws of Learning," *English Journal*, Vol. 35 (May, 1946), pp. 247–52
A consideration of the learning of grammar as a part of the whole educative process.

SMITH, J. HAROLD: "A Plan for Presenting Grammar," *English Journal*, Vol. 48 (October, 1959), pp. 404–06

"The plan herewith proposed is intended as a basis of study and a core-reference for learners, all the way from grade school through college. This form may be either simplified for the lower levels or rendered more complex for the higher levels. But a chart form should be available always and referred to constantly."

TIDYMAN, WILLARD F. and BUTTERFIELD, MARGUERITE: *Teaching the Language Arts*, McGraw-Hill, 1951

See Chapters 1 and 2 for an interesting general discussion of functional grammar.

WARD, CHARLES H.: *What Is English?* Scott, Foresman, 1925

A trenchant style and superior insight make Mr. Ward as readable and timely now as he was four decades ago. The chapter on grammar (pp. 157–210) is an engrossing statement, however controversial. "In one respect," writes Mr. Ward, "opinion about the place of grammar is unanimous: teach it before the pupils come to me."

WEINSTOCK, ESTHER M.: "The Syntax Twins," *English Journal*, Vol. 42 (February, 1953), p. 97

How one teacher used famous couples, Antony and Cleopatra, Napoleon and Josephine, to clarify grammatical constructions.

WOLFE, DON M.: "A Grammatical Autobiography," *English Journal*, Vol. 49 (January, 1960), pp. 16–21

A comprehensive review of grammar may be personalized in a grammatical biography all about oneself beginning with simplest sentences and ending with most complicated ones. See below, pages 497–505.

———: "Grammar and Linguistics: A Contrast in Realities," *English Journal*, Vol. 53 (February, 1964), pp. 73–78

Weaknesses of structural linguistics when applied to writing problems on the high school level.

14   Creative Patterns in Teaching Grammar

A CREATIVE APPROACH to grammar I would define as any teaching device that calls into play the unique student's language resources to dramatize a grammatical principle. Any time a student applies a free word choice or phrase choice from his own experience to a problem in grammar, he is using a creative pattern of learning. For instance, in the sentence below, an eighth- or ninth-grade student may be asked to supply his own adjectives to answer the questions:

A _____ _____ dog ran across the porch.
    What size?   *What color?*

To initiate the discussion, we may ask our thirty students to write this sentence, each choosing two adjectives of his own. In response, though we shall not have thirty different adjectives for each blank, we shall have a variety for discussion and evaluation. Who has the liveliest, most original adjectives? Meanwhile other sentences, such as the ones below, may be used to the same end:

In the refrigerator we found _____ _____ bottles.
                    How many?   *What kind?*

Up the tree ran _____ _____ _____ squirrels.
          How many? *What size?* *What color?*

Thus the student may learn the specific questions that adjectives answer. Because he learns the specific answers to these questions in terms of his own vocabulary, he is much more likely to grasp and apply the definition of *adjective* than if he works only with adjectives in the textbook.

Similarly, in finding specific adjectives to use in place of such vague and unsatisfactory words as *nice, good, fine* and so on, the class may supply, perhaps, ten or twelve different adjectives to use in the blanks below instead of *nice* and *good:*

Because it was such a _____ day, we had a _____ time.

In classes from the seventh through the tenth grade, the student may approach verbs, nouns, and adverbs in the manner described above. His interest in the part of speech is immediate, personal, and individual. He sees the range of adjectives or verbs in his own vocabulary. When his adverb or adjective is named by someone else, he chooses still another word of his own. Moreover, he evaluates the strength and weakness of the adjectives or adverbs under discussion.

Building Four-Word Sentences

After the class has studied adjectives, nouns, and verbs, an interesting exercise is to put them together into sentences. This is creative grammar in the sense that, although the student is not using his own words, he does make up his own sentences. The combination of words that he uses is likely to be different from that of anyone else in the room. We may ask that each member of the class, for example, compose ten sentences from the list of words below. In each sentence he is to use only four words: two adjectives, one noun, and one verb. Using only four words may seem too restrictive, but it is surprising how many different sentences may come from a small number of words. We may, of course, change the assignment to permit five words per sentence. My own advice would be to use either four-word or five-word sentences, but not both.

Adjectives	Nouns	Verbs
blue, two	truck	blew
cold, a	wind	flickered
an, American	lights	fluttered
big, old	stars	crashed
several	men	chattered
million	flag	twinkled

Teaching Prepositional Phrases

The approach to creative grammar described above may be applied to many different situations. For example, let us consider the use of prepositional phrases. After identifying the parts of a prepositional phrase and putting a list of prepositions on the board, we may ask the student to experiment with two or three different prepositions in each blank below to complete the phrase:

_____ the room	_____ my friend
_____ the moon	_____ the window
_____ the floor	_____ that day
_____ the school	_____ the people

Another device in teaching prepositions which I would consider creative is acting out prepositional phrases such as those in the sentences below:

1. Martha sat *at* the teacher's desk.
2. Martha walked *around* the teacher's desk.
3. Martha stood *beside* the teacher's desk.
4. Martha stood *by* the window.
5. Martha looked *out* the window.
6. Martha ran *to* the door.

This exercise is designed for the eighth-grade level, but any exercise which requires acting in front of the class may be carried on successfully in the early high school years as well. At the ninth-grade level the students might be asked to write four sentences themselves that could be acted before the class. The actions and personality of each person would serve to emphasize the meaning of a preposition, especially one showing direction, or position.

To show how prepositional phrases act as adjectives or adverbs, we may begin with sentences like the following:

A man _____ passed _____.
         What kind?   *Where?*

We may ask the students to use in the first blank above an adjective prepositional phrase such as *in a blue suit*. Many students may speak similar phrases telling *what kind*, the more humorous the better for classroom morale:

| with a black eye | with a scared look | on a purple cow |
| on a brown horse | in a black Mercury | in a pink shirt |

To answer the question *where*, the class may contribute a number of adverb phrases like the following:

| across the icy street | down the stairs | toward the pickle jar |
| into the auditorium | into the hot mill | to the pitcher's mound |

Each contribution by the class gives an opportunity to test the meaning of the words *prepositional phrase*. We have an opportunity further to clarify the concept of a group of words acting as a single part of speech, even though it contains within itself three parts of speech. We may also break down one of the phrases to show that though it does not contain an adverb, it has an adverbial function.

An Hour's Action in Prepositional Phrases

Once the idea of a prepositional phrase is thoroughly established, several lively exercises are possible. For instance, we may ask each student to write a story made up simply of ten or twelve prepositional phrases on topics such as the following:

1. Just Before the Kickoff	6. Getting Ready to Study
2. Washing the Dishes	7. After the Bell Rings
3. When I Make Brownies	8. Getting Dressed after Gym Class
4. When I Press My Dress	9. When I Paint the Kitchen
5. Mowing the Lawn	10. Helping Dad Wash the Car

Here is one boy's response to this assignment, a story in prepositional phrases about his actions in the hour after awakening:

ONE HOUR TO GO

1. out of bed	5. at the table	9. across the street
2. into the bathroom	6. into my mouth	10. on my bike
3. into my clothes	7. on the front step	11. toward school
4. down the stairs	8. for my friends	12. at my desk

Jerry Rabow

An Assembly Speech

This exercise may be varied by asking each student to place a verb before each prepositional phrase in his new story:

AN ASSEMBLY SPEECH	OFF TO SCHOOL
1. walked to the stage	1. jumped from my bed
2. looked at many faces	2. looked out the window
3. trembled with fear	3. leaped into my clothes
4. stared at my feet	4. rushed out the door
5. spoke in a cracked voice	5. hopped on my bike
6. stumbled out every word	6. raced down the street
7. rushed off the stage	7. sat on the grass
Philip Agnew	*George Krouse*

Building Ten-Word Sentences

A constructive final step in the teaching of prepositional phrases is the building of ten sentences of ten words each, using only words from the list below. In each sentence the student is asked to use a verb, a subject, an adjective modifying the subject, and two prepositional phrases, one an adjective phrase, the other an adverbial phrase. This exercise requires the student to examine carefully the function of each word he uses in the sentence. It is creative in the sense that he is making his own combination of words, even though the word choices themselves are not his own.

Example: A boy in a red cap sat on the roof.

A man with a haggard face limped down the street.

Nouns	Verbs	Adjectives	Prepositions
car	ran	haggard	in
man	crept	broken	on
dog	limped	shaggy	up
house	stole	new	along
face	rose	worn	under
boy	lay	a	without
cap	sat	the	to
coat	raced	blue	down
book	spoke	red	with
roof	stood	ten	into

The Class' Own Present Participles

In teaching the present participle, we may begin by asking the class to suggest five or six different present participles for each blank in the sentences below:

_____ around, the policeman blew his whistle.
_____ and _____, the girls ran down the hill.

In the first sentence above, we may point out as we go along the livelier, more intense word choices among those the students suggest. For example, *swerving* around or *swinging* around would suggest action much more exactly than the participle *turning*. Thus when the students themselves suggest many words to illustrate one principle, we have an opportunity for creative evaluation of the words they may wish to use in their themes. From the exercise above we may advance to one such as the following, in which the student describes an action of someone in his own family or his own classroom:

Tying his apron around his fat stomach, my father dipped his hands in the dish water.
Tapping his pencil on the desk, my friend Joe looks out the window.
Flashing a stern glance at the class, Miss Henry rose from her chair.

In terms of correctness the most important problem, of course, is the dangling participle. To teach our students to avoid danglers, we may ask them to complete sentences such as the following:

1. Skating across the pond, _____.
   Who skated?
2. Howling mournfully, _____.
   Who or what howled?
3. Whispering in the dark, _____.
   Who whispered?
4. Laughing and shouting, _____.
   Who laughed and shouted?
5. Racing up the hill, _____.
   Who or what raced?

The completion of such sentences in class discussion or in written work allows limited creative ingenuity. The important thing is that each student realize that the subject of the sentence must be able to perform the action described by the participle.

Another creative approach to participles is to ask the students to tell a brief story in present participles, each of which is followed by an object or a modifier. As in the exercise on prepositional phrases, we may first suggest a number of topics such as the following:

When We Painted the Car   My Dog's Antics on the Lawn
My Mother in the Kitchen   Traffic at the Green Light
My Little Sister at Play   In the School Cafeteria

Here is an illustration of a story told in participles followed by objects and modifiers as suggested above:

IN THE SCHOOL CAFETERIA

1. swishing open the door   6. lifting a bottle of milk
2. hearing the clatter of dishes   7. balancing my tray
3. sliding my tray along   8. waiting for my check
4. laughing with friends   9. slipping out my napkin
5. choosing a ham sandwich   10. chattering with the gang

Helen Geronimo

The Student's Own Infinitive Phrases

As in previous problems we may introduce the infinitive by asking the class to supply a number of different phrases that might fit into one construction:

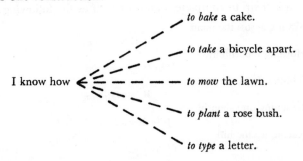

I know how
to *bake* a cake.
to *take* a bicycle apart.
to *mow* the lawn.
to *plant* a rose bush.
to *type* a letter.

Below are a few sentences to call forth the class' own infinitive phrases. Since infinitive phrases may be nouns, adverbs, or adjectives, the question under each blank points to the use of the infinitive phrase. Of course, in these situations it is necessary to explain to the class that an infinitive phrase, being always half verb, may take an object or be followed by a predicate adjective or predicate nominative.

1. ____ _____ _____ _____ is my greatest ambition.
            What?

2. This is the way ____ _____ _____ _____.
   To do what?
3. My friend has a need ____ _____ _____ _____.
   What kind?
4. I turned around ____ _____ _____ _____.
   Why?

At any time we can spontaneously associate grammar with a meaningful experience for the student, we are helping him to learn grammar creatively. For instance, we may ask the student to write ten infinitive phrases which express ten of his ambitions, small or large, as shown in this example:

MY TEN AMBITIONS

1. To play center for South High.
2. To buy an old car for forty dollars.
3. To win a game of checkers from my Dad.
4. To make a B in English just once.
5. To read *Great Expectations*.
6. To take a grip to California.
7. To ask a certain girl for a date.
8. To be admitted to Benton College.
9. To get an interesting job next summer.
10. To make my big brother proud of me.

Harold Jackson

Some students in the class may not wish to read or discuss all ten ambitions. The more meaning these ten ambitions have for the student the less he may be inclined to discuss them unless he feels especially friendly to the class. But when a discussion of this topic is possible, an evaluation of ambitions is especially fruitful in the junior or senior year of high school. At the ninth- or tenth-grade level, however, it can also be a fascinating topic. In the ideal lesson of this kind, the grammatical principle becomes more and more incidental to the definition of various ambitions. The more remarkable the discussion, however, the more intensely the student is likely to remember the technical aspects of grammar which he associates with it. If he is able to read to the class a couple of his ambitions that provoke exciting discussion or deepening thought, then a technicality of grammar takes on new meaning. The more personal and individual the language any person uses, the more vital become the technical means and elements of communication.

Teaching Complex Sentences

The first problem in the teaching of complex sentences is the definition of a dependent clause. It is easy to teach recognition of dependent clauses by using a list of fifteen or twenty dependent clause openers as shown in the list below:

DEPENDENT CLAUSE OPENERS

as (as soon as)	if	than	while	which
after	since	unless	that	who
although	why	until	whom	
before	how	when	whose	
because	though	where	what	

Once we have this list before the class and have drilled on recognition of dependent clauses, we are ready to break down the concept of the dependent clause into its various classifications. This we may do by asking the class to use its originality in supplying different *who* clauses which describe their classmates. The concept of the adjective clause takes on a new meaning. For instance, several members of the class may speak *who* clauses like these:

> I am thinking of a girl *who has red hair*. Who is she?
> I am thinking of a boy *who won a mile race yesterday*. Who is he?
> I am thinking of a boy *who wants to be a lawyer*. Who is he?
> I am thinking of a boy *who always uses green ink*. Who is he?
> I am thinking of a girl *who is wearing a red sweater*. Who is she?

From the teaching of *who* clauses, we may go to adverbial clauses with *while* or *because*. At each point in the teaching of complex sentences we begin with the invention of the construction under discussion by different members of the class. The best way for any student to learn a grammatical construction is to speak or write examples from his own language resources.

Imitation of Distinguished Sentences

Another creative activity in learning grammar is for the student to write sentences of his own imitating the structure of distinguished models. Consider this sentence from Conrad's *Nigger of the "Narcissus"*: "Streaming with perspiration, we swarmed up the rope, and, coming into the blast of cold wind, gasped like men plunged into icy water." In the upper years of high school, after studying participles, we may ask each student to write a sentence like this one, using experience and words of his own, but following Conrad's structure, opening with a present participle, and tucking another one in parenthetically, as Conrad does. We may place this or another sentence on the board and work out a cooperative imitation with the class, showing the problems involved. We may say, "What is a participle as strong and visual as *streaming*? Let us make a picture of boys shovelling snow or climbing into a bus. Who has an idea for a picture and an opening participle?" To imitate this sentence well, the student must consider other problems than the participles, his main concern. What is a verb as vivid as *swarmed*? As *gasped*? What image will be as intense as "blast of cold wind" or "icy water"? It is creative to require oneself to choose visualizing words and phrases as intense as those of the sentence we have chosen.

Here are some sentence patterns worthy of imitation, patterns that help the student see grammatical elements acting to make language more vivid and intense:

1. Opening with two adverbs:

Wistfully, admiringly, the old voice added, "It's snug in here, upon my word!" — Katherine Mansfield, "The Fly."

2. Using an adjective after the subject:

A half-moon, *dusky-gold*, was sinking behind the black sycamore tree. — D. H. Lawrence, *Sons and Lovers*.

3. Using a pair of co-ordinated adjectives:

Round the decay of that colossal wreck, *boundless and bare*, the lone and level sands stretch far away. — Percy B. Shelley, "Ozymandias."

4. Opening with an infinitive, ending with a simile:

To remove want and the fear of want, to give all classes leisure and comfort, the decencies and refinements of life, would be *like turning water into a desert.* — Henry George, *Progress and Poverty.*

5. Opening with one adverbial clause:

Whenever she rose easily to a towering green sea, elbows dug ribs, faces brightened. — Joseph Conrad, *Nigger of the "Narcissus."*

6. Opening with two adverbial clauses:

When lilacs last in the dooryard bloom'd,
And the great star early droop'd in the western sky in the night,
I mourned, and yet shall mourn with ever-returning spring.
— Walt Whitman, *Leaves of Grass*

In making this assignment, we may say: "Here are sentences I like, with the grammatical elements we need to work on further. But if you don't like these sentences, choose your own; *only be sure they have quality.* Get your sentences from good books." It is fun to write both the chosen sentences and the imitations on the board, in order to discuss word choices, rhythms, punctuation. Reading both original sentences and imitations aloud is very instructive on a number of language fronts, not the grammar front only.

*   *   *

This exploration of creative patterns in learning grammar is suggestive only, not inclusive. I have tried to present approaches from the simplest beginnings with parts of speech to the manipulation of grammatical elements in mature, memorable sentences. We may recapitulate the patterns as follows: (1) The student is creative when he uses his own adjectives, adverbs, etc., to illustrate first principles. (2) From this initiation he next builds sentences in various patterns, consciously using some one else's nouns, verbs, adjectives, and adverbs, pinning down parts of speech. (3) When the student comes to prepositional phrases, he takes another creative step, writing a little story about an experience, in prepositional phrases only. (4) He takes similar steps with infinitive phrases and participial phrases. (5) In learning adjective clauses, he describes members of his own class. (6) Finally, he sees grammatical elements in action in distinguished sentences from great books. He writes sentences similar in structure, endeavoring to make his diction as intense and alive as the language of his model. These six patterns are creative in varying degrees, and no two teachers will use them in the same way. The present exploration may lead, we hope, to other experiments whereby the teaching and learning of grammar may become year by year a more creative experience than we have known it in the past.

To the Student Teacher: Suggested Activities

1. Read *Living Language 9* (Harcourt, 1954), pp. 248–51, 338–50, and *Enjoying English 9* (Singer, 1954), pp. 250–70. Copy two or three exercises that you think are most effective in teaching adjectives and adverbs. Make a critical comment on each exercise to show why you selected it.
2. Ask a seventh- or eighth-grade friend to try the exercise on p. 205. Then make a report on whether or not this exercise is really practical.
3. With the same seventh- or eighth-grade pupil, work out the exercises on p. 204 and a story of twelve prepositional phrases as shown on p. 205. Show the participle exercise on p. 207 to a ninth- or tenth-grade teacher. Ask her if you might try it in her class. Does it really work?
4. Ask a ninth- or tenth-grade pupil to write a story in present participles like that on p. 208.
5. Write ten sentences opening with adverbial dependent clauses. Use a different dependent clause opener with each sentence. Put a comma after each introductory adverbial clause. For a further explanation of this exercise, see "A Student's Grammar Profile" (below, p. 464, sentence 21).
6. Write five sentences in imitation of five selected from pp. 211–12. In your sentences use words of visual intensity comparable to those of the original.

15   Style Through Grammar: Sentence-Building and Transformation[1]

THE SENTENCE-BUILDING process, as used in thousands of classrooms across the nation, is a realistic means of improving style by use of traditional grammar, such as the expansion of a kernel sentence into a longer, more sophisticated sentence. Let us begin with a kernel sentence, such as "My father spoke," and build it up with steps such as the following:

1. *Expand the verb of the sentence with an adverbial phrase of time.*

   Last evening my father spoke.

2. *Now use a past participle that gives an image of the father's physical position.*

   Last evening, *settled in his armchair*, my father spoke.

3. *Add an image in the form of an absolute construction.*

   Settled in his armchair, *his brown eyes glowing in the firelight*, my father spoke.

4. *Add a color and a prepositional phrase of further explanation.*

   Settled in his old red armchair, his eyes glowing, my father told *of his boyhood days on an Iowa farm.*

---

[1] For applications of transformational grammar in the sentence-building game, see below, pp. 224–26.

5. Use a more specific word for one of the words in your sentence.

Settled in an old red armchair, his brown eyes glowing, my father told of his boyhood *winters* on an Iowa farm.

Kernel Sentences Ready to Grow

The students in your class or mine may select one of the kernel sentences below and first expand it orally by using the sequence of steps described above. At each step in the sequence, several students may suggest a differently worded sentence. "Which sentence is best of all?" you and I may say, and then, "Why?" The main element of stylistic riches in this exercise is structure, arrangement of grammatical elements within the sentence. But diction impinges upon structure, and often the sentence becomes too long and cumbersome. Sometimes a single phrase, however picturesque, must be sacrificed to the rhythm each student's ear can recognize when alternatives are spoken by his classmates.

1. A bell rang.	7. My father knocked.
2. The car swerved.	8. A pony galloped.
3. The girl ran.	9. The player leaped.
4. A plane roared.	10. A bird flew.
5. A leaf fluttered.	11. My sister sang.
6. The baby crawled.	12. A fire blazed.

Sentence Building and Style

When we analyze sentences in the manner shown above, we see that many of the elements of transformational grammar are fundamentally identical with corresponding elements of traditional grammar. It is true that transformational grammar does not give attention to parts of speech as such. Nor does it deal with improvement of diction, such as the substitution of a vivid verb like *hopped* for a weak verb like *moved*. It deals fundamentally with expansion of kernel sentences and the shifting of elements of the sentence from one position to another. This approach, however, has been used extensively in sentence building, especially in recent years, without the burden of any new terminology. All sentence building embodies the principles of expansion, substitution, and transformation.

One of the main aims of the English teacher is to use grammar, however defined, for the improvement of style. Within the framework of familiar terms, the student of traditional grammar may work with one sentence, shifting, adding, and subtracting words, as a painter experiments with oils, thus becoming more and more aware of the grammatical identity of his materials. At the same time his sense of style suddenly sharpens; he becomes conscious of smooth and awkward rhythms, of varied openings, of subtle changes in meaning induced by a single change in word position.

Improvement of diction, as in the substitution of a strong adverb for a weak one, is a part of the resources of traditional grammar in the sentence-building game. Thus far transformational grammar has not emphasized such improvements in diction. To open a sentence-building experiment at the junior high school level, for instance, we begin with a sentence such as "The little bird hopped from branch to branch." We may say to the class, "Now let us first add an adverb telling *how*." As various students suggest adverbs, we may write them on the board. Here are some possibilities that might emerge from such a discussion: *nimbly, nervously, cautiously, fearfully, saucily*. Choosing adverbs that might go into this sentence is in itself a creative process. We may ask the class, "Of the adverbs suggested, which do you consider the liveliest? Which is the most exact? Which makes the clearest picture?" Thus any discussion of adverbs in context may lead to an evaluation of diction and the reason for our choices.

The next step, once the adverb is chosen, is to decide where to place it most advantageously within the sentence. This depends in part, of course, on the exact shade of meaning and effect the writer wishes to achieve. Here are some possibilities that may be suggested by the class:

1. *Saucily* the little bird hopped from branch to branch.
2. The little bird hopped *saucily* from branch to branch.
3. The little bird *saucily* hopped from branch to branch.

Reading the sentence aloud each time the adverb changes position allows us to examine more realistically the slight shift in meaning or emphasis. It helps train the ears of the class to recognize the position, if any, in which the adverb sounds awkward or forced.

If it sounds forced to the ear, would it also sound forced to a person reading it silently? In such a discussion the student sees the stylistic variants possible with the shifting of just one word. If this process appears to be stimulating, we may choose another adverb and repeat the procedure.

Making Diction More Exact

The next step is to show how the sentence may be improved by making the language more exact. We may say to the class, "What noun is more exact than the noun *bird?*" Members of the class may suggest possible noun substitutions such as *bluebird, redbird, goldfinch,* or *robin.* Any one of these nouns would be an improvement over the generic word *bird.*

Adding a Prepositional Phrase

A sentence, like a dress or a necktie, always looks more appealing with a touch of color. If the discussion thus far has been as lively as we hope, we may carry it a step further by saying, "Would anybody like to add to the sentence a prepositional phrase to make the picture of the tree and the bird more complete?" Perhaps we have been studying prepositional phrases. Perhaps we are ready to review prepositional phrases. If some sudent says, "Yes, I would add a prepositional phrase to tell what kind of branch. I would suggest adding the phrase, *of the apple tree,* to the sentence," we now have a sentence reading as follows:

The bluebird hopped saucily from branch to branch *of the apple tree.*

We call for other prepositional phrases and write them on the board: *of the plum tree, of the peach tree,* etc. Each of these prepositional phrases tells *what kind* of branch; they are adjective prepositional phrases. We now carry the manipulation of the sentence a step further by asking for a prepositional phrase telling *where.* Various answers may come, such as: *above my head, in the July sunset, during the April shower.* These phrases may also be written on the board for identification and evaluation. We now have a sentence that may read like this:

During the April shower a bluebird hopped saucily from branch to branch of the apple tree.

Other questions may now arise. Is the sentence now too long and cumbersome? If you wanted to make the sentence shorter, would it be better to eliminate the adverbial phrase telling *where* or the adjective phrase telling *what kind?*

The pattern sentence, "A little bird hopped from branch to branch" is suited to a seventh- or eighth-grade class. The following sentences will have more mature challenge for pupils of high school levels:

The coach paced up and down.	A puppy raced across the lawn.
An old man hobbled along.	The fire blazed.
The principal spoke.	The lights flickered.

This discussion of a sentence-building exercise shows how it is possible to use grammatical elements for stylistic emphasis and variety. In such a discussion the more adverbs and prepositional phrases suggested by the class, the more creative participation we have in learning grammar. By this procedure we link the technicalities of parts of speech to a sense of the vivid phrase, the emphatically well-placed word, and the rhythmical patterns of the sentence.

Concentration on the Verb

To begin a sentence-building experiment with emphasis on the verb, we may write on the board a sentence like the following:

A boy walked across the porch.

We may say to the class, "What is a more exact verb than *walked?* Let us write a list of more exact words on the board." Then we may have a series of verbs like the following: *skipped, sauntered, dashed, weaved, skated, toddled.*

Now we say, "Let us turn the sentence around, putting the verb before the subject." Then we have a sentence like this:

Across the porch toddled a little boy.

Completing the Picture

Finally, we may give our attention to making the picture of the boy more complete. We may ask the class to use adjectives or phrases that will help to individualize the little boy. Here are some possibilities:

1. *Add an adjective:*

> Across the porch toddled a skinny little boy.
> Others: *a rosy little boy, a little Mexican boy, a laughing little boy, a ragged little boy.*

The more adjectives selected by the class, the more creative the discussion. Again we have a chance to evaluate the adjective. Which adjective differentiates the boy most completely from all other boys?

2. *Experiment with two adjectives following the subject in normal order.*

> A little boy, *rosy and chubby,* toddled across the porch.

3. *Experiment with adding a prepositional phrase describing the boy:*

> Across the porch toddled a little boy *with bright blue eyes.*

Other phrases like these: *with a blue rubber elephant in his hand; in a red swim suit; with tousled yellow curls; with a black cocker puppy in his arms.*

Building a Sound and Color Sentence: Accent on Verbs Again

1. To teach sensory intensity as a part of grammar for style, we may open a class experiment with a short sentence like this:

> The water gurgled.

2. Now we have a sound verb, *gurgled.* Does it also describe action? What verb can we use that would suggest both action and sound? Perhaps a word like *splashed* would suggest both sound and action. If not, perhaps we could use two verbs, like this:

> The water splashed and gurgled.

We may have other verbs suggested, such as *babbled, trickled, foamed, swirled, roared, moaned, leaped, tumbled.*

3. Next we may add an adjective or an adjective phrase describing the water:

> The ice water gurgled into the glass.
> The water of the brook splashed and gurgled.

4. Now we say to the class, "How can we add color to our sentence"? Some one may suggest:

> The water of the brook gurgled along the green banks.
> The water gurgled into the green glass.

5. Change the water to some other liquid to give color to the sentence in a different way:

> The green medicine splashed into the spoon.
> The brownish "coke" foamed into the glass.

This outline of steps for class discussion is meant to be suggestive only. If at any time the discussion falters, and we feel that each student should proceed individually, we direct each member of the class to begin with a small sentence of his own and build it up in successive steps, as outlined on the board. The last sentence should include sound and color in the smallest number of words. Here are some short sentences the class may use as openers:

The horse neighed.	The wind whistled.
The old hen clucked.	The car screeched.
The pen scratched.	The train flashed by.

Building a Picture Sentence: Using Participles

To concentrate on the use of participles, we may suggest that each pupil build a sentence about some one in his family. To show what we mean by this experiment, we may work it out with the class in the following steps at the board:

1. Write a sentence about your father, using a vivid verb. *Example:* My father slumped in his chair.

We may say to the class, "What other verbs could we use in this sentence, verbs that would make clear pictures of action?"

2. Open the sentence with a present participle. *Example:* Striking a match lazily, my father slumped in his chair.
3. Now instead of a present participle, use an absolute construction which gives a picture of the father. *Example:* His blue eyes twinkling, my father slumped in his chair.
4. Now change the position of the participial phrase: My father, striking a match lazily, slumped in his chair.

5. Change the position of the absolute construction. *Example:* My father, his blue eyes twinkling, reached for an apple.
6. Now use a past participle in an absolute construction. *Example:* My father, his face wreathed in smiles, lazily lighted his pipe.

In this sentence-building exercise, even though the student can not always recognize a present participle or a past participle, we may teach him how to use them in various positions in the sentence. The best way to identification is actual usage of one's own participles. But improvement of style is more important than mere identification. Nothing is more helpful in the visualization of people than the use of participles. What we achieve is an extra verb which is the soul of action and visualization, especially of people. If we can teach the student to use an absolute construction, in a few sentences of his own, even though the terminology still eludes him, we may find effective absolute constructions turning up in themes.

When the student writes six sentences of his own, following these six steps, we urge him to describe his father, mother, or close friend realistically in his sentence, choosing a typical action that serves to individualize the personality. Such sentences, when read aloud to the class, will not only be helpful in teaching grammar for style, but also in teaching the visualization of people and acquainting the students with interesting members of each other's families.

Building a School-Experience Sentence

We may ask the class to choose a small sentence, such as "My teacher embarrassed me," and make it more colorful and exact, as shown in the examples below:

1. Begin with the words that name the month and time of day.
   ALLEN: *One January afternoon* my teacher embarrassed me.

2. Follow the opening words with a *when* construction that tells how old you were or what grade you attended.
   SUSAN: One January afternoon, *when I was in the sixth grade*, my teacher embarrassed me.

3. Add a prepositional phrase with a gerund, telling *how* or *why*.
   FRANK: One January afternoon, when I was in the sixth grade, my teacher embarrassed me *by asking me to leave the room*.

The sentence-building exercise above is useful not only in teaching the adverbial clause or adverbial phrase, but also in teaching the elements of a topic sentence, when we wish the students to write a theme about a school experience. The finished sentence tells not only *when* and *where*, but also *how* and *what*. Any time we can teach the student to use phrases and clauses that make the meaning more complete or more explicit we are teaching both grammar and style in a highly effective manner.

Building a Friendship Sentence: Using Two Dependent Clauses

We may ask the class to begin with a sentence, such as "I made a friend," and build it up step by step.

1. Add a prepositional phrase telling *where*.
   HANK: I made a friend *in Charley's bicycle shop*.

2. Open your sentence with a phrase telling *when*.
   GEORGE: *One Saturday afternoon in May*, I made a friend in Charley's bicycle shop.

3. After your opening phrase, use an adverb clause beginning with *when, while,* or *as*.
   MAX: One Saturday afternoon in May, *while Charley was fixing a flat tire on my bike*, I made a friend in his repair shop.

4. Add an adjective clause beginning with *who* to describe the friend.
   HANK: One Saturday afternoon in May, while Charley was fixing a flat tire on my bike, I made a friend *who came from a farm in Alabama*.

Small Sentences to Expand

1. I lost a friend.
2. My friend helped me.
3. I saw a friendly act.
4. I made an enemy.
5. I met a friend.
6. George hurt his friend.

Building a Quotation Sentence

We may ask the class to choose a short sentence, such as "Help me," or "Wait a minute." Write it so that we hear and see the speaker, like this:

"It's mine!" cried my sister, as she grabbed the rag doll.

1. Tell who is speaking. Use a conversational tag, such as *he said* or *he whispered:*
   "I'm sorry," *my brother said.*
2. Add an adverb telling how it is said:
   "I'm sorry," my brother said *shyly.*
3. Add a word picture in an absolute construction to describe the speaker:
   "I'm sorry," my little brother said shyly, *his blue eyes full of tears.*
4. Add a gesture or some other bit of action. Use a participial phrase:
   "I'm sorry," my little brother said shyly, *hanging his head and turning away.*

This exercise is extremely useful in any writing project which involves the use of dialogue, particularly in the upper levels of high school English. When we ask our students to write a description of a person or a bit of characterization, we may use this kind of sentence-building to show how a skillful writer can combine dialogue with descriptive images and bits of action. In this exercise the key constructions are the adverbs, the absolute constructions, and the participial phrases.

*   *   *

The use of the sentence-building process in the teaching of grammar may be adapted to the most elementary problems or the most advanced. In the average seventh-grade class it might be used as effectively as in a twelfth-grade college-preparatory group. The secret of the effectiveness of this approach is that each student is able to provide his own grammatical elements and shape them into his own sentences. It is true that each sentence and its grammatical elements may loosely or exactly follow a pattern set by the teacher. In this process the student is both imitative and creative. He has to provide his own words, but the sequence of grammatical elements is set up for him by the teacher. The student sees that his own choices are identical in function, and therefore in name, with the parts of speech used in the original sentence. Best of all, this approach to grammar has its immediate impact upon stylistic improvement. At each point in the process, the student is compelled by his very freedom of choice to compare a strong with a weak verb, an exact adjective with a general one. He learns to prefer the specific to the generic word, realizing that the specific word incorporates the general meaning but that the generic term does not communicate the individualized impression or the exact image that is the essence of vivid diction. Another decisive asset in the sentence-building process is the re-arrangement of words to achieve variations in sentence rhythms and sentence patterns. Once a student has written a single sentence in which, for example, two adjectives follow the subject, as on pages 361–62 above, he is very likely to use this same construction in his papers. He is also likely to notice this construction in the literature that he reads. Gradually he becomes aware of a number of mature sentence patterns which he also may learn to identify in grammatical terms. The sentence-building process then is creative for the student not only in teaching him to identify grammatical elements, but also in showing him through his own language resources some of the mature elements of stylistic excellence.

TRANSFORMATIONAL GRAMMAR: COMPARISONS AND CONTRASTS [2]

As Noam Chomsky himself points out, "Neither the theory of transformational grammar nor the description of English structure that has been and is being developed in accordance with its principles can be regarded as a closed and fixed system." [3] In such a situation it is inevitable that authorities on transformational grammar differ among themselves. The English teacher, meanwhile, wishing to find elements of pragmatic usefulness in all new theories, searches for down-to-earth applications in the classroom. One of the useful elements of transformational grammar is the conception of the expansion of a kernel sentence. Let us again consider expansion of the two fundamental elements of a kernel sentence such as "A boy walked." This kind of expansion has been used for many years by

[2] For modified applications of transformational grammar in sentence-building games, see *Enjoying English 7* (1965), pp. 11–12, 27, 140–41; *Enjoying English 8* (1965), pp. 19–20, 34–35, 265–66; *Enjoying English 9* (1966), pp. 152, 196–97, 286–87; *Enjoying English 10* (1966), pp. 301, 318–19; *Enjoying English 11* (1966), pp. 160–61, 169, 312–13; *Enjoying English 12* (1966), pp. 101, 230, 336–48.

[3] Introduction to Paul Roberts' *English Syntax* (Harcourt, Brace, and World, 1964), p. xiii. Mr. Roberts' work is highly instructive, particularly when he reverts to the nomenclature of traditional grammar.

gifted teachers, using the terminology of traditional grammar. The transformational grammarian follows somewhat the same steps, as we have seen at the beginning of this chapter:

1. The subject of the sentence is expanded:

A boy *in blue dungarees* walked.

This kind of expansion of one of the two fundamental sentence parts, subject and verb, is called by some authorities a *transformation.*[4]

2. The verb is expanded:

A boy in blue dungarees walked *across the grass.*

3. Now the form of the sentence is changed to a question:

Did a boy in blue dungarees walk across the grass?

The change from a statement to a question is a special kind of transformation called a *substitution.* Here the substitution is one of a question in place of a statement.

4. Now the form of the verb is changed for emphasis:

A boy in blue dungarees *did walk* across the grass.

5. Expanding the sentence with an adverbial clause opener works still another kind of transformation:

As we sat at the kitchen window, a boy in blue dungarees walked across the grass.

6. Still another kind of expansion is this:

A boy in blue dungarees walked across the grass, *whistling a tune from* Oklahoma!

To some authorities, however, a transformation cannot be authentic

---

[4] To the teacher using traditional grammar, "in blue dungarees" is simply enriching the sentence by the use of a modifier. To some transformationalists, however, this insertion of "in blue dungarees" represents the "imbedding" of a second kernel sentence, "A boy wore blue dungarees," in the matrix sentence. To many teachers this conception of one kernel sentence absorbing another is a needless encumbrance in realistic classroom applications of grammar to the sentence-building resource.

unless it represents a synthesis of two or more kernel sentences which show some one structural item in common.[5] Here is an example:

> A bell rang.
> A bell was sonorous.
> A bell was in the tower.

These kernel sentences may be combined in forms, then, such as the following:

> A sonorous bell in the tower rang.
> A bell rang sonorously in the tower.
> A sonorous bell rang in the tower.

Such a conception of combining one or more kernel sentences with the matrix sentence is awkward and artificial for the student as compared with the step-by-step expansion of one kernel sentence.

The principles of transformational grammar, especially the key concept of expansion of the subject and verb of kernel sentences, are already tried and tested in many classroom experiments with the sentence-building process rooted in traditional grammar. The impact of transformational grammar is salutary in classroom application to the extent that it encourages sentence building from the simplest kernel sentences to more complex and sophisticated sentences. Experience shows that sentence building can be used with great effectiveness in oral discussion as well as in written steps from the third grade through the twelfth. What is now needed from the experts is not further proliferation of new theories in transformational grammar, but practical applications to classroom situations. So far only Enola Borgh and Verna Newsome have dealt with the ultimate test: the application of sentence building to style by means of examples from literary sentences, the framing of sophisticated sentences, and the intensification of diction. For the future the key dilemma is this: However much advanced specialists need a more exact and systematic description of the language, the student does not need it at all; he needs to have easily-learned new ways and means to improve his sentences. Only when the transformational grammarians focus their energies on this need shall we have the fruit of their labors.

---

[5] See Dr. Gladys Haase, "Transformational Grammar: A Synthesis," below, pp. 360–71.

To the Student Teacher: Suggested Activities

1. Develop a school experience sentence in three steps like those on pp. 221–22.
2. Develop a picture sentence with participles in six steps like those on pp. 220–21.
3. Develop a quotation sentence in four steps like those on pp. 222–23.
4. See *Enjoying English 8* (1966), pp. 6, 19–20, 28, 34–35, etc. Develop one of these sentence-building games on the board for your teaching-of-English class. Other sentence-building games of the same kind may be found in *Enjoying English 9* (1966), pp. 128, 152, 309; *Enjoying English 11* (1966), pp. 160–61, 169, 312–13, etc.
5. Select a sentence you like especially from Hardy's *The Mayor of Casterbridge* and write a sentence of your own with the same construction and comparably intense language.
   Example from *The Mayor:* "And in autumn ... innumerable tawny and yellow leaves skimmed along the pavement, and stole through people's doorways into their passages, with a hesitating scratch on the floor like the skirts of timid visitors."
6. Read a passage from *Lord Jim* or *Youth*, by Joseph Conrad. Write a sentence in structural imitation of a sentence you liked especially. Try for comparably intense diction.
   Example from *Youth:* "Now I see it always from a small boat, a high outline of mountains, blue and afar, in the morning; like faint mist at noon; a jagged wall of purple at sunset."

Suggested Readings

ANDERSON, HAROLD A.: "Critical Thinking through Instruction in English,' *English Journal*, Vol. 36 (February, 1947), pp. 73–79
   Helping students to connect their own experience with the meaning of words and the structure of sentences. Excellent examples are used in the article.

BATEMAN, DONALD R.: "More Mature Writing through a Better Understanding of Language Structure," *English Journal*, Vol. 50 (October, 1961), pp. 457–60
   Intriguing analysis of an approach to sentence structure by analysis of "layers of modification."

BORGH, ENOLA M.: "The Case for Syntax," *Elementary English*, Vol. 42 (January, 1965), pp. 28–34
   The author makes many suggestions for practical exercises in which sentences "can be expanded by inserting modifiers before the subject, after the subject, before the verb, and after the verb," also for the use

of transformational principles to help students rewrite sentences in various ways.

————: *Grammatical Patterns and Composition*, Wisconsin Council of Teachers of English, 1963

Practical and imaginative study of sentence patterns, illustrated by excellent passages from significant writers. Most useful when least encumbered by new terminology, as in exercises on sentence sense, subjects and predicates, expansion of verbs.

DAVISON, ETHEL B.: "Power from Sentence Patterns," *English Journal*, Vol. 39 (September, 1950), pp. 379–84

How to let the student get a "picture" of the structure of a sentence.

HOOK, J. N.: *The Teaching of High School English*, Ronald Press, 1950

See Chapter 10 for practical suggestions to the teacher in helping the student see the *growth* of a sentence.

NEWSOME, VERNA L.: "Expansions and Transformations to Improve Sentences," *English Journal*, Vol. 53 (May, 1964), pp. 327–35

The main benefit of this article is its application of theory to particular problems of style. The expansion principle is especially well handled. The author realizes that application of principles is a hundred times more needed than new grammatical theory or terminology. She returns often and effectively to the nomenclature of traditional grammar.

ST. PETER, MARY: "A Sentence Strikes Out," *English Journal*, Vol. 50 (April, 1961), pp. 271–72

Delightful personification of Mr. Sentence by a graduate student. The mechanical teacher, says Sentence, "wants me paralleled, punctuated and varied!"

TEER, MARGARET: "Building Sentence Patterns by Ear," *English Journal*, Vol. 38 (April, 1949), pp. 197–200

Letting the students hear good sentences. Interesting suggestion about the use of a recording machine in the classroom.

TICHENOR, HELEN: "The Sentence: A Basis for Grammar and Composition," *English Journal*, Vol. 37 (September, 1948), pp. 361–64

How to make the actual composition of sentences by the students the basis of illustrating grammatical principles.

THOMAS, OWEN: *Transformational Grammar and the Teacher of English*, Holt, Rinehart and Winston, 1965

An attempt to clarify the principles of transformational grammar and put it in perspective of the new learning. The author realizes that scientific grammar must somehow be adapted to make it pedagogically usable.

WOLFE, DON M., with ELLEN M. GEYER and DON F. MAHAN, *Enjoying English 12*, Singer, 1966, "Golden Sentences from the Masters," pp. 349–52

16 Reminder Words and Vocabulary Exactness

IN DEVELOPING reading skill, each of us, child or adult, must learn new words at his own pace and in his own way. Each of us has a somewhat different experience when confronted with an unknown word, whether in a novel, a magazine article, or a treatise on astronomy. Sometimes we look up the word in the dictionary, only to find that it has half a dozen meanings from which we must choose one. In reading literature, we may find it especially disturbing to turn from a poem or a story to the bleak pages of the dictionary in search of a meaning. Even when we religiously track down a word we are eager to know, we may find that in context it has a meaning slightly different from the dictionary definition. Word meanings, then, depend so much upon context that often we find that we can guess at their connotations and save time from dictionary hunting for a little more enjoyable reading. No two people increase their reading vocabulary in quite the same way or at the same pace, nor do any two people feel the need for knowing exactly the same words. One person may want desperately to know a chemistry or mathematics vocabulary, another the words of biology, or art, or the names of automobile parts. It seems a fruitless task, then, to make the building of a reading vocabulary a main aim of an English program. I am certain that some teachers make word roots and histories a fascinating enterprise to each one in the class; the same teacher often inspires the class with the new words in *Silas Marner*, *The Return of the Native*, or Burke's *On Conciliation with America*. But to many teachers such a task is as cold and lifeless as the words themselves out of their context on the magic page. Few such drills, however appealing, can meet the reading vocabulary needs of all students in the class.

Choosing the Most Exact Word

If the enlargement of reading vocabulary is not a practical aim, what shall we call a vital element of vocabulary training? That part of vocabulary training which helps us to speak and write *more exactly* is the heart of the matter. The high school boy or girl knows a great many words which are specific rather than general, concrete rather than abstract, which he never uses. Our task is to make him aware of his resources for speaking and writing exactly what he means in the fewest possible words. On the eighth- or ninth-grade level, for example, we may teach him to write a number of different verbs more exact than *walked*, as in the sentences below:

> A man *tottered* down the street.
> A man *limped* down the street.
> A man *wobbled* down the street.

Every boy or girl possesses a number of active image-making verbs that he may use instead of generic verbs. He may use, for example, *grabbed*, *snatched*, *seized*, instead of *took*. Even among these three more active verbs, he can see instantly that *snatched* is more exact than *seized*. We may ask our class to think of those exact verbs that describe the movements or sounds of the students in the class. One student may write that he sees or hears people *wriggle*, *gasp*, *cough*, *snort*, *sneeze*, *twitch*, *groan*, *whisper*. We must, therefore, awaken in the student a sense of the hierarchy existing in any group of similar words, from the most vivid and exact to the haziest and most general.

Exactness through Sensory Phrasing

On the eighth- and ninth-grade level one of the most effective ways of bringing exact words into focus is to ask, "What words does the word *Christmas* suggest to you?" The child may write a number of words such as "white snow," "tinkling bells," "red mittens," "green holly," "squealing children," "ringing bells." Instantly the class sees that those words which electrically appeal to the senses are more exact than general words such as *Christmas.* When we take such a word as *kitchen* and ask our class to set down twelve or fifteen specific picture words that the word *kitchen* reminds them of, we may get such a list as this:

blue flame	ice cubes	white curtains
red linoleum	crisp toast	crinkly bacon
melting butter	burnt fudge	sizzling grease
cinnamon smell	dirty dishes	frothy orange juice

Of course it is true that the word *kitchen* is not equivalent to these words. But in asking for words which the word *kitchen* or *breakfast* calls to mind, we are requiring our students to think in more specific terms and therefore to write more vividly.

This principle may be applied to all training in the use of sensory language. Take, for example, such a word as *noise.* How can we make the word *noise* specific? The noise of running water, the noise heels make on the sidewalk, the noise of pencils writing, the noise a door makes, the noise of voices? We may ask our students of the eighth or ninth grade to list many specific sounds for the word *noise,* as in the following exercise:

The _____ of water	The _____ of a puppy
The _____ of heels	The _____ of a kitten
The _____ of a ball	The _____ of a window
The _____ of pencils	The _____ of a shoe
The _____ of a door	The _____ of breaking glass
The _____ of voices	The _____ of a motor
The _____ of brakes	The _____ of a bee
The _____ of a whistle	

Reminder words offer an unlimited field for making students aware of more exact vocabulary resources. In choosing reminder words, we shall be wise to use as specific a starting-point as possible. In this sense *street* is preferable to *city,* *kitchen* is preferable to *house,* *refrigerator* is preferable to *kitchen,* *classroom clothes* or *classroom sounds* is preferable to *classroom.* By the very word we name as a reminder word we can require our students to be more specific or less specific.

In making our students aware of more exact adjectives that appeal to the five senses, we may use an exercise such as this one:

Adjectives of the Five Senses

Choose a word which will appeal to one of the senses as you describe each noun in the list below.

Example: sweet peach (taste)

1. _____ apple (taste)		9. _____ sweater (touch)
2. _____ burrs (touch)		10. _____ sweater (sight)
3. _____ leaf (sight)		11. _____ grapes (sight)
4. _____ bird (sound)		12. _____ grapes (taste)
5. _____ bird (sight)		13. _____ frost (sight)
6. _____ bonfire (sight)		14. _____ frost (touch)
7. _____ bonfire (sound)		15. _____ air (smell)
8. _____ bonfire (smell)		16. _____ air (touch)

Search for the Specific Word

When we assign descriptions of places and people, we have another opportunity to teach the usefulness of exact diction. We may ask our students to use specific words for such general adjectives as *beautiful, ugly, happy, strong, weak, small*. Instead of *ugly* face, we may ask them for more exact adjectives, such as *scarred, pitted, swollen, craglike, sallow, pimply*. The word *beautiful* as applied to *face* is more difficult to reduce to specific terms, but our students may suggest *rosy, glowing, smiling, luminous, dimpled*. Words such as *wonderful, beautiful, lovely, ugly, nice, bad, good* are too general to be descriptive. When it seems necessary to use such a word, we must provide for the reader other words which really visualize a particular kind of beautiful face or nice person. Only by the use of specific image-making words can the reader visualize the person described as ugly or beautiful, sad or weak. Consider this student theme, for instance, in which John's intense images make the place and the mother come alive:

DECEMBER NIGHTS IN BROOKLYN

On December nights in our cold tenement on St. Paul's Street in Brooklyn, Mama would sit for hours before the square black iron stove. With the oven door swung open, her feet in worn slippers like scarred and battered ships would rest on a rectangular silvery plate just below the door. Mama would rock back and forth to a measured squeak in the frail mahogany rocker staring into dazed thoughts; a stare that had no eyes; rocking to the tick-tock counterpoint of an unkempt fading clock that idled its time away on a mantel above the stove. The gray mantel was covered with bright yellow oilcloth, its scalloped edges curling from the heat of the precious stove. Sometimes Mama would lay an elbow-torn maroon sweater of mine across her round heavy shoulders; for no matter how much heat the burning heart of the stove gave off, it never seemed quite enough. There were times when a white damask napkin, a napkin of earlier dreams, was knotted tight around Mama's head.

John P. Brady

Students who learn the use of such specific words soon see the relationship between their own exact vocabulary and that of the writers they are coming to know. To read Hamlin Garland afresh, for instance, with a background of exact image-making words in one's own writing, is a revelation. Among modern American writers Garland is one of the most consistent in using words exact enough to differentiate each face, each place, each mood from others of its kind.[1] Consider, for example, this passage from "Up the Cooly":

FARMHOUSE IN THE RAIN

The rain was still falling, sweeping down from the half-seen hills, wreathing the wooded peaks with a gray garment of mist, and filling the valley with a whitish cloud.

It fell around the house drearily. It ran down the tubs placed to catch t, dripped from the mossy pump, and drummed on the upturned milk pails, and upon the brown and yellow beehives under the maple trees. The chickens seemed depressed, but the irrepressible blue-jay screamed amid it all, with the same insolent spirit, his plumage untarnished by the wet. The barnyard showed a horrible mixture of mud and mire, through which Howard caught glimpses of the men, slumping to and fro without more additional protection than a ragged coat and a shapeless felt hat.

In analyzing this passage, we may point out to our class the use of such images as "gray garment of mist," "mossy pump," "brown and yellow beehives," "slumping to and fro." Only by such electric

[1] See also the description by Joseph Conrad beginning, "And this is how I see the East," page 398.

images is Garland able to make us feel the exact mood of his character as he watches the scene.

When we deal with dialogue, we have an opportunity to make our students conscious of the multitude of verbs that may be used in place of the word *said*. On any level from the seventh grade through the twelfth it is instructive to make a cooperative list in class of verbs that might be used in the writing of dialogue. A few of these are: *whispered, babbled, hissed, grunted, mumbled, murmured, gasped.*

Pinning Down Meanings

The more concrete and the less abstract a word, such as "tinkling bell," the less likely it is to be misunderstood. A term such as "three red roses" creates an image instantaneously, and the same image simultaneously in the mind of everyone who hears it. The moment we speak an abstract word, however, such as *kindness, courage, cowardice, American*, we must immediately pin down a particular meaning of the abstraction in order not to be misunderstood. As pinning down meanings is the heart of the semantic search, so it is also the core of vocabulary growth. To show a class how difficult it is to pin down meanings of abstract words, we may use such an example as "nice person," and ask the class to help us define the term. The class may respond with a number of definitions like the following:

a person with good manners	a church member
a member of a good family	an outspoken person
someone who agrees with me	a friendly person
someone with stimulating ideas	a widely traveled cosmopolite
someone who always does the conventional thing	a discriminating person
	an American
someone with a good disposition	an attractive looking person

Once we present the complications of defining such a concept, we demonstrate to our class that we cannot give too much thought to using exact adjectives rather than generalized ones. For the word *nice*, we may also ask the class to suggest single adjectives that are more exact, such as *amiable, courteous, thoughtful, cheerful, helpful*.

How vital it is to citizenship to train our young people to use specific words instead of general words, especially in abstract language, we may hear for ourselves in political speeches and read in editorials in the public press. Scarcely a political campaign passes without one candidate or another stamping himself as a hundred-per-cent American without pausing to define his term. When we consider such terms as *Americanism* and *democracy*, we need especially rigorous training in our classrooms. We need to put before our young people examples of political theorizing which fail lamentably to specify the most important terms used. Here is an example, with questions at the right, showing what persons trained in vocabulary exactness would be asking.

MY CREED IS AMERICANISM	WHAT THE CRITICAL THINKER IS ASKING
I believe in Americanism. No country is so glorious as America in her traditions and ideals. The spirit of liberty and freedom. for which our forefathers fought in the Revolution is still implanted in the hearts of the millions of citizens who live in this great land. For my part, I am happy that I was not born in an alien country where no liberty prevails. I am thankful that I can, in some degree, pass on to my children, undiminished, the spirit of Americanism in which I believe. If I am elected, I pledge myself to uphold Americanism in the halls of Congress.	What does he mean by "Americanism"? He does not say. Now he's generalizing. What does he mean by liberty and freedom? What is he driving at? What do alien countries have to do with Americanism? He has changed the subject again, and I'm still puzzled. What does he mean by the "spirit of Americanism"? He has left his audience completely in the dark.

Unfortunately the words of greatest meaning to us are those which require the most rigorous analysis in order to pin down meanings. If we ask our students what they mean by the words *love, beauty, patriotism, religion, brotherhood, maturity,* they are hard-pressed to reply and still more hard-pressed to come to any agreement on the exact meaning of any one of these words. Yet few things are more important at any level from the seventh grade through the twelfth and beyond than pinning down the meanings of words we live by. As set forth elsewhere in this book, we may ask our students to pin down the meaning of such vital words as *marriage, family, success, son, daughter, father, high school, college, student, courage, propaganda, prejudice, poverty, creativity.*

*   *   *

The addition of new words to one's reading vocabulary is infinitely less essential than the rediscovery and persistent use of the exact words we already know. The more concrete a word, such as *red apple*, the more quickly and easily it is visualized and the less chance for misinterpretation on the part of the hearer. On the other hand, the more abstract the word, the more difficult it is to pin down its precise meaning. We must train our students, therefore, to use abstractions with great caution, attempting at each use to specify the exact meaning of the word used. Since abstractions are the words we live by, each of us needs to re-assess each year the meanings they have for us. Hence, as teachers we cannot give too much time in the classroom to the definition of key words in our daily speech. When we call upon each member of the class to rise and speak his definition of a word such as *hate* or *peace*, we require each member of the class to rethink the definition he has hitherto held. Nothing is more important in arriving at exact definitions than hearing a number of meanings none of which exactly fits one's own preconception of the word's essential meaning.

The more persistently our students describe places and people from close, accurate observation, the more chance they have of individualizing those people and places, studying a tree or a face until they can communicate its uniqueness in exact images. This is one way to originality in art. It is also one way to originality in science. At the point where the writer, the artist, and the scientist observe an object until it becomes differentiated from all other objects — at that point they possess in common the fruit of exactness in observation and expression.

To the Student Teacher: Suggested Activities

1. Take a word such as *Christmas, kitchen, drugstore, dinner,* and make a list of specific sensory words the original word reminds you of. Try for at least twenty-five words, divided among touch, taste, smell, color, and sound images.

2. Choose a single word such as *face*, *sister*, or *college*. In rapid succession write the first ten words that come to your mind as you concentrate on the original word. Then write a short paper tracing your thoughts from word to word. The thoughts you trace may run too deep into your experience to permit you to hand in your paper. If so, choose a new word and try again. This is a fascinating experiment you and your future students will want to try more than once.

3. Make a list of the twenty most exact words on a page of Joseph Conrad or Willa Cather or Charles Dickens. Arrange the words in order from the most specific to the least specific. Make notes on your first few words to show why you place them high in your scale. Do the same with a few of the least specific words. *Note:* Remember to give the name of the story or novel in your report.

4. Leaf through a book on vocabulary building, or read one of the articles on vocabulary building in the *English Journal*. Write a brief report on one idea of value you found.

5. Read several editorials (or columns by Reston, Alsop, Lippman, etc.) in the local newspaper. Paste one on a sheet of paper and underline the words you consider least specific in meaning. Write a brief note on each of these words to show why it is used too loosely.

6. "Prejudice is a loose idea, tightly held." Explain the meaning of this statement as applied to a particular word or phrase.

Suggested Readings

ALLEN, ANDREW E.: "An Individual Vocabulary-Building Device," *English Journal*, Vol. 51 (March, 1962), pp. 205–07

A practical and imaginative word-a-day vocabulary-building program.

BRITAIN, JAMES C.: "Magic Words," *English Journal*, Vol. 41 (November, 1952), pp. 491–94

The use of one word a week to elicit inquiry, investigation, or experience in order that the student may come to understand it.

COHLER, JENNY: "Say What You Mean," *English Journal*, Vol. 43 (February, 1954), pp. 84–86

A stimulating and rewarding approach to vocabulary building: classroom discussions of groups of similar words which aim for mastery of 500 new words as well as recognition of semantic inferences in words through emphasis on the substitution of exact for approximate meanings.

CONRAD, LAWRENCE: "Intensive Vocabulary Study," *English Journal*, Vol. 29 (December, 1940), pp. 794–99

Teaching the students to grasp the meaning of words through their use in a variety of exercises. Examples given.

COWING, AMY: *Writing Words That Work*, U.S. Printing Office, 1961
> A guide to techniques of writing with a view toward enhancement of readability. "Personal Words Sell," the author says, and so do personal sentences.

DELL, WILLIAM C.: "Creativity and the English Curriculum," *English Journal*, Vol. 52 (March, 1963), pp. 200–05
> The section on definition of happiness in this rich and vital article is superb. Other topics suggested are: What is fear? When is hate? What is most valuable to me? Where is fun?

GREEN, J. C.: "Modernizing the Teaching of Vocabulary," *English Journal*, Vol. 34 (June, 1945), pp. 343–44
> Interesting new methods are suggested in this article for teaching the building of a vocabulary.

MILLER, WARD S.: "Word Hobbies," *English Journal*, Vol. 37 (January, 1948), pp. 31–35
> How the use of the dictionary can become a real adventure in learning.

MIRRIELEES, LUCIA B.: *Teaching Composition and Literature in Junior and Senior High School*, Harcourt, Brace, 1952
> See Chapter 5. This chapter discusses motivation for word study, the different levels of speech, and the application of semantics at the high school level.

O'QUINN, GLORIA: "Vocabulary Panels for the Talented," *English Journal*, Vol. 52 (February, 1963), pp. 114–15
> Use of panels in which wit and humor are used by pupils and teacher as incitements to vocabulary growth.

RAGLE, JOHN W.: "Something Old, Something New, Something Borrowed: A Vocabulary Program," *English Journal*, Vol. 45 (April, 1956), pp. 208–11
> As an answer to dreaded lists of "book words," this teacher provided a practical incentive for vocabulary building by choosing suitable words from current magazine and newspaper clippings.

TREANOR, JOHN H.: *Treanor's English Series*, Pamphlet Number Two, "Vocabulary Study in the Elementary School," Boston, 1953
> The present author owes much to Mr. Treanor's imaginative and realistic methods. This invaluable pamphlet may be secured directly from Mr. Treanor at 3 Agassiz Park, Boston 30.

Part III

THE TEACHING
OF LITERATURE
AND SEMANTICS

17 Selecting and Teaching a Classic Novel

To SELECT A NOVEL for one's class (let us say, to begin with, an average ninth-grade class) is a privilege more often denied than granted to the high school teacher. If we are faced, then, with the requirement of a course of study, not our own choice, how can we interest an average ninth-grader without any aspirations to college, in a book such as *Ivanhoe*, unrelated to his world of movies, jazz, sports, girls, his world of swagger and uneasiness and violent moods? We cannot disregard the remoteness of the class experience, of the thoughts and feelings of even the brightest students, from the world of Ivanhoe, Cedric the Saxon, and the lovely Rebecca. We must search our students for the clue to our attack. Perhaps they have seen the film of *Ivanhoe;* perhaps, even though some have seen it, the class would be willing to see it again as a class party, at a neighborhood theatre. This failing, perhaps the school can secure the movie for use in its own auditorium. The movie, at any rate, is our strongest ally in the whetting of interest. But let us say that this ally of sound and color and movement and glamor may be found only at a remote unreachable town. We must depend upon our own resources.

Introducing a Classic Novel

To introduce the assignment, we may speak to the class somewhat as follows: "Boys and girls, our next literature reading is the novel *Ivanhoe,* by Sir Walter Scott. I have thirty copies of this book on my desk and shall pass out one to each pupil before the end of this class hour. For some students this novel is not easy reading. But since it is a required book, I shall do my best to make it interesting, and I know you will want to learn why it is an important novel and much worth the time you spend in reading it. I am asking you to finish this story by one month from today. On that day we shall have a test on the book. But while you are reading (and I hope you will begin this week-end), I want to tell you some fascinating things about this masterpiece and its author, Sir Walter Scott. I hope you will read his novel, not only because the test is coming up, but also because you are really excited about the characters.

"Nobody reads every word of *Ivanhoe* or any book. Each of us skips words or paragraphs or pages or chapters, but none of us exactly the same ones. You may skip descriptions. I may skip conversation or even part of a tournament duel, such as the one in *Ivanhoe.* We often skip when our interest lags and read every word when for some reason a passage or a chapter electrifies us and we can't stop.

"This is one of the great books of English literature, but that does not necessarily mean it is a great book for you. If you are a serious reader, however, and love good novels, you will come back to *Ivanhoe.* It is a story of Norman knights whose ancestors, twenty thousand of them, had defeated the Saxons in the battle of Hastings in 1066. The scene of *Ivanhoe* is about a hundred years later. The Saxons are still deeply rebellious and resentful. They have not yet intermarried with the Norman knights. The Normans took possession of their lands and made laws to perpetuate Norman ownership of England. In fact, even now a great deal of the land of England is in the possession of the descendants of the same knights pictured in *Ivanhoe.*

"One of the characters in this novel is Richard the Lion Hearted, who has just returned to England from the Crusades. As you read *Ivanhoe,* you will want to know more about Richard and his great victories in Palestine over the Saracens. He was a great warrior, but he had no love for the arts of peace. The hero Ivanhoe has also just returned from the Crusades. He is a fine warrior, the son of Cedric the Saxon, who hated the Norman oppressors. The Normans regarded the Saxons as barbarous and uncouth. When they visit Cedric's house, they do not dry their hands with a towel, as the Saxons do; they wave them in the air until they are dry. Cedric's house does not have a chimney; the smoke goes out a hole in the roof above the open fire. In France the Normans had been accustomed to fine buildings, lovely music, stately churches. But they find none of these things in Saxon England."

Presenting the Background: Manners and Customs

As background for the study of *Ivanhoe*, we may find it useful to discuss with the class a contrast of the Saxon and Norman civilizations which were forced to mingle in England after the conquest of 1066. This amalgamation of the two cultures, in which the Saxons emerged dominant in national character but deprived of most of their land, required about three centuries. The Normans assigned the land to their followers, wrote the laws in Latin, and set up courts in which the Saxons were always at a disadvantage. The Saxons, however, though forced down into a huge middle class, gradually imposed many of their ancient local democratic customs upon the invaders. By 1400 the conquerors and the conquered were more English than either Norman or Saxon.

The younger our students, the more we are forced to simplify all subjects, but especially history. The contrast below needs hundreds of qualifications for the advanced student of history; but simplified as it is, it can be very helpful to our students of *Ivanhoe* in helping them to visualize the mingling of habits and social backgrounds Scott was so aware of in the telling of his tale. Scott himself is forced to simplify history in order to make Cedric the Saxon a compelling contrast to his Norman guests. The outline as it appears below can hardly fail to interest the student at some point. We find a mingling of such characteristics not only in our own language and literature, but in our lives and culture as well. We find also certain parallels between this contrast and that of the Cavaliers and the Puritans, and of the Southerner and the Yankee, as pictured, for example, in *The Crisis*, by the American novelist Winston Churchill.

A lively discussion of the contrast below may result from such questions as: "Are you more Saxon than Norman in your philosophy? In your religious outlook, do you find more in common with the Normans than with the Saxons? In your choice of words in conversation, are you more inclined to Saxon vocabulary than Norman?"

NORMANS	SAXONS

Appearance and Personality

NORMANS	SAXONS
Mainly tall and slender	Mainly short and stocky
Mainly dark-haired and blue-eyed	Fair-haired and blue-eyed
Quick and lithe of movement	Slow and resolute
Fun-loving and optimistic	Serious and pessimistic
Expressive	Reserved: "unlocked his word hoard"
Adventurous	
Fond of gay music	Adventurous
Fond of joyous moods	Fond of sad music
Refined in manners	Fatalistic
Temperate in drinking habits	Crude in manners
Yeast of the English people	Intemperate in drinking habits
Eagle of the race	Dough of the English people
	Ox of the race

Religion and Church Architecture

NORMANS	SAXONS
Beauty of sound and color	Emphasis on conscience
Love of ritual	Love of moral instruction
Pageantry and ceremony	Sermon and admonition
Stone churches	Wooden churches
Stained glass windows	Ordinary windows

Literature

NORMANS	SAXONS
Musical Verse	Rough language rhythms
Stories of love and chivalry	Stories of war and hardship
French influence in sound and tone	German influence in sound and tone
Chaucer	*Beowulf*
Gawain and the Green Knight	*Battle of Brunanburh*
Strain of gaiety, charm, delight	Strain of seriousness, morality, fatalism, suffering

Government

NORMANS	SAXONS
Inclined to feudal customs	Inclined to local self-government
Obedience to prince or king	Democratic influence of individual soldier and farmer
Inclined to conformity and obedience	Individualistic and rebellious

Language

| Ornamental words: *verdure, beauti-ful* | Everyday words: *the, work, you, find, find, apple* |
| 75 per cent of English vocabulary | 25 per cent of English vocabulary |

NOTE: On any page of fiction, we are likely to find more Saxon-derived words than words derived from Latin, French, and Norman French. This is because Saxon-derived words are the ones more often used, even though they are much less numerous in the total vocabulary.

During the month's time we have allotted for an extensive reading we are sketching in the historical background of the book; we are also pointing out from week to week certain exciting passages in *Ivanhoe* in the hope of arousing more curiosity and concentration of effort. The approaching test ideally should impose no fear or dislike of the book; it is only for the laggards that we would set a deadline at all, though we realize of course that an assigned test is often a necessity in competing with other courses for the student's time. My own view is that *Ivanhoe* is one of the most difficult of all books for average ninth-graders. Hence we must work particularly hard to build up an interest. In this task no other motivation would be quite so strong as seeing *Ivanhoe* in a color film. The ingenious boys of the class may like to construct a Norman castle or a replica of the tournament court. Others may like to paint pictures of Rebecca or Brian or Rowena. Still others may make reports on historical background or on particularly vivid moments they have found in the novel.

An Intensive Reading for Analysis

After the test on the extensive reading of the novel, we may give to the class an outline of study questions for the intensive rereading to come. Each pupil should review several chapters of the book for each date the assignment is due, and set up goals, by the questions we ask, for his analysis of the story. We may choose to give a few brief tests on the daily assignments, or ask for summaries in which each student quotes several passages to show his particular interest in the action, description, characterization, or dialogue of the chapters he has reread. Such summaries could not be copied, since no two students would want to hand in the same quotations. In this kind of more intensive reading we may wish to spend from one to three weeks, depending on the requirements of the course of study and perhaps also on the intensity of class interest in the novel. For us the extensive reading is the heart of the achievement; but now we have a chance to discuss narrower points of style, characterization, and details of Scott's historical treatment. In these daily discussions we may call first on a group of three or four pupils for two-minute talks on the chapters assigned. These pupils may plan the discussion as a panel, if they wish, drawing the class into the conversation after they have spoken and exchanged views. By asking for two-minute talks from three or four pupils each day, we assure a freshness of impression and call forth from the class many ideas and shades of judgment, especially when the speakers differ among themselves. We may ask one panel to begin each talk with a quotation and to say why it is arresting; we may ask another to begin each talk with an interesting sidelight on one of the characters. Still another group may wish to act out an exciting scene, adapting their own script from the novel, changing it to suit their interpretation. Often the group may be named well in advance and thus have an opportunity to plan an exciting approach of their own.

This, then, is a recommended program for teaching a novel required of all students of our class by the course of study. First, we distribute the books and allow about one month for an extensive reading of the novel, during which time we endeavor, (in perhaps a half hour's time each week), while proceeding with other units of writing, poetry reading, or usage, to build up an interest in the novel. In this our aim is to dissolve the resistance to required reading and substitute the student's curiosity as a motive for returning to the book until it is finished. Second, we outline for the class study questions for five to fifteen assigned dates for intensive reading of specified chapters. Third, for recitations on these dates we plan varied programs, with our key resource the panel of three or four students who will lead the discussion each day. To make certain that the class as a whole is following along with the intensive reading, we may give a few tests or require answers to a number of key questions to be written in theme form. Nothing is more unsettling to a speaker or a panel than to discuss episodes and characters forgotten or hazily remembered by many members of the class.

Selection by Grade Level

I do not minimize the difficulties confronting a teacher required to teach *Ivanhoe* or *Silas Marner* or *David Copperfield* or *Pride and Prejudice*. In no one of these novels, but particularly in *Ivanhoe*, can the American student today identify himself with the hero or heroine. A boy's most desperate need in reading is to feel that he is sharing the hero's dilemmas and that the book is therefore helping the reader with his own. When the interest in a novel is mainly historical and intellectual, and when literary appreciation *per se*, however vital to us as specialists in English, receives great emphasis in the classroom, the deepest meaning of reading a novel is lost upon the class. For the deepest meaning is that electric identification that makes the reader live and weep and laugh and suffer with his hero or heroine and emerge from the reading experience with a sense of profound emotional expansion. This kind of experience, however, is one that most teachers and students do not expect from the classic novels of Austen, Scott, Eliot, or Dickens. Memorable works though they are, we cannot expect our students in high school to feel the intellectual fascination we experienced with these novels in college and graduate courses. Fortunately, we no longer ask our students to scale such bleak and inaccessible peaks as *The Last of the Mohicans*. Fond as I am of Eliot and Dickens, I doubt that we are justified in requiring them for any but college-preparatory students. When we are required to assign novels remote from our students' thoughts and feelings and dilemmas, we shall, of course, communicate our own enthusiasm as fully as possible, even as we do in teaching a Shakespearian play.

When we have the opportunity to help select novels for a course of study, our aim should be to find works of undoubted literary merit with a high degree of readability and interest for the class. On the ninth-grade level, such books as *My Antonia*, *A Lantern in Her Hand*, *Martin Eden*, or *The Prince and the Pauper* are possibilities; on the tenth-grade level, *Arrowsmith*, *The Red Badge of Courage*, *O Pioneers!*, *Giants in the Earth*. Perhaps none of these can equal the literary merit of *Silas Marner;* but for the average class, even of college-preparatory sophomores, they possess more intense and permanent reading excitement. By the eleventh year we have a wider choice of master novels our students will like. In American literature we may confidently choose *Huckleberry Finn* and *The Scarlet Letter,* both of which present burning problems still unsolved. Of all of Dickens, *Great Expectations* is the easiest for the average reader, and opens with scenes of remarkable contrast and intensity. I should prefer it for these reasons to *A Tale of Two Cities,* which has the advantage intellectually of vivid historical interest. It is much easier for the average American youth to identify himself with Pip's childhood than with Sidney Carton's sacrifice. Yet Dickens' pictures of the Revolution are of immense value from the point of view of general education. For easier reading, a book such as *The Crisis* may be used profitably in the tenth or eleventh year, though not literature at all on the same plane with Hawthorne, Hardy, or Meredith. Many high schools are using *The Return of the Native* in the eleventh year, a book appallingly inferior to and harder to read than either *Tess of the D'Urbervilles* or *The Mayor of Casterbridge.* In all of Hardy, *Tess* is the most moving and powerful novel to high school juniors and seniors, and closest to their feelings and problems. For teaching the structure and essence of classic tragedy, *The Mayor* is much easier for students to absorb than *Oedipus the King* or *Othello.* Moreover, the tragedy of Michael Henchard, concurrent with his immense spiritual growth toward the end of the story, when his fortunes are lowest, deepens the student's insight into those pitless impersonal forces that sometimes warp and betray us to catastrophe from birth onward. But these same forces also gave Henchard a spirit large enough to sustain his devotion "to the edge of doom," and this is his greatness in the midst of his descent.

*   *   *

Ideally, we select a required novel to meet our definition of the word *literature* and at the same time meet the need of the student to read a book of intense and permanent meaning in his life. If the book does not illumine a dark part of himself, if it does not carry him into the story and make him feel the hero's problem as his own, it is not meeting his need. This need is more imperative than our own desire to introduce to the class a great book of English or American literature. If some selections lean to our need for high literary standards in the course of study, others may perhaps meet the needs of the students without possessing the standard of literary merit we should like to maintain.

Once the novel is selected, we allow the students a month to read it in their own various ways, meanwhile arousing their curiosity anew from week to week, while proceeding with other units of the course of study. Following a test on the extensive reading, we distribute mimeographed outlines for the intensive reading, and proceed with discussions of particular chapters from day to day, shortening or prolonging the intensive reading according to the response of our class to the novel at hand. To many students nothing is so disagreeable as a *required* novel; one of our aims must be, therefore, to create enthusiasm for and curiosity about the master work we have selected.

To the Student Teacher: Suggested Activities

1. Examine five courses of study for the ninth grade in your library. What novels are taught in the ninth year? Examine these novels and then show in a brief essay which one you would prefer to teach.
2. Compare the first chapters of *Ivanhoe* with the first chapters of *Giants in the Earth* or *The Prince and the Pauper*. Which of the three novels is easiest to read? Which of the three novels would you recommend for your course of study? Give reasons for your selection.
3. For the tenth year compare *Silas Marner* with *Arrowsmith*, *The Red Badge of Courage*, and *The Crisis*. Which of these novels has the greatest literary value? Show which one you would choose as a requirement in the tenth grade and give reasons for your answer.
4. For the junior level compare *A Tale of Two Cities* with *Great Expectations* and *Huckleberry Finn*. Of these three novels, which would be of greatest interest to juniors? Which to you is of greatest literary value? Give reasons for your answers.
5. For the senior level compare *The Scarlet Letter* with *Tess of the D'Urbervilles* and *The Mayor of Casterbridge*. Granting the high literary quality of all three novels, which would be the most absorbing to high school seniors?
6. Compare *The Return of the Native*, a novel which appears often in courses of study, with *Tess of the D'Urbervilles* and *The Mayor of Casterbridge*. Show which one of the three novels you would choose for a senior class and show why your choice would benefit your students.

Suggested Readings

BURTON, DWIGHT L.: *Literature Study in the High Schools*, Holt, Rinehart and Winston, 1963
    Lively and perceptive essays on the teaching of literature. Helpful for practical hints for the classroom teacher, especially in assignments for home reading. An invaluable book.

COTTER, JANET M.: "*The Old Man and the Sea:* An 'Open' Literary Experience," *English Journal*, Vol. 51 (October, 1963), pp. 459–63

> Miss Cotter describes *The Old Man* as a "natural for the high school," as I am sure it is. But would it fall into better perspective if it were combined with *Billy Budd* or *Lord Jim* or *The Mayor of Casterbridge?*

EDWARDS, ANNE: "Teen-Age Career Girls," *English Journal*, Vol. 42 (November, 1953), pp. 437–42

> Arresting plan for an English course given to ninth-grade commercial students, with a suggestive list of novels and non-fiction reading.

English Evidence, ed. C. H. Ward, Scott, Foresman, 1925

> See "Ways of Approaching Certain Classics," pp. 29–53.

Essays on the Teaching of English, ed. Robert M. Gay, Harvard University Press, 1940

> In this rich collection two novelists and teachers, Mary Ellen Chase and John Erskine, write with much insight about the teaching of literature. Do not miss another essay in this collection, "Yesterday," by Alfred M. Hitchcock.

FELICE, SISTER MARY, F.S.P.A.: "An Approach to Teaching *A Tale of Two Cities*," *English Journal*, Vol. 48 (January, 1959), pp. 31–33

> Concrete and illuminating suggestions for assignments suited to pupils' interests. Rich in classroom wisdom.

Good Reading, Mentor Book, New American Library, New York, 1964

> Lists of memorable novels selected and annotated by specialists, pp. 75–114.

LITTLE, GAIL B.: "Three Novels for Comparative Study in the Twelfth Grade," *English Journal*, Vol. 52 (October, 1963), pp. 501–05

> Comparison of the characters of Huckleberry Finn, Holden Caulfield, and Chick Mallison: "Huck Finn is an escapist; Holden Caulfield, a near casualty; Chick Mallison absorbs his problem and grows."

MARCUS, FRED H.: "*Cry, the Beloved Country* and *Strange Fruit:* Exploring Man's Inhumanity to Man," *English Journal*, Vol. 51 (December, 1962), pp. 609–16

> A perceptive and illuminating contrast.

MARCUS, FRED H.: "*A Farewell to Arms:* The Impact of Irony and the Irrational," *English Journal*, Vol. 51 (November, 1962), pp. 527–35

> A perceptive analysis of Hemingway's best novel. I see its values more clearly than ever before. But I miss a comparison in terms of the highest reach of the artist. Is it a greater novel than *War and Peace* or *Lord Jim?*

MEISEL, PEGGY R.: "An English Curriculum for the Eleventh Grade," *English Journal*, Vol. 52 (March, 1963), pp. 186–95

> Useful outline of eleventh-grade readings with the theme "We end by asking ourselves 'Who am I?'" The course concludes then with an analysis of self in terms of literature analysis.

MORRIS, HARRY: "*The Pearl:* Realism and Allegory," *English Journal*, Vol. 52 (October, 1963), pp. 487–95

   Illuminating analysis: highly useful to teachers of *The Pearl*.

Reading Ladders for Human Relations, American Council on Education, Washington, D.C., 1964

   Arresting essay, "Ways of Using Books," pp 1–14..

SCHUSTER, EDGAR H.: "Discovering Theme and Structure in the Novel," *English Journal*, Vol. 52 (October, 1963), pp. 506–11

   Analysis of an experiment with *To Kill a Mockingbird*.

STEARNS, GERTRUDE B.: *English in the Small High School*, Lincoln: University of Nebraska Press, 1950

   Chapter 16, "The Reading Program," is rich and informative, with dozens of specific helps and titles.

THOMAS, CHARLES S.: *Teaching of English in the Secondary School*, Houghton, Mifflin, 1927

   "The Teaching of Prose Fiction," pp. 249–81, contains many specific helps and insights for the teaching of the classic novels.

18 The Teaching
of Poetry

WHAT POEMS SHALL I CHOOSE?

WE COME to the classroom with a body of poems that have set us singing in golden moments of other years. Perhaps we have had in high school or college a single inspiring teacher who made *Paradise Lost* breathe and sing for us, even though we were prepared to resent and resist the Miltonic idiom. Perhaps we were fortunate enough to have a remarkable teacher of Shakespeare's sonnets, or Shelley's "Indian Serenade," Tennyson's "Rizpah," or the lines of Rossetti:

> Your hands lie open in the long fresh grass,
> The finger points look through like rosy blooms . . .

We come with hundreds of moments we should like to recapture for our students, to distill for them the precious insight and the echoing magic of Donne, Keats, Browning, Whitman, Housman, Millay: of such lines as

> Remember me when I have gone away,
> Gone far away into the silent land;
> When you can no more hold me by the hand
> Nor I half turn to go, yet turning stay.

To the classroom each of us brings a love of poetry unique in its passion because it represents a unique youth harried and borne aloft by dreams and visions no one else could believe in, all in all. If this passion does not exist, we can neither read poetry with a voice of magic nor bring to the class the insight only the poet can make unforgettable.

Nothing, then, is more important for teaching poetry than the long emotional preparation infused with a passion for song and image, color and idea; infused also with a memory of sudden revelations which Edmund Wilson has called "the shock of recognition." Yet before we read and discuss a poem with the class, we must make a new emotional preparation. Usually a rereading of the poem, parts of it aloud, will sustain and refresh our passion, calling up the impressions and ideas of other years. Without this refreshening we cannot capture for the class the enthusiasm that we felt the first time an inspired teacher read the poem aloud to us.

Meanwhile, however, we have made a decision; we have chosen poems to read first to our class. Let us say it is a ninth-grade class, and we are free to choose from a number of short poems the one poem that will give the class confidence in our choice and in our capacity to make them see and hear and touch. What will our students like? What first poems will inspire, fascinate, or delight them? To make such a choice, we need to understand some of the capricious feelings that wash over them daily like waves over a beach of sand. To make the poem real, we must know whether or not our students can identify themselves with the feelings of the poem. Only if it passes this test will it be real enough to take root in the deeper levels of personality.

Poems for the Ninth-Grade Level

In considering poems that we might introduce in the ninth grade, we are less likely to err with a poem of humor and delight than with one of high seriousness. Perhaps the boys will not hear or read Nathalia Crane's "The Flathouse Roof" so eagerly as the girls, but in a later moment, with another poem, we shall hope to capture fixed attention from our boys of thirteen and fourteen. Many of them will like "The Flathouse Roof," too. Even if the poem is not in our book, we may read it aloud with assurance that they can follow the story. Perhaps we say to the class, "Boys and girls, for our first poem I have chosen one written by a girl in her early teens.

Almost all of us remember some experience like that described in this poem. Here it is." Then we may read the opening lines:

THE FLATHOUSE ROOF

I linger on the flathouse roof, the moonlight is divine.
But my heart is all a-flutter like the washing on the line.

I long to be a heroine, I long to be serene,
But my feet, they dance in answer to a distant tambourine.

And, oh! the dreams of ecstasy. Oh! Babylon and Troy.
I've a hero in the basement, he's the janitor's red-haired boy.

There's the music of his mallet and the jigging of his saw;
I wonder what he's making on that lovely cellar floor?

He loves me, for he said it when we met upon the stair,
And that is why I'm on the roof to get a breath of air.

He said it! Oh! He said it! And the only thing I said
Was, "Roger Jones, I like you, for your hair is very red."

The class may be a little self-conscious in discussing this poem, but we may begin with a few easy questions like the following: "How old do you think the heroine is?" "How old is the hero of this poem?" "What line or phrase I have read seems most original to you?" From a critical point of view the best line in the poem is, of course, "But my heart is all a-flutter like the washing on the line." Usually even a ninth-year student will pick out the best line among a dozen and the most striking phrase within the most poetic line. But we should be careful not to make our discussion too intellectual. If they enjoy the poem and wish to discuss it, well and good. If not, we go on to another. We read this poem to capture their interest more than to show the essence of poetic skill. Particularly we are mindful of Milton's dictum that "rhyme is no necessary Adjunct or true Ornament of Poem." Unfortunately most of our students come to us with a notion fixed by many years that rhyme is indispensable to poetry. Hence in discussing "The Flathouse Roof" we avoid the subject if possible, not being ready yet to break down the idea that lines must rhyme in order to achieve poetic intensity.

Another first poem appealing to the ninth grade is "The Sleeper," by Walter de la Mare. Every child has felt a momentary dread of a mother's death or the death of a little brother or sister.

Like the young mother who looks at a sleeping child and then listens for his breathing, each of us at some time identifies death with sleep. "The Sleeper" tells a story that can be read aloud to the class even though the poem may not be represented in the class anthology. We deliberately choose a poem such as "The Sleeper" that tells the story of a moment. Here are the first lines of the poem:

THE SLEEPER

As Ann came in one summer's day,
   She felt that she must creep,
So silent was the clear cool house,
   It seemed a house of sleep.
And sure, when she pushed open the door,
   Rapt in the stillness there,
Her mother sat, with stooping head,
   Asleep upon a chair;
Fast — fast asleep; her two hands laid
   Loose-folded on her knee,
So that her small unconscious face
   Looked half unreal to be:
So calmly lit with sleep's pale light
   Each feature was; so fair
Her forehead — every trouble was
   Smoothed out beneath her hair.

So far among our first poems we have had nothing especially for the boys of the class, many of whom think poetry is a peculiarly feminine obsession. Let us hope that Vachel Lindsay's beautiful poem, "The Broncho That Would Not Be Broken," is in their anthology. We may say to the class, "Here is a story of a broncho that has so much liveliness and spirit that he is always dancing in the sheer joy of being alive. Then one day he is lent to a farmer who wants to break his spirit and change him into a meek horse who will pull a wagon or a plow. Finally, when the broncho keeps on dancing, the farmer and his men bring whips to break his spirit. Even when they harness him to three mules pulling a big red reaper, he still keeps dancing. Then, on a day of very hot winds, the broncho dies suddenly of a broken heart." As we read the poem to the class, we try to make them hear the broncho dance in the very cadence of the poem. To the very end he dances, until the moment he is released from the three mules in front of the red reaper. Of this poem we may ask questions like the following: "What line makes the spirit of the broncho most real to you? Why does Vachel Lindsay have the grasshoppers cheer the broncho? Why do the crows say, 'Nobody cares for you'? In what lines does Vachel Lindsay tell us the physical cause of the broncho's death? What line suggests most vividly the actual movement of the broncho's legs and feet?"

In choosing our first poems, we must be careful, then, to mingle those moods and topics that appeal to boys as well as to girls. For boys we must have poems of action like "The Broncho That Would Not Be Broken" or Alfred Noyes' "The Highwayman," which is liked by almost all seventh, eighth, ninth, and tenth graders, not only for its intense action but also for its memorable images of color and sound.

In the realm of family relationship, a poem instantaneously appealing from the seventh grade onward is Langston Hughes' "Mother to Son." It is easy for the class to put itself in the place of a humble mother of indomitable will, her speech, like that of many working people, full of striking metaphor. The poem reads as follows:

MOTHER TO SON

Well, son, I'll tell you:
Life for me ain't been no crystal stair.
It's had tacks in it,
And splinters,
And boards torn up,
And places with no carpet on the floor —
Bare.
But all the time
I'se been a-climbin'·on,
And reachin' landin's,
And turnin' corners,
And sometimes goin' in the dark
Where there ain't been no light.
So, boy, don't you turn back.
Don't you set down on the steps
'Cause you finds it kinder hard.
Don't you fall now —
For I'se still goin', honey,
I'se still climbin',
And life for me ain't been no crystal stair.

There are few adolescent boys and girls who cannot respond from their own experience to the admonitions of the mother in this poem. If the mother is pictured as a Negro, she must communicate to her son an even greater fortitude to overcome obstacles than a white mother in the same dilemma.

A valuable teaching asset of this poem is that it contains no rhyme. What is it, then, that makes it poetry? Poetry, we may say, is the electrification of language. In what lines of this poem does language become electric and incandescent? Why are *tacks* and *splinters* more electric than *floor?* Hughes made language more electric when he put words in the mouth of a mother in this dramatic situation. A dramatic monologue, concentrating on a moment of crisis, by its very form and selection intensifies language. "Mother to Son" has the added advantage of being completely comprehensible to the average student except, perhaps, for the symbol of luxury and magnificence, the "crystal stair."

Another poem well liked by ninth- and tenth-grade youngsters is "Songs for My Mother," by Anna Hempstead Branch:

> My mother's hands are cool and fair,
>   They can do anything.
> Delicate mercies hide them there
>   Like flowers in the spring.
>
> When I was small and could not sleep,
>   She used to come to me,
> And with my cheek upon her hand
>   How sure my rest would be. . . .
>
> My mother has the prettiest tricks
>   Of words and words and words.
> Her talk comes out as smooth and sleek
>   As breasts of singing birds. . . .

Still another appealing poem among those first read aloud may well be "The Old Woman," by Joseph Campbell:

> As a white candle
> In a holy place,
> So is the beauty
> Of an aged face.
>
> As the spent radiance
> Of the winter sun,
> So is a woman
> With her travail done.

The significance of the poem and the most intense image appear in the last stanza:

> Her brood gone from her
> And her thoughts as still
> As the waters
> Under a ruined mill.

Such poems as "Songs for My Mother" and "The Old Woman" need little explanation. It is easy for us to discuss the significance of the last stanza of "The Old Woman." Many boys and girls of fourteen will have a strong sympathy with elderly people and are eager to understand their problems. In such a poem as "The Old Woman" we draw away, it is true, from the thoughts and feelings of the class to a comprehension of the thoughts and feelings of an older generation. The poem presents an opportunity to teach the need for imaginative insight into the problems of elderly people and suggestions of how we may make their lot easier and happier. At fourteen, moreover, though often sympathetic with grandparents, many boys and girls are beginning to believe that their mothers and fathers are difficult, dull, or obtuse. Such a poem as "Songs for My Mother" gives us an opportunity to discuss attitude toward parents as one of the most important signs of growing up. "How can I be more mature in my attitude toward my mother and father?" "How can I be mature in my attitude toward my grandmother?" "What is maturity in these relationships?" These are questions that may well form a part of the discussion, whether on a personal or an impersonal basis. The discussion of the problem, if it turns out well, is pretty certain to evoke personal illustrations more vital to the class than the poem itself.

FIRST ASSIGNMENTS:
HOW TO USE MEMORY READINGS

In introducing poetry for the first time, our primary aim, then, must be to prove to our class that we can bring to them poems that have lucid and profound meaning in terms of their own experience. If the poems we choose cannot electrify their senses and feelings, we cannot expect them to be interested in the technicalities of form, stanza, or verse. But in order to intensify the delight and expectancy our choices have inspired in the class, we must be ready with practical assignments. I am aware that many experts advise against the memorizing of poems as militating against true enjoyment. If the pupil hates an assigned poem, he is certain to hate it more if he is required to memorize it. But if he loves a poem, and the lines keep ringing in his ears, then to memorize it may be a delight. In assigning memory work in an eighth- or ninth-grade class, we may say, "Boys and girls, for the past week we have been reading aloud a number of poems about people and problems and humorous situations that we are all familiar with. Now I ask that for tomorrow you memorize a few lines of your favorite poem among those we have studied and speak the lines to the class. In this first assignment I would advise you to select no more than ten lines. If you have had trouble in memorizing poetry, take only three or four lines. The number of lines is not important. What is important is the expressiveness with which you speak them to the class. When you are troubled about remembering words, you cannot speak expressively. Therefore the first task is to memorize the lines so well that in speaking them to the class you can give your fullest attention to expression, not to memory. If some of you take the same lines from the same poem, so much the better. We shall have a chance to compare various interpretations of the same line. We have found in class, as you know, that three of us may emphasize a different word in the same line of poetry and each thereby produces a slightly different meaning."

This kind of preliminary assignment may be given after the first two or three days of class discussion. From this time on our memory work assignments may take many forms. We may ask each pupil to join with another pupil or even with several friends to arrange a poem for choral speaking. It is surprising how ingenious and observant boys and girls can be in this kind of work. They soon learn to recognize what quality of voice best fits a particular line. For choral speaking, it is true, we need some preparation in class. We may select several boys and girls to read a poem before the class, arbitrarily assigning to each student the line he is to speak, experimenting until we are satisfied that the best choral arrangement possible has been selected for the voices at hand. A team working on a poem together may choose, however, to assign its members to various stanzas without regard to voice quality. Any kind of cooperation in memorizing and reciting a poem is to be preferred to none at all.

A sound general principle in the memorizing of poetry is to keep the recitations very brief until after the class has recited several times and each of the reluctant or embarrassed members has had a chance to prove to himself that he can speak a few lines with ease. Half a dozen recitations of four or five or ten lines each are often worth many times more than one recitation of a longer poem. When we come to longer poems, however, we may offer special credit to those who wish to recite a complete poem such as "The Harpweaver" or "Elegy Written in a Country Churchyard" or "Maud Muller"; or, in the junior and senior years, "Ben Jonson Meets a Man from Stratford" or "Michael" or "The Death of the Hired Man."

Many teachers disapprove of reciting memorized verse in the junior and senior years of high school. The advice of other experienced teachers, however, is quite the contrary. It is a very valuable experience for juniors and seniors to speak selected lines of poetry before the class. To do this well, each speaker must make an emotional preparation. He must be in love with the lines he speaks. Then he must give dedicated energy to the memorizing of the poem. Finally he must work at it with his voice until he has exactly the emphasis and intonation he wishes to achieve. This mastery of a few lines is one of the richest experiences a teacher of English can initiate for his students regardless of the grade level. An important advantage to this kind of assignment that has not been sufficiently recognized is this: the true music inherent in everyone's voice is not apparent except in the reading of poetry. Unconsciously a student will very often select those lines to which the music of his voice is best suited. Very often lines that he had not expected to produce music will show to himself and to the class a radically different side of his personality.

One great hazard, however, in the memorizing of poetry is the tendency to select too many lines. Most students become ambitious to encompass more lines than they can both memorize and read aloud with superb expression. We must therefore caution our classes, especially in the upper years of high school and in the first years of college, to select a few lines for perfect recitations rather than many lines for halting ones. The moment a student forgets his lines in reciting poetry to the class, his listeners become distracted from the striking ideas, phrases, images, or sounds of the poem to an embarrassment for the speaker's forgetfulness.

THE ESSENCE OF POETRY UNDER GLASS

After the first poems and the first assignments, we are ready for a more systematic analysis of the essence of poetry. We must remember, too, that as teachers of broad background we must reveal to our students something of the range of great poets and incandescent moments within their work. Many English teachers of today, unfortunately, know a great deal about T. S. Eliot but have never discovered the magic of Longfellow's "Evangeline" or Tennyson's "Rizpah." The more concerned we are with this perspective of historical greatness in poetry, the more we shall require ourselves to make a list of the great poets in both English and American literature, seeking some one masterpiece from each poet that we can present to our classes. If by some chance we are assigned ninth and tenth grades one year, eleventh and twelfth the next, we need two or three masterpieces from each poet to fit the range of interests of our various groups. It is true that in introducing poetry on any level we must often choose the poems of our own time and idiom. Nevertheless each poet of the past has a great poem timeless and dramatic in its significance. To a junior or senior a poem such as Byron's "Prisoner of Chillon" or Gray's "Elegy Written in a Country Churchyard" will have a significance much more pertinent to today's problems than Eliot's "The Wasteland" or "The Love Song of J. Alfred Prufrock." To select from each great poet a masterpiece permanent in its theme but appealing and timely in its idiom: this is our goal. For such selection every teacher needs in his background full, rich survey courses in English and American literature.

The essence of poetry is the intensification of language, ideas, or experience. By this I mean the acceleration of thought transference: the more quickly a few lines of poetry can take hold of the reader's senses or focus his emotional energy into one overwhelming surge of feeling, the more concentrated its essence. The essence of poetry derives from many kinds of language magic. It also derives from the magic of plot or situation, which Aristotle called "the soul of tragedy." In some dramatic monologues, such as Browning's "The Laboratory" or Sandburg's "Mag," we have poetic intensification with little electrification of phrase. On the other hand, in the sonnets of Shakespeare and the lyrics of Wordsworth, we have the magic of language without the magic of story or dramatic scene. A poet may electrify the word music of his language as well as its images. In the first stanzas of Gray's "Elegy" or Lowell's "The First Snowfall" we see the magic of word music combined superbly with the magic of image. When I use the word *image* in this discussion, I refer to exactness and completeness of visualization, as in Hughes' use of the words *splinters* and *tacks* in his poem, "Mother to Son." *Floor* is a general image and hard to visualize because there are many kinds of floors; but *tacks* and *splinters* are easily visualized, hence more forceful in their impact. To some lovers of poetry, its word music has a much more profound impact than its imagery. But it should be noted that even in Shakespeare, who wrote poetry to be spoken in plays, the image is more important than the music of meter or mingling of syllables. When I speak of word music, I do not include, of course, the suggestion of actual sounds, as in "surly sullen bell" or "wheels his droning flight." Alliteration in "surly sullen bell" is a means to word music; the sound of the word *bell* is a part of word music, but the actual sound of the bell ringing is to me a sense image like "yellow leaf" or "tarnished with rust" or Whitman's "I press with slow rude muscle." Imagery that appeals instantaneously to the senses is the primary means of intensifying language; word music, achieved by the use of rhyme, meter, rhythm, alliteration, assonance, is to me a secondary means. However, the more varied the means used of electrifying language, word music, and dramatic scene, the more intense becomes the poetry. This is why Shakespeare, who combines these elements of poetic essence more consistently than any other poet, reaches over the centuries and brightens life's page with irresistible incandescence.

The Means of Intensification

Two main resources by which the poet intensifies language may be summarized in two categories, imagery and word music. Within each category are a number of technical devices:

Imagery	*Word Music*
1. Images of color	8. Rhythm
2. Images of sound	9. Rhyme
3. Images of touch	10. Meter
4. Images of smell	11. Alliteration
5. Images of action	12. Assonance
6. Similes	13. Mingling of vowels
7. Metaphors	

The poet accelerates communication in still other ways: by defining a word dramatically, as Masters defines *silence* in the poem, "Silence"; by having a character speak in a crisis, as in "Ulysses"; by having a man speak from the dead, as in *Spoon River Anthology;* by personifying inanimate things, as in "Blow, blow, thou winter wind," or "far-swooping elbow'd earth," or "Sweet sounds, O beautiful music, do not cease"; by concentrating on one moment of time, as in T. S. Eliot's "Six O'clock"; by the use of repetitive phrase, as in the sonnet, "Tired of all these, for restful death I cry."

Prose and Poetry: What Then Is the Difference?

Often the student will ask, "Doesn't the prose writer do all of these things, too?" The answer is, "Yes." The novelist and short-story writer electrify language, but not so consistently or so fully as the poet. In every good novel we find many nuggets of poetry. Many of the most intense passages from Thomas Wolfe's books have been arranged in verse form in *A Stone, a Leaf, a Door.* On the other hand, most poems contain lines or phrases or passages of prose, that is, language that does not awaken the senses. *Paradise Lost* itself contains hundreds of lines of prose. Not even the finest poem can strike lightning in every word, if only because it must use articles, prepositions, and conjunctions, which fall flatly and dully on the mind. It is true that an idea can be intellectually electrifying, and many poets today blithely by-pass sensory phrasing for the sting and sway of ideas. The logic of this approach would be irresistible if all readers were philosophers or mathematicians. The intellectual in man is only a small segment of his personality. The poet needs to involve the whole man. Hence one of his main aims is to reduce ideas to the language of the senses, "to give to airy nothings a local habitation and a name." The poet knows he must take hold of man's emotions before he can reach his mind; and there is no sure way to seize the reader's emotions except through the language of the senses.

Finding the Electric Images

The most effective way of showing the class the essence of poetry is to say: "What words in this poem make you see something instantly? What words make you hear a sound with electric force? What words make you feel you are touching or tasting or smelling something?" Let us consider for such an analysis this passage from Whitman's "Song of Myself":

I AM HE THAT WALKS

I am he that walks with the tender and growing night,
I call to the earth and sea half-held by the night.

Press close, bare-bosom'd night! Press close, magnetic, nourishing night!
Night of south winds! night of the large few stars!
Still, nodding night! mad, naked, summer night.

Smile, O voluptuous, cool-breath'd earth!
Earth of the slumbering and liquid trees;
Earth of departed sunset! earth of the mountains, misty-topt!
Earth of the vitreous pour of the full moon, just tinged with blue!
Earth of shine and dark, mottling the tide of the river!
Earth of the limpid gray of clouds, brighter and clearer for my sake!
Far-swooping elbow'd earth! rich, apple-blossom'd earth!
Smile, for your lover comes!

Some students may say that they can see most clearly the "full moon, just tinged with blue," others "far-swooping elbow'd earth," or "limpid gray of clouds." Our aim is to help them see that they can choose the most intense phrases, whether or not we can agree on *the* most intense one. For images of touch they may point to "Press close, bare-bosom'd night." For an image of smell, "apple-blossom'd earth" is easy to identify. The only colors are *gray* and *blue;* we have often explained that colors always intensify language. But what of sounds? Whitman has no sounds in this passage. "What sound might he have used?" we may ask.

How Figures of Speech Electrify Language

In the Whitman passage, when Whitman writes, "far-swoop elbow'd earth," he compares the hills to elbows. This kind of comparison, we explain, is called a metaphor; it does not use the word *like* or *as* to complete the comparison. Does the metaphor of the elbow make us see the contours of the earth more vividly? Does it make the language more electric? Whitman speaks to the night as if it were a woman. He continues this idea in "bare-bosom'd night." This gives us an opportunity to explain the apostrophe, which is a special kind of metaphor, in this phrase likening the night to a woman. "When the poet addresses the night as a person," we may ask, "does this make the language of the poem or the situation more intense and dramatic?"

For reinforcing the concept of sensory language and the use of metaphor, we may refer to poems we have already studied, such as "Mother to Son," in which the poet compares the stairs to the life struggle upward and the tacks and splinters to the obstacles. We may point out the beautiful similes in "Songs for My Mother" and "The Old Woman." We may read to the class Harriet Monroe's beautiful lines from "Love Song," beginning, "I love my life, but not too well."

Still another kind of figure is personification of an inanimate object, as used in Sandburg's "I am a copper wire slung in the air" and his lines about steel, "Beat me and hammer me into a crowbar." All figures of speech intensify language partly because they make us see and hear and touch the objects that convey the ideas.

Suggested Assignment: Write a Short Poem about One Moment

Nothing teaches appreciation of poetry more concretely than the writing of a few lines of verse derived from standards agreed upon by the class. Let us say we ask the class to write a poem of five to ten lines about a moment in a particular place. In each line we ask for an image appealing instantaneously to the senses. We may summarize on the board the requirements of this assignment as follows:

What to Try For

1. Time of day
2. Season of the year
3. Particular place
4. Color words, sound words, action words

5. An image in each line
6. No use of rhyme
7. A simile if possible
8. A metaphor if possible

We prefer that our students avoid rhyme because we want to concentrate on the image of sensory intensity in each line. We explain that the season of the year and the time of day can be communicated only indirectly. To dramatize the assignment, we may read a poem like the following:

SNOW TOWARD EVENING

Suddenly the sky turned gray,
The day,
Which had been bitter and chill,
Grew soft and still.
Quietly
From some invisible blossoming tree
Millions of petals cool and white
Drifted and blew,
Lifted and flew,
Fell with the falling night.

Melville Cane

We may analyze "Snow Toward Evening" to show how Mr. Cane has achieved a concentration on one moment, using an image in almost every line, and weaving into his poem the incidental information we need about time and place. Was this poem experienced or imagined? Does a poet have to see what he describes? We may stress the need for observing realistic moments and places like the following:

A Moment in Church   In a Hospital Room
A Moment on Our Street   At Our Dinner Table
When the Rain Began   When the Band Marched
When the Light Turned Red   At Our Library Table
The Ambulance Came Along   In the Cafeteria Line

When we have read the papers in response to this assignment, it is an arresting and informative experience to go through each poem in class, reading aloud the word, the phrase, or the line that comes nearest to poetry. The class can help decide. Perhaps only a few in the class will achieve an image in each line, but achievement in making their own images will go further to explain this poetic requirement than the discussion of many poems not their own. We must emphasize in this assignment the importance of writing, as Wordsworth did, with eyes on the object. Observation is the only path to originality for most amateur poets, and our students are not attempting a professional achievement. Even so, the young poets who do develop in our classes must root their best first achievements in close, exact observations such as students required of themselves in these poems:

ESCAPE

In the long sweaty afternoon
   the city sprawls on the
   grass in its shirtsleeves.
Little dancing heat waves sizzle
   along the street-car line.
   Kids play in the streets,
Wishing for ice cream, sit on the curbs,
   Silent and
   hot.

Ruth Bachman,
West Seattle High School,
Seattle, Washington

CHILDREN

Beside a gutter frothing in the sun
Sit little savages with icy hands.
They laugh because the waters bravely run
Their splinter sail-boats off to distant lands.
They laugh with laughter crisp with curses, for
The wind is tearing splinter sail-boats down
Before they reach the corner grate; before
They find the river underneath the town.
The river's treachery they do not know,
They only see the sun-touched gutters foam.
They only watch the gray, soot-coated snow
Ebb from the narrow street that is their home.

In winter they will borrow courage from
Remembered gutters frothing in the sun.

Donna Bowen,
Roosevelt High School,
Minneapolis, Minnesota

Suggested Assignment: The Passage of Personal Meaning

But the most important image or line to each reader is the one which reminds him of an intense moment in his own life. The moment the passage calls to mind need not be a moment of parallel meaning; the validity of the memory is more important than any similarity of idea. For example, the passage from "Song of Myself" may call to mind a significant moment of another kind or another season, though most students have vivid memories of intoxicating summer nights, as Whitman had. When students feel free to describe such moments, poetry suddenly possesses for them an intimate meaning. What poems will be real to our students? What poems will call up the parts of themselves that no friend has fully understood? These are questions every dedicated teacher of poetry knows he must answer. Consider, for example, such a poem as this one by Carl Sandburg:

PRIMER LESSON

Look out how you use proud words.
When you let proud words go, it is not easy to
    call them back.
They wear long boots; they walk off proud;
    they can't hear you calling —
Look out how you use proud words.

When we read this poem in class, we may ask first, "How does Carl Sandburg personify proud words? What is the most original line or metaphor?" Then we may say, "Almost everyone here has had an experience of using proud words. What moment can you call up from the past in which you were sorry you had used proud words?" Then we may read to the class a student theme like the following:

A QUARREL WITH MY BROTHER

As a small boy, in those hot August days along the Tennessee River, I often spoke proud words and even inflicted blows I couldn't call back. Joe was only nine. I was two years older, but he often beat me in checker games, which we played in the dusty grass on the shady side of the house. I would get angry when he beat me and say, "I can whip you," and turn over the checker board on the grass. He would jump up to fight, and then I would sometimes hit him fiercely in the middle of the spine. He would sit down, his back to the house, and begin to cry. I can still see him as he sat there, tears overflowing his brown eyes and spilling down his cheeks. But this I could not stand. I could not bear at all to see him cry. I would sit down beside him and put my arm around his shoulders and say, "Don't cry, Joe. Please don't cry," over and over again. At last he would stop and consent to go with me to hunt meadowlarks (with one bean-shooter), and we would be friends again. But I never forgot my cruel words, or the look of reproach in his brown eyes, or my joy when he forgave me.

Henry Marston

In making this assignment, we ask that the student quote one or more lines from the poem, as shown above. Then he must take pains to build up his moment and place as the poet does, by the use of color and sound and touch words, also by letting the reader know the season, the time of day, the particular place within the general place, with a bit of dialogue to make the moment still more realistic to the reader.

*   *   *

On each level from seventh grade through high school, our first aim in the teaching of poetry is to know our students so well that we can select poems that will light fires in their memories and electrify their feelings. Our selection of the most vivid and readable poems can banish scorn and boredom with a delight they had not thought possible. After this delight is a reality, we show, step by step, the means by which the poet makes language incandescent, rooting the eye of the reader to his image and taking the ear captive with his music.

These resources of the poet for intensifying communication the student can learn most effectively by writing a few lines of his own about a particular moment in a place he knows, using images of color and sound and touch from actual observation, preferably writing his lines with his eyes and ears open at the spot he is describing, capturing an image in each line and foregoing rhyme, a "thing of no true musical delight," for whatever internal word music he can muster. There are few students who cannot write a phrase, a figure, an image, of genuine merit when they compose under the spell of deep feeling for a particular place or moment. To describe a place as one would take a snapshot, one must inevitably describe a moment. Any attempt to suggest the mood of a moment in a series of lines based on honest, exact observation is certain to create some originality of image. By following the method of the poet, even in writing one or two poems, whether or not his success is remarkable, the student often perceives the essence of poetic diction, mood, and situation more concretely than he would by discussing a hundred poems.

In the study of poetry what is the kernel of reality for each reader? Where can he take hold of it and apply it to a problem in his own life? What crisis or joy or moment of beauty in his memories does it describe or express? These questions direct us to the poems our class will first respond to. The best traditional poems, like Gray's "Elegy," Whitman's "When Lilacs Last . . . ," Longfellow's "Evangeline," Browning's "Fra Lippo Lippi," Tennyson's *Idylls of the King,* have many passages of personal meaning as well as intellectual and historical significance. The quotation of a few lines by the student, followed by a description of a life moment which these lines call to his mind, is the most valuable kind of identification, unique in its application and purely individual in its selection. But this kind of impression may be broadened to include reminiscences of moments in books or movies or other poems as well as in life. As teachers we must be ready to dramatize from our own experiences, personal or intellectual, the meaning of many passages that will suggest to the class their own unique applications. The more abstract and difficult a poetic idea, the greater the necessity for transforming it into a dramatic scene from a life experience.

The following poems have been selected mainly from the considerations presented above, poems which from experience easily involve our senses and sympathy, poems which the average reader enjoys and remembers. With these it is easy to teach the principles of poetic diction and techniques set forth in this chapter. To this list each reader of this book will of course add many favorites of his own. What a teacher feels about a poem no one else cares for he can often communicate to the class, and this passion is a resource to be diligently cherished. In the teaching of poetry perhaps each of us blossoms more fully into a unique individual than in any other **experience in the teaching of English.**

Seventh and Eighth Grades

Rosemary and Stephen Vincent Benét, "Pocahontas," "Wilbur Wright and Orville Wright," and "Johnny Appleseed"

William Cullen Bryant, "To a Waterfowl" and "Robert of Lincoln"

Robert P. Tristram Coffin, "Tom Was Just a Little Boy"

Thomas A. Daly, "Between Two Loves"

Louise Driscoll, "Hold Fast to Your Dreams"

Robert Frost, "The Pasture" and "Stopping by Woods on a Snowy Evening"

Thomas Gray, "Elegy Written in a Country Churchyard"

Theodosia Garrison, "April"

Rudyard Kipling, "The Thousandth Man"

Sidney Lanier, "Tampa Robins"

Henry Wadsworth Longfellow, "Evangeline," "Courtship of Miles Standish," and "The Children's Hour"

James Russell Lowell, "The First Snowfall"

Edna St. Vincent Millay, "Afternoon on a Hill"

Alfred Noyes, "The Highwayman"

Carl Sandburg, "Theme in Yellow"

Sara Teasdale, "Barter"

Celia Thaxter, "The Sandpiper"

Walt Whitman, "The Greatest City"

Ninth and Tenth Grades

Conrad Aiken, "Music I Heard"

Robert Browning, "The Laboratory"

George Noel Gordon, Lord Byron, "The Prisoner of Chillon"

Melville Cane, "Snow toward Evening"

Elizabeth Coatsworth, "Swift Things Are Beautiful"

Robert P. Tristram Coffin, "The Secret Heart"

Robert Frost, "Stopping by Woods on a Snowy Evening"

Thomas Gray, "Elegy Written in a Country Churchyard"

Oliver Wendell Holmes, "The Last Leaf"

Langston Hughes, "Dreams" and "Mother to Son"

Bret Harte, "Her Letter"

Vachel Lindsay, "The Broncho That Would Not Be Broken" and "The Leaden-Eyed"

Edwin Markham, "Lincoln, Man of the People"

Edna St. Vincent Millay, "The Harpweaver"

Alfred Noyes, "The Highwayman"

Carl Sandburg, "Primer Lesson"

Alan Seeger, "I Have a Rendezvous with Death"

Sara Teasdale, "The Philosopher"

Alfred Tennyson, "Ulysses"

Francis Tichnor, "Little Giffen"
John Greenleaf Whittier, "Maud Muller" and "In School Days"
William Wordsworth, "The Daffodils"

Eleventh and Twelfth Grades

Robert Browning, "Soliloquy in a Spanish Cloister" and "My Last
    Duchess"
George Noel Gordon, Lord Byron, "The Prisoner of Chillon"
T. S. Eliot, "Prelude"
Robert Frost, "The Death of the Hired Man" and "Dust of Snow"
Thomas Hardy, "The Man He Killed"
Oliver Wendell Holmes, "The Last Leaf"
Edgar Lee Masters, "Doc Hill," "Anne Rutledge," and "Mollie McGee"
John Milton, "On His Blindness" and *Samson Agonistes*
Alfred Noyes, "The Barrel Organ"
Lizette Woodworth Reese, "Tears"
Edwin Arlington Robinson, "Richard Cory," "Miniver Cheevy," and
    "Ben Jonson Meets a Man from Stratford"
Christina G. Rossetti, "Uphill"
Carl Sandburg, "Masses" and "Mag"
Percy Bysshe Shelley, "Ode to the West Wind," "When the Lamp Is
    Shattered," and "Ozymandias"
Alfred Tennyson, "Break, Break, Break" and "Rizpah"
Dylan Thomas, "The Hunchback in the Park" and "Fern Hill"
John V. A. Weaver, "Drug-Store"
Oscar Wilde, "Requiescat"
William Wordsworth, "Michael," "The Solitary Reaper," and "Lines
    Written in Early Spring"

To the Student Teacher: Suggested Activities

1. Explore Whitman's *Leaves of Grass*, Sandburg's *Collected Poems*, Robert
   Frost's *Collected Poems*, or a volume by Tennyson, Browning, or Christina
   Rossetti, to find three or four poems not mentioned in this chapter that
   you think would be suitable for one grade level from the seventh through
   the twelfth. Under each poem you select write a paragraph or two showing what particular things in this poem would appeal to the grade level
   you have chosen.
2. Read an essay or preface on poetry, such as *The Name and Nature of
   Poetry*, by A. E. Housman, Walt Whitman's preface to *Leaves of Grass*,
   Wordsworth's preface to *Lyrical Ballads*, or Milton's prefaces to *Samson
   Agonistes* and *Paradise Lost*. Write several paragraphs showing what two
   or three particular ideas you liked in the essay or preface, quoting passages to illustrate.
3. Make a list of ten poems, some of them mentioned in this chapter, that

you would like boys and girls to read. Under the name of each poem write an annotation of several sentences to show how you would create interest in this poem before the student reads it.

4. Read to the class from memory a poem of ten lines or more. Ask each member of your class to write a one-sentence impression of the best line or the best quality of your reading. A member of the class may be appointed to bring 4 × 6" slips of paper to class for this purpose. Each student of your class who also reads a poem will have some bit of criticism from every fellow member.

5. Join with several other members of the class to arrange a poem for choral speaking. Practice several times before you come to class. Memorize your poem, if possible, in order to insure maximum concentration on expression when you give the reading.

6. Read Lizette Woodworth Reese's remarkable poem, "Tears." In a paragraph or two show how you would present it to the class. What elements of the essence of poetry could you reveal to your class in this poem alone?

7. Try the experiment of telling the synopsis of a narrative poem, such as Wordsworth's "Michael," a synopsis so individual that only you could write it. This you may do by interweaving the synopsis with quotations from the poem that push the story forward, quotations that you feel are very important in poetic essence or characterization. No two people would write such a synopsis in exactly the same way. Hence it makes a valuable kind of assignment for the outside reading of poetry.

8. Read a portion of Hughes Mearns' *Creative Youth*. What approach to the writing of poetry did Mr. Mearns use that you think would be especially fruitful? In your analysis quote one or two passages from Mr. Mearns.

Suggested Readings

BECK, WARREN: "Poetry's Chronic Disease," *English Journal*, Vol. 33 (September, 1944), pp. 357–64
Some practical methods are suggested for interesting young students in writing poetry.

BRADLEY, A. C.: *Shakespearean Tragedy*, Meridian Books, 1955
Considered by many authorities the most illuminating book of Shakespearean criticism available.

CIARDI, JOHN: *How Does a Poem Mean?* (Boston: Houghton Mifflin Company, 1959).
A spirited and helpful introduction to critical analysis of poetry.

Conducting Experiences in English, National Council of Teachers of English, New York, 1939
See Chapter 12, "Choral Speaking and Oral Reading," pp. 208–18

DEBOER, JOHN, and others: *Teaching Secondary English*, McGraw-Hill, 1951

See pp. 27–30 for an interesting account of how one teacher stimulated the writing of poetry in her class.

GLECKNER, ROBERT F.: "*The Lamb* and *The Tiger* — How Far with Blake?" *English Journal*, Vol. 51 (November, 1962), pp. 536–43

Exciting analysis of the use of Blake's poems applied to life here and now. *Example:* the hard dilemma of savagery and love in the same person. But a fascinating dilemma, as embodied in "The Little Black Boy," is surely an omission the author did not intend.

HARRISON, G. B.: "The Teaching of Shakespeare," *English Journal*, Vol. 52 (September, 1963), pp. 411–19

Pertinent and helpful analysis of *Julius Caesar.* As Harrison writes, "No other author wears so well or lasts so long."

HUGHES, LANGSTON: *The Dream Keeper*, Alfred A. Knopf, 1949

A volume of many uniquely appealing poems for grades seven to twelve.

KATZ, MARTIN R.: "A Poetry Unit in Action," *English Journal*, Vol. 35 (December, 1946), pp. 536–40

Interesting account of how students were introduced to poetry and the results in their own writing.

LABRANT, LOU: *We Teach English*, Harcourt, Brace, 1951

For some useful and perceptive remarks on the writing of poetry, see pp. 150–52.

LODGE, EVAN: "Poetry: A Springboard Approach," *English Journal*, Vol. 43 (October, 1954), pp. 357–62

A successful means of introducing poetry to a high school class includes reading aloud dialect selections and parodies, making a scrapbook of students' favorite poems, and writing "cooperative class limericks" before delving into serious creative writing and reading.

MCGOLDRICK, JAMES H.: "The Back Door to Poetry," *English Journal*, Vol. 43 (May, 1954), pp. 257–59

With skillfully chosen examples, this ninth-grade teacher proved that all poetry is not somber, "intellectual," sentimental, or effeminate, before delving into a more fundamental study of poetry.

MARTZ, LOUIS L.: "The Teaching of Poetry," in *Essays on the Teaching of English*, ed. Edward J. Gordon and Edward S. Noyes (Appleton-Century-Crofts, 1960)

Excellent technical analysis of "Stopping by Woods on a Snowy Evening."

MEARNS, HUGHES: *Creative Youth*, Doubleday (1925)

The most valuable single book on poetry writing by high school students. Rich in illustrative student poems.

SISTER M. BERNETTA QUINN, O.S.F.: "Modern Poetry and the Classroom," *English Journal*, Vol. 50 (December, 1961), pp. 590–95

Unusually rich and helpful insight on the teaching of recent poetry.

Full of specific impressions of particular poems and ways to present them.

SISTER M. PHILLIPS, C.S.C.: "Piloting into Poetry," *English Journal*, Vol. 32 (December, 1943), pp. 563–65

A useful step-by-step outline showing how students may be stimulated to the writing of poetry.

SISTER MARY HELEN, C.S.C.: "Living Shakespeare," *English Journal*, Vol. 54 (January, 1965), pp. 48–51

Illuminating description of the aims, organization, and values of the Shakespeare annual festival at the Academy of St. Catherine in Ventura, California.

"Some of the Best Illinois High School Poetry of 1962," *Illinois English Bulletin* (March 1963), 109 English Building, Urbana, Illinois

Stories in Verse, ed. Max T. Hohn, Odyssey Press, 1943

Excellent introduction to narrative poetry. Selections varied in mood and technique. Many useful helps.

THORNLEY, WILSON R.: "Developing the Creative Process in Poetry," *English Journal*, Vol. 38 (September, 1949), pp. 375–79

This is an account of an experiment in helping students to write poetry. Useful suggestions and some illuminating examples of students' work.

WALTER, NINA WILLIS: *Let Them Write Poetry*, Holt, Rinehart and Winston, 1962

A book rich in practical and imaginative suggestions for teachers of both elementary and high school levels. The pupil poems quoted are rich in original images.

WOLFE, DON M., with JOSIE LEWIS and LELA T. HAMILTON: *Enjoying English 9*, Singer, 1966, "Analyzing a Poem: Proud Words," pp. 296–303

Yesterday and Today, ed. Louis Untermeyer, Harcourt Brace, 1926

Still the most useful and appealing introductory volume of poems for ninth and tenth graders. Excellent teaching helps.

19   How to Teach the Short Story

THE CRUCIAL PRINCIPLE of the short story is deceptively simple but profound, a principle that may be understood and dramatized on many levels. When, as in many a movie, the hero overpowers the villain and the audience cheers for the triumph of righteousness, this is no art and no short story. A short story rather is a study of two parts of the same hero, one part of him at war with another. Take a story, for example, such as "Split Cherry Tree," by Jesse Stuart, in which Dave's father, Mr. Sexton, is presented as a gun-toting Kentucky-mountain farmer whose son is in the local high school. When the principal keeps Dave in after school to earn a dollar to help pay for the broken cherry tree, the son arrives home late to do the chores and is forced to tell his father the truth. The farmer believes the principal, Mr. Herbert, has been unfair to Dave, and goes to school the next morning to dispense justice in his own way: "A bullet will go in a professor same as it will any man. It will go in a rich man the same as it will a poor man." Dave dreads the meeting of the principal and his father, but there is no escape. When Mr. Sexton comes to school, however, laying the gun on the office chair beside him, another part of him begins to take form. He is almost illiterate but very imaginative. He takes an interest in Mr. Herbert, who is afraid, but not too afraid, to explain his stand and defend his idea of punishment and his belief in the dissection of lizards as a valid educational experience. When Mr. Herbert sees that the father is interested, he persuades the older man to stay for the school day and see the microbes under the microscope scurrying about in the tartar scraped from his own teeth. After school Mr. Sexton insists on helping his son sweep the school to earn the rest of the dollar he owes Mr. Herbert.

Thus one sees two sides to Dave's father, one might say his gun-totin' side and his desire to be amicably fair. In a way both sides of him are parts of the same sense of justice. When he first hears of Dave's punishment, a part of him is afire with the quick justice of the pistol. But as he talks with Mr. Herbert, the justice-reasoning part of him wins out and he comes quickly to an understanding with the principal and a comprehension of values he has never hitherto recognized.

This principle of the short story, that it is essentially a crisis in which two parts of the same man are at war, is almost as easy to explain to a seventh-grade class as to a twelfth. "Split Cherry Tree" is consistently visual, full of fiery images that bring the reader to the school and make him feel a part of the drama of father, teacher, and son. For the slow, backward reader, such a story is ideal; for the older, sophisticated reader, it is full of riches in problems and ideas.

Giving the Principle Reality

To make this key principle of inner conflict a reality, we may ask our students questions such as the following: "Can you remember a moment in which two parts of your own personality were at war with each other? Consider, for example, a moment in which you may have been angry at your brother or your mother. One part of you in a moment of anger may have felt an intense dislike of your brother. Another part of you loved him deeply. When this happens, you have the kernel of a short story. The drama of these two parts of one personality struggling with each other makes a good novel and a good play, too." We may extend this idea by asking the student to tell about a moment in which two parts of himself struggled against each other on the same day or in the same week. Such realistic accounts of actual inner conflicts provide excellent material for original short stories. Indeed the most vital kind of short story stems from a recognition of inner conflict either in the writer's own experience or in the experience of someone he knows well. Many students who study short stories and try to write them have the conception of a short story as a sally of imagination unrelated to realistic observation of character in ourselves and the people around us. If this is not always a flight from the necessities of art, it is a flight from reality by young people who are with our help attempting to face their problems, not run from them. In teaching the writing of short stories, as in showing how to probe their structure and meaning, the English teacher must help the student grapple with the stark and painful in life, knowing that only then will he have the resources to emerge triumphant from his own dilemmas.

We should train our students, then, as they read a short story, to look for the inner conflict rather than the conflict between man and man. In many stories we see two characters at war within themselves because an internal crisis in one man's life often produces also a crisis for another. For example, in "Sheener," by Ben Ames Williams, a story well loved by high school students, the central figure is a drunken Englishman by the name of Evans, who is befriended by a Jewish newsboy named Sheener. Sheener believes not only in Evans the man but in Evans' stories about his aristocratic heritage which he boasts of while in his cups. Sheener takes Evans off the Boston streets to his own lodging, where he watches over him, providing him with food, clothing, and medical care. When Evans hears that his son is coming to America to see him, he he begins to take hold of himself anew. Sheener helps him make himself presentable and even goes with him to the railway station when he meets his son. There Evans says to Sheener, "I say, I want to meet my boy alone. You won't mind standing back a bit when the train comes in." Sheener dutifully stands back. When the young man gets off the train and sees his father, Sheener walks toward them, looking at Evans and his son expectantly. The son is puzzled. Then Evans cuts Sheener cold and Sheener walks away. In Sheener's words, "A gentleman like him can't let on he knows a guy like me."

In this story we do not realize until near the end that Evans, now that he is sober, is ashamed of his friend Sheener, not only because he is Jewish but also because his clothes are rather disreputable-looking as compared to the new clothes which he has purchased for his friend. One part of Evans is full of gratitude to

Sheener, who has rescued him from alcoholic oblivion. But another part of Evans is snobbish and anti-Semitic, particularly when he wishes to make a good impression on his son, whom he has not seen for many years. One of the technical weaknesses of "Sheener" is that we do not see the two parts of Evans struggling with each other early enough in the story. We see only the effect of the struggle in the dramatic conclusion in which Evans, his face flushing, pretends not to know his friend.

This crisis in Evans' life is also a crisis for Sheener. When the old man rejects him, the greatness of his spirit still makes him a champion of the man he believed in.

The greater the short story, the more profound the dilemma in which the hero finds himself. When we can sympathize with each side of a person in the turmoil of inner conflict, when we can see that each part of him has a justification, then the short story poses a more profound dilemma than in such a story as "Split Cherry Tree," in which the gun-justice side of Mr. Sexton is wholly destructive. Consider, for example, one of the great short stories of English literature, "The Apple Tree," by John Galsworthy, a story well loved by high school students, especially by juniors and seniors. In this story Frank Ashurst, an English college student on a summer walking tour, suffers an injury and is carried to a nearby farmhouse, where he is nursed and cared for by Megan, the niece of the farmer. Megan is beautiful but almost illiterate; she soon falls in love with Frank, and he with her. Almost every night they meet in the apple orchard beside a brook. When he realizes that he is desperately in love with Megan, Frank decides to marry her despite the disparity in education and family background. He goes to town to buy her some wedding clothes. There he meets a college friend and three girls from his own social circle. Suddenly another part of Frank, the part of him that is conventional and realistic, begins to loom in his thoughts, struggling against that part of himself which he had thought irrevocably in love with Megan. After leaving his college friends, Frank walks along the beach in a mood of despair. When he sees Megan looking eagerly for him, he lies down on the beach, hiding his face, struggling to resolve his perplexity. At last, when he decides to look for Megan, she has disappeared. He lets her go, does not seek her at her house, cannot bear to return even to tell her good-bye. Many years later, when he is married to a conventionally educated woman, Frank discovers that Megan had drowned herself in the brook under the apple tree.

In this story, depending upon one's sense of values, we may say that neither part of Frank's personality is evil or hateful. The part of him that is in love with Megan has the sympathy of almost every reader. The part of him which rejects Megan has the sympathy of many readers also. I have discussed this story with dozens of classes of college freshmen and sophomores. To my amazement I have found only a few young men who felt that Frank did the wrong thing in leaving Megan. The average American youth is much more realistic about marriage than is normally supposed. Despite the romantic elements in our tradition, most American boys consider many factors other than love in selecting a wife. Many boys have said in class, "I think Frank did the right thing in leaving her, but he should have gone back at least to tell her good-bye."

"The Apple Tree," then, is superior to both "Sheener" and "Split Cherry Tree" in the sense that the opposing elements of the internal crisis are more evenly balanced. If Frank had decided to marry Megan, the reader could sympathize with him and see at the same time the disadvantages the marriage would entail. On the other hand, the reader can also sympathize with Frank for leaving Megan, if not with his abrupt desertion. Each of the directions in a really searching story, then, one of which the hero must choose, has a penalty for the hero and also a reward. When the alternatives of action in a short story are thus evenly balanced in beneficent and destructive concomitants, we are likely to have a dilemma which pierces so deep that the reader finds himself forced to resolve the crisis in his own thoughts. Indeed the best kind of short story is one which reflects for each of us an internal struggle of our own. There are few men who have not known their Megans and few women who have not had opportunities to marry men whom their friends or families thought to be unsuitable.

The principle thus far exemplified may be used as the focus of criticism both of literature and life in dozens of classic stories: in Steinbeck's "Leader of the People," in which a little boy wavers between hero-worship of his grandfather and a more mature acceptance of his grandfather's worth, symbolized at the end when he makes a glass of lemonade for the great leader; in Mary Wilkins Freeman's "Revolt of Mother," in which a New England mother, torn between acceptance and revolt toward her husband's parsimony, moves her family into the new barn she prefers to her old farm house; in Willa Cather's remarkable story, "A Wagner Matinee," in which Aunt Georgiana leaves her bleak farm in Nebraska to return to Boston and the music circumstance has denied her for a quarter of a century, torn at the end between the beauty of her Boston milieu and the ugliness of her Nebraska world, her children notwithstanding; in Katherine Mansfield's unforgettable story, "The Fly," in which the London business man who has lost his son in World War I wavers between a determined forgetfulness of his sorrow and the last wave of despair that will destroy his reason. In such crises a man's unique character stands revealed more explicitly than any conflict with human or natural forces outside himself could achieve. In teaching these stories, we need to be prepared to ask, "Did the hero or heroine make the right choice? If you had been in Aunt Georgiana's place, what would you have done?" A story such as Irwin Shaw's "The Girls in Their Summer Dresses" reveals one of the most troubling conflicts within man, the biological desires impelled by nature and the desire dictated by society and his ideals to live the life of a faithful husband. Such a story few teachers would feel appropriate to discuss in high school classes. Despite the relative freedom to deal with such themes, the conflict depicted by Shaw is still a rarity in short stories of preeminent literary worth.

Great Stories That Deviate from the Rule

In our rich American literature, as well as in world literature, we have a number of distinguished stories that do not fulfill the central principle I have illustrated in the preceding pages. From the seventh grade through the tenth grade, we like to read sketches and stories that may not portray an internal struggle. Such a beautiful sketch, for example, as Stephen Crane's "Dark Brown Dog" is infinitely appealing to classes from the seventh grade onward, if only because it pictures a little boy deprived of his dog by a drunken father. The sympathy of the reader from the first sentence of this sketch is focused on the little boy and his dog. Though the story ends with the death of the dog, it is not a story of internal crisis, nor is it a story to shock or horrify.

Stories of sudden shock, violence, and murder often attempt to substitute horror for insight, whereas a quiet story such as Morley Callaghan's "All the Years of Her Life" is infinitely more instructive than the pretentious violence of Hemingway's "The Killers." Stories of sudden shock and violence appear every day in movies and magazines, but whether they may be called art or not is still to be decided. Most literature of insight and permanence does not depend upon such conventional trappings.

Such a great story as "Tennessee's Partner," by Bret Harte, achieves a distinction rare in American letters, though it does not portray a character in conflict with himself. The partner sticks closer than a brother to the very end of Tennessee's life, never faltering in his devotion. Nor does Albert Maltz' memorable story, "Man on the Road," about a West Virginia miner near death of silicosis, show any deep conflict or clear alternatives of action. I have never found a class which did not respond to this beautiful character sketch. From the first sentence it holds the attention fast through its electric images of action, face, gestures, place, sound.

In all stories of classic structure, however, we look for the inner struggle and the projection of alternatives in the march of scenes, as in "Paul's Case," by Willa Cather. Paul has a deep conflict within himself. The love of beauty, for the fulfillment of which some money is necessary, struggles against another part of his personality, that of sensible action symbolized in his parents' way of life and the expectations of his high school teachers. In the end his love of beauty triumphs over his sense of orderly conduct and thus precipitates his suicide. To my mind "A Wagner Matinee" and "The Sculptor's Funeral" are infinitely superior to "Paul's Case" in their reflection of values and dilemmas which we can discuss in the classroom and apply to problems of today. It is true that the three stories have a similar theme, the rebellion some people feel against the ugliness and bleakness of many elements of the American scene. But "Paul's Case" portrays a sick personality, whereas in Aunt Georgiana we see a person of sturdy mental health struggling with her dilemma.

Like the Greek play, the short story takes a character when a crisis of his life is nearing crystallization. The object of the short story is to compress the crisis and the action within a few pages, in order to bring illumination of great intensity upon the hero's dilemma. A sketch of his own which Oscar Wilde called "The Greatest Short Story of the World" is a profound and arresting example of this essence of compression:

PARABLE

Christ came from a white plain to a purple city, and as He passed through the first street, He heard voices overhead, and saw a young man lying drunk upon a window-sill. "Why do you waste your soul in drunkenness?" He said. "Lord, I was a leper and You healed me, what else can I do?" A little further through the town He saw a young man following a harlot, and said, "Why do you dissolve your soul in debauchery?" and the young man answered, "Lord, I was blind, and You healed me, what else can I do?" At last in the middle of the city He saw an old man crouching, weeping upon the ground, and when He asked why he wept, the old man answered, "Lord, I was dead, and You raised me into life, what else can I do but weep?"

Discussion and Analysis

The teaching of the short story has many practical applications and rewards. In the first place it is the form of literature that often can be read aloud and hold the rapt attention of the class. A number of the stories I have cited, such as "Man on the Road" and Mansfield's "The Fly," we may read aloud and discuss in one class period. Similarly Crane's remarkable sketch, "Experiment in Misery," the story of a night Crane actually spent in a New York flop house, and "The Dark Brown Dog" are short enough to be read aloud within fifteen or twenty minutes, leaving time for exciting discussion. Once we have shown the class, let us say, a class weak in reading skill, that we can select a story they will like, we can then with some confidence assign them stories to read silently. Many students are willing to read short stories when a novel looms like a mountain peak remote and inaccessible. One good way to get students interested in reading longer stories outside of class is to tell them fragments or beginnings. If we should assign, for example, in the junior or senior year, Anderson's "I Am a Fool," Maureen Daly's "Sixteen," Galsworthy's "Quality," or "The Apple Tree," it is excellent motivation to tell the class the situation in brief before the action really begins. The whetting of class curiosity is an art that each English teacher must learn for himself. We must learn not to tell too much of the story or novel we are assigning. We must also learn not to tell so little that the inkling of excitement and suspense is not quite crystallized.

As in teaching the drama and the novel, so in teaching the short story: the important thing is the illumination of the life of the student, not the mastery of form or technique or the comprehension of complicated plots. When we know the problems which agitate the minds of our class, we may select short stories that dramatize similar dilemmas. When we see that the idea of an internal crisis in a novel or a play is difficult for our students to comprehend, we may read a classic short story to illustrate the principle. Always, however, we return to the searching questions of personal application: "What does this story mean in my life? How does it help me to become a more mature, responsible person? What dangers does it reveal that I also may have to face? What handicap is there in my personality that I can overcome as the hero did? Are there people around me that this story can help me to understand? Can it help me to understand my parents, my friends, my school?" These questions and many others like them are always more rewarding and fruitful in the study of literature than the whole armament of literary criticism.

To the Student Teacher: Suggested Activities

1. Read Galsworthy's "The Apple Tree." Then write a report telling what you would have done in the hero's place and giving reasons for your decision.
2. Select five passages from "The Apple Tree." Write each passage on your paper. Then under each quotation describe a moment from your own experience that this passage called to your memory. Or: Under each quotation write a paragraph to show why you selected it. Analyze each passage stylistically if you wish, or compare your passages with those of another author.
3. Read Joseph Conrad's *Heart of Darkness*. Then make a ten-minute report to the class in which you analyze the hero as a man divided within himself. How does Conrad gradually sharpen the reader's focus on his hero's dilemma? Since this is not a story usually read by high school students, you may choose alternatives from any of the stories named in this chapter.

4. In a long paragraph (200–300 words) describe a moment of crisis in your own life when two parts of you were drawn in opposite directions. Use images to make the time and place real. Use bits of monologue to show what your thoughts were.
5. Read Joseph Conrad's novel, *Lord Jim*. State in a paragraph your conception of Jim's internal struggle and its final resolution.
6. Select a story which can be read in fifteen or twenty minutes, such as "Split Cherry Tree," "A Wagner Matinee," or "Man on the Road." Read it in a high school class if possible, or read it to your own college class and lead the discussion.

Suggested Readings: Short Story Collections

American Vanguard, ed. Don M. Wolfe, Cornell, 1948
Contains first professional stories of Sigrid de Lima, William Styron, and John Burress.

GLICKSBERG, CHARLES I.: *Writing the Short Story*, Hendricks House, 1953
An incisive and perceptive analysis of the art of the short story.

Great American Short Stories, ed. Wallace and Mary Stegner, Dell paperback, 1957
Contains Harte's "Tennessee's Partner," Crane's "The Open Boat," Faulkner's "Wash."

Great Modern Short Stories, ed. Bennett Cerf, Modern Library
Contains Galsworthy's "The Apple Tree," Conrad's "Heart of Darkness."

Masters of the Modern Short Story, ed. Walter Havighurst, Harcourt, Brace, 1945
Includes Conrad's "Youth," Faulkner's "Barn Burning," and Mansfield's "The Stranger."

Pocket Book of Modern American Short Stories, ed. Philip Van Doren Stern, Pocket Books, 1954
Contains "Babylon Revisited," "Profession Housewife," "Leader of the People."

Short Stories for Our Times, ed. Simon Certner and George H. Henry, Houghton Mifflin, 1950
Contains "Sheener," "Split Cherry Tree," "All the Years of Her Life." A collection for high school use, with helpful study suggestions.

Short Studies for Study and Enjoyment, ed. Harold T. Eaton, Odyssey Press, 1959
Contains Butler's "Pigs Is Pigs," Galsworthy's "The Pack."

Short Story Reader, The, ed. Rodney A. Kimball, Odyssey Press, 1961
Contains Thurber's "The Catbird Seat," Crane's "The Upturned Face," Suckow's "The Man of the Family."

SIMPSON, RAY H. and SOARES, ANTHONY: "Best- and Least-Liked Short

Stories in Junior High School," *English Journal*, Vol. 54 (February, 1965), pp. 108–111
> A significant survey of pupil response to 862 short stories; 4250 seventh and eighth graders participated in the survey.

Stories for Youth, ed. A. H. Lass and Arnold Horowitz, Harper, 1950
> Contains "Sixteen," by Maureen Daly, "Weep No More, My Lady," by James Street, and "Quality," by John Galsworthy.

Story Essays, ed. Harriet L. McClay, Henry Holt, 1931
> Humorous and interesting tales about animals, science, fashion, pioneers, and Indians.

Twenty Stories by Stephen Crane, World Publishing Company, 1945
> Contains "Experiment in Misery," "The Blue Hotel," "The Open Boat."

Twenty-two Short Stories of America, ed. Edith R. Mirrielees, D. C. Heath, 1937
> Contains "Miss Letitia's Profession," "After Twenty Years," and "Mr. Brownlee's Roses."

WOLFE, DON M., with RUTH NELSON and LAURADA K. OSBORN, *Enjoying English 11*, Singer, 1964. "Reading a Great Short Story," pp. 356–67

SUGGESTED READINGS: *English Journal*

BURTON, DWIGHT L.: "Teaching Appreciation of Fiction," *English Journal*, Vol. 42 (January, 1953), pp. 16–20
> Arresting analysis of appreciation growth and senior preferences of ten short stories grouped under the topic, "Personal Problems."

DOMINCOVICH, H. A.: "Composition in the Short Short," *English Journal*, Vol. 30 (April, 1941), pp. 294–97
> How a study of the short story can lead to the student's writing of autobiography.

GILL, NAOMI B.: " 'Depth' Reading," *English Journal*, Vol. 42 (September, 1953), pp. 311–15, 323
> Hints on the interpretation of symbolism and phrases of implication. Useful references to particular stories and novels.

HENNING, ALICE B.: "Teaching an 'Idea' Story," *English Journal*, Vol. 42 (May, 1953), pp. 256–59
> Concrete and exciting suggestions for making short-story reading more fruitful.

HENRY, GEORGE: "How to Get Interesting Themes," *English Journal*, Vol. 33 (September 1944), pp. 348–55
> Interesting examples, with useful suggestions, of autobiographical material written by students.

TILFORD, ELINOR: "Nothing Happens as Interesting as a Story," *English Journal*, Vol. 29 (September, 1940), pp. 563–67

The student diary as a source of material for the student's creative efforts. Contains a long list of published diaries that are of interest to students.

VICKERY, THYRA: "Narration Recollected in Tranquillity," *English Journal*, Vol. 30 (April, 1941), pp. 299–306

Preparing for the writing of a short story by a series of related exercises and the keeping of a notebook. A useful article.

20 Novels
for the Classroom Shelf:
Grades Nine and Ten

ONE OF THE IDEALS of the imaginative English teacher of an average ninth-grade class is to find a novel for each student that keeps him eager and excited from the first page to the last. The fourteen-year-old who is only ten years of age in reading development deserves our insight and devotion as much as the college-preparatory student. We must take him where we find him, perhaps a lad with no stimulation from family or peers, and find for him a novel that becomes a moving and shaking experience. The key factor at first is not the literary excellence of this book but its power to sweep him emotionally into the author's world. Once a student has read a novel with this profound effect on his personality, we shall find it easy to guide him to stories of more permanent worth. Of all the forms of literature the novel, in its wealth of sensory language, is nearest to the tenacious grip of the motion picture in its hold on the reader's psyche. Biographies and autobiographies fall next in order in the degree of sensory appeal. Until a student feels this electric grasp of his whole being that only sensory language can achieve, he has not found that joy in reading which magically opens a hundred doors to the education he needs.

Our problem, then, with boys and girls of an average class, is to find a group of novels or true-life stories, perhaps no more than fifteen or twenty of them, that the students will see daily on the classroom shelf and gradually recommend to each other. In our reading guidance program, the first book we suggest to each student is the most crucial. It is the student's test of our insight as well as our test of his response. Often a student will not accept a teacher's recommendation of a book to be read at home; but when he does accept our suggestion, then it is his response to this first book that counts most in the year's program. To suggest a book, we need to have some inkling of our student's out-of-classroom thoughts, of his problems at home, his capacity to read, and of his resistance to English in past years. Has he actually ever read a book thoroughly, from the first page to the last? Many students boast at the end of high school that they made many book reports in four years without reading a single book. This makes our reading guidance a mockery and a delusion to the young citizens who need it most.

Easy Books for Boys

For a boy weak in reading skill, I would recommend as a first book a short animal tale fresh and green in our own memory, such as Curwood's *Kazan*, Ramee's *Dog of Flanders*, or London's *Call of the Wild*. *Smoky*, by Will James, is also appealing to many boys of thirteen or fourteen who do not yet feel they have to act tough and read only about war and gangsters, if at all. For the weak reader, an animal book of literary value, such as *The Yearling*, is too sophisticated in style and thought. A book about a country school, bears and dogs, and adventures in country life, such as Connor's *Glengarry School Days* and Stuart's *The Thread that Runs so True* is often appealing to boys of all backgrounds. For weak readers who already feel superior to animal books, Gunther's story of the death of his son, *Death Be Not Proud*, is short, painful, and full of the drama of father and son. To many a boy casually picking up this book, its brevity would be its most telling recommendation, but only until he has spent a couple of hours with it. For the weak student, we need to think of the least formidable looking volume, avoiding, of course, such a book as *The Nigger of the "Narcissus,"* which many a weak student chooses for its brevity, struggles through parts of it, fakes his report, and hates English anew. Wright's *Black Boy*, on the other hand, not much longer than Conrad's masterpiece, is a highly readable and exciting story of one youth, a book rapidly becoming a classic of contemporary literature. We must not let our weak student know that a certain book is a classic; in many cases this is almost certain to send him flying away. *After* he has enjoyed it, then we laugh and say, "Did you know that book is already to some people a classic in American literature? You wouldn't have believed it, would you? A classic is sometimes easy to read you know; it doesn't *have* to be hard and unreadable just because it's a classic."

For many retarded as well as superior students, some Civil War stories are perenially certain to take mind and senses captive. The best one I know for countless conquests is Fox's *The Little Shepherd of Kingdom Come*, now almost half a century young. The early chapters of this story, the scenes of Chad and his dog Jack setting out from a fatherless and motherless cabin in the mountains, Chad's growing-up years with the Tolliver family, Jack on trial for killing a sheep, Chad's love for Margaret and Melissa's love for him, his going to war and coming back — these scenes form an ideal blending of youthful struggle, action, and romance. Who can forget Chad's cherished footprint in the yard, preserved by Melissa under a box? I have known few readers who, once well started in this story, could resist its spell. When an imaginative teacher knows even half a dozen such books, and finds that they have a magic power over her weakest students, she has the brightest possible beginning for a home-reading program.

Books That Appeal to Girls

Girls of the ninth-grade, it is true, have a very different outlook from the boys', though the story of *The Little Shepherd* has its magic for them too. But a story of first love, such as Maureen Daly's *Seventeenth Summer*, is more likely to appeal to them than a good animal story or an exciting war story. To some girls of urban background a love story of the mountains, such as *Trail of the Lonesome Pine*, may be a memorable reading experience. Cather's *My Antonia* is short and easy to read for girls, memorable for its bright images of the Nebraska farmlands, delicate, realistic shadings of character, and lovely cadences unique in the American language. I doubt that for most girls Willa Cather is more difficult to read than *Sue Barton, Student Nurse*, which is appealing to many eighth- and ninth-grade girls. It is infinitely preferable, of course, to read *Sue Barton* with zest

than to read Willa Cather with calm pulse and wavering mind.
Books such as Dorothy Fisher's *Understood Betsey* and Mary Ellen
Chase's *Silver Shell* are appealing to many ninth-grade girls, the first
because it shows a city girl becoming self-reliant on a farm, the
second because it excites and releases the imagination and that love
of beauty intensified by adolescent strivings. The advantage that
Sue Barton has over these two books is that it allows the reader to
project herself into a vocation which many girls even in the ninth-
grade visualize as a door opening to marriage opportunities.

The Main Goal: A Love of Reading

Our first aim is to help each member of the class develop a love
of reading, a conviction that many books await the eager mind to
give endless hours of pleasure and illumination. Yet every student
has emotional problems that a good book may help to solve. We
may say to a student, "How is the heroine of this book like you?
How is she different? What is the most important thing she taught
you?" A girl who feels sorry for herself might gain a perspective of
her weakness by reading *A Lantern in Her Hand*, by Bess Streeter
Aldrich, or *Sunshine and Shadow*, by Lorraine and Jerrold Beim. What
are the main problems of the ninth-grade girl? Of the ninth-grade
boy? We may ask a committee of girls and a committee of boys to
make a list of their key problems. Then comes a golden opportunity
in classroom reading guidance. What good books can they read to
help them solve these problems? We may make a list on the board
of the favorite novels read thus far. Then we may ask those who have
read each book to tell what problems it may help to solve. Of course,
no one of us wants to feel that reading should resolve itself into a
problem-solving discipline. A breathless hunger for what happens on
the next page is perhaps a more valuable goal in the ninth-grade
than prolonged self-analysis with a problem hovering darkly in the
back of one's mind. An hilarious book, such as *The Egg and I* or
Cheaper by the Dozen, is often a pearl without price to the harassed
teacher who knows the peril of separating from the classroom the
joy of laughter or the precious memories of silent reading in the
living-room chair. If we can help each student find a sense of joy in
reading, we have helped him win a life-long asset in solving both his

own problems and those he has in common with all American citizens.

In every average class we find many reading preferences already established. We take each student where he stands in the world of books and push him forward. For the boy accustomed to adventure stories and wanting no other, we may recommend for our classroom shelf *Mutiny on the Bounty* or *Kon-Tiki*, the latter a true story of a handmade raft crossing the Pacific from Peru to Polynesia. For the reader who is curious about life on the frontier, and does not wish it dished up with romantic sauce, we may suggest *Giants in the Earth*, one of the most haunting novels of American literature, a book full of sensory language that heightens its readability on almost every page. What is life like in the coal towns of Wales? The family story of *How Green Was My Valley* has many facets of appeal: conflicts between father and son, between young hero and teacher; the struggle against poverty and ugliness; his own first love and a brother's marriage viewed through the eyes of the young hero. Not the first book, nor the easiest, *How Green Was My Valley*, but we cherish its vivid scenes for our students, and perhaps read a few pages to the class. *City Boy*, by Herman Wouk, which opens with grade-school boys talking about grammar and baseball on the steps (a delightful scene to read aloud), will bring many a shock of recognition to boys and girls who have grown up in large cities. To each student, at first, according to his preferences, if possible. Gradually, as he hears about other books from members of the class, he may widen his perspective.

For the average ninth or tenth grade, we are looking primarily for books of rich concentration of sensory language. The nearer the language is to color photography and the sound track of a movie, the more surely it will appeal to a slow reader, especially if the book is short. Such a book as Wharton's *Ethan Frome* has these two immense advantages. Yet many a teacher would rightfully hesitate to suggest such a book on the early high school level. Certainly it would not be the first book suggested; but by the second semester we know our students well enough to decide which ones are ready for the stark tragedy of *Ethan Frome:* a New England farmer married to a woman ugly in spirit, in love with a simple farm girl who comes to help with the household chores. The problems arising in this book perhaps cannot be discussed in many classes, but the question, "What should Ethan have done in this situation?" may easily come up in conference. Many students in the ninth and tenth grades, especially among the less privileged groups, have known the tragedy of broken homes or miserably unhappy parents. The danger of shocking the sensibilities of our students is less than the danger of omitting from our private discussions with them the anguish of their own lives. Such a book as *Ethan Frome*, which to my mind loses some of its power by the dramatic incident of the attempted suicide, will in many cases encourage the student to talk over some of his own home problems with a sympathetic teacher. More often than not the English teacher of the average ninth or tenth grade has been more sheltered than his students. He must somehow let his students know that he is at least no less than they aware of the destructive influences at work in their lives. A realistic book that dramatizes these dilemmas and shows counter forces at work may be a turning point in a youth's life, especially when the reading is followed by a discussion with a perceptive teacher.

True Stories and Social Problems

A true story such as *Diary of a Young Girl*, by Anne Frank, has a deep fascination for both boys and girls of the average ninth grade. Anne was only thirteen when the Nazis entered Holland and she and her family hid themselves in an abandoned warehouse in Amsterdam. The language of Anne Frank, as well as her memorable insight into the personalities of her family and friends, are already making this book a classic in the psychology and literature of adolescence. This is a painful book to read, but its sensory vividness alone makes it unforgettable. Few boys and girls will not recognize in this book some of their own thoughts and problems or those of their friends. In Anne's situation, these problems are heightened immeasurably by the danger of capture that can lead only to the concentration camp and death from gas or starvation.

In the field of social problems, one easily read novel can lend more illumination to the average boy or girl than many textbooks. Many teachers would not assign a book such as *The Good Earth* to ninth- or tenth-graders. But this easy-to-read book portrays as no other about China the desperate poverty in the midst of which two-thirds of the people of China and many other countries go to bed hungry every night. Some teachers delicately brought up may be shocked by the marital behavior of the hero but not at all shocked by Pearl Buck's images of a people stricken with famine. The test of a book for the average student is not whether we or some of our students are shocked by it, but whether or not they read it in mental and emotional tension sustained over a number of hours. In any book of literary value the reader is likely to face bitter realities. We cannot protect our students from the horror and spiritual ugliness of many moving pictures. In any book of social illumination we may suggest, such as *The Good Earth* or *All Quiet on the Western Front*, or *The Grapes of Wrath*, we must weigh the shock of ugliness as against the sum of illumination that the young citizen may acquire; we must also weigh the shock of ugliness as against his not reading at all or reading a book of inferior worth or no fascination for him. No one who has read Sinclair's *The Jungle* can forget the scenes of stockyard butchery, the workers with their feet wrapped in burlap and soaked with the blood of the slaughter house, frozen and soaked again. This book more than any other helped to arouse the nation and Congress to pass the Pure Food and Drug Act of 1906. *The Jungle* is valuable as history; it is also valuable as one of the minor classics in American fiction. For our puposes, it is especially valuable because many retarded students find it fascinating reading after they become accustomed in the opening chapters to the strange names of the main characters. The vivid pictures of the slaughter houses and of child labor make it one of the most instructive and easy-to-read novels in American literature. Though the scenes pictured in *The Jungle* have small relevance now to American life, the suffering and poverty portrayed are still a pervasive phenomenon in most of Asia. The conditions described in *The Grapes of Wrath* are still a vivid memory in the minds of living people, and mild or extreme poverty is still a bitter reality among one-fifth to one-eighth of our citizens. According to the 1962 *Statistical Abstract* over seven millions of America's fifty-six million families received in 1960 an annual income of $2000 or less.

*   *   *

Whether or not the particular titles suggested in this chapter are all applicable to the average classroom, we have examined together certain useful principles by which we may select books for the reading shelf. They may be summarized in the order of declining validity as follows: (1) A book must be sufficiently easy to read so that if he is interested the student will devour it hungrily. (2) The book should relate when possible to the student's problems in his home, his school, his community. (3) If these two conditions can be met, then the book chosen should also have literary value. (4) For correlation with social studies, important novels picturing social conditions, especially those abroad, are desirable. In applying these principles, we must remember that the most powerful motivation to read is the recommendation of a classmate. If we can get two or three students to recommend a book, this is our most vital resource in reading guidance. If by the end of the year we have proved to each student that many other good books wait for him to keep him reading far into many nights, we may have achieved an influence of life-long impact on the growing child.

To the Student Teacher: Suggested Activities

1. Read the opening chapters of Ramee's *Dog of Flanders*, London's *Call of the Wild*, Curwood's *Kazan*, James' *Smoky*, Rawlings' *The Yearling*, and Knowles' *A Separate Peace*. Which of these books would be most appealing to weak readers of the ninth grade? Write a brief comment on each book.
2. Read the opening chapters of Connor's *Glengarry School Days*, Stuart's *The Thread That Runs So True*, Aldrich's *A Lantern in Her Hand*, and Lee's *To Kill a Mockingbird*. Of these three stories, which would be most interesting to average ninth-grade boys? Which would be most interesting to girls? Write a brief comment on each of these three books.
3. Read with care the early chapters of John Fox's *The Little Shepherd of Kingdom Come*. Show how this story would or would not be appealing to average ninth-grade youngsters you know.
4. Read the opening chapters of *Mutiny on the Bounty* and *Kon-Tiki*. Of these two adventure stories, which would be most interesting to average ninth-grade boys?
5. Make a list of five or six books not named in this chapter that you feel would be of interest to ninth-grade girls or boys. Write a brief annotation on each book.
6. Read the opening chapters of Richard Wright's *Black Boy*. In the community you know could you put this book on your classroom shelf and

encourage your students to read it? A more important question: Do you think boys and girls, both Negro and white, should be encouraged to read this book? Give reasons for your analysis.

7. Read Gunner Myrdal, *Challenge to Affluence* (New York, Random House, 1963), particularly Chapter 4, "Unemployment and Poverty," and mimeograph a sheet of statistics for your classmates to have before them as you make a brief report to them. See also Michael Harrington, *The Other America* (New York, Macmillan, 1962), and for a World view Paul G. Hoffman, *World Without Want*, (New York, Harper and Row, 1962). Give the class your definition of the word *poverty*.

SUGGESTED READINGS

Books for You, published by the NCTE, 508 South Sixth Street, Champaign, Illinois, 1959

BRATTON, DOROTHY: "Reading for Therapy," *English Journal*, Vol. 46 (September, 1957), pp. 339–46
    An exciting article for showing how one gifted teacher related reading assignments realistically to student problems.

BULMAN, LEARNED T.: "Biographies for Teenagers," *English Journal*, Vol. 47 (November, 1958), pp. 487–94
    A study of highly readable biographies which fascinate teenagers.

BURTON, DWIGHT L.: "Literature for Social Development," *English Journal*, Vol. 43 (May, 1954), pp. 231–34
    A discussion of the value of literature in creating social awareness and improving human relations, with excellent suggestions for books to answer these needs.

BURTON, DWIGHT L.: *Literature Study in the High Schools*, Holt, 1959
    Rich and informative suggestions on reading guidance and the relation of literature to adolescent experience.

CRABBE, JOHN K.: "On the Playing Fields of Devon," *English Journal*, Vol. 52 (February, 1963), pp. 109–11
    On gifted teacher's experiences with John Knowles' *A Separate Peace*.

EDWARDS, ANNE: "Teen-Age Career Girls," *English Journal*, Vol. 42 (November, 1953), pp. 437–42
    Arresting plan for an English course given to ninth-grade commercial students, with a suggestive list of novels and non-fiction reading.

GILL, NAOMI B.: " 'Depth' Reading," *English Journal*, Vol. 42 (September, 1953), pp. 311–15, 323
    Hints on the interpretation of symbolism and phrases of implication. Useful references to particular stories and novels.

Good Reading, Mentor Book, New American Library, New York, 1956
    Indispensable manual of reading guidance. See p. 300.

GRANITE, HARVEY R.: "Good Books for 'Lower-Class' Students," *English Journal*, Vol. 54 (October, 1965), pp. 585–91

Excellent choices of some books of realistic, appealing literary quality for slow learners.

HACKL, LLOYD: "Honor and Fame: A Tenth Grade Unit," *English Journal*, Vol. 52 (November, 1963), pp. 628–29

An illuminating analysis of the experiment with the theme of honor and fame in masterpieces from *Samson Agonistes*, through *Lord Jim* to Spender and Frost.

KING, CARLYLE: "Conrad for the Classroom," *English Journal*, Vol. 47 (May, 1958), pp. 259–62

The author praises Conrad's portrayal of such divided characters as Heyst in *Victory*, who cannot "defend himself from compassion." Another virtue of Conrad is that he shows expressions of nobility in ordinary men. A distinguished article, rich in its analysis of Conrad's philosophy of art and superb value for the high school student.

LEPS, FANNIE B.: "Our American Heritage: A Reading-Centered Language Arts Unit," *English Journal*, Vol. 43 (April, 1954), pp. 187–90

A valuable experiment in free reading by average seventh-grade pupils. Suggestive list of novels used.

MC COLLY, WILLIAM: "Teaching *The Red Badge of Courage*," *English Journal*, Vol. 50 (November, 1961), pp. 534–38

How students analyze the subtleties of style, mood, and iron in a great novel.

MOSING, MALCOLM: "Appreciation through Units," *English Journal*, Vol. 44 (February, 1955), pp. 80–86

Literature taught within meaningful frameworks: units on drama and the motion picture, "The Influence of Environment on Personality and Thought," and "Developing a Personal Philosophy." Suggestive list of books for each unit.

Patterns in Reading, An annotated Book List for Young Adults, by Jean Carolyn Roos. American Library Association, Chicago, 1961. paperbound

A judicious and authoritative list with brief annotations classified by themes such as "Family Fun and Laughter," "Greece — Her Glory," and so forth.

PETITT, DOROTHY: "The Junior Novel in the Classroom," *English Journal*, Vol. 52 (October, 1963), pp. 512–20

An exciting analysis of various novels' successful use on the seventh- and eighth-grade levels.

POTTER, ROBERT E.: "Reading Unlimited," *English Journal*, Vol. 42 (January, 1953), pp. 28–32

One class period per week devoted to free reading successfully encouraged more "outside" reading, and proved that reading is not just a required classroom activity, but a rewarding one for leisure time as well.

Reading Ladders for Human Relations, American Council on Education, Washington, D.C., 1964

Invaluable manual for reading guidance with seven reading ladders from easy books to the more difficult. Grouped around central problems such as, "Patterns of Family Life," "Community Contrasts," "Differences between Generations." Valuable on every level of reading guidance.

ROSENBLATT, LOUISE M.: "Literature: the Reader's Role," *English Journal,* Vol. 49 (May, 1960), pp. 304–10, 315

"Through literature, the business of self-discovery and self-organization can go hand-in-hand with imaginative participation in the cumulative experience, the keenest sensitivities, the highest aspirations of our culture."

Senior Book List, ed. Lois Markey for National Association of Independent Schools, Concord Public Library, Concord, N.H., 1963

An authoritative, up-to-date annotated list compiled for private secondary schools, grades nine through twelve. Yearly selection of ten best adult books.

SHEHAN, LAWRENCE P.: "Course Content for Slow Learners in Ninth Grade," *English Journal,* Vol. 53 (March, 1964), pp. 196–201

Reviews basic elements of usage, grammar, and literature that slow learners can absorb easily.

STEARNS, GERTRUDE B.: *English in the Small High School,* University of Nebraska Press, 1950

Strikingly rich chapters on reading and library resources in the small high school, with carefully prepared lists of books, pp. 238–93.

SWADOS, HARVEY: "The World of Upton Sinclair," *Atlantic,* Vol. 208 (December, 1961), pp. 96ff.

A perceptive and vital analysis of the uses of *The Jungle* in the high school classroom.

21 Finding the Readable Great:
Guidance for
College Entrance

IN 1894 THE UNITED STATES COMMISSIONER OF EDUCATION reported that the average American had finished only four years of elementary school. By 1917, when America entered World War I, the average American soldier had completed eight years of schooling. By World War II, 1941–1945, the typical American soldier was a high school graduate. Now the time is not many decades distant when the average American will have had two years of college training, general or specialized, usually with some emphasis on masterpieces of literature. This state of affairs is already a reality in many communities, notably those of California. From past and present trends we must assume that the proportion of students preparing for college will continue to expand. This means that reading guidance for college requirements will become each year an increasingly vital part in high school education. The influence, moreover, of the great books reading program in thousands of American communities is making it inevitable that high school teachers of English must lay new stress on the books commonly accepted as masterpieces, preparing our young people not as technicians but as broadly read citizens competent to compare the greatness of past civilizations with the genius of creative thought and achievement in our own communities. It stands to reason that America cannot raise its level of vision without a growing cognizance of the great visions and achievements embodied in the literature, art, and science of our predecessors. The greatness of Florence cannot be understood fully even by seeing its masterpieces. One must go to Vasari's *Lives of the Painters* for a touchstone of what a small American city intoxicated by the creative life might achieve in our time. To understand the greatness of Athens, one must go to Thucydides, Plutarch, and Xenophon, just as to understand Concord, one must go to Emerson, Hawthorne, and Thoreau.

Introducing the Readable Great: Samson Agonistes

As high school teachers, we often feel it is impossible to give the kind of reading guidance that our college preparatory students desperately need even to compete with the graduates of the better private schools. I have known only a few high school teachers who can take the time, for example, to meet their students for oral book reports after school. To my mind, until the present teaching load is cut a third to one-half, this is the only way that a genuine reading-guidance program can come into existence. Only after school can we meet our students individually and take them to the library and pick out for each one another great book suited to the reading capacity of his mind. When we have the strength and energy to carry out such a program, we can look forward to our most fruitful and enriching experiences with our students. In meeting students individually after school, we come to know them, to understand their dreams and conflicts, their hopes and frustrations. We have a chance to say, as Jesse Stuart's teacher said to him, "I would just like to be around to see what is coming out of that head of yours."

One of the secrets of successful reading guidance is the knowledge of how to pry open a great author at the most readable point in his formidable array. For instance, we usually think of introducing Milton's poetry with "Lycidas" or "Il Penseroso." These are very difficult poems for college students, much more so for teen-agers, however bright. Moreover, these poems often seem relatively cold, statuesque, and unmoving to the high school boy or girl of our time. To introduce our bright youngsters to Milton, we may say something like this: "Boys and girls, I recommend John Milton as one of the great minds of world literature. When Milton was forty-one years old, England abolished her king and established a republic, as America was to do fourteen decades later. At the same time, she abolished her House of Lords and did away with bishops. Milton was heart and soul for this English republic. He served his republican government as Secretary of Foreign Tongues. But in a few years, when Milton was fifty-one years old and blind, the English people supported a counter-revolution and took back their king. They brought back their bishops; they set up again the House of Lords. Milton had to hide for his life. At night he would hear the roistering cavaliers ride past his house, laughing and drinking and hooting at the Puritans and their serious way of life. Milton felt like an exile from his own land. But he had a strong will. He was still determined to write the three great poems he had dreamed of long ago: one a great epic like that of Homer or Virgil, one a dialogue like the book of Job, and one a play like the great tragedies of the ancient Greeks.

"Milton is generally hard to read, but every great author has at least one easy opening to his mind and art. The opening to Milton's mind is the great play he wrote in his old age. This play is called *Samson Agonistes;* it tells the story of Samson that we all know from the Old Testament. In the first lines of the play we see the blind Samson sitting by the roadside in the sun, and we hear him speak,

> A little onward lend thy guiding hand
> To these dark steps, a little further on.

"In this play Milton tells about Samson working as a slave for the Philistines, turning the great stone that grinds the corn. He tells about Delilah coming to plead with Samson to take her back, and about Samson's old father, Manoah, coming to urge him not to give up hope that he may yet escape to freedom. This play is much shorter and easier to read than anything by Shakespeare. One can read it through in a couple of hours. Unlike other poems by Milton, there is not a single classical reference in *Samson Agonistes.* Moreover, it is the most personal poem that Milton ever wrote, for in some ways Milton was like Samson. Like Samson, Milton was blind. Like Samson, at the end of his life, Milton felt himself imprisoned among his enemies. Then, too, surprisingly enough, Milton felt that, like Samson, he had been betrayed by a woman. This woman was Mary Powell, his first wife, who left him and then returned to him a few years later and bore him four children. Milton took her back, but we cannot believe that he ever forgave her or loved her fully. Milton felt that his need for a wife had tricked him into marriage with a girl unworthy of his great creative dreams. So, when we read *Samson*, we are also reading something about Milton himself. Listen, for example, to these lines about Samson's blindness:

> Why was sight
> To such a tender ball as the eye confin'd
> And not as feeling through all parts diffus'd
> That she might look at will through every pore?

After recommending *Samson* in this manner to the class, we may also encourage our eager students, in chats after school, to read the play and give us their impressions. Perhaps we can find a number of copies of *Samson* so that our bright people can read parts of the play aloud in class. We may ask several of the advanced students to give a panel discussion of their impressions of *Samson*. Still another team might join together to tell the story, inter-weaving it with quotations from memory. If there are enough copies of *Samson*, the whole class can easily read and discuss the play. Once *Samson* is read, the better students may well have a passion for Milton. They will ask us what to read next. What to read next after *Samson?* This is a puzzle. Nothing in all Milton's prose or poetry is as easy as *Samson Agonistes*. But once a student has become enamored of the author, he will find his way, perhaps in the *Areopagitica*, perhaps in the invocation to light in Book III of *Paradise Lost*, or in the whole of Book VIII, which, of all the parts of the epic, is the easiest to read and the most delightful. What *Samson Agonistes* is to all of Milton's poetry, Book VIII is to *Paradise Lost:* a door that swings easily open to one of the most beautiful interiors in world literature.

What Great Novels Are Most Readable?

This means of guiding a student to that work of an author most easily absorbed is one that we may extend to many fields. Of all the types of literature the most easily read is the novel. When we come to Melville, for example, we do not recommend *Moby Dick* as the opening book. It is too long and too symbolic. Instead we recommend *Typee*, a fast moving tale of cannibal life on a South Sea island. Fortunately, to open Mark Twain, we come at once to his masterpiece, *Huckleberry Finn*. Nothing in Mark Twain, except perhaps *Tom Sawyer*, is easier to read than *Huckleberry Finn*. When we turn to Dickens, the easiest novel to most young people, by testimony of long experience, is not *Oliver Twist* or *David Copperfield* but *Great Expectations*. If the student can read anything of Dickens with pleasure, the book for enjoyment is *Great Expectations*, with its remarkably intense images of the graveyard, the criminal Magwitch in chains, and Joe's blacksmith shop in the opening chapters. In Scott, unfortunately for high school students, no book is easy. The bright student who may read *Ivanhoe* at seventeen with utter despair will often re-read it ten years later with a gasp of delight on many pages. Among George Eliot's novels, *Adam Bede* is one of the easiest. Although, of course, *Silas Marner* is much shorter, it cannot compare with *Adam Bede* for intensity of interest to the average college-preparatory junior or senior. Among the great masterpieces of English fiction, most students would have had a taste of *Robinson Crusoe* in high school. But the best of Defoe, for the opening wedge to his mind and art, is *A Journal of the Plague Year*, with its unforgettable images of London life paralyzed by fear and the smell of death. In George Meredith the best choice is *The Ordeal of Richard Feverel*, with its portrayal of father and son and sweetheart painfully real, despite Meredith's poetic style.

When we turn to Thomas Hardy, no book is so easy to dramatize as *The Mayor of Casterbridge*. Of this book we may speak somewhat as follows: "I hold in my hand one of the memorable novels of English literature, some would say the greatest of all. At the beginning of the story, the hero, an almost illiterate young peasant of twenty-one, walks unhappily along a country road with his wife and child. Coming to a country fair, he enters a refreshment tent and begins to drink. After he gets drunk, he offers to sell his wife to the highest bidder. This may sound absurd, but as late as 1800 it is known that the sale of wives was not an uncommon act among poor and ignorant families in remote parts of England. The name of the man who sells his wife is Michael Henchard. The next morning, when he discovers what he has done, he looks everywhere for his wife and child, but in vain. Finally, struck with remorse and horror, he goes into a church and takes a vow that he will not drink again for twenty-one years. Twenty years later Michael Henchard has become the mayor of the rural town of Casterbridge. He is presiding at a dinner in the town hotel. On this very day his wife Susan comes back seeking for him, accompanied by her daughter Elizabeth Jane. Susan cannot approach him at the dinner, but later she sends him a message by her daughter. How will he receive them? You will never forget this book. It will keep you awake all night. It is a haunting story of what Hardy calls 'a vehement gloomy being who has quitted the ways of vulgar men without light to guide him on a better way.' "

Unfortunately, the book of Hardy most often read in high school is *The Return of the Native*, a book depressingly inferior to both *The Mayor of Casterbridge* and *Tess of the D'Urbervilles*. *Jude the Obscure* unfortunately cannot be assigned; it is too difficult and too iconoclastic for high school seniors. But if a student is ready for *Tess*, it may become one of the great reading experiences of his life. When Tess, in her naïveté, believes that Angel Clare will forgive her for having mothered a child out of wedlock, he having fathered such a child himself, Hardy dares to bring to an unforgettable focus a tragedy as real in our day as in his. Few juniors and seniors in high school today are not ready to grapple with this problem. But if we consider only Hardy's characterization of Tess' unique psyche in the setting of the Dorset farm country, his memorable images of the blossoming woods and fields, the book is a choice for which our best students will be grateful.

Among the European novelists, the two most vital in a world view of great books are Tolstoy and Dostoievsky. In preparing students for college, we do well to direct them to *Resurrection* as the most readable of Tolstoy's novels. No other book Tolstoy wrote gives such a clear picture of Czarist Russia or a hero's dilemma as this one. We may say to the class, "In this book, while a young Russian aristocrat is visiting his relatives in the country, he casually seduces a servant girl and goes on his way back to the city. When it becomes known that the girl is going to have a child, she is driven away, still refusing to name the father. Ten years later, while working in a house of prostitution, the girl commits a crime and is brought to trial. On the jury trying her is the aristocrat who had fathered her child. She does not recognize him, but he remembers her, and his conscience works a revolution in his mind. He goes to see her in her prison cell. When he talks over his problem with his high-born friends, they all laugh at him. The woman he wronged is about to be sent to Siberia. What should he do? This is the beginning of one of the great novels of the world."

Often in guiding students to prepare them for college, we know that we may fire their curiosity by letting them hear just a part of the story. In speaking of *Resurrection*, we may wish to read aloud the scene in which the prisoners are led away to Siberia after going to a blacksmith's shop to have chains riveted to their wrists and ankles. *Resurrection* was written after Tolstoy had in effect renounced his art to become a reformer. Yet, try as he might, he could not reject his great art. His characterizations have the shadinsg, the complexities, of unforgettable drama. *Resurrection* is much easier to read than *Anna Karenina* or *War and Peace*. If the student has been interested in *Resurrection*, he will want to go on to Tolstoy's other masterpieces. One of his great works of timeless insight is the little book, *What Is Art?* A brilliant high school senior will find in Tolstoy's synthesis of art and ideas of social reform a touchstone book to which he will return again and again.

The open door to Dostoievsky is *The House of the Dead*. *Brothers Karamazov*, *The Idiot*, and *Crime and Punishment* are all much too difficult to be used as introductions to the art of Russia's greatest novelist. In college, where he belonged to a liberal political club, Dostoievsky and his companions were arrested for discussing reforms of the Czarist regime. After their arrest they were thrown into jail and brought before the firing squad. At the last moment an officer galloped up with a reprieve from the Czar. Dostoievsky and his friends were sentenced to ten years in prison. *The House of the Dead* is the poignant record of these ten years, full of insight and compassion, a readable revelation of the mind of a genius.

Is the Student Ready for the Problems Portrayed?

I realize that the high school teacher must bear in mind many considerations in acting as a guide to the reading of his students. He must ask himself if the student is ready for the problems described in the book he recommends. A student may be highly endowed intellectually but still lack that understanding which would enable him to absorb a book such as *Resurrection* or *The House of the Dead*, without making him feel that all great literature is morbid or depressing. In view of the influences of screen, comic strip, and television to which the young people of today are subjected, it is highly unlikely that the student will be shocked by *Tess*, for instance, or *Madame Bovary*. Nevertheless, many brilliant students have been sheltered from the harsh realities which the greatest literature often portrays. Therefore we must be careful to time each recommendation according to the psychological as well as the intellectual outlook of the student involved. Many years after college a boy who had idealized me in his freshman year reproached me for recommending *Of Human Bondage*. He did so on the assumption that this book made the relationship between Philip Carey and his mistress unusually attractive and appealing. I took his admonition seriously. Although he was indeed naïve as a freshman, his heart could not accept a book that would push him ahead intellectually while inflicting a shock to his moral code. Of course, we cannot always be aware of these complexities in the sensibilities of our students, but each teacher does to some extent realize when he is being idealized by his students. The more a student idealizes his teacher, the more likely he is to identify the teacher's ideas with those of the novelist; hence the teacher bears more than an intellectual responsibility in recommending the great books he knows the student will need for his intellectual growth.

The fiction of French literature is less in demand for college entrance than that of Russia or England. Most students are not yet ready for Flaubert's terrifying inspection of the soul of Madame Bovary. Nor is Flaubert so important a novelist in world literature as Dickens or Dostoievsky. Sooner or later the student will need to read Hugo's *Les Miserables* or Balzac's *Pere Goriot*, although even in college he will find them hard going. If we believe that a title from Zola should be chosen, it probably should be *Germinal* or *The Dram Shop*. But infinitely preferable to these as a readable classic in French literature, although not so great a literary masterpiece, is Rousseau's *Émile*. Few French literary works lose as little in translation as *Émile*. Full of bright, intense images, it is the story of a boy growing up, of his tutor teaching him new things from month to month and year to year. Many of our students who go on to college will become teachers. *Émile* is one of the great masterpieces in education as well as in the history of ideas.

Using the Readable Utopias

Among prose masterpieces many of the most exciting and the most permanent in intellectual value are the utopias. One of the shortest and easiest to read is More's *Utopia*, if one can secure a translation in modern English. This book is especially fascinating if read in connection with Roper's *Life of Thomas More*. Among the many exciting things in More's *Utopia*, the students are most likely to be interested in his treatment of religion. "In Utopia," we may explain, "all religions are allowed. Some citizens worship the moon or other planets. Each person worships according to his own conscience. The search for beauty and art is a daily enterprise after the six-hour workday. The young and the old mingle together and learn from one another."

In some ways the most stimulating of utopias, though not so well written, is Edward Bellamy's *Looking Backward*, which pictures a socialistic American society in the year 2000. Many students find in *Looking Backward* a life-long fascination. It is less important as an outline of socialism than as a searching examination of our present society. "In this book," we may say, "a Bostonian goes to sleep in a subterranean bedroom built especially to keep out city noises. When he awakens, it is in the year 2000. Bit by bit, the hero explores a new America. Each American family is receiving an annual income from the state, an income not in money but in credit cards. Each year he must spend all his income. In Bellamy's utopia each boy and girl has a college education suited to his needs. But he must study until he is twenty-one. This book, written in the form of a novel, is one of the most influential books in American thought. It has been a best seller for half a century. Dozens of utopias have been written to continue its story or to attempt to prove its ideas unsound."

Except for the particularly brilliant student, the *Republic* of Plato is much too difficult to assign. But the story of Socrates' life is fascinating to high school juniors and seniors. The story of his trial we may tell to the class and invite them to read his great speech, the *Apology*, justifying his way of life before the jury of five hundred Athenian citizens. This is one of the great speeches in world literature, about thirty pages in length, and it is thought to transmit fairly accurately what Socrates actually said. We may read a portion of this to the class. Many students will be encouraged to take out several of Plato's dialogues, now available in the Modern Library edition, and read the rest of the *Apology* for themselves. After we have discussed the trial of Socrates, we may tell about his last days in prison and read to the class the last few pages of the *Phaedo*, the story of Socrates' final conversations with his disciples and his drinking of the hemlock, one of the most dramatic and poignant passages in the literature of the West.

Introducing Greek Literature

I have never known a high school or college class that was not interested in the trial and death of Socrates and in the writings of Plato which vividly describe these happenings. These records by Plato of the life and death of Socrates are the best introduction to the riches of Greek genius. Whether or not our students will be encouraged to read the *Symposium*, we may tell them something of the story: how Socrates and a group of his friends decide to spend the night together, talking and drinking. Their subject is a definition of love. Each of the men at the party defines love in a different way. These definitions in themselves are fascinating, especially the one by Aristophanes, who declares that originally the earth was inhabited by creatures made up of two people, their backs fastened together, with four arms, four legs, and two faces. Jove became angry with these people and cut them all in two parts. One half of each creature was a man or a woman with one face, two arms, and two legs. Since that time, according to Aristophanes, the spirits of these creatures have been wandering over the earth, each seeking for his lost mate. Socrates and his friends talk on through the night. In the morning Socrates leaves his friends, the last one of whom falls asleep at sunrise. Socrates goes the gymansium where he spends the day as usual. The *Symposium* is much too difficult and perhaps too bizarre for the average college preparatory student. But for the brilliant student who is eager to grasp the essence of Greek genius, the *Symposium* is one of the easier dialogues for him to cope with.

I have never known any group of high school students who did not respond to Plato's story of the trial of Socrates and his speech to the court of five hundred Athenians, as set down in the *Apology*. "The difficulty, my friends," said Socrates to the court, "is not to avoid death, but to avoid unrighteousness; for that runs faster than death. I am old and move slowly, and the slower runner has overtaken me, and my accusers are keen and quick, and the faster runner, who is unrighteousness, has overtaken them. And now I depart hence condemned by you to suffer the penalty of death. . . . The hour of departure has arrived, and we go our ways—I to die, and you to live. Which is better God only knows." The eloquence of the *Apology* is intensified by the dramatic situation of Socrates speaking to the court as his own attorney. It is said that his pupil, Plato, took down his words, and most scholars believe that the speech of Socrates to the court is an authentic record. Only forty short pages long, it may be easily read and the dramatic situation absorbed and understood by the average student. The dedicated teacher, however, wishing to introduce this peak of Greek literature to his scholars, may wish to tell a part of the story in his own words and read passages from the *Apology*.

Plato's *Phaedo* is a discussion of immortality between Socrates and his disciples, a discussion that took place, according to Plato, in the prison cell where he was to drink the poison hemlock. The *Phaedo* is much too philosophical to be appealing to the average student, but the end of the *Phaedo*, beginning with the passage "Now the hour of sunset was near," has a lifelong impact on the sensitive student, portraying the last hour of one of the world's greatest men, Socrates drinking the hemlock in the midst of his disciples. You and I may read the last two or three passages of this marvelous tract to the class, beginning with the words "Now the hour of sunset was near, for a great deal of time had passed while he was within." When the jailer brings the poison for Socrates to drink, he says to him, "To you, Socrates, whom I know to be the noblest and gentlest and best of all who ever came to this place, I will not impute the angry feeling of other men, who rage and swear at me, when, in obedience to the authorities, I bid them drink the poison." After the jailer has spoken thus to Socrates, he bursts into tears, turns away, and goes out. Socrates then asks for the cup of poison to be brought. The sun still has not set, but Socrates does not wish to postpone his own execution, saying, "I do not think that I should gain anything by drinking the poison a little later . . . saving a life which is already forfeit." Crito signals to the servant, who brings the poison. Then follows the unforgettable description of Socrates actually drinking the hemlock and the gradual steps by which his body becomes stiff and yields to death.

In recommending the riches of Greek intelligence to high school students, I have been constantly amazed at their capacity to read Greek plays. The two plays easiest for them to read are Sophocles' *Oedipus the King* and *Antigone*. A third play that is almost as easy is Euripides' *Medea*. Often even a high school freshman or sophomore is able to read these plays, not of course grasping them fully, but often comprehending their essential meaning with surprising acumen. After all, the plays of Shakespeare which we teach in the freshman and sophomore years of high school are much more difficult in many ways than the dramas of Sophocles and Euripides.

At each step in our discussion of Greek genius we may point out that no people in the history of the world has produced as many creative minds in so short a time as the Greeks. They produced sculptors whom the world has never excelled. They built temples so beautiful that we imitated the Greeks to build a memorial to our great Abraham Lincoln. They produced two historians, Thucydides and Herodotus, who are models of historical scholarship. Who can forget the story of Herodotus which tells how Darius counted his soldiers by tracing huge circles in the sand and filling each circle with one thousand warriors, repeating the process time after time until the army was counted? Thucydides' *History of the Peloponnesian War* is so accurate that after twenty centuries archeologists have made excavations according to his description of walls and temples. The Greeks also produced the greatest book on public speaking, the *Rhetoric* of Aristotle, a book eminently readable, now available in the Modern Library edition as well as in an excellent translation by Lane Cooper. America has produced no philosopher comparable to Aristotle, no architect equal to the designer of the Parthenon, no sculptors comparable to Phidias and his students. Two books peculiarly useful to the English teacher who wishes to introduce to his students the genius of Greek civilization are *The Greek View of Life*, by G. Lowes Dickinson, and the easily read *Story of Philosophy*, by Will Durant. The usefulness of Durant lies partly in the succinct little biographies of the various philosophers.

The possibilities of guidance, not only for college entrance but also for a lifetime of intellectual growth, are inestimable, though limited, it is true, by the amount of time the high school teacher can devote to conferences. But when conditions are such that the teacher can hear reports after school hours, then take the student to the library to select new books, the best students may develop more fully intellectually in one year than most others in all four years of high school. One teacher I know said this: "My bright freshmen read more books in one year than I read all through college." The more time and energy one feels he can give to reading guidance, the more cumulative the riches he bestows. Each enthusiastic student becomes a reading counselor himself. Time spent here we know will count in full measure. Time spent on grammar or punctuation may or may not achieve the end we hope for. A final benefit of the guidance program is the intellectual stimulation it promises for us teachers. We cannot recommend books unless we know them. We cannot hear reports intelligently unless we have read and enjoyed the books ourselves. My advice is not to recommend any books that one has not read. Let us keep our list small, if necessary, but choice. We may make a collection of the books that have kept us awake at night, if only twenty-five or thirty of them, and keep copies of them on our shelves in the classroom. Often students who are enthusiastic about books will donate copies of them to the classroom library. When great books are actually on the shelves of the classroom, it is possible to take a book down, holding it temptingly in one's hand, and read a few passages. To an eager mind no recommendation is more memorable or dramatic than this; such an invitation to read is often irresistible.

A BRIEF CHECKLIST OF GREAT BOOKS

In the foregoing outline of reading-guidance principles, I have omitted, by necessity, a number of key authors. The following list is, therefore, intended to supplement titles of works mentioned in this chapter. For the sake of convenience in examining these subjects,

I have also included almost all the authors and books previously referred to in this discussion.

I. GREEK LITERATURE

Aeschylus, *Agamemnon*
Aristotle, *Ethics*, Book X (on happiness), *Rhetoric* (on the psychology of the young, the middle-aged, and the old)
Euripides, *Medea*
Plato, *Apology*, last pages of *Phaedo*, last pages of *Symposium*
Sophocles, *Antigone*, *Oedipus the King*

II. RENAISSANCE

Bacon, *Essays*
Milton, *Samson Agonistes*, *Areopagitica*
Montaigne, *Essays* (selections about his education and home life)
More, *Utopia*
Vasari, *Lives of the Painters* (Leonardo da Vinci)
Comenius, *The Great Didactic*

III. ENGLISH NOVELS

Conrad, *Lord Jim*, *Victory*
Defoe, *A Journal of the Plague Year*
Dickens, *Great Expectations*
Eliot, *Adam Bede*
Fielding, *Tom Jones* (early chapters)
Galsworthy, *The Apple Tree*
Hardy, *The Mayor of Casterbridge*, *Tess of the D'Urbervilles*
Huxley, *Brave New World*
Lawrence, *Sons and Lovers*
Llewellyn, *How Green Was My Valley*
Maugham, *Of Human Bondage*
Meredith, *The Ordeal of Richard Feverel*
Moore, *Esther Waters*
Paton, *Cry, the Beloved Country*
Scott, *Ivanhoe*
Thackeray, *Vanity Fair*
Wells, *Tono Bungay*

IV. EUROPEAN NOVELS

Barbusse, *Under Fire*
Dostoievsky, *The House of the Dead*
Hamsun, *Hunger*
Mann, *Buddenbrooks*
Remarque, *All Quiet on the Western Front*

Rolland, *Jean-Christophe*
Rousseau, *Émile*
Tolstoy, *Resurrection*
Werfel, *Forty Days of Musa Dagh*
Zola, *The Dram Shop*

V. AMERICAN NOVELS

Allen, *Anthony Adverse*
Bellamy, *Looking Backward*
Buck, *The Good Earth*
Cather, *My Antonia, O Pioneers*
Dreiser, *Jennie Gerhardt*
Hawthorne, *The Scarlet Letter*
Hemingway, *The Old Man and the Sea*
Lewis, *Arrowsmith*
Melville, *Typee*
Norris, *The Octopus*
Rolvaag, *Giants in the Earth*
Sinclair, *The Jungle*
Steinbeck, *The Grapes of Wrath*
Wharton, *Ethan Frome, House of Mirth*
White, *A Certain Rich Man*
Wilder, *The Bridge of San Luis Rey*

VI. UTOPIAS

Bacon, *Essays, New Atlantis*
Bellamy, *Looking Backward*
Comenius, *The Great Didactic*
More, *Utopia*
Morris, *News from Nowhere*
Plato, *Republic*, Book III (on the education of young philosophers)

VII. HISTORY, BIOGRAPHY, AND AUTOBIOGRAPHY

Bradford, *Damaged Souls*
Franklin, *Autobiography*
Gandhi, *Autobiography*
Jefferson, *Notes on the State of Virginia*
Lee, *Great Englishmen*
Plutarch, *Lives* (Mark Antony, Caesar, Alexander the Great)
Renan, *Life of Jesus*
Sheean, *Personal History*
Steffens, *Autobiography*
Tolstoy, *What Is Art?*
Van Paassen, *Days of Our Years*

Wells, *Experiment in Autobiography*
Wells, *Outline of History*
Wilde, *De Profundis*

To the Student Teacher: Suggested Activities

1. Ask a high school junior or senior to read with you the first chapters of Tolstoy's *Resurrection*. Then discuss the book with him to see if he finds it readable. Make a written report of your findings to your teacher.
2. Carry out the same experiment with *The Mayor of Casterbridge.*
3. Read Galsworthy's "The Apple Tree." Ask permission of a high school teacher to introduce this story to her class in a way that would make the students want to read it. Ask the teacher to evaluate your presentation. Then present a report of the experience to your professor.
4. Read Milton's *Samson Agonistes* and make a ten-minute oral report on it to your teaching-of-English class. Show why you believe academic juniors or seniors would or would not be interested in reading this masterpiece.
5. Read Thomas More's *Utopia* in modern English. Read also the first chapters of Edward Bellamy's *Looking Backward.* Which of these two utopias would be of greater interest to the academic junior or senior? Write a brief comparison of these two books in terms of readability on the upper high school levels.
6. Ask a ninth- or tenth-year student to read with you Sophocles' *Oedipus the King.* Exchange impressions of this play with your high school friend. Then ask him to come to your teaching-of-English class to give his impressions of the play as a readable great. Could the average college-preparatory student read this play with interest?
7. Perform the experiment described above with Meredith, *The Ordeal of Richard Feverel;* Dickens, *Great Expectations;* or Melville, *Typee.*
8. Memorize a sentence or a short passage from Plato's *Apology, Phaedo,* or *Symposium,* and speak it to the class. Or read the remarkable passage in the *Republic* (III, 415; use Jowett's translation in the Modern Library edition) beginning, "Citizens, we shall say to them in our tale, you are brothers, yet God has framed you differently. Some of you have the power to command, and in the composition of these he has mingled gold, wherefore also they have the greatest honour; others he has made of silver, to be auxiliaries; others again to be husbandmen and craftsmen he has composed of brass and iron; and the species will generally be preserved in the children. But as we are all of the same original stock, a golden parent will sometimes have a silver son, or a silver parent a golden son." Speak a part of this or another passage from memory. What is the significance of this passage for us today? Is it valid in a democratic society?

SUGGESTED READINGS

BILLINGS, JANE K., and PAULSON, JOAN A.: "Honors Reading Program in a Senior High School," *English Journal*, Vol. 54 (May, 1965), pp. 425–28

> How one English department initiated a successful honors reading program, which the authors speak of as "the most personally rewarding experience we have had in the field of education."

BLAIR, GLENN MYERS: "The One Hundred Books Most Enjoyed by Retarded Readers in Senior High Schools, *English Journal*, Vol. 30 (January, 1941), pp. 42–47

> This still valuable list contains a surprising number of reputable novels, among them *Lorna Doone, Robinson Crusoe, Tom Sawyer, The Jungle Book, Alice Adams, Call of the Wild.*

BUNYAN, JOHN: *Grace Abounding to the Chief of Sinners*, Everyman Library, 1963, edited by G. B. Harrison

> Bunyan's spiritual autobiography in unforgettable images.

BURTON, DWIGHT L.: "Teaching *The Secret Sharer* to High School Students," *English Journal*, Vol. 47 (May, 1958), pp. 263–66

> Perceptive analysis of the values in Conrad for high school seniors.

"But What Are We Articulating With?" *English Journal*, Vol. 51 (March, 1962), pp. 167–79

> The NCTE committee reports on the freshman English offerings in ninety-five colleges and universities. A valuable, realistic article.

CAULEY, THOMAS: "Learning to Understand the 'Other Fellow' Better," *English Journal*, Vol. 43 (May, 1954), pp. 249–52

> What would you have done in his place, with his problem? Mr. Cauley's students searched through novels and stories of merit with this question in mind, and others such as, "How does it feel to be a member of a broken family?" "How does a person get over the deep hurt of losing a friend?"

English For the Academically Talented Student in the Secondary School, ed. Arno Jewett, NCTE and the National Education Association Project on the Academically Talented Student, 1960

ESTES, HELEN J.: "College Level English in High School," *English Journal*, Vol. 48 (September, 1959), pp. 332–34

> Miss Estes outlines a concrete and workable plan whereby students in her high school and others have earned college credit or advanced placement under the University of Connecticut's Cooperative Program for Superior Students.

FREDERIKSEN, MILDRED: "Honors Enrichment in the Eleventh Grade," *English Journal*, Vol. 50 (December, 1961), 620–23

> Themes illuminated by comparative study of *Moby Dick, The Scarlet Letter, The Crucible*, the life and works of Gandhi, and Tolstoy's *My Religion*.

HACKL, LLOYD: "Honor and Fame: A Tenth Grade Unit," *English Journal*, Vol. 52 (November, 1963), pp. 628–29

An illuminating analysis of the experiment with the theme of honor and fame in masterpieces from *Samson Agonistes*, through *Lord Jim* to Spender and Frost.

HARRISON, G. B.: "The Teaching of Shakespeare," *English Journal*, Vol. 52 (September, 1963), pp. 411–19

Pertinent and helpful analysis of *Julius Caesar*. As Harrison writes, "No other author wears so well or lasts so long."

HAVIGHURST, ROBERT J., with EUGENE STIVERS and ROBERT F. DEHANN: *A Survey of the Education of Gifted Children*. University of Chicago Press, 1955.

Concrete and representative statements about community programs for gifted children.

HUNT, KELLOGG W.: "*Lord Jim* and *The Return of the Native*: A Contrast," *English Journal*, Vol. 49 (October, 1960), pp. 447–56

"The great difference in the effectiveness of the two novels lies in the degree to which one subject, one theme, interpenetrates all aspects, all the interrelated technical components, of the work. The moral and psychological theme of *Lord Jim* interpenetrates all its components."

JOHNSON, FRANCES: "A Unifying Theme for the Year," *English Journal*, Vol. 52 (February, 1963), pp. 97–101

"Each period has its peculiar image of man," as indeed does each student and each author. In this exciting article the author shows how she related both the writing and the reading of her senior classes to this single theme.

MARCUS, FRED H.: "*The Scarlet Letter*: the Power of Ambiguity," *English Journal*, Vol. 51 (October, 1962), pp. 449–58

An illuminating analysis of central problems in Hawthorne's great novel, with many practical applications to classroom teaching.

MORICONI, RALPH JOHN: "Eleventh Grade Honors Program," *English Journal*, Vol. 51 (March, 1961), pp. 193–95

A refreshing emphasis on themes as opposed to types of literature. Sample themes: Man inside his shell, right intention, the road not taken, man versus ignorance, man versus misfortune, serenity, conformity.

O'NEAL, ROBERT: "World Literature in High School: Lusty Orphan," *English Journal*, Vol. 52 (February, 1963), pp. 94–96

O'Neal shows that the advent of paperbacks has given a new impetus and validity to the reading of world classics, of which he lists twenty-five favorites, chosen by teachers of some 167 schools. A suggested single image theme: what image of man does the masterpiece present to the reader?

Reading Guidance for the Gifted, Proceedings of the 1960 Library Institute, directed and edited by Lillian L. Batchelor, School of Library Science, Immaculate Heart College, Los Angeles

Reading Ladders for Human Relations, ed. Muriel Crosby, American Council on Education, Washington, D.C., 1963

Reading List for College-Bound High School Students, Wisconsin Council of Teachers of English, 3700 N. 75th Street, Milwaukee 16

ROBINSON, R. D.: "The Odyssey: Style and Structure," *English Journal*, Vol. 54 (November, 1965), pp. 694–97

> The importance of *The Odyssey*, its style and structure, for the present-day classroom.

The Search for Talent, College Entrance Examination Board, New York, 1960. Copies may be ordered from the Board, Princeton, New Jersey, or Box 27896, Los Angeles 27, California.

> This book contains invaluable articles on the definition of talent, problems of disadvantaged students (Kenneth B. Clark), ways in which loss of talent occurs, means of talent identification in foreign countries, and ways to break down barriers to the development of talent.

WERTENBAKER, THOMAS J.: "A Surfeit of Surveys," *English Journal*, Vol. 52 (January, 1963), pp. 9–15

> The author shows that the use of dominant themes is not inconsistent with chronological presentation of literature. The two approaches used together provide "a compelling structure for what must else seem a hopelessly amorphous mass of writing."

WILLEY, WILBUR: "A Thematic Approach to the Teaching of English," *English Journal*, Vol. 51 (December, 1962), pp. 643–45

> Refreshing use of the readable great in analysis of vital themes.

Writers and Their Work. A descriptive leaflet giving titles of over 160 titles of pamphlets about British authors. Each pamphlet is a valuable introduction to the life and works of the author, with scholarly bibliographies. Write to British Book Centre, 122 East 55 Street, New York 22, for leaflet containing titles of all pamphlets available.

WRIGHT, LOUIS B.: "Shakespeare for Everyman," *English Journal*, Vol. 53 (April, 1964), pp. 229–39

> An incisive review of the resources of special appeal which Shakespeare has for the average person.

22   Book Reports That Stretch the Mind

A BOOK REPORT that does not inspire other boys and girls to read is like an electric current that on a long street lights only one lamp out of thirty. The ideal book report is one that stretches not only the mind of the reader but also arouses the eager curiosity of the class. Hence, impractical though it may sometimes be, we need to have many book reports given in short talks to the class. This does not preclude, of course, a written report from which the student may extract ideas and images for a short talk, avoiding of course, the exact language of his paper.

The Exploratory Book Report

The first book report of the year may be assigned somewhat like this: "Boys and girls, we have an official book list, and we are going to have book reports. But I have not read all the books on this list; I can hear reports intelligently only on those books that I have read. For our first report, then, I ask you to choose from among the books I have listed in the mimeographed sheet I just passed around. The first book report may sound peculiar to you. I do not ask you to read the whole book or even a certain number of pages. What I do ask is that you read until you come across a *scene*, a dramatic situation which you think would make this class eager to read the book. Then I should like you to tell the story of that *one scene* to the class. The idea is to make that one scene very real by building it up with word pictures — sights, sounds, movements, and colors.

"Let me illustrate what I mean by giving you a report about a book I like. Will some one please time me? I shall take only two minutes for this report, and I should like each person in the class to complete his report in two minutes, too. Are you ready? Then I shall begin:

A MOMENT FROM *LORD JIM*

"In *Lord Jim*, by Joseph Conrad, the hero is an idealistic young Englishman working as first mate on a ship crossing the Indian Ocean. It is a dark summer night. On board the ship a thousand Mohammedan pilgrims are sleeping on the decks. Suddenly the crew faces an emergency: they find that rust from one of the great steel bulkheads is breaking off in great flakes. The ship appears to be sinking. Knowing that the lifeboats will not hold the thousand pilgrims, the crew, including the captain, decides to desert the ship. Jim stands at the rail of the boat as the sailors and their officers lower the boats and pull away in the darkness. Whatever other men may do, Jim knows his duty well. He has decided without hesitation, almost without reflection, to stay with the ship. Then from the dark sea below, one of the crew in the lifeboat calls up to him. A moment afterward something happens to Jim that he never expected. He leaps over the rail, plunges down into the sea, swims toward the lifeboat, and joins the crew. This is a critical and ineffaceable moment in Jim's life. Everything that happens to him afterward goes back somehow to this one moment of cowardice for which he bitterly reproaches himself."

This kind of exploratory book report is an appropriate and constructive opener in our home-reading program. Usually the student needs to read only a few chapters in order to find a moment that will interest the class. If he finds the book not to his liking after that, he is not bound to continue in order to fulfill our requirement. If he likes the book, he reads on from curiosity, which is the strongest and most fruitful of all motivations, the force indeed that we hope will keep him reading all his life. Another reason such a first report is desirable lies in the concentration on a single episode. Only through such limitation of topic can a report of two minutes embody dramatic force and vividness. With a very strict timekeeper, we can perhaps get around the class in two or three meetings, allowing some time for discussion and comments of our own. Still another benefit of this approach is that almost at once we see how many students really like the books we especially want them to read and recommend to each other. Moreover, with as many as fifteen or twenty books sampled and savored, the class has a chance to become curious about some of the books we hope they will read during the semester. Furthermore, if we wish a written report at this juncture, the student is better prepared after hearing some thirty talks to write the story of one moment and give his comments upon it. What did he learn from this moment? This is something he does not have time to put into his speech, but in a separate paragraph of his theme he can explain why this moment is significant to him.

A series of such oral reports, when vividly presented (and the description of a moment is likely to be more dramatic than any other impression), is likely to whet the curiosity of many other readers in the class. An eager curiosity about a book is the stimulant we seek most persistently; when it stems from another student's enthusiasm, it is the most powerful catalytic agent in the whole field of reading guidance. Several moments from the same book make it more exciting, not less. In two or three periods of such reports, a group of fifteen or twenty recommended novels may set the tone and create the motivation for a semester's reading. That is why our own preliminary recommendations, based on the novels we have actually read, must be made with consideration for both reading enjoyment and literary worth. When enjoyment and worth conflict, we yield to enjoyment because we must take our students at the level we find them and push them forward; our aim is to recommend the most readable books with genuine literary merit, providing for both the weak and the strong readers of our class.

Another type of exploratory report, requiring an evaluation of some episode or passage of searching personal relevance, may be presented in such terms as these: "In your next book report, I should like you to select a book that you believe from our discussions will have some parallel patterns or opposite patterns to your own life. Unless a book reminds you of something in your own thoughts or your own experience, it is not likely to be worth reading. A family novel like *How Green Was My Valley* or *Look Homeward, Angel* has episodes, sad or comical, trivial or critical, that remind you of your own family in some way. Perhaps you have had the experience, as I had in grade school and in high school, of selling papers in your home town. In selling papers, a boy learns to watch a customer's face. Is the man going to buy, or not? If he does buy, will he have the right change? If not, will he say, 'Keep the change'? In his novel called *Tar*, Sherwood Anderson tells about a man to whom he sold papers in a little town in Ohio. He would take the paper from Tar and then say, 'I'll pay you tomorrow.' The next day the same thing would happen. About this time Tar came across this same man in the cemetery, weeping at his wife's grave. After that he had a very different idea of the man. This episode reminded me not of any such sad episode or contradictory personality, but simply of the habit I got into as a boy of watching the man's face to see if he was going to buy. In a similar way, almost any good book you read will at some point remind you of a moment in your own experience. Did you ever have a teacher who treated you unfairly? Did you ever have a fight with a friend? Did you fall in love in the third grade, the fourth grade, the sixth or seventh? Read on in your chosen book until you find a sentence that reminds you of something in your own life. Copy down this sentence. When you come to make your report, read this sentence to the class and tell something about the situation in the book in which it is spoken or used. Find more than one sentence if you can. But when you come to give your report, use only one sentence. Then describe the moment in your life that this sentence reminds you of."

This kind of book analysis has several striking advantages for class morale and stimulation of reading curiosity. From the student's point of view, it permits exploration without great expenditure of time. If he is interested, he will come back to the book compelled by his curiosity, not by our stern requirement. In class, moreover, he may hear several other students speak about this book in a way to whet his interest and make him see how little he has probed the marrow of the story. If three or four or even more people report on the same book in class, his interest may rise sharply with each new perspective. In this kind of report no two people are likely to choose the same passage. To be given at all, the report must be honest and searching and based on some actual reading analysis. First the student reads the sentence to the class; then he explains the circumstances that lead up to it. Finally, he describes a moment from his own experience that this sentence reminds him of.

The First Written Report

After a number of two-minute reports on well-liked books, we may ask each student to make a written report based on one passage only. We may explain the assignment thus: "On your paper copy the passage from the story at the top of the page. Put quotation marks around it and the name of the book underlined beneath the passage. Then leave a whole line of space and start a new paragraph. This paragraph contains your story of a moment in your life that this sentence in the book reminds you of. In your passage about yourself, tell when and where the experience took place, the name of the town and the month of the year. You can make your story even more readable by telling the name of the street and the time of day. As you describe the experience, use sound words and color words. Build up the scene as the writer of your book would do." The decisive advantage of this kind of written report is that each impression is highly individual and each passage is a unique choice. It is hard to write a "phony" book report for this assignment. Moreover, the students themselves like such reports. They like to write about themselves in relation to episodes or ideas from good books.

One benefit we are seeking in this kind of reading and discussion is a close identification of the student with an idea, a character, or an episode in the story. This approach to a good book may be adapted to the weakest as easily as to the most brilliant student in the class. We do not seek to make detached literary critics out of our students, but rather to find those stories in which they may act and feel and think with the hero or heroine. The more often they can do this in a novel, the more profound and moving the reading experience.

Still another benefit from such a series of brief oral and written reports, the centers of which are autobiographical parallels, is the easy way by which the students become partly acquainted with one another's backgrounds. Such exploratory reports we assign at the beginning of the year or semester, when we are getting acquainted with our students and they with each other. We want them to feel friendly to one another so that each becomes a respected teacher of every other pupil, bringing a "sum of illumination," in Milton's phrase, unique among his fellows. A report in which the student tells something about his own experience as related to an idea or an image in the book provides a natural and easy access to the speaker's values and childhood patterns.

Credit for Length and Quality

When we assign a report on a whole book, we cannot expect our students to be mature enough to select the best books, not the shortest ones. In the ninth grade it is very natural even for the best students, who are very busy people, to choose *A Dog of Flanders* rather than *Jane Eyre* or *Great Expectations.* To equalize the time factor as much as possible, we may give points to each of our books and estimate fifty points for a semester's reading. For *A Dog of Flanders* we might suggest seven points, for *Jane Eyre* twelve or fourteen, for *The Little Shepherd* the same number, for *Great Expectations* sixteen, based on relative length and difficulty. When reports on completed books are given orally, we may say, "I can see you had a grand time with *Great Expectations* and read it very thoroughly. I think it should be twenty points instead of sixteen." Or: "That report on *Jane Eyre* was weak. I'd count it about eight points. Do you want to read those middle chapters again, or go on to another book?" If the student has not enjoyed the book, he will ordinarily much prefer to make a fresh start with a new book. The use of a flexible point evaluation makes it possible to give high points to those books we are eager to have read. We may, for example, choose to rate *Mill on the Floss* or *Death Comes for the Archbishop* or *Lord Jim* as sixteen or eighteen points in the senior year if we want our best students to read them for college preparation, always of course, with the understanding that the point evaluation depends on the quality of the report.

The After-School Conference

For reports on completed books, nothing avails so much for teaching effectiveness as conversation at our desk after school. Such reports may take as much or as little time as we wish, depending upon the day's demands on our time and energy. When a number of students appear, and we wish to concentrate on the few who have shown up for the first time, we may ask a single question of second or third comers, such as (of *The Little Shepherd*) "What finally happened to Rebel Jake and Yankee Jerry?" To ask such a question, we must have the book fresh in mind. If the student answers promptly, that is enough for us, and the report has taken only a couple of minutes. He may leave for the day or wait awhile for us to go with him and several classmastes to the library for new books. When we hear a vague answer to a specific question in a report, we ask a few more questions. Failure to answer correctly or answering too generally may derive from a lapse of memory or a lapse of reading. Only a few try to bluff us in a face-to-face chat, especially when they know that we have assigned them only the books we have read ourselves. After each student has made a report or two, we know which students read thoroughly, and which ones, if any, will try to bluff with only a half reading dictated by boredom or the pressure of time. These private chats about books have several solid advantages. One is that the student does not ordinarily show up unless he has actually read the book. Another advantage is that we see from the reports how the student reads, what he skips, what scenes fascinate him, and how thoroughly he remembers. We may ask him questions on any level, factual or philosophical, social or personal. Still another advantage is that we thus discover the student's reading preferences and are able to recommend other good books that he will like. If he is willing to wait, we go with him and several classmates to the library to help them choose other novels. Finally, at these moments we have a chance to give each student a little attention in private; we may take the opportunity to ask him about a school problem or a difficulty at home. If he finds us receptive and sympathetic, he may have the courage to ask us about a new problem that nags at his psyche every day. If fact, coming for the book report may be the chance he has made to have a chat with us. For these reasons the brief after-school conference has more integrity and richer rewards for teacher and student than any other kind of report. In these times we have our best opportunities not only for reading guidance, but also for those moments of jollity and companionship and private understanding that do more than a thousand class admonitions to build a morale of deep educational meaning.

The Group Report: Panel Discussions

To hear book reports for an hour after school several nights a week, however far-reaching and satisfying the intrinsic rewards, may require a prohibitive expenditure of time and energy. But in my experience it is the only way to be completely certain that our students read the books; it is the only sure way of giving a little individual attention to every student. However, if the cost in energy seems prohibitive, then we have other ways than those already described of capturing the curiosity of the class. Several of our best juniors or seniors, for example, may enjoy reading a single provocative book such as *Looking Backward*, by Edward Bellamy, or *The Geography of Hunger*, by Josué de Castro, and reporting on it cooperatively in the form of a panel discussion. A panel discussion of this kind may be intensely exciting, especially when the group has planned the panel with the aim in mind of persuading everyone in the class to read the book: one member may begin by telling how *Looking Backward* opens in the year 2000; another may speak on the industrial army, one on the equal division of national income, another on the justification of everyone attending college, still others on the position of woman and the attitude toward crime in Bellamy's utopia. The panel's experience in planning the discussion is in itself a memorable one, and few books are better preparation for college than *Looking Backward*. Other seminal books that might be used for such a cooperative report are *The Mayor of Casterbridge*, *Lord Jim*, *Look Homeward, Angel*. The group may choose to relate such a book as *Look Homeward, Angel* to family problems of today's youth, of their own, combining with their discussion such relevant novels as *A Tree Grows in Brooklyn* and *East of Eden*. A panel on *The Geography of Hunger* would direct the class' attention to the primary social dilemma of feeding the world's increasing population. The decisive advantage of the cooperative report is the intense education deriving from the preparation by superior students and the sharpening of class curiosity not only about the books discussed but also the issues involved.

*   *   *

A few inspired teachers can make reading an irresistible pursuit.

They may bring six or eight books into class every week or so, read a passage from each one, hold it up tantalizingly, describe another of its moments with an eager, expectant air, until several hands go up and one boy or girl comes forward for the prize. This is an ideal classroom excitement. Most teachers, however, must rely upon a mixture of coercion and inspiration, especially those who look upon the weakest third of the class as redeemable citizens still plastic and teachable, even when a little unwilling to read and write and think through the problems of the citizen. In reading guidance especially, we need a variety of resources in technique and approach. But the imaginative teacher will prepare herself thoroughly in novels easily read by the weak third and novels she knows the gifted ones will need; she will possess that contagious enthusiasm for books which is the soul of reading guidance. If she also loves youngsters and wants to see them grow, she will add to the suggestions of this chapter effective devices of her own for the stretching of minds and hearts in book-report hours.

To the Student Teacher: Suggested Activities

1. Make an oral book report to the class in which you describe a moment in the story that to you was memorable and dramatic.
2. Make a book report to the class in which you merely give an outline of a moment in the book or read a passage from the book, and then go on to describe a moment from your own experience which this passage in the story reminds you of.
3. Join with several of your friends in the teaching-of-English class to have a panel discussion of an important book, such as *Looking Backward*, by Edward Bellamy, *Look Homeward, Angel*, by Thomas Wolfe, *The Geography of Hunger*, by Josué de Castro, or *The Grapes of Wrath*, by John Steinbeck. Each panel should have a leader who calls the group together and works out the panel program.
4. Bring to class a single passage from a book you have not yet read fully but have always wanted to read. Read this passage to the class and explain why you selected it.

Suggested Readings

Books for the Teen Age, The New York Public Library, 1962
   A valuable bibliography of titles with interest and appeal in many

departments of life: science, poetry, mathematics, archeology, and sports, as well as fiction.

BOSSONE, RICHARD M.: "The Book-of-the-Week Club," *English Journal*, Vol. 42 (April, 1953), pp. 205–07

How a seventh-grade class organized small groups for informal discussions and panel discussions of particular books. A clear guide to discussion techniques.

BROCHICK, ANNA: "Improving Oral Reports," *English Journal*, Vol. 42 (May, 1953), pp. 262–64

Hints on how to make oral book reports lively and appealing.

CAMPBELL, JEAN L.: "The Use of Quotations in Language Arts Classes," *English Journal*, Vol. 49 (December, 1960), pp. 638–39

"Quotations are stepping-stones to recommending books, stories, and articles written by or about the people whose words are quoted."

COFFIN, GREGORY: "Improving Book Reviews," *English Journal*, Vol. 42 (December, 1953), pp. 510–11

Practical and explicit form for written book reviews, setting up admirable critical standards. Suggestive pupil model.

English for the Academically Talented, ed. Arno Jewett, NCTE, 1960

Rich in ideas for enriching the reading and writing of superior minds. Emphasis on great books related by themes, such as the nature of evil, the sacrifices great men have made, the role of conscience in great decisions. Compare Aeschylus' *Agammemnon* with O'Neill's *Mourning Becomes Electra*.

FORD, NICK AARON: "What High School Students Say about Good Books," *English Journal*, Vol. 50 (November, 1961), pp. 539–45

Revealing quotations from student papers submitted for NCTE awards. A Kentucky student wrote that literature is "an outcry from one spirit to another." Literature is "a path of escape," but it "supplies courage and wisdom to face adversities."

GOLDSTONE, HERBERT: "*Wuthering Heights* Revisited," *English Journal*, Vol. 48 (April, 1959), pp. 175–85

"The world of *Wuthering Heights* is far from being strange — unless to love intensely and completely is strange. In its intensity and completeness the world of the book has, as already suggested, much in common with that of tragedy."

Good Reading, Mentor Book, New American Library, New York, 1964

Ideal for stimulation of student reading and discussion of good books.

GOWAN, JOHN C.: "The Underachieving Gifted Child, A Problem for Everyone," *Journal of Exceptional Children*, XXI (April, 1955), pp. 247–49

HOLBROOK, DAVID: *English for Maturity*, Cambridge University Press, 1961

A book rich in ideas and resources by a master secondary school teacher of English. The chapter titled "The Very Culture of the Feelings" lies at the heart of Mr. Holbrook's philosophy. His chapter, "Poetry in the Classroom," is also excellent. There are few hints on ways and means of helping the child to write about himself, however. The great heritage of autobiographical writing, which the student may emulate with lifelong profit, is neglected.

JOHNSON, FRANCES: "A Unifying Theme for the Year," *English Journal*, Vol. 52 (February, 1963), pp. 97–101

"Each period has its peculiar image of man," as indeed does each student and each author. In this exciting article the author shows how she related both the writing and the reading of her senior classes to this single theme.

Language Arts for Superior and Gifted Students, Grades 1–12. Curriculum guide in English mimeographed. Send to Mr. G. Alfred Helwig, Baltimore County Schools, Aigburth Manor, Towson 4, Maryland.

"Library," article from the *World Book Encyclopedia*. Send for copy to Field Enterprises Educational Corp., Merchandise Mart Plaza, Chicago 54, Illinois

Reading Ladders for Human Relations, American Council on Education, Washington, D.C., 1964

Invaluable manual for reading guidance with seven reading ladders from easy books to the more difficult. Grouped around central problems such as, "Patterns of Family Life," "Community Contrasts," "Differences between Generations." Valuable on every level of reading guidance.

ROSENBLATT, LOUISE: *Literature as Exploration*, Appleton Century, 1938

The most fruitful and suggestive book known to the present author for showing ways and means of self-understanding through imaginative selection of readings from literature.

SCHWARZ-BART, ANDRE: *The Last of the Just*, Atheneum, 1961

The story of Jewish suffering and idealism which begins with a pogrom in the twelfth century and ends with the experiences of the hero in the French resistance. A great work of art, unforgettable in its vividness, a story that "uncovers the grieving thread in your soul."

23 Practical Semantics:
Social Ideas under Glass

How CAN ONE train high school students in the elementary principles of semantics? This is the question many teachers without formal training in semantics would like to have answered. This chapter is an attempt to meet that need. The basic meaning of the word *semantics*, which the dictionary defines as "the science of meanings, as contrasted to the science of sounds," is applied daily in every English classroom. Every time we look up a word or attempt to define one in class, we engage in a semantic search. The more ways we understand of pinning down meanings, the more fully we have mastered semantics, at least in the elementary meaning of the word I have quoted above. One of the teacher's problems, then, is to learn how to define words by various methods: by the logical definition, by use of a single synonym, by description, by illustration and comparison, by use of a homonym and contrasting meaning. If these ways of pinning down a meaning sound abstract and difficult, it is not because they are complicated. We can easily train ourselves and our students in some of the basic principles of the science of meanings.

DEFINITIONS: HEART OF SEMANTIC SEARCH

Primary Tool: The Logical Definition

We turn, first, then, to the logical definition in a single sentence, the most elementary tool in the science of meanings. A logical definition is a short concise equation in the form of a statement, like this: "A pencil is a slender cylinder or strip of black lead, usually encased in wood, for writing or drawing." Such a logical definition has four parts: (1) the name of the term to be defined: *pencil*, (2) the sign of the equation: the word *is*, (3) the general classification, or "genus": *strip of lead*, (4) the specific classification, called the "differentia": *usually encased in wood, for writing or drawing*. For convenience, the four parts of a definition may be placed in a chart:

Name	Sign	General Classification	Specific Classification
A table	is	an article of furniture	consisting of a smooth, flat board fixed on legs
Badminton	is	a game	similar to tennis, played with shuttlecocks
Healthy	is	an adjective	that means *robust, hale*, or *free from illness*

The logical definition is an indispensable tool for the student in each one of his subjects; teachers in other fields will be grateful to us if we can help eliminate such definitions as "Polio is when . . . ," "The Gulf Stream is where . . . ," etc. We are justified in reviewing the logical definition each year and using it to pin down the meaning of as many words as possible, if only to fix it anew in the pupil's mind as a primary resource of semantics.

Another semantic tool is the expansion of a logical definition into a paragraph, with the original definition used as the topic sentence. The paragraph may often be developed by description, by use of statistics or details, by illustration, by comparison and contrast, perhaps also by a combination of these methods. Here is an expanded definition developed by description:

THE TEST TUBE

The test tube is a hollow, thin-walled glass container, used mainly in chemical experiments, cylindrical in shape and sealed at one end. The length of a test tube varies from four inches to ten inches. The diameter of the cylinder, which also varies, is usually dependent upon the length of the tube. As the length increases, the diameter increases. For example, a tube 75 mm. long will have a diameter of about 10 mm., and a tube 100 mm. long would have a cylindrical diameter of 13 mm. The sealed end is rounded. Furthermore, the open end is turned out and flattened in order to allow for a more efficient pouring of a liquid contained in the tube.

Emanuel Schapiro

When assigning the expansion of a logical definition, we may use such terms as *orange, pigeon, glue, California, Chicago, adverb, letter, whale, violet, Memphis, Grand Canyon*. Such words would require a variety of paragraph development. Statistics would be used in describing some places. When we wish expansion by description only, we can say, "Answer such questions about your object as *what shape, what size, what material, what color.* Tell what common object it resembles. Tell what it is used for." Breaking down the elements of an expansion helps the student to make his definition more complete. The more technical the word, the greater the necessity of using comparison to some common object to suggest shape and size.

We have said that the primary purpose of semantics is to pin down meanings. We have begun mainly with concrete words because it is easy to pin down the meanings of such words as *banana, fork, grasshopper, toad, triangle, ruler, scissors.* Concrete words are more fixed in meaning than abstract words. The more concrete a word, such as *grasshopper*, and the less changeable the image it calls up in most people's minds, the less controversial its meaning. On the other hand, the more abstract the word, such as *father* or *love* or *democracy*, and the more changeable and varied the images it calls up in people's minds, the more controversial is its meaning. We teachers should begin, therefore, with definitions of concrete words in order to establish first the skill of stating logical definition, avoiding words of emotional involvement.

Abstractions under Glass

The most vital words are often those abstractions the meanings of which we can never pin down fast and tight. To each boy or girl the words *son, daughter, brother, sister, father, mother* have different meanings from those written or thought by any other person. Nothing is more instructive to a high school boy than to write definitions of the words *son* and *father*. At the beginning of a period, we may say to the class, "If you are a boy, write your definition of the word *son* in one sentence. I do not want the dictionary definition but rather your picture of a son, either what he is or what you would like him to be. If you are a girl, write your definition of the word *daughter*." We may allow ten minutes for the writing of this one definition, the single sentence (or several sentences) to be on theme paper, to be marked and handed back like any other theme. When the themes are complete, we may ask each student to read his or her definition. As one student after another reads or speaks, a heated discussion ensues; there is scarcely a definition of *son* or *daughter* that some one in the class does not challenge. Even more heated is the discussion next day, when we ask each person to write two definitions in the first ten minutes of the class: *father* and *mother*.

Making definitions of these and similar words is one of the most searching (and sometimes painful) learning processes a schoolroom can provide. At the same time, the unique emotional coloring that each student brings from his own experience shows why no two definitions of the word *father* or the word *mother* can ever be quite identical. A student may write, "A father is a man whose wife bears him a child," thus evading the issue of shaping his own definition. Another may say, "A father is a man in the house who seldom talks to his sons." Still another may say, "A father is a man who watches over his son and tries to be there when the son needs him." Whether the definitions set down are evasive, realistic, or idealistic in tone, they reflect the individuality of each student and help the class to rethink their own private definitions. In the search for a science of meanings, this approach to family words shows how each abstraction must bear the unique coloring of the speaker's home life.

Clarifying Social Ideas with Definitions

In helping students to clarify social abstractions, we find again that the definition is the most important intellectual tool. When we come to define such words as *democracy, Americanism, patriotism, citizen,* we strike very emotional differences of opinion. Again we may ask each member of the class to write in a single sentence at the beginning of the class period a definition of *democracy* or *American* or *citizen*. After these statements are written, many students in the class, if not all, may read their definitions for discussion. This exchange of views helps each student to examine and test his own definition.

In defining such a word as *democracy*, each student will give not a dictionary definition but his own individual definition, thereby expressing a particular meaning from among many possible interpretations. For example, one student may say, "Democracy to me is the chance I have had to attend a free public high school." Another student may say, "Democracy to me means freedom of speech in the classroom, on the street, in public meetings." Still another student may say, "My father escaped from Europe after years of fear that a knock on the door might land him in a concentration camp. Democracy to me is freedom from this fear of a knock on the door." These definitions differ in emphasis rather than in essence. In defining any word, such as *democracy* or *Americanism*, each student expects to see the emphasis or slanting in his own definition tested or challenged by other members of the class. This makes for a natural yet disciplined kind of intellectual growth.

Definition in Focus: One Moment

It is often not enough, however, to define one of the great words that symbolizes American freedom. The more generalized the abstraction, as in *freedom, peace,* or *Americanism,* the greater the semantic necessity for an illustration. It is an excellent plan for each student to describe a moment which illustrates his definition. The more complete and explicit such a description of a moment or an experience, the more differentiated becomes the abstraction the student has chosen to define.

SCHOOL-PAPER DILEMMA

Last year we had an amazing thing happen on our school paper, the *Sportsman.* Joe Richards wrote an article criticizing the school policy of forcing everybody to walk single file while changing classes. Neither the principal, Mr. Hooper, nor our sponsor, Miss Evans, wanted us to run this article, which was called, "Lock Step at Bellevue High." I admit the language was pretty harsh, but it expressed what all of us felt, especially the staff, which was unanimous in opinion. Mr. Hooper said, "If you run this article, it will be a slap in the face, not only to the superintendent and me, but also to the school board, which approves of this policy." Miss Evans said, "We are older than you. We can see the effects of this article. You can't." Well, we had a long meeting of the staff at which all these ideas were brought out, with Miss Evans present. We said to Miss Evans: "What will happen if we decide to run it?" At this Miss Evans smiled and said, "Mr. Hooper and I have talked this over. You are citizens in the making, some of you will soon be drafted, and as an experiment we shall let your decision stand." When Miss Evans said that, I realized how much she believed in freedom of speech. The American tradition of free speech and free press suddenly became a reality to me, and I understood Milton's words: "Give me the liberty to know, to utter, to argue freely according to conscience, above all liberties."

Walter Benson

WHEN DEMOCRACY WENT TOO FAR

I was on the *Sportsman* last year along with Walter Benson. That was a great American moment for me, too, when Miss Evans told us we could print the article. No one could have been more fair or democratic than she was. But now I believe she carried democracy too far. We were not old enough or wise enough to make this decision in spite of her advice. Miss Evans knew the principal and superintendent; she knew the men on the school board and the spirit of the community. She knew the reasons why the single file in the hall was required. Unfortunately, our class did not have this background. We could not foresee the practical results of our idealism; we were young Americans acting on a good principle that is not always workable. When my dad heard about our action, he said, "You kids made a mistake. There will be trouble about this. Miss Evans will be on the carpet." Well, my dad was right. Miss Evans was harshly criticized, and this year the newspaper has a new adviser who is required to censor everything severely. So I would say that though it was a great moment for us when Miss Evans allowed us to decide the issue, we seniors have to understand that some of our great principles are still not workable. We have to know when and how far the American dream can work.

Joyce Harvey

On the day our students describe particular moments or situations, the application of the word *democracy* or *Americanism* immediately becomes individualized. This particularizing of the context of an idea is a very necessary step in exact thinking. Only when we have the circumstances described, the context fully known, is it possible to see the exact meaning of the abstraction under glass. The difficulty with a generalized term such as *democracy* or *Americanism*, when it is not resolved in terms of particular moments, is that some members of the class, though using the same word, may be thinking of entirely different applications. Similarly with such a word as *success*. Certainly a definition of the word *success* is a part of everyone's philosophy of life; yet if one asks a class of thirty seniors to describe the word *success*, specifically, "What Success Means to Me," he will receive a number of different generalizations, such as, "Success to me is getting married and raising a family." "Just now success to me is being admitted to the college of my choice." These definitions of *success*, though very different, can be made still more exact if each student, after giving his generalization and discussing it with the class, then describes a moment which symbolizes to him his abstraction.

Often a teacher of juniors or seniors may hear the question, "In defining such a vague word as *democracy* or *citizen* or *success*, isn't it just a question of opinion? Isn't one man's judgment as good as another's?" When this question comes, we have a chance to show that there is always a relative maturity or immaturity in the shaping of definitions. No one would claim that a boy of eight and the same boy at seventeen or eighteen would have the same definition of *success* or *student* or *freedom*. Our aim in shaping and comparing definitions is to develop a more mature outlook than the one of yesterday, last month, or last year. The more time and thought one gives to a definition, whether of *electricity*, *peace*, *creativity*, *fission*, or *magnetism*, the more likely he is to make a more mature definition. In the tenth book of his *Ethics*, Aristotle defines happiness as the art of contemplation over a lifetime, carried on without the necessity of making a living. Though we may not agree with Aristotle, we cannot stamp his definition as hasty or immature. Aristotle said his kind of happiness was superior because creative thought, unlike sensory pleasure, could be almost continuous; moreover, his happiness depended only upon himself, not upon the presence of a friend or loved one. When we compare the great definitions through the centuries, Aristotle's definition possesses a maturity the serious thinker must reckon with. The aim of definition-making is growth, not finality, and shaping a definition brings two kinds of intellectual growth. One kind of growth arises from the comparing of values and ideas; the other kind derives from a comprehension of semantic difficulties in pinning down meanings.

For fruitfulness in semantic search, then, no tool has so many useful functions as the definition. Beginning with the single-sentence definition of the concrete word, we may ask our students to expand their definitions by use of description, illustration, and the use of facts and figures. Coming gradually to abstractions, we show our students how to define them first in single sentences, encouraging each one to set down his *differentiae*, and speaking or reading his definition for discussion with the class. Few discussions prove so conducive to intellectual growth as those dealing with a single abstraction, when each student can speak freely his differences of judgment and emphasis. In our aim to make a definition completely explicit, nothing is so final as the description of a moment in which the full context of the word in question may be so described as to be fully individualized.

Here is a list of significant abstractions we may wish to try with our classes:

father	success	maturity	democracy	love
mother	student	happiness	freedom	hate
daughter	work	creativity	Americanism	peace
son	friend	propaganda	pacifism	war
brother	anger	semantics	poverty	race

Tracing the Origins of Ideas

Semantics as the "science of meanings" has come to have many applications to our study of language other than the shaping of definitions. One application is a search for the origins of our ideas. If a boy had an idea in the seventh grade that "all Italians carry knives," where did the idea come from? What was it in his experience that gave him this impression? In early youth many people have heard and believed the statement that "you always get cheated in a Jewish store." What is the origin of this superstition and a hundred others of its kind which we lap up as easily, says James Harvey Robinson, as a kitten laps milk? For each one of us to examine his ideas and pin down his irrational assumptions one by one is an indispensable element of personal growth and citizenship, whether or not this search has a strict relevance to the science of meanings.

One fruitful assignment is to ask each student to take any idea he once held, not necessarily what we would call a social superstition, and then let him show how it began and how it was changed. Here are sample statements from the tenth-grade level:

Girls can't do arithmetic.
Scotsmen are all stingy.
Negroes are all lazy.
Teachers don't understand.
Redheads have hot tempers.

Novels are all hard to read.
I never could do English.
Policemen are mean to you.
I would always knock on wood.
You can't change human nature.

Here are two student themes to illustrate the result of this assignment:

WHAT PEOPLE SAID

When I was a boy of about eight, one of my playmates said to me, "Didn't you know the Jews killed Christ?" When I asked my mother about this, she said, "No, it isn't true." But I believed the playmate rather than my mother. When I came to know a few Jewish boys, this stayed in the back of my mind. Then I read *The Robe*. I began to see that this idea I had long held was a mistake, a horrible injustice against the Jewish people. The Romans killed Christ; he was too dangerous to their rule to be left alive.

Sherman Dickson

WHAT MY MOTHER SAID

When I was a little girl, my mother, who grew up in Vermont, said very casually, "Southerners are lazy." We were then living in Connecticut. I kept this idea in mind and continued to believe it, even though I had never seen a Southerner. Then when I was in the eighth grade, we moved to South Carolina. It took only a little time in South Carolina for me to see that this idea was just a superstition. Now, when I know so many hard-working South Carolinians, I kid my mother and say, "Well, Mom, do you still think Southerners are lazy?" She just laughs and says, "I certainly did bring you up wrong on that, didn't I?"

Joyce Wendell

Testing Generalizations

Perhaps no intellectual habit is more vital to citizenship than a persistent testing of one's own generalizations. The more practical ways and means we can evolve for teaching this intellectual habit, in English classes from the seventh grade onward, the safer and surer the democratic process. One approach is to ask the class, let us say a ninth-grade class, how each generalization like those below would be challenged, tested, and qualified.

1. Young people today expect jobs to be handed to them on silver platters. (All young people?)
2. No one on relief would work if he had a chance. (Is everyone on relief a chiseler?)
3. Labor union leaders are racketeers. (All of them? A few of them? How many have you known?)
4. The Chinese are a sly people. (How many have you known?)
5. All high school students cheat when they have a chance.
6. Young people today have no respect for their parents.
7. Seventh-graders can't sit still.
8. Southerners are cruel to colored people.
9. Northerners don't understand Negroes.
10. Californians are more friendly than New Englanders.
11. Republicans are all unfair to union labor.
12. Democrats are unfair to employers.

Such generalizations may be chosen and discussed for any grade level. We may ask the boys and girls of the class to contribute for discussion generalizations they make at home or on the playground. Our approach to the problem cannot be completely realistic until each student tests a number of his own generalizations and shows how he would qualify them.

How Would You Prove It?

One effective way of showing the weakness of generalization is to ask a class of juniors or seniors how, given unlimited funds for research and experiment, they would prove or disprove certain assumptions, such as the ones below. Which statements would be the hardest to prove or disprove? Which the easiest?

1. Success in athletics means success in later life.
2. The yellow race is inferior to the white.
3. Negroes did not make good combat soldiers in World War II.
4. Russia has closed all the churches.
5. The Italians are cowardly soldiers.

6. The average miner's life is five years shorter than the average farmer's.
7. Babe Ruth made more home runs in the major leagues than Lou Gehrig.

In the field of medicine or road-building, we usually accept statements only upon the evidence of long experiment and research. But in the field of social ideas, many citizens are still governed by assumptions that have not yet been proved or disproved. How can we overcome this deficiency in social reasoning? This question alone shows the need for exercises and applications of the kinds suggested above.

USING LANGUAGE CONSTRUCTIVELY

Seeking the Constructive Reply

Another application of applied semantics is to the constructive use of language in social situations of everyday. On the ninth-grade level, we may begin by asking the class to give a constructive and destructive reply to each remark in the following situations:

1. "Why did the coach take Harry out?" (A constructive answer might be, "He wants to rest him for the last quarter." A destructive answer: "I'll bet he has a grudge against Harry.")
2. A student asks: "Why did we lose the game?"
3. A father asks his son: "Where are you going?"
4. A customer says to a clerk: "I can't get any service in this store."
5. A young sister says, "Will you do the dishes for me so I can study for my test?"

Handling Epithets

How can one handle epithets? This is another practical problem of every day. The epithet is a dangerous and misleading generalization, compressing a complex, many sided personality into one small pigeonhole. Discuss epithets such as the following in class. What could one say in response to each one?

That referee was a robber!   George is a bookworm.
Mary Ann is a real brain.   Don't be a sap!

He has a yellow streak down his back.
Joe's a tightwad.

Joe's just a drip.
She's a shrinking violet.

The Tone of Voice Tells a Story

We may ask the class to read each sentence below in two tones, one unfriendly, to the listener, the other neutral or friendly.

Will you close that door?
Turn that light out.
Don't come late.
I cannot tell you.

That's my tennis racquet.
Hold still, please.
Step all the way in.
Who recommended this book?

Using the Language Profile

One effective device to help a student analyze his own language behavior is to ask him to make what we call a Language Profile. A Language Profile is simply a record the student keeps of his own spoken words at various moments of the day. The idea is to select words spoken in as many situations and with as many emotional attitudes as possible. This kind of record may be written in ink and handed in as a theme. We may discuss several profiles in class; then we may ask each student to write an analysis of his Language Profile. What does it show about his personality? Has he used language constructively or destructively in the main? What various or contradictory feelings has he expressed? Such an analysis might close with an idea of how he can use language in daily situations more constructively. Here is an example of a Language Profile:

JACK WEBER: A DAY IN SPOKEN SENTENCES

7:00 A.M.	"What time is it, Mom?"
7:15	"Aw, gee, I don't want two eggs!"
8:00	"Hi, Joe! Say, lend me your pen a minute."
8:30	"Sorry I'm a little late, Miss Brunson."
9:00	"Sure I'll go with you to the principal. I saw the whole thing. I'll stick by you."
12:00 P.M.	"The coach looks as if he were up pretty late last night."
2:30	"How about letting me use your bike tonight, Ted? I have to go across town to see a friend, and I hate to ride buses."
2:45	"Don't get tough now, Butch. You were *so* out of bounds."

Using Language to Help Solve Problems

Still another application of practical semantics is the analysis of student problems, with a discussion of the kinds of language activities that might be used to clarify the problems or create good will between two people. Here are three examples of problem moments that might be discussed in class. Still more effective would be discussion of problem moments of their own that members of the class might describe in writing.

THE TEACHER WAS SUSPICIOUS

Fanny and Dolores sat together during an algebra test. Each made the same mistake. The next day, the teacher called Fanny and Dolores to her desk. "You two girls who were sitting together were the only ones in the class to make this mistake," she said. "That looks quite suspicious to me." Dolores had not cheated, and she had not seen Fanny look at her paper. Yet the teacher was suspicious. What action should Dolores have taken?

A STOLEN JERSEY

At the last game of the Varick High football season, George Hood, the regular end, was taken out in the last ten minutes of play. Very angry at the coach, George in desperation stole a jersey that he should have returned to the manager. Later, as he cooled off, he regretted his action. What should he have done?

LATE TO CLASS

Victor, who had a widowed mother, had a job that made him late to his first class two days a week. His teacher, Mr. Brooks, was very stern. Victor didn't want to tell him why he was late. What should he have done?

*   *   *

Among the rich and varied resources for teaching practical semantics in the classroom, we find always that the definition is our primary tool. It is our indispensable tool not only in priority of timing and approach but also in its incitement to intellectual growth. The definition, whether brief or extended, has a multitude of practical applications. Among these applications, its use at the beginning of a period to invite twenty-five or thirty differentiated meanings of one abstraction is of superlative practicality in inducing an exciting discussion. When the applications of semantics shade into analysis of social ideas, we can provide each student with ways of tracking down the questionable assumptions and generalities that have formed an integral part of his thinking. The opportunities for the application of semantics to the field of social ideas are expanding each year. Finally, when we apply semantics to language used in social situations, we can help each student not only to identify the destructive elements of his own conversation day by day but also to see the ways in which he can make language more creative in human relations. No adolescent problem is without its semantic significance or beyond reach of constructive language action. Hence the necessity for an increasing awareness of the conscious and unconscious relations between speech and personality patterns, both in the student's own conversations and in those of the people he talks with daily.

To the Student Teacher: Suggested Activities

1. Choose any four concrete words and write logical definitions of them as illustrated on pp. 330–31.
2. Write a definition of one of these words: *daughter, son, father, mother*. Put your key idea in the opening sentence. Then expand your definition into a paragraph.
3. Write a similar paragraph in which you define the word *democracy, citizen*, or *patriotism*.
4. Write a similar paragraph in which you define the word *maturity, success*, or *creativity*.
5. At the beginning of the hour in your teaching-of-English class, everyone may write a sentence defining the word *happiness*. Then each person in the class may speak briefly, reading his definition and giving reasons for his emphasis.
6. Make a Language Profile of one of your own days, like that shown on pp. 340–41. Then write an analysis of your profile, showing what it reveals about your use of language on this particular day.
7. Read *Living Language 10* (Harcourt, 1954) and *Enjoying English 10* (Singer, 1966) on the use of problem situations like those described on p. 341. Do you believe that discussion of these hypothetical situations in an English class can be constructive? Give reasons for your analysis.
8. Make a list of ten generalizations that you make in your own thoughts or speech (see pp. 336–37). Then rewrite these statements to show how you would qualify them to make them more accurate.

Suggested Readings

BENS, JOHN H.: "The Birth of an Idea," *English Journal*, Vol. 41 (October, 1952), pp. 415–20

This article examines the ideas students hold as necessary for living happily today, the sources from which these ideas come, and how these ideas were "pumped" from their sources into the students' minds.

BILSKY, MANUEL: *Patterns of Argument*, Holt, Rinehart and Winston, 1963

A valuable introduction to elementary rhetorical and semantic principles.

BURTON, DWIGHT L.: "Literature for Social Development," *English Journal*, Vol. 43 (May, 1954), pp. 231–34

Excellent specific suggestions of readable novels of social insight, with emphasis on the problems of American teen-agers.

COTTRELL, BEEKMAN W. and JOSEPHS, LOIS S.: "Love in the Tenth Grade,' *English Journal*, Vol. 52 (September, 1963), pp. 430–33

Analysis of an excellent unit on the theme of love in world literature.

GOMBAR, WILLIAM: "International Interview," *English Journal*, Vol. 38 (March, 1949), pp. 153–54

How foreign students in the classroom were used as an opportunity to break down prejudices and provincialisms.

Intergroup Relations in Teaching Materials, Report of the Committee on the Study of Teaching Material in Intergroup Relations, American Council of Education, 1949

This is an important study of the tensions and problems, with helpful suggestions, of the wide variety of groups that makes up American life today. Invaluable for the teacher.

KILPATRICK, WILLIAM H. and VAN TIL, WILLIAM: *Intercultural Attitudes in the Making*, Harpers, 1947

See Chapter VII, "The High School Teacher." What does "democratic human relationship" mean so far as the teacher and his classroom are concerned?

OPPENHEIM, MAE G.: "Teach It Wrong First," *English Journal*, Vol. 51 (February, 1962), p. 122

Intriguing definition of a précis, with practical procedure for teaching it.

ROSENBLATT, LOUISE M.: *Literature as Exploration*, Appleton-Century-Crofts, 1933

The development of literary appreciation in the study of the classics, with problems of social significance.

RYAN, H. H.: "Social Aims in the English Program," *English Journal*, Vol. 29 (January, 1940), pp. 26–32

The use of "personal relations" in novels to bring home to the students the meaning of social responsibility.

SMITH, DORA V.: "Basic Considerations in Curriculum-making in the Language Arts," *English Journal*, Vol. 37 (March, 1948), pp. 115–26

Critical analysis of the means of communication (radio, television, newspapers) as a way of training students for a more democratic life.

TABA, HILDA: *Reading Ladders for Human Relations*, American Council on Education, 1964

Useful listing of books with brief reviews on problems of human and social relations.

THOMAS, CLEVELAND A.: *Language Power for Youth*, Appleton-Century-Crofts, 1955

An important source book of tested teaching methods in semantic problems. Twenty teachers have collaborated in supplying classroom procedures and exercises.

THOMAS, CLEVELAND A.: "Semantic Concepts for Secondary School English," *English Journal*, Vol. 49 (March, 1960), pp. 186–91

"The ability to interpret the language usage of others is a necessary means of winnowing the truth from the half-truth and the falsehood."

TURNER, MINNIE P.: "Living through Early American Literature," *English Journal*, Vol. 45 (February, 1956), pp. 92–95

A creative project dramatizing historical scenes provided deeper understanding of the basic democratic values expressed in early American political writings.

WATTS, MARJORIE S.: "Intercultural English. An Experiment," *English Journal*, Vol. 34 (February, 1945), pp. 81–87

An account of a successful attempt of a class of high school students to establish cultural and racial tolerance.

WOLFE, DON M., with JOSIE LEWIS and LELA T. HAMILTON, *Enjoying English 9*, Singer, 1966, "How to Build a Definition," pp. 373–74

ZAHNER, LOUIS: "The Teaching of Language," *English Journal*, Vol. 44 (November, 1955), pp. 443–50

An illuminating analysis of practical applications of semantic principles, stressing discrimination between value judgments and statements of fact, degrees of generalization, concrete and abstract words, kinds of questions, etc.

24   Grammar and Linguistics:
A Contrast in Realities

leaders in the National Council deplored the emphasis given to formal grammar throughout the nation. Almost every teacher knew grammar; very few teachers felt the competence or the enthusiasm or the energy to teach writing. The very schedule of English teachers, five or six classes daily, two hundred pupils a week, made writing assignments impossible to cope with. The fault with the teaching of grammar was the failure to apply grammatical knowledge to punctuation and style. Many critics felt, indeed, that no great amount of grammar teaching could be applied to style. Hence the teaching of grammar as such was discouraged. To such an extent as the leaders of the Council held to a party line, it was a hard position against formal grammar; indeed the teaching of any grammar was in the minds of many somewhat suspect. Grammar appealed to a small intellectual part of a student only; it did not take into account his need for letting his deep feelings and thoughts flow into language. When grammar flourished in the classroom, the sympathies of both teacher and students somehow dried up; before such a limited analysis of the power of language the student stood alien and hostile to the teacher's idea of English. The deep and violent emotional life of the high school student found in many if not most English classrooms no link to expressive reality as encouraged by the teacher. The more grammar, the less self-expression; it was grammar that defined the student's attitude toward English, not

From *English Journal*, Vol. 53 (February, 1964), pp. 73–78.

themes which opened the deep streams of his life and let them flow into burning images. Life seldom invaded the classroom; it was a separate compartment of cars and girls and friends and midnight hours.

Nevertheless, many gifted teachers combined expert teaching of grammar with remarkable power to draw forth the student's deep thoughts. They saw that once a grammatical concept was taught, the student should immediately use his own prepositional phrases in a story, his own predicate adjectives to express his moods, his own participles, infinitives, and adverbial clauses. When thus taught, grammatical constructions became personal possessions that found continuing expression from theme to theme. Many teachers assigned grammatical autobiographies to combine mastery of grammatical concepts with self-expression.[1] Meanwhile they assigned themes from week to week which tapped the explosive powers of self-expression about those topics that the *student*, not the teacher, defined as experience with deepest meaning. In such a teacher's classroom learning grammar was not inconsistent with the flow of original thoughts and feelings. To such a teacher the relation between the teaching of grammar and the teaching of writing was not one of mutual hostility and rejection; the student accepted both. Indeed the more personal became his weekly themes, the more grammar took on new and vital significance.

Then came linguistics, or a new zeal for linguistics, an interest in which was fostered by outstanding college professors and leaders within the National Council. To almost every enthusiast for linguistics, traditional grammar had failed to describe the language with those minute and accurate qualifications necessary to scientific analysis. Unlike the traditional grammar, the new science incorporated the sounds of language as well as the function of each element of structure. Instead of eight parts of speech, the linguists followed Fries in defining four parts of speech as Class 1, Class 2, Class 3, and Class 4 words and denominating fifteen to seventeen groups of structure words. In the midst of proliferating linguistic theory, Paul Roberts and others attempted in a series of books to bring linguistics within reach of the average classroom teacher.

[1] See Don M. Wolfe, "A Grammatical Autobiography," *English Journal*, Vol. 49 (January, 1960), pp. 16–21.

Lou La Brant in her exciting series, *Your Language*, adopted and expanded the new linguistic terminology. If the terminology of the old grammar was antiquated and inexact, the terminology of structural linguistics was so extensive and so difficult to define that even those teachers most eager to comprehend the new science found it impossible to adopt in the classroom or teach with any degree of assurance, especially in the midst of a new surge of the writing and usage assignments to college-bound students. When an eager classroom teacher tried to teach linguistics to a class oriented in traditional grammar, he more often than not found the task baffling and fruitless. Indeed he was now taking a dozenfold as much time to teach a new grammar as he had taken to teach the old, meanwhile neglecting his far more important task of assigning college essays and analyses of great books to those students preparing for college. If the old grammar brought lethargy and boredom to the classroom, the new grammar to some teachers brought sickness of spirit and a more colossal waste of precious time than the old grammar had ever mustered. Meanwhile, where was English? What new insight did linguistics bring to an appreciation of style, to the rhetoric of beautiful sentences? Where was the visualization of the incandescent moment from a great book, from the student's life — a moment of fear, hope, happiness, despair, discovery?

II

My own view is that those who believe in structural linguistics for the average classroom must show how the new science can be used to improve both punctuation and style: the same test that they justly believed should be applied to the teaching of grammar. I believe that traditional grammar has a hundred times as great a potential for improving punctuation and style as structural linguistics. I wish to present again some concrete principles by which formal grammar can be used by the average teacher. I am not defending grammar as a wholly economical resource; I am defending it as a resource of limited benefits that no person of professional training can afford to dispense with. Consider the five sentence patterns below and the classroom assignments based on them. Traditional grammar can help the student to understand these patterns. Creative imitation of these sentences can enhance the student's comprehension of grammar while improving his appreciation and command of literary diction.

Pattern 1. *Introductory Prepositional Phrases for Background*

On the pleasant shore of the French Riviera, *about halfway* between Marseilles and the Italian border, stands a large, proud, rose-colored hotel.

> *F. Scott Fitzgerald*, from *Tender Is the Night*

Assignment: Describe a building you know in a sentence constructed like the one above. Begin with a background image in a prepositional phrase naming state or country or town; then, as Fitzgerald does, use another prepositional phrase to identify the place more exactly. Finally, use the verb and subject of the sentence, with the subject at or near the end.

Example: Among the mountains of West Virginia, on a steep road between Elkins and Parsons, stands a lonely, roofless house of gray stone.

Pattern 2. *An Adjective Following the Subject*

A half moon, *dusky-gold*, was sinking behind the black sycamore tree.

> *D. H. Lawrence*, from *Sons and Lovers*

Assignment: Write a sentence like this one in construction and intensity of diction. In your imitation use two color adjectives following the subject, as Lawrence does; also use one other color in your sentence.

Example: A high sail, chalk white, was dipping toward the blue water.

Pattern 3. *A Past Participle Following the Subject*

The lazy October afternoon, *bathed in a soft warmth of a reluctant sun*, held a hint of winter's coming chill.

> *Ruth Firor*

Assignment: Describe an afternoon, a morning, a house, a yard. In your imitation try for personifying words such as *lazy* and *reluctant*.

Example: The raw December air, showered with gusts of swirling snow, swept down the long alley.

Pattern 4. *Two Participles; Two Verbs, a Simile*

Streaming with perspiration, we *swarmed* up the rope, and coming into the blast of cold wind, *gasped like men plunged into icy water*.

> *Joseph Conrad*, from *The Nigger of the Narcissus*

Assignment: Write a sentence with grammatical elements parallel to the one above, opening with a participle as Conrad does, using two verbs as visual and dynamic as *swarmed* and *gasped*. Conclude your sentence with a simile as intense in diction as Conrad's. This is the most challenging assignment thus far.

Example: Shivering with cold, I jumped into bed, and wrapping myself in the warmth of the blanket, drew my head under it like a turtle shrinking back into its shell.

Pattern 5. Adverbial Clause Followed by an Absolute Phrase

Even as she was falling asleep, head bowed over the child, she was still aware of a strange wakeful happiness.

> *Katherine Anne Porter*, from "María Concepción"

Assignment: Opening with an *as* clause, as in the sentence above, use an absolute phrase to give an image of the person, as Katherine Porter does.

Example: As he stood before the class, head tilted toward the window, the sunlight brightened the brown of his freckles and the blue of his eyes.

By analyzing these five patterns and then writing sentences containing for each pattern the same sequence as in the original, the student is required to use grammatical elements in a way that makes them memorable. The principle of creative imitation, a highly neglected art of explosive possibilities, relies here upon a realistic knowledge of grammatical elements. They become memorable to him because they are combined with intense diction. In order to do well, the student must use a verb or an absolute phrase or a participle as electric as the original words. The teachers who have tried this method know that each sentence imitation instantly shows both the good taste and the grammatical knowledge of the pupil at work. Is there any element of structural linguistics that makes such a direct application of theory to style as is found in this application alone of traditional grammar?

The principle applied above to short sentences may be further extended to passages like the one below from Thomas Hardy.

SPHERES OF THISTLEDOWN

And in autumn airy spheres of thistledown floated into the same street, lodged upon the shop fronts, blew into drains; and innumerable tawny and yellow leaves skimmed along the pavement, and stole through people's doorways into their passages with a hesitating scratch on the floor, like the skirts of timid visitors.

Thomas Hardy, from *The Mayor of Casterbridge*

Merely analyzing this passage for its remarkable resources, its use of background, middleground, and foreground images, its use of the blending elements of the spheres of thistledown and the flying leaves, its images of color and sound and touch, its simile at the end: all of this is not enough. The teacher must then ask the class to write a sentence similar step by step in grammatical construction to Thomas Hardy's original. Once a student has used his own diction, his own visualization, in constructing a sentence exactly like Hardy's in grammatical order, he has applied grammar to style in the most realistic way possible:

IN THE WINTER DUSK: IMITATION OF HARDY

And in the winter dusk, long gusts of wind whispered secrets to the windows, wailed under the door, sighed across the carpet to the fire; and delicate purple-white snowflakes danced around the treetops, pitted the roof, and trickled down the cottage with wistful resignation, like the tears of silent lovers.

Frances Dyller

The student perforce extends his command of grammar for style in imitating this sentence: by the use of three parallel verbs in the first independent clause as electric as those of Hardy; by the use of parallel prepositional phrases in each clause; meanwhile he tries in his own diction for a combination of consonant sounds as beautiful as the *l*'s, *m*'s, and *n*'s in "innumerable tawny and yellow leaves" or the use of the *s* sound in such words as *passages*, *scratch*, *skirts*, and *visitors*. The beginning of the achievement is the student's ability to imitate the structure of the sentence; the end is beauty of rhetoric and diction.

This approach to style we have described presupposes a long apprenticeship in the elements of grammar. This apprenticeship is often wasteful of time and energy that might be devoted to writing experiences without emphasis on variety of sentence structure or punctuation according to grammatical rules. However, for that increasing proportion of students who intend to go on to college, the knowledge of grammatical constructions for both style and punctuation is in the opinion of many college teachers indispensable. The more the student aspires to attend college or prepare for a profession, the more he needs a knowledge of elementary grammar in both speech and writing. If the student is not going on to college and does not expect to enter a profession, certainly he does not need a knowledge of grammar. He can get along perfectly well in conversation. Even though he punctuates incorrectly, he can write letters well enough to make himself understood. He can, indeed, make his meaning clear without punctuating sentences. The growing acceptance, however, of the necessity of some college work in addition to high school for the average student makes a knowledge of elementary grammar increasingly vital as the years pass.

For whatever purposes the teacher uses grammar, whether or not the time he spends on it is justified, he needs a stable and consistent description of the language. Traditional grammar provides such a classification, however weak and inconsistent much of its terminology and applications. Traditional grammar presents a rough and often inconsistent classification of word function. As Vena Newsome points out in *Structural Grammar in the Classroom*, the word *brother's* in such a phrase as "My brother's classmate" defies exact analysis in terms of formal grammar. Certainly fundamental grammar is a crude instrument. It depends for definition now upon meaning, as in definition of nouns, and now upon structure, as in definitions of adjectives and adverbs. Nevertheless, despite such weaknesses this grammar *does* function better than *any other* because it is simpler, it has fewer terms, it has a long history of pragmatic effectiveness. Moreover, its description of language is used not only by teachers of English, but also by teachers of French, German, Spanish, and Italian. Each of these languages has roughly the same formal classification of the parts of speech. So far there is no attempt in any of the European countries to make a new science of structural linguistics a substitute for formal grammar on the secondary school level. This fact alone should give pause on the American scene to those scholars now attempting to make structural linguistics a consistent system of language analysis to replace formal grammar.

One of the curious deficiencies of some structural linguists is their refusal to recognize the intricate difficulties of descriptions of structure in which scholars of the new science take refuge. May I call attention, for example, to a sentence in one of the great works on structural linguistics, Fries' *The Structure of English* (p. 183):

> The subject itself is simply that Class 1 word that is bound to a Class 2 word to form the basic arrangement of the sentence, and it is identified and distinguished from other Class 1 words not by meaning but by certain contrastive arrangements.
>
> Charles Carpenter Fries, *The Structure of English*

How anyone involved in a classroom situation could explain to the class such a sentence as this, or paraphrase the sentence in understandable diction, I cannot see. Fries, it is true, did not intend this sentence to be used in a high school classroom. He was writing for scholars who would, in turn, translate his principles into comprehensible terms. Nevertheless, the very nature of the principles involved in structural linguistics, of breaking down the old terminology and substituting new terms for old conceptions, makes it difficult for the scholar to devise a nomenclature as simple and easy to use as the old one.

Is there any teacher in a practical classroom situation who prefers the term, "Class 1 word," to the word *noun* or the word *pronoun?* Is there any teacher in a practical teaching situation who prefers the term, "Class 2 word," to the word *verb?* Whatever may be the deficiencies of such terms as *noun, pronoun, verb,* or *adverb,* are they more vague or difficult to teach than such terms as "Class 1 word," *determiner, intensifier?* Each time the structural linguist adds a new term to his description of the language, he may be adding new knowledge to the world of subtle and sophisticated scholars. Necessarily, however, he is reducing the area of fundamental communication of language principles in the average classroom situation. Whereas structural linguistics shows the weaknesses of the simple classification of parts of speech, at the same time it provides a dramatization of the dangers of a complex, highly rarefied nomenclature which only a few scholars can be expected to understand fully.

Whatever the weaknesses of formal grammar, the terminology is at present to many teachers more consistent and stable than the terminology of structural linguistics. If it is uneconomical of time and energy to apply formal grammar to style, as many of its critics claim, then it is many times more uneconomical to apply structural linguistics to style. Indeed I have not found, among the many proponents of structural linguistics, any claim that it can be applied realistically to classroom writing for college-bound students. Every new book on structural linguistics presents the teacher with new terms, often new terms for old concepts, new terms which he is forced to translate into terms provided by traditional grammar. All the objections that the opponents of traditional grammar have made to a nomenclature barren of stylistic fruitfulness can be applied a hundredfold to the nomenclature of structural linguistics in terms of the average high school classroom. One cannot find in the history of English teaching on the American scene so many conceptions on a high intellectual level set forth and described with so little effective application to classroom writing problems as in the many books written on structural linguistics. This does not mean that the study of structural linguistics is barren or fruitless for advanced students of language. Indeed this is where the study of linguistics belongs — in the comparative study of language on the graduate level. Structural linguistics belongs to those scholars who have a profound knowledge of the roots of English in Anglo-Saxon and Norman French and Latin, to those teachers who have lived for years in each of several European countries, mastering the spoken tongue. Structural linguistics involves inherently a knowledge of phonetics which is virtually useless in the average high school classroom. It involves a comparative evaluation of speech sounds in various languages, an evaluation totally foreign to the problems of the average English teacher. Indeed there is no department of structural linguistics that the average high school teacher can take hold of and make practical in his own classroom.

Those who have, like Mr. Paul Roberts, applied structural linguistics to classroom teaching have been most successful in this effort when they have returned bluntly to traditional grammatical terms. They have been least successful when they have been drawn into strange terminology for old principles. Almost all the vocabulary of structural linguistics can be translated into the traditional vocabulary of grammar. Why, then, do we need a new vocabulary at all?

We need rather to simplify the terminology of traditional grammar and agree upon nomenclature, as has been done in France. Instead of reducing the nomenclature, however, to a minimum number of terms agreed upon by publishers, scholars, and textbook writers, we are expanding grammatical nomenclature by leaps and bounds. The proliferate nomenclature of structural linguistics alone is sufficient reason why it cannot become an effective instrument of classroom teaching on the American scene. Only in the teaching of traditional English grammar is it possible to prepare the student for his increasing need to learn foreign languages. The nomenclature of structural linguistics has no counterpart in the teaching of French, Spanish, German, or Italian on the secondary school level. This does not mean that structural linguistics is a useless pursuit. It is extremely useful, as I have suggested, for advanced scholars of comparative languages.

There is more waste of time and energy in the teaching of grammar than in any other aspect of American education. Our problem, however, is not to abolish traditional grammar in favor of a rarefied new science, but to devise new ways of dramatizing the parts of speech and the grammar of the simple sentence in daily lessons of *one year* or *one semester*. Let us have the help of a gifted cartoonist, an artist of the quality of Bill Mauldin, to help us dramatize grammar. Let us have dedicated teachers who *know* they can make grammar stick. Each of us can recall *one* teacher and one classroom when grammar became a reality. Only one such teacher is needed. In some excellent New England high schools years ago, grammar was taught as a separate subject to those going on to college. The basic course should always be a separate subject. We have the resources to make traditional grammar a workable reality. Meanwhile, let those scholars who believe in structural linguistics continue their quest, not to make the new science a high school resource, but to trace on the post graduate level a more complete and accurate description of the language, spoken and written, than any group of scholars has thus far created.

A BRIEF DICTIONARY OF TERMS USED IN STRUCTURAL LINGUISTICS

Structural linguistics is a broad study of the parts of speech, sentence structure, and voice patterns. The structural linguist believes that many of the traditional grammatical concepts are inadequate to describe the functions of words in the immense range of uses in English speech. In his analysis of the forms of speech the structural linguist often uses new terms for old concepts. He may call a demonstrative adjective a *determiner*, verbs *Class 2* words, an adverb of degree an *intensive*.

One main aim of the structural linguist is to clarify the structure of the sentence in terms of its grammatical elements. When you diagram a sentence, you may justly call yourself a structural linguist. The structural linguist also graphs sentences to show structure, but he uses his own kind of diagram and perhaps some new terminology of his own. He may call a demonstrative adjective a *marker*, a co-ordinate conjunction an *equalizer*, a noun modified by a prepositional phrase a *noun cluster*, etc. The structure of a few basic sentence patterns is an important element of structural linguistics, as it has always been an important element of traditional grammar. The manipulation of sentence elements for improvement of style has always been emphasized in *Enjoying English* and by thousands of effective teachers of grammar. Structural linguistics is adding some new resources, especially in the work of the advanced scholar of speech patterns, to the study of language.

Class 1 words	Nouns and pronouns. *We* have read three *plays*.
Class 2 words	Verbs. Carlyle sometimes *wrote* obscurely.
Class 3 words	Adjectives other than articles, possessive adjectives, and demonstrative adjectives. Shelley was *fearless*. *Young* Keats was full of dreams.
Class 4 words	Adverbs telling *how, when, where*. Fred spoke *disdainfully*. The rocket shot *upward*, etc.
Auxiliaries	Auxiliary verbs, such as *am, are, is, may*, etc.
Conjunctions	Co-ordinating conjunctions, such as *and, but, or,* and *nor*

Determiners	Adjectives that tell *whose* or *which one*, such as *a, an, the, those, this, our*
Equalizers	Co-ordinating conjunctions
Form classes	Nouns and pronouns (Class 1); verbs (Class 2); adjectives other than determiners (Class 3); adverbs except adverbs of degree (Class 4). Only a few hundred words in the language (of about half a million words in all) do not belong to one of these four parts of speech.
Form features	Changes in any word required by its use in the sentence; in nouns, use of plurals; in verbs, change of tenses; in adjectives, addition of *ly* to form adverbs; changes in spelling required by comparison of adjectives and adverbs
Function words	(See *structure word groups*)
Headword	Noun in a noun cluster or verb in a verb cluster: *captain* of the ship; *reached* for a cup; *come* when you can
Intensifiers	(See *intensives*)
Intensives	Adverbs of degree, such as *very, too, really, quite*, etc.
Mark	To identify
Marker	Sometimes a modifier that identifies the function of the word to follow: *this* book. Sometimes an auxiliary verb: *would* come. Sometimes a syllable, such as *ly*, that identifies an adverb: careful*ly*
Morpheme	Any suffix, prefix, or word of one syllable, such as *book* or *with*, which cannot be divided into smaller parts and maintains a constant meaning in various contexts: *book*ish, *book*man, *book*worm. Also the smallest meaningful unit such as the *s* for plural nouns or the third person singular of verbs: book*s*, cup*s*, take*s*, talk*s*.
Noun cluster	A noun and its modifiers, such as *a tall man in a black hat, a boy whom I like*
Prepositions	Prepositions, such as *with, at, under*, etc.
Question words	Dependent clause openers when used with questions, such as *who, where, what* (sometimes called *question markers*)
Sentence connector	Adverbial conjunction. Joan was ill; *therefore* she could not sing the part.

Sentence pattern   Any persistent sequence of grammatical elements in speech or writing.

Roberts lists four basic patterns in *Patterns of English*, (pp. 70–76):

1. Noun-verb (Roses bloomed.)
2. Noun-linking verb-adjective (Parents were patient.)
3. Noun-linking verb-noun (Poets are seekers.)
4. Noun-transitive verb-noun (John liked rockets.)

Newsome, *Structural Grammar in the Classroom* (p. 14), lists four basic patterns as follows:

1. Noun-intransitive verb-adverb (Planes flew low.)
2. Noun-linking verb-adjective (The book was tedious.)
3. Noun-linking verb-predicate noun (Our ship is a carrier.)
4. Subject-transitive verb-object (Fred wrote a poem.)

The *Enjoying English* series stresses three basic patterns (see "The Six Helpers," above, pp. 184–86):

1. Subject-transitive verb-object (Fred knew electronics.)
2. Subject-linking verb-predicate noun, pronoun, or adjective (Books are weapons. It was I. Birds are graceful.)
3. Subject-intransitive verb-adverb or prepositional phrase (The car lurched forward. The car lurched toward the curb.)

Sentence patterns   As related to style. See above, "Learning Grammar Through the Sentence-Building Process," pp. 207–16. See also *Enjoying English 11*, "Ten Distinguished Sentence Patterns," pp. 268–72; *Enjoying English 12*, "Sentence Patterns: The Spice of Style," pp. 335–48; and "Golden Sentences from the Masters," pp. 349–54.

Sentence structure   The arrangement of grammatical elements within the sentence. The study of such arrangements for clarity, emphasis, and classical order of images from background to middleground to foreground, etc. See chapters on sentence structure, above, pp. 164–216.

Structure word groups   Determiners (demonstrative and possessive adjectives), auxiliaries (auxiliary verbs), prepositions, intensives (adverbs of degree), conjunctions, subordinators (adverb clause openers and [sometimes] relative pronouns), question markers, and interjections.

Subordinators   Subordinating conjunctions, such as *because, since, while, although:* and relative pronouns, such as *who, which*, and *that*. A subordinator signals a subordinate noun-verb pattern.

Verb cluster

A verb and its modifiers, such as *leaped away from the fire.*

Terms used to Describe Voice Patterns Only

Intonation

Intonation is the combined effect of stress, pitch, and juncture on the tone and meaning of a sentence. Notice the changes in meaning in each sentence below.

When will Morrison fly?   When *will* Morrison fly?

When will *Morrison* fly?   When will Morrison *fly?*

Juncture

A pause in speech. *Plus juncture* (+) is the suggestion of a pause, as in the voiced distinction between "I struck" and "ice truck." *Single-bar juncture* (|) is the pause after the loudest stress in the sentence: "When you leave | I leave too." *Double-bar juncture* (||) is usually a pause one uses with an interrupter: "At that moment || seeing a bright light || Tom stopped." *Double-cross juncture* (#) is a pause usually signalling a full stop in the thought of the speaker: "We waited an hour # however, Major Walker did not appear#

Pitch

Rising or falling tones in the voice. When the voice sound has a high rate of vibration, it has a high pitch. When the vibration rate is low, the sound has a low pitch. Lowest to highest pitch might be represented as 1, 2, 3, and 4:

2   2   2   4 3   4   3   2   2
Why are you leaving? Why did you resign?

Phoneme

A variable speech sound symbolized by a certain letter or combination of letters. The letter *t*, for example, is a variable speech sound, depending on what letters precede or follow it: *took, at, city, still.* Here the variations in the *t* sound arise from its immediate environment of other letters or sounds, but it is still the same phoneme. The total number of phonemes in English speech is estimated as forty-one (Francis), forty-five (Roberts), and forty-three (Gleason). Gleason identifies twenty-four consonant phonemes and nine vowel phonemes.

Stress   Loud or soft voice emphasis on a particular syllable or word: We saw a *few* turkeys. We saw a
few *turkeys*. We *returned* home.

Suggested Readings

BARNETT, LINCOLN: "Who is Behind the Assault on English?", *Horizon*, July,
1963, pp. 33–48
    Excerpts from *The Treasure of our Language*, by Lincoln Barnett, Knopf,
    1963. Mr. Barnett attacks most of the assumptions of the structural
    linguists. One passage reads as follows: "From the study of primitive
    tongues, linguists derived a rule: Usage is all that counts."
BERTSCH, RUTH E.: "Linguistic Birds and Sentence Structure," *English
Journal*, Vol. 52 (January, 1962), pp. 46–49
    New terms for the study of basic grammatical patterns. Uses the old
    grammar for realistic and profitable applications.
BLOOMFIELD, LEONARD: *Language*, Holt, Rinehart and Winston, 1933
BORGH, ENOLA M.: *Grammatical Patterns and Composition*, Wisconsin Council of
Teachers of English, Wisconsin State College, Oshkosh, Wisconsin, 1963
    One of the most realistic applications thus far evolved of structural
    grammar to composition. The approach is most successful when it
    relies frankly upon such terms as subjects and predicates, compound
    sentences, clauses, coordination, subordination, basic sentence patterns
    from literature, sentence sense.
CORBIN, RICHARD: "Grammar and Usage: Progress but Not Millennium,"
English Journal, Vol. 49 (November, 1960), pp. 548–55
    "Structural grammar, by the admission of its authors, is far from a
    perfect description of our language at work, but we, as teachers, will
    be remiss if we do not give a careful scrutiny before we accept or reject
    it. Here is one positive suggestion, at least, in answer to the question,
    "What grammar shall we teach?" Thousands of sympathetic teachers
    will have to test it in hundreds of thousands of classrooms before we have
    the proof of its worth — and before we can answer with certainty the
    question that then logically follows, "How can we teach it?"
    "Whatever system of grammar finally emerges, we must keep sturdily
    in mind the fact that its sole purpose, first, last, and all of the time, is to
    help create livelier, clearer, more accurate speakers and writers of
    English."
FRANCIS, W. NELSON: *The Structure of American English*, Ronald Press, 1958
FRIES, CHARLES CARPENTER: *The Structure of English*, Harcourt, Brace and
World, 1952
GLEASON, H. A., JR.: *An Introduction to Descriptive Linguistics*, Holt, Rinehart
and Winston, rev. ed., 1961

HILL, ARCHIBALD A.: *Introduction to Linguistic Structures*, Harcourt, Brace & World, Inc., 1958

HOCKETT, CHARLES F.: *A Course in Modern Linguistics*, Macmillan Company, 1958

HUGHES, JOHN P.: *The Science of Language*, Random House, 1962

LEES, ROBERT B.: "The Promise of Transformational Grammar," *English Journal*, Vol. 52 (May, 1963), pp. 327–30
> This article pins down some elements of transformational grammar without attempting to show how they may be applied in writing problems.

Linguistics and Composing and Verbal Learning, Conference on College Composition and Communication, October, 1962, NCTE
> Contains especially illuminating though sparsely illustrated article titled, "What is English?" by H. A. Gleason, Jr., and an exciting essay called "The Voice of the Writer," by Walker Gibson.

NEWSOME, VERNA: *Structural Grammar in the Classroom*, Milwaukee, Wisconsin Council of Teachers of English, 1961

ROBERTS, PAUL: *Patterns of English*, Harcourt, Brace and World, 1956; *English Sentences*, Harcourt, Brace and World, 1962
> Like all scholars who attempt realistic applications of structural linguistics, Mr. Roberts makes his best contributions to classroom realism when he turns bluntly to traditional terminology. Both these books, like Mr. Roberts' *English Syntax* (Harcourt, Brace and World, 1964), which applies the principles of transformational grammar, reflect the benefits of a keen experimental mind, reaching toward new ideas with a sound base in the old.

ROBERTS, PAUL: "Linguistics and the Teaching of Composition," *English Journal*, Vol. 52 (May, 1963), pp. 331–35
> As usual with articles on linguistics, the practical applications are few and far between.

RYCENGA, JOHN A., and SCHWARTZ, JOSEPH: *Perspectives on Language*, Ronald Press, 1963. Several excellent chapters on structural linguistics

SCHUSTER, EDGAR H: "How Good Is the New Grammar?" *English Journal*, Vol. 50 (September, 1961), pp. 392–97
> "I strongly suspect that when the research is done, we will find that writing will be improved little indeed by grammar study, whether structural or traditional."

SMITH, HENRY LEE, JR.: *Linguistic Science and the Teaching of English*, Harvard University Press, 1956

THOMAS, OWEN: "Generative Grammar: Toward Unification and Simplification," *English Journal*, Vol. 51 (February, 1962), pp. 94–99.
> Plausible in theory, weak in realistic applications.

25 Transformational Grammar: A Synthesis

By Dr. Gladys Haase, Brooklyn College

TRANSFORMATIONAL GRAMMAR is a point of view and a method. It is not easy to give a succinct definition of either of these characteristics. Transformational grammar may be likened to qualitative analysis in chemistry in that it offers a means of analyzing and specifying the elements of which a complex substance—in the case of grammar, the sentence—is composed.

The transformational grammarian views a sentence like the following,

What secrets remain under the gigantic ice cap are fast being exposed,

as a fusion of "kernel" sentences, simple, indicative, declarative statements, such as:

1. They expose the secrets fast.
2. The secrets remain under the cap.
3. The cap is ice.
4. The cap is gigantic.

The application of specific transformational rules can, step by step, produce the complex sentence quoted above. First, sentences three and four can be reduced to attributive adjectives and embedded in sentence two:

2a. The secrets remain under the *gigantic ice* cap.

Then sentence 2a can be given the form of a question:

2b. *What* secrets remain under the gigantic ice cap?

This question can, in turn, be nominalized and embedded in sentence one, by being substituted for the object, *the secrets:*

　1a. They exposed *what secrets remain under the gigantic ice cap* fast.

To emphasize this embedded question, the transformation for the passive will produce:

　1b. What secrets remain under the gigantic ice cap *are exposed* fast.

Finally to express the notion of continuative action, still another rule will give the formula for altering the form of the verb:

　1c. What secrets remain under the gigantic ice pack *are* fast *being exposed.*

In other words, the transformational grammarian views this primary sentence as a rearrangement of originally separate and basically simple linguistic elements. These elements, here, were not only the four kernel sentences, but also notions of relative importance, of question, of continuative action. The rules of transformational grammar describe the process of deriving the basic kernel sentences as well as the methods by which the structural elements within these sentences can be manipulated.

In 1957, Noam Chomsky published his *Syntactic Structures,*

. . . one of the first serious attempts on the part of a linguist to construct within the tradition of scientific theory-construction a comprehensive theory of language which may be understood in the same sense that a chemical, biological theory is ordinarily understood by experts in those fields.[1]

This study was the first publication of the theory and the statement of rules of transformational grammar. In the succeeding nine years Chomsky himself and other linguists (Emman Bach, Jerrold Katz, Robert B. Lees, Paul M. Postal, Robert P. Stockwell and others) have sought to apply this method of grammatical description to English, and to other languages as well. It seems by all standards to be a more accurate, comprehensive and concrete method of stating the facts of English grammar than any now existing. The work of the linguists in the field, however, is generally technical and difficult to understand unless one has some knowledge of linguistics. Therefore, efforts are now being made to make the concepts and

[1] Robert B. Lees, review of *Syntactic Structures* by Noam Chomsky, *Language*, Vol. 33 (July-September, 1957), pp. 377–78.

rules of transformational grammar more accessible to the general student, and even to seventh and eighth graders. Works by Ralph Goodman, John C. Mellon, Owen Thomas and James Sledd should probably be studied before going on to the more scientific presentations of the subject.

Any grammar is essentially a set of rules purporting to describe the structure of a language. The difference between the systems of grammar by which English has heretofore been described and that proposed by the transformational grammarians lies in the nature of the material they seek to describe, the point of view from which linguistic structure is described and the terminology of such statements.

Transformational grammar has rules that deal with linguistic structures (not with rhetoric, semantics, or sounds and parts of speech viewed in isolation). It profits from the evidence about English the scholars working in other fields of linguistics have recorded, especially from the work of structural grammarians. Transformational grammar takes as its starting point the sentence, a construction that represents a fusion of linguistic structures. To take the sentence as a basis for developing its rules seems sensible enough, though the explanations that the transformational grammarians give for doing so are not always easy to follow. They do not attempt to define such elements as sentence, part of speech, word, object. They assume that those for whom English is a natural language recognize such elements intuitively. They believe that some of these elements are probably indefinable—as are many of the natural phenomena upon whose existence physicists, chemists or biologists have built various workable scientific theories that permit the understanding of how these phenomena can be used. The fact is that it is quite possible to learn and to use the rules of a transformational grammar of English without a thorough understanding of the reasons for the assumptions on which it is based.

In seeking to find the simplest and most direct process of constructing all of the grammatical utterances of the English language (and none of the ungrammatical ones), transformational grammarians have devised a series of rules which are given an algebraic-like statement and which are applied in a rather strict order. The most significant of these rules are of two sorts which are called respectively phrase-structure rules and transformational rules.

Phrase-structure rules are statements, progressively more specific, about the essence of English sentence structure: the first of them indicates the bipartite nature of sentences: $S = NP + VP$. Succeeding rules specify in turn the elements that may compose the NP (noun phrase) and the VP (verb phrase), respectively. Phrase-structure rules enable the transformational grammarian to derive what he calls "kernel" sentences: basic, active, declarative sentence patterns.

The second category of rules is that which gives its name to the system as a whole. Transformational rules are applicable only to elements within the phrase-structure grammar. A given transformational rule is a direction for altering the form of a given element in a kernel sentence, or the order in which it appears. Still other transformations may permit the embedding of one kernel sentence in another. These phrase-structure and transformational rules enable the grammarian to make clear the "deep" structures of English. His rules are concepts that give coherence to the multiplicity of facts that are now known about English. His rules are like the labeled compartments of an old-fashioned pigeon-hole desk. They show us where the structural elements of English (the parts of speech), the basic formal elements (inflections for plurality, tense, non-finite verbs, etc.), and the basic notional elements (number, gender, time, importance, negation, etc.) are to be "filed" in the sentence.

The system of transformational grammar is especially noteworthy for the fact that it gives rules to describe the syntactic effects of what has heretofore been loosely termed notional grammar and relegated, for want of a clear understanding, to the category of semantics. We have forms for the singular or plural of nouns, and we also have notions of number that are attached to nouns, or to nouns when they have certain meanings. The words *gold* and *beauty* for instance, may be singular in form, but they certainly do not carry the notion of "one-ness" that other nouns, called countables, may do. Rather, *gold* has the notion of a mass, a quantity of that metal, and *beauty* suggests a concept made up of many pleasing qualities. Such words have been called "mass" words, because of the notion they convey. When they are used in this way, there are certain syntactic effects. They cannot be modified by an article;

they cannot be made plural, and this in turn will affect the form of the verb or of pronoun references. Transformational rules are the first to give specific expression to this aspect of grammar.

I should like to illustrate the generalizations I have just made by showing the phrase-structure derivation of a simple sentence pattern, and, later, of the operation of a transformational rule on one element of this pattern.

The following three sentences: *the men hear the sounds, the architect mentions the plan,* and *the bird-watchers see the orioles* all represent a given pattern, a kernel sentence that may be created by the application of phrase-structure rules. The process may be listed or diagrammed:

1. S [Sentence]
2. $NP + VP$ [Noun phrase + Verb phrase]
3. $D + N + VP$ [Determiner + Noun + Verb phrase]
4. $D + N + V + NP$ [Determiner + Noun + Verb + Noun phrase]
5. $D + N + V + D + N$ [Noun determiner + Noun + Verb + Noun determiner + Noun]

The final series of symbols (terminal string) indicates a sentence in which the verb is transitive. The diagram makes clear the structural analysis of each of the elements of the terminal string as well as showing that the second NP (noun phrase), although made up of the same parts of speech as the first, plays a subsidiary role in the whole sentence. A way of expressing these elements in a manner which would permit transitive sentences of the type illustrated above, and only of this type, would be to apply what the transformational grammarian calls "expansion rules":

Art	Count	vNP	Art	Count
D -	$+ N$ - Hum	$+ V$ - vNP - Tpas	$+ D$ -	$+ N$ - Nhum
Sg or Pl	Sg or Pl	Tfac	Sg or Pl	Sg or Pl [2]

[2] Ralph Goodman, "Transformational Grammar," in Norman C. Stageberg, *An Introductory English Grammar* (New York: Holt, Rinehart and Winston, Inc., 1965), p. 343.

This "string" now makes specific limitations: the subject must be a noun designating a human, it may be singular or plural and must be modified by the definite article; the verb is transitive, but must be one capable of being followed only by a direct object, one capable of being given the passive form or of taking its direct object in the form of a factual clause; the noun used as direct object must designate a non-human, may be either singular or plural and must be modified by the definite article.

The passive voice is an element of "notional" grammar, in that it is a device to subordinate, or even to eliminate, the statement of the subject notion of the sentence. It does this by giving emphasis to some other noun-element in the sentence, usually the direct object. This is raised from its subsidiary level in the predicate and given emphasis by being made the formal subject of the sentence. There is a necessary change in the form of the verb because of this shift in emphasis. Most grammars describing English treat the passive as though it were a category of the verb. Transformational grammar more properly shows that it should be a rule governing the noun elements in the sentence, that the change in the verb is the result of the shifting of the subject and object in the sentence. Chomsky states the rule in the following way.[3]

Structural analysis:
NP - Aux - V - NP [Noun phrase - Auxiliary - Verb - Noun phrase]

Structural change:
X_1 - X_2 - X_3 - X_4 [X = each principal structural item]
$\rightarrow X_4$ - $X_2 + be + en$ - X_3 - by $+ X_1$

In the sentences I used above, where there were three principal items, NP - V - NP, the passive transformational rule would require that I state the third element in the sentence as the formal subject and that I subordinate the notional subject as an adverbial phrase. They would become respectively: *the sounds are heard by the men, the plan is mentioned by the architect,* and *the orioles are seen by the birdwatchers.*

Transformational rules may apply to several elements in a sentence and, as can be seen from my opening illustration, once one

[3] Noam Chomsky, *Syntactic Structures* ('s Gravenhage, The Hague: Mouton and Company, 1957), p. 112.

element has undergone a transformational change, it is capable of being acted on in another way by still another transformation. For instance, another transformation may give the formula for eliminating from the sentences above any statement whatsoever of the notional subject.

In addition to the phrase-structure rules and the transformational rules, this system makes use of lexical rules and morphophonemic rules.

Lexical rules identify words by phonetic symbols and by specifying the changes in form the words undergo and the syntactical notions they may have. *Cheese* /t ʃiz/, for instance, would be classified as a noun, and, in one of its meanings, as a mass word, non-human, singular in form and incapable of being modified by the indefinite or definite article. *Give* /gɪv/ would be classified as a verb, transitive, capable of taking both indirect and direct objects and of being given a passive form. The specifications given for a word in the lexicon are primarily syntactic ones that play their role in making it possible to construct only grammatical sentences in the transformational system.

Morphophonemic rules are statements of the change in sound that may take place when inflections are added to words: the phonetic form of the word, particularly the sound in which it ends, affects the pronunciation of the inflectional ending. The use of the inflection for plural can involve morphophonemic changes such as: *man - men; horse - horses* / - ɪz/; *task - tasks* / - s/; *saw - saws* / - z/; *wife - wives* / - vz/. The inflection for past tense can cause such changes as *give - gave; walk - walked* / - t/; *lag - lagged* / - d/; *parade - paraded* / - ɪd/. Morphophonemic rules become applicable after the kernel sentence has been attained, after the transforms have been achieved and after the appropriate lexical elements have been selected. The "lexical terminal string" *the girl give* + Sg *those boy* + PL *milk* becomes *the girl gives the boys milk* /ðə gərl gɪvz ðə bɔiz mɪlk/.

I find myself in the position of having tried to define or characterize transformational grammar, a system that itself dispenses with definitions. Certainly no real concept of it can be given briefly. I suspect that what I have actually done in the preceding paragraphs is to suggest what I find interesting about it—or at least to emphasize some of its valuable qualities. It is a formulation of the structure of English that takes full cognizance of the findings of linguistic research. It affords generalizations that reveal the grammatical relationships of the disparate elements of English. It is succinct in its statements, and the rules that must be learned are relatively few in number, even though the number of rules is being increased as a result of further development of the system.

Unfortunately, transformational grammar is not easy to learn. Because they wish to state their axioms and theorems without ambiguity, transformational grammarians make use of mathematical terminology and algebraic formulations of the rules. As I said above, for a person like myself, who knows little of mathematical terminology, these formulations seem at first obscure and difficult— one has to learn a language in order to study his own language. Then, as understanding grows, these formulations and the rigid step-by-step order in which one must apply them seem to get in the way: one's intuitive knowledge leads him to the "solution" before the process of working out the rules gets him there. Hence he is apt to miss the implications of some of the steps he has skipped over and must review them in order to gain full knowledge of the system and all that it shows about the structure of English. Yet, the exactness and brevity of the mathematical terminology is one of the virtues of the system, for it causes the eye to focus on the few structural elements we use in infinitely varying combinations to state the pedestrian or to stir the imagination.

At times transformational grammar seemed a very arbitrary system to me. I cannot deny that its rules serve to lead one to construct grammatically correct sentences in English, but I find it exasperating, for instance, to have to accept the division that is made in this system between what are called "determiners" (indefinite and definite articles, demonstrative adjectives, possessive pronouns) and the adjective, or at least, attributive adjectives. Historically all such words, except the pronouns, were noun modifiers and had inflections for case, number and gender so that they could mirror the grammatical categories of the nouns they modified. But, as I showed briefly at the beginning, transformational grammar traces the attributive adjective to a rule which causes a sentence—or part of it—to be embedded in another which has one of its major structural elements in common:

1. The boy is tall.
2. The boy runs.

In these two sentences the *NP* (noun phrase) serving as subject is identical. Given this identity, the rule permits the elimination of all but the predicate adjective of sentence one, and the embedding of this adjective in the noun phrase subject (which is identical to that of sentence one) giving the result:

2a. The *tall* boy runs.

Chomsky calls this the *nominalizing transformation* T_{adj}.[4] (I cite his formula here as a further illustration of the appearance of the rules of transformational grammar.)

Structural analysis: of S_1 (sentence 1)

      T - N - is - A [definite article - noun - is - adjective]

        of S_2 (sentence 2)

X - NP - Y [X, Y = major structural elements unspecified; noun phrase]
      (X or Y may be null)

Structural change:

$(X_1 - X_2 - X_3 - X_4; X_5 - X_6 - X_7)$ [X's = major structural elements of
                                   each of the sentences above]

        $\rightarrow$ [can be rewritten as]
        $X_5 - X_1 + X_4 + X_2 - X_7$
        [0   the   tall   boy runs]

This transformational rule works; it is capable of general illustration and application. But it seems a terribly cumbersome method of getting an adjective before a noun. There are other aspects of transformational grammar which my intuitive knowledge of English or my knowledge of linguistics cause me to question, and this was for me, one of the greatest difficulties in studying it. But the fascinating fact remains: no matter how I expostulate or object, I find myself obliged to make use of transformational grammar and to accept its rules.

SUGGESTED READINGS

BACH, EMMON, *An Introduction to Transformational Grammars*, New York: Holt, Rinehart and Winston, Inc., 1964.

[4] Noam Chomsky, *Syntactic Structures*, p. 113.

CHOMSKY, NOAM, *Syntactic Structures*, 's Gravenhage, The Hague: Mouton and Company, 1957

GOODMAN, RALPH, "Transformational Grammar," in Norman C. Stageberg, *An Introductory English Grammar*, New York: Holt, Rinehart and Winston, Inc., 1965.

LEES, ROBERT B.: "Grammatical Analysis of the English Comparative Construction," *Word*, Vol. 17, no. 2, August 1961, pp. 171–85.

LEES, ROBERT B., review of *Syntactic Structures* by Noam Chomsky, *Language*, Vol. 33 (July-September 1957), pp. 375–408.

MELLON, JOHN C.: *A Grammar of English Sentences*, Culver, Ind.: Culver Military Academy, 1964. [textbook for 8th and 9th grade]

THOMAS, OWEN: *Transformational Grammar and the Teacher of English*, New York: Holt, Rinehart and Winston, Inc., 1965.

Part IV

RESOURCES IN BOOKS AND IDEAS

26 First Days of the Class: Professional Problems and Opportunities

THE FIRST FEW DAYS of class, whether one is an experienced teacher or not, present problems to solve and opportunities to grasp, especially in the field of human relations. To show oneself firm yet friendly, definite yet permissive; to set a pattern of classroom procedure that the students recognize as predictable yet pregnant with surprise and delight; to feel out the problem students and place them near us if possible, psychologically and physically; to prove that our assignments can be provocative and practical; to invite orderly discussion and draw out the timid ones — all these we must do in rapid succession, perhaps all in the one short hour in the first day of class or the five short hours of the first week.

Settling the Class in Place

Before going to class, let us say an average ninth-grade class, we prepare to make the wheels of adaptation run smoothly. In these first days especially we do not fail to come to class on time, before the first pupils if possible; we know that even on the first day discipline problems may gather steam if two or three jokesters can get into a huddle before we arrive. To secure an orderly seating arrangement and learn names quickly, we bring to class three-by-five cards or slips of paper. We allow the class to take the seats they wish. When everybody is present, however, and a few stragglers sit in the back row (almost always the ones with flamboyant resistance to

English), we ask these stragglers to take the vacant seats in the first or second row. We know that we must always leave the back row vacant rather than the first; we keep our class in a compact group, equally close to each other, no one pupil or group isolated or set apart.

When the class is seated, we immediately pass out three-by-five cards or slips of paper and ask the student to write the following information:

1. Name, last name first
2. Time and number of the class
3. Row in which you are seated (A, B, C, etc.)
4. Number of your seat (counting number 1 as the seat nearest the window)
5. Address
6. Telephone number

Even though we may have the information elsewhere, we ask the student to write his address and telephone number, the latter especially important when a pupil is absent because of illness, accident, or personal crisis.

E						
D						
C						
B						
A	Jerry Martin	Frances McKee	Tony Carillo	Laura Stone	Jack Brown	Ralph Mais

Window Side

We now have at hand the names of the whole class and may even be able to call upon individuals and look directly at them, having before us the desk location of each boy or girl. This approach we may now reinforce by calling the roll and asking in advance that the individual pupil correct us if we mispronounce his name. This recognition of the pupil's individuality in the emphasis we give to addressing him correctly is the first actual relationship we achieve. Before the next class we may be able to make a chart of the class (on a sturdy filing folder) with the name of each person in his seat box as appears in the diagram on page 374. We can mark absences in the spaces if we wish. Experienced teachers have found that this procedure has a sharply beneficial effect on the relations between the teacher and the pupils in the first few days of class.

Making the First Assignment

The first assignment shows the class whether or not we understand not only their interests, but also their limitations of time and resources. Still more important, it tells them whether we understand how to dramatize assignments so that they will act from interest rather than from compulsion. The time to make almost all assignments is *at the beginning of the hour*, when we know the bell is not about to jangle in the offing and the pupils have time to ask questions. We let the pupils know that this will be the usual procedure. Generally speaking, the more time we spend on assignments, and the more fully we anticipate pupil difficulties, the better the performance of the class, and the easier our own task of marking papers. For the first assignment (due tomorrow or the next day, as we choose) we need a project that (1) requires no more than a half hour to complete, (2) requires individual judgment and selection, (3) gives a sense of immediate accomplishment in the enthusiasm of first efforts, and (4) must be handed in and graded.

Let us say we are opening the junior year with a study of *The Crisis*, by Winston Churchill, or *A Tale of Two Cities*. We may say to the class: "Boys and girls, in a few days we are beginning our first book of the semester, *A Tale of Two Cities*. This novel is one of the great works of English literature. But what is *literature*, anyway? What do you think it is? What is one thing literature does? I am not speaking of poetry now, but of prose literature, and specifically the novel. For tomorrow, I should like you to begin your exploration of literature with a sentence. Yes, just one sentence, and that a sentence quoted from a novel you have liked, not necessarily from a novel English teachers like, a sentence that excited you or gave you an idea or brought you to the spot and made you break out in a sweat. I should like you to write this sentence in pen and ink on theme paper in the way I shall show you here on the board, with your name and class number and the time in the upper right-hand corner, margins on four sides, and the name of your book underlined just under your sentence. Do not use quotations marks unless the author uses them in the book."

Thus we present the mechanics of the assignment, but this is just the beginning. We bring to class several novels and read a sentence from each one. We choose them on various levels: *Lord Jim, Gone with the Wind, Arrowsmith, The Grapes of Wrath*. After reading each sentence, we say why we like it, why in our judgment it has something of literary value, what chord it strikes in our experience. If we have had time to have these several sentences mimeographed for the class to see as well as to hear, so much the better. We may choose a philosophical passage like this one from *Middlemarch:* "Her office was not to claim justice, but to give tenderness." "This is one picture of a wife's duty in marriage," we may say. "Perhaps this is the way George Eliot looked at it. Is it your idea of a wife's duty? Is it a husband's duty as well?" Or we may take a passage like this from *The Ordeal of Richard Feverel:* "When nature has made us ripe for love, the gods are not long in providing a temple for the flame." On the junior or senior level, nothing is of more interest than sentences about love and marriage. As examples we shall want to use also sentences of visual intensity, like this one from *The Apple Tree:* "He caught hold of her hands, but she shrank back, till her passionate little face and loose dark hair were caught in the pink clusters of the apple blossoms." To make this assignment in a way to show the class its potentialities requires probably twenty minutes to a half hour. We may conclude by asking the class to name some novels they have liked. We must caution them to be ready with choices; also to go to the library promptly to be sure they have one or two books of their choice for doing this assignment.

Class Relaxation with Oral Autobiographies

In making the first assignment, especially one involving the library, we must allow sufficient time, partly because we may want to use parts of the next class period or two for oral autobiographies. If even a few students can speak a few brief sentences about themselves, this helps create a rapport in most classes, a rapport based on the most basic of understandings: Each pupil is a unique teacher if we can get out of him and into the minds of the class something vital about his life. The fundamental things may not come yet. But these autobiographies, however superficial at first, pave the way for more basic self-revelation. We may ask each student to say a few things about himself, in answer to questions like these:

When and where were you born?
What elementary school did you attend?
What do your father and mother do?
What about your brothers and sisters?
Have you tentatively chosen your career?

If some students avoid the third question above, it is wise not to press for an answer. Let these first autobiographies be brief, a few each day as the time permits, until gradually we may feel free to ask more fundamental questions, and the students will feel free to answer them, knowing that in this class the members are respectful of each person and expectant of illumination from his experiences.

Meeting Problems of Discipline

In the first few days may come a crisis in discipline, perhaps with a rowdy boy in the back row or a group of two or three cronies who egg each other on in testing the new teacher. When we are interrupted by such pupils, it is often effective to stop in the middle of a sentence, saying nothing to them, but waiting until they are quiet, then starting again. We may stop thus another time or two. If the trouble persists, one good plan is to go quietly to the seat of the offender and ask him to leave the room and wait for us at the principal's office. A written note to this effect may be even more effective. The important thing is to use *action, not words*. This action we may follow by meeting the pupil in the office and having a quiet, pleasant chat with him, asking him questions about himself, avoiding the issue of the incident.

Another important action is to move a pupil to a different seat. This assures us that the clique is broken for the time being and one of the chief offenders placed near the desk. This breaking up of a group is often necessary and usually should be done just before the next class starts and not during the class. We like to be permissive about seats; it is natural for students to want to be near their friends. But we must be firm, once our patience is exhausted. The offender must keep his new seat for the term or until he is convinced he must conduct himself well.

Responsibility to Our Colleagues

By the end of the first week, we have met perhaps 150 to 200 students, each with his bundle of energy straining for release, while we come home dog-tired. Our first duty is to understand and help our students. We have responsibilities also, however, to our principal and our colleagues. We must stand ready to welcome the principal to our classroom as a friendly critic and adviser. If he has not visited the room after the first month or two, we may say, "Are you going to visit me one day soon?" just to make it easier for him to come. For the day he designates, we have chosen the kind of assignment or lesson we can carry out with the greatest assurance. If the discussion becomes lively, we may even ask the principal for his opinion on a point or two. After the principal's visit, it is courteous to ask him for a conference in which we can discuss with him his suggestions and our questions. Perhaps he has had difficulties with some of our problem children; in this department alone his experience will be very helpful. Nothing is more constructive in any conversation than a question that helps the other fellow to express himself on a topic he knows well.

Often the more conscientious and effective the teacher, the less time and energy he wishes to spend on the inevitable weekly, monthly, and even daily records that differ from system to system except in one respect: they get heavier each year. If we are original or unorthodox or individualistic as a teaching personality, we should take particular pains to be consistently cooperative in answering the requests for records and special reports of every kind. To some principals the ideal teacher is the one who never bothers him with problem students and never fails to turn in records and reports precisely at the hour named. Whether or not our principal is such a person, he will much appreciate our cooperation in these less important professional functions that make his school run smoothly and save him from embarrassing moments with his assistants who must be mainly concerned with facts and figures and not with those golden moments when minds swing open or a child with a sorrow has found in us a willing ear and doesn't want to leave. I remember a master teacher who said once, "Conform in the little things. Dress as you are expected to. Be consistent and unfailing in little courtesies. Be prompt. Turn in everything on time. Then you can be very much of a nonconformist in the way you think and the way you teach and no one will mind." We need to be friendly in a courtesy sense with everyone: the janitor, the secretary in the office, the school nurse, the distributor of textbooks and supplies — all of whom are a part of the school system in which it is our duty to help the wheels run smoothly.

What is a professional attitude toward one's fellow-teachers? We can be completely friendly, impartially friendly, for the first few months without concentrating on one colleague's friendship, however *sympathique* he may be. In some communities, where teachers are constantly thrown together, we may find it difficult to avoid being too dependent on a single friend (I am considering friends, for the moment, of the same sex). A teacher, like every human being, has a right to a close friendship, and no one will question this right. But it is unwise in a professional sense to permit one friendship to so absorb our energies as to prevent our coming to know and cherish our other colleagues in school and out. We must avoid incurring jealousies, especially when we are highly successful as a teacher and attractive to colleagues as a personality. Where jealousy does arise, we may combat it by showing kindness to the victim, starting the kind of rumor that flies almost as fast as its opposite; I mean a word of praise. When we have a student who has been helped by a colleague, it is considerate and constructive in human relations to let the colleague know that we know about his good work. When we hear about a destructive action by a colleague, it is most unwise and unprofessional to repeat it, even to a close friend in the school system. On the other hand, when we know of a constructive action, it helps build school morale to send out a little current of good report. Most of us need above all things a little success; and no praise is sweeter with the honey of success than a sentence commending our life's work. Each of us has untapped resources of mind or spirit that a word fitly spoken may instantly unlock. Who can forget the casual unexpected phrase of approval spoken perhaps in the long-ago years when one was always moody and ill at ease, such as, "You move like a good basketball player," or "You know, the back of your head has a beautiful shape," or "I've always liked the perky tilt of your chin; I just like to watch that chin when you get up to speak." The art of compliment deserves the energy of our imagination also in our association with our colleagues; a compliment is the most powerful of stimulants because it leaves in the memory indelible sustaining images for lonely evenings or chill winter mornings. Most important of all, in any school it is the mark of a good teammate, a teacher who performs her professional duties beyond the cold letter of the law.

Relations with the Community

Teaching is more difficult and demanding on the junior high school level than on any other; next in factors of tension we may place the high school and elementary grades, last the college years, which require less imagination and energy in classroom relations than any others. As high school teachers, we are subjected to more stresses and strains than our fellow-professionals handling the most advanced graduate classes. Hence, in reality the work load of the high school teacher should be cut in half, from thirty hours of classroom or study-hall duty to twelve or fifteen hours, which are now considered a rather heavy work load for a college teacher. To be sure, the excuse is given that college work requires more preparation and more work at home than high school classes. But this is not true of the conscientious high school teacher; he gives less time to preparation than the college teacher only because his days and nights are too short for marking papers and reading the books he desperately needs to know.

Nevertheless, the high school teacher, in addition to all his school burdens, must bear as well the responsibility of representing his school to the community. "When school is over," said Ellen Geyer long ago, "you must go to the drug store, drink an ice-cream soda, and forget about school until the next day." This is sound advice, especially for the teacher who finds himself nervous or distraught at the day's end, and one should resist responsibilities that subtract heavily from vitality for classroom teaching.

Each teacher must decide for himself what portion of his energy he can devote to community life. When a student is in trouble in our class, however, it is imperative to talk with his parents and, if possible, go to see them. This kind of visit unites community and school in the most creative way possible. As often as one can, it is constructive to take an interest in community activities, in plays given by teachers, in community projects such as the Red Cross and the Y.M. or Y.W.C.A., and in the various school clubs that link the school and the citizens. In many communities teachers have worked on committees to make surveys of school needs. To show how far America is lagging behind in crucial educational planning, we may point out that Russia reportedly is spending fourteen per cent of her national income on education, where America is spending only one or two per cent. Every teacher, as a citizen, has a right to agitate for those school improvements that he considers most essential. If the proper emphasis were placed on school needs, America would now be paying her teachers, especially elementary teachers, $10,000 to $20,000 a year, placing all her children in beautiful classrooms, no more than fifteen or twenty together. In high school, not only does the number of teaching hours need to be cut in half, but the number of students in each class needs also to be cut in half. Ideally speaking, a high school teacher should teach no more than three classes meeting five days a week, and in each of these classes fifteen or twenty pupils. If each teacher had no more than sixty pupils to meet each week, instead of one hundred and fifty or two hundred, we should be able to give individual attention comparable to that given in the best colleges. To achieve these aims is not only within our resources; it is imperative in order to meet the challenge of Russia to the free world. We must make this investment whether or not some say we are in debt and do not have the money.

Our national debt is now (1966) more than 300 billion dollars. Certainly a few billions may be more constructively added to this debt to raise salaries and build schools than to provide a few more rockets to reach the moon. Education does not go out of date like jet engines and long-range bombers. We are in more danger of competition from Russia in the field of skillfully trained men and women than we are in the field of space ships.

Each high school teacher, then, needs to develop a credo of citizenship whereby he joins with enlightened citizens in the community to improve not only his school but the schools of the future in which his successors will teach. As a respected leader of the community, the teacher can have a profound influence on the actions of its citizens in raising educational standards. Nothing is more precious than words of insight spoken by a dedicated teacher to a child who loves him; no words have a more lasting influence than these. America cannot afford to have any but superb teachers. The best minds and the richest personalities belong in this field. Whatever our beliefs about school improvement, is it not our responsibility as teachers to represent graciously and spiritedly the school system which we serve as fully and often as we conscientiously can? We do not assume that it is a perfect instrument, but we must keep our minds open to opportunities not only to improve the school itself but also to strengthen the ties that bind the citizen to the teacher and child in the classroom.

It is not necessary to go out of our classroom to meet the parents of our students. We can begin in a small way by having a class party to which parents are invited. With the permission of the principal, we may exhibit at this party the work of our students and let them make charts to show the parents what we are doing. In the exhibit we may include the textbooks we use and the novels we have enjoyed. Such a party in which the parents meet other children, each other, and the teacher, can hardly fail to be successful. In some schools the first report card for each class is given to the parent by each teacher at a reception for parents. In this way the parent has a chance to go from teacher to teacher and exchange a few words about his child's work in each class. But when our principal and our colleagues are unwilling to try such a broad experiment, we as individuals can try a small one. If an exhibit is objected to, we can have a party, if not at the school, then at some place off the school grounds. At some point, in a manner acceptable to the community, we can create a social situation in which we can understand our children more fully by exchanging ideas with their parents.

*   *   *

In summary, then, the teacher faces problems and opportunities in human relations at a number of different levels in the very first week of class. One is the classroom level, about which we have written at length. Another level is that of our associations with our colleagues and supervisors. Still another is that of our associations with the community by which our school is evaluated. Of these categories of professional relations, that involving the student in the classroom and out is, of course, the most crucial. But the teacher of English, to be most effective, must be conscious every day of his responsibilities to other teachers and supervisors, and to the community at large.

To the Student Teacher: Suggested Activities

1. Interview two teachers in their classrooms after school. Ask them what their main professional problems are during the first week of class. Make a written report to your teacher summarizing your findings.
2. Interview another teacher in the grade level of your choice, asking her what she has found to be a good first assignment in her English class.
3. Interview still another teacher, asking her what problems of discipline she usually encounters during the first week of class. How does she deal with one of these problems? Make a written report to your teacher.
4. Ask a teacher what she feels about responsibilities to the community. Does she feel it necessary to give a certain amount of time to community work other than school work? Make a written report analyzing the teacher's response.

Suggested Readings

ANDERSON, LORENA A., and BENSON, EUNICE P.: "Organization of an English Department," *English Journal*, Vol. 48 (March, 1959), pp. 145–47

"We found that some of our ills were only organizational; teachers left things undone since no one was directly responsible; some were afraid of overstepping authority or leaving hurt feelings, and consequently important details dangled."

BLAISDELL, THOMAS C.: *Ways to Teach English*, Doubleday, 1930
> Blaisdell's chapters of questions to the English teacher are especially bracing and provocative. See Chapters 12, 23, and 43.

BRUNER, JEROME S.: *The Process of Education* (Harvard University Press, 1963), pp. 17–32
> Though lacking in specifics, the chapter on "The Importance of Structure" has valuable insight for the English teacher. "Unless detail is placed into a structured pattern," writes Dr. Bruner, "it is rapidly forgotten."

"But What Are We Articulating With?" *English Journal*, Vol. 51 (March, 1952), pp. 167–79
> The NCTE committee reports on the freshman English offerings in ninety-five colleges and universities. A valuable, realistic article.

CARLSEN, G. ROBERT: "Conflicting Assumptions in the Teaching of English," *English Journal* Vol. 49 (September, 1960), pp. 377–86
> An article of electrical significance. For example:

Traditional	*Modern*
That aesthetic values in a piece of literature are to be found by studying such things as rhythmic patterns, the precision of structure, word pictures, and the like.	That aesthetic values exist in terms of the significance of the synthesis of experience that a piece of literature evokes in the reader."

CONANT, JAMES B.: *The American High School Today*, McGraw-Hill, 1959
> An analysis of the present weaknesses and strengths of the American high school. Indispensable commentary and statistical analyses.

DIEDERICH, PAUL B.: "The Rutgers Plan for Cutting Class Size in Two," *English Journal*, Vol. 49 (April, 1960), pp. 229–36
> Essentially a plan to meet students less often in smaller classes. Analyzed realistically by Lawrence Niblett in the October, 1960, issue of the *Journal*.

Directory of Assistantships and Fellowships for Graduate Study in English and the Teaching of English, edited by Donald R. Tuttle.

DUSEL, WILLIAM J.: "Determining an Efficient Teaching Load in English," *Illinois English Bulletin*, (October, 1955), 121 Lincoln Hall, Urbana, Illinois.

End-of-Year Examinations in English for College-Bound Students, Grades 9–12, published by the College Entrance Examination Board, Box 592, Princeton, N. J., 1963

Essays on the Teaching of English, ed. Robert M. Gay, Harvard University Press, 1940
> A book rich in suggested directions and values for the professional teacher of English. Essays by Dora V. Smith, Angela Broening, Howard Mumford Jones, Reed Smith, Mary Ellen Chase, John Erskine, and others.

Four Quarters (ed. Brother Edward Patrick, La Salle College, Philadelphia 41), Vol. 12 (November, 1962)

> This distinguished issue deals entirely with the writings of Katherine Anne Porter. Rich in ideas for the teacher of writing.

HENRY, GEORGE H.: "Only Spirit Can Measure Spirit," *English Journal*, Vol. 43 (April, 1954), pp. 177–82

> A superb expression of the fundamental ideas and forgotten ideals through which every English teacher can become "a means of bringing the sons of the masses into a realization of their true worth."

HOOK, J, N.: *The Teaching of High School English*, Ronald Press, 1950

> See Chapter 11, "The Responsibilities and Problems of a Teacher of English," Note particularly the section on the teacher of English in a democratic society.

JEWETT, ARNO, ed.: *English for the Academically Talented Student*, published by the NCTE, and the National Education Association Project on the Academically Talented Student, 1960

JEWETT, ARNO: *English Language Arts in American High Schools*, U. S. Printing Office, 1961

> Analysis and sampling of courses of study in almost all states and many cities of the Union. Answers the questions: "What are other states and communities doing? What new emphasis is gaining ground? What emphasis is diminishing?"

JOHNSON, FRANCES: "Unifying Theme for the Year," *English Journal*, Vol. 52 (February, 1963), pp. 97–101

> "Each period has its peculiar image of man," as indeed does each student and each author. In this exciting article the author shows how she related both the writing and the reading of her senior classes to this single theme.

LOBAN, WALTER, RYAN, MARGARET, and SQUIRE, JAMES R.: *Teaching Language and Literature*, Harcourt, Brace & World, 1961

> Detailed and suggestive analysis of main problems of the teaching of English. Excellent bibliographies.

LUCAS, F. L.: *Style*, Collier, 1962.

> One of the most vital essays for the English teacher's shelf. Sample passage: "We are all serving life sentences of solitary confinement within our bodies; like prisoners, we have, as it were, to tap in awkward code to our fellow men in their neighboring cells." Another book one should not miss is John Middleton Murry's *The Problem of Style* (London: Oxford University Press Paperback, 1961). Murry writes: "In literature there is no such thing as pure thought; in literature thought is always the handmaid of emotion."

MC GUIRE, EDNA: "College Freshmen on Writing in High School," *English Journal*, Vol. 51 (April, 1962), pp. 256–58

> A valuable sampling of opinion in response to specific questions, such as,

"How often should high school students write? How should the teacher mark the themes?"

NIBLETT, LAWRENCE: "The Rutgers Plan: Not Enough or the Right Kind of Help," *English Journal*, Vol. 49 (October, 1960), pp. 481–82

"English teachers, instead of wringing their hands over the problems they face, can take heart by joining together, as they are doing in nearly every state, and creating public awareness of the kind of job they would like to do for their students. The public will respond favorably if it knows the facts."

Paperbacks for High School, 1963–64, ed. by Norman R. Lee. Obtainable from the author at: Reading Centre, Syracuse University, Syracuse 10, N. Y.

A list of the 500 best paperback books recommended for junior and senior high school students. Published annually.

POOLEY, ROBERT C.: "The Professional Status of the Teacher of English," *English Journal*, Vol. 48 (September, 1959), pp. 309–41

"I think the best way to describe what the professional status of the English teacher ought to be is to describe the functioning of a school in which this ideal English teacher has earned the respect of colleagues, the administration, and the public, by reason of his education, his competence, and his professional leadership."

RINKER, FLOYD: "Priorities in the English Curriculum," *English Journal*, Vol. 51 (May, 1962), pp. 309–12

This article names the development of the teacher as the first priority: ability to write is a fundamental element in teacher preparation. Writing by the students should take one-third of the school week. Grammar is not high in the list of priorities, but: "The Commission recommends that grammar be retained as an essential part of the English curriculum."

SAUER, EDWIN: *English in the Secondary School*, Holt, Rinehart, and Winston, 1961

Dependable guide lines in analyzing the main problems of the teaching of English.

SHERMAN, STUART: *Shaping Men and Women*, ed. Jacob Zeitlin, Peter Smith, 1932

Essays by a master critic of greatness in literature and men.

SMITH, SIR WILLIAM, ed., revised by E. H. Blakeney and John Warrington: *Smaller Classical Dictionary*, E. P. Dutton & Co., 1958

An invaluable reference book every English teacher and college-bound student should have on his shelf.

SQUIRE, JAMES R. and others: *The National Interest and the Teaching of English*, NCTE, 1961

An indispensable analysis of English teaching in America: deficiencies, achievements, perspectives based on answers to questions by teachers in every state. Selected conclusions: (1) Teachers are not receiving quality training in English proper (2) Sixty percent of high school courses in English are now taught by teachers who lack even the minimum requirements of a major in English (3) Only forty-one percent of the colleges require prospective teachers to take an advanced course in composition.

STEARNS, GERTRUDE B.: *The Teacher of English in the Small High School*, University of Nebraska Press, 1950

The professional advantages and opportunities for the English teacher in a small high school are analyzed with clarity and perception.

STROM, INGRID M.: "Summary of Investigations Relating to the English Language Arts in Secondary Education — 1958–1959," *English Journal*, Vol. 49 (February, 1960), pp. 119–30

First of a series of summaries published each February in the *Journal*.

STROM, INGRID M.: "Summary of Investigations Relating to the English Language Arts in Secondary Education: 1960–61," *English Journal*, Vol. 51 (February, 1962), pp. 123–40.

Filled with interesting facts, such as: of 476 high schools then listed in California, only 4 percent of 4,000 English teachers were using structural grammar in any degree.

The Education of Teachers of English, ed. Alfred H. Grommon, The Commission on the English Curriculum of the NCTE, Appleton-Century-Crofts, 1963

The Portable Greek Reader, ed. by W. H. Auden, published by the Viking Press, 1960

THRALL, WILLIAM FLINT and HIBBARD, ADDISON; revised and enlarged by C. Hugh Holman, *A Handbook to Literature*, Odyssey Press, Inc., 1962

The most valuable single compact book on literary terms for teachers and college-bound students. Reliable definitions in alphabetical arrangement, with valuable references for extended study.

WONNBERGER, CARL G.: "A Report on a Report: Preparation In English for College-Bound Students," *English Journal*, Vol. 50 (May, 1961), pp. 321–26

The author feels that the preparation asked for by the Commission on English of the College Entrance Examination Board is too traditional and conservative. A reply to "A Report on a Report," by Dr. Harold C. Martin, chairman of the Commission on English, may be found on pp. 327–28 of the May issue of the *Journal*.

Writers and Their Work, a catalog published by Longmans, Green & Co., England (Write to British Book Centre)

A series of pamphlet introductions to over 160 writers in English literature. Each pamphlet is an invaluable summary of biographical and critical commentary. Available at The British Book Centre, Inc., 122 East 55th Street, New York 22, N. Y.

27 Professional Growth: Books of Permanent Meaning

LOOKING BACK on high school or college years, we remember perhaps one or two teachers who left us with a gift beyond price: an intellectual awakening. Perhaps this intellectual awakening was so electric that our eagerness to read the masterworks is habitual and permanent. If such is our continuing mood, and if such a teacher inspired us, we are fortunate in two ways: in the impact on our own personal and professional growth, and in the likelihood that we can similarly electrify our students. In his reminiscences Stuart Sherman recalls such a teacher, whom he overheard speaking to a colleague at a football game. "I read themes till three in the morning," said Sherman's teacher. "Then I wanted something to take the taste out of my mouth. And so I took down the *Antigone* of Sophocles and read it; *and do you know, it was so beautiful that I couldn't sleep.*" Stuart Sherman never forgot this moment: his teacher watching the game, speaking very casually, and eating peanuts all the while. Sherman writes, it is true, in the intellectual idiom of an earlier generation; we are not likely to read and reread *Antigone* as did the best trained among our predecessors; and more's the pity: nothing in world literature prepares us for the essence of tragedy in Shakespeare, Ibsen, and O'Neill, or Hardy and Tolstoy, as do Sophocles and Aeschylus. In graduate or undergraduate school, we can take nothing more fundamental for professional growth than a course in Greek tragedy in translation, whether or not we can later recommend all the plays we read to the most gifted among our students.

At this point we must read and reread also the *Poetics* and *Rhetoric* of Aristotle, the *Poetics* for its definitions of tragedy and the meaning of *pity* and *fear*. A simplified meaning of the former term is that an audience feels *pity* when a man's suffering is out of all proportion to his fault; a noble man comes to his downfall through a flaw in his character that should not rightfully destroy him. And *fear* we feel for ourselves, that such a tragic flaw might destroy us, too; and thus the audience in the Greek sense becomes a part of the play. On the theme of audience participation in the hero's dilemma no book is so exciting in its modern applications as Shaw's *The Quintessence of Ibsenism*, a kind of modern counterpart to some of the themes in the *Poetics*, and in this respect Shaw's prefaces are remarkably informative, too.

Making Seminal Books Our Own

In every field, then, but especially in the classics, we seek a few seminal books that help us lay cornerstones to our intellectual structure, whether or not our future students will be able to share the lines and movement of our growth. A major in English should properly place its initial emphasis, as in England, on Greek and Roman classics; two courses extending over the first or second year of college would not be too much. In English literature we find such a constant stream of references to Greek and Roman greats that no piecemeal reading will illuminate. We need an organized, systematic mastery especially of Greek mythology, Greek history, Greek literature, Greek philosophy, to *precede* the study of the great books of England and America. The Bryant translations of the *Iliad* and the *Odyssey* should be on every English teacher's shelf; Edith Hamilton's excellent book, *Mythology*, with its careful citation of sources; parts of Thucydides and Xenophon; selections from Plato and Aristotle; the complete Greek tragedy and a volume of Aristophanes. Failing to have this grounding in college, we must try to acquire it for ourselves; graduate courses in the classics will reinforce and direct our individual search.

Our intellectual growth is communicable only in part to our students; yet concurrent with our reading of seminal books in courses or out, we need to build a realistic perspective of the points at which our students can profit from our advances. In grappling with the great books and achievements of the Renaissance, for example, we can easily interest the student in the drawings, paintings, and sayings of Leonardo. There is something in Leonardo to fascinate every type of mind; we find plans and drawings of airplanes, tanks, battering rams, submarines, model cities, and in the man himself a range of professions and talents undreamed of in former ages: aviation engineer, sanitary engineer, artist, poet, sculptor, mathematician, biologist, anatomist, chemist, a man so strong he could twist a horseshoe as if it were lead; a man handsome in carriage, delightful in conversation, generous to friends. If we can borrow even an abridged copy of Leonardo's *Notebooks*, edited by Edward McCurdy, we shall find this source inexhaustible in interest, with its hundreds of drawings and scientific commentaries, bits of philosophy, and an extraordinary little essay on comparison of the arts. Even the weak student cannot fail to find a fascination at some point in Leonardo. We shall find his paintings alone an education in art appreciation with more and more color prints available each year. The best biography of Leonardo is the one by Antonina Vallentin. The Merejkowski *Romance* is not nearly so well-rounded a portrait as this one. Every biography of Leonardo is of course indebted to Vasari's *Lives of the Painters*, which is a whole storehouse not only of Renaissance greatness, but also of ideas useful to us in the development of every kind of talent. To Vasari the genius of the men he describes was a result in good part of the ferment of the age, not of genetic magic. Time after time he shows how one man caught fire from another and forthwith committed all his energies to the realization of his dream.

Each student in a class can share such a fascination with us; of a time in Italy, in a small city called Florence, when hundreds of men from ordinary families suddenly grew into genius which we still cannot explain. Great men always seem to appear in clusters. Each person can bring to class a quotation from Leonardo, from Vasari, from John Addington Symonds' great book, *History of the Renaissance in Italy*, or from Jacob Burckhardt's masterpiece, *The Civilization of the Renaissance in Italy*. Even a quotation from a biography or an encyclopedia requires him to select a value, an idea, that appeals to him. What have we done in America, what ferment can we point to, comparable to the ferment in Florence that produced Leonardo and Michelangelo? In every exploration we make a realistic application to America and, at last, to the life of each member of the class. "What does all this mean to me, my life, my ambitions, my future?" This is the key question the student keeps asking, silently or aloud, and this question we must always try to answer, both for ourselves and for our students.

Choosing Renaissance Masterpieces

In the Renaissance period appear peaks of literature and thought which we can gradually scale and make our own, often leading our students after us. To spend even two hours with the first chapters of *Don Quixote* reveals why it brings the world perpetual delight. To read Shakespeare (after a start in college, let us hope, with a master teacher), we need a single volume for each play, slowly making each our own, filling it with notes and reminders and choice passages on interleaved pages. Some teachers have a small black notebook of sonnets and quotations from Shakespeare, arranged by topics. Emerson wrote of Shakespeare, "What king had he not taught state? . . . What maiden has not found him finer than her delicacy? What lover has he not outloved?" In social thought we have More's *Utopia*, one of the most provocative books of world literature, and easy to read. *Utopia* shows the democratic faith of the Renaissance, a new look at plastic man and his creative reach, whereas Machiavelli's *The Prince* traces the bleak trail of repression and hatred and the shriveling of man's spirit in the imposition of tyranny. It is significant that the two books appeared within three years of each other, *The Prince* in 1513, *Utopia* in 1516, embodying the extremes of despair and hope in Renaissance man. One of the great Renaissance classics, which no training in educational theory should omit (along with Plato's *Republic* and Rousseau's *Émile*) is John Amos Comenius' *The Great Didactic;* this masterpiece anticipates the ideas of Horace Mann and John Dewey; it also prefigures the still expanding vitality of a democratic outlook.

Another Renaissance author we can share with our students is Bacon, who is inexhaustible. In his early years he wrote, "I have taken all knowledge to be my province." I never knew a student in high school who did not find in Bacon's *Essays* something exciting and memorable and applicable to his own experience. The *Essays* range over many subjects, from "Marriage and Single Life" to "Gardens" and "Of Nature and Man." The style is easy, the meaning clear, the subject units short and pithy. Bacon touches no idea that he does not illuminate with a unique light. The story of Bacon's life is full of drama and genius: a lawyer-statesman who loved fine clothes and great dinners and the touch of royalty, following in secret his great dream of creating a scientific method. In his last years, disgrace: his honors stripped from him one by one, leaving him only one great dream which he never betrayed. His death was a fitting symbol of his deepest passion: Getting out of a coach on a winter day, Bacon bought a chicken, had it killed, dressed, and filled with snow. Would this snow save the flesh from putrefaction? Bacon wanted to know. The experiment brought him death from pneumonia a few weeks later. In *Novum Organum*, which no English teacher can afford to pass by, Bacon showed men how to gain certain knowledge through science, avoiding the pitfalls of hasty generalizations. Book I of the *Organum* is filled with illumination on every page. Three inventions, writes Bacon, have transformed society: gunpowder has revolutionized warfare, the compass has revolutionized navigation, and the printing press has transformed the world of literature. To Bacon cooperative science could enormously expand men's energies. He was convinced that "a great mass of inventions yet remains" that would make for peaceful revolutions throughout the globe. If Bacon were alive today, what would he say about the atom bomb? Would he say, "What if the atom bomb should put an end to war when no other invention could? The world may yet find in its dread new weapons the only way to a lasting peace; a peace based on mutual fear, perhaps, but this peace men everywhere prefer to mutual annihilation." Such applications of key ideas to contemporary dilemmas are a necessity for intellectual growth in the classroom or out.

Seeking Breadth of Outlook and Resources

Thus gradually one may build for himself an intellectual structure, extended by other cloisters, walled gardens, or lofty doorways, each intrinsic to our plan. Many English teachers make the error of limiting themselves to aesthetics, loving the metaphysical intricacies of Donne's poetry or the subtleties of versification without tracing the links that bind the master's mind to the solid earth and the comprehension of the average boy or girl. When Donne spoke, in a sermon, of a fly buzzing round his head as he knelt in supplication to his God, he showed that he knew how to speak to humble people; and there is no one of us who has not experienced such an ironical happening in his religious meditations. Even such a profound insight as "Never send to ask for whom the bell tolls; it tolls for thee" was real to the audience of Donne's day, who knew the plague and the many death carts, each with its tolling bell. We must search in each author for that part of him which is real to us, which has parallels we can point to in the life around us; only as we do this can we make the author real to our students. The more rarefied in meaning or technical in form a line of verse, the more imperative it becomes to "give to airy nothings a local habitation and a name." For every book of aesthetics, we need to turn to a book of ideas or fictional realism, such as the sermons of Donne, the *Leviathan* of Hobbes, the first chapter of *Don Quixote*, the first chapter of *Robinson Crusoe* or *A Journal of the Plague Year*. Beyond each metaphysical idea is a personal experience, and beyond each personal experience is a social condition. But unless we can illuminate a passage of poetry in terms of today's personal experience or today's social condition, we cannot usually induce our students to find in literature a continuing fascination. Beautiful sounds have a magic that does not fully compensate for obscurity of meaning. Only the meaning of poetry, not the sound, can call up a parallel in personal experience that makes a lasting imprint on the memory or bears fruit in daily action.

One condition of professional growth is an awareness of the gaps in our reading; no intellectual satisfaction is quite like that which comes from the gradual mastery of the great minds we have hitherto been forced to pass by. In the seventeenth century, if we have missed Hobbes' *Leviathan*, Sir Thomas Browne's *Religio Medici*, or Dryden's *All for Love*, or a leisurely reading of *Paradise Lost*, we come to them prepared and expectant, as we are prepared to see the Michelangelo murals in the Sistine Chapel for the first time, or the Ghiberti doors in Florence, or the room full of Blake etchings in the Tate Gallery in London, or Emerson's hat still on the wall in his Concord house.

To be aware of the great books we have missed is in itself a token of reward and delight. The day comes at last when we sit down in our fresh hours, the house quiet, the spirit calm, the mind expectant. If the field is the eighteenth century, we may turn to *Tom Jones, Amelia,* or Jefferson's *Notes on the State of Virginia.* In a new framework of ideas we may reread "Elegy Written in a Country Churchyard," precursor of romantic and revolutionary ideas of later decades. The "Elegy" is ideal for the classroom, and its comment on the origin of great men is in the tradition of democratic guesses which as the decades pass take on more and more surely the aspect of scientific fact. No poem is easier to teach than "The Elegy" or more fondly remembered by the mass of high school students. Though the "Elegy" is not a gap in the intellectual growth of most teachers, we may have missed Rousseau's *Émile,* Boswell's *Life of Johnson,* Johnson's *Lives of the Poets,* Blake's *Songs of Innocence,* and especially, at the end of the century, William Godwin's *Political Justice,* which is the key to Shelley's thought and a great book in its own right. Unfortunately, many survey courses in English literature no longer introduce us to Wordsworth, Coleridge, Shelley, Keats, and Byron as a group that help to explain each other. We may come to teaching, therefore, without having had either a thorough survey course or, what every English teacher needs, a solid course in the romantic poets. For Wordsworth and Coleridge we need especially the preface to *Lyrical Ballads* and the illuminating replies by Coleridge in *Biographia Literaria.* Of the five poets, Keats and Byron are the easiest to comprehend; and in classroom discussion perhaps "The Prisoner of Chillon" is the most appealing to the average boy or girl without a special interest in literature. Among the romantics, Shelley is the most complex in mind and achievement. His prose, particularly his prefaces to *Prometheus Unbound* and *The Cenci,* contains memorable passages of classic worth. Sooner or later we must come to *The Cenci,* one of the most remarkable closet dramas of English literature, written in a style utterly unlike the Shelley we find in his poems or prose.

Reading for professional growth requires many detours for intellectual pleasure and profit, such as an exploration of the revolutionary period in American history, a period rich in social classics, though poor in literature of the first rank. Biographies of

Jefferson, Franklin, Hamilton, and John Adams lead us to their letters and their papers of permanent worth in American thought. Among these are the *Federalist Papers* by Hamilton and Madison; Paine's *The Rights of Man* and *The Crisis;* Jefferson's *Notes on the State of Virginia* and *Bill for Establishing Religious Freedom.* Perennial classics are *The Journal of John Woolman* and Crèvecoeur, *Letters from an American Farmer.* It is advantageous to relate American revolutionary literature to that of England and France. Americans may remember that Robert Burns and William Blake were extremely sympathetic with the American revolutionists, whereas Samuel Johnson was doggedly hostile. In violent protest against England's attitude toward the French, Blake wore a red cap through the streets. Though many Americans deplored the excesses of the French Revolution, they had read Rousseau, Voltaire, and Montesquieu with profit. Jefferson was especially fond of Condorcet's classic written in the shadow of the guillotine, *Sketch of the History of the Human Spirit.*

*   *   *

The suggestions thus far set forth might be extended to many fields of literature, and I hope that the annotated lists of Appendix 1 will be found to be of permanent worth to the teacher who wishes to prepare himself in those seminal books which will be of special benefit to his students. Each of us must set his own goals of intellectual purpose and delight. To know the seminal books is not enough. Each time we can communicate a great book's essence to another, it assumes a new stature in our own meditations. But these reflections are only shadows of what might be in the world of action. The great books help us to grow internally and to represent in our actions the essence of our heroes and heroines. However frequent our failures in the classroom and out, we must foster an expectancy of greatness in ourselves — greatness of spirit, talent, or educational action that will ultimately nourish crop after crop of American youth informed by the world's great books and inspired by the dreams of the world's choice spirits.

To the Student Teacher: Suggested Activities

1. Make a list of fifteen or twenty masterpieces mentioned on pp. 312–14 or pp. 425–43 that you would like to read in college or soon after. In a brief annotation on each book, show why you are curious about it and why you want to read it eventually.
2. Read the life of Michelangelo and the life of Leonardo in Vasari's *Lives of the Painters*. Quote three passages from each life, showing what ideas or facts about these artists were most significant to you. [See also Irving Stone's remarkable book *The Agony and the Ecstasy*.]
3. Read the opening pages of Dostoievsky's *Crime and Punishment* and his *House of the Dead*. Which of these books would you prefer to read further? Give reasons for your choice.
4. Read Plato's *Apology*. Write an impression of this oration, quoting several passages from Socrates' language.
5. Dip into Comenius' *The Great Didactic*. Then write an impression in which you quote several passages from the masterpiece, passages you believe are still timely and constructive.
6. Read several chapters of Rousseau's *Émile*. What ideas do you find here that are still provocative? Make a list of the most arresting passages.
7. In what department of great books do you feel that your background is most deficient? Write a brief analysis of this deficiency, showing what books you wish to read eventually to overcome it.

28   Classical Principles
in Action: The Teacher
as Writer and Critic

IN ORDER TO INTERPRET literature to his class, each teacher aspires to be a gifted critic. In the midst of today's *avant garde* writing and criticism, he may conclude that there are no certainties of literary analysis which he may attain for his own satisfaction or communicate to his students. To arrive at such a conclusion is to thwart one's growth as a teacher and lover of literature. We have at hand a body of judgments and principles which enable us to evaluate the quality of a writer, whether we are studying *The Odyssey*, *The Leopard*, or *The Pearl*. Such a body of critical knowledge is attainable by the average teacher. The gaining of such knowledge, moreover, is full of delight and illumination of literature as well as rich in practical ways to teach it. Let no teacher, therefore, despair of becoming a judicious literary critic. Each one of us with enough patience and persistence can gain the knowledge necessary to analyze a passage of literature and explain in specific terms of diction and structure why the passage possesses or does not possess literary value. I realize there are many critics and writers who say today that there are no certain rules by which a work of art may be judged. This is the kind of nonsense that sometimes burns away the noble aspirations of an English teacher. We can master step by step a large body of critical theory by which a work of art may be judged with certainty and assurance.

What Is Classical in Writing Art?

To describe this body of theory, we use the term "classical principles." By classical principles we mean those theories of creative

397

writing adhered to by the great masters of the past from Homer and Chaucer to Conrad and Cather. When, for example, the writer wishes to describe a place, how does he begin? What elements of information does he present to the reader in the opening sentences? In describing a place, does he use a progression of far to near objects, or is the progression from near to far satisfactory? Should there be such a thing as a culminating image in describing a place or a person? If so, what is the function of the culminating image? The classicist has specific answers to these questions. We may see the answers by analyzing even one passage, such as the following from Joseph Conrad:

THIS IS HOW I SEE THE EAST

And this is how I see the East. I have seen its secret places and have looked into its very soul; but now I see it always from a small boat, a high outline of mountains, blue and afar in the morning; like faint mist at noon; a jagged wall of purple at sunset. I have the feel of the oar in my hand, the vision of a scorching blue sea in my eyes. And I see a bay, a wide bay, smooth as glass and polished like ice, shimmering in the dark. A red light burns far off upon the gloom of the land, and the night is soft and warm. We drag at the oars with aching arms, and suddenly a puff of wind, a puff faint and tepid and laden with strange odours of blossoms, or aromatic wood, comes out of the still night — the first sigh of the East on my face.

Joseph Conrad, from *Youth*

The classicist believes in coming to the point in the opening sentence of his paragraph, his novel, his poem, as Conrad does in the passage above, as Milton does in the first sentence, even the first line, of *Paradise Lost*. In the second sentence above, Conrad accomplishes several aims of the classicist's creed. We know that the hero is looking at the shoreline from a small boat. Like every good painter, Conrad sketches in first the background of mountains and makes them real to us. Then he writes, "I have the feel of the oar in my hand," with this image of touch bringing the reader into the boat, so that he can look at the scene with the hero's own eyes. The phrase, "feel of the oar in my hand," is incidental to the story, but highly significant from the artist's point of view in helping the reader catch the mood of the moment. Then Conrad sketches in the middle-ground images of the bay and returns for a moment to the far-off background, where a red light burns. For a third time Conrad reminds us of the point of view, this time with another touch image, "drag at the oars with aching arms." Then comes the culminating image, an image of smell, a smell "laden with strange odours of blossoms, or aromatic wood." A classicist rarely uses an image of smell to bring his passage to a climax, but we feel that Conrad in this instance is justified. From the five senses he chooses the one most acute at that moment to suggest to us the mystery of the East. Conrad's use of intense imagery is also in the classical tradition. One may say the more intense the concentration of imagery and the fewer terms of interpretation used, the more completely the diction of a passage is in the classical tradition.

The best way to become a critic is to *try the classical principles in your own writing.* Write first a description of an outdoor place that you can observe afresh, as presented on pages 401–02. We may summarize in a chart the key principles, somewhat as follows:

Try For	Avoid
1. One moment of time: season and time of day	1. Interpretive adjectives, such as *beautiful, remarkable, wonderful,* etc. These words should be used by the reader as he reads, not by you.
2. One point of view definitely stated	2. Passive voice, such as "could be seen." The use of the passive voice weakens your style.
3. Order: a. Background images b. Intervening details c. Foreground details d. Most conspicuous detail	3. The verbs *is, are, was,* etc. These weak, watery forms of the verb *to be* you should carefully weed out of your description before handing it in.
4. Definite placing of all objects in the picture	4. Generalizing statements at the end of your theme. Use a vivid concrete detail.
5. Active, suggestive verbs	5. Change in point of view. Keep one position as you describe your place.
6. Elimination of images that do not suggest the mood	6. Negative statements, such as "The moon was not shining," or "The river was not wide."

The Professional Need of a Writing Course

How does a teacher in service or a prospective teacher acquire a body of critical principles in the classical tradition by which to judge the quality of a novel, a short story, or a poem? The best and most practical way is to *follow the footsteps of the masters* in a writing course under a gifted teacher, who brings to the classroom a long background in the study of the classics of world literature. Such a teacher knows that the best way to become a critic is by writing descriptions, stories, and sketches in the tradition of the masters. Such a series of assignments represents the accumulated wisdom of the classical tradition. In carrying through such a program, it is not necessary to become a writer of distinction oneself. It is necessary to retrace the masters' steps in writing apprenticeship and thus to face their dilemmas of style and structure. Only then does a serious student of literature become securely grounded in the best critical thought of his field.

How did Conrad and Crane and Dickens come to know the secrets of classical art? They read and studied the master works of their great predecessors. But they learned more about the classical principles *by writing than by reading.* You and I can learn similarly, even by writing the assignments one by one that we make in turn to our gifted students.

PROGRESSION OF ASSIGNMENTS: THE TEACHER AS WRITER

The progression of assignments in the following pages is from the personal and the concrete to the social and the abstract. Many such writing experiments you and I have already carried out in college classes or in graduate courses. Choose the assignments you think most fruitful in the development of your own writing and growth of critical insight. The first aim is to relearn the first great principle of the classical tradition: the use of intense sensory diction, as in Homer's "rosy-fingered dawn" and Milton's "winged with red lightning." A part of the magic of writing is seeing the familiar world anew, this time for the purpose of making a record: the bend of black branches outside one's window on a snowy day; the smell of burning wood in the fireplace, the red hot ash below, the flames of red and gold crackling above the black log; the wrinkles in the eye corners of a loved one's face. "No man ever forgot," wrote Emerson, "the visitations of that power to his heart and brain, which created all things new; that was the dawn in him of music, poetry, and art." Observing the world afresh, forcing oneself to sit at one spot and make a record of the sights and sounds of the moment, this creates all things new. When one finds a fascination with this achievement, all else follows. Each of us possesses a unique vision. "A man is born into the world with his own pair of eyes," wrote Crane, "and he is not at all responsible for his vision — he is merely responsible for his quality of personal honesty." No street or face or store window honestly observed is ever quite the same to two people. No impression of a room made with one's eye on the objects can be without a touch of originality. The unique vision selects the unique image if not the unique phrase.

Describing an Outdoor Place

Choose a place out of doors that you can go to and observe afresh. Take notes as you observe. Then, before putting your theme in final shape, study carefully Mildred King's "Night Scene" below, and Maurice Posner's sketch, "Ryker Alley." How does Mildred make you stand beside her as she observes the Seagram Building? How does she establish a point of view? How does she show time and place? Does Mildred give you a picture of the whole building before she describes particulars? What is her culminating image? In Maurice Posner's sketch, how does he tell us at the very beginning the time of day and point of view? Does he begin with images of background and then go to middleground and foreground objects?

NIGHT SCENE

Across Park Avenue, in the quiet November night, I see the Seagram Building. Lighted windows shine like gleaming dominoes, lend a shadowy luster to the tall bronze sheath. Behind wide glass frames on the ground floor, hidden lamps illumine a sand-colored structure resembling the walls of the Egyptian tomb. Eight fountains, wreaths spraying silvery water, sit symmetrically on either corner of the diamond-dusted pavement. To one side, two trees, long-stemmed chalices, sway in soft concert with the wind.

They raise their filigree branches, whisper their hosannas to the heavens. The midnight-blue sky, an infinite feathery quilt, blankets everything. Only the full moon glows, pale and ethereal, mid the trees' fragile limbs.

Mildred King

RYKER ALLEY

I threw my barracks bag over my shoulder and, mounting the El steps, looked back over Ryker Alley. In the October afternoon shadows, I saw for the last time the Manhattan tenement ravine that I had called home. It twisted its narrow, winding way as if noise and soot, and the ant-activity of thousands of people, had cut a gorge between the overhanging gray-brown buildings. On the cobble-stoned street fell the patterned shadow of the overhead railway ties. Above me loomed the vaulted stone towers of the Brooklyn Bridge, its thin tracery of gray steel webbing the sky, the roadway in a swift arch soaring over the East River to the banks of Brooklyn. From rust-red escapes hung white bedsheets, billowing in the wind, and in their roundness looked like fungus clinging to a cliff side. As far as I could see, pushcharts lined the gutters. Vendors hawked their wares of pink calico and blue jeans, of plum blue grapes and brown-speckled bananas, and of brined herring and scaly carp on a bed of chopped ice. In the afternoon breeze wafted the salt, sewered smell of the East River. From below, I heard the honking of yellow, checkered taxicabs, the double-clutching grind of Mack trucks, their drivers cursing and bullying a path through the strangulated traffic; and from above, the anger of the subway trains. Across the street two young men in shiny garbardines and brown felt hats, their long black locks curling devoutly at their ears, entered a basement synagogue. Through the door which swung brokenly from one hinge, before the flickering candle flames of a seven-branched candelabrum, I briefly glimpsed gray-bearded men wrapped in striped, fringed prayer-shawls, rocking in prayer. Next to the El stairs, from behind a broken wood fence, seeped the smell of urine, acid and stinging. Through the fence I saw the empty lot where once stood the tenement in which I was born, now filled with un-drained puddles of water, shining with the green glisten of broken bottles, and where frightened yellow cats foraged among the rusty tin cans. On a brown, moldering brick wall hung a tattered poster urging a vote for Fiorello H. La Guardia.

Maurice Posner

The Five Senses in Action

Write five brief paragraphs in each of which you concentrate on one of the five senses. Appeal to the other four senses as well in each sketch if you can. Try especially for sounds and colors. Tell *when* and *where* in each paragraph. It is always economical to begin, "On this November afternoon," as Marjorie does in her theme on smells, naming the month and time of day in two words. Why are smell and taste more difficult to describe than sight and sound? Which is the easiest of the five senses to describe?

SOUNDS: AFTER-DINNER MUSIC

Not from the radio, but from the dish-pan, rises the after-dinner music. The selection begins in light, airy moods and ends with sorrowful, deep bass notes. First, there is the *tinkle, clink, clink, tinkle* of the crystal glasses, which grows into a stronger, resounding tone — *kling, ping, kling, ping* — as the silverware flies from pan to drainboard. For variation the milk bottle adds its *glug, glug, glick* as it drowns in the foamy water and sinks to the bottom of the sudsy depths. The rather flat monotones of the everyday dishes are followed by the fierce, crashing notes of the pots and pans, and the final crescendo of the frying pan as it *bongs* upon the hook from which it is to hang. But wait, with the last piece completed and the water sliding from the tilted pan, one last spoon adds a tinkling note of hope as it slips into the sink. New hope — for what? It is a hope that someone other than I will enjoy the pleasure of the dish-pan music tomorrow evening.

Virginia C. Barber

TOUCH: THE BARBER'S CHAIR

As I sat miserably in the barber's chair that August day, some short pieces of hair slid down my back. They tickled, itched, scratched, and burned; as though filled with life, they wriggled, squirmed, and bit furiously at my skin.

Charles Turek

TASTE AND SIGHT: COOL PAUSE

It was a hot day. I climbed up on the red and chrome stool before the fountain, glad of the damp breeze which the humming electric fan blew my way. The clerk swept away a chocolate-smeared glass with a reddened hand and rubbed a sour cloth across the cold surface of the marble counter. His other hand hovered expectantly over the shiny row of taps as he waited for me to give my order. I said, "A lemon coke, please," because I was thirsty; then I watched his deft hands push in the proper taps. First came a spurt of brown syrup, next the hiss and splash of carbonated water, then a dash of lemon, a scoop of crushed ice, and the whole was whipped into foaming delectability by a long-handled spoon. He set down the drink with a flourish, offered me two straws popped from a clean, wrinkled paper jacket, ignored my grateful, "Thanks!" and left me to enjoy the "pause that refreshes."

Lucie Dowling

SMELLS

On this November afternoon a patch quilt of smells greets me as I open the door to the school building. I identify them as I walk to my room. As I climb the stairs, I know the drab gray smell of a sour mop. Mimeograph ink makes the black patches, surrounded by the lavender of the ditto fluid. As I pass the lavatory, the acid smell of yellow makes me turn my head. The pastel-colored smells flow to meet me as I open the door of the teachers' lounge. I walk across the rug, and the brown smell of dust assails my nostrils. The clean smell of white drifts from the health office, and the green comes from the cleaning compounds in the janitor's closet. From the heat of the radiators comes a smell of rusty red.

Marjorie Jayson

Describing a Classroom

This assignment calls for immediate, unforgettable practice in writing with the eye upon colors, movements, faces; the ear open to classroom sounds; the finger tips touching desks, pencils, erasers, handkerchiefs; the nose open to varied smells in the classroom air. Read the models, "Barbara to My Left," p. 66, "May Morning," below, or write a better one of your own. List the requirements on the board as shown above, p. 66.

MAY MORNING

As I sit at my desk this May morning, the yellow sunlight swirls round the green walls and brightens Jane's golden hair under the open window at my left. Through the window comes a breeze laden with spring and the smell of flowering earth. In front of me Joe suddenly turns round to borrow my eraser. As he sees me glance again toward the window, his freckled red face widens in a grin. I hear the squeak of wheels as Mr. French rolls back his chair and walks slowly toward the windows, his back very straight, his black hair shining in the sun, his full lips curved in an expectant smile. I hear the far-off cries of children, high and shrill, the honking of a horn, the sudden screech of brakes. Jane goes forward to ask Mr. French something, her voice tinkling out a short question, her red nails glinting as she holds up her paper. Joe turns and grins at me again, his white teeth gleaming, his blue eyes dancing. I give his shoulder a sharp little punch. Struggling to write, I feel my fingers sweating around my pen. It is a warm day, and spring comes in through the window.

Harold Fontanella

Describing a Room at Home

Years ago, after World War II, I taught a class of disabled veterans at American University. They wrote a book called *The Purple Testament*. Eleven of the fifty-three men and women were amputees; all were somewhat tense and shaky, though the healthiest group psychologically I have ever taught. Not having had any military experience, I felt humble and sad and unprepared as I looked into their faces; but I soon saw, as they spoke and wrote each week, that they trusted me. I began with objective assignments of descriptions of home-town moments and places: I remember a backyard tree in Minnesota, a moment at a Coney Island hot-dog stand, Grandma's cookies in a quiet New England town.

Finally, after descriptions of outdoor places, I asked them to describe a room at home. Any such theme, if written from honest observation, pierces deep and unlocks streams of energy. So it was with John Regan, nineteen years old, a short, quiet boy with blue eyes and red hair; he had lost his leg in a tank battle. Here is his story:

MY ROOM AT THE LILAC INN

As I look around this room in this third-rate boarding house, my eyes are greeted first by the entrance to its gloomy interior. The door is painted a dirty cream color. There is a crack in one panel. The ceiling is the same dingy color with pieces of adhesive tape holding some of the plaster in place. The walls are streaked and cracked here and there. Also on the walls are pieces of Scotch tape that once held, I presume, some sexy girls, pictures of *Esquire Magazine* origin. Across the room runs a line; upon it hang a shirt, a grimy towel, and washed stump socks belonging to my roommate, Jack Nager. By the door near the top sash juts a piece of wood on which is hung — it looks like an old spread. It is calico, dirty, and a sickly green color.

Behind that is a space which serves as our closet; next to that is the radiator, painted the same ghastly color. The landlady must have got the paint for nothing. On top are Jack's black suitcase, his green soap dish, and a brightly colored box containing his hair tonic. Over by the cracked window are a poorly made table and chair. On top of the table, a pencil, shaving talcum, a glass, a nail file; one of my socks hangs over the side. Above the table is our window, the curtains of cheese cloth held back by a string. There is also a black, fairly whole paper shade to dim such little sunlight as might enter.

This window is my only promise of a better future. Through it, I can see the well-lit and nicely furnished living room of a modern apartment house across the street. Someday I'll live like that.

There, next to the window, leaning against an aged bureau, as if resting, are my faithful crutches. On the oilcloth covering the top of the bureau lie some seventeen-odd books. These I used at the _____ University here in Washington, D.C. I am attending a six-month course, getting the fundamentals needed to be a Service Officer for veterans. There are enough books on that bureau to take at least a year's reading for absorption. Beard's *American Government and Policy, Anatomy, How to Interview, Soldier to Civilian*, government laws, manuals, textbooks, a public-speaking guide and what-have-you are all reflected in the cloudy mirror. On the bureau stands a picture of my love, my faithful wife. I think of her. I wish I were with her tonight.

Standing alongside this bureau is this *thing*. A leather cup, straps and buckles dropping from it. Below this cup, the flesh-colored *thing* and calf, and on its foot a brown sock and oxblood shoe. This is a prosthesis. I've called this wooden leg a lot of other things. This is the replacement for the real one that was shot off in France. O, what the hell! A leg isn't everything. You've got to keep living. There are a lot worse things in this world to reckon with than an artificial leg.

On the parlor chair, here probably because there's no other place for it, my brown pants are thrown, together with my old khaki shirt. On the floor my recently painted foot locker that was in many an army camp with me is still doing service.

Jack Nager grunts alongside me in the double bed as he turns over; he is getting a good sleep tonight. His below-the-knee stump quivers as he touches some close-to-the-skin nerve on the bed. His foot was also a donation for democracy. I reach to turn out the twenty-five-watt bulb on the shadeless lamp; I find the light switch. The room is in darkness. From the street three stories below comes the sound of a motor car; it fades away. Occasionally a click, click of heels hitting the pavement as someone passes by. Within the house the sound of muffled voices, the flushing of a toilet, someone blowing his nose.

I forget everything and concentrate on sleep.

John J. Regan, *The Purple Testament* (1949)

The discussion of John Regan's theme with the class is a highly creative experience. We may wish to progress from the central meaning to the structure, asking the students their impressions of John's outlook at this moment, and what passages best show his state of mind. What phrase best shows his attitude towards his wound? Turning to points of style, we may say, "What is the connotation of the phrase, *twenty-five-watt bulb?*" No two teachers will lead such a discussion in the same way, but it can hardly fail to be searching and instructive in many ways.

HELPS AND POINTERS: CLASSICAL PRINCIPLES IN FOCUS

As for the structure of such a theme, we may write on the board a list of aims for the assignment such as follows:

1. Point of view. Where were you standing as you observed the room?
2. Put in images and colors of background as John does in describing the walls.
3. Describe any significant pictures on the walls.
4. Describe the articles of furniture.
5. Describe the bed in which you sleep.
6. Describe clothes hanging up or thrown over chairs as John does. Visualize most fully significant clothes or shoes.
7. What can you see from the window?
8. What is the object in the room most important in your life? Put it last for emphasis among the objects you describe.
9. What sound do you hear as you sit in your room or look at it from the doorway? Why do the sounds at the end of John's theme become so emphatic and memorable?

Using a Blending Element

By describing the movement of light or smoke or rain or color as it touches a person or a place, the writer can blend several images into one sentence and one mood.

SUMMER RAIN

Rain drops splattered the dusty asphalt, struck the scattered wind-tossed papers, plopped against the sides of wood-planked sheds.

Ellen Juro

BIRD SONG

A bird shivered its song down the length of a tree, and the note trembled a moment on the edge of my hearing; the muscles in my stomach tightened; I ran down the street like a child.

Laura Chernev

THE CANDLE FLAME

The wavering flame dances brightly in the quiet blue eyes, glows yellow on the simple frames, transforms the rolling tears into drops of gold.

Evelyn Gross

THE YELLOW-WHITE GLOW

The yellow-white glow from the ceiling lamp splashed on John Meehan's boyish face, brightening the reddened forehead, the clean-shaven pink cheeks, and causing a faint pattern of squares to form on his horn-rimmed glasses.

Carole Busby

A PURPLE BATHROBE

A torn purple bathrobe clings to drooping shoulders, slides over a protruding stomach, and spreads apart at the bottom over spindly white legs.

Sheila Kanowitz

ALARMING REDNESS

The first and most violent impression was his redness. Everything about him was red — hair, large protuberant ears, eyebrows, even his bony, knuckly hands. . . . Moreover, it was a most alarming redness. His face was so red that it seemed to throw off heat, and if at that moment smoke had begun to issue from his nostrils and he had burst out in flames all over, George would hardly have been surprised.

Thomas Wolfe, *You Can't Go Home Again*

Describing a Person You Know Well

Choose a person you know well and feel deeply about. Describe this person as he sits near you or across the table at home or in a restaurant.

MY GRANDMOTHER

I sit at the table with my grandmother. As the wrinkled white hands, trembling slightly, light the next candle, the yellow-blue flame casts a dark shadow on the gray walls. A pair of blue-veined hands caress the ancient silver, fondle the delicate carving, then rise to a tired face in fervent prayer. Wisps of white hair flecked with brown peek from a silk kerchief adorning the quivering head, now covered for the holy blessing. The wavering flame dances brightly in the quiet blue eyes, glows yellow on the simple frames, transforms the rolling tears into drops of gold. Swaying gently, the plump figure prays, blesses her children, and their children and theirs to come, blesses her dead mother and her dead babies. The yellow gleam illuminates the solemn gray dress enfolding the worn body, the round face uplifted. A full warm smile appears on the wrinkled face, and the whisper, "Good shabbos," echoes against the peaceful walls.

Evelyn Gross

The Classical Principle in Describing a Person

In her theme about her grandmother Evelyn establishes at once the point of view with the phrase, "at the table"; then the reader can sit with her and look across at the grandmother. With the word *grandmother* and the "blue-veined hands" and "white hair" we have a sense of approximate age; from the candles we know the time of day. The candle flames form a wonderful blending element, giving action to the light and bringing eyes, glasses, and tears together in symbolic unity. The blending sentence beginning "The wavering flame" is a work of art in itself. Already we have images of the grandmother's dress; then the writer has the grandmother move and act and speak, with the whispered sound of "Good shabbos" the culminating image.

In Stevenson's description of Black Dog in the sketch below we have the classicist ideal exemplified with dramatic compression: first the point of view exactly established and the *frame* of the man: "a tall, strong, heavy, nut-brown man." This phrase shows the coloring of Black Dog as well as his stature; it also shows his approximate age with the word *heavy*. Notice how skillfully Stevenson uses the image of the pigtail (establishing his occupation) with the image of the coat. Within this framework of imagery Stevenson now comes to particularizing images that establish a *dominant impression of character:* "hands ragged and scarred, with black, broken nails"; these images are foreboding, but do not in themselves suggest a violent or evil man. But when we come to the saber cut and particularly, "a dirty, livid white," we have a strong dominant impression of a violent man prone to evil action. Yet Stevenson has not used a single interpretive expression except perhaps the word *dirty*.

BLACK DOG AT THE DOOR

I remember him as if it were yesterday, as he came plodding to the inn door, his sea-chest following behind him in a hand barrow; a tall, strong, heavy, nut-brown man; his tarry pigtail falling over the shoulders of his faded blue coat; his hands ragged and scarred, with black, broken nails; and the saber-cut across one cheek, a dirty, livid white.

Robert Louis Stevenson, from *Treasure Island*

ANTICIPATING WEAKNESSES

As you edit your description, weed out rigorously the weak phrases listed on the following page:

1. The verb *to be: was, is, had been, were*
2. The passive voice, especially *was seen, was heard*
3. Colorless verbs such as *seem* and *appear*
4. Time-frayed adjectives such as *silver, silver-haired*
5. Interpretive adjectives such as *beautiful, menacing, handsome.* Use other interpretive adjectives sparingly: depend rather on the suggestiveness of your images of form, color, or movement, such as *round, smooth face, bristling red hair, his cane haltingly tapping the sidewalk.*
6. Statements that tell what you did *not* see, such as "He needed a hair-cut," or "he was not a tall man."
7. Large words for small occasions, such as "resumed progress."

EVALUATING THEME ACHIEVEMENT

1. Do I have a blending device that fuses several images? Do I have at least three images in the blending sentence?
2. Have I used images to fit the impression of the person I am trying to create? Have I eliminated all images that might suggest a different impression?
3. Have I made clear the physical position of my character in relation to my own? Is my point of view completely clear?
4. Have I made clear the time of day, season of the year, place, subordinating this information in phrases?
5. In the last sentence of my description have I concentrated on the most vivid detail of my character's appearance? Is it a detail that emphatically suggests my impression of his personality? Is it in keeping with the mood of my portrait?
6. Have I avoided stylistic weaknesses common to descriptive writing as listed on page 399?

Describing a Person in a Setting

The next step in describing a person is to put your character in a specific setting, as Helen does in the sketch below, "Mr. Wilson." As you read this sketch, notice how deftly Helen establishes the mood of the setting with sharp, clear images in the opening sentence. She carefully interweaves the time of day and season of the year with two words, "November evening." Then Helen begins her sketch of Mr. Wilson, establishing several points of information in her sentence beginning, "A glance at his tall, spare figure. . . ." We have first a suggestion of Mr. Wilson's stature, his age, his professional background. Then comes one of the most remarkable blending elements I have ever found in either professional or student writing. In the sentence beginning, "Flakes of mud were in his hair, . . ." Helen uses a blending element of rain and mud with consummate skill, weaving into the blending sentence images of Mr. Wilson's eyes, his overalls, even his shoes. Like a painter, Helen then comes to more significant particularizing images. As Mr. Wilson leans on his shovel, he suddenly begins to cough. Helen visualizes the impact of this cough and concludes her description of Mr. Wilson with a culminating image of the small splotch of blood. The sequence of images in this sketch from the pictures of background to the culminating image fulfills in a superb way the classical progression from general to specific, from less significant to more significant. The culminating image of the handkerchief with the splotch of blood suggests the mood of despair and frustration in Mr. Wilson's life.

MR. WILSON

All was gray and miserable — dark clouds hanging motionless over sombre hills, the low bank along the road shaggy with dead grass, the uneven cinder road running along the gutter where men were wearily digging, and the steady, monotonous drizzle of rain blurring the desolate landscape. As I walked home from school that November evening, I paused to watch the C.W.A. workers. In the midst of the sturdy-looking laborers Mr. Wilson was conspicuous. A glance at his tall spare figure, graying hair, stooped shoulders, and long sensitive hands that were revealed in spite of the disfiguring gloves told me that some irony of circumstance had placed him in the ditch. The dripping rain and the sloshing and shoveling of the other workers splattered mud all over Mr. Wilson. Flakes of mud were in his hair, in the corners of his passionless blue eyes, spots of it on his face, long smudges on his baggy blue-denim overalls; mud crusted the edge of his trouser legs and caked in awkward lumps on his heavy working shoes. Every few moments he paused, exhausted, to lean on his shovel. Suddenly a racking cough convulsed his frail form, a feverish blotch of red burned on his haggard cheeks, water filled his eyes, and a small splotch of blood stained one end of the handkerchief held to his lips.

Helen Trempus

Recalling a Crystal Moment

Call up and describe a memorable moment in your life, a moment of joy, sorrow, sadness, repose, anticipation, self-doubt, wonder, love, hate, ecstasy. How can you make this moment a burning memory in language, unforgettable to the reader?

The paragraph below is from *Of Human Bondage*, by Somerset Maugham. Philip, the boy here, who is afflicted with a club foot, has been away to boarding school for the first time. Curious about his affliction, the boys of the school have persecuted him, tearing off his shoe and stocking in the locker room to gaze and deride. Philip comes home for Christmas vacation in a fever of despair. But then at the dinner table he hears his uncle, who is a minister, say that "prayer can remove mountains." Immediately Philip decides to pray for a miracle that will make his club foot whole.

PHILIP'S PRAYER

He prayed with all the power of his soul. No doubts assailed him . . . he went up to bed tremulous with excitement. There was snow on the ground, and Aunt Louisa had allowed herself the unaccustomed luxury of a fire in her bedroom; but in Philip's little room it was so cold that his fingers were numb, and he had great difficulty in undoing his collar. His teeth chattered. The idea came to him that he must do something more than usual to attract the attention of God, and he turned back the rug which was in front of his bed so that he could kneel on the bare boards; and then it struck him that his nightshirt was a softness that might displease his Maker, so he took it off and said his prayers naked. When he got into bed it was so cold that for some time he could not sleep, but when he did, it was so soundly that Mary Ann had to shake him when she brought in his hot water next morning. She talked to him while she drew the curtains, but he did not answer; he had remembered that this was the morning for the miracle. His heart was filled with joy and gratitude. His first instinct was to put down his hand and feel the foot which was whole now, but to do this seemed to doubt the goodness of God. He knew that his foot was well. But at last he made up his mind, and with the toes of his right foot he just touched his left. Then he passed his hand over it.

Somerset Maugham, *Of Human Bondage*

Now read and compare this moment from Maugham with "Through the August Night" below. Which of the two moments is more vivid to you? Which of the five senses does Maugham appeal to most often to bring his reader into Philip's room? Which image makes you and me feel almost a part of Philip? In Charles' moment below, does he emphasize images of touch as much as Maugham? What sentence is most vivid in Charles' theme? Does it capture your imagination, make you feel closer to the hero than to Philip in his little room?

THROUGH THE AUGUST NIGHT

I squirm deeper into my seat as the bus races through the rain-soaked August night, its lights bouncing from the filmed highway and jutting into the mist drifting from the black Jersey swamps. I'm leaving behind a part of myself, a part I'll never get back again. The asphalt ribbon is broken by the flaring neon mosaic of passing roadhouses and drive-ins, and as these patterns of light flash past me. I wonder if that's all a man is: a series of sections scattered through the world with only memories to pull the threads together. Threads. Threads twining through time, threads of love, truth and aloneness; the threads of one's self — wrapped by the elusive thread of dreams. This is the last run from Washington to New York; the bus is almost empty. A few passengers occupy the red-covered seats; their heads roll against the chair-backs and nod with the lurching of the darkened bus. My leg jostles the seabag propped alongside me, leaving a smudge on my starched uniform. I move my hand slowly toward my knee, then stop and lean back in the seat. Why should I bother? Who's going to chew me out? I've got my discharge from the Navy; there's no need to worry about a clean uniform any more — no need at all — I'm free. I'm going home. I should be happy — that's for sure. But free for what? A tired melancholy fills me as I rest my head on the cool window glass.

Charles Edward Bryan

TO MAKE A MOMENT REAL

1. Pinpoint the moment in place and time. Use the name of the month, as Charles does in his first sentence. How does Maugham suggest season and cold air in the house?
2. *Appeal to all five senses if possible.* What do you see most vividly in Maugham's moment? What do you hear in Charles' moment? Which moment puts greatest emphasis on images of touch? Identify the best image of touch in each moment.
3. Which moment has better images of action? Discuss the ones you like best. Use several striking images of action in your own paper.
4. Which moment has the most vivid language? What are the five or six most vivid words in each moment?
5. Use a bit of dialogue to make your moment real. Would either of the themes above be more vivid if the author had used spoken words? Are the stories better without dialogue?

What Is Happiness?

Describe a moment from your life that symbolizes for you the essence of happiness. Build up the moment with images so that the reader can enter into it and feel the setting as well as the thoughts.

A Theme about Religion

Write a theme about a deeply felt religious moment in your life. Use many images to let the reader share your experience in the setting you visualize for him. For an example of a story about a religious moment, see "My Confirmation," "Morning Watch," and "The Rosary," pp. 116–17, or the moment from *Of Human Bondage*, p. 412, or "Parable," by Oscar Wilde, p. 283.

Writing a Family Theme

Write a theme about a member of your family, describing preferably a single moment. The deeper the feelings expressed in this theme, the more certainly unique sentence rhythms and diction of dignity and originality will appear. For examples of family themes see "Desert of Silence" and "My Father's Pipe," pages 58 and 59.

Introspection: Mingling of Interior and Exterior

Describe an intense mood you have felt, a surge of feeling lasting five or ten minutes. Begin with images of the setting to let your reader feel the mood of the exterior world in which your thoughts took place. Interweave thoughts with irrelevant interruptions from the setting, particularly interruptions of sounds. For an example of such a mood sketch, read "Six O'clock," on pages 57–58.

Connotative Images

Write a series of images suggested by one word, such as *black, July, yellow, autumn, washday, night, gray, winter, summer, gold, father, mother, love, beauty.*

DECEMBER

An old man selling chestnuts on the corner; soft hair blowing back from faces, falling limply, caressing cheeks and foreheads; bundled up children roller skating over sidewalks; red, blue, yellow, green streamers flapping over a used car lot; the clanging of a fire engine; the Salvation Army band playing Christmas carols with wrong brass notes; white sea-gulls and black water splashed over a green and brown field; brown leaves clinging to a wet street; clumps of bushes huddling before a row of city white houses; the year's first snowflakes melting on the sidewalk; hot chocolate steaming in thick blue mugs; long scarves and woolen mittens.

Susan Bogdanow

YELLOW

A plush carpet of dandelions around a forgotten house; a fluffy canary singing to the morning sun; the thousand winking eyes in a field of bobbing daisies; the cool shimmer of lemon pie in August; the silk-soft fur of a plump, tawny cat; a dazzling organdy dress on a little girl with brown eyes; a tapered brass vase reflecting candlelight; the mellowed gold of an old wedding band.

Catherine DeBaerstrand

BLACK

Black: the dead locust limb that scrapes my bedroom window; crows, hundreds of them, perched like clothespins in the branches of a bare tree; the crooked lines of tar that fill the cracks on a concrete highway; the tip of Buddy's nose when it is wet; seven black swans, floating on a leaf-flecked pond; twisted Italian tobies in a yellow box; leeches squirming in a white earthen jar; burned gunpowder from my shotgun on the flannel cleaning rag; the lacquered Eaglerock biplane at Rogers Field; tiny cloves stuck in a baked Virginia ham; licorice, in elastic sticks and lozenges and squares; cloud shadows on fields of ripening grain.

University of Pittsburgh, *Student Themes*

Definitions in Images

Define an abstract word in an image. Use a word such as *beauty, joy, love, sadness, cruelty, tenderness, hope, religion, winter, spring, loneliness, old age, youth.*

LONELINESS

Loneliness is a curled brown leaf in the December twilight, now tumbling over and over, now lying still on the black pavement.

Howard Brettler

HOPE

Hope is a flapping yellow apron hung on a black fire escape above a dismal alley.

Esther Lacroix

HAPPINESS

Happiness is a ten-year-old boy standing over a blazing fire, watching small yellow kernels burst into snowflakes of popcorn.

Steve Golo

Defining Words to Live By

Define the words *adult, son, daughter, student, work, college, education, creativity,* in single sentences.

A MAN MATURE ENOUGH

A son is a man mature enough to show tenderness to an inarticulate father in the father's proud, angry moments.

Joseph Baron

FLASH OF INSIGHT

Creativity is the flash of insight that the thinker can communicate instantly in a poem, a painting, or a page of music that the world will wish to preserve.

Sandra Richards

Words to Define and Redefine

Define five of the words below in single sentences. Or, define one of these words at the beginning of a class. Then each student may read his definition to the class. Compare your definition with others. The words: *maturity, beauty, ambition, grace, kindness, man, woman, courtesy, magnanimity.*

A Turning Point in Your Life

Write a theme about a happening, an accident, a decision, an event, that you can now call a turning point in your life. Read Mark Twain's essay, "The Turning Point of My Life."

Writing a Short Poem

Write a poem of eight or ten lines, concentrating on one moment as does Melville Cane in his poem, "Snow Toward Evening," p. 226.

Suggest a particular time and place. Show the season of the year. Use an image in each line. Make each line suggest the mood you wish to achieve. Make each line appeal to the reader's ear, eye, or finger tips. Use sounds and colors. Use an original comparison, simile, or metaphor. Avoid rhyme.

Describing Things You Like

In a series of images describe things you like, as is done in the essay called "Quiet Things," p. 55. Here are a few suggested topics:

1. The Things I Like Best Are Blue
2. I Like Moving Things Best
3. Green Is My Favorite Color
4. The Things I Like Best Are Soothing
5. Things I Love to Touch
6. The Sounds I Like Best
7. Smells I Remember Best
8. The Things at Home I Like Best

Describing a Meal: Its Symbolic Meaning

Describe a meal that you recall vividly, not perhaps for the pleasure the food gave you but for its symbolic importance in your life: a last meal with someone you loved, a meal at home as your older brother was leaving, a meal when someone cried, a meal when everyone was happy and joyous.

Writing a Long Paper

Write a theme about yourself in six or seven paragraphs that defines for you one of these words: *beauty, pain, sadness, courage, college, growth, insight, teacher, boyhood, home, friendship*. Select six or seven moments that symbolize for you the meaning of the word you select. Describe each of these moments vividly, using many images, telling the time and place of each happening, building up the action with sensory language, bits of dialogue, images of action, similes and metaphors.

A Theme about an Idea

Write a theme about a passage from a distinguished book, such as one of the following. George Meredith's *Ordeal of Richard Feverel:*

"When nature has made us ripe for love, the gods are not long in providing a temple for the flame." Thomas Hardy's *Mayor of Caster-bridge:* "Happiness is but the occasional episode in a general drama of pain." George Eliot's *Middlemarch:* "Her purpose [in marriage] was not to claim justice but to give tenderness."

Pretend You Are an Animal

If you could become an animal for an hour, what animal would you choose to be? Describe one moment of your new life.

Writing a Book Review

Write a review of one of the following books: Hardy's *Mayor of Casterbridge*, Meredith's *Ordeal of Richard Feverel*, Dickens' *Great Expectations*, Eliot's *Felix Holt* or *Daniel Deronda*, Dostoievsky's *House of the Dead*, Tolstoy's *Resurrection*, Rousseau's *Émile*.

The Words That Mean Most to You

Name five words that you need most urgently to define to make your life what you want it to be. Then define each word in a single sentence.

The Words That Mean Most to Our Country

Name five words that our country needs to define most urgently. Then define each of these words in a single sentence. Compare your definitions with those of your classmates.

Writing an Autobiography[1]

Write an autobiography about one part of your life, selecting six or seven intense episodes or scenes that contribute to your central idea. Unify your theme by centering it on one person, one

[1] See above, pp. 78ff. For other illustrative themes of autobiography, see Don M. Wolfe, *The Freshman and His World*, pp. 107–109.

time, one feeling, one problem, one summer, one place, one impression of yourself. In each main episode include one dramatic moment in which you use many images of place and person to sweep your reader into your story. Build up each moment with the following resources:

1. Time of day, season of year
2. Images of place
3. Images of person
4. Images of action
5. An image of touch
6. Bit of dialogue
7. Colors
8. Sounds
9. Introspection
10. Similes and metaphors

AUTOBIOGRAPHY TOPICS

1. My Dad and I: Five Moments
2. How a Friendship Grew: Five Moments
3. My Definition of Love
4. Our Kitchen: A Place of Happy Moments
5. My Ambition and How It Grew
6. A Teacher in My Life
7. A Job I Disliked: Five Moments
8. The Greatest Influence in My My Life
9. My Great Decision and How I Made It
10. My First Meeting with Death
11. The Most Important Year of My Life
12. A Turning Point in My Life

Theme on Disposition: My Peculiar Self

Describe a moment or use a series of images which suggest a vital aspect of your personality. Begin, "I am a staunch friend," "I cannot resist panhandlers," "I am slow to anger," "I harbor resentments," "I have lost my sensitivity," "I am cheerful when I awake."

I LOVE OLD THINGS

The old things that never change are those which I love. I love to glance over and to feel the softness and daintiness of my baby shoes. I love to visualize the woman that my grandmother was after looking at her beautiful picture in its antique frame. I love our silver candle holders that were brought from Russia and have been faithfully used every Friday night for over a hundred years. I love to sit in the sagging comfort of our oldest chair and feel as if it were a part of myself. I love to talk to elderly people who appreciate talking to someone and do so naturally. I love the exquisite old decorations of our synagogue which help to create for me the solemn and holy atmosphere of ancient Israel. I love to roam through a spacious old house enjoying a sense of freedom because there is so much room. I love to slip into my favorite and most comfortable old woolen robe. I love to skim through old magazines looking for something which I might have missed. I love my grandmother's brooch which has now become an heirloom, resting in its protective velvet box, not noticing the changing world around it. I love my house at Passover time when its yearly atmosphere is always the same. Yes, these are the things I love.

Frances Topolsky

Personification for Originality

Personify an inanimate object you know well, as Catherine does in the sketch below, "The Old School Bus." Is Catherine's personification more personal in style than Peggy's story about the maple?

THE OLD SCHOOL BUS

The school bus lumbered slowly down the road and stopped beneath an elm tree for three small children. It gathered them in, and they climbed into the soft seats so perfect for nestling, like a grandmother's ample lap. The children laughed and shouted, and the bus mingled in its own familiar sounds: creaking, snorting in its efforts to start up after each stop, wheezing as it carried them steadily up the steep hill. The children traced pictures on the old bus's steamed glasses on cold mornings, and rushed into the warmth of its open arms on frosty afternoons. And sometimes, at the end of a long day, it rocked them to sleep, humming softly.

Catherine DeBaerstrand

OUR MAPLE

Our maple is a shameless lover, reaching out to each season, tangling it in her branching arms. Spring caresses her with soft warm breath, gently ruffling her rigid branches. Helplessly her branches swell. Her bark grows plump and tender. Shyly she brings forth tentative green buds. Summer turns her into a woman, full-blown with green, surrounded by sunny lazy warmth, compounded of mysterious leafy groves shadowing each other in secret grottos. But autumn is full of demands and wild promises. "Wake up!" says the impatient racing wind. "Come with me." But she is rooted in the grey black dusk, and the golden globes of street lights can only stream forth beams of silent compassion. Left behind, her aching leaves curl around the wind. They cannot clutch it and soon fall disconsolately to the ground. Her branches stiffen, numb with loneliness and sorrow. Winter takes the discarded lover fiercely, then mocks her with raucous shrieks. Her branches are black and dead. She no longer feels the taunting gusts which break off her twigs. She can only snap hollowly with bitter protest. Vicious blasts callously toss her back and forth. Only the soft wet snow soothes her tormented, unresisting skeleton.

Peggy Dicker

What Am I? A Part of All That I Have Met

How does a poem such as Whitman's "There Was a Child Went Forth" speak for you and me? How does it speak for our students? The first lines of the poem give the clue to Whitman's meaning:

There was a child went forth every day,
And the first object he look'd upon, that object he became,
And that object became part of him for the day or a certain part of the day,
Or for many years or stretching cycles of years.
The early lilacs became part of this child,
And grass and white and red morning-glories, and white and red clover,
  and the song of the phœbe-bird, . . .

Like Whitman, each of us call up sights and sounds and moments of taste and touch that answer the question, "What am I?" Such a theme (which may be assigned with assurance on many levels from seventh grade to graduate school) may have a selection of images from a single moment or from many moments. The first theme below was written by a teacher, the second by a seventh-grade pupil, each of them following Whitman's key idea.

MY FATHER AND I

As my thoughts fly back, I am a boy of ten again, living at the edge of a little town in Oklahoma. It was a dark November morning, only a few months before my father left his family. I was lying in bed waiting; it was still dark. Suddenly I heard my father's steps; then he touched me on the shoulder saying, "Let's go, son." I rose quickly and slipped on my cold overalls, an old blue shirt, and sneakers. We set out across the dewy prairie grass, my father holding his gun in the crook of his arm. At last we came to Beaubean's Pond. We clambered up the high bank and looked over into the black water. Four or five ducks sat there peacefully, swaying with the wash of the waves. Suddenly a loud flapping of wings! They flew upward. My father raised his gun and fired; one duck fell into the water, giving out a shrill cry. After a moment it gathered strength and suddenly flew up across the water. My father raised his gun but did not fire again. I could see his reddened face and his brown eyes now, looking at me with a question. I followed him as he clambered down the bank of the pond; I held on to his shoulder. The eastern horizon was now red-streaked, the clouds bathed with fire. We walked back through the grass, my father's hand on my shoulder. I am this moment, this boy of ten, the wet grass around my legs, the feel of my father's hand, and the question in his eyes.

Christopher Morland

WHAT AM I? A DARK AND LONELY NIGHT

I am the white Good Humor truck with jingling bells on a humid August night that sends me pleading to Dad for a nickel and a dime. I am the peeling green paint on the squeaky seesaw in our backyard. I am the painful splinter embedded in my palm, a gleaming needle in my arm, and the salty tears that flow in the doctor's office. I am a dark and lonely night in a hospital bed overlooking the East River, whose surface shimmers with reflected lights, red and silver and green, and the fear of the operation the next day. On the day beginning our vacation, with every inch of the car packed neatly, I am the despair in my father's eyes with the flat tire at the intersection of Nassau and Witherspoon Streets. I am the surprise when a pink worm wriggles across our sidewalk after a sudden summer storm. I am the stillness of a mole on the wet green grass. I am the caress in my mother's eyes when I skip home from the first day in school or as I kneel and say my bedtime prayers. On a hot summer night I am the chill of the ice cube I suck, most of which drips down my arms and stains my blue jeans. I am the stillness of a Little League game that I ended by striking out, and the feel of my father's arms across my shoulder and his voice saying, "We can't win them all, can we?" I'm the miseries I've suffered, the joys I've known, and the things I've done.

Michael Ladner

APPENDICES

Appendix 1

Elements of a Reading Program

[The annotated list below may be useful to English teachers, to juniors and seniors preparing for college, and to superior freshmen and sophomores who have a curiosity about great books.]

A. Introduction to Greek Genius

The riches of Greek intelligence, even in the fragmentary mirror of their preserved literature, sculpture, and architecture, appear inexhaustible. It is difficult for us to realize that Athens in a few centuries cradled more geniuses than has Paris, or London, or New York in later eras. True, we are superior in scientific achievement, but we have produced no such versatile genius as Aristotle, no philosopher who is Plato's equal, only one tragic poet comparable to Sophocles, no sculptor like Phidias. The Greeks established an architecture so beautiful, so symmetrical, that twenty-five centuries later America has built a Greek temple as a shrine for the martyred Lincoln. In art, in philosophy, in drama, in bodily grace, the Greeks created patterns of perfection that all the world still seeks to emulate or surpass. To any young American, then, who seeks for himself, his family, and his city the riches of past cultures, a study of Greek civilization becomes an adventurous necessity. The following books are some of the most important milestones chosen for their readability and intrinsic value among the many Greek classics.

The Greek View of Life   G. LOWES DICKINSON

To the teacher who wants to understand the genius of the Greeks, this book is indispensable, especially the chapter on Socrates. It is a short book, very readable, with meaty quotations from the great Greek classics of philosophy, history, drama.

The Story of Philosophy   WILL DURANT

Durant's chapters on Socrates, Plato, and Aristotle are a lively, informal introduction to Greek thought. Probably you will not want to read the whole book; but require yourself to read the first three or four chapters. Facile style, lively interpretive comments.

Apology   PLATO

The *Apology* is really a speech made by Socrates when he was on trial for his life before five hundred Greek citizens. It is thought to be a fairly accurate transcript of Socrates' actual words. In places the *Apology* is difficult reading; for the most part, however, it is easy for the average reader to follow. Only thirty pages long, this masterpiece of world literature may be read in less than an hour.

Crito   PLATO

After Socrates had been condemned to death, he remained in prison for several days discussing with his disciples practical and philosophical questions, one of which was the advisability of an attempted escape. In this dialogue Socrates considers this question, eventually deciding not to flee his punishment. The *Crito*, even shorter than the *Apology*, may be read with ease and profit.

Phaedo   PLATO

On the last day of Socrates' life he engaged in a long conversation with his disciples about the immortality of the soul. Much of this dialogue is difficult for the layman in philosophy. No one should miss, however, the last four or five pages, which tell in graphic detail the story of Socrates' last hour with his friends: the coming of sunset, the grief of the jailer, the preparation and drinking of the poison, its gradual effect on Socrates' body, his last words and movements.

Symposium   PLATO

At a drinking party lasting through the night, Socrates and a group of friends present their definitions of love, each with the peculiar emphasis of his personality. Socrates speaks last. This dialogue contains intimate revealing glimpses of Socrates' remarkable character. Though in places somewhat abstract and difficult, this dialogue contains some of the most beautiful passages in world literature.

The Republic   PLATO

The Republic, written at the height of Plato's remarkable powers, is a blue print of his ideal commonwealth. *The Republic* is the flower and summation of Plato's philosophy; it contains in dramatic form expression of the main currents of his political and philosophical thinking.

Book III, on the integration of athletics and music in the young man's education, is one of the easier chapters. Book V, on the position of women in Plato's utopia, has many fascinating passages.

Ethics   ARISTOTLE

Aristotle did not write with either the vivid phrasing or the dramatic illustrations of Plato. Consequently some readers find his books abstract and colorless. You can profit, however, by spending even an hour with this remarkable book, which, like the *Politics*, has been required reading for centuries at the universities of Cambridge and Oxford.

Politics   ARISTOTLE

Aristotle was a realistic conservative who believed in governmental control by an aristocracy of brains and natural talent. He accepts slavery, condemns democracy; he defines the various types of government and traces their rise and fall. The *Politics* remains an indispensable classic to students of government, sociology, philosophy. It was diligently studied by James Madison and Alexander Hamilton.

Rhetoric   ARISTOTLE

The *Rhetoric* was the first great handbook on public speaking. It is still studied assiduously by specialists in speech and debating. The *Rhetoric* is much more fascinating to the average reader than either the *Politics* or the *Ethics*. Aristotle shows that the first necessity of the speaker is to understand human nature, to be able to analyze his audience and appeal to their dominant motives. His analysis of the psychology of the young, the middle-aged, and the old is as fresh and vital as if written yesterday. A readable edition of the *Rhetoric* is that by Lane Cooper.

Agamemnon   AESCHYLUS

Aeschylus was born in Greece in 525 B.C. He was thirty years older than Sophocles, forty-five years older than Euripides. Like Sophocles, he was a soldier as well as a poet. He is said to have written seventy tragedies, of which only seven remain. In this story Agamemnon, one of the leaders of the Greek expedition to Troy, has sacrificed his daughter Iphigenia. This act awakens inextinguishable hatred in the heart of his wife, Clytemnestra. The play pictures Agamemnon's return to his palace where a murderous revenge awaits him.

Oedipus the King   SOPHOCLES (495–406 B.C.)

Sophocles wrote about a hundred dramas, of which only seven remain. At Oedipus' birth, it is prophesied that he will some day murder his father and marry his own mother. To prevent such a catastrophe, his parents have him exposed on a hillside to die. A kindly shepherd, however, saves Oedipus from death and rears him to boyhood. Some years later, when Oepidus is passing along a narrow hillside road, he meets a warrior accompanied by servants. Neither Oedipus nor the warrior will give way. In the bloody melee that follows, Oedipus kills the warrior and goes on his way. Many years later. . . . Considered the greatest of Greek tragedies, and by some critics the greatest tragedy ever written. *Oedipus the King* traces the profound effect of ironic circumstance on Jocasta, his wife and mother, and Oedipus himself.

Antigone   SOPHOCLES

Antigone, the daughter of Oedipus, braves the wrath of one of her brothers to administer the traditional burial rights to another. The story of a brave, idealistic woman destined to dire suffering for noble action.

Medea   EURIPIDES

For Medea's assistance in stealing the Golden Fleece, Jason has brought her back as his wife to the city of Corinth. Ten years later Creon, the king, orders Jason to put away Medea and marry the daughter of the king. The play depicts Medea's fantastically cruel revenge for this treachery. Nowhere in Greek literature are the rights of woman more persuasively elaborated than in this play. Of the three great Greek tragedians, Euripides is the most realistic in tone, if less stately and poetic. Of his seventy-five plays, eighteen have survived.

The Frogs   ARISTOPHANES

In the extant thirteen plays of Aristophanes, one finds pictured the gay hedonism of the Greeks, their love of laughter and satire, their debauchery and coarseness. In *The Frogs*, Bacchus and Xanthias descend into the eternal shades to bring back Euripides. Hercules shows them the way, and after crossing the river Styx, Bacchus disguises himself as Hercules and demands entrance. A hilarious scene of this play, and the most informing, is the argument between Euripides and Aeschylus as to which is the greater playwright.

B. FIVE GREAT BOOKS OF THE RENAISSANCE

Utopia   SAINT THOMAS MORE

Published in 1516, *Utopia* reflects a social idealism utterly contradictory to Machiavelli's *The Prince*, classic of Renaissance political realism. It is a picture of an ideal society, prefaced by an incisive analysis of the social evils of More's England. *Utopia* was immediately acclaimed by humanist intellectuals of all Europe.

Essays   MONTAIGNE

Montaigne lived a life of leisure and contemplation in sixteenth-century France. He set out in his *Essays* to report himself, to record his prejudices, his enthusiasms, his ideas of men and books. Montaigne's buoyant humor, his honesty and frankness, his insight into human nature have endeared him to readers of four centuries. "I speak the truth," he wrote, "not enough to satisfy myself, but as much as I dare speak. And I become a little more daring as I grow older." If you buy a Montaigne, ask for the excellent Trechmann translation (Oxford University Press).

Autobiography BENVENUTO CELLINI

This book is a curious blend of Renaissance and personality: a highly developed artistic sense and creative impulse, coupled with savagery and meanness in personal relationships. Vivid reflection of the life and manners of an Italian artist.

Advancement of Learning FRANCIS BACON

This book teems with surprisingly modern ideas of education. Bacon shows what societies in the past have done to advance learning. He then demonstrates what remains to be done, emphasizing observation and recording of natural phenomena, comparative anatomy in the study of medicine, the reconciliation of science and religion. This is a difficult book, but one well worth coming back to every few years.

Aeropagitica JOHN MILTON

The most comprehensive and penetrating essay ever written on freedom of speech and freedom of discussion. It is hard going, especially the first few pages, and you may not be interested in Milton's historical references to censorship in Greece and Rome. But there are many memorable passages in this essay; its arguments are the very stuff and substance of democratic liberties.

C. TWENTY-FIVE ENGLISH NOVELS

Journal of the Plague Year DANIEL DEFOE

In 1664 the plague broke out in London and continued until late in 1665. Over 100,000 persons, between one-half and one-third of London's whole population, were carried away. Defoe's remarkable pictures of life in London during this terrifying epidemic are fiction; but historians are agreed that they give the modern reader a suggestive conception of the plague's effect on the populace.

Tom Jones HENRY FIELDING

Fielding traces the fortunes of Tom Jones, a robust, irrepressible youth of many virtues, none of them traditional. A mature, rich novel, one of the great stories of the language. Long, rather difficult for the immature reader. Fielding introduces each new section of the book with a delightful essay.

Kenilworth   WALTER SCOTT

Not for subtle characterization, but for its remarkable description of life in Elizabethan England, especially the pageantry at Kenilworth castle, we recommend this book. Scott includes the Earl of Leicester and Sir Walter Raleigh in his gallery of *Kenilworth* portraits.

Emma   JANE AUSTEN

Men do not usually like this book. It is a novel of manners, of parties, and dinner conversations, of courtship in eighteenth-century England. The language is delightfully spry and lively, the characters are very real, though we never see their deepest thoughts.

Great Expectations   CHARLES DICKENS

Pip, the boy hero of this story, has great expectations of becoming a gentleman in London. He receives money unexpectedly, falls in love, makes new friends, becomes ashamed of his best friend, Joe Gargery. This story is alive with fascinating, unforgettable characters: Jaggers, the lawyer, Wemmick, his clerk, Miss Havisham, the rejected bride. Dickens' warm humanity, his delightful sense of the comic and absurd are nowhere more alive than in this book.

Bleak House   CHARLES DICKENS

Perhaps Dickens' most ambitious novel, *Bleak House* tells the story of Lady Dedlock's efforts to keep from her husband the story of her unacknowledged daughter, Esther; the story also of long delays in the old Court of Chancery, in an actual case settled long after Dickens' death. Rich in suspense, low comedy, gusto, variety of portraiture. The description of the fog in the opening chapter Conrad thought as •superb as any writing in English fiction.

Vanity Fair   WILLIAM M. THACKERAY

One of the world's great satirical novels. The scheming, unscrupulous heroine, Becky Sharp, captures the sympathy and reluctant admiration of the reader. Thackeray gets inside his people, lets us see the gradual and inevitable changes in their personalities.

The Ordeal of Richard Feverel   GEORGE MEREDITH

An aristocratic English boy watched over by his philosophical father in vain, Richard falls in love with a beautiful, uneducated peasant girl, marries her despite his father's anger. An unforgettable chronicle of an idealistic boy breaking himself on life's inexorable windmills.

The Mill on the Floss   GEORGE ELIOT

This book tells in part the story of George Eliot's own girlhood. Vivid account of the childhood problems of Maggie and Tom Tulliver.

Like all of Eliot's novels, it is rich in description, psychological analysis, philosophical overtones.

Adam Bede   GEORGE ELIOT

A story of village life in Victorian England with Adam Bede, a carpenter, Dinah Morris, an itinerant preacher, and Hatty Green, a pretty, impulsive dairymaid, as the principal characters. Mrs. Poyser, a farm wife of buoyant humor and much linguistic imagination, is an unforgettable character.

The Mayor of Casterbridge   THOMAS HARDY

Michael Henchard, the hero of this story, is an impulsive peasant youth, "a vehement, gloomy being," says Hardy, "who had quitted the ways of vulgar men without light to guide him on a better way." In a drunken stupor he sells his wife to a sailor. Twenty years later she returns to him; now he is the mayor of Casterbridge . . . Put *The Mayor* on your *must* list. It is one of the great novels of world literature.

Tess of the D'Urbervilles   THOMAS HARDY

Moving story of a simple, faithful peasant girl betrayed by a relative, scorned by society, condemned by the church. A novel of intense dramatic power and rich description of the English countryside.

The Woodlanders   THOMAS HARDY

This is a tender and beautiful story depicting the enduring loyalty of simple, woodland peasants: Giles Winterborne, Marty South.

The Picture of Dorian Gray   OSCAR WILDE

A young man's search for sensual pleasure changes only his portrait, not his face. The subtle, gradual deterioration of his soul Wilde traces in the lines of the portrait.

Esther Waters   GEORGE MOORE

Story of a servant girl's misfortunes. Moore paints her character realistically but sympathetically.

The Light that Failed   RUDYARD KIPLING

The story of an artist who goes blind, then finds himself unable to cope with the problems of a dark world. The story traces the gradual disintegration of his confidence.

The Apple Tree (a long short story)   JOHN GALSWORTHY

An aristocratic young Englishman, having fallen in love with an uneducated but beautiful peasant girl, resolves to marry her. Then he passes through many days of tormenting indecision, especially after observing again a cultivated girl of his own class who would know how to supervise his home and entertain his gifted friends. Finally he gives up his peasant girl. Many years later he returns.

The Man of Property   JOHN GALSWORTHY

A scathing, subtle satire of Soames Forsyte, an English businessman who calculates every possession in life in terms of property. So also he evaluates his wife Irene, who cannot accept his sense of values.

Lord Jim   JOSEPH CONRAD

A sensitive young Englishman, who has always pictured himself a hero, jumps from his ship, deserts his post, to save his life. Finally, after a long quest for the assurance of courage, he gains a costly victory. This is a great book, the most penetrating study of courage and cowardice ever written.

Of Human Bondage   SOMERSET MAUGHAM

Forever conscious of his club foot, Philip Carey passes through bitter boyhood struggle, attempts to become a painter, finally succeeds as a physician. Meanwhile, he fails to find the love and happiness he had hoped for. A rich, full-bodied book, one of the greatest English novels.

Sons and Lovers   D. H. LAWRENCE

Remarkably clear and colorful chronicle of a boy's early life in an English mining village. Lawrence traces in detail the early love life of his hero and the piercing conflict between his jealous mother's love and that of his sweethearts.

Tono Bungay   H. G. WELLS

The story of George Ponderevo, an English youth of great scientific curiosity who allows his life to be diverted to moneymaking. The wastes of English business life as symbolized in the manufacture and sale of Tono Bungay, a patent medicine, are the central theme of this story. The hero's love life, however, Wells depicts with even more conviction than his educational and commercial adventures.

If Winter Comes   A. S. M. HUTCHINSON

A story of idealistic Mark Sabre, in England of World War I. Unhappily married, victimized by convention, Sabre finally finds the happiness he deserves. Rich in humorous sallies and philosophical overtones.

Point Counter Point   ALDOUS HUXLEY

A brilliant satirical analysis of London society: its hypocrisy, its coarseness, its shallowness, its smugness.

Brave New World   ALDOUS HUXLEY

A satire on scientific advances carried to ridiculous lengths in a utopia.

How Green Was My Valley   RICHARD LLEWELLYN

A chronicle of irresistible conviction of family life in a Welsh mining valley. Family frictions, school struggles, and early romance, Llewellyn pictures with unerring fidelity.

D. Famous American Novels

The Scarlet Letter   NATHANIEL HAWTHORNE

In this remarkable book Hawthorne contrasts two marriages, that of Hester and Chillingworth, sanctioned by society, but uncemented by love; and, on the other hand, that of Hester and Dimmesdale, sanctioned by love, but utterly condemned by society. This is a subtle book, probably the greatest American novel thus far written — a book forever timely and arresting. Was Hawthorne bitterly satirizing the Puritan conception of sin? Or was he concerned with the psychological effects of sin, whether real or imagined? Even today critics differ heatedly on Hawthorne's purpose in writing *The Scarlet Letter.*

Moby Dick   HERMAN MELVILLE

This is a story of whaling life — of sailors capturing whales, cutting them up, boiling the blubber, storing away the precious oils. Melville's genius for complete and satisfying visualization of ships and men and whales is well worth your leisurely reading and reflection. Melville somehow expresses the heights of man's yearnings and the depths of his sufferings—in language closer to Shakespeare's than any other American has risen to.

Typee   HERMAN MELVILLE

A white man seeks contentment on a South Sea island, describes sympathetically the life of his cannibal friends. An authentic picture of island life from Melville's own experience.

Anthony Adverse   HERVEY ALLEN

A book of many unforgettable scenes: Boyhood days in a convent, duels, slave trading in Africa, crucifixion of a valiant priest, the march of refugees into Mexico.

Looking Backward   EDWARD BELLAMY

The hero of this remarkable story, awaking in a subterranean bed-room, finds that he has slept for over a hundred years. It is America in the year 2000 A.D., his country transformed into an amazingly different society. One of the most influential American classics.

The Good Earth
PEARL BUCK

Epic story of a poor Chinese farmer and his loyal wife. The farmer gains wealth: his soul and body lose touch with the good earth, but the wife is ever faithful.

A Lost Lady
WILLA CATHER

In some ways the most moving of all Cather's memorable novels: a young man's idealization of an older woman and the gradual cracking of the image.

Death Comes for the Archbishop
WILLA CATHER

Beautiful story of two courageous priests and their missionary efforts in the American Southwest of pioneer days.

Jennie Gerhardt
THEODORE DREISER

A sensitive working girl as the victim of a harsh environment, Jennie possesses remarkable capacity for loyalty and self-sacrifice. An unforgettable heroine.

Sister Carrie
THEODORE DREISER

A woman of mediocre caliber rises from poverty to stage prominence. The decline of her lover, Hurstwood, is pictured with moving veracity. Dreiser's realistic detail in *Sister Carrie* caused such widespread protest that general distribution of the book was delayed seven years after its original publication.

A Farewell to Arms
ERNEST HEMINGWAY

Into harshly realistic episodes of the first world war in Italy, Hemingway weaves a compelling love story at once brutal and tender.

Arrowsmith
SINCLAIR LEWIS

Vivid story of an idealistic American doctor and of his determination to seek scientific truth at the cost of material success. Lewis' finest novel.

The Octopus
FRANK NORRIS

Compelling story of the struggle of California farmers against the political and economic power of the railroads.

Giants in the Earth
O. E. RÖLVAAG

A remarkable story of Norwegian pioneers on the Dakota prairies. Per Hansa, the hero, is well suited physically and mentally to the rigors of pioneer hardships. Rölvaag traces the delicate adjustments of married life against a background of primitive struggle.

The Jungle   UPTON SINCLAIR

An intensely realistic story of a Lithuanian immigrant family struggling for existence in the shadow of Chicago stockyards. Unforgettable
images of meat-packing processes, family life in the stockyard slums,
deterioration of the hero's powers.

The Grapes of Wrath   JOHN STEINBECK

An impressively realistic chronicle of the Joad family, their misfortunes
in Oklahoma, their trek westward to California, their gripping daily
struggle for food and shelter.

Ethan Frome   EDITH WHARTON

Tragic history of an idealistic farmer caught in the web of ironic circumstance. The background of bleak New England hillsides and farm
houses Mrs. Wharton paints with a full-embodied vividness unequaled
in her other novels.

The House of Mirth   EDITH WHARTON

Trained to indolence and pursuit of a wealthy husband, Lily Bart
finds herself unable to play this game to its appropriate conclusion.
She is caught between two modes of life, suitable to neither one. Mrs.
Wharton treats her heroine with sympathy, Lily's friends with restrained
irony.

A Certain Rich Man   WILLIAM ALLEN WHITE

Eager for riches, John Barclay rises to unprecedented economic power,
directing political machines, disregarding the pleas of his friends. A
moving story of uneven merit but remarkable power. Memorable
portraits: Colonel Culpepper, General Ward, Jake Dolan.

The Woman of Andros   THORNTON WILDER

The scene of this finely etched tale is the island of Andros; the time,
several centuries before the birth of Christ. Wilder pictures the social
and intellectual life of Chrysis, an hetaira feared and frowned upon by
the fathers of the young men who attend her discussions. Philosophical
in tone, beautiful in language.

The Bridge of San Luis Rey   THORNTON WILDER

Over a South American canyon runs a slender bridge. Seven people
of different ages and vocations are walking across. Suddenly it crashes
into the depths of the canyon; the seven lose their lives. The hero of
the story muses, "Does God have a plan for each person's life? If so,
in this catastrophe, did each of the seven meet his fate in accordance
with God's pattern of his life?" *The Bridge* traces his investigation of
this problem.

E. Twelve Famous European Novels

Don Quixote   CERVANTES

This delightful novel, contrasting the romantic with the realist, the visionary with the practical, the conservative with the utopian, is rich in philosophical satire and buoyant comedy. If you don't like it now, come back to it in your senior year.

Émile   JEAN-JACQUES ROUSSEAU

An educational classic in novel form, filled with sparkling, image-laden language, unexpected philosophical notions. Rousseau traces the ideal education of a youth, beginning with the care of the newborn child and ending with the selection of a suitable wife.

The House of the Dead   FYODOR DOSTOYEVSKY

When Dostoyevsky was a young man, he was arrested for discussing reforms of the czarist regime, thrown into prison, and finally brought before the firing squad. At the last moment his sentence was commuted to ten years in Siberia. This book is an unforgettable chronicle of his life in Siberian prisons. Not so mature a novel as *Crime and Punishment* or *Brothers Karamazov*, *The House of the Dead* is an easier, more readable introduction than either of those two to Dostoyevsky's genius.

Anna Karenina   LEO TOLSTOY

Tragic story of Anna Karenina's love for her son, hatred for her husband, fear of losing the man she loved, and finally self-destruction. The character of Levin reflects in part Tolstoy's own life and ideas. A book remarkable for its excellent portraits and revelation of Russian life. One of the great books of world literature.

Resurrection   LEO TOLSTOY

An aristocratic Russian youth loves a servant girl casually, leaves the neighborhood without realizing she is to become a mother. Ostracized by society, the girl flees to the city without revealing the name of her lover, finally becomes a girl of the streets. Years later the hero sees her in court, recognizes his responsibility for her plight, transforms the pattern of his own life.

War and Peace   LEO TOLSTOY

An unforgettable picture of Russia in the early years of the nineteenth century. We come to know the heart of shambling, awkward Pierre, the heart, too, of reserved, intellectual Andrey, both aristocrats. The Napoleonic invasion Tolstoy pictures with panoramic sketches alternated with amazing visualization of hospitals, battle scenes, deaths, moods of the great and humble.

Thaïs   ANATOLE FRANCE

The story of a monk of early Christian days who persuades an actress, Thaïs, to enter a convent and to become a nun. Thoughts of Thaïs prey so heavily on the monk's mind that he finds himself unable to continue his calling. A biting satire on celibacy, with engaging philosophical digressions.

The Dram Shop   ÉMILE ZOLA

The story of a poverty-stricken laundress and husband, their gradual disintegration under the weight of persistent drinking. Finally, disease and death overtake the husband, hunger and death the wife. Unforgettable images of poorer quarters of Paris, of kitchens and saloons, streets and hosqitals. Zola's method of unceasing reporting of detail evident in every page of this depressing but fascinating novel.

Under Fire   HENRI BARBUSSE

Impressive delineation of the effects of war on French soldiers of 1914–16. Many critics regard this book as the greatest of the war novels.

All Quiet on the Western Front   ERICH REMARQUE

Chronicle of a German youth's training for war, life in the trenches, love for his comrades, devastation of spirit, shattering of his hopes, disillusionment with the war aims of his country. Intensely human, painfully realistic. A book forbidden by Hitler in his war on books inimical to Nazi tyranny.

Hunger   KNUT HAMSUN

An intensely realistic analysis of a hungry man's sensations and moods. Short, easy to read; unforgettable episodes.

F. A GALLERY OF UTOPIAS

Only a few choice spirits among all the great men of literature (such as Aristotle, Montaigne, Samuel Johnson) have regarded the world in which they lived as the best man is capable of creating. To show their conception of the society men might eventually build, many men of genius have projected utopian blueprints, tracing patterns of perfection that have inspired the most intelligent and imaginative men of succeeding generations. By reading a number of these utopias, therefore, the reader of today inevitably grapples with the persistent ideals of a civilized culture that have agitated men's minds for twenty centuries.

A good starting point in the reading of these masterpieces is More's *Utopia*. It is one of the shortest of dream societies, and Book II, which describes the new society, has many vivid, arresting passages. Book I reflects More's impressions of the abuses in sixteenth-century England.

The most interesting utopia from the American point of view is not More, however, but *Looking Backward*, by Edward Bellamy, which pictures an American society of the year 2000. Unlike the earlier utopias, *Looking Backward* is in the form of a novel; it was a best seller in 1888, and its influence in American life has been remarkably persistent. Dissatisfied with the mechanization of production pictured in *Looking Backward*, William Morris wrote his provocative *News from Nowhere*, also in the form of a novel; Morris pictures the new life as individualistic and creative, especially in the arts and crafts. Of all the utopias, Plato's *Republic* is still in some respects the greatest of all, not in its anticipation of modern problems, many of which arise from industrialization, but in its rich psychological and philosophical insight.

The Republic   PLATO

A commonwealth governed by philosophers carefully selected from all ranks of society, nurtured in common dining halls, educated intensively in music, gymnastics, mathematics, astronomy, and the art of discussion. Then they withdraw from society to search again for the highest truth.

The New Testament

Not the concrete outlines of human institutions, but the spirit of human brotherhood permeating all relationships and obliterating all artificial distinctions, is the distinctive quality of the earthly utopia pictured by Jesus of Nazareth. The concept of an earthly utopia Jesus called the kingdom of heaven. In his *Outline of History*, H. G. Wells writes about it as follows: "This doctrine of the Kingdom of Heaven, which was the main teaching of Jesus, and which plays so small a part in Christian creeds, is certainly one of the most revolutionary doctrines that ever stirred and changed human thought."

The City of God   SAINT AUGUSTINE

A religious utopia written to justify the superiority of Christianity to the pagan cults.

Utopia   SAINT THOMAS MORE

A commonwealth of democratic annual elections with its citizens creating wealth cooperatively, providing economic security for the whole nation, exchanging houses by lot every ten years; a people loving gardens and music, given to tolerance and contempt for gold.

The New Atlantis   SIR FRANCIS BACON

In this remarkable essay (the shortest of utopias) Bacon is not concerned with the economic and social welfare of all classes; rather he pictures the benefits derived from a great university of scientists working cooperatively for the common good. This university Bacon called Salomon's House, "the noblest foundation," he wrote, "that ever was upon the earth, and the lantern of this kingdom is dedicated to the study of the works and creatures of God." The passion of Bacon's life was the scientific method and the organization of scientific research. In his epoch-making *Novum Organum*, he delineated with startling clarity the defects of preceding scientific research and illustrated with remarkable concreteness how a truly scientific method could be projected.

The Law of Freedom in a Platform   GERRARD WINSTANLEY

This remarkable blueprint for an English commonwealth, which Winstanley presented to Cromwell in 1652, called for the abolition of buying and selling, the establishment of common storehouses, the annual election of rulers, common ownership of land. Winstanley's criticism of the social abuses of his day is pregnant with meaning for modern readers. *The Law of Freedom* is now available for the first time in *The Works of Gerrard Winstanley*, edited by Professor Sabine of Cornell University (Cornell University Press).

Looking Backward   EDWARD BELLAMY

Three years of college for all, three years of manual labor, choice of vocation (with fewest hours on the most unpleasant job), equality of incomes, elimination of want, efficient distribution of society's goods — these are Bellamy's claims for the society of the future, with no change in human nature. A book to read skeptically and critically; yet the questions it raises are still to be answered. When the hero looks back, check his diagnosis carefully with your own reading and observation.

Equality   EDWARD BELLAMY

This book is a continuation of *Looking Backward*. Many of the topics touched on lightly in *Looking Backward* Bellamy elaborates in *Equality*. Chapter XXIII, "The Parable of the Water Tank," has become a classic in American social literature.

News from Nowhere   WILLIAM MORRIS

Morris is more of an artist than Bellamy in the creation of scenes and characters. As a novel more interesting, as a social tract less illuminating, than *Looking Backward*. Morris stresses the individual freedom possible in a commercial society, especially in artistic endeavor.

Erewhon   SAMUEL BUTLER

This satirical novel describes a society in which life is made attractive for most people by simple reversal of the attitudes, manners, and customs of nineteenth-century England. Especially provocative is the section speculating on the possibility that instead of being freed by machines, man may too easily be enslaved by them.

G. History and Biography

Lives   PLUTARCH

These biographies of the famous men of Greece and Rome are filled with illuminating detail and arresting anecdote. In an hour you can read the life of Mark Antony and taste Plutarch's life of Caesar or Alexander the Great. Give yourself at least this taste of Plutarch. Emerson wrote, "Go with mean people, and you think life is mean. Then read Plutarch, and the world is a proud place, peopled with men of positive quality, with heroes and demigods standing around us, who will not let us sleep."

The Decline and Fall of the Roman Empire   EDWARD GIBBON

No teacher with a curiosity about history or the sonorous rhythms of English prose should pass by the rich, full mind of Gibbon. Read him skeptically and critically (as he also read and thought), if only Chapter XV on the rise of Christianity amid the glories of pagan Rome.

The Outline of History   H. G. WELLS

The early chapters of this book, dealing with the origin of vegetable and animal life, the emergence of mammals and the ancestry of man, are a fascinating record. If they seem too technical, pass them by for the chapter on writing, or Chapter XVIII on serfs, slaves, and free men, or the excellent chapter on the rise of Buddhism. Read also Chapter XXIX on the rise of Christianity and Chapter XXXIV on the Renaissance.

Life of Jesus   ERNEST RENAN

Renan was first a Catholic, then an idealistic skeptic; the personality of Jesus, however, held a life-long fascination for him. He spent years in Palestine in preparation for his biography of Jesus, whom he characterizes as a man, not as a divinity. Renan's introductory analysis of his sources and methods of historical research is a classic document.

The Mind in the Making   JAMES HARVEY ROBINSON

This remarkable book, the quintessence of a great historian's wisdom, describes the psychology of our savage and barbaric ancestors and traces the effect of this psychology upon our present-day thinking. Do not pass by the chapter on creative thought as a power for transforming the world. An abstract, highly compressed book that forces us to re-examine our prejudices and social assumptions.

Democracy in America   ALEXIS DE TOCQUEVILLE

Written in 1830, this remarkable book is a timeless, eloquent, and perceptive analysis of the strengths and weaknesses of the American experiment. An indispensable handbook on American life, customs, literature, thought. Available in two-volume Vintage paperback (Knopf).

Leonardo de Vinci   ANTONINA VALLENTIN

In this book Vallentin has distilled for us the thought of the most versatile and creative mind of the Renaissance. Leonardo directed the building of canals and the military defense of city walls; he studied the flight of birds and built the first airplanes. He was a great scientific genius, an amazing engineer. This book describes his scientific and artistic achievements in felicitous and colorful language.

Elizabeth and Essex   LYTTON STRACHEY

An old story told with new interest and insight by one of the greatest of modern biographers. Clear, crisp prose. Read also *Orlando*, Virginia Woolf's fictionalized biography of Queen Elizabeth.

Great Englishmen   SIR SIDNEY LEE

Deft portraits of Sir Walter Raleigh and other great Elizabethans.

Damaged Souls   GAMALIEL BRADFORD

Brief sympathetic portraits of Aaron Burr, Thomas Paine, Benedict Arnold, and others. Fascinating sketches by a master biographer.

Autobiography   BENJAMIN FRANKLIN

In this book one finds reflected Franklin's early childhood, the growth of his interest in books and writing, his amazing activities in scientific research, diplomacy, public finance, organization of schools and colleges.

Life of Samuel Johnson   JAMES BOSWELL

A rich, detailed biography recorded from the daily observations of the persistent Boswell. A great bear of a man, the most learned of his day, surrounded and admired by talented poets, actors, statesmen. As Franklin represents a dynamic, progressive America, so Johnson reflects the tenacity of English institutions.

The Education of Henry Adams   HENRY ADAMS

An autobiography for sophisticated readers; to college students it often seems long and tedious. A great, rich autobiography that should be read late rather than early in the college course.

Confessions of an English Opium-Eater   THOMAS DE QUINCEY

The story of De Quincey's addiction to drugs he tells with unforgettable humility and in beautiful stately prose.

A Son of the Middle Border   HAMLIN GARLAND

A biography describing in vivid, picturesque language the hardships and ugliness of pioneer life. A sturdy, salty book that illuminates a distinctive personality.

The Making of an American   JACOB RIIS

A Danish boy immigrates to America, has various vocational adventures before becoming a reporter in New York. Riis' vivid observations of New York life he recorded in *How the Other Half Lives*.

Men and Politics   LOUIS FISCHER

Vivid and illuminating record of the education of a young American who becomes a foreign correspondent.

Autobiography   LINCOLN STEFFENS

Unforgettable pictures of his early life in California, his experience in American and German universities, his first reporting days in New York, his gradual understanding of the roots of crime and political graft, the widening of his intellectual horizons, and the deepening of his understanding of society — all these help to make this autobiography one of the most fascinating records of modern American life.

Experiment in Autobiography   H. G. WELLS

An utterly frank and highly descriptive account of Wells' early childhood, his intellectual advances, his sicknesses as turning points in his career, his preoccupation with biological research, his development as a novelist and historian.

Madame Curie   EVE CURIE

The story of an iron-willed woman, highly talented, unswervingly loyal to scientific endeavor, devoted wife and mother. Illuminating glimpses of her early life in Poland, her student years in Paris, her sorrows, her gradual triumph and recognition in the world of science.

H. THE ENGLISH TEACHER'S SHELF: INDISPENSABLE HANDBOOKS

1. *Oxford Companion to English Literature*, ed. Sir Paul Harvey (Oxford University Press, London and New York, 3rd ed., 1956), 911 pages, $10.00

   The superb value of this book (in addition to that of its reliable short biographies) is its summaries of particular poems, novels, large critical ideas. Incitements to intellectual growth on every page.

2. *Oxford Companion to American Literature*, ed. James D. Hart (Oxford University Press, London and New York, 3rd ed., 1956), 890 pages, $10.00

   Follows the same alphabetical plan as the English *Companion*. Exciting summaries, not only of books, poems, plays, long stories, but also of such ideas as *Puritanism, transcendentalism, romanticism, antinomianism*, etc. Deals also with history, sociology, theology.

3. *A Handbook to Literature*, revised edition, ed. Thrall, Hibbard, and Holman (Odyssey Press, New York, 1960), 608 pages, clothbound $4.25, paperback $2.50

   The most reliable and detailed dictionary of literary terms, such as *epic, free verse, classicism, taste, stress, rondel*, etc. References given in each article. A book the teacher needs every day, especially in training college-bound students.

4. *Familiar Quotations*, ed. John Bartlett, revised by Christopher Morley (Little, Brown and Company, Boston, 13th ed., 1951), 1831 pages, $10.00

   Rich in teaching resources, incitements to reading, phrases and ideas that capture the imagination. See also *New Dictionary of Thoughts* (Hanover House, Garden City, New York, 1961), 794 pages, $10.00; *Dictionary of Shakespeare Quotations* (Dutton paperback), $2.15

5. *Smaller Classical Dictionary*, ed. Sir William Smith, Everyman ed. (E. P. Dutton Company, New York, 1952), paperback, $1.45

   An indispensable guide to myths, personalities, drama, sculpture, monuments, battles, art of ancient Greece and Rome.

6. *Shakespeare's Imagery*, by Caroline Spurgeon (Cambridge University Press, Cambridge, England), $2.45 paperback

   An illuminating study of permanent worth, not only in understanding Shakespeare but also in interpreting the genius of sensory diction which make's Shakespeare's style incandescent.

Appendix 2

Four Course-of-Study Patterns: Ninth Year

When we sit down with a committee to plan a course of study for the ninth grade, our first aim is to agree upon fundamental requirements. What shall be the proportion in time spent between composition and literature? Are we to concentrate on literature in one semester and composition in another? How many themes should we ask pupils in the first semester to write? How many should they write in the second semester? Are the themes to be assigned regularly, whether once a week, once every two weeks, or once a month? Once such fundamental questions are answered, it will be relatively easy to agree upon the content of composition and grammar and the content of literature to be offered.

A course of study, when finally agreed upon, should not be an inflexible requirement upon the teacher, but rather a general guide representing the collective judgment of the teachers involved. No teacher can do justice to a classic or a composition topic about which she is not enthusiastic. In general, though we should prefer that each teacher give each recommendation of the course of study a fair trial, we would advise deviation with enthusiasm rather than observance with reluctance. One value of constructing a course of study together, however, is that each teacher may learn a great deal from the experience of other members of the group.

PLAN I

School requirements and circumstances.

A. The semesters are eighteen weeks in length.

B. The students are to write once a week or once every two weeks.

C. Composition and literature are alternated during the semester. The course of study calls for three classics each semester. The school uses single classics in separate volumes.

D. The proportion of time spent on literature and composition is left to the discretion of the teacher.

E. The program calls for thorough groundwork in grammar.

F. Speech training is emphasized in composition work.

First Semester

Materials used:

1. Seven or eight theme assignments, one every two weeks. On Tuesday of the theme week a period is taken to read through and discuss the theme assignment of the week (due on Thursday). On Wednesday the themes of the preceding assignment are returned, the errors put on the board, and some of the best themes read. On Thursday the students hand in their themes, no time on Thursday being used for theme writing or discussion. The total time spent in class is two periods a week, or about eighteen periods a semester.

2. *Difficult Words* (*its, it's, too, to,* etc.), first three weeks of the semester (about 11 periods when theme days are deducted).

3. Collection of contemporary short stories, 4th and 5th weeks.

4. *Capital Letters,* 6th week.

5. *Spelling,* 7th week.

6. *The Man without a Country,* or similar classic, 8th week.

7. *Verbs,* 9th and 10th weeks.

8. Novel such as *Treasure Island, Call of the Wild,* or *Giants in the Earth,* 12th, 13th, and 14th weeks. (Complete in two weeks, if possible.)

9. *Simple Sentences,* 14th, 15th, 16th, 17th, and 18th weeks.

Second Semester

Materials used:

1. Seven or eight theme assignments. Same plan to be used as outlined for first semester.

2. *Compound Sentences,* first two weeks.

3. Anne Frank, *Diary of a Young Girl,* Lincoln Steffens, *Boy on Horseback,* or similar autobiography, 3rd and 4th weeks.

4. *Complex Sentences,* 5th, 6th, and 7th weeks.

5. *Yesterday and Today,* ed. Louis Untermeyer (or similar collection of modern and older poetry), 8th and 9th weeks.

6. *Punctuation,* 10th, 11th, 12th, and 13th weeks.

7. *Sentence Errors,* 14th and 15th weeks.

8. *Julius Caesar,* or similar classic, 16th, 17th, and 18th weeks.

PLAN II

School requirements and circumstances:

A. The students are to write only once a month — four or five times a semester.

B. Semesters are eighteen weeks in length.
C. Anthology of literature and composition work are alternated.
D. The teacher must give approximately equal time to composition and literature.
E. The program calls for thorough groundwork in grammar.
F. Emphasis is on class discussion and speech training.

First Semester

Materials used:

1. The teacher uses four or five theme assignments. In the same manner as we have recommended for the fortnightly themes, she hands back the corrected themes just before the new themes are due. A day is used each month for putting errors on the board and for reading good themes. Thorough discussions precede each assignment.
2. *The Lady of the Lake, The Vision of Sir Launfal,* or similar classic, first three weeks.
3. Short stories and essays in anthology, 4th, 5th, and 6th weeks.
4. *Verbs* and *Nouns,* 7th and 8th weeks.
5. *Simple Sentences,* 9th, 10th, 11th, 12th, 13th, and 14th weeks.
6. *Compound Sentences,* 15th week.
7. *Julius Caesar,* or similar classic, 16th, 17th, and 18th weeks.

Second Semester

1. Four or five theme assignments.
2. *Complex Sentences,* first three weeks.
3. *Ivanhoe, Tom Sawyer, The Crisis,* or similar classic, 4th, 5th, and 6th weeks.
4. *Punctuation,* 7th, 8th, and 9th weeks.
5. Story poems and story essays in anthology, 10th, 11th, and 12th weeks.
6. *Sentence Errors,* 13th, 14th, and 15th weeks.
7. Sherwood's *Abe Lincoln of Illinois,* Shakespeare's *Twelfth Night,* or other full-length play, last three weeks.

PLAN III

School requirements and circumstances:

A. Speech training is to receive marked emphasis.
B. No groundwork in grammar is required.
C. A main aim is to attack common errors in speech and writing.
D. Composition is taught the first semester, literature the second.
E. In the semester devoted to composition the students are to write every two weeks, seven or eight themes a semester.

Semester of Composition

Materials used:

1. Seven or eight theme assignments, one every two weeks (or weekly assignments if desired). Emphasis on speech projects suggested in assignments.
2. *Sentence Errors*, two weeks.
3. *Difficult Words*, two weeks.
4. *Capitals*, one week.
5. *Spelling*, two weeks.
6. *Fun with the Dictionary*, two weeks.
7. *Business Letters*, one week.
8. *Friendly Letters*, one week.

PLAN IV

School requirements and circumstances:

A. Composition is taught in the first semester, literature the second.
B. In the semester devoted to composition the students are to write every two weeks, seven or eight times a semester.
C. The semester is twenty weeks in length.
D. The students will not receive much training in grammar after the ninth year.
E. Training in class discussion is emphasized.

Semester of Composition

Materials used:

1. Seven or eight theme assignments, one every two weeks. If themes are due on Friday, the themes written two weeks before are returned on Thursday. Thursday is given to reading good themes and drilling on common errors. Tuesday or Wednesday is spent in class discussion.
2. *Verbs* and *Nouns*, first two weeks.
3. *Simple Sentences*, six weeks.
4. *Compound Sentences*, 9th, 10th weeks.
5. *Complex Sentences*, 11th, 12th, and 13th weeks.
6. *Punctuation*, 14th, 15th, 16th, and 17th weeks.
7. *Sentence Errors*, 18th, 19th, and 20th weeks.

Suggested Readings

BURTON, DWIGHT L., editor: "A Check List for Evaluating the English Program in the Junior and Senior High School," reprint from the *English Journal*, Vol. 51 (April, 1962), pp. 273–82

DYER, PRUDENCE: "An Expression, a Possession, and a Dream," *English Journal*, Vol. 53 (September, 1964), pp. 442–44

This article describes a six-year literature program in a rural consolidated junior and senior high school. Suggestive thematic progression.

HARRISON, WERNA: "Fusion in the English Curriculum," *English Journal*, Vol. 50 (May, 1961), pp. 341–43

A delightful and informative article, written with zest and insight. A victory: when a junior boy learns that he can learn chemistry from an experiment with nail polish in an English classroom!

MALMSTROM, JEAN: "A Progress Report on a Textbook Analysis," *English Journal*, Vol. 51 (January, 1962), pp. 39–43

A useful summary of main and minor points of textbook analysis, without any agreement on the weighting of items.

Appendix 3

Newspaper and Magazine: Two Suggested Units

A. EXPLORING NEWSPAPERS

Assignments

1. Find a good newspaper article about a current event. Paste the article on a sheet of paper. Underline the words that tell *who, what, where,* and *when.* Has the writer communicated this information in his first few sentences?

On a separate sheet of paper tell what part of the article you liked best and why.

2. Find a comic strip in your local paper in which you think the humor has a lot of "punch." Paste this clipping on a sheet of paper. On a separate sheet of paper write a short paragraph in ink about the comic situation. Why does it appeal to you? Why is it humorous?

3. Read what two newspapers have to say about the same event. Paste the clippings dealing with this happening on a sheet of paper. On another sheet of paper write a comparison of these two accounts. Which one is more complete? Which one deals with the event in a more factual tone? Which one in your opinion is more accurate in reporting the news?

4. Select five headlines from one or more newspapers. Paste them on a sheet of paper. Give the name and the date of each paper under the clipping.

On a separate sheet of paper tell which words in these headlines, if any, are slanted to appeal to the emotions of the reader before he has a chance to read the article for himself.

5. Cut out a clipping from a newspaper about an athletic game that you have seen. Paste the clipping on a sheet of paper. On another sheet of paper analyze the news article. Show at what points, in your opinion, it is inaccurate. Show also at what points, in your judgment, the writer reported accurately what really happened.

449

6. The New York *Times* is generally regarded as America's best newspaper. If you can do so, buy a copy of the *Times* and cut out an article about an event in the foreign news. Paste this clipping on your paper. On the same sheet of paper place a clipping from another paper which describes the same event.

Now compare the two articles. In what way, in your opinion, is the *Times* superior in its writing of the news?

7. Many newspapers believe that "news is anything that makes a person sit up and say, 'Gee whiz!'" Find what you consider to be a sensational news item. Cut out the clipping about the sensational happening and paste it on a sheet of paper. How does the newspaper writer appeal to the reader's love of the sensational? What word pictures does he use to appeal to the average reader's curiosity about sensational happenings?

8. From your local newspaper cut out five headlines. Arrange these headlines in the order of their importance to American citizens. Post your sheet of five headlines on the bulletin board. When your turn comes, explain why you placed the headlines in the order you have chosen. Why is one event more far-reaching in its effect on American life than another? For example, is an announcement about a new peaceful use of atomic energy more important than a supreme court decision about segregation? What event named in your five headlines is of least importance?

B. EXPLORING MAGAZINES

Assignments

1. Cut out the beginning of an article from your favorite magazine. Paste it on a sheet of paper. On another sheet of paper write a paragraph in ink explaining why this article represents your favorite magazine reading.

2. Paste two pictures from your favorite magazine on a sheet of paper. In a short paragraph show why these pictures appeal to you.

3. Make a list of five features in the current issue of one of the following magazines: *Time, Coronet, Saturday Evening Post, Reader's Digest, Look, Life,* or any magazine recommended by your teacher. In a brief paragraph about each feature, tell why you find it valuable or interesting.

4. Cut out six good passages from a magazine. Paste each passage on your paper and underline the sentence you like best. Under each passage leave enough space for several sentences of your own. In these sentences tell why you like the sentence you have underlined.

5. Find a magazine article or story with many word pictures. Cut out several paragraphs and paste them on your paper. Underline the most vivid word pictures. Then write a brief paragraph explaining why the word pictures you have chosen are the most appealing.

6. Read an article in one of the following: *Harper's, Atlantic, Fortune, Commentary, Reporter, Virginia Quarterly Review,* or any other magazine recommended by your teacher. Write a brief paragraph telling what you read and why it did or did not interest you.

7. In your town or school library look briefly at ten magazines you have not become acquainted with. Write the name of each magazine on your paper and under it list the type of material it contains, such as news articles, personality portraits, color pictures, editorials, essays about literature, essays on politics, essays on economics, humor page, short stories, novelettes. At the end of your paper set down the ten magazines in the order of your preference.

8. Copy five sentences on your paper from a magazine of your choice. Be sure that each sentence contains at least one comma. Then in a brief explanation under the sentence show why the author uses the comma. What comma rule that you have learned does he apply in his sentence?

SUGGESTED READING

JORDAN, LEWIS: *News: How It is Written and Edited,* New York Times, 229 West 43 Street, New York, New York 10036
Invaluable professional hints and practical directions.

Appendix 4
Audio-Visual Aids

The advances in visual aids in the past three decades are so overwhelming as to reduce almost to irrelevance the appeal to the ear of the pupil. Imagine a class choosing between a cartoon film strip of any kind without sound and a radio program, however humorous and appealing. Learning is many times more visual than auditory. The extent to which listening can be taught or learned is still a puzzle. But one cannot imagine a pupil *not* listening to some teachers and some members of the class. The responsibility for listening attention rests always with the fascination of the speaker, not with the listening habits of the audience.

The number of film strips available for teaching purposes is incredibly rich, as any teacher may see by examining even one of the state-sponsored catalogs of aids available at nominal rentals. So far, unfortunately, we have no excellent film strips for the teaching of grammar. Effective films used systematically in this field, produced with the same imagination accorded our finest color cartoons, could reduce the burden and the weariness of grammar teaching to a degree not yet imagined on the American scene.

REFERENCES AND SUGGESTED READINGS

Audio-Visual Guide: William Lewin, ed., 172 Renner Avenue, Newark 8, N. J.

BURKHARD, R.: "Radio Listening Habits of Junior High School Pupils," *Bulletin of the National Association of Secondary-School Principals*, Vol. 25 (1941), pp. 45–48

Educational Motion Pictures for School and Community, 1956–57. Department of Audio-Visual Services, College of Adult and Extension Education, University of Kentucky, Lexington

Though the film rental service is available only to Kentucky teachers, this remarkable catalog is a mine of information about audio-visual aids. Excellent annotation of each resource listed.

Educational Screen: Paul C. Reed, ed., 64 East Lake Street, Chicago 1, Ill.

ELLIFF, GERTRUDE: "A Direct Approach to the Study of Listening," *English Journal*, Vol. 46 (January, 1957), pp. 20–27
Concrete suggestions for improvement of listening habits. Recommends the *Brown Carlsen Listening Comprehension Test.*

Experiencing the Language Arts, Bulletin No. 34, 311 pp. Bulletin Production Workshop, Florida State University, 1948. Angela M. Broening, Consultant. Write to State Department of Education, Capitol Building, Tallahassee, Fla.

GLICKSBERG, CHARLES I.: "Practical Logic in the Classroom," *English Journal*, Vol. 35 (1946), pp. 14–21
Excellent suggestions on the art of discussion and types of discussion "starters."

GOLDEN, RUTH I.: "The English Language Laboratory," *English Journal*, Vol. 46 (January, 1957), pp. 28–31
Fruitful suggestions about the use of the tape recorder in speech activities. Lively and realistic suggested topics and assignments.

LAMSON, MARY V.: "Finding the Right Poem," *English Journal*, Vol. 46 (March, 1957), pp. 148–53
Cites poems and collections that brought enthusiastic response in her classes.

MURI, JOHN T.: "The Use of Recordings in High School English Classes," *English Journal*, Vol. 46 (January, 1957), pp. 32–39
Excellent summary of available recordings based on survey of teacher preferences. Analysis of difficulties teachers have found in using recordings.

SHELLENBERGER, ELFRIEDA, and OSCAR M. HAUGH: "Wichita Revises Its Language Arts Program," *English Journal*, Vol. 46 (May, 1957), pp. 269–74
A study of procedures and principles in one city's cooperative revision of its English program.

STARR, CECILE, ed.: "Ideas on Film," *Saturday Review of Literature*, Vol. 27 (January 27, 1951), pp. 32 a–d
Gives the names of 215 film libraries, located in thirty-seven states, for consultation on the rental or sale of 16 mm. films.

STERNER, ALICE P.: "Radio Appreciation," first eight units of a course in the subject, *Audio-Visual Guide*, November and December, 1950. Also available: course in "Television Appreciation." For reprints write to *Audio-Visual Guide*, 172 Renner Avenue, N. J.

SULLIVAN, G. W.: "Listening Behavior in the Secondary Schools," *American Teacher*, Vol. 31 (1946), pp. 12–13

TYLER, I. KEITH: "The Listening Habits of Oakland (California) Pupils," *English Journal*, Vol. 25 (1936), pp. 206–15

Appendix 5

Representative English Tests

Grammar and Mechanics

Cooperative English Test. Test A, Mechanics of Expression Test. Grades 7–12; college. Length, forty minutes. Cooperative Tests for the East: 20 Nassau Street, Princeton, N. J.; for the West: 4641 Hollywood Boulevard, Los Angeles, Calif.

English Usage. Every Pupil Test. Grades 7, 8, 9. Ohio State Department of Education. Columbus 15, Ohio. A new test, balanced and inexpensive, is constructed annually. Available to teachers and pupils in all states.

English Usage. Every Pupil Test. Grades 10, 11, 12. A new test annually. Ohio State Department of Education, Columbus 15, Ohio.

Essentials of English Tests. Dora V. Smith and Constance McCullough. Grades 7 through 12. Educational Test Bureau. Minneapolis (720 Washington Avenue), Nashville (2106 Pierce Avenue), Philadelphia (3433 Walnut Street).

CROSS, E. A.: *Cross English Test.* Grades 9–12. Two forms.

SMITH, DORA V., and C. MCCULLOUGH: *Essentials of English Tests.* Grades 7–12; college entrance. Three forms. Length, forty-five minutes. Educational Test Bureau, Oak Street and Washington Ave., S.E., Minneapolis, Minn.

Survey Test of English Usage, Form H. L. J. O'Rourke, Ph.D. The Psychological Institute, P.O. Box 1118, Lake Alfred, Florida. This is one of the simplest and easiest tests to administer yet devised. The vast experience of the author on a nation-wide basis makes this test especially valuable. For Grades 9 through 13.

TRESSLER, J. C.: *Revised Tressler English Minimum Essentials Test.* Grades 8–12. Three forms. Public School Publishing Company, Bloomington, Ill.

454

Composition

Effectiveness of Expression: Test B. Grades 7–12; college. Length, forty minutes. Determines sense of style, structure, organization, and language. Cooperative Tests for the East: 20 Nassau Street, Princeton, N. J.; for the West: 4641 Hollywood Boulevard, Los Angeles, Calif.

POLEY, IRVIN C., *Poley Precis Test.* Grades 9–12. Tests reading comprehension. Public School Publishing Company, Bloomington, Ill.

PRESSEY, S. L. and L. C.: *Pressey Diagnostic Tests in English Composition.* Grades 7–12. Four forms. Tests sentence structure and grammatical skill. Public School Publishing Company, Bloomington, Ill.

Vocabulary and Reading

Cooperative Vocabulary Test. Grades 7–9; college. Aims to determine vocabulary range rather than rapidity of recognition. Length, thirty minutes (attempted scales may be limited if desired). Cooperative Tests for the East: 20 Nassau Street, Princeton, N. J.; for the West: 4641 Hollywood Boulevard, Los Angeles, Calif.

HAGGERTY, M. E.: *Haggerty Reading Examination*, Sigma 3. Grades 6–12. Two forms. C. A. Gregory Company, 345 Calhoun Street, Cincinnati, Ohio
Iowa Silent Reading Test. Grades 4–8, 9–12. Two forms. Length, forty-five minutes.

Literature Appreciation

Cooperative Literary Comprehension and Appreciation Test. Grades 10–12. Two forms. Length, forty minutes. Cooperative Tests for the East: 20 Nassau Street, Princeton, N. J.; for the West: 4641 Hollywood Boulevard, Los Angeles, Calif.

LOGASA, HANNAH, and MARTHA JANE MCCOY WRIGHT: *Logasa-Wright Tests for Appreciation of Literature.* Grades 9–12; college. Public School Publishing Company, Bloomington, Ill.

College Entrance Examinations

End of Year Examinations in English for College-Bound Students, Grades 9–12, 1963, College Entrance Examination Board, Box 592, Princeton, N. J. A highly valuable presentation of sample questions, student responses, and analysis of ratings.

Appendix 6

Suggested Letter-Writing Unit: Ninth or Tenth Grade

[The most important thing about letter writing is *mailing the letter*. If we assign letters only to stamp and mail, the motivation is relatively unfailing and realistic. Almost no one wants to write carelessly when he knows a stranger or friend is really going to read his letter. Moreover, when the replies come in, the motivation is heightened immeasurably, especially when vitally important free materials begin to decorate our walls. For motivation in business letters we cannot recommend too highly two pocket books, *A Wonderful World for Children*, by Peter Cardozo (Bantam) and *1001 Valuable Things Free, No. 2*, by Mort Weisinger (Bantam).]

A. FRIENDLY LETTERS

Assignments

1. Write a letter to a friend or relative. First make a rough draft in pencil. Punctuate the letter according to standard usage as shown in your textbook. Copy the letter in ink. Bring an envelope and stamp from home, or send one boy of your class to the post office for stamped envelopes. Show both letter and envelope to your teacher. Appoint a boy or girl to mail all the letters.

One of the hardest things to learn about writing letters is to fold a letter properly. Be sure you know how. Ask your teacher to show you how to do it. Practice folding a letter before you fold the one you are going to mail.

2. Write a postcard to a friend. Write it first in rough draft on a piece of paper exactly the size of a post card. Leave a neat margin all the way around. Avoid such general words as *nice, fine, good, the same*. Then copy your message on a real stamped post card. Appoint a member of the class to mail all the cards.

3. Write a letter to your mother or dad, brother or sister. Even though you will address it to your own home, send it through the mail. It will mean more to the receiver than if you should hand it to him. In your letter tell your father or mother something about your English class, about a friend or two in the class, about one or two interesting things you have done this term.

4. Write a letter to your teacher. Tell her what you have enjoyed about the course. What part of your English course has meant most to you? How do you think the course could be strengthened? Tell her what specific assignments you think would give more meaning to the course. In what way have you failed to make the most of your opportunities in English? In what assignments have you done your best work?

Be sure you mail all letters you write for these assignments. Assign a friend in the class to buy envelopes for the whole class. A letter addressed, sealed, and stamped will mean much more to your teacher than one handed to her in class.

5. Find a pen pal in another city, state, or country. Your teacher may know a teacher in another city who could help find a boy or girl of your interests. To find a pen pal abroad, write to one of the following:

   a. Pen Friends Committee, English-Speaking Union, 19 East 54th Street, New York 22, New York. Write A. B. Grant. Letters from a class preferred. State age and number of applicants.

   b. Council for Education in World Citizenship, Overseas Correspondence Section, 11 Maiden Lane, London, W. C. 2, England.

   c. Karl Knutason, 27 B. Lastmakarogatan, Stockholm, Sweden.

[For the teacher's use: "World Peace Through Friendly Letters," motto of Dyer's Pen-Pal Service Organization, R.F.D.3, Sequin, Texas. A nonprofit agency, service to teachers only, supplying the names of foreign students, ages 12–16. The organization invites teacher enquiries.]

B. BUSINESS LETTERS

Assignments

6. Write a letter in block form making a request for free materials, such as a map, a booklet, a poster. You will find hundreds of free things described you may write for by looking at the pocket book called, *1001 Valuable Things Free, No. 2* (Bantam Books).

When you receive your free map or booklet, bring it to class and show it to your classmates. Pin interesting free materials on your bulletin board.

7. Arrange a trip to the post office for the class. Find out how the post office works, what its problems are. Arrange a talk with the

postmaster or one of his assistants. Ask him questions like these: What is the biggest weakness in addresses? How important is the zip code? How important is the return address? How can a citizen speed up the delivery of an important message? Is it true that European postal systems are more efficient than ours?

8. Write a post card asking for a catalog or other free information in answer to an advertisement. Write a first draft in pencil, the card itself with pen and ink.

9. Write to a college or special school you might like to attend after graduation from high school. See a list of colleges in any good dictionary such as *The American College Dictionary*. Ask the college for a catalog and any pictures showing scenes of the campus and its buildings.

When you receive a reply, bring the catalog to class and discuss the entrance requirements with your classmates. Paste or pin interesting pictures on your bulletin board.

10. Write a neat business letter to a company in whose work you are interested. Ask the company if it would be willing to let you see an application form for employment. You can explain that you want this application form not to apply for a job, but to use for discussion in your English class. What do companies ask of applicants for jobs? This is a good way to compare questions that various companies think are significant in application forms.

Appendix 7

A Student's Grammar Profile

[The grammar profile below is designed as a review for high school juniors and seniors. One value of this review is that it may be used over and over again, with the student writing different sentences. When he knows his basic errors, he may concentrate on those errors to the exclusion of all others. The student who is weak in transitive verbs, for example, might illustrate #4 with fifteen or twenty verbs, each used both transitively and intransitively. This profile is taken verbatim from *Skills and Practices, Book B* (L. W. Singer Company, 1955), pp. 177–83.]

In the four tests that follow you will find a profile of the main points of grammar, sentence structure, and punctuation. By testing yourself with each problem, you can see where you are weak and where you are strong in the mastery of English skills. After testing yourself, you can make yourself strong by doing the assignment under each problem imaginatively and repeatedly. As you write the sentences asked for, be sure to punctuate each construction correctly according to the comma reminders.

BASIC SENTENCE PATTERNS

1. Predicate pronouns in nominative case follow verb *to be:*

   It was Tom and (he, she, they, we, I).

Assignment: Write five sentences using the five pronouns above with five forms of the verb *to be* (was, will be, etc.). Underline each predicate pronoun and label it.

EXAMPLE: It was _he_. (*predicate pronoun*)

2. The verb *to be:* intransitive copulative verb.

   It (is, was, will be, would have been) an easy victory.

459

3. Predicate adjectives follow verb *to be*, as well as sense verbs:

The cake *was* sweet.   The cake *tasted* sweet.

Sense verbs: taste, seem, appear, smell, feel, look, sound

Assignment: Use the seven sense verbs above in seven sentences with seven different predicate adjectives. Underline each predicate adjective and label it.

EXAMPLE: The sky looked _blue_. (*predicate adjective*)

4. A transitive verb takes an object. An intransitive verb does not.

TRANSITIVE	INTRANSITIVE
The policeman *stopped* our car.	Our car *stopped* suddenly.

Assignment: Use each of the following verbs in two sentences, first transitively, then intransitively. Underline and label each verb transitive or intransitive.

stopped, opened, ran, plopped, hammered, sang, painted

       (*trans.*)   (*intrans.*)
EXAMPLE: I _stopped_ the clock. The clock _stopped._

5. A transitive verb often takes a noun as a direct object.

A motorist hailed our *car*.   Matthew cut the *screen*.

Assignment: Write five sentences using nouns as objects of transitive verbs. Underline and label each object.

EXAMPLE: Henrietta baked a chocolate _cake_. (*noun object*)

6. A transitive verb often takes a double object consisting of noun and pronoun.

The officer stopped *John and me*.

Assignment: Write five sentences in which you use a noun and a pronoun as objects of each transitive verb. Use five different pronouns. Underline and label each object.

                 (*noun object*)
EXAMPLE: The teacher praised _Barbara_ and _me_. (*pronoun object*)

Reminder: Pronoun objects in objective case: *me, us, him, her, them, whom.*

7. A preposition often takes a pronoun as its object.

Dad bought the car for *me*.

Assignment: Write ten sentences in which you use a prepositional phrase with a pronoun as the object of the preposition. Underline and label each prepositional phrase. Use six different pronouns. Use ten different prepositions.

EXAMPLE: Randy's uncle solved the problem *for him*. (*prep. phrase*)

8. A preposition often takes a noun and pronoun as its direct object.

> The frightened dog ran toward *Carl* and *me*.
> Rebecca bought the tickets for *Nancy* and *me*.

Assignment: Write fifteen prepositional phrases in which each preposition has both a noun and a pronoun object. Use six different pronouns as objects. Use fifteen different prepositions from the list on page 179. Underline and label each object.

$$\qquad\qquad\text{(noun object) (pronoun object)}$$
EXAMPLES: between *Eunice* and   *her*

$$\qquad\qquad\text{(noun object) (pronoun object)}$$
with *Andy* and   *him*

PARTICIPLES, INFINITIVES, AND GERUNDS

9. A present participle often makes an effective sentence opener.

Reminder: A present participle ends in *ing: coughing, cleaning, throbbing*.

> *Stalking* from the room, he slammed the door.

Assignment: Write three sentences opening with present participial phrases. Underline and label each present participle. Use a comma after an introductory participial phrase.

10. A mature writer often opens a sentence with a past participle.

Reminder: A part participle usually ends in *ed: helped, discouraged, slashed*.

(*past participle*)
EXAMPLE: *Battered* by repeated blocks and tackles, he limped slowly off the field.

Assignment: Write five sentences opening with past participles. Underline and label each past participle.

Reminder: Use a comma after an introductory participial phrase.

(*past participle*)
EXAMPLE: *Quieted* by the hot bath, he quickly fell asleep.

11. As we grow up stylistically, we like to open a sentence with an absolute

construction. An absolute construction consists of a noun modified by a participle.

His head aching fiercely, he stumbled toward the door.

In this sentence the noun *head* is modified by a participle *aching*.

Assignment: Write two sentences opening with absolute constructions. Underline and label each one.

Reminder: Put a comma after an absolute construction.

(*noun, present participle*)
EXAMPLE: <u>*Her mind working quickly,*</u> she realized the danger.

12. An absolute construction may be formed with a past participle.

His courage bolstered by this small success, he strolled to work with a slight swagger.

In this sentence the noun *courage* is modified by the past participle *bolstered*.

Assignment: Write two sentences opening with absolute constructions. Underline and label each one. Put a comma after an absolute construction.

(*noun, past participle*)
EXAMPLE: <u>*Her health restored by the operation,*</u> she resumed her studies.

13. A sentence is often opened by a prepositional phrase with a gerund as object of the preposition.

By fitting the boxes deftly together, he made room for his knapsack.

In this sentence the gerund *fitting* is object of the preposition *by*.

Assignment: Write three sentences opening with prepositional phrases with gerunds as objects of the prepositions. Underline and label each one. Put a comma after the prepositional phrase.

(*prep., gerund*)
EXAMPLE: <u>*By solving the problems quickly,*</u> he passed the examination.

14. Usually only a sophisticated stylist opens his sentence with an infinitive phrase like the following:

To calculate the results most efficiently, he used his new slide rule.

In this sentence *to calculate results most efficiently* is an infinitive phrase of purpose. Infinitive = *to* and *verb*.

Assignment: Write two sentences opening with infinitive phrases of purpose. Underline and label each one.

Reminder: Use a comma after the infinitive phrase.

(*infinitive phrase of purpose*)
EXAMPLE: <u>*To finish the task quickly*</u>, she used a machine.

15. Another mature construction is the infinitive used as the subject of a sentence.

    <u>*To anchor the boat*</u> was surprisingly difficult.

    Assignment: Write three sentences opening with infinitive phrases used as subjects of the sentences. Underline and label each one.

    (*infinitive phrase as subject*)
EXAMPLE: <u>*To become an engineer*</u> was his main ambition.

16. Below is an infinitive phrase used as object of the transitive verb *wanted*. There is nothing distinctive or unusual about this construction.

    He wanted <u>*to see the Metropolitan Museum*</u>.

    Assignment: Write two sentences using infinitive phrases as objects of transitive verbs. Underline and label each one.

    (*infinitive phrase as object*)
EXAMPLE: They planned <u>*to climb the mountain*</u>.

17. Often an infinitive phrase is used as an adjective to describe a noun. In the sentence below, *to speak persuasively* describes the noun *ability*.

    He had the ability <u>*to speak persuasively*</u>.

    Assignment: Write two sentences using infinitive phrases as adjectives. Underline and label each one.

    (*infinitive phrase as adjective*)
EXAMPLE: Ella had a reason <u>*to object strongly*</u>.

18. In the sentence below, the infinitve phrase is an adverbial phrase of purpose, telling why, and is used at the end of the sentence.

    He wrote home <u>*to ask his father's advice*</u>.

    Assignment: Write three sentences with infinitive phrases used as phrases of purpose. Underline and label each one.

    (*infinitive phrase of purpose*)
EXAMPLE: She telephoned the lawyer <u>*to learn the verdict*</u>.

19. A noun in apposition is usually set off by commas.
    My uncle, *a bank cashier*, knows the business world thoroughly.

    Assignment: Write two sentences using nouns in apposition. Underline and label each one.

(*noun in apposition*)
EXAMPLE: The car, *a black Buick sedan*, crashed through the fence.

20. An appositive makes an effective sentence opener.
     An idealist, *Alan disliked his harsh father*.

Assignment: Write two sentences using appositives as sentence openers. Underline and label each one.

(*appositive*)
EXAMPLE: *A beautiful site*, the Cloisters is visited each year by thousands.

USING DEPENDENT CLAUSES

21. An adverbial dependent clause always opens with one of these words: *although, though, if, unless, until, before, when, as, as soon as, while, since, because, after, in order that, so that, than.*
     As he sat down, he struck a match.

Reminder: Use a comma after an introductory adverbial clause.

Assignment: Write ten sentences, each of which opens with an adverbial clause. Open each adverbial clause with one of the words above. Be sure to underline, label, and put a comma after each adverbial clause.

(*introductory adverbial clause*)
EXAMPLE: *Although the problem was difficult*, we solved it.

22. An adverbial clause coming at the end of a sentence is usually restrictive. Do not set it off with commas.
     I shall see him *if he arrives on the five o'clock train*.

Assignment: Write five sentences each of which ends in an adverbial clause. Use a different opener for each adverbial clause. Underline and label each clause.

(*adverbial clause*)
EXAMPLE: I cannot study *when I am tired*.

23. Adjective Clauses: When identification of a person or thing depends on the clause only, it is restrictive and therefore not set off by commas.

Reminder: Words that introduce adjective clauses are *who, whom, which, whose, that*.
     The woman *who is wearing the blue dress* is my cousin.

Assignment: Write five sentences containing restrictive adjective clauses. Underline and label each one.

(restrictive adj. clause)

EXAMPLE: The car *that struck the dog* was a blue Plymouth coupe.

24. A nonrestrictive adjective clause is set off by commas because it is parenthetical in meaning.

   Tom Gallagher, *who is president of the fraternity,* led the grand march.

   Assignment: Write five sentences containing nonrestrictive adjective clauses. Underline and label each one.

   (nonrestrictive adj. clause)

EXAMPLE: Marie, *who is working out of town,* did not hear the news.

25. Noun Clauses: A noun clause is always restrictive. Words that open clauses are *that, who, whom, whoever, which, whomever, why, what, how, where, whether.* A noun clause may be used as:

   a. Subject of the sentence
        Why he had left was a mystery.
   b. Object of a transitive verb
        I believe *that she will come.*
   c. Predicate noun
        This is *what I mean.*
   d. Object of a preposition
        Give ice cream to *whoever comes.*

   Assignment: Write four sentences using the four different noun clause constructions shown above. Underline and label each of the clauses.

   (noun clause used as pred. noun)

EXAMPLE: The decision was *that we would have to forfeit the game.*

A FEW POINTS OF PUNCTUATION

26. A comma is used between two independent clauses when a conjunction is expressed.

        Jonathan knew the secret, but he wouldn't disclose it.

   Reminder: Co-ordinating conjunctions are *and, but, or,* and *for.*

   Assignment: Write four compound sentences using a different coordinating conjunction in each one.

27. A comma is used to separate words in a series. By a series we mean at least three words.

        She was preparing fresh string beans, carrots, and new peas.

Assignment: Write two sentences using words in a series. Use commas to separate the words in the series.

28. When a conversational tag comes after a spoken sentence, begin the tag with a small letter.

   Reminder: A conversational tag is such an expression as *he said, I replied,* etc.

   "We turn down this road," said Jack.

   Assignment: Write two conversational sentences, putting the tags after the sentences.

29. When a conversational sentence is broken by a tag, begin the second part of the quotation with a small letter.

   "Marilyn," she said, "when can you return my book?"

   Assignment: Write two conversational sentences, each sentence broken by a tag. Punctuate correctly.

30. When two conversational sentences are broken by a tag, begin the second sentence with a capital letter:

   "That is true," answered Jack. "We saw the whole thing happen."

   Assignment: Write two conversational sentences broken by a tag. Punctuate correctly.

Appendix 8

Tests in Usage Essentials

[The advantage of the test below is that it requires each student to apply the principle with his own language rather than merely making a choice or correcting a sentence. It may be used over and over again. When a student has a continuing weakness, we may ask him to write ten or fifteen sentences to illustrate one principle. This usage test is taken from *Skills and Practices, Book B* (L. W. Singer Company, 1955), pp. 184–86.]

High school students have most difficulty in their written work with the problems below. First, read over the essentials tests and ask your teacher questions. As you write each sentence in the tests, underline the part that is the key to the usage problem.

> EXAMPLE: *It's* too early for *its* leaves to sprout.
>
> He said, "*You're* a real friend."

After you have taken the tests, perhaps you can exchange papers with a friend to make corrections. Then take the test again, repeating only those problems with which you have made mistakes. The second time, write more than one sentence for each problem. Write two, three, or more sentences, depending upon the difficulty you have with it. If you take a test three or four times, you will increase your mastery of the minimum essentials of written usage.

POSSESSIVES AND CONTRACTIONS

1. Write five sentences, using in each the possessive of *it* at least once. Use the possessive of *who* once in a sentence.
2. Use the contraction of *it is* in three sentences. Use the contraction of *who is* once.
3. Use the possessive of *it* and the contraction of *it is* in one sentence.
4. Use the contraction of *you are* in a bit of conversation.

467

5. Use the possessive of *you* and the contraction of *you are* in one sentence.
6. Use the contraction of *they are* five times, writing five sentences.
7. Use the contractions of *do not, does not, would not,* and *could not* in three or four sentences.
8. Use *their* and *there* correctly in one sentence.
9. Write the contractions meaning *I would, I have,* and *I will.*
10. Use *their* correctly five times in three sentences.
11. Write two sentences in which you use the possessives of *Burns* and *Dickens.*
12. Write sentences using the possessives of *sailor, sailors, farmer, farmers, class, John, Jones.*

NAMES, TITLES, AND NUMBERS

13. Write one or two sentences containing the names of one or more trees, flowers, or birds.
14. Write a sentence containing the names of two games.
15. Write a sentence containing the title of an article, an essay, or a poem.
16. Write a sentence containing the names of several magazines.
17. Write a sentence containing the name of a book with a phrase such as "by Charles Dickens" to show the name of the author.
18. Write in one sentence the titles of two books and in another the titles of two poems, two short stories, or two essays.
19. Write a sentence containing the names of three motion pictures.
20. Write the complete names of three streets, three rivers, two mountains, and two theaters.
21. Write in a sentence the names of three school subjects.
22. Write in a sentence the names of three colleges or universities.
23. Write a sentence containing two names of college courses followed by numbers referring to year or level.
24. Write five numbers that can be spoken in two words.
25. Write five numbers that require three words to speak.
26. Write a sentence containing a fraction written as two words and separated by a hyphen.

WRITING CONVERSATION

27. Write one sentence of conversation preceded by a conversational tag.
28. Write a sentence of conversation followed by a conversational tag.
29. Write a sentence of conversation divided by a conversational tag.
30. Write two sentences of conversation divided by a conversational tag.
31. Putting the conversational tag at the beginning, write a bit of conversation containing an exclamation, a question, a command, and a statement. Let only one person speak. Use only one set of quotation marks.
32. Write a bit of conversation expressing a question in three words and another sentence in not more than three words. Let only one person speak.

The Fragment and the Run-together Sentence

33. Write a sentence fragment; then show how you would add or subtract words to make it a complete sentence.
34. Use the word *however* between two complete thoughts. Punctuate it correctly. Do not use *also, and,* or *but.*
35. Use the word *however* in the middle of a simple sentence.
36. Write two complete thoughts, the second of which opens with *suddenly.*
37. Use the word *then* between two complete thoughts. Do not use *also, and,* or *but.*
38. Write two complete thoughts, the second of which opens with the word *he.*
39. Write two complete thoughts, the second of which opens with the word *now.*
40. Write two complete thoughts, the second of which opens with the word *there.*
41. Write two complete thoughts, the second of which opens with the word *she* or the word *they.*
42. Write two complete thoughts, the second of which opens with the word *finally,* the word *consequently,* or the word *moreover.*

Sentence Openers and Modifiers

43. Write a sentence opening with a participial phrase.
44. Write a sentence opening with a dangling participle. Keeping the participle as it stands, change the rest of the sentence to eliminate the dangler.
45. Write a sentence opening with an adverbial clause.
46. Write a sentence opening with an absolute construction.
47. Write a sentence opening with a past participle.
48. Write a sentence opening with an infinitive phrase of purpose.
49. Write a sentence with an infinitive phrase as the subject.
50. Write a sentence opening with a prepositional phrase. Do not set it off with a comma.
51. Write a sentence opening with an adverb. Do not set it off with a comma.
52. Write ten two-word adjectives connected by hyphens.
53. Write a sentence containing three coordinate or parallel adjectives.
54. Write a sentence containing three adjectives not parallel.

Phrases and Clauses

55. Write twelve prepositional phrases, each opening with a different preposition. Draw circles around the prepositions.
56. Write five sentences, each of which contains two dependent clauses. Underline the dependent clauses, and draw circles around the subordinating conjunctions.

57. Write a sentence containing an appositive.
58. Write a sentence containing (in this order) an adverb, a prepositional phrase, an adverbial clause, and an independent clause.
59. Write four compound sentences, using each of the coordinating conjunctions: *and, but, or,* and *for.*
60. Write a sentence in which two independent clauses are separated by a semicolon.
61. Write four compound sentences. Begin the second clause in each sentence with one of the following words: *his, them, our, we, I,* or *whose.*

Punctuation and Usage

62. Write sentences using the word *too* correctly three times.
63. Write a sentence using the word *to* correctly, one time before a noun, one time before a verb.
64. Write a sentence containing a date: month, day, and year.
65. Write a sentence containing an address (house number and name of street).
66. Write three complimentary endings of business or friendly letters. Capitalize the correct words.
67. Write three salutations for business or friendly letters. Punctuate each correctly.
68. Write a sentence containing a series preceded by a colon.
69. Write three sentences using the word *lie* (to recline) in the past tense.
70. Write three sentences using the participle *lying* (reclining).
71. Write three sentences using the word *see* in the past tense.

Appendix 9

Speech Errors under Fire: Grades 7 to 12

[The following invaluable guide from Pooley, *Teaching English Usage* (Appleton-Century-Crofts, 1946), pp. 194–98, 218–23, shows the most persistent errors in speech and in what years they should be attacked.]

I. Errors to Be Attacked for Elimination in the Junior High School
   A. *Pronouns*
      1. Case forms
         a. *Him*, (*her*) and *me* went.
         b. It was *him, her, them.*
         c. Will you wait for John and *I?*
         d. Did you see her and *I?*
         e. Let him and *I* do the work.
         f. *Us* boys want to go.
         g. She invited *we* girls to the party.
         h. This is the man *which* did the work.
   B. *Verbs*
      1. Principal parts
         a. He *ask* me to go. (other *-ed* forms)
         b. They have *ate* all the melon.
         c. He has *began* to read the book.
         d. We *begun* the work at three o'clock.
         e. I have *broke* my pencil.
         f. I *brung* my lunch.
         g. My pencil is *busted.*
         h. He has *came* here before.
         i. He *done* the work well.
         j. I have *drank* all the milk.
         k. I *drunk* it all.
         l. She *give* me the picture.

471

     m. The bell has *rang.*

     n. He *run* all the way.

     o. Then he came to me and *says.* ...

     p. He *seen* the accident.

     q. My dress is *tore.*

     r. The boys have *went* home.

     s. My dress is *wore* out.

     t. I have *wrote* two letters.

2. Agreement with subject

     a. Her hair *are* long.

     b. One of the books *are* lost.

     c. Each of the books *are* interesting.

     d. He *don't* play tennis.

     e. There *is* two holidays this month.

3. Miscellaneous

     a. Jim *ain't* here now.

     b. Please *borrow* me a pencil.

     c. If he *had* of come, he would have built the fire.

     d. You *had* ought (*you'd* ought) to do that.

     e. He *laid* in the shade, *was laying* in the shade, wants to *lay* in the shade.

     f. *Learn* us a new game.

     g. *Leave* me see the butterfly.

     h. *Set* in this chair; he *set* in this chair, has *set* in this chair, etc.

C. *Adjectives and adverbs*

1. Is he eating *a* apple?

2. He writes *good.*

3. This *here* book is mine.

4. That *there* one is yours.

5. Do you know *them* boys?

6. I don't like *these kind* (*those kind*, or *sort*) of stories.

D. *Double negatives*

1. He hasn't *neither* book.

2. Haven't you *never* been to Chicago?

3. Jane hasn't *no* pen.

4. I haven't *nothing* to do.

E. *Miscellaneous*

1. My brother *he* went to the football game. (and other double subjects)

While a great many of the forms listed in this outline will be taught as the need arises in composition, speech, reports, recitations, and so forth, some of them can be introduced or reinforced by instruction connected with grammar. For this reason they have been arranged in grammatical categories. But note well that from all the evidence available, *the study of grammar in itself has practically no effect on usage habits*, at least in the junior high school. When the child's desire to improve himself has been aroused, when certain specific faults have been made clear, and the desirable substitutes have been practiced, then he may be helped by a grammatical explanation of the fault and its correction. Grammatical reasons may strengthen changes already begun. However, it may be stated as an axiom for the junior high school: *grammar alone does not establish sound usage habits*.

In order to concentrate upon the forms most needed by junior high school pupils, the teacher will have to neglect a variety of usage items which will ultimately need correction as the pupil matures. Outline II below is presented to suggest the type of usage deviations which may be ignored. Superior pupils whose usage has eliminated all errors in Outline I may be individually guided concerning items in Outline II. Such pupils tend to ask for such guidance and profit by corrections or suggestions made on compositions. The items in Outline II, however, will usually not receive class instruction in the junior high school. Indeed, many of them represent good current usage.

II. Forms to Receive No Class Instruction in the Junior High School

    A. *Pronouns*

        1. Case forms

            a. It is *me, us.*

            b. Tim is taller than *me, her, him.*

            c. Mary is as tall as *me, her, him.*

            d. Everybody (everyone) had *their* lesson.

            e. When *you* are driving a car *you* should be able to act quickly.

            f. *Who* did you invite?

            g. *Who* did you go with?

            h. Invite *whoever* you choose.

    B. *Verbs*

        1. Agreement with subject

            a. The kind of games you like *are* too simple.

            b. Athletics *are* important in our school.

            c. Neither of the boys *are* here.

            d. Neither John nor George *are* here.

            e. The father with his two sons *were* here.

        2. Miscellaneous

            a. I *guess* I'll go.

            b. I haven't *got* any paints.

            c. I *got* home early.

            d. It *says* in my history book. . . .

            e. I *will* probably go to the party.

            f. If I had time I *would* be glad to help you.

    C. *Adjectives and adverbs*

        1. He's *awfully* rich.

2. I feel *badly* about the accident.
3. You walked *further* than I did.
4. I am *kind of* tired.
5. This is the *largest* of the two apples.
6. *Most* anyone can do this work.
7. I *only* saw her once.
8. His work is *pretty* good.
9. Come here *quick*.
10. Drive *slow*.
11. He's *sort of* angry.

D. *Conjunctions and prepositions*
1. He isn't *as* tall as his brother.
2. Divide the work *between* the four groups.
3. Study your lesson *like* I do.
4. It looks *like* it will rain.
5. He fell off *of* the roof.
6. Your book is *different than* mine.

EFFECTIVE TEACHING PROCEDURES

To teach usage effectively in the junior high school, the following principles should be understood and applied in the planning of courses of study, the organizing of usage units, and the teaching of daily lessons. As an introduction to these principles it is suggested that the junior high school teacher read the discussion of "popular fallacies in the teaching of usage" presented in Chapter IX.

PRINCIPLES FOR TEACHING USAGE IN THE JUNIOR HIGH SCHOOL

1. Individualize instruction in usage so as to meet the most urgent needs of each pupil at the moment of his recognition of the need.
2. Emphasize desirable patterns of oral language, and by training the ear to be alert to language forms, assist the child in making his own corrections.
3. Place all usage instruction so far as possible in situations calling for the natural use of language in speech and writing.
4. Teach usage positively as well as negatively; develop sensitivity to appropriate forms of language for various needs in life.

Individualized instruction. To the teacher in the typical junior high school meeting five or six classes a day with an average of thirty pupils to a class, the idea of individualized teaching in usage may seem preposterous. Yet with a clear notion of the goals to be reached, a strategic plan of action, and some materials worked out in advance, any teacher can individualize instruction in usage to a considerable degree.

I. Errors to Be Attacked for Elimination in the Senior High School

A. *Pronouns*

1. Case forms
   a. It was her, him, them.[1]
   b. I am as tall as him, her, or taller than him, her.
   c. Did you see John and I?
   d. Give the book to John or I.
   e. Let him and I go.
   f. Everyone came but she and John; or, John and I.
   g. Us fellows went early.
   h. The candy was meant for we girls.

2. Agreement with antecedent
   a. Everybody brought their friends.
   b. Has everyone their hats?
   c. Everyone helped themselves.
   d. He is the one which did it.

B. *Verbs*

1. Principal parts
   a. The fender is broke.
   b. He begun the work early.
   c. Has the mail came?
   d. He come early.
   e. He has did the work well.
   f. I done the work alone.
   g. He has drank all of the water.
   h. I drunk the pop.
   i. The water was froze.
   j. He give me the book.
   k. Has the bell rang?
   l. He run a mile.
   m. Have you saw the movie?
   n. He handed me the letter and says. . . .
   o. I seen it last night.
   p. He is suppose to go. (and other -d forms)
   q. We have went three times.
   r. He has wrote the letter.

2. Agreement with subject
   a. Either Jack or Ed are going.
   b. One of these sports are especially popular.
   c. My hair are straight.
   d. It don't matter when we go.

[1] The only exceptions which usage makes to the pattern of the nominative following the verb, *to be* are "It is me" and the less frequent "It is us."

    e. Every one of the boys have come.

    f. She is one of those girls who is easily offended.

    g. There is several magazines on the table.

    h. We, you, they, Jim, and Henry was there.

3. Miscellaneous

    a. Fred ain't here now.

    b. Will you borrow me a pencil? [2]

    c. She et her lunch.

    d. He had ought (hadn't ought) to go.

    e. If he had of come, he would have had a good time.

    f. He lays down, laid down, was laying down, has laid down, wants to lay down, etc.

    g. Learn us the game.

    h. Leave him go now.

    i. The river raised last night.

    j. Let me set at the head table.

    k. If he would have done the work, he wouldn't have failed.

    l. If he hadn't studied, he would of failed.[3]

C. *Adjectives and adverbs*

1. I am a admirer of art.
2. He does his work good.
3. This here pencil is broken.
4. That there pen scratches.
5. These kind (those kind or sort) of books don't appeal to me.
6. Them books are all yours.

D. *Double negatives*

1. She can't hardly carry a tune.
2. I haven't hardly any paper.
3. We haven't never been late before.
4. He hasn't no book of his own.
5. They haven't nothing to do now.

E. *Miscellaneous*

1. Where is the party at?
2. That is all the farther (further) I went.
3. Then this man he tried to escape. (and other double subjects)

The expressions that follow in Outline II are either established in present usage or are still in dispute. If the forms are established, there can be no reason for trying to correct them; if they are in dispute, few pupils have time to bother with them. A more favorable attitude toward good English can be created by concentrating attention upon a relatively small

---

[2] This misuse of *borrow* is common in certain parts of Wisconsin.

[3] *Would of* is, of course, an error that occurs only in writing. The oral elision, *would've*, appears frequently in the conversation of educated people.

number of language forms. A few defects may be cured, but to be told that nearly all of one's language habits are bad is merely discouraging. Although the forms in the following list do not deserve class attention, individuals who inquire about any of them should certainly be given as accurate information as possible and should be urged to observe how the forms are used. They may be told that an expression is acceptable for colloquial but not for more formal English, that even for colloquial use a given form seems to be preferred, or that no preference can be indicated.

II. Forms to Receive No Class Instruction in the Senior High School

    A. *Pronouns*

        1. Case forms
            a. It is me.
            b. Who did you invite?
            c. Who is it for? [4]
            d. I will work with whoever you suggest.

        2. Agreement with antecedent
            a. They had a bad earthquake in San Francisco last week.
            b. Everyone was here, but they all went home early. [5]
            c. I failed to answer his question, which was thoughtless of me.
            d. If you are going to make a windmill, you need tools. [6]
        3. Unclassified
            a. They invited my guests and myself.

    B. *Verbs*

        1. Agreement with subject [7]
            a. Athletics are stressed in most schools.
            b. The kind of tools you want are hard to find.
            c. Neither of the boys were here.
            d. None were willing to oppose the bill.

        2. Miscellaneous
            a. I've got to write the letter.

[4] For colloquial use the interrogative *who* may be used instead of *whom* unless the pronoun in the sentences follows immediately its verb, verbal, or preposition. The relative *whom* presents practically no problem because of the common tendency to omit the pronoun or to use *that*, e.g., "a girl I know," "a girl that I know."

[5] The plural pronoun may have a singular antecedent if in the sentence the pronoun is far removed from its antecedent, especially if the plural idea is very strong. If the pronoun is placed near its antecedent, good usage follows the grammatical rule for agreement, e.g., "Everyone brought his friends."

[6] In informal speech and writing, the indefinite *you* is permissible. It also appears frequently in literary English.

[7] There is an increasing tendency for a verb to agree with the meaning rather than with the form of the subject.

      b. I got home early.

      c. I will probably be at the party.[8]

      d. Will you want this book tonight?

      e. I would go if I were you.

      f. Would you go if I stayed at home?

      g. He said that New York was a large city.[9]

C. *Adjectives and adverbs*

1. It was awfully kind of you to come.
2. I feel badly.
3. He ran further than I did.
4. Most everyone came.
5. I only have fifty cents.
6. Come quick.
7. It is pretty cold today.
8. The wind is real strong.
9. You'd better drive slow.

D. *Conjunctions and prepositions*

1. He isn't as old as Henry.
2. The reason he wrote a poor test was because he was ill.
3. Arrangements were made to divide the work between the four girls.
4. I don't know if I can go.
5. It looks like it would rain.
6. I tried to swing the racket like you do.[10]

E. *Miscellaneous*

1. Try and finish the work on time.
2. What was the reason for Henry objecting? [11]
3. He tried to thoroughly understand the problem.[12]

---

[8] Very little distinction is made between the uses of *shall* and *will* and *should* and *would*. "Shall I," however, is regarded as being more courteous than "Will I?"

[9] Such attraction to the past tense is common and probably established.

[10] *Like* for *as* or *as if* is generally permitted in conversation and informal writing but not for formal use.

[11] Either the possessive or accusative case of a noun seems to be accepted before a gerund. The accusative case of a pronoun in this position is open to dispute.

[12] The split infinitive is permissible except when the use of it produces an awkward construction.

Appendix 10

O'Rourke's Sequence:
Introduction of Points of Usage

[The selection below is Appendix A of Mr. L. J. O'Rourke's *Rebuilding the English Curriculum to Insure Greater Mastery of Essentials* (Washington, 1934), pp. 97–98. Mr. O'Rourke lists here seventy-eight items of usage, of which twenty-seven have application only in writing. One high value of Mr. O'Rourke's listing, especially to curriculum planners, is his sequential arrangement of the usage items.]

It was not a purpose of this study to make fixed assignments of points of usage to each grade; rather, it was desired to determine a sequence for the introduction of points of usage which would serve as a flexible course of study, adaptable to the needs and abilities of each class.

The list that follows shows the sequence in which phases of usage are presented in the suggested course of study for the elementary grades. As stated on page 23, three factors have been considered in determining this sequence: (1) the practical utility of each phase of usage; (2) the difficulty of each phase of usage; and (3) the relation of each phase of usage to other phases.

The findings of this study indicate that by limiting instruction to those essentials of usage which make up this list, and by presenting them in the order here indicated, the effectiveness of English-usage instruction in the elementary grades should be greatly increased.

Sentence recognition
Sentence development
* Capitalization: first word in a sentence
* Punctuation: period
* Punctuation: question mark
* Capitalization: names of persons

* Asterisks indicate phases of usage that apply to written work only.

479

* Capitalization: initials
* Capitalization: *I*
  Use of *I* with name words:
    John and *I*, Mary and *I*, My brother and *I* (not *me*)
    John and I (not *I and John*)
* Capitalization: names and places
  Pointing words: *these* and *those* (not *them*)
  Correct use of *came* and *come*
  Correct use of *saw* and *seen*
  Correct use of *did* and *done*
  Correct use of *went* and *gone*
  Correct use of *ran* and *run*
  Correct use of *sit* and *set*
  Correct use of *let* and *leave*
  Correct use of *doesn't* and *don't*
  Correct use of *is* and *are*, especially *you are*
  Correct use of *was* and *were*, especially *you were* and *they were*
  Words that say "No" (*not, n't, none, nothing, no one, nobody, nowhere*)
  Correct use of *teach* and *learn*
* Capitalization: names of days and months
* Punctuation: period following abbreviations of days and months
* Punctuation: comma in dates
* Capitalization: names of holidays
  Use of *himself* and *themselves* (not *hisself* and *theirselves*)
  Correct use of *eat, ate,* and *eaten*
  Use of *this* and *that* (not *this here* and *that there*)
  Avoiding unnecessary words, as, my brother *he*
* Punctuation: comma (or colon) after salutation of a letter
* Punctuation: comma after friendly close of a letter
* Capitalization: *Doctor, Street, Avenue, Dr., St., Ave.*
* Punctuation: comma in address
  Correct use of *there is* (*was*) and *there are* (*were*)
* Capitalization: titles of books, poems, etc.
* Capitalization: first word in each line of poetry
  Correct use of *give, gave,* and *given*
  Correct use of *took* and *taken*
  Correct use of *bring* and *brought*
  Correct use of *good* and *well*
  Making words mean *more* (not *more taller*, etc.)
  Making words mean *most* (not *most loveliest*, etc.)
  Use of *I, he, she, we,* and *they* with one another or with names, as *He and I, John and she, Mary and he, We and our friends,* etc.
  Use of *are* and *were* with *He and I, John and she, Mary and he,* etc.
* Punctuation: comma in series
* Capitalization: titles of persons

* Correct use of *two, too,* and *to*
* Punctuation: apostrophe in contractions
  Use of *have* in such phrases as *could have, ought to have,* etc. (not *of*)
  Correct use of *wrote* and *written*
  Correct use of *grew* and *grown, knew* and *known, threw* and *thrown*
* Punctuation: quotation marks
* Punctuation: comma before or after quotation
* Capitalization: first word of quotation
* Punctuation: comma after *yes* and *no*
* Punctuation: comma to set off name of person spoken to
  Use of *me, him, her, us,* and *them* with one another or with names, as, *She asked him and me, They asked John and her,* etc.
  Use of *me, him, her, us,* and *them* after *with, between, to, for*
  Correct use of *we children* and *us children*
  Correct use of *spoke* and *spoken, broke* and *broken, froze* and *frozen, chose* and *chosen, stole* and *stolen*
  Correct use of *drank* and *drunk, sang* and *sung, rang* and *rung*
  Correct use of *a* and *an*
  Correct use of *rise* and *raise*
  Correct use of *lie* and *lay*
  Use of different forms of *sit, sat, rise, raise, lie,* and *lay*
  Correct use of *began* and *begun*
  Use of *ought* (not *had ought*)
  Use of *shall I* (not *will I*) in asking questions
  Use of *he said* (not *he says*)
  Correct use of *rode* and *ridden*
  Correct use of such words as *careful* and *carefully*
* Punctuation: apostrophe to make word show ownership
  Avoiding unnecessary words, as: *where to, off of, where is it at, from off*
  Correct use of *like* and *as*
  Use of *I, he, she, we,* or *they* after *as* or *than,* as *I am older than she*
  Use of *hardly* and *scarcely* (not *haven't hardly,* etc.)

In addition to the phases of usage listed, the suggested course of study provides repeated opportunity for oral and written composition, including the writing of friendly letters. Frequent drills on enunciation, pronunciation, and vocabulary building are included. Throughout the entire course constant attention is given to sentence structure, the pupil being taught to recognize and use complete sentences and to avoid "run-on" sentences. A system of cumulative reviews tends to reenforce the teaching of each point throughout the entire elementary-grade English course.

Appendix 11

Relation between Use and Error

[The list of usage items below is taken from Stormzand and O'Shea, *How Much English Grammar?* (Baltimore, 1924), p. 191. The listing is especially valuable because it shows the number of errors which occur in pupil themes out of one thousand chances. Notice that in writing, pronouns are used incorrectly only on rare occasions, whereas confusion between *its* and *it's* occurs in 290 chances out of a thousand. As we should expect, comma errors with quotations have a very high frequency.]

Error Quotients, Arranged in order of Importance
(The figures indicate the number of errors that may be expected in school compositions in 1,000 chances)

Rank	Description	Quotient
1	Comma setting off dependent clause out of its natural order omitted	650
2	Name of city and state written without punctuation	600
3	Independent clauses of compound sentences not separated	578
4	Hyphen omitted in compound word	507
5	Non-restrictive clause not set off	495
6	Members of series not separated	492
7	No punctuation after introductory expression	458
8	Comma before, after, or in broken, quotation	447
9	Use of objective for possessive with gerund	444
10	Wrong form of possessive nouns	427
11	"You" used indefinitely	390
12	Failure to capitalize proper nouns and adjectives	316
13	Failure to distinguish "it's" and "its"	290
14	Interrogation mark omitted	259

Rank	Description	Quotient
15	"Only" misplaced in sentence	237
16	"O'clock" written without apostrophe	231
17	Use of "most" for "almost"	222
18	Miscellaneous misuses of apostrophe	211
19	No period after titles	193
20	No period after abbreviation	147
21	Misuse of quotation marks	110
22	Wrong number of verb with expletive "there"	76
23	Wrong form in past participle	42
24	No period (group total)	30
25	Predicate nominative pronoun in wrong case	22
26	Misspelling of "there" or "their"	21
27	No period at end of sentence	19
28	Failure to use capital at beginning of sentence	10
29	Pronoun object of verb in wrong case	6
30	Pronoun object of preposition in wrong case	4
31	Incomplete sentence	4
32	Misspelling of "to," "too," or "two"	4
33	Wrong form in past tense	2
34	Pronoun subject of verb in wrong case	.3

Appendix 12

The Most Common Grammatical Errors

HENRY HARAP

[The selection below is a reprint of Mr. Harap's article in the *English Journal* (Volume XIX, 1930), pp. 440–46. It is still the most complete summary of grammatical errors in both written and oral usage.]

There is in existence an accumulation of thirty-three investigations of written and oral errors made by pupils. None of these is complete or comprehensive due to one of several causes. The investigation may have failed to include a sufficiently large number of persons. It may have been limited to a locality which revealed certain unique errors and failed to reveal others. The treatment of the data may have concealed certain specific items.

The composite of thirty-three investigations given below does not pretend to be an original contribution. However, it has several advantages over preceding lists. First, it is more comprehensive than any preceding list of common grammatical errors; second, each error is given specifically, that is, as it should be treated in class work; third, nearly every error is followed by a specific illustration.

The frequency of occurrence of these errors is not given because of the lack of uniformity in recording them by various investigators. Some were recorded by types of error, some by rules of grammar and some by illustrations of the error itself. It would not be wise to undertake to teach all of the cases included in the list but no inventory test which is not purely local can afford to neglect to include all of them.

The following is a list of the most common errors in grammar, punctuation, and sentence structure. The logical arrangement and numeration were arrived at with great care, although the latter may not suggest it. The arabic numerals represent items which should be treated as separate units for purposes of instruction.

I. Verbs

1. Disagreement of a verb with its subject in person.
   don't for *doesn't.*
   Disagreement of a verb with its subject in number.
2. Wrong number of verb with expletive *there.* *There remains three boys to see.*
3. Agreement with a singular noun that has a plural ending. *Athletics are.*
4. When separated from subject by a phrase. *Not one of our friends were there.*
5. Singular verb with a compound subject joined by *and.* *How is John and his brother?*
6. After a pronoun whose antecedent is overlooked. *She is one of those who is easily overlooked.*
7. After *neither.* *Neither of us deserve the prize.*
8. Hair *are; was* for *were; is* for *are.*
   Wrong past tense.
9. *seen* for *saw;* 10. *come* for *came;* 11. *begun* for *began;* 12. *done* for *did;* 13. *give* for *gave;* 14. *run* for *ran;* 15. *laid* for *lay;* 16. *swum* for *swam;* 17. *drunk* for *drank;* 18. *would run* for *ran;* 19. *use* for *used;* 20. *sung* for *sang;* 21. *says* for *said;* 22. *dove* for *dived;* 23. *was* for *were.*
24. Failure to use the past perfect tense. *I found him almost recovered though he was quite ill.*
25. Failure to use present perfect tense. *See me after you see Mr. Smith.*
26. Change of tense in main clause.
   Wrong past participle.
27. *went* for *gone;* 28. *did* for *done;* 29. *saw* for *seen;* 30. *froze* for *frozen;* 31. *came* for *come;* 32. *broke* for *broken;* 33. *laid* for *lain;* 34. *swam* for *swim;* 35. *tore* for *torn.*
36. Use of double negative.
   could not hardly for *could hardly;* use of *didn't have no; ain't got no; didn't do nothing; hadn't no* for *hadn't.*
   Use of wrong verb.
37. *lay* for *lie;* 38. *leave* for *let;* 39. *lend* for *borrow;* 40. *sat* for *set.* 41. *set* for *sit;* 42. *learn* for *teach;* 43. *can* for *may.*
44. Use of *have got* for *have; have not got* for *have not.*

II. Pronouns

45. Subject not in nominative case. *John and me are going to camp this summer.*
46. Predicate nominative not in nominative case. *It is him. It is me.*[1]
47. The use of wrong cases of pronouns after *than* and *as* and *as well as.* *He is taller than me. This misfortune falls more heavily upon you than I.*

---

[1] Usage permits either "It is *I*" or "It is *me*". "It is *me*" is almost universal, at least in the Middle West, except among teachers on parade.

48. Object of a preposition not in objective case. *Mother gave the ball to John and I.*
49. Object of a verb not in objective case. *Mother sent John and I.*
50. *Whom* for *who; who* for *whom.*
51. Wrong formation of compound pronouns. *They hurt theirselves.*
52. Use of objective for possessive with gerund. *I'm tired of him complaining.*
53. Disagreement of pronoun with its antecedent. *Will everyone bring their paper?*
54. Confusion of *its* and *it's. Its hard to tell. The dog hurt it's paw.*
55. Use of *which* for *who* and vice versa. *He is the man which I meant. This is a dog who knows his tricks.*
56. Lack of clear reference of pronoun to antecedent. *Mary told her friend that she was mistaken.*

III. Adjectives and Adverbs

57. Incorrect comparison of adjectives.
58. Use of adjective for adverb when modifying an adjective. *Awful* for *very; real* for *very.*
59. Use of adjective for adverb when modifying a verb. *He is most done. Everyone will be treated fair.* This error also involves many other specific cases including the misuse of *good, easy, careless, fine, safe, different, neat, bad.*
60. Use of adverb for adjective after a copulative verb. *He feels badly.*
61. *Only* misplaced in the sentence. *He only helped the boys.*
62. Use of *those* and *these* for *that* and *this. I like those kind of grapes.*
63. Use of expression *that there* and *this here. That there man is my neighbor.*
64. Use of *them* for *these* and *those. Them things are ours.*

IV. Prepositions and Conjunctions

Use of superfluous preposition.

65. *in back of* for *back of* or *behind; off of* for *off; start in* for *start; add up* for *add; end up* for *end;* 66. *where are you at; return back.*

Use of wrong preposition.

67. *off me* for *from me; by my aunt* for *to my aunt; to home* for *at home;* 68. *different to* for *different from; in* for *into; between* for *among.*

Use of wrong conjunction.

69. Use of *like* for *as* or *as if.*
70. *Where* and *how wrongly* used as a conjunction. *Did you read where the boy was saved from drowning in the creek? Did you read how a man was killed?*

V. Nouns

Wrong number in nouns.

71. Nouns ending in *y* preceded by a consonant.
72. Nouns ending in *o* preceded by a consonant.
73. Nouns ending in *is* (*basis*).

74. Plural of proper nouns.
75. Nouns which change their form in forming the plural (*phenomenon*).
76. Nouns which have no plural (*athletics*).
77. Nouns which have no singular (*scissors*).
78. Compound nouns (*brother-in-law*).
    Wrong form of possessive case in nouns.
79. After plural nouns ending in *s*. *Teachers' dining room.*
80. Compound nouns (*court-martial*).

VI. SENTENCE STRUCTURE

81. Omission of subject. *Received your letter.*
82. Omission of predicate.
83. Dangling participle. *The boy gazed as his father, trembling with anger.*
84. Misplaced modifier. *She claimed she had paid her admission several times.* (meaning one admission).
85. Wrong handling of parallel structure. *He taught piano, violin, and vocal* (should be voice).
86. Double subject. *John, he went. Why there was.*

VII. PUNCTUATION

87. No period at the end of a sentence.
88. No period after abbreviations.
89. No ? at the end of a sentence.
90. Failure to set off a restrictive clause by a comma.
91. Failure to set off a series by commas.
92. Failure to set off a parenthetical element by commas.
93. Failure to set off an appositive by commas.
94. Failure to set off a quotation by a comma.
95. Failure to use quotation marks.
96. Failure to use a semicolon when there is no conjunction between clauses of a compound sentence.
97. Failure to use a semicolon to set off a series.
98. Failure to use parentheses.
99. Failure to use a colon.
100. Failure to use an exclamation point.
101. Apostrophe not properly used to show a contraction.

VIII. CAPITALIZATION

102. Failure to capitalize proper nouns.
103. Failure to capitalize title of a book; articles; newspapers; chapter headings.
104. Failure to capitalize the first word of a direct quotation.
105. Wrong use of capital for title of a person when it is used as a common noun.
106. Wrong use of capitals for the names of school subjects other than languages.

The following is the list of sources which were used in making the consolidated list of common grammatical errors:

Betz, A., and Marshall, E., "Grammar Based on Errors," *English Journal*, June, 1916, pp. 491–500. A study of errors made by Kansas City pupils.

Bobbitt, S. A., "Shortcomings in the Written English of Adults," in F. Bobbitt, *Curriculum Investigations*, chap. xii. A study of 362 letters to discover errors in punctuation, grammar, etc.

Special Report of the Boise, Idaho, Public Schools, June, 1915. Also in *Sixteenth Yearbook of the National Society for the Study of Education*, Part I, pp. 89–91. A study of oral errors for a semester, made by C. S. Meek.

Charters, W. W., and Miller, E., "A Course of Study in Grammar," *University of Missouri Bulletin*, Vol. XVI, No. 2 (Education Series 9), 1915. A course based on the errors actually made by the children of Kansas City.

Charters, W. W., "Minimal Essentials in Elementary Language and Grammar," *National Society for the Study of Education, the Sixteenth Yearbook* (1917), chap. vi. Summary of several studies.

Charters, W. W., *Curriculum Construction* (Macmillan, 1923), p. 204. A table showing the comparison of percentages in oral errors made by children in Kansas City, Detroit, Hibbing, and Pittsburgh.

Charters, W. W., "Language and Grammar," *Department of Superintendence, Third Yearbook* (1925), chap. viii. Summary of several studies.

Clapp, F. L., "A Test for Habits in English," *Elementary English Review*, February, 1926, pp. 42–6. Contains a list of most common errors made on a comprehensive test designed by the author.

Connersville, Indiana, School Board Report, 1908. Contains a study by G. M. Wilson of oral errors made by children.

Fairmont (West Virginia) *Normal School Bulletin*, Vol. III, No. 1. A study of language errors.

Fillers, H. D., "Oral and Written Errors in Grammar," *Educational Review*, December, 1917, pp. 458–70. Grammatical errors made by 900 pupils in Bonham, Texas, in oral and written language.

Guiler, W. S., "Analysis of Children's Writings as a Basis for Instruction in English," *Journal of Educational Method*, February, 1926, pp. 259–64. A study of errors in punctuation and capitalization in 1,731 children's themes.

Hermans, M. C., *Teaching Grammar by Problems*. A prospectus published by Henry Holt & Co. Contains summary of errors found in investigations made by Charters and Starek.

Johnson, R. I., "The Persistency of Error in English Composition," *School Review*, October, 1917. Pp. 555–80. A study of errors found in 132 exercises of high school freshmen and 66 exercises of college freshmen.

King, V. R., "Study of the Persistency of Grammatical Errors in English Compositions of Oakland High School Pupils," Report in the *Cali-*

fornia Curriculum Study by W. C. Bagley, and G. C. Kyte (University of California, 1926), pp. 118–20. Errors found in 306 compositions of ninth-grade pupils in Oakland.

Leonard, S. A., "The Wisconsin Tests of Grammatical Correctness," *English Journal*, June, 1926, pp. 430–32. Contains a list of 31 most common errors made by pupils in a comprehensive test designed by the author.

Lyman, R. L., "Fluency, Accuracy, and General Excellence in English Composition," *School Review*, February, 1918, pp. 85–100. A study of errors contained in 322 high school freshman exercises.

McPhee, Clare, "The Teaching of Language Forms," *Elementary School Journal*, October, 1925, pp. 137–46. Selects and grades language forms designed to eliminate most common language errors.

Potter, W. H., and Touton, F. C., *Achievement in the Elimination of Errors in the Mechanics of Written Expression throughout the Junior-Senior High School*. "University of Southern California Studies," 2d ser., No. 3 (1927), p. 3. Contains sixty-four errors summarized from previous studies.

Pressey, S. L., "A Statistical Study of Children's Errors in Sentence-Structure," *English Journal*, September, 1925, pp. 530–35. A study of the types of errors in sentence-structure based on a total of 980 papers written by pupils of Grades VII–XII.

Pressey, S. L., "A Statistical Study of Usage and of Children's Errors in Capitalization," *ibid.*, December, 1924, pp. 727–31. An analysis of letters, magazines, and newspapers to discover what capitalization is most frequently used.

Randolph, E. D., "Analysis of Errors of Children in Speyer School," *Sixteenth Yearbook of the National Society for the Study of Education*, Part I (1917), pp. 98–100. A study of 1,040 pages of stenographic reports of the oral schoolroom language of New York children.

Randolph, E. D., "Conventional Aversions Versus Fundamental Errors in Spoken English," *Pedagogical Seminary*, September, 1917, pp. 318–36. A study of 1,040 pages of stenographic reports of the oral language of New York children.

Ruhlen, H., and Pressey, S. L., "A Statistical Study of Current Usage in Punctuation," *English Journal*, May, 1924, pp. 325–31. An analysis of letters, magazines, and newspapers to discover what punctuation marks are most commonly used.

Sears, I., and Diebel, A., "A Study of the Common Mistakes in Pupils' Oral English," *Elementary School Journal*, September, 1916, pp. 44–54. A collection of 2,200 oral errors over a period of four days.

Stormzand, M. J., and O'Shea, M. V., *How Much English Grammar*. Baltimore, Md.: Warwick & York, 1924. A study of constructions in compositions of children and adults including writers of fiction.

Sunne, D., "The Effect of Locality on Language Errors," *Journal of Educa-*

tional Research, October, 1923, pp. 239–51. A study of the oral and written errors of Louisiana children.

Tenth Yearbook of Superintendents' and Principals' Association of Northern Illinois (May, 1915), ("Essentials of Elementary English"). Also in the *Sixteenth Yearbook of the National Society for the Study of Education*, Part I, pp. 88–9. A study of oral and written errors made by O. S. Thompson.

Tressler, I. C., "High School Grammar: An Investigation." *English Journal*, December, 1917, pp. 645–57. A study of the 700 oral and written errors made by high school pupils in six weeks. Twenty-four types of general errors are included.

Willing, M. H., "Valid Diagnosis in High School Composition," Teachers College Bureau of Publications, 1926, pp. 55–64. This is a table of common errors in composition consisting of the author's and other error lists.

Wilson, G. M., "Errors in Language of Grade Pupils," *Educator-Journal*, December, 1909. A study of the errors of Connersville children.

Wilson, G. M., "Locating the Language Errors of Children," *Elementary School Journal*, December, 1920, pp. 290–96. A summary of errors in five language studies.

Wiswall, Z. E., "A Study of Sentence Structure in Eighth Grade Composition," *ibid.*, February, 1926, pp. 441–48. An analysis of 800 compositions to discover defects in sentence structure.

Appendix 13

How to Judge a Textbook

The most vital element of an English textbook is motivated assignments in speaking and writing that derive from basic patterns of experience in adolescent life. But to tell a ninth or a twelfth grader, "Write a story about a friend," or, "Describe a moment of deep happiness in your life," without setting up standards of vividness, limitation of topic, and variety of approach, is to bring to our desks dull and lifeless themes. The motivated assignment requires student models that define quality of achievement and teach more in a few minutes by suggestion than we can teach in an hour by admonition. Some authorities have a strange distrust of pupil models. But is any textbook worth its salt that teaches students to write without showing them the language that our materials have inspired other students to use? Very little of the student's own language gets into the books that teach him to speak and write. It is not generally realized that the gifted student, and very often the average student, can write stories containing sentences of professional quality. It is our job as teachers to prove to our students that they can write as well *at times* as Jesse Stuart or Charles Dickens or Stephen Crane. Such heightened achievement is the pulsing life of a motivated assignment. No teacher who has used a variety of such stories in making an assignment believes for a moment that some students will imitate the content of the stories before him. Such an assumption would suggest that the student does not have his own unique story to tell, an assumption which we know is false. But in a student model our class has a standard of visualization before them, of sentence appeal and variety of sentence beginnings. We can show the student by means of the model how to achieve this same intensity. There are, of course, other elements of motivated assignments, as we have shown in such charts as those on pages 79–83, but the student theme is the heart and soul of motivation. The greater the proportion of the student's own authentic language we find in a textbook, the richer the stories that emerge from our use of it. When experience patterns are carefully selected, the response of each student to such writing assignments is certain to be highly individual in quality of diction and depth of self-expression. The best writing assignment excites the most gifted student in the class to a high peak of achievement; he surpasses himself. Similarly, in response to the best assignment, particularly when we use high quality student models, the least gifted student reaches a peak he has not hitherto visualized he can attain. Thus for appeal to an expression of individual differences the written assignment is the most important key to attainment in English.

The best writing assignments have a progression from the personal and the concrete to the social and the abstract. Beyond each student lies a family situation, and beyond each family situation lies a social condition. Each assignment dealing with personal experience provides an opportunity, therefore, for exploration of intellectual concomitants. The best textbooks in English will contain problems of critical analysis of stories, novels, and plays, preferably not in opening units, but in the natural progression from personal experience to intellectual applications. The more deeply the student feels about autobiographical writing, the more certain he is to have an interest in novels, stories, poems, and plays which penetrate deeply into life's meaning in a perspective beyond his own family, school, and community.

Speaking and writing assignments give the teacher an opportunity to diagnose the special needs of his class in the field of usage. A textbook must have incidental treatment of spelling, capitalization, and sentence sense within a speaking and writing unit. But it must also have full units on the various aspects of usage, to which the teacher may turn at any time, units in plurals and possessives, sentence sense, dictionary practice, special common errors such as *too-to, it's-its, there-their*. About seventy percent of all written errors may thus be eliminated without any knowledge of grammar. Therefore thorough usage units, in which the practices are copious and varied and weighted in proportion to frequency of error and difficulty of the problem involved, are the second most important resource of a language textbook in the secondary school.

A textbook should be adaptable to various kinds of English teachers. Many teachers unable to elicit sparkling stories are adept at teaching important language jobs, such as letter writing and report writing, précis writing, interviewing, taking steps in research, introducing people, making an outline, speaking about a book, reciting a poem, speaking a poem with a speech choir. A textbook must have many resources to meet multiple needs and extend the effectiveness of different kinds of teacher training. An intellectual skill much needed in American schools is the art of answering a question; another vital skill is that of framing a formal definition in a single sentence. Such language skills are indispensable in the teaching of English as a tool subject. The art of asking a question of a fellow student to show one's interest in him and his opinions has a lifelong application to human relations, more honored in the breach than in the observance. A textbook must select such a vital language job for insistent and continuing emphasis.

A textbook should have thorough, consecutive chapters in grammar, not an incidental treatment with a page of nouns on page forty-five and a section about verbs beginning on page seventy. There are talented teachers who are successful, I am sure, in teaching grammar a few days each month; such a teacher can turn to the grammar chapters as he needs them. The teacher who wants to spend consecutive weeks on grammar, however, should have consecutive chapters. The greatest weakness in most textbooks is the lack of sufficient practice sentences in usage and grammar. I have never met an English teacher who said that his textbook had too many drills. Publishers, however, despite the insistent pleas of textbook authors, often strive mightily to reduce practice materials on any one grammatical problem to the minimum used by their competitors. A much needed resource in grammar teaching is a series of fifty or one hundred master sentences from novelists and poets that can be used five or six times over for different purposes: recognition of nouns, verbs, adjectives, adverbs; then for diagraming or parts-of-speech analysis in other forms.

TEXTBOOK RATING CHART: GRADES 7 THROUGH 12

A. *Organization* (20 points)

1. Do speaking and writing assignments receive initial emphasis in the book?
2. Are such skills as sentence sense, spelling, and capitalization included for incidental practice in the speaking and writing assignments?
3. Are usage skills treated also in separate systematic units?
4. Are there units on sentence sense, spelling, capitalization, levels of usage, vocabulary enlargement?
5. Is grammar presented in a separate and consecutive series of units?
6. Are there annotated lists of books arranged according to experience topics, some of which are found in writing assignments?
7. Does the gifted student have specially designed and challenging assignments in each chapter?
8. Are summaries of skills and principles brought together in a separate handbook at the end of each text?
9. Does the book contain passages of superb literature as well as remarkable single sentences for study of diction and sentence structure?

B. *Motivated Assignments in Speaking and Writing* (50 points)

1. Are the assignments based on basic experiences of the student, including family life?
2. Does each assignment provide for class discussion, an opportunity for an oral paragraph preceding the actual writing?
3. Does each assignment provide at least three pupil models?
4. Are the pupil models varied in mood and paragraph development?
5. Does each assignment provide fifteen to twenty suggested theme topics?
6. Does each assignment provide treatment of correctness, including spelling?

7. Does each assignment provide a special exercise in improvement of diction or sentence structure?

C. *Thorough Presentation of Usage* (25 points)

1. Is there copious drill on a few problems rather than sparse drill on many problems?
2. Is the amount of drill on each problem proportionate to difficulty of the problem and persistence of error?
3. Do sentence errors receive more drill than any other usage problem?
4. In capital-letter drills, does the sentence error again receive attention? Is there drill also on what *not* to capitalize?
5. Is there a chapter on spelling? Is there a selection of the most difficult words, numbering twenty to fifty? Are the hard spots in these "demons" dramatized?
6. Is dictation used effectively in drills on usage?
7. Is the proportion of space given to practice at least five times the proportion of space given to explanation of principles?

D. *Incitements to Intellectual Curiosity* (10 points)

1. Does the text relate the vividness of concrete language in student themes to the vividness of concrete language in great books?
2. Does the text contain passages and stories for analysis from the great books, such as *Moby Dick, The Red Badge of Courage,* Cather's "A Wagner Matinee?"
3. Does the text contain a rich sprinkling of master sentences for study, imitation, and discussion?
4. Does the text contain helpful annotated booklists?
5. Are book reports limited in scope to one scene, one moment, one idea, one character?
6. Is motivation for the writing and research papers concrete and appealing, with a student model to illustrate and an analysis of step-by-step procedures?
7. Does the book contain invitations to define key words such as *happiness, American, love, citizen, ambition, education,* etc.?

E. *Presentation of Language Jobs: Written* (10 points)

1. Does the author emphasize mailing a friendly letter as the most important motivation to write it well?
2. Does the pupil mail the business letters he is requested to write?
3. Is research for reports and long papers based upon the student's curiosity?
4. Does analysis of literature correlate well with analysis of science and social studies?
5. Is the student taught how to answer a question in a sentence, a paragraph?
6. Is the student taught how to write a formal definition in one sentence?

7. Is the student taught how to write a summary or a précis of several paragraphs in a few sentences?

F. *Presentation of Grammar* (25 points)

1. Is the grammar concentrated in one part of the book, so that the teacher can use it systematically or incidentally, as he chooses?
2. Are the practices so copious that the teacher will not have to make up his own?
3. Are cartoons used to dramatize grammatical principles?
4. Are students directed to act out certain definitions, such as prepositions?
5. Is diagraming used to visualize grammatical concepts?
6. Is there copious drill on diagraming?
7. Is there a body of fifty or one hundred sentences from literature that can be used for several purposes, such as recognition of nouns, verbs, adjectives, and adverbs, as these chapters are studied; then for diagraming? Are these sentences arranged in order of difficulty?

G. *Testing Program and Resources for Gifted Pupils* (10 points)

1. Is there a test at the end of each unit of usage and grammar? Is there a second test, of greater difficulty, but covering the same problems?
2. Does each chapter contain a project of special challenge for the gifted student: a suggestion of a book to read or an idea to investigate?
3. Are students referred throughout the book to master sentences recommended for creative imitation or grammatical analysis?
4. Are gifted students called upon to analyze or dramatize important statistical statements?
5. Are assignments provided which specifically anticipate college requirements in writing?

H. *Sentence Building and Sentence Structure* (10 points)

1. Does the student have repeated opportunities to build a longer, more sophisticated sentence from a short one?
2. Is he told what to add step by step: an adverb telling *when* or *where*, an adjective or a noun naming a color, an image of sound, etc.?
3. Does the text provide practices in re-arranging sentence structure, opening sentences in a variety of ways?
4. Does each student then have an opportunity to build his own sentence in six or seven steps in written form?
5. In building a single sentence, does the student have an opportunity to enhance vividness of diction, also use of metaphor and simile?
6. Does the student have an opportunity to imitate a number of distinguished sentence patterns from literature?
7. Does the student have a special chapter requiring analysis of weaknesses in sentence structure?
8. In visualizing places, is the classical principle taught of progression of

images from far to near, background to foreground, in a single sentence as well as in a paragraph?

I. *Quality of Language* (20 points)

1. Is the diction of the author specific and concrete, as opposed to abstract and general?
2. Is the language of the exercises concrete, image-making?
3. Does the author suit his language and his examples to the age level the book is designed for?
4. Is the language of the student models concrete, image-making?
5. Are the poems used in the text of genuine literary quality? Has the author been able to bring forth from his students language of distinctive visual quality?

J. *Illustrations* (20 points)

1. Does the book have a high proportion of teaching illustrations as opposed to decorative ones?
2. Does the book have at least sixty cartoon-like drawings that dramatize principles of usage and grammar?
3. Do at least half the cartoon drawings make use of the personification of objects or animals?
4. Does the book have a good sampling of student art, in full color?
5. From the viewpoint of the art critic, do the illustrations have distinction?

Using the Chart

The relative importance of each criterion in the Chart is shown above in terms of points, which total 200 as a perfect rating. Within each criterion a teacher may wish to answer each question with a grade of 100 to 0. On the criterion of illustrations, for example, the ratings might run as follows: 1–70, 2–50, 3–0, 4–0, 5–30. The average of these ratings would be 30. The score on illustrations would then be 30 percent of 20 points, or 6 points.

In rating a book, answering each question as shown above, we may have a picture somewhat as follows:

Organization	15 points
Motivated Assignments	20 points
Presentation of Usage	25 points
Incitements to Intellectual Curiosity	7 points
Language Jobs: Written	6 points
Grammar	15 points
Testing Program; Gifted Pupils	5 points
Sentence Building	4 points
Quality of Language	13 points
Illustrations	6 points
	119 points

Appendix 14

A Grammatical Autobiography[1]

As English teachers we are aware that no bigger gap exists between life and the schoolroom than that between life and grammar. Language is easy, fluent, spontaneous; feelings are often fire and ice; but grammar is abstract, difficult, at times insurmountable. To overcome the inertia of the student in his response to grammar, we must find some way to relate grammar to his experience. A solution to this problem becomes increasingly imperative as more and more seniors aspire to enter college and the professional world beyond. More than any other series of abstractions, we need to give grammar "a local habitation and a name," pinning its various elements to the student's own experience. But how can this be accomplished? What methods or devices can we use?

Any student from the seventh grade through the twelfth can write a series of fifty or a hundred sentences about himself to illustrate certain grammatical principles. This assignment I call a grammatical autobiography. The number of sentences and the difficulty of concept may vary from year to year, from class to class. But the principle of making grammatical abstractions not only concrete but riveted in meaning to the student's own experience would apply on every level of attainment or maturity. The idea of such an autobiography is not one of systematic progression in the teaching of grammar but of comprehensive review that will allow the student to concentrate on those elements in which he finds himself most vulnerable to repeated error.

As a part of a student's grammatical autobiography, we may say, for example, "Write eight or ten sentences each containing a predicate adjective describing your personality. At the beginning of each sentence use a prepositional phrase, such as '*At home* I am usually *talkative.*' " A tenth-grader's sentences may run something like this:

[1] From *English Journal*, January 1960, pp. 16–21.

497

1. *At school* I am usually *jolly.*
2. *With a close friend* I am *expansive.*
3. *At home* I am usually *quiet.*
4. *In English class* I am *discouraged.*
5. *On sunny days* I am *optimistic.*
6. *On Sunday morning* I am *blue.*
7. *On the telephone* I am sometimes *witty.*
8. *With my boy friend* I am *coquettish.*
9. *In a car* I am *nervous.*
10. *With my dad* I am *talkative.*
11. *With my mother* I am sometimes *evasive.*

Such an assignment may, of course, bring in its wake superficial answers or searching ones, depending upon the relationship of the teacher to his class. When, however, the student is asked to write his grammatical autobiography in a special notebook to which we shall ask him to add from time to time, the project assumes the validity we want: a fusion of vital experience with the difficult abstractions we are trying to clarify.

In teaching the infinitive, we may ask the student to make a record of his ambitions in infinitive phrases only, as Harold Jackson did in the following:

MY TEN AMBITIONS

1. To play center for South High.
2. To buy an old car for forty dollars.
3. To win a game of checkers from my dad.
4. To make a B in English just once.
5. To read *Great Expectations.*
6. To make a trip to California.
7. To ask a certain girl for a date.
8. To be admitted to Benton College.
9. To get an interesting job next summer.
10. To make my big brother proud of me.

When the class has written phrases in response to this assignment, we may profitably read and compare ambitions, infinitives meanwhile appropriately forgotten. But after reading selected sentences to the class or having them written on the board, we return to the grammatical problem. This time we may ask the student to write complete sentences opening with infinitive phrases of purpose: "To achieve this ambition, I must, etc." We can also extend the same personalizing principle to sentences using the infinitive as subject and predicate noun. At the same time, finding memorable infinitives in Shakespeare or Milton may be an exciting adventure to those who have also personalized infinitives in their own experience. "Give me the right to know," wrote Milton, "to utter, to argue fully according to conscience, above all liberties." The nuances of literature take on more meaning when a student uses a grammatical structure like that of a master he admires.

As we teach the science of definition, which is the heart of the semantic search, we may couple the shaping of definition not only with the student's personal experience but also with the use of predicate nouns he will find it hard to forget. Emerson is rich in such definitions: "Man is the facade of a temple." "Man is a stream whose source is hidden." "Man is a dwarf of himself." "Man is a fagot of thunderbolts." Each student may profitably write a definition of the word *man*, answering the question "What is man *to you?*" using a predicate noun as every good definition requires. If the word *man* is too difficult, we may ask the student to define the word *citizen*, *maturity, grace, beauty, son, daughter*.

The grammatical autobiography may contain stories told in prepositional phrases, such as the following one by Jerry Rabow:

ONE HOUR TO GO

1. out of bed
2. into the bathroom
3. into my clothes
4. down the stairs
5. at the table
6. into my mouth
7. on the front step
8. for my friends
9. across the street
10. on my bike
11. toward school
12. at my desk

In teaching the distinction between the adjective and adverb prepositional phrases, we may ask the pupil to tell a story about himself in verbs and adverb phrases only, such as those below by Philip Agnew and George Krouse:

AN ASSEMBLY SPEECH

1. walked to the stage
2. looked at many faces
3. trembled with fear
4. stared at my feet
5. spoke in a cracked voice
6. mumbled out each word
7. rushed off the stage

OFF TO SCHOOL

1. jumped from my bed
2. looked out the window
3. leaped into my clothes
4. rushed out the door
5. hopped on my bike
6. raced down the street
7. sat on the grass

Still another combination is that of participial phrases followed by objects and modifiers, telling the story of a personal experience:

IN THE SCHOOL CAFETERIA

1. swishing open the door	6. lifting a bottle of milk
2. hearing the clatter of dishes	7. balancing my tray
3. sliding my tray along	8. waiting for my check
4. laughing with friends	9. slipping out my napkin
5. choosing a ham sandwich	10. chattering with the gang

Helen Geronimo

As we meet new needs and dilemmas in the teaching of grammar, the possibilities of grammatical autobiography expand. For example, in teaching the restrictive adjective clause we may ask the student to write a number of sentences about friends and family, beginning as follows:

1. I know a friend who . . .
2. I am a friend who . . .
3. I know a brother who . . .
4. I am a brother who . . .

We also ask our students to write sentences about the use of money, each one beginning with *although*, such as:

1. Although I have worked three summers, I have saved no money.
2. Although my dad gives me a weekly allowance, I am usually broke.
3. Although I borrow frequently, I pay back promptly.

As students write such sentences, the restrictive *who* clause and the introductory *although* clause cannot help but take on a new and emphatic personal meaning in the context described. Our aim is *not to teach more grammar,* but to make what we do teach indelible in the memory. I cannot imagine a student really hating grammar who searches out forty nouns in Lincoln's "Gettysburg Address." Nor can a student hate those grammatical terms by which he has expressed some indelible facts and impressions of himself.

One of the most fascinating approaches to grammatical autobiography in the eleventh or twelfth grade is to select passages from literature which describe in part the student's own experience. He is then prepared to write a sentence similar in construction to a master sentence he has chosen for himself. For example, consider this sentence from the *Mayor of Casterbridge:*

And in Autumn airy spheres of thistledown floated into the same street, lodged upon the shop fronts, blew into drains, and innumerable tawny and yellow leaves skimmed along the pavement, and stole through people's doorways into their passages with a hesitating scratch on the floor, like the skirts of timid visitors.

Looking at this remarkable sentence from a grammatical point of view only, we see first a series of three active verbs, each followed by a prepositional phrase; then an independent clause with a compound verb, *skimmed* and *stole*, followed by six consecutive prepositional phrases. The student who is able to construct a sentence of his own like this one, with the same series of grammatical constructions in sequence, pulls together in one passage many elements of his grammatical knowledge.

However, the grammatical construction of this sentence cannot be disassociated from its imagery or its rhetoric. Here Hardy presents us first with a frame of a village street in autumn through which thistledown is floating. Within the frame of the street he places images of shop fronts and drains. Within the frame of shop fronts he shows us innumerable tawny and yellow leaves, stealing into people's doorways. Beyond each doorway is a passage, and we hear the scratch of the leaves upon the floor "like the skirts of timid visitors." This passage is a remarkable synthesis of the art of the novelist. The simile, preceded by color images, sound images, active verbs, and a touch image, comes appropriately at the climax of the sentence. None of this analysis of Hardy's sentence can be separated from its grammatical construction. For those students whose minds need stretching, it is an ideal task for them to write sentences of this same grammatical construction. Where Hardy has prepositional phrases, the student uses prepositions. Where Hardy has active verbs, the student follows Hardy's example. Where Hardy uses sounds and colors and images of touch, the student does likewise. I grant that in writing such a sentence the student may depend less upon autobiography than upon imagination. But there are many kinds of autobiographies, and to the student who can write such a sentence, we may say, "This is a good sign, not only of your knowledge of grammar but also of your understanding of intense sensory diction. Moreover, your simile at the end is almost as striking and original as that of Hardy himself." I have had college students who have profitably spent half a day in paraphrasing this sentence, achieving not only the same sequence in grammatical constructions, but also an equally intense diction.

Here is an example of a college student's imitation of the master sentence from Hardy's *Mayor*. Notice how carefully the structure follows that of the original sentence.

IN THE WINTER DUSK: IMITATION OF HARDY

And in the winter dusk, long gusts of wind whispered secrets to the windows, wailed under the door, sighed across the carpet to the fire; and delicate purple-white snowflakes danced around the treetops, pitted the roof, and trickled down the cottage with wistful resignation, like the tears of silent lovers.

Frances Dyller

The selection of a master sentence that the junior or senior thinks worthy of imitation begins of course with the idea of the sentence, not its structure. Nevertheless, within the fascinating sentence, the student finds particular constructions he would like to make a part of his language resources. When even a few students can bring such sentences to class, write them on the board, and then copy for comparison their own sentences, the class can make a long step forward in a more sophisticated appreciation of grammar. Consider, for example, this sentence from Anzia Yesierska, "How I Found America":

> More and more the all-consuming need for a friend possessed me. In the street, in the cars, in the subways, I was always seeking, ceaselessly seeking for eyes, a face, the flash of a smile that would be light in my darkness.

This passage represents a common experience. What part of it is worthy of imitation? We may say, "Choose the most distinguished part of the passage. Imitate that part only in terms of your own experience." The student would hardly select the first sentence as an example of distinguished diction or structure. But the second sentence, ah, that is different. But what is best in the second sentence, its series of prepositional phrases or its series of noun objects? And are these objects more distinguished than the metaphor at the end of the sentence? In some such classroom situation lies the ideal fusion of literary appreciation, writing skill, and grammatical realism.

SUGGESTED SEQUENCE: GRAMMATICAL AUTOBIOGRAPHY

The sequence of questions below is from easy to difficult. The questions are suggestive rather than inclusive. If some questions seem too elementary for our grade, we may pass them by. The teacher of grade seven or grade twelve will wish to modify the sequence to suit her needs. Many students will think of autobiographical ideas that they would like to express in grammatical form. Others will think of grammatical constructions they have always found baffling. Autobiographical sentences may help them to fix the constructions in mind, especially when the ideas are exchanged with those of fellow-students.

1. In what state were you born? Use and underline a prepositional phrase. *Example:* I was born *in Nebraska.*
2. When were you born? Use and underline a prepositional phrase. *Example:* I was born *on October 24, 1943.*
3. What is your father's name? Use and underline a predicate noun. *Example:* My father's name is *Nathan.*
4. On what street do you live? Use and underline a prepositional phrase. *Example:* I live *on Rogers Avenue.*
5. What color are your eyes? Use a predicate adjective. *Example:* My eyes are *blue.*
6. What color is your hair? Use a predicate adjective. *Example:* My hair is *brown.*

7. Write ten sentences that describe your personality. Begin each sentence with a prepositional phrase. *Example: At school* I am *friendly.*

8. What did you see when you first awakened this morning? Use the word *saw* with a noun object. Mark *saw* as a transitive or intransitive verb. *Example:* I *saw* the pink *curtain.*

9. What clothes did you put on this morning that you especially like? Use and label a transitive verb. *Example:* I *put* on my corduroy *jacket.*

10. What did you eat for breakfast this morning? Use three objects of a transitive verb, label it, and punctuate the series of nouns correctly. Underline and label each noun. *Example:* I ate *oatmeal, toast,* and *butter.*

11. Who is your closest friend in this room? Use a predicate noun. *Example:* My closest friend is *Harry.*

12. Define the word *son, daughter, maturity, beauty, friendship, citizen,* or *student* in one sentence. Use a predicate noun. Open your sentence with the words "To me." *Example: To me* a *son* is a boy who tries to understand his father's struggles.

13. What river have you crossed? Open with a prepositional phrase telling when. Mark your verb transitive or intransitive. *Example:* In October 1956, I *crossed* the Colorado *River.*

14. Describe an action of yours that took place today. Open with a present participle. *Example: Opening* the garage door, I backed out the car.

15. Write a sentence describing your dad or mother at the dinner table. Use at least one nominative absolute. *Example:* My dad ate slowly, laying down his fork now and then, smiling at my mother, *his laughing blue glance sweeping around the table.*

16. What occupations do several of your family follow? Name four relatives and tell what occupation each follows. Use predicate nouns and underline them. *Example:* My uncle is a locomotive *engineer.*

17. What three sounds do you like? Use three gerunds as objects of your verb. *Example:* I like the *pattering* of rain on my window, the *crackling* of a wood fire, the *humming* of a motor.

18. What activity did you enjoy most as a child of ten or twelve? Use a gerund as the object of your verb. *Example:* I liked *swimming* in the Y.M.C.A. pool.

19. What are ten ambitions you cherish? Use infinitive phrases only. (See above, pp. 208–209.)

20. What job have you held that you like best? Use an intransitive verb. *Example:* I *worked* in a clothing store.

21. What three colors did you see today? Answer with the transitive verb *saw. Example:* I *saw* the blue of the sky, the green of the grass on our front lawn, the black of the tar on the roadway.

22. Write a sentence about your use of money beginning with *although. Example: Although* I do not make money easily, I always spend it fast.

23. Write a sentence opening with an *as* or *even as* clause, followed by a nominative absolute. Describe a moment you recall, in a sentence like

the following from Katherine Anne Porter, "Maria Concepcion":
"Even as she was falling asleep, head bowed over the child, she was still
aware of the strange, wakeful happiness."

24. Describe an action you remember, in a sentence constructed like the
following from Joseph Conrad, *Nigger of the Narcissus:* "Streaming with
perspiration, we swarmed up the rope, and, coming into the blast of
cold wind, gasped like men plunged into icy water."

25. Choose a sentence or passage from a book that represents to you an
experience you recall vividly. Write a sentence of your own about the
experience, using the same grammatical construction that your writer
used. Here are examples:

"A half moon, dusky-gold, was sinking behind the black sycamore
tree."

D. H. Lawrence, *Sons and Lovers*

"The moonlight fell upon the earth like a magic unearthly dawn. It
wiped away all rawness, it hid all sores. It gave common and familiar things
— the sagging drift of the bar, the raw shed of the creamery, the rich curve
of the lawyer's crab-apple trees — a uniform bloom of wonder."

Thomas Wolfe, *Look Homeward, Angel*

Appendix 15

The Dramatization
of Statistics

A single page of statistics discussed in class or used as theme topics may bring a very intense educational experience to our students. In presenting such a page of statistics to the class, we may say, "Which statistical statement below is most important to your occupational success? Which is most important to you as an American citizen? Which is most important to you as a thoughtful observer of world problems?

1. In 1962 one-half of all high school graduates went to college.
2. In the past three decades the Soviet Union has produced 1,117,800 engineers. America has produced, in the same period, 620,200.
3. Russia spends 5% of the gross national income on education. We spend about 3.6% of the national income on education.
4. Between 1951 and 1961 the number of college students increased 83%, whereas the total school population increased 51%.
5. College graduates between the ages of forty-five and fifty-four earn an average of $7,907 annually, whereas high school graduates earn an average of $4,519 annually during those years.
6. In the upper 5% of most talented students only 63% are in the college preparatory group. Of the upper 25% in ability only 50% are taking college preparatory work.
7. Two-thirds of the people of the world go to bed hungry each night.
8. Two-fifths of the brides, in American marriages in 1962, and one-eighth of the grooms were in their teens.
9. In 1935 the poorest 20% of the families received only 4% of the income. Their share rose to 5% in 1944 and has remained at that level ever since.
10. In 1960 the lowest 20% of American wage-earners made less than $2,800.00 annually. The top 5% made $16,250.00.
11. In 1962, though 70,000,000 people were employed, there were still 1,000,000 youngsters out of school and out of work. Unemployment among teenagers was 12.5 per cent, as compared to overall unemployment of 5.3 per cent.

PINNING DOWN STATISTICAL MEANING

We may ask our students, let us say a class of juniors or seniors, to write a theme applying statistical facts to their own experience, personal or intellectual. Here are two such papers, from *Enjoying English 12* (1966), pages 27 and 29.

WHY COLLEGE FACTS BRING ME A JOLT

The facts about college in this body of statistics have given a jar to my complacency. Up to this time I have not considered seriously going to college. I am in the upper 25% of my class, but so far I have not taken much college preparatory work. My parents have not stressed it, and I know my father is not really able to send me. But I see as never before that college is very vital in rearing a family. A college graduate at forty-five makes almost twice as much as a high school graduate. If my dad were a college graduate he would now, according to these figures, be prosperous enough to send me to college. I now have a new purpose: to work at night and go to school during the day. My friend Sam has a job in a box factory, working from midnight to 8:00 A.M. Then he goes to college, taking a reduced schedule. It is hard, but he is determined. Sam has often assured me that he is going to college not to enjoy an education but to make a better living when he gets married. These statistics help me to put Sam's case and mine in perspective. We do not seek culture as such or read great books for love of learning. We simply want the skill and training with which to earn a comfortable living for ourselves and our families.

Fred Dickson

THE MOST IMPORTANT FACT

To me the most important fact cited in these pages is the one from *Geography of Hunger:* "Two thirds of the people of the world go to bed hungry every night." I grant this fact is more important from a world point of view than from a national or a personal point of view. I have never experienced hunger beyond the hours that pass between meals. Yet I have an imagination. My uncle has lived in Calcutta. He has pictured to me the hungry people who sleep in the streets, many thousands of them refugees. As long as these people, or any people, are hungry, how can they think of reading a good book, hearing a great poem, sitting still in a classroom, or helping their brothers and sisters? I think of Gandhi's saying, "To a hungry man democracy is a loaf of bread." The first task of this world is collectively to abolish hunger. In his *Geography of Hunger* Josue de Castro shows that this is possible. In our own great land we have virtually abolished hunger. Our next task is to be our brother's keeper and help other nations to rid the world of its greatest plague.

Harry Anderson

Appendix 16

Golden Sentences
for Grammatical Analysis

The use of golden sentences for grammatical or rhetorical analysis has a significance far beyond its present limited application in American school rooms. When a student analyzes or diagrams a memorable sentence, he absorbs both consciously and unconsciously the excellence of its diction and rhythm. Such an approach both enhances literary appreciation and intensifies grammatical meaning. The intricacies of grammar take on a fresh dignity when they are analyzed in the language of Abraham Lincoln, Henry Thoreau, or Walt Whitman. A final step is the creative imitation of a golden sentence, in which the student uses the same structure but not the same diction or meaning as the master (see pp. 500–501).

The sentences below are arranged in a progression from the simplest sentences to the most complex. When a teacher has such a collection of golden sentences on hand, he may assign them either as advanced work for the gifted students or as further intensive analysis for the whole class. Furthermore, the use of such sentences encourages the individual student to find passages of his own for analysis in masters of both poetry and prose.[1]

1. Low hangs the moon. *Walt Whitman*
2. Spring came on forever. *Vachel Lindsay*
3. The silence surged softly backward. *Walter de la Mare*
4. Happiness too swiftly flies. *Thomas Gray*

[1] Sentences 1–10 contain nouns, intransitive non-linking verbs, adjectives, and adverbs. In sentences 11–20, prepositional phrases appear; in sentences 21–30, transitive verbs; in sentences 31–40, copulative verbs; in 41–50, compound sentences; in 51–60, complex sentences; in 61–70, infinitives and participles. For other such sequences of master sentences, see *Enjoying English 7*, pp. 322–24; *Enjoying English 8*, pp. 328–30; *Enjoying English 9*, pp. 402–403; *Enjoying English 10*, pp. 402–404; *Enjoying English 11*, pp. 426–29; *Enjoying English 12*, pp. 419–21.

5. The game fish swims upstream. *John Moore*
6. The stars pale silently. *Conrad Aiken*
7. Down swept the chill wind. *James Russell Lowell*
8. Here might the red bird come. *Ralph Waldo Emerson*
9. Now the sun had stretched out. *John Milton*
10. That wreck shall lie forever. *John Greenleaf Whittier*
11. The keen sparkle of frost is on the sill. *Conrad Aiken*
12. The angel spirit of rain laughed . . . in the night. *Robert Louis Stevenson*
13. I must go down to the seas again. *John Masefield*
14. Part of the moon was falling down the west. *Robert Frost*
15. She floats upon the river of his thoughts. *Henry Wadsworth Longfellow*
16. Into each life some rain must fall. *Henry Wadsworth Longfellow*
17. The gray back of winter was broken. *Thomas Wolfe*
18. With rue my heart is laden. *A. E. Housman*
19. I am involved in mankind. *John Donne*
20. The winter evening settles down
    With smells of steaks in passageways. *T. S. Eliot*
21. Spring rides no horses down the hill. *Edna St. Vincent Millay*
22. Any man's death diminishes me. *John Donne*
23. The curfew tolls the knell of parting day. *Thomas Gray*
24. The scarlet of the maples can shake me like a cry of bugles. *Bliss Carman*
25. Quick leaves cast a shimmer of green against our whited walls.
                                                    Christopher Morley
26. . . . I behold, upon the night's starred face,
    Huge cloudy symbols. *John Keats*
27. Stunted birches hug the shallow water line. *Sidney Lanier*
28. The mass of men lead lives of quiet desperation. *Henry Thoreau*
29. I had a lover's quarrel with the world. *Robert Frost*
30. Before winter I built a chimney, and shingled the sides of my house.
                                                    Henry Thoreau
31. We are the hollow men. *T. S. Eliot*
32. The only gift is a portion of thyself. *Ralph Waldo Emerson*
33. A whale ship was my Yale College and my Harvard. *Herman Melville*
34. The woods are lovely, dark and deep. *Robert Frost*
35. Her voice was ever soft, gentle and low. *Shakespeare*
36. It was night, in the lonesome October
    Of my most immemorial year. *Edgar Allan Poe*
37. A rose is pink by the fountain's brink. *Christina Rossetti*
38. The report of my death was an exaggeration. *Mark Twain*
39. A good book is the precious life-blood of a master spirit. *John Milton*
40. Every man . . . is eloquent once in his life. *Ralph Waldo Emerson*
41. A king may make a nobleman, but he cannot make a gentleman.
                                                    Edmund Burke
42. Heard melodies are sweet, but those unheard
    Are sweeter. *John Keats*
43. Therefore never send to know for whom the bell tolls; it tolls for thee.
                                                    John Donne

44. The bud may have a bitter taste, but sweet will be the flower.
    William Cowper
45. Men may come and men may go, but I go on forever.
    Alfred, Lord Tennyson
46. The bush burned with fire, and the bush was not consumed. *Exodus*
47. Ice is the silent language of the peak; and fire [is] the silent language of the star. *Conrad Aiken*
48. A boy's will is the wind's will,
    And the thoughts of youth are long, long thoughts.
    Henry Wadsworth Longfellow
49. Dust thou art, and unto dust shalt thou return. *Genesis*
50. I do not sound your name, but I understand you. *Walt Whitman*
51. My heart is like a rainbow shell that paddles in a halcyon sea.
    Christina Rossetti
52. He prayeth best, who loveth best
    All things both great and small. *Coleridge*
53. Be ashamed to die until you have won some victory for humanity. *Mann*
54. Time the ruined bridge has swept down the dark stream which seaward creeps. *Emerson*
55. Yet each man kills the thing he loves. *Oscar Wilde*
56. I dipt into the future, far as human eye could see. *Tennyson*
57. Parting is such sweet sorrow
    That I shall say good-night till it be morrow. *Shakespeare*
58. As we resumed work in the field, the memory of its splendors went with us like a golden cloud. *Garland*
59. No spring nor summer beauty hath such grace
    As I have seen in one autumnal face. *John Donne*
60. He today that sheds his blood with me shall be my brother. *Shakespeare*
61. One day, about noon, going towards my boat, I was exceedingly surprised with the print of a man's naked foot on the shore, which was very plain to be seen in the sand. *Daniel Defoe*
62. My definition of a free society is a society where it is safe to be unpopular.
    Adlai E. Stevenson
63. Fame is the spur that the clear spirit doth raise . . .
    To scorn delights, and live laborious days. *Milton*
64. I should have been a pair of ragged claws
    Scuttling across the floors of silent seas. *T. S. Eliot*
65. Here was a man to hold against the world,
    A man to match the mountain and the sea. *Edwin Markham*
66. . . . that was my long scythe whispering to the ground. *Robert Frost*
67. When the lamp is shattered
    The light in the dust lies dead. *Percy Bysshe Shelley*
68. To have faith is to have wings. *James M. Barrie*
69. To live in hearts we leave behind,
    is not to die. *Thomas Campbell*
70. Precious memories may remain even of a bad home, if the heart knows how to find what is precious. *Dostoievsky*

Appendix 17

Aspirations under Glass

Early in his youth Milton compared aspirations, deciding at last to be a minister or a poet. At Cambridge, when he found himself "church-outed by the prelates," he turned more and more to the study of poetry. But still his vision of himself, as shown in "Comus" and "Lycidas," was not that of a poet who would shake the world for all the centuries to come. Only gradually, as he tells us, did his dream evolve: "To leave something so written to aftertimes as they should not willingly let it die." Day by day Milton pondered and expanded his aspiration: He would be a poet, yes, but his definition of the word *poet* now assumed the most explosive dimension of all. He would be a poet representing his native England as David had spoken for Israel, Homer for Athens, Virgil for Rome. He would write an epic as great as *The Iliad*, a Greek play as great as *Oedipus*, a dialogue like the *Book of Job*. This gradual elevation of an aspiration in Milton's life alone has not yet received the scholarly study it deserves as applied to incitements to greatness on the American scene. What is difficult to realize is that no act of greatness is suddenly born whole, like Minerva from the head of Zeus. Every creative action has a beginning deep in one's youth that the average teacher or parent would consider at the time an event of insignificance.

So far in American high schools we teachers have given almost no study to the comparison of aspirations. An aspiration has a seed, a womb, a birth, a childhood, a maturity. Almost every boy or girl in high school is involved in analysis of several aspirations, but he almost never places them in historical perspective, comparing his aspiration, for example, with that of the boy Jesse Stuart, the boy Thomas Jefferson, the boy John Kennedy, the boy John Milton, or the boy Robert Oppenheimer. When Jesse Stuart was in high school, an English teacher, passing him in the hall one day, reached up and patted him on the head, saying, "I'd just like to be around long enough to see what's coming out of that head of yours." The proportion

510

of great men on the American scene is thus far only a trickle as compared to the proportion in Periclean Athens, when one man in every four thousand achieved greatness by the standards of later ages.[1] So far America has produced no sculptor comparable to Phidias, no philosopher of the stature of Aristotle or Plato, no historian as great as Thucydides or Herodotus, no genius in mathematics comparable to Euclid, no poet of tragedy comparable to Sophocles or Aeschylus. For our memorial to Abraham Lincoln we selected a Greek temple. Our scholars and foundations have established no institute to study the means by which the proportion of great men in American life can be increased. But certainly the known events in the lives of great men and women all point to particular moments of illumination in the presence of beloved friends, parents, or ideas. If through our help an aspiration to be a poet, a sculptor, a great historian, grows in a student's mind where no dream previously dwelt, this represents an elevation of ambition that may be decisive in his destiny. Nor do we know yet to what extent an indomitable purpose and superior resources of energy may compensate for a lack of superior intelligence in reaching a goal of creative distinction. Among the thousand selected children of genius I. Q. studied by Terman and his associates, the low achievement of the 150 least successful as men and women in later years could be traced only to *differences in aspiration.*[2]

There can be no greatness without an early dream planted by a discerning father, friend, teacher, or an exciting idea. It is hard for even the English teacher to realize that Hawthorne's sentences were once pale and listless, that even the incandescent images of Shakespeare and Keats were not inborn, but grew from early weak stabs at poetic expression. Like aspiration itself, all greatness begins with a seed that may flower or wither, a seed that the imaginative teacher watches over in a realistic expectancy. No great man has come to light whose early comrades and elders did not undervalue his potential genius. How often do people say of you and me and our students, "I didn't know he had it in him!" Every youth has more potential greatness in him than even the most imaginative teacher can perceive or enhance.

[1] The great anthropologist, Alfred Kroeber, could not believe that nature was more generous in bestowing genius upon the Athenians than upon the men and women of other times and countries. He thought it unreasonable to believe that "heredity turned itself on and off again . . . like a playful faucet." To Kroeber heredity might account for one genius "in many hundred thousand or million births." Yet three-fourths of these geniuses born are lost to civilization by virtue of unfavorable environment. "Only a fraction," then, says Kroeber, "of all the men congenitally equipped for genius ever actualize as such." Kroeber's conclusion is that only in environment can we find the secrets by which large numbers of men, as in Periclean Athens, suddenly emerge as great men in many fields. See Alfred Kroeber, *Anthropology* (New York: Harcourt, Brace and Company, 1948), pp. 337–40.

[2] Don M. Wolfe, *Image of Man in America* (New York: McGraw-Hill Book Company, 1963).

One final test of any civilization is the birth it gives to the clustering of great men, as in the Athens of Pericles, the Florence of Michelangelo, the London of Queen Elizabeth, and the Boston of Emerson. It is futile to say that such a clustering of genius is no concern of the high school English teacher. Each of us can make a beginning in the high school classroom by comparing one aspiration with another. What does one want from life? Does he want a car, a fine house, beautiful children? All these are laudable. But does he, like Milton or Shakespeare, aspire to a life beyond life, an "immortality of fame"? Does he aspire to be read as long as the English language endures? Almost every day the English teacher has an opportunity to compare and elevate aspirations. The English teacher is a miner of greatness, greatness in his students and in himself.

Biography the Key: What Happened in Youth?

One realistic way to compare aspirations is to study the aspirations of childhood in great men. What were the books and who were the people, for example, who inspired Jefferson as a boy? Jefferson has left us an exciting program of studies which he recommended to Bernard Moore and John Minor. At William and Mary, which Jefferson entered at sixteen, he studied fifteen hours a day. His closest friend, John Page, wrote that "Jefferson could tear himself away from his dearest friends and fly to his studies." Studies of the childhood of John Stuart Mill, Mark Twain, George Washington Carver, or John Bunyan are equally revealing. What explosion of energy in John Bunyan's life made possible the moving and highly original images of his biography, *Grace Abounding to the Chief of Sinners?* When Isaac Newton was a boy in school, he was at first just average in accomplishment. Then one day when he was only nine, he had a victorious fight with a boy of fourteen. All at once he found himself the hero of the school. Almost as suddenly and violently his intellectual life underwent a revolution. From that time forth his scholastic accomplishments advanced apace until he was the school's most distinguished student. The English teacher is one who understands the meaning of such an episode. He understands also that the unlocking of energy in a creative direction is the most precious of all gifts he can bestow on the boys and girls in his class. One useful book for examining the childhood of genius is Catherine Cox, *The Early Mental Traits of Three Hundred Geniuses* (Stanford University Press, 1926). The childhood of Michelangelo, as traced imaginatively in *The Agony and the Ecstasy*, is also full of illumination for the searcher of aspirations and the miner of greatness.

MAKING AN ASPIRATION LADDER [3]

Someone has defined education as "the comparison and selection of an aspiration." No great achievement is possible without an aspiration. Discuss the aspirations below.

[3] *Enjoying English 12* (1966), p. 16.

1. To go to college
2. To serve in the Peace Corps
3. To be a teacher
4. To play on a college football team
5. To write a great novel
6. To become a nuclear physicist
7. To marry and have beautiful children
8. To read the great books of the world
9. To serve on an international court of law
10. To become a leader in abolition of poverty in India
11. To write a biography of a hero I admire
12. To have my own car and visit many states of the United States
13. To become a journalist-historian and write books about various countries, as John Gunther and Louis Fischer have done
14. To live in England and gradually explore its historic monuments and beautiful countryside
15. To learn Greek, read Greek literature, and explore Greek ruins
16. To become an archeologist investigating the ruins of countries and cities mentioned in the Bible
17. To become a moving picture actor or actress
18. To fly a jet plane
19. To become a poet like Robert Frost or Carl Sandburg
20. To own a big house and ride in a Continental
21. To have a secretarial job in a beautiful office
22. To be a great poet expressing American hopes and dreams and individuality, as Milton spoke for England and Dante for Florence

****

Four-Star Challenge: Three Problems

Problem 1. Choose five of the aspirations in order of importance that you believe you should consider as possible of fulfillment in your own life. Write a paragraph about your first choice.

Problem 2. What aspiration, if achieved, would have the greatest influence on future Americans? Which would have the least influence? Arrange six or seven aspirations in order of your choice. Write a paragraph justifying your first choice and last choice.

Problem 3. Investigate the growth of an aspiration in the life of a great man you admire. What steps in thought or experience led finally to the crystallization of his aspiration?

Appendix 18

A Realistic Writing Program for Culturally Diverse Youth [1]

Two centuries ago, before anyone dreamed of the political upheavals in America and France, Thomas Gray wrote a poem profoundly revolutionary. As he wandered among the stones of the country churchyard, he said to himself, "Why did no great man come from this village? Why was there no John Milton, no John Hampden, no Oliver Cromwell?" Gray's revolutionary answer to his own questions appears in the key stanza of his poem "Elegy Written in a Country Church-Yard":

> But knowledge to their eyes her ample page
>   Rich with the spoils of time did ne'er unroll;
> Chill penury repressed their noble rage,
>   And froze the genial current of the soul.

Even much later in history, when every American town had not only a free elementary school but a free high school as well, this notion of Gray's appeared to be romantic nonsense. Poverty and ignorance indeed! In the minds of conservative thinkers it was not poverty and ignorance that barred the way to talent and great achievement; it was genetic limitation. Was not every man's destiny determined at his birth? It was nature, not environment, that made him a great man. But as early as 1634, America had set a revolutionary precedent that was to upset this pattern of thinking: Our forefathers in New England established free public schools, the essence of which was, "Every child can learn, and no one knows how much." In the ideal classroom we have an explosive force that breaks through all genetic limitations.

[1] By the author. Reprinted from *Improving English Skills of Culturally Different Youth*, a publication of the U. S. Department of Health, Education, and Welfare, Office of Education.

514

I speak particularly now of learning to write in a classroom of children of mixed backgrounds, a classroom still close to poverty, bound by the limitations of the parents. Can we convince each student in this class that he can learn to read and write well, notwithstanding any genetic lack of intelligence? We are gradually seeing that the release of energy in the adolescent toward a specific academic goal is a far greater factor in his success than any genetic endowment. The experience in New York City of Junior High School 43 alone shows how explosive is our power to help children move on to college. Most of the graduates of J.H.S. 43 attend George Washington High School. Now "the dropout rate of . . . students attending George Washington High School has been cut in half. . . . The percentage of these graduates eligible for college has leaped from about 9 percent to 36 percent. IQ scores . . . have risen sharply." [2]

When a boy or girl in a mixed classroom sees that he has a chance, sees that the teacher believes in him, sees that the teacher really means it when he says, "I am here to prove to you that you can write," something happens to that boy. When a teacher takes him to a Shakespearean play in Central Park, when a teacher spends 15 or 20 minutes writing helpful comments on his theme, when a teacher holds up his paper in class, even a single sentence, as an achievement any college teacher would be proud of, something happens to that boy: a release of energy, which in decades past we have come to think of as coming only from the inherently gifted child. We are seeing more clearly every year that this assumption of inherent gifts is more illusion than reality. Every child is gifted, depending upon the extent to which his energy is released in intellectual directions: learning to write, learning to read, learning to work mathematical problems.

This energy is released in a deprived youth only when he sees that those opportunities which he thought were open only to the "bright kids" are now opening to him. Maybe his father was born in Puerto Rico and still speaks hardly a word of English. Maybe his mother was born in Mexico and never even learned to read and write. A gifted teacher can still prove to that child that he can read, that he can write, that he can go on to college. It is not the IQ that stands in his way; it is the indifference of society to the conditions that have hitherto held him back. His enemy is not his IQ, but a classroom of 35 or 40 as opposed to a classroom of 20. His enemy is not his IQ, but a teacher who fails to show week after week that this child is in a unique way her teacher and the teacher of every other child in the class. The way this child becomes a teacher is by writing well, and the teacher is there to prove that he can write well.

The first step in a writing program for the future is to keep the class of mixed youngsters to 20. Twenty-five are too many. Often even 22 are too many. It depends on the teacher, but let us say, as a rule of thumb, that the smaller the class, the friendlier its members are likely to be to each

[2] Arthur D. Morse, *Schools of Tomorrow*. New York: Doubleday and Company, 1960, p. 46.

other. A loving, expectant classroom of peers and teacher is indispensable to the flowering of intelligence. The smaller the class, the more attention the teacher can give to each student, the more time she can spend on each theme. Not only must we keep the class to 20, but we must not give the teacher more than four of these classes, or a total of 80 students. She has to live with them, take them to plays, take them to museums. She has to visit their homes. She has to get their parents into the classroom. She has to take these youngsters to various colleges. She has to take them to visit courts and jails. She must take them to Emerson's house and Hawthorne's Old Manse at Concord, Jefferson's Monticello, the Lincoln Memorial—all the time proving to them that they can mint fresh and memorable images of moments and places.

Given this ideal situation, a teacher can be successful, not only proving to the youngsters that they can write, but also proving to them that they can read the best books, that they can go on to college, that they can "amount to something" in the great American tradition. Each one of us has had this experience. Somewhere, maybe in the 6th, 7th, or the 10th grade, we had such a teacher. Why did we respond? Was it because we had a promising IQ? Did anyone ever say about you, as many people have said about me, "I didn't think he had it in him"? Well, America is a country which proves all such predictions fallacious and misleading. Every boy "has it in him" if we release that inexhaustible energy in the adolescent years in the direction of books and ideas and preparation for college.

The first step the English teacher can take toward this end is to make a weekly writing assignment. The more time that is spent on this assignment, the better the result. It has to be a topic on which everyone in the class can write with deep feeling. Unless the assignment calls forth deep feeling, none of that precious energy will go into it. Only when great energy is released does the student surpass himself. Only then can we prove to him that he can write.

The first question, then, is, "What topic will appeal to everybody in the class?" Let us say we choose an assignment such as *proud words*. Everyone speaks proud words. You remember Carl Sandburg's poem on this topic, which we read to the class:

Look out how you use proud words.
When you let proud words go, it is not easy to call them back.
They wear long boots; they walk off proud; they can't hear you calling—
Look out how you use proud words.

The most important motivation is not, however, a poem by a great writer, but a theme by one of our own students from the year before or a theme written, perhaps, by the teacher himself in preparation for this assignment—a theme about a moment in his own early life. Perhaps for this special assignment he writes a theme like this one:

MY BROTHER FRED

One July morning several years ago, when we lived along a West Virginia creek, I used proud words I couldn't call back. I was sitting on the back porch, getting ready to go trout fishing, when my little brother Fred came out and sat down on the steps. He was about 8 years old, a chubby yellow-haired boy with big blue eyes. When he looked up at me with a pleading look, I knew what he was going to say. He was always asking to go with me somewhere. I guess I was angry at him because he couldn't climb along the creek banks as fast as I. So I blurted out, "No, you can't go, and don't ask me again." He sort of crumpled up and began to sniffle. Then without a word he walked down the steps and across the yard, his head down and the sunlight splashing over his yellow hair. All day I felt jumpy inside and didn't enjoy the fishing. At supper that evening, Fred just looked away when I sat down, and I didn't eat much trout. But I couldn't ask him to forgive me, and I couldn't call back my proud words.

Joe Breckinridge

In such an assignment one of our purposes is to help the class to talk. The more the class talks following the reading of themes, the more likely the students are to reach deep into their own feelings and experiences when they begin to write. In order to carry on such a discussion, the teacher must from the first day create a friendly classroom. If this is not done, the writing program somehow goes awry. We do not yet know the relation of love between the teacher and class and love among fellow students to the release of intelligence. But no underprivileged boy or girl learns to write exceptionally well from a teacher who does not respect him and look upon him with an eye of faith and affection.

As the writing assignments continue week after week, the students come to see each other's problems. They write about fathers and mothers, they write about moments of decision, they write about moments of love and hate. They write about favorite books and favorite movies. They write about moments of religious faith. One thing the teacher can do is to ask the student to write down anonymously what he considers his most important problems. Here is a sampling of problems described anonymously in various classrooms:

How can I keep from quarreling with my mother?

Why do parents object because a boy is not of my religion?

How can a girl be popular with boys without making the boys think she's wild?

I am afraid to face the world. All of a sudden I have become very self-conscious, and I don't know why.

What is the best way of finding out what job I'm best fitted for?

The mere self-listing of student problems shows the appalling gap that exists between the invitations to write and speak in the English class and the problem realities of each individual student. Each student has a right to expect that he can write or speak about some deep realities of his life for this reason: Until he describes the conflicts that torture him and drain his emotional energy, he has not realized the writing power and talent of which he is capable.

When Emerson said, "Every man is eloquent once in his life," he was too restrictive of man's creative energies. Were he alive today, he might well change his dictum to read: "Every man is eloquent each time he speaks from a deep cavern of himself as if to his only trusted friend." Until English teachers in America assume, then, a responsibility for finding out the deep-running problems, fears, and obstacles of each student and encourage him to express his feelings as freely as he can about each one, the student cannot find the natural level of his writing power nor make the first crucial step toward the mature answers to the questions that rack his brain and plague his sleepless hours.

Let us say we are teaching a 10th-grade class of mixed backgrounds. Most of the students in the class do not expect to go on to college. We have been working to convince them they can go on, but we have several obstacles. One is the IQ record in the principal's office. Another is the poor grades the class has had in the past. Another, of course, is the temptation of taking a job. Most of our students need spending money, especially the boys. Now 15 or 16, they want to take their girls to movies, but their fathers and mothers are poor. How can we keep them in school? How can we even present the dropout problem? One way to present the dropout problem is to assign a theme on this topic. We never compel a class to write on the topic we assign. We want each one to write on the topic that draws on the deepest well of his emotional energy. This is the dynamo that provides the power by which he works and thinks. The deepest feelings call forth the most eloquent language. Let us read, then, to the class a theme like the following:

LAST NIGHT AFTER SUPPER

Last night after supper my Dad and I sat in the living room of our railroad apartment, which overlooks the Allegheny River here in Pittsburgh. In the October dusk the street lights were blinking on. From far off came the moan of a fog horn: a coal barge chugging upriver. My Dad has a blast furnace job at J&L Steel Corporation. He doesn't work long hours, but it's very heavy labor, and his paycheck is never enough to take care of a family of five. Suddenly my Dad said to me, "Son, in 1 month you'll be 16. What are you going to do?" I look at Dad's thick graying hair and warm brown eyes, wide with concern for me, his oldest son. I knew what he meant. He didn't want me to drop out of school.

Well, I don't want to drop out either, but I know what Dad is up against. His paycheck is $75 a week. It sounds big, but it isn't enough. I make about $10 a week delivering groceries after school. My boss, Mr. O'Brien, says he'll give me a full-time job at $40 a week any time I want it. I hate to ask Dad for money. I need money every week for lunches, for carfare, for an evening at the movies with my friends. I'm good in math, and my math teacher wants me to stay on in school and go to college. But how can I go to college? I'm not good enough to get a scholarship, and Dad can't possibly send me. All these thoughts went through my mind as I sat there in the living room, Dad looking out at the river and back at me again. I said to him, "Well, Dad, I know you don't want me to quit, but I think it's time I helped myself, and help the family a little bit, too. It won't be long before Joe will need spending money the way I do now." Then I saw the hurt look in Dad's eyes, and I said, "But I'll talk it over with Mr. Trembly. Y'know, he's my math teacher. I'll see what he says." But I knew even at that moment, and I think Dad knew, too, that I just had to drop out.

George Belicheck

Such a theme brings not only a vital class discussion; it may also bring in its wake several breakthroughs to superior achievement in the same class. This is the event we hope for most: a theme that sets off chain explosions in self-expression.

The more deeply they feel, the more eloquently they write. The more eloquently they write, the more vital to them becomes *the concern for correctness*. When a boy or girl struggles desperately to express his deepest thoughts, then he has the most valid reason of his life to punctuate and spell and write with clarity and elegance. At that time he has the greatest need also to make his reader see, touch, smell, taste, and hear just as he did at a critical moment of his life.

No assignment is more of a challenge than an autobiography, but you and I need to be dogmatic and restrictive, not in subject matter but in ways and means. We need to say, "Limit the topic of your autobiography. Write about you and one girl, you and your father, you and your friend. Write about you in one summer, your experiences in one room or one school, your experiences in one day or night: five moments of experience." We illustrate the structure of an autobiography to show the introductory paragraph, five paragraphs describing five moments, and the concluding paragraph this way:

Intro-duction	Moment 1	Moment 2	Moment 3	Moment 4	Moment 5	Con-clusion

As in other assignments, we read to the class autobiographies or portions of autobiographies such as the following:

AUTOBIOGRAPHY

I squirm deeper into my seat as the bus races through the rain-soaked August night, its lights bouncing from the filmed highway and jutting into the mist drifting from the black Jersey swamps. I'm leaving behind a part of myself, a part that I'll never get back again. The asphalt ribbon is broken by the flaring neon mosaic of passing roadhouses and drive-ins, and as these patterns of light flash past me I wonder if that's all a man is: a series of sections scattered through the world with only memories to pull the threads together. Threads. Threads twining through time; threads of love, truth, and aloneness; the threads of one's self—wrapped by the elusive thread of dreams. This is the last run from Washington to New York; the bus is almost empty. A few passengers occupy the red-covered seats; their heads roll against the chairbacks and nod with the lurching of the darkened bus. My leg jostles the seabag propped alongside me, leaving a smudge on my starched uniform. I move my hand slowly toward my knee, then stop and lean back in the seat. Why should I bother? Who's going to chew me out? I've got my discharge from the Navy; there's no need to worry about a clean uniform any more . . . no need at all . . . I'm free. I'm going home. I should be happy—that's for sure. But free for what? A tired melancholy fills me as I rest my head on the cool window glass.

Charles Bryan

The wise teacher prefers the term "autobiographical writing" to the term "creative writing." Autobiographical writing is the only democratic art capable of achievement in the schools at large. The time will come when we shall ask each citizen, young or old, to speak an autobiography for the education of future Americans, a record transmitted to posterity, that our descendants might hear not only our words, our life stories, but also our voices. We cherish for each child the "relief of utterance," the "dropping of the stones of memory into the pool of language." We believe in the search for the child's unique vision, in fragments coined in language every other child can understand. We believe in the comparison of aspirations, such as the aspirations of other great men with that of Milton, who wanted to leave "something so written to aftertimes, that they should not willingly let it die." We believe that there is no child, no man or woman who is not disabled, no one who has not suffered a unique bitterness and a unique sorrow. We believe in the plasticity of the child and the man to recoil from bitterness and sorrow into healing and hope. We believe that one way to health in the life of each boy and girl is to write about himself, his unique moments of joy, love, and frustration. The good English teacher is one who draws forth, week by week and month by month, stories that reveal to each member of the class a unique and unforgettable personality that he wishes to cherish the rest of his life.

What America needs is a searching, comprehensive program of writing that reveals to the student the unique dignity of his own experiences and the unique coloring of his personality; a program that helps the student identify some of his main dilemmas and the words he needs most urgently to define in years to come; a program that links writing realistically to appreciation of literature. For the teacher a program is needed that brings immense rewards in professional growth and insight, justifying her belief in the still untallied capacity for talent and achievement in American boys and girls.

In the writing program which I have described, the most important language tool is sensory language. The use of sights and sounds, colors and smells, images of touch is particularly vital in the description of a single moment of action.

We believe, then, in the magic of the child's plasticity, the most precious genetic ingredient of all. I like that statement in John Pfeiffer's wonderful book, *The Human Brain*, "Man is not anything except teachable." We believe that the habit of original thought can be engendered in the classroom, an expectancy of originality in one's fellow pupils. We believe that love in the classroom is indispensable to the flowering of intelligence, love not only between teacher and class, but also between student and student. We believe in the daily record of life in sensory language, a record that persists day after day and week after week until the boy and girl see all life anew. As Emerson wrote, "No man ever forgot the visitations of that power to his heart which created all things new; which was the dawn in him of music, poetry, and art." Perhaps you remember that wonderful passage from *The Brothers Karamazov*, "Precious memories may remain even of a bad home, if the heart can learn to know what is precious." We believe in a continuous record of precious memories of home life.

We believe that the student's own record of his life is the best introduction to the incandescent moments of great books. We are not content, and the student is not content, with a writing program that touches only his superficial life. We believe in a writing program that grapples relentlessly and lovingly with the deepest dilemmas of the student's experience, those dilemmas that teach him to be a better son, a better brother, a better friend and neighbor. The teacher of writing is a liberator, a miner of greatness. As described in Emerson's lines, "We are now men, and must accept in the highest mind the same transcendent destiny, not minors or invalids lying in a protected corner, not cowards fleeing before the revolution, but guides, redeemers, benefactors, obeying the Almighty effort and advancing upon chaos and the dark."

Suggested Readings

HARRINGTON, MICHAEL: *The Other America, Poverty in the United States*, The Macmillan Company, 1962

> As defined by Mr. Harrington, nineteen per cent of America's families are in the low income category. A dramatic and forceful book with many concrete illustrations of deprivation.

KEYSERLING, LEON H.: *Progress or Poverty*, Conference on Economic Progress, December, 1964

> In this valuable and dramatic study, Mr. Keyserling estimates that 34,000,000 Americans live in poverty. He discusses the steps taken to raise the income level of the poorest families by means of education and employment opportunities, especially through the Economic Opportunity Act of 1964. This volume is most extant and readable, has many charts and pictures to dramatize its statistics, is available for only $1.00 per copy (Conference on Economic Progress, 1001 Connecticut Avenue, N.W., Washington 6, D.C.).

LICHTER, SOLOMON O., RAPIEN, ELSIE B., SEIBERT, FRANCES M., SKLANSKY, MORRIS A., M.D.: *The Drop-Outs*, The Free Press of Glencoe, 1962

> A careful scholarly study of drop-out boys and girls and the destructive forces at work to stop the school career of intellectually capable students. Excellent case illustrations and reliable conclusions.

MYRDAL, GUNNAR: *Challenge to Affluence*, Pantheon Books, 1962

> The Swedish author of *An American Dilemma* reviews the economic stagnation of an affluent society and its failure to solve social problems.

RIESSMAN, FRANK: *The Culturally Deprived Child*, Harper & Row, 1962

> This volume discusses the sociological and psychological aspects of children who are culturally deprived.

Appendix 19

Suggested Theme Topics

[The theme topics below embody a rough progression from the sensory record to the abstract, from the personal and immediate to the intellectual and philosophical. The word *moment*, as in previous suggested topics refers to a pin point of time, whether a few minutes or a half hour, as exemplified in Virginia Woolf's memorable essay, "The Moment: Summer's Night," or the first pages of *The Grapes of Wrath*, picturing a turtle crossing a road. The shorter the time span embodied in a single paragraph or sketch, and the more fully expanded the sensory record, the more individualized becomes the student's language. The more abstract the topic, the greater the necessity for concentration on a single moment to dramatize his meaning in a unique manner. Does the topic call up in the student's mind an electric moment, and with that recollection a sudden flow of emotional energy? This is the ideal consequence and the most severe test of the suggested theme topic.]

1. From My Bedroom Window
2. Our Kitchen at Breakfast
3. Sounds I Like at Night
4. The Moment I Was Afraid
5. My Biggest Worry
6. A Classroom Moment: Sights and Sounds
7. The Yellow Things I Like
8. A Moment of First Love
9. A Golden School Moment
10. A Moment with My Favorite Teacher
11. A Moment with My Dad
12. When Dad Was Angry
13. Why I Admire My Mother
14. My Definition of *Son*
15. My Definition of *Daughter*
16. Angry Words to My Best Friend
17. My Definition of *Success*
18. One Moment: A Turning Point in My Life
19. What Love Means to Me
20. One Moment in a Great Book
21. A Moment When I Found Joy
22. My Definition of *Science*
23. A Moment of Aspiration
24. The Power of Music: A Moment I Remember

25. The Last Two Minutes
26. A Moment of Triumph
27. My Definition of *Freedom*
28. When I Was Proud of Dad
29. The Turning Point of My Life
30. My Definition of *Happiness*
31. Why I Want to Go to College
32. A Moment of Sudden Growth
33. My First View of Death
34. A Mood I Vividly Remember
35. I Thought I Was Drowning
36. A Moment of Decision
37. My Toughest Dilemma
38. A Day of Discovery: Myself
39. Why I Admire My Brother
40. A Moment of Religious Faith
41. One Thing I Believe
42. Why I Believe in Laughter
43. The Best Book in My Life
44. One Moment: Learning to Drive
45. Driver at the Wheel: Danger
46. The Circus: A Moment of Wonder
47. World Series Moment
48. My Goal Is to Go to College
49. The Moment I Awoke
50. What Makes Me Afraid
51. I Began a New Life
52. A Job I Hated
53. The Place I Want Most to See
54. My Image of Human Nature: One Moment
55. A Wonderful Story and Why: "The Bride Comes to Yellow Sky"
56. Why I Like the Ending of "A Wagner Matinee"
57. Lord Jim's Great Decision
58. Why Milton's Samson Preferred Death to Life
59. How Milton Was Like Samson
60. How Stephen Crane Uses Color
61. The Most Unforgettable Character I Ever Met
62. What Is an American?
63. Plato's Idea of Heredity
64. Aristotle's Definition of *Happiness*
65. When Tess Put the Note under Angel's Door
66. Why Othello Was Susceptible to Jealousy
67. A Moment of Crisis in *Brothers Karamazov*
68. The Moment I Most Needed Money
69. What Is Greatness?
70. When Michael Henchard Became a Great Man
71. Plato's Horses: Black and White
72. The Tragic Flaw in Oedipus
73. Why Ahab Wanted to Kill Moby Dick
74. The Moment in Gandhi's Life I Admire Most
75. A Revelation to Me: Leonardo's *Notebooks*
76. The Sentence in Emerson I Like Best
77. Jefferson's Most Revolutionary Idea
78. Why Man Is Perfectible
79. Why Gray's "Elegy" Is a Revolutionary Poem
80. America's True Greatness

Appendix 20

Spelling: Hard Spots in Hard Words

[This drill may be used over and over again until each student has identified his problem words and spelled them correctly several times. Students enjoy drill as a diagnostic test. It may be used six or seven times in mimeographed form: two or three times in the first month, twice in the second month, and twice in the fourth month. To slow down decisions, we may ask the students to fill in the missing letters only in pen and ink.]

1. a   ross the river
2. unti   eight o'clock
3. very defi   te conclusion
4. sep   rate the papers
5. proof of exist   ce
6. found it   voice
7. is tr   ly foolish
8. know w   ther you are going or not
9. against his princip   s
10. an unusual experi   nce
11. loss of i   agination
12. study of gramm   r
13. come immed   ly
14. he is very independ   nt
15. a w   rd lighting effect
16. a new bu   ness
17. see the   r home
18. bill was rec   ved
19. when op   rtunity knocks
20. a point quickly de   ided
21. an at   letic girl
22. they went tog   ther
23. a hasty appear   nce
24. contro   the floods
25. an apt d   cription
26. work is nec   sary
27. bel   ved in prayer
28. on that oc   sion
29. do it befo   tomorrow
30. a nice s   prise
31. a sad occu   nce
32. usu   ly he goes home
33. the mirage dis   peared
34. the effect was dis   pointing
35. a princip   question
36. the water was a   right
37. then the   are other boys
38. house ac   modates thirty
39. took fifteen min   s
40. to l   se money
41. a suc   sful career
42. an accident oc   red
43. legible wr   ting

525

44. Where? Directly over th
45. much knowl   ge
46. W   re are they now?
47. an excel   nt scholar
48. he proc   ded to reply
49. defective sp   ch
50. bills were pa   d
51. very good fr   ds
52. the baby tr   s to walk
53. constant comp   tition
54. many people com   ng
55. she was stud   ng
56. the begin   ng
57. autocratic gov   ment
58. avoid rep   tion
59. prob   y they did
60. final   left home
61. a pleas   nt talk
62. sim   l   r reaction
63. a noble wom   n
64. we do   t know
65. he does   t know
66. argu   g is useless
67. an ang   l of God
68. a notic   ble error
69. advi   e him
70. gave good advi   e
71. new acquaint   ce
72. d   vide the money
73. a good lab   tory
74. perm   ent address
75. before the alt   r
76. alt   r this copy
77. Jim l   d the way
78. bel   ve in him
79. a superintend   nt
80. great priv   leges
81. prec   ding day
82. conc   ve an idea
83. a high c   ling
84. she ch   se this yesterday
85. Why ch   se at all?
86. awary consc   ce

87. words are chang   ble
88. of fo   ty men
89. well-equip   d
90. in the cemet   ry
91. easy prof   sor
92. car   ing a bag of cement
93. r   thm of music
94. str   ch the line
95. p   form his duty
96. canva   all towns
97. d   scribe his hat
98. never dec   ve me
99. it   my fault
100. a depend   t person
101. the des   rt was good
102. live in the de   rt
103. the rain des   nds
104. call a doct   r
105. animated disc   ion
106. always embar   sed
107. dim   g room
108. a qu   t church
109. stylish clo   s
110. unusual op   nions
111. it   color
112. six feet in heig
113. could not breat   fresh air
114. you r   too late
115. the re   coming soon
116. the vill   n
117. hop   ng to see you
118. shin   g stars
119. shi   y metal
120. She said, "   ou must go."
121. ask what you r   doing
122. the police stop   d us.
123. it   leaves are gone
124. princip   reasons
125. princip   and rules
126. a great lon   l   ness
127. the wheel is l   se
128. an opt   mistic person

Appendix 21

An Excellent Test for College-Bound Students

The test below is reprinted with permission from *End-of-Year Examinations in English for College-Bound Students, Grades, 9–12* (Princeton, 1963), published by the Commission on English and copyrighted by its parent organization, the College Entrance Examination Board. It is Question 3 of the examination for grade 10. Forty minutes were allowed on this test. It is one of the most practical, searching, and comprehensive of all the new tests devised by the College Entrance Examination Board. The directions to the teacher appear at the end of this question, on pp. 81–83 of the volume. The examination board writes, "The advantages of this kind of language question are the chances it offers for variety, range, and novelty in the items themselves; the demands it makes upon the active thinking and active writing skill of the student; and the fact that this kind of testing avoids the common practice of confronting the student with bad writing to which he is to apply first aid."

Examination for Grade 10: Question 3

Rewrite each sentence according to the directions which follow it. Make as few changes as necessary.

1. Jack and Ben are waiting for us at the gate. (Begin with words *Either Jack or Ben.*)
2. George was elected president of his class because of several characteristics. (Enumerate several of George's characteristics without making a second sentence or changing what is already written.)
3. The new boys have finished their work. (Change *The new boys* to *Each of the new boys.*)
4. If you ever dare to come into my nice clean kitchen again with those muddy boots, your father's going to hear about it. (Rewrite, making the sentence a gentle plea instead of an angry threat.)

527

5. All the students who plan to attend the dance must buy their tickets in advance. (Change *All the students who* to *Each of the students who*.)

6. Men, who are egotistical, are always wanting to be flattered by women. (Use punctuation which any man would prefer.)

7. Between the officials and you, there must be no misunderstanding. (Change *you* to the first person personal pronoun.)

8. Jack asked his parents why he couldn't have a car. (Rewrite so as to give Jack's direct words to his parents.)

9. If Alan had had more practice diving, he would have been awarded the medal. (Rewrite, changing *If* to *Because* and keeping as close as possible to the meaning of the given sentence.)

10. John, who is the manager of a large department store, filed the complaint. (Change *John* to *Only the man*.)

11. The teacher was pleased that for once each and every single one of all her students had punctually handed in on time his or her book report on Catherine Bowen's biograghy of the life of Justice Holmes. (Rewrite, cutting out all unnecessary words.)

12. Mary completed the work ahead of schedule, whereas John barely finished on time. (Rewrite, changing *whereas* to *however*.)

13. While Walt was shopping in the square, a peddler sold him a Turkish rug. (Change *While Walt was shopping* to *While shopping*.)

14. John is known as an excellent ballplayer. (Change *is* to *you are*.)

15. For successful teaching, knowledge of the subject should be linked with the desire and ability to share that knowledge. (Rewrite, changing *For successful teaching* to *To be a successful teacher*.)

16. Divide the money between the Girls' Athletic Association and the Boys' Service Club. (Add *and the Students' Publication Committee*.)

17. My older nephew is doing well, but his younger brother wants to go to a less demanding school. (Rewrite, inserting *who has always been a real scholar* after *nephew*, and inserting *a less able student* after *brother*.)

18. Springfield is the capital city of Illinois. It is the burial place of Abraham Lincoln. (Change to one sentence, omitting one *is* and not using a conjunction.)

19. Opportunity seldom knocks twice. (Begin with *The golden gate of opportunity*.)

20. The burglar's final shot missed its target and embedded itself in one of the ancestral portraits, improving it beyond all recognition. (Change the tone of this sentence by altering just *one* word.)

Appendix 22

Publishers' Addresses

American Book Company, 55 Fifth Avenue, New York, N.Y. 10003
Appleton-Century-Crofts, Inc., 60 East 42 Street, New York, N.Y. 10017
Bantam Books, Inc., 271 Madison Avenue, New York, N.Y. 10016
Bobbs-Merrill Company, 4300 West 62 Street, Indianapolis, Ind. 46206
Bowker, R. R., Co., 1180 Avenue of the Americas, New York, N.Y. 10036
Columbia University Press, 2960 Broadway, New York, N.Y. 10027
Crowell, Thomas Y., Company, 201 Park Avenue South, New York, N.Y.
10003
Dodd, Mead & Co., 432 Park Avenue South, New York, N.Y. 10016
Dryden Press, Inc. (Write to Holt, Rinehart and Winston, Inc., 383 Madison Avenue, New York, N.Y. 10017)
Dutton, E. P., & Co., Inc., 201 Park Avenue South, New York, N.Y. 10003
French, Samuel, Inc., 25 West 45 Street, New York, N.Y. 10036
Funk & Wagnalls Co., 360 Lexington Avenue, New York, N.Y. 10017
Ginn & Company, Statler Building, Back Bay P.O. 191, Boston, Mass.
02117
Harcourt, Brace & World, Inc., 757 Third Avenue, New York, N.Y. 10017
Harper & Row, Publishers, 49 East 33 Street, New York, N.Y. 10016
Harvard University Press, 79 Garden Street, Cambridge, Mass. 02138
Heath, D. C., & Company, 285 Columbus Avenue, Boston, Mass. 02116
Holt, Rinehart and Winston, Inc., 383 Madison Avenue, New York, N.Y.
10017
Houghton Mifflin Co., 2 Park Street, Boston, Mass. 02107
International Textbook Co., Scranton, Pa. 18515
Iroquois Publishing Company, Inc., Route 9W, Englewood Cliffs, N.J.
Knopf, Alfred A., Inc., 501 Madison Avenue, New York, N.Y. 10022
Laidlaw Brothers, Thatcher & Madison Streets, River Forest, Ill. 60305
Lippincott, J. B., Co., East Washington Square, Philadelphia, Pa. 19105
Little, Brown & Co., 34 Beacon Street, Boston, Mass. 02106

Liveright Publishing Corp., 386 Park Avenue South, New York, N.Y. 10016

Longmans, Green & Co., Inc. (Write to David McKay Co., Inc., 750 Third Avenue, New York, N.Y. 10017)

Lothrop, Lee & Shepard Co., Inc., 419 Park Avenue South, New York, N.Y. 10016

Lyons & Carnahan, 407 East 25 Street, Chicago, Ill. 60616

McGraw-Hill Book Co., 330 West 42 Street, New York, N.Y. 10036

Macmillan Co., 60 Fifth Avenue, New York, N.Y. 10011

Merriam, G. & C., Co., 47 Federal Street, Springfield, Mass. 01101

Merrill, Charles E., Books, 1300 Alum Creek Drive, Columbus, Ohio 43216

Metropolitan Museum of Fine Arts, Fifth Avenue at 82 Street, New York, N.Y. 10028

National Council of Teachers of English, 508 South 6 Street, Champaign, Ill. 61820

Nelson, Thomas, & Sons, 18 East 41 Street, New York, N.Y. 10017

Noble & Noble, Publishers, Inc., 67 Irving Place, N.Y. 10003

Norton, W. W., & Company, Inc., 55 Fifth Avenue, New York, N.Y. 10003

Odyssey Press, Inc., 55 Fifth Avenue, New York, N.Y. 10003

Oxford University Press, Inc., 417 Fifth Avenue, New York, N.Y. 10016

Pitman Publishing Co., 20 East 46 Street, New York, N.Y. 10017

Prentice-Hall, Inc., Englewood Cliffs, N.J. 07632

Putnam's, G. P., Sons, 200 Madison Avenue, New York, N.Y. 10016

Rand McNally & Co., 8255 Central Park Avenue, Skokie, Ill. 60076

Regents Publishing Company, Inc., 200 Park Avenue South, New York, N.Y. 10003

Rinehart & Company, Inc. (Write to Holt, Rinehart and Winston, Inc., 383 Madison Avenue, New York, N.Y. 10017)

Ronald Press Company, 15 East 26 Street, New York, N.Y. 10010

Row, Peterson & Company (Write to Harper & Row, Publishers, 49 East 33 Street, New York, N.Y. 10016)

Sadlier, William H., Inc., 11 Park Place, New York, N.Y. 10007

Saunders, W. B., Co., West Washington Square, Philadelphia, Pa. 19105

Scott, Foresman & Company, 433 East Erie Street, Chicago, Ill. 60611

Scribner's, Charles, Sons, 597 Fifth Avenue, New York, N.Y. 10017

Silver Burdett Company, Park Avenue & Columbia Road, Morristown, N.J. 07960

Singer, L. W., Company, Inc., 249–259 West Erie Boulevard, Syracuse, N.Y. 13202

South-Western Publishing Co., 5101 Madison Road, Cincinnati, Ohio 45227

Standard Publishing Co., 8121 Hamilton Avenue, Cincinnati, Ohio 45231

University of Chicago Press, 5750 Ellis Avenue, Chicago, Ill. 60637

University Publishing Company, 1126 Q Street, Lincoln, Neb.   68508
Van Nostrand, D., Co., Inc., 120 Alexander Street, Princeton, N.J.   08541
Wiley, John, & Sons, Inc., 605 Third Avenue, New York, N.Y.   10016
Winston, John C., Co. (Write to Holt, Rinehart and Winston, Inc. 383 Madison Avenue, New York, N.Y.   10017)
World Book Co. (Write to Harcourt, Brace & World, Inc., 757 Third Avenue, New York, N.Y.   10017)

INDEX